Students learn best when they att[end]
keep up with their reading and [do]
but learning shouldn't end when class is over.

MyEconLab *Picks Up Where Lectures and Office Hours Leave Off*

Instructors choose MyEconLab:

"MyEconLab offers them a way to practice every week. They receive immediate feedback and a feeling of personal attention. As a result, my teaching has become more targeted and efficient."

—Kelly Blanchard, Purdue University

"Students tell me that offering them MyEconLab is almost like offering them individual tutors."

—Jefferson Edwards, Cypress Fairbanks College

"Chapter quizzes offset student procrastination by ensuring they keep on task. If a student is having a problem, MyEconLab indicates exactly what they need to study."

—Diana Fortier, Waubonsee Community College

Students choose MyEconLab:

In a recent study, 87 percent of students who used MyEconLab regularly felt it improved their grade.

"It was very useful because it had EVERYTHING, from practice exams to exercises to reading. Very helpful."

—student, Northern Illinois University

"It was very helpful to get instant feedback. Sometimes I would get lost reading the book, and these individual problems would help me focus and see if I understood the concepts."

—student, Temple University

"I would recommend taking the quizzes on MyEconLab because they give you a true account of whether or not you understand the material."

—student, Montana Tech

Get Ahead of the Curve

MICROECONOMIC STRUCTURE

The organization of the microeconomics chapters continues to reflect the authors' belief that the best way to understand how market economies operate—and the best way to understand basic economic theory—is to work through a simple model of a perfectly competitive market system first, including discussions of output markets (goods and services) and input markets (land, labor, and capital), and the connections between them. Only then do the authors turn to noncompetitive market structures such as monopoly and oligopoly. When students have worked through a simple model of a perfectly competitive market system, they begin to understand how the pieces of the economy "fit together." Learning perfect competition first also enables students to see the power of the market system. It is impossible to discuss the efficiency of markets as well as the problems that arise from markets until students have seen how a simple perfectly competitive market produces and distributes goods and services. The accompanying visual gives you an overview of the structure.

CHAPTERS 6–8 provide an overview of firm and household decision making in simple perfectly competitive markets.

CHAPTERS 9–11 show how firms and households interact in output markets (goods and services) and input markets (labor, land, and capital) to determine prices, wages, and profits.

CHAPTER 12 is a pivotal chapter that links simple perfectly competitive markets with a discussion of market imperfections and the role of government.

CHAPTERS 13–19 cover the three noncompetitive market structures (monopoly, oligopoly, and monopolistic competition), externalities, public goods, uncertainty and asymmetric information, and income distribution as well as taxation and government finance.

▲ Understanding the Microeconomy and the Role of Government

ECONOMICS IN PRACTICE FEATURE

To help pique students' interest in the economic world, the authors include the chapter feature entitled *Economics in Practice*. This feature either (1) describes a personal observation or a research idea and provides an analysis using the concepts of the chapter or (2) presents a newspaper excerpt that relates to the concepts of the chapter.

TENTH EDITION

Principles of
Microeconomics

The Pearson Series in Economics

Abel/Bernanke/Croushore
*Macroeconomics**

Bade/Parkin
*Foundations of Economics**

Berck/Helfand
The Economics of the Environment

Bierman/Fernandez
Game Theory with Economic Applications

Blanchard
*Macroeconomics**

Blau/Ferber/Winkler
The Economics of Women, Men and Work

Boardman/Greenberg/Vining/Weimer
Cost-Benefit Analysis

Boyer
Principles of Transportation Economics

Branson
Macroeconomic Theory and Policy

Brock/Adams
The Structure of American Industry

Bruce
Public Finance and the American Economy

Carlton/Perloff
Modern Industrial Organization

Case/Fair/Oster
*Principles of Economics**

Caves/Frankel/Jones
World Trade and Payments: An Introduction

Chapman
Environmental Economics: Theory, Application, and Policy

Cooter/Ulen
Law & Economics

Downs
An Economic Theory of Democracy

Ehrenberg/Smith
Modern Labor Economics

Ekelund/Ressler/Tollison
*Economics**

Farnham
Economics for Managers

Folland/Goodman/Stano
The Economics of Health and Health Care

Fort
Sports Economics

Froyen
Macroeconomics

Fusfeld
The Age of the Economist

Gerber
*International Economics**

Gordon
*Macroeconomics**

Greene
Econometric Analysis

Gregory
Essentials of Economics

Gregory/Stuart
Russian and Soviet Economic Performance and Structure

Hartwick/Olewiler
The Economics of Natural Resource Use

Heilbroner/Milberg
The Making of the Economic Society

Heyne/Boettke/Prychitko
The Economic Way of Thinking

Hoffman/Averett
Women and the Economy: Family, Work, and Pay

Holt
Markets, Games and Strategic Behavior

Hubbard/O'Brien
*Economics**

*Money, Banking, and the Financial System**

Hughes/Cain
American Economic History

Husted/Melvin
International Economics

Jehle/Reny
Advanced Microeconomic Theory

Johnson-Lans
A Health Economics Primer

Keat/Young
Managerial Economics

Klein
Mathematical Methods for Economics

Krugman/Obstfeld/Melitz
*International Economics: Theory & Policy**

Laidler
The Demand for Money

Leeds/von Allmen
The Economics of Sports

Leeds/von Allmen/Schiming
*Economics**

Lipsey/Ragan/Storer
*Economics**

Lynn
Economic Development: Theory and Practice for a Divided World

Miller
*Economics Today**

Understanding Modern Economics

Miller/Benjamin
The Economics of Macro Issues

Miller/Benjamin/North
The Economics of Public Issues

Mills/Hamilton
Urban Economics

Mishkin
*The Economics of Money, Banking, and Financial Markets**

*The Economics of Money, Banking, and Financial Markets, Business School Edition**

*Macroeconomics: Policy and Practice**

Murray
Econometrics: A Modern Introduction

Nafziger
The Economics of Developing Countries

O'Sullivan/Sheffrin/Perez
*Economics: Principles, Applications and Tools**

Parkin
*Economics**

Perloff
*Microeconomics**

*Microeconomics: Theory and Applications with Calculus**

Perman/Common/McGilvray/Ma
Natural Resources and Environmental Economics

Phelps
Health Economics

Pindyck/Rubinfeld
*Microeconomics**

Riddell/Shackelford/Stamos/Schneider
Economics: A Tool for Critically Understanding Society

Ritter/Silber/Udell
*Principles of Money, Banking & Financial Markets**

Roberts
The Choice: A Fable of Free Trade and Protection

Rohlf
Introduction to Economic Reasoning

Ruffin/Gregory
Principles of Economics

Sargent
Rational Expectations and Inflation

Sawyer/Sprinkle
International Economics

Scherer
Industry Structure, Strategy, and Public Policy

Schiller
The Economics of Poverty and Discrimination

Sherman
Market Regulation

Silberberg
Principles of Microeconomics

Stock/Watson
Introduction to Econometrics

Introduction to Econometrics, Brief Edition

Studenmund
Using Econometrics: A Practical Guide

Tietenberg/Lewis
Environmental and Natural Resource Economics

Environmental Economics and Policy

Todaro/Smith
Economic Development

Waldman
Microeconomics

Waldman/Jensen
Industrial Organization: Theory and Practice

Weil
Economic Growth

Williamson
Macroeconomics

---

* denotes myeconlab titles

Log onto www.myeconlab.com to learn more.

TENTH EDITION

Principles of
Microeconomics

Karl E. Case

Wellesley College

Ray C. Fair

Yale University

Sharon M. Oster

Yale University

Prentice Hall

Boston   Columbus   Indianapolis   New York   San Francisco   Upper Saddle River
Amsterdam   Cape Town   Dubai   London   Madrid   Milan   Munich   Paris   Montreal   Toronto
Delhi   Mexico City   Sao Paulo   Sydney   Hong Kong   Seoul   Singapore   Taipei   Tokyo

Dedicated To
Professor Richard A. Musgrave
and
Professor Robert M. Solow
and
Professor Richard Caves

Editor in Chief: Donna Battista
AVP/Executive Editor: David Alexander
Editorial Project Managers: Melissa Pellerano, Lindsey Sloan
Editorial Assistant: Megan Cadigan
AVP/Executive Marketing Manager: Lori DeShazo
Marketing Assistant: Kimberly Lovato
Managing Editor: Nancy Fenton
Senior Production Project Manager: Nancy Freihofer
Senior Manufacturing Buyer: Carol Melville
Senior Art Director: Jonathan Boylan
Cover Design: Jonathan Boylan

Image Manager: Rachel Youdelman
Photo Researcher: Diahanne Lucas Dowridge
Full-Service Project Management/Composition: GEX Publishing Services
Typeface: 10/12 Minion
Text Permission Project Supervisor: Michael Joyce
Director of Media: Susan Schoenberg
Content Lead, MyEconLab: Noel Lotz
Senior Media Producer: Melissa Honig
Supplements Production Coordinator: Alison Eusden
Printer/Binder: Courier, Kendallville
Cover Printer: Lehigh Phoenix

Credits and acknowledgments borrowed from other sources and reproduced, with permission, in this textbook appear on appropriate page within text.

Library of Congress Cataloging-in-Publication Data

Case, Karl E.
  Principles of microeconomics / Karl E. Case, Ray C. Fair, Sharon M. Oster. -- 10th ed.
    p. cm.
  Includes index.
  ISBN 978-0-13-138885-7 (0-13-138885-1) 1. Microeconomics. I. Fair, Ray C. II. Oster, Sharon M. III. Title.
  HB172.C36 2012
  338.5--dc22

                    2010049924

10 9 8 7 6 5 4 3 2

Prentice Hall
is an imprint of

www.pearsonhighered.com

ISBN 13: 978-0-13-138885-7
ISBN 10: 0-13-138885-1

About the Authors

Karl E. Case is Professor of Economics Emeritus at Wellesley College where he has taught for 34 years and served several tours of duty as Department Chair. He is a Senior Fellow at the Joint Center for Housing Studies at Harvard University and a founding partner in the real estate research firm of Fiserv Case Shiller Weiss, which produces the S&P Case-Shiller Index of home prices. He serves as a member of the Index Advisory Committee of Standard and Poor's, and along with Ray Fair he serves on the Academic Advisory Board of the Federal Reserve Bank of Boston.

Before coming to Wellesley, he served as Head Tutor in Economics (director of undergraduate studies) at Harvard, where he won the Allyn Young Teaching Prize. He was Associate Editor of the *Journal of Economic Perspectives* and the *Journal of Economic Education*, and he was a member of the AEA's Committee on Economic Education.

Professor Case received his B.A. from Miami University in 1968; spent three years on active duty in the Army, and received his Ph.D. in Economics from Harvard University in 1976.

Professor Case's research has been in the areas of real estate, housing, and public finance. He is author or coauthor of five books, including *Principles of Economics, Economics and Tax Policy*, and *Property Taxation: The Need for Reform*, and he has published numerous articles in professional journals.

For the last 25 years, his research has focused on real estate markets and prices. He has authored numerous professional articles, many of which attempt to isolate the causes and consequences of boom and bust cycles and their relationship to regional and national economic performance.

Ray C. Fair is Professor of Economics at Yale University. He is a member of the Cowles Foundation at Yale and a Fellow of the Econometric Society. He received a B.A. in Economics from Fresno State College in 1964 and a Ph.D. in Economics from MIT in 1968. He taught at Princeton University from 1968 to 1974 and has been at Yale since 1974.

Professor Fair's research has primarily been in the areas of macroeconomics and econometrics, with particular emphasis on macroeconometric model building. He also has done work in the areas of finance, voting behavior, and aging in sports. His publications include *Specification, Estimation, and Analysis of Macroeconometric Models* (Harvard Press, 1984); *Testing Macroeconometric Models* (Harvard Press, 1994); and *Estimating How the Macroeconomy Works* (Harvard Press, 2004).

Professor Fair has taught introductory and intermediate macroeconomics at Yale. He has also taught graduate courses in macroeconomic theory and macroeconometrics.

Professor Fair's U.S. and multicountry models are available for use on the Internet free of charge. The address is http://fairmodel.econ.yale.edu. Many teachers have found that having students work with the U.S. model on the Internet is a useful complement to an introductory macroeconomics course.

Sharon M. Oster is the Dean of the Yale School of Management, where she is also the Frederic Wolfe Professor of Economics and Management. Professor Oster joined Case and Fair as a coauthor in the ninth edition of this book. Professor Oster has a B.A. in Economics from Hofstra University and a Ph.D. in Economics from Harvard University.

Professor Oster's research is in the area of industrial organization. She has worked on problems of diffusion of innovation in a number of different industries, on the effect of regulations on business, and on competitive strategy. She has published a number of articles in these areas and is the author of several books, including *Modern Competitive Analysis* and *The Strategic Management of Nonprofits*.

Prior to joining the School of Management at Yale, Professor Oster taught for a number of years in Yale's Department of Economics. In the department, Professor Oster taught introductory and intermediate microeconomics to undergraduates as well as several graduate courses in industrial organization. Since 1982, Professor Oster has taught primarily in the Management School, where she teaches the core microeconomics class for MBA students and a course in the area of competitive strategy. Professor Oster also consults widely for businesses and nonprofit organizations and has served on the boards of several publicly traded companies and nonprofit organizations.

Brief Contents

Contents

8 Short-Run Costs and Output Decisions 167

9 Long-Run Costs and Output Decisions 189

14 Oligopoly 293

15 Monopolistic Competition 313

16 Externalities, Public Goods, and Social Choice 329

17 Uncertainty and Asymmetric Information 353

Preface

Our goal in the 10th edition, as it was in the first edition, is to instill in students a fascination with both the functioning of the economy and the power and breadth of economics. The first line of every edition of our book has been "The study of economics should begin with a sense of wonder." We hope that readers come away from our book with a basic understanding of how market economies function, an appreciation for the things they do well, and a sense of the things they do poorly. We also hope that readers begin to learn the art and science of economic thinking and begin to look at some policy and even personal decisions in a different way.

What's New in This Edition?

- In microeconomics, there has been a good deal of exciting new work in the areas of economic development, behavioral economics, and experimental economics. This edition has added material in various places throughout the microeconomics chapters that describe this work. A particular highlight is Chapter 21, which carefully lays out the methodological approach used by researchers doing randomized experiments in the economic development area and describes some of the results of that work.

- This edition has augmented the current research focus of many of the *Economics in Practice* boxes. Historically, the boxes have focused principally on newspaper excerpts related to the subject of the chapter. Beginning last edition and pushed through more strongly this edition, we have added boxes that we hope will demonstrate more clearly the ideas that lie at the heart of economic thinking. Thus, two thirds of the boxes in the chapters relate an economic principle either to a personal observation (why does Denzel Washington get paid what he does?) or to a recent piece of economic research (new work by Emmanuel Saez on the fact that much of modern wealth comes from wages rather than interest, Carola Frydman's work on executive compensation, and Rachel Croson's work on gender and trust). When possible, we focus on work by younger scholars and on more recent research. It is our hope that new students will be inspired by the wide breadth and exciting nature of the research currently going on in economics as they read these boxes.

- Many graphs and tables have been heavily revised and updated to include the most recent data available from 2008 to as recent as the fall of 2010. The inclusion of up-to-date studies and data is essential to promoting a better understanding of recent microeconomic developments.

- A number of the chapters have been reworked to improve their readability. Chapters 9, 12, and 18 have been most affected.
- We have added many new problems in the end-of-chapter materials, aiming for more text-specific questions.

Economics is a social science. Its value is measured in part in terms of its ability to help us understand the world around us and to grapple with some of the social issues of the times: How do markets work, and why are they so powerful? Why do firms earn profits, and how are wages determined? Does it matter to consumers if there are many firms in an industry or only one? In 2006, the top 20 percent of the households in the United States earned 48 percent of all income generated. Why do we see this income inequality, and why has it been growing? There is enormous poverty in many parts of the world. Are there ways to intervene, either at the country level or the individual level? In almost any marketplace in the United States we see goods that were produced in countries from all over the world. U.S. goods also travel to far corners of the world to be sold to consumers in Europe, Asia, and Latin America. Why do we see the pattern we do? Across the globe, people are increasingly worried about global warming. What tools can an economist bring to the table in helping to solve this complex problem? These questions are microeconomic questions. To answer them, we need to learn how households and firms make decisions and how those decisions are interconnected. As we begin to see the way in which market outcomes—like prices, profits, industry growth, and the like—emerge from the interplay of decisions made by a legion of households and firms, acting largely in their own interests, we hope that the reader's sense of wonder will grow.

The Foundation

The themes of *Principles of Microeconomics*, 10th edition, are the same themes of the first nine editions. The purposes of this book are to introduce the discipline of economics and to provide a basic understanding of how economies function. This requires a blend of economic theory, institutional material, and real-world applications. We have maintained a balance between these ingredients in every chapter. The hallmark features of our book are its:

1. Three-tiered explanations of key concepts (*stories-graphs-equations*)
2. Intuitive and accessible structure
3. International coverage

Three-Tiered Explanations: Stories-Graphs-Equations

Professors who teach principles of economics are faced with a classroom of students with different abilities, backgrounds, and learning styles. For some students, analytical material is difficult no matter how it is presented; for others, graphs and equations seem to come naturally. The problem facing instructors and textbook authors is how to convey the core principles of the discipline to as many students as possible without selling the better students short. Our approach to this problem is to present most core concepts in the following three ways:

First, we present each concept in the context of a simple intuitive *story* or example in words often followed by a table. Second, we use a *graph* in most cases to illustrate the story or example. And finally, in many cases where appropriate, we use an *equation* to present the concept with a mathematical formula.

Microeconomic Structure

The organization of the microeconomic chapters continues to reflect our belief that the best way to understand how market economies operate—and the best way to understand basic economic theory—is to work through the perfectly competitive model first, including discussions of output markets (goods and services) and input markets (land, labor, and capital), and the connections between them before turning to noncompetitive market structures such as monopoly and oligopoly. When students understand how a simple, perfectly competitive system works, they can start thinking about how the pieces of the economy "fit together." We think this is a better approach to teaching economics than some of the more traditional approaches, which encourage students to think of economics as a series of disconnected alternative market models.

Learning perfect competition first also enables students to see the power of the market system. It is impossible for students to discuss the efficiency of markets as well as the problems that arise from markets until they have seen how a simple, perfectly competitive market system produces and distributes goods and services. This is our purpose in Chapter 6 through 11.

Chapter 12, "General Equilibrium and the Efficiency of Perfect Competition," is a pivotal chapter that links simple, perfectly competitive markets with a discussion of market imperfections and the role of government. Chapter 13 through 15 cover three noncompetitive market structures—monopoly, monopolistic competition, and oligopoly. Chapter 16 covers externalities, public goods, and social choice. Chapter 17, which is new to this edition, covers uncertainty and asymmetric information. Chapters 18 and 19 cover income distribution as well as taxation and government finance. The visual below (Figure II.2 from page 118), gives you an overview of our structure.

International Coverage

As in previous editions, we continue to integrate international examples and applications throughout the text. This probably goes without saying: The days in which an introductory economics text could be written with a closed economy in mind have long since gone.

▲ FIGURE II.2 **Understanding the Microeconomy and the Role of Government**

Tools for Learning

As authors and teachers, we understand the challenges of the principles of economics course. Our pedagogical features are designed to illustrate and reinforce key economic concepts through real-world examples and applications.

Economics in Practice

As described earlier, the *Economics in Practice* feature presents a real-world personal observation, current research work, or a news article that supports the key concept of the chapter and helps students think critically about how economics is a part of their daily lives. The end-of-chapter problem sets include a question specific to each *Economics in Practice* feature. Students can visit www.myeconlab.com for additional updated news articles and related exercises.

Graphs

Reading and interpreting graphs is a key part of understanding economic concepts. The Chapter 1 Appendix, "How to Read and Understand Graphs," shows readers how to interpret the 200-plus graphs featured in this book. We use red curves to illustrate the behavior of firms and blue curves to show the behavior of households. We use a different shade of red and blue to signify a shift in a curve.

Problems and Solutions

Each chapter and appendix ends with a problem set that asks students to think about and apply what they've learned in the chapter. These problems are not simple memorization questions. Rather, they ask students to perform graphical analysis or to apply economics to a real-world situation or policy decision. More challenging problems are indicated by an asterisk. Additional questions specific to the *Economics in Practice* feature have been added. Several problems have been updated. The solutions to all of the problems are available in the *Instructor's Manuals*. Instructors can provide the solutions to their students so they can check their understanding and progress.

MyEconLab 💹 myeconlab

Both the text and supplement package provide ways for instructors and students to assess their knowledge and progress through the course. MyEconLab, the new standard in personalized online learning, is a key part of Case, Fair, and Oster's integrated learning package for the 10th edition.

▶ **FIGURE 3.9 Excess Demand, or Shortage**
At a price of $1.75 per bushel, quantity demanded exceeds quantity supplied. When excess *demand* exists, there is a tendency for price to rise. When quantity demanded equals quantity supplied, excess demand is eliminated and the market is in equilibrium. Here the equilibrium price is $2.50 and the equilibrium quantity is 35,000 bushels.

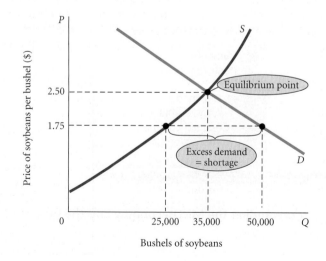

For the Instructor

MyEconLab is an online course management, testing, and tutorial resource. Instructors can choose how much or how little time to spend setting up and using MyEconLab. Each chapter contains two Sample Tests, Study Plan Exercises, and Tutorial Resources. Student use of these materials requires no initial setup by their instructor. The online Gradebook records each student's performance and time spent on the Tests and Study Plan and generates reports by student or by chapter. Instructors can assign tests, quizzes, and homework in MyEconLab using four resources:

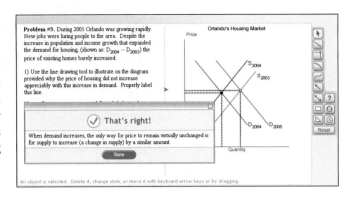

- Preloaded Sample Tests
- Problems similar to the end-of-chapter problems
- Test Item File questions
- Self-authored questions using Econ Exercise Builder

Exercises use multiple-choice, graph drawing, and free-response items, many of which are generated algorithmically so that each time a student works them, a different variation is presented. MyEconLab grades every problem, even those with graphs. When working homework exercises, students receive immediate feedback with links to additional learning tools.

Customization and Communication   MyEconLab in CourseCompass™ provides additional optional customization and communication tools. Instructors who teach distance learning courses or very large lecture sections find the CourseCompass format useful because they can upload course documents and assignments, customize the order of chapters, and use communication features such as Digital Drop Box and Discussion Board.

Experiments in MyEconLab

Experiments are a fun and engaging way to promote active learning and mastery of important economic concepts. Pearson's experiments program is flexible and easy for instructors and students to use.

- Single-player experiments allow your students to play an experiment against virtual players from anywhere at anytime with an Internet connection.
- Multiplayer experiments allow you to assign and manage a real-time experiment with your class. In both cases, pre- and post-questions for each experiment are available for assignment in MyEconLab.

For the Student

MyEconLab puts students in control of their learning through a collection of tests, practice, and study tools tied to the online interactive version of the textbook, as well as other media resources. Within MyEconLab's structured environment, students practice what they learn, test their understanding, and pursue a personalized Study Plan generated from their performance on Sample Tests and tests set by their instructors. At the core of MyEconLab are the following features:

- Sample Tests, two per chapter
- Personal Study Plan
- Tutorial Instruction
- Graphing Tool

Sample Tests   Two Sample Tests for each chapter are preloaded in MyEconLab, enabling students to practice what they have learned, test their understanding, and identify areas in which they need further work. Students can study on their own, or they can complete assignments created by their instructor.

Personal Study Plan
Based on a student's performance on tests, MyEconLab generates a personal Study Plan that shows where the student needs further study. The Study Plan consists of a series of additional practice exercises with detailed feedback and guided solutions that are keyed to other tutorial resources.

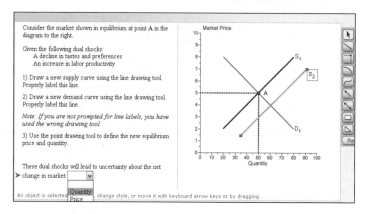

Tutorial Instruction
Launched from many of the exercises in the Study Plan, MyEconLab provides tutorial instruction in the form of step-by-step solutions and other media-based explanations.

Graphing Tool A graphing tool is integrated into the Tests and Study Plan exercises to enable students to make and manipulate graphs. This feature helps students understand how concepts, numbers, and graphs connect.

Additional MyEconLab Tools MyEconLab includes the following additional features:

1. **Economics in the News**—This feature provides weekly updates during the school year of news items with links to sources for further reading and discussion questions.

2. **eText**—While students are working in the Study Plan or completing homework assignments, one of the tutorial resources available is a direct link to the relevant page of the text so that students can review the appropriate material to help them complete the exercise.

3. **Glossary**—This searchable version of the textbook glossary provides additional examples and links to related terms.

4. **Glossary Flashcards**—Every key term is available as a flashcard, allowing students to quiz themselves on vocabulary from one or more chapters at a time.

5. **Research Navigator (CourseCompass™ version only)**—This feature offers extensive help on the research process and provides four exclusive databases of credible and reliable source material, including the *New York Times*, the *Financial Times*, and peer-reviewed journals.

MyEconLab content has been created through the efforts of:

Charles Baum, Middle Tennessee State University; Sarah Ghosh, University of Scranton; Russell Kellogg, University of Colorado–Denver; Bert G. Wheeler, Cedarville University; and Noel Lotz and Douglas A. Ruby, Pearson Education.

Resources for the Instructor

The following supplements are designed to make teaching and testing flexible and easy.

Instructor's Manuals

Prepared by Tony Lima of California State University, East Bay (Hayward, California), the *Instructor's Manual* is designed to provide the utmost teaching support for instructors. It includes the following content:

- Detailed *Chapter Outlines* include key terminology, teaching notes, and lecture suggestions.

- *Topics for Class Discussion* provide topics and real-world situations that help ensure that economic concepts resonate with students.

- Unique *Economics in Practice* features that are not in the main text provide extra real-world examples to present and discuss in class.

- *Teaching Tips* provide tips for alternative ways to cover the material and brief reminders on additional help to provide students. These tips include suggestions for exercises and experiments to complete in class.

- *Extended Applications* include exercises, activities, and experiments to help make economics relevant to students.
- *Excel Workbooks*, available for many chapters, make it easy to customize numerical examples and produce graphs.
- *Solutions* are provided for all problems in the book.

Three Test Item Files

We have tailored the Test Item Files to help instructors easily and efficiently assess student understanding of economic concepts and analyses. Test questions are annotated with the following information:

- **Difficulty:** 1 for straight recall, 2 for some analysis, 3 for complex analysis
- **Type:** Multiple-choice, true/false, short-answer, essay
- **Topic:** The term or concept the question supports
- **Skill:** Fact, definition, analytical, conceptual
- **AACSB:** See description in the next section.

The Test Item Files include questions with tables that students must analyze to solve for numerical answers. The Test Item Files also contain questions based on the graphs that appear in the book. The questions ask students to interpret the information presented in the graph. Many questions require students to sketch a graph on their own and interpret curve movements.

Microeconomics Test Item File 1, by Randy Methenitis of Richland College: Test Item File 1 (TIF1) includes over 2,700 questions. All questions are machine gradable and are either multiple-choice or true/false. This Test Item File is for use with the 10th edition of *Principles of Microeconomics* in the first year of publication. TIF1 is available in a computerized format using TestGen EQ test-generating software and is included in MyEconLab.

Microeconomics Test Item File 2, by Randy Methenitis of Richland College: This additional Test Item File contains another 2,700 machine-gradable questions based on the TIF1 but regenerated to provide instructors with fresh questions when using the book the second year. This Test Item File is available in a computerized format using TestGen EQ test-generating software.

Microeconomics Test Item File 3, by Richard Gosselin of Houston Community College: This third Test Item File includes 1,000 conceptual problems, essay questions, and short-answer questions. Application-type problems ask students to draw graphs and analyze tables. The Word files are available on the Instructor's Resource Center (www.pearsonhighered.com/educator).

The Test Item Files were checked for accuracy by the following professors:

Leon J. Battista, Bronx Community College; Margaret Brooks, Bridgewater State College; Mike Cohick, Collin County Community College; Dennis Debrecht, Carroll College; Amrik Dua, California State Polytechnic University, Pomona; Mitchell Dudley, The College of William & Mary; Ann Eike, University of Kentucky; Connel Fullencamp, Duke University; Craig Gallet, California State University, Sacramento; Michael Goode, Central Piedmont Community College; Steve Hamilton, California State Polytechnic University; James R. Irwin, Central Michigan University; Aaron Jackson, Bentley College; Rus Janis, University of Massachusetts, Amherst; Jonatan Jelen, The City College of New York; Kathy A. Kelly, University of Texas, Arlington; Kate Krause, University of New Mexico; Gary F. Langer, Roosevelt University; Leonard Lardaro, University of Rhode Island; Ross LaRoe, Denison University; Melissa Lind, University of Texas, Arlington; Solina Lindahl, California State Polytechnic University; Pete Mavrokordatos, Tarrant County College; Roberto Mazzoleni, Hofstra University; Kimberly Mencken, Baylor University; Ida Mirzaie, Ohio State University; Shahruz Mohtadi, Suffolk University; Mary Pranzo, California State University, Fresno; Ed Price, Oklahoma State University; Robert Shoffner, Central Piedmont Community College; James Swofford, University of South Alabama; Helen Tauchen, University of North Carolina, Chapel Hill; Eric Taylor, Central Piedmont Community College; Henry Terrell, University of Maryland; John Tommasi, Bentley College; Mukti Upadhyay, Eastern Illinois University; Robert Whaples, Wake Forest University; and Timothy Wunder, University of Texas, Arlington.

The Association to Advance Collegiate Schools of Business (AACSB)   The authors of the Test Item File have connected select Test Item File questions to the general knowledge and skill guidelines found in the AACSB assurance of learning standards.

What Is the AACSB?   AACSB is a not-for-profit corporation of educational institutions, corporations, and other organizations devoted to the promotion and improvement of higher education in business administration and accounting. A collegiate institution offering degrees in business administration or accounting may volunteer for AACSB accreditation review. The AACSB makes initial accreditation decisions and conducts periodic reviews to promote continuous quality improvement in management education. Pearson Education is a proud member of the AACSB and is pleased to provide advice to help you apply AACSB assurance of learning standards.

What Are AACSB Assurance of Learning Standards?   One of the criteria for AACSB accreditation is quality of the curricula. Although no specific courses are required, the AACSB expects a curriculum to include learning experiences in areas such as the following:

- Communication
- Ethical Reasoning
- Analytic Skills
- Use of Information Technology
- Multicultural and Diversity
- Reflective Thinking

Questions that test skills relevant to these guidelines are appropriately tagged. For example, a question testing the moral questions associated with externalities would receive the Ethical Reasoning tag.

How Can Instructors Use the AACSB Tags?   Tagged questions help you measure whether students are grasping the course content that aligns with the AACSB guidelines noted. In addition, the tagged questions may help instructors identify potential applications of these skills. This in turn may suggest enrichment activities or other educational experiences to help students achieve these skills.

TestGen

The computerized TestGen package allows instructors to customize, save, and generate classroom tests. The test program permits instructors to edit, add, or delete questions from the Test Item Files; create new graphics; analyze test results; and organize a database of tests and student results. This software allows for extensive flexibility and ease of use. It provides many options for organizing and displaying tests, along with search and sort features. The software and the Test Item Files can be downloaded from the Instructor's Resource Center (www.pearsonhighered.com/educator).

PowerPoint® Lecture Presentations

Three sets of PowerPoint® slides, prepared by Fernando Quijano of Dickinson State University and his assistant Shelly Tefft, are available:

- A comprehensive set of PowerPoint® slides that can be used by instructors for class presentations or by students for lecture preview or review. The presentation includes all the figures, photos, tables, key terms, and equations in the textbook. Two versions are available—the first is in step-by-step mode so that you can build graphs as you would on a blackboard, and the second is in automated mode, using a single click per slide.

- A comprehensive set of PowerPoint® slides with Classroom Response Systems (CRS) questions built in so that instructors can incorporate CRS "clickers" into their classroom lectures. For more information on Pearson's partnership with CRS, see the description below. Instructors may download these PowerPoint presentations from the Instructor's Resource Center (www.pearsonhighered.com/educator).

- Student versions of the PowerPoint presentations are available as .pdf files from the book's MyEconLab course. This version allows students to print the slides and bring them to class for note taking.

Instructor's Resource CD-ROM

The Instructor's Resource CD-ROM contains all the faculty and student resources that support this text. Instructors have the ability to access and edit the following three supplements:

- *Instructor's Manuals*
- Test Item Files
- PowerPoint® presentations

By clicking on a chapter or searching for a key word, faculty can access an interactive library of resources. Faculty can pick and choose from the various supplements and export them to their hard drives.

Classroom Response Systems

Classroom Response Systems (CRS) is an exciting new wireless polling technology that makes large and small classrooms even more interactive because it enables instructors to pose questions to their students, record results, and display the results instantly. Students can answer questions easily by using compact remote-control transmitters. Pearson has partnerships with leading providers of classroom response systems and can show you everything you need to know about setting up and using a CRS system. We provide the classroom hardware, text-specific PowerPoint® slides, software, and support; and we show you how your students can benefit. Learn more at www.pearsonhighered.com/crs.

Blackboard® and WebCT® Course Content

Pearson offers fully customizable course content for the Blackboard® and WebCT® Course Management Systems.

Resources for the Student

The following supplements are designed to help students understand and retain the key concepts of each chapter.

MyEconLab

MyEconLab allows students to practice what they learn, test their understanding, and pursue a personalized Study Plan generated from their performance on Sample Tests and tests set by their instructors. Here are MyEconLab's key features. (See page xx of this preface for more details on MyEconLab.)

- Sample Tests, two per chapter
- Personal Study Plan
- Tutorial Instruction
- Graphing Tool

Study Guide

The Study Guide, prepared by Thomas M. Beveridge of Durham Technical Community College, provides students with additional applications and exercises.

Each chapter of the Study Guide contains the following elements:

- **Point-by-Point Chapter Objectives** A list of learning goals for the chapter. Each objective is followed up with a summary of the material, learning tips for each concept, and practice questions with solutions.
- *Economics in Practice* **Questions** A question that requires students to apply concepts of the chapter to the *Economics in Practice* feature. The answer accompanies the question.

- **Practice Tests**   Approximately 20 multiple-choice questions and answers and application questions that require students to use graphic or numerical analysis to solve economic problems.
- **Solutions**   Worked-out solutions to all questions in the Study Guide.
- **Comprehensive Part Exams**   Multiple-choice and application questions to test students' overall comprehension. Solutions to all questions are also provided.

CourseSmart

CourseSmart is an exciting new *choice* for students looking to save money. As an alternative to purchasing the print textbook, students can purchase an electronic version of the same content and save up to 50 percent off the suggested list price of the print text. With a CourseSmart eTextbook, students can search the text, make notes online, print out reading assignments that incorporate lecture notes, and bookmark important passages for later review. For more information or to purchase access to the CourseSmart eTextbook, visit www.coursesmart.com.

Student Subscriptions

Staying on top of current economic issues is critical to understanding and applying microeconomic theory in and out of class. Keep students engaged by packaging, at a discount, a semester-long subscription to the *Financial Times* or Economist.com with each student text. Contact your local Pearson Prentice Hall representative for more information about benefits of these subscriptions and how to order them for your students.

Acknowledgments

We are grateful to the many people who helped us prepare the 10th edition. We thank David Alexander, our editor, and Lindsey Sloan and Melissa Pellerano, our project managers, for their help and enthusiasm.

Lori DeShazo, Executive Marketing Manager, carefully crafted the marketing message. Nancy Freihofer, production editor, and Nancy Fenton, our production managing editor, ensured that the production process of the book went smoothly. In addition, we also want to thank Marisa Taylor of GEX Publishing Services, who kept us on schedule, and Diahanne Dowridge, who researched the many photographs that appear in the book.

We want to give special thanks to Patsy Balin, Murielle Dawdy, and Tracy Waldman for their research assistance.

We also owe a debt of gratitude to those who reviewed and checked the 10th edition for accuracy. They provided us with valuable insight as we prepared this edition and its supplement package.

Reviewers of the Current Edition

Mohsen Bahmani, University of Wisconsin—Milwaukee
Klaus Becker, Texas Tech University
Jeff Bookwalter, University of Montana
Suparna Chakraborty, City University of New York—Baruch
Scott Cunningham, Baylor University
Elisabeth Curtis, Dartmouth
Erwin Ehrhardt, University of Cincinnati
Barbara Fischer, Cardinal Stritch University
Bill Galose, Drake University

Brett Katzman, Kennesaw State University
Heather Kohls, Marquette University
Daniel Lawson, Drew University
Ming Lo, St. Cloud State University
Nathan Perry, University of Utah
Joe Petry, University of Illinois-Urbana-Champaign
Chris Phillips, Somerset Community College
Jeff Phillips, Morrisville Community College
David Spigelman, University of Miami
John Watkins, Westminster
Janice Weaver, Drake University

Reviewers of Previous Editions

The following individuals were of immense help in reviewing all or part of previous editions of this book and the teaching/learning package in various stages of development:

Cynthia Abadie, Southwest Tennessee Community College
Shawn Abbott, College of the Siskiyous
Fatma Abdel-Raouf, Goldey-Beacom College
Lew Abernathy, University of North Texas

Rebecca Abraham, Nova Southeastern University

Basil Adams, Notre Dame de Namur University

Jack Adams, University of Maryland

Douglas K. Adie, Ohio University

Douglas Agbetsiafa, Indiana University, South Bend

Sheri Aggarwal, University of Virginia

Carlos Aguilar, El Paso Community College

Ehsan Ahmed, James Madison University

Ferhat Akbas, Texas A&M University

Sam Alapati, Rutgers University

Terence Alexander, Iowa State University

John W. Allen, Texas A&M University

Polly Allen, University of Connecticut

Stuart Allen, University of North Carolina at Greensboro

Hassan Aly, Ohio State University

Alex Anas, University at Buffalo, The State University of New York

David Anderson, Centre College

Joan Anderssen, Arapahoe Community College

Jim Angresano, Hampton-Sydney College

Kenneth S. Arakelian, University of Rhode Island

Harvey Arnold, Indian River Community College

Nick Apergis, Fordham University

Bevin Ashenmiller, Occidental College

Richard Ashley, Virginia Technical University

Birjees Ashraf, Houston Community College Southwest

Kidane Asmeron, Pennsylvania State University

Musa Ayar, University of Texas, Austin

James Aylesworth, Lakeland Community College

Moshen Bahmani, University of Wisconsin-Milwaukee

Asatar Bair, City College of San Francisco

Diana Bajrami, College of Alameda

Mohammad Bajwa, Northampton Community College

Rita Balaban, University of North Carolina, Chapel Hill

A. Paul Ballantyne, University of Colorado, Colorado Springs

Richard J. Ballman, Jr., Augustana College

King Banaian, St. Cloud State University

Nick Barcia, Baruch College

Henry Barker, Tiffin University

Robin Bartlett, Denison University

Laurie Bates, Bryant University

Kari Battaglia, University of North Texas

Leon Battista, Bronx Community College

Amanda Bayer, Swarthmore College

Klaus Becker, Texas Tech University

Richard Beil, Auburn University

Clive Belfield, Queens College

Willie J. Belton, Jr., Georgia Institute of Technology

Daniel K. Benjamin, Clemson University

Charles A. Bennett, Gannon University

Emil Berendt, Siena Heights University

Daniel Berkowitz, University of Pittsburgh

Kurt Beron, University of Texas, Dallas

Derek Berry, Calhoun Community College

Tibor Besedes, Georgia Institute of Technology

Thomas Beveridge, Durham Technical Community College

Anoop Bhargava, Finger Lakes CC

Eugenie Bietry, Pace University

Kelly Blanchard, Purdue University

Mark Bock, Loyola College in Maryland

Howard Bodenhorn, Lafayette College

Bruce Bolnick, Northeastern University

Frank Bonello, University of Notre Dame

Jeffrey Bookwalter, University of Montana

Antonio Bos, Tusculum College

Maristella Botticini, Boston University

G. E. Breger, University of South Carolina

Dennis Brennan, William Rainey Harper Junior College

Anne E. Bresnock, California State Polytechnic University, Pomona, and the University of California, Los Angeles

Barry Brown, Murray State University

Bruce Brown, California State Polytechnic University, Pomona

Jennifer Brown, Eastern Connecticut State University

David Brownstone, University of California, Irvine

Don Brunner, Spokane Falls Community College

Jeff Bruns, Bacone College

David Bunting, Eastern Washington University

Barbara Burnell, College of Wooster

Alison Butler, Willamette University

Charles Callahan, III, State University of New York at Brockport

Fred Campano, Fordham University

Douglas Campbell, University of Memphis

Beth Cantrell, Central Baptist College

Kevin Carlson, University of Massachusetts, Boston

Leonard Carlson, Emory University

Arthur Schiller Casimir, Western New England College

Lindsay Caulkins, John Carroll University

Atreya Chakraborty, Boston College

Suparna Chakraborty, Baruch College of the City University of New York

Winston W. Chang, University at Buffalo, The State University of New York

Janie Chermak, University of New Mexico

David Ching, University of Hawaii – Honolulu

Harold Christensen, Centenary College

Daniel Christiansen, Albion College

Susan Christoffersen, Philadelphia University

Samuel Kim-Liang Chuah, Walla Walla College

Dmitriy Chulkov, Indiana University, Kokomo

David Colander, Middlebury College

Daniel Condon, University of Illinois at Chicago; Moraine Valley Community College

Karen Conway, University of New Hampshire

Cesar Corredor, Texas A&M University

David Cowen, University of Texas, Austin

Tyler Cowen, George Mason University

Amy Cramer, Pima Community College, West Campus

Peggy Crane, Southwestern College

Barbara Craig, Oberlin College

Jerry Crawford, Arkansas State University

James Cunningham, Chapman University

James D'Angelo, University of Cincinnati

David Dahl, University of St. Thomas

Sheryll Dahlke, Lees-McRae College

Joseph Dahms, Hood College

Sonia Dalmia, Grand Valley State University

Rosa Lea Danielson, College of DuPage

David Danning, University of Massachusetts, Boston

Minh Quang Dao, Eastern Illinois University

Amlan Datta, Cisco Junior College

David Davenport, McLennan Community College

Stephen Davis, Southwest Minnesota State University

Dale DeBoer, Colorado University, Colorado Springs

Dennis Debrecht, Carroll College

Juan J. DelaCruz, Fashion Institute of Technology and Lehman College

Greg Delemeester, Marietta College

Yanan Di, State University of New York, Stony Brook

Amy Diduch, Mary Baldwin College

Timothy Diette, Washington and Lee University

Vernon J. Dixon, Haverford College

Alan Dobrowolksi, Manchester Community College

Eric Dodge, Hanover College

Carol Dole, Jacksonville University

Michael Donihue, Colby College

Shahpour Dowlatshahi, Fayetteville Technical Community College

Joanne M. Doyle, James Madison University

Robert Driskill, Ohio State University

James Dulgeroff, San Bernardino Valley College

Kevin Duncan, Colorado State University

Yvonne Durham, Western Washington University

Debra Sabatini Dwyer, State University of New York, Stony Brook

Gary Dymski, University of Southern California

David Eaton, Murray State University

Jay Egger, Towson State University

Ann Eike, University of Kentucky

Eugene Elander, Plymouth State University

Ronald D. Elkins, Central Washington University

Tisha Emerson, Baylor University

Michael Enz, Western New England College

Erwin Erhardt III, University of Cincinnati

William Even, Miami University

Dr. Ali Faegh, Houston Community College, Northwest

Noel J. J. Farley, Bryn Mawr College

Mosin Farminesh, Temple University

Dan Feaster, Miami University of Ohio

Susan Feiner, Virginia Commonwealth University

Getachew Felleke, Albright College

Lois Fenske, South Puget Sound Community College

William Field, DePauw University

Deborah Figart, Richard Stockton College

Mary Flannery, Santa Clara University

Bill Foeller, State University of New York, Fredonia

Fred Foldvary, Santa Clara University

Roger Nils Folsom, San Jose State University

Mathew Forstater, University of Missouri-Kansas City

Kevin Foster, The City College of New York

Richard Fowles, University of Utah

Sean Fraley, College of Mount Saint Joseph

Johanna Francis, Fordham University

Roger Frantz, San Diego State University

Mark Frascatore, Clarkson University

Amanda Freeman, Kansas State University

Morris Frommer, Owens Community College

Brandon Fuller, University of Montana

David Fuller, University of Iowa

Mark Funk, University of Arkansas, Little Rock

Alejandro Gallegos, Winona State University

Craig Gallet, California State University, Sacramento

N. Galloro, Chabot College

Bill Ganley, Buffalo State College

Martin A. Garrett, Jr., College of William and Mary

Tom Gausman, Northern Illinois University

Shirley J. Gedeon, University of Vermont

Jeff Gerlach, Sungkyunkwan Graduate School of Business

Lisa Giddings, University of Wisconsin, La Crosse

Gary Gigliotti, Rutgers University

Lynn Gillette, Spalding University

Donna Ginther, University of Kansas

James N. Giordano, Villanova University

Amy Glass, Texas A&M University

Sarah L. Glavin, Boston College

Roy Gobin, Loyola University, Chicago

Bill Godair, Landmark College

Bill Goffe, University of Mississippi

Devra Golbe, Hunter College

Roger Goldberg, Ohio Northern University

Joshua Goodman, New York University

Ophelia Goma, DePauw University

John Gonzales, University of San Francisco

David Gordon, Illinois Valley College

Richard Gosselin, Houston Community College

Eugene Gotwalt, Sweet Briar College

John W. Graham, Rutgers University

Douglas Greenley, Morehead State University

Thomas A. Gresik, University of Notre Dame

Lisa M. Grobar, California State University, Long Beach

Wayne A. Grove, Le Moyne College

Daryl Gruver, Mount Vernon Nazarene University

Osman Gulseven, North Carolina State University

Mike Gumpper, Millersville University

Benjamin Gutierrez, Indiana University, Bloomington

A. R. Gutowsky, California State University, Sacramento

Anthony Gyapong, Penn State University, Abington

David R. Hakes, University of Missouri, St. Louis

Bradley Hansen, University of Mary Washington

Stephen Happel, Arizona State University

Mehdi Haririan, Bloomsburg University of Pennsylvania

David Harris, Benedictine College

David Harris, San Diego State University

James Hartley, Mount Holyoke College

Bruce Hartman, California Maritime Academy of California State University

Mitchell Harwitz, University at Buffalo, The State University of New York

Dewey Heinsma, Mt. San Jacinto College

Sara Helms, University of Alabama, Birmingham

Brian Hill, Salisbury University

David Hoaas, Centenary College

Arleen Hoag, Owens Community College

Carol Hogan, University of Michigan, Dearborn

Harry Holzer, Michigan State University

Ward Hooker, Orangeburg-Calhoun Technical College

Bobbie Horn, University of Tulsa

John Horowitz, Ball State University

Daniel Horton, Cleveland State University

Ying Huang, Manhattan College

Janet Hunt, University of Georgia

E. Bruce Hutchinson, University of Tennessee, Chattanooga

Creed Hyatt, Lehigh Carbon Community College

Ana Ichim, Louisiana State University

Aaron Iffland, Rocky Mountain College

Fred Inaba, Washington State University

Richard Inman, Boston College

Aaron Jackson, Bentley College

Brian Jacobsen, Wisconsin Lutheran College

Russell A. Janis, University of Massachusetts, Amherst

Jonatan Jelen, The City College of New York

Eric Jensen, The College of William & Mary

Aaron Johnson, Missouri State University

Donn Johnson, Quinnipiac University

Paul Johnson, University of Alaska Anchorage

Shirley Johnson, Vassar College

Farhoud Kafi, Babson College

R. Kallen, Roosevelt University

Arthur E. Kartman, San Diego State University

Hirshel Kasper, Oberlin College

Brett Katzman, Kennesaw State University

Bruce Kaufman, Georgia State University

Dennis Kaufman, University of Wisconsin, Parkside

Pavel Kapinos, Carleton College

Russell Kashian, University of Wisconsin, Whitewater

Amoz Kats, Virginia Technical University

David Kaun, University of California, Santa Cruz

Brett Katzman, Kennesaw State University

Fred Keast, Portland State University

Stephanie Kelton, University of Missouri, Kansas City

Deborah Kelly, Palomar College

Erasmus Kersting, Texas A&M University

Randall Kesselring, Arkansas State University

Alan Kessler, Providence College

Dominique Khactu, The University of North Dakota

Gary Kikuchi, University of Hawaii, Manoa

Hwagyun Kim, State University of New York, Buffalo

Keon-Ho Kim, University of Utah

Kil-Joong Kim, Austin Peay State University

Sang W. Kim, Hood College

Phillip King, San Francisco State University

Barbara Kneeshaw, Wayne County Community College

Inderjit Kohli, Santa Clara University

Heather Kohls, Marquette University

Janet Koscianski, Shippensburg University

Vani Kotcherlakota, University of Nebraska, Kearney

Barry Kotlove, Edmonds Community College

Kate Krause, University of New Mexico

David Kraybill, University of Georgia

David Kroeker, Tabor College

Stephan Kroll, California State University, Sacramento

Joseph Kubec, Park University

Jacob Kurien, Helzberg School of Management

Rosung Kwak, University of Texas at Austin

Sally Kwak, University of Hawaii-Manoa

Steven Kyle, Cornell University

Anil K. Lal, Pittsburg State University

Melissa Lam, Wellesley College

David Lang, California State University, Sacramento

Gary Langer, Roosevelt University

Anthony Laramie, Merrimack College

Leonard Lardaro, University of Rhode Island

Ross LaRoe, Denison University

Michael Lawlor, Wake Forest University

Pareena Lawrence, University of Minnesota, Morris

Daniel Lawson, Drew University

Mary Rose Leacy, Wagner College

Margaret D. Ledyard, University of Texas, Austin

Jim Lee, Fort Hays State University

Judy Lee, Leeward Community College

Sang H. Lee, Southeastern Louisiana University

Don Leet, California State University, Fresno

Robert J. Lemke, Lake Forest College

Gary Lemon, DePauw University

Alan Leonard, Wilson Technical Community College

Mary Lesser, Iona College

Ding Li, Northern State University

Zhe Li, Stony Brook University

Larry Lichtenstein, Canisius College

Benjamin Liebman, Saint Joseph's University

Jesse Liebman, Kennesaw State University

George Lieu, Tuskegee University

Stephen E. Lile, Western Kentucky University

Jane Lillydahl, University of Colorado at Boulder

Tony Lima, California State University, East Bay, Hayward, CA

Melissa Lind, University of Texas, Arlington

Al Link, University of North Carolina Greensboro

Charles R. Link, University of Delaware

Robert Litro, U.S. Air Force Academy

Samuel Liu, West Valley College

Jeffrey Livingston, Bentley College

Ming Chien Lo, St. Cloud State University

Burl F. Long, University of Florida

Alina Luca, Drexel University

Adrienne Lucas, Wellesley College

Nancy Lutz, Virginia Technical University, Virginia Tech

Kristina Lybecker, Colorado College

Gerald Lynch, Purdue University

Karla Lynch, University of North Texas

Ann E. Lyon, University of Alaska Anchorage

Bruce Madariaga, Montgomery College

Michael Magura, University of Toledo

Marvin S. Margolis, Millersville University of Pennsylvania

Tim Mason, Eastern Illinois University

Don Mathews, Coastal Georgia Community College

Don Maxwell, Central State University

Nan Maxwell, California State University at Hayward

Roberto Mazzoleni, Hofstra University

Cynthia S. McCarty, Jacksonville State University

J. Harold McClure, Jr., Villanova University

Patrick McEwan, Wellesley College

Rick McIntyre, University of Rhode Island

James J. McLain, University of New Orleans

Dawn McLaren, Mesa Community College

B. Starr McMullen, Oregon State University

K. Mehtaboin, College of St. Rose

Randy Methenitis, Richland College

Martin Melkonian, Hofstra University

Alice Melkumian, Western Illinois University

William Mertens, University of Colorado, Boulder

Randy Methenitis, Richland College

Art Meyer, Lincoln Land Community College

Carrie Meyer, George Mason University

Meghan Millea, Mississippi State University

Jenny Minier, University of Miami

Ida Mirzaie, The Ohio State University

David Mitchell, Missouri State University

Bijan Moeinian, Osceola Campus

Robert Mohr, University of New Hampshire

Shahruz Mohtadi, Suffolk University

Amyaz Moledina, College of Wooster

Gary Mongiovi, St. John's University

Terry D. Monson, Michigan Technological University

Barbara A. Moore, University of Central Florida

Joe L. Moore, Arkansas Technical University

Myra Moore, University of Georgia

Robert Moore, Occidental College

Norma C. Morgan, Curry College

W. Douglas Morgan, University of California, Santa Barbara

David Murphy, Boston College

John Murphy, North Shore Community College, Massachusetts

Ellen Mutari, Richard Stockton College of New Jersey

Steven C. Myers, University of Akron

Veena Nayak, University at Buffalo, The State University of New York

Ron Necoechea, Robert Wesleyan College

Doug Nelson, Spokane Community College

Randy Nelson, Colby College

David Nickerson, University of British Columbia

Sung No, Southern University and A&M College

Rachel Nugent, Pacific Lutheran University

Akorlie A. Nyatepe-Coo, University of Wisconsin LaCrosse

Norman P. Obst, Michigan State University

William C. O'Connor, Western Montana College

Constantin Ogloblin, Georgia Southern University

David O'Hara, Metropolitan State University

Albert Okunade, University of Memphis

Ronald Olive, University of Massachusetts, Lowell

Martha L. Olney, University of California, Berkeley

Kent Olson, Oklahoma State University

Jaime Ortiz, Florida Atlantic University

Theresa Osborne, Hunter College

Donald J. Oswald, California State University, Bakersfield

Mete Ozcan, Brooklyn College

Alexandre Padilla, Metropolitan State College of Denver

Aaron Pankratz, Fresno City College

Niki Papadopoulou, University of Cyprus

Walter Park, American University

Carl Parker, Fort Hays State University

Spiro Patton, Rasmussen College

Andrew Pearlman, Bard College

Richard Peck, University of Illinois at Chicago

Don Peppard, Connecticut College

Elizabeth Perry, Randolph College

Nathan Perry, University of Utah

Joseph A. Petry, University of Illinois

Mary Ann Pevas, Winona State University

Chris Phillips, Somerset Community College

Frankie Pircher, University of Missouri, Kansas City

Tony Pizelo, Spokane Community College

Dennis Placone, Clemson University

Mike Pogodzinski, San Jose State University

Linnea Polgreen, University of Iowa

Elizabeth Porter, University of North Florida

Bob Potter, University of Central Florida

Ed Price, Oklahoma State University

Abe Qastin, Lakeland College

Kevin Quinn, St. Norbert College

Ramkishen S. Rajan, George Mason University

James Rakowski, University of Notre Dame

Amy Ramirez-Gay, Eastern Michigan University

Paul Rappoport, Temple University

Artatrana Ratha, St. Cloud State University

Michael Rendich, Westchester Community College

Lynn Rittenoure, University of Tulsa

Brian Roberson, Miami University

Michael Robinson, Mount Holyoke College

Juliette Roddy, University of Michigan, Dearborn

Michael Rolleigh, University of Minnesota

Belinda Roman, Palo Alto College

S. Scanlon Romer, Delta College

Brian Rosario, University of California, Davis

Paul Roscelli, Canada College

David C. Rose, University of Missouri-St. Louis

Greg Rose, Sacramento City College

Richard Rosenberg, Pennsylvania State University

Robert Rosenman, Washington State University

Robert Rosenthal, Stonehill College

Howard Ross, Baruch College

Paul Rothstein, Washington University

Charles Roussel, Louisiana State University

Jeff Rubin, Rutgers University

Mark Rush, University of Florida

Dereka Rushbrook, Ripon College

Jerard Russo, University of Hawaii

Luz A. Saavedra, University of St. Thomas

William Samuelson, Boston University School of Management

Allen Sanderson, University of Chicago

David Saner, Springfield College – Benedictine University

Ahmad Saranjam, Bridgewater State College

David L. Schaffer, Haverford College

Eric Schansberg, Indiana University – Southeast

Robert Schenk, Saint Joseph's College

Ramon Schreffler, Houston Community College System (retired)

Adina Schwartz, Lakeland College

Jerry Schwartz, Broward Community College

Amy Scott, DeSales University

Gary Sellers, University of Akron

Atindra Sen, Miami University

Chad Settle, University of Tulsa

Jean Shackleford, Bucknell University

Ronald Shadbegian, University of Massachusetts, Dartmouth

Linda Shaffer, California State University, Fresno

Dennis Shannon, Southwestern Illinois College

Stephen L. Shapiro, University of North Florida

Paul Shea, University of Oregon

Geoff Shepherd, University of Massachusetts Amherst

Bih-Hay Sheu, University of Texas at Austin

David Shideler, Murray State University

Alden Shiers, California Polytechnic State University

Gerald Shilling, Eastfield College

Dongsoo Shin, Santa Clara University

Elias Shukralla, St. Louis Community College, Meramec

Anne Shugars, Harford Community College

Richard Sicotte, University of Vermont

William Simeone, Providence College

Scott Simkins, North Carolina Agricultural and Technical State University

Larry Singell, University of Oregon

Priyanka Singh, University of Texas, Dallas

Sue Skeath, Wellesley College

Edward Skelton, Southern Methodist University

Ken Slaysman, York College

John Smith, New York University

Paula Smith, Central State University, Oklahoma

Donald Snyder, Utah State University

Marcia Snyder, College of Charleston

David Sobiechowski, Wayne State University

John Solow, University of Iowa

Angela Sparkman, Itawamba Community College

Martin Spechler, Indiana University

Arun Srinivasa, Indiana University, Southeast

David J. St. Clair, California State University at Hayward

Sarah Stafford, College of William & Mary

Richard Stahl, Louisiana State University

Rebecca Stein, University of Pennsylvania

Mary Stevenson, University of Massachusetts, Boston

Susan Stojanovic, Washington University, St. Louis

Courtenay Stone, Ball State University

Ernst W. Stromsdorfer, Washington State University

Edward Stuart, Northeastern Illinois University

Chris Stufflebean, Southwestern Oklahoma State University

Chuck Stull, Kalamazoo College

Della Sue, Marist College

Abdulhamid Sukar, Cameron University

Christopher Surfield, Saginaw Valley State University

Rodney B. Swanson, University of California, Los Angeles

James Swofford, University of Alabama

Bernica Tackett, Pulaski Technical College

Michael Taussig, Rutgers University

Samia Tavares, Rochester Institute of Technology

Timothy Taylor, Stanford University

William Taylor, New Mexico Highlands University

Sister Beth Anne Tercek, SND, Notre Dame College of Ohio

Henry Terrell, University of Maryland

Jennifer Thacher, University of New Mexico

Donna Thompson, Brookdale Community College

Robert Tokle, Idaho State University

David Tolman, Boise State University

Susanne Toney, Hampton University

Karen M. Travis, Pacific Lutheran University

Jack Trierweler, Northern State University

Brian M. Trinque, University of Texas at Austin

HuiKuan Tseng, University of North Carolina at Charlotte

Boone Turchi, University of North Carolina, Chapel Hill

Kristin Van Gaasbeck, California State University, Sacramento

Amy Vander Laan, Hastings College

Ann Velenchik, Wellesley College

Lawrence Waldman, University of New Mexico

Chris Waller, Indiana University, Bloomington

William Walsh, University of St. Thomas

Chunbei Wang, University of St. Thomas

Bruce Webb, Gordon College

Ross Weiner, The City College of New York

Elaine Wendt, Milwaukee Area Technical College

Walter Wessels, North Carolina State University

Christopher Westley, Jacksonville State University

Joan Whalen-Ayyappan, DeVry Institute of Technology

Robert Whaples, Wake Forest University

Leonard A. White, University of Arkansas

Alex Wilson, Rhode Island College

Wayne Winegarden, Marymount University

Jennifer Wissink, Cornell University

Arthur Woolf, University of Vermont

Paula Worthington, Northwestern University

Bill Yang, Georgia Southern University

Ben Young, University of Missouri, Kansas City

Darrel Young, University of Texas

Michael Youngblood, Rock Valley College

Jay Zagorsky, Boston University

Alexander Zampieron, Bentley College

Sourushe Zandvakili, University of Cincinnati

Walter J. Zeiler, University of Michigan

Abera Zeyege, Ball State University

James Ziliak, Indiana University, Bloomington

Jason Zimmerman, South Dakota State University

We welcome comments about the 10th edition. Please write to us care of David Alexander, Executive Editor, Pearson Economics, 75 Arlington Suite 300, Boston, MA 02116.

Karl E. Case

Ray C. Fair

Sharon M. Oster

Save a Tree!

Many of the components of the teaching and learning package are available online. Online supplements conserve paper and allow you to select and print only the material you plan to use. For more information, please contact your Pearson Prentice Hall sales representative.

The Scope and Method of Economics

1

The study of economics should begin with a sense of wonder. Pause for a moment and consider a typical day in your life. It might start with a bagel made in a local bakery with flour produced in Minnesota from wheat grown in Kansas and bacon from pigs raised in Ohio packaged in plastic made in New Jersey. You spill coffee from Colombia on your shirt made in Texas from textiles shipped from South Carolina.

After class you drive with a friend on an interstate highway that is part of a system that took 20 years and billions of dollars to build. You stop for gasoline refined in Louisiana from Saudi Arabian crude oil brought to the United States on a supertanker that took 3 years to build at a shipyard in Maine.

Later you log onto the Web with a laptop assembled in Indonesia from parts made in China and Skype with your brother in Mexico City, and you call a buddy on your iPhone with parts from a dozen countries. You use or consume tens of thousands of things, both tangible and intangible, every day: buildings, music, staples, paper, toothpaste, tweezers, pizza, soap, digital watches, fire protection, banks, electricity, eggs, insurance, football fields, buses, rugs, subways, health services, sidewalks, and so forth. Somebody made all these things. Somebody organized men and women and materials to produce and distribute them. Thousands of decisions went into their completion. Somehow they got to you.

In the United States, over 139 million people—almost half the total population—work at hundreds of thousands of different jobs producing over $14 trillion worth of goods and services every year. Some cannot find work; some choose not to work. Some are rich; others are poor.

The United States imports over $200 billion worth of automobiles and parts and about $300 billion worth of petroleum and petroleum products each year; it exports around $62 billion worth of agricultural products, including food. Every month the United States buys around $25 billion worth of goods and services from China, while China buys about $5 billion worth from the United States. High-rise office buildings go up in central cities. Condominiums and homes are built in the suburbs. In other places, homes are abandoned and boarded up.

Some countries are wealthy. Others are impoverished. Some are growing. Some are not. Some businesses are doing well. Others are going bankrupt. As the 10th edition of our text goes to press, the world is beginning to recover from a period during which many people felt the pain of a major economic downturn. In the United States at the beginning of 2010 more than 15 million people who wanted to work could not find a job. Millions around the world found themselves with falling incomes and wealth.

At any moment in time, every society faces constraints imposed by nature and by previous generations. Some societies are handsomely endowed by nature with fertile land, water, sunshine, and natural resources. Others have deserts and few mineral resources. Some societies receive much from previous generations—art, music, technical knowledge, beautiful buildings, and productive factories. Others are left with overgrazed, eroded land, cities leveled by war, or polluted natural environments. *All* societies face limits.

economics The study of how individuals and societies choose to use the scarce resources that nature and previous generations have provided.

> **Economics** is the study of how individuals and societies choose to use the scarce resources that nature and previous generations have provided. The key word in this definition is *choose*. Economics is a behavioral, or social, science. In large measure, it is the study of how people make choices. The choices that people make, when added up, translate into societal choices.

The purpose of this chapter and the next is to elaborate on this definition and to introduce the subject matter of economics. What is produced? How is it produced? Who gets it? Why? Is the result good or bad? Can it be improved?

Why Study Economics?

There are four main reasons to study economics: to learn a way of thinking, to understand society, to understand global affairs, and to be an informed citizen.

To Learn a Way of Thinking

Probably the most important reason for studying economics is to learn a way of thinking. Economics has three fundamental concepts that, once absorbed, can change the way you look at everyday choices: opportunity cost, marginalism, and the working of efficient markets.

Opportunity Cost What happens in an economy is the outcome of thousands of individual decisions. People must decide how to divide their incomes among all the goods and services available in the marketplace. They must decide whether to work, whether to go to school, and how much to save. Businesses must decide what to produce, how much to produce, how much to charge, and where to locate. It is not surprising that economic analysis focuses on the process of decision making.

Nearly all decisions involve trade-offs. A key concept that recurs in analyzing the decision-making process is the notion of *opportunity cost*. The full "cost" of making a specific choice includes what we give up by not making the alternative choice. The best alternative that we forgo, or give up, when we make a choice or a decision is called the **opportunity cost** of that decision.

opportunity cost The best alternative that we forgo, or give up, when we make a choice or a decision.

When asked how much a movie costs, most people cite the ticket price. For an economist, this is only part of the answer: to see a movie takes not only a ticket but also time. The opportunity cost of going to a movie is the value of the other things you could have done with the same money and time. If you decide to take time off from work, the opportunity cost of your leisure is the pay that you would have earned had you worked. Part of the cost of a college education is the income you could have earned by working full-time instead of going to school. If a firm purchases a new piece of equipment for $3,000, it does so because it expects that equipment to generate more profit. There is an opportunity cost, however, because that $3,000 could have been deposited in an interest-earning account. To a society, the opportunity cost of using resources to launch astronauts on a space shuttle is the value of the private/civilian or other government goods that could have been produced with the same resources.

scarce Limited.

Opportunity costs arise because resources are scarce. **Scarce** simply means limited. Consider one of our most important resources—time. There are only 24 hours in a day, and we must live our lives under this constraint. A farmer in rural Brazil must decide whether it is better to continue to farm or to go to the city and look for a job. A hockey player at the

University of Vermont must decide whether to play on the varsity team or spend more time studying.

Marginalism   A second key concept used in analyzing choices is the notion of **marginalism**. In weighing the costs and benefits of a decision, it is important to weigh only the costs and benefits that arise from the decision. Suppose, for example, that you live in New Orleans and that you are weighing the costs and benefits of visiting your mother in Iowa. If business required that you travel to Kansas City, the cost of visiting Mom would be only the additional, or *marginal*, time and money cost of getting to Iowa from Kansas City.

> **marginalism** The process of analyzing the additional or incremental costs or benefits arising from a choice or decision.

Consider the video game business. It has been estimated that to create and produce a complex multiplayer role-playing game like World of Warcraft (WOW) costs as much as $500 million. Once the game has been developed, however, the cost of selling and delivering it to another player is close to zero. The original investment (by Activision) made to create WOW is considered a **sunk cost**. Once the game has been developed, Activision cannot avoid these costs because they have already been incurred. Activision's business decisions about pricing and distributing WOW depend not on the sunk costs of production, but on the incremental or *marginal* costs of production. For Activision, those costs are close to zero.

> **sunk costs** Costs that cannot be avoided because they have already been incurred.

There are numerous examples in which the concept of marginal cost is useful. For an airplane that is about to take off with empty seats, the marginal cost of an extra passenger is essentially zero; the total cost of the trip is roughly unchanged by the addition of an extra passenger. Thus, setting aside a few seats to be sold at big discounts through www.priceline.com or other Web sites can be profitable even if the fare for those seats is far below the average cost per seat of making the trip. As long as the airline succeeds in filling seats that would otherwise have been empty, doing so is profitable.

Efficient Markets—No Free Lunch   Suppose you are ready to check out of a busy grocery store on the day before a storm and seven checkout registers are open with several people in each line. Which line should you choose? Usually, the waiting time is approximately the same no matter which register you choose (assuming you have more than 12 items). If one line is much shorter than the others, people will quickly move into it until the lines are equalized again.

As you will see later, the term *profit* in economics has a very precise meaning. Economists, however, often loosely refer to "good deals" or risk-free ventures as *profit opportunities*. Using the term loosely, a profit opportunity exists at the checkout lines when one line is shorter than the others. In general, such profit opportunities are rare. At any time, many people are searching for them; as a consequence, few exist. Markets like this, where any profit opportunities are eliminated almost instantaneously, are said to be **efficient markets**. (We discuss *markets*, the institutions through which buyers and sellers interact and engage in exchange, in detail in Chapter 2.)

> **efficient market** A market in which profit opportunities are eliminated almost instantaneously.

The common way of expressing the efficient markets concept is "there's no such thing as a free lunch." How should you react when a stockbroker calls with a hot tip on the stock market? With skepticism. Thousands of individuals each day are looking for hot tips in the market. If a particular tip about a stock is valid, there will be an immediate rush to buy the stock, which will quickly drive up its price. This view that very few profit opportunities exist can, of course, be carried too far. There is a story about two people walking along, one an economist and one not. The non-economist sees a $20 bill on the sidewalk and says, "There's a $20 bill on the sidewalk." The economist replies, "That is not possible. If there were, somebody would already have picked it up."

There are clearly times when profit opportunities exist. Someone has to be first to get the news, and some people have quicker insights than others. Nevertheless, news travels fast, and there are thousands of people with quick insights. The general view that large profit opportunities are rare is close to the mark.

> The study of economics teaches us a way of thinking and helps us make decisions.

To Understand Society

Another reason for studying economics is to understand society better. Past and present economic decisions have an enormous influence on the character of life in a society. The current state of the physical environment, the level of material well-being, and the nature and number of jobs are all products of the economic system.

To get a sense of the ways in which economic decisions have shaped our environment, imagine looking out a top-floor window of an office tower in any large city. The workday is about to begin. All around you are other tall glass and steel buildings full of workers. In the distance, you see the smoke of factories. Looking down, you see thousands of commuters pouring off trains and buses and cars backed up on freeway exit ramps. You see trucks carrying goods from one place to another. You also see the face of urban poverty: Just beyond the freeway is a large public housing project and, beyond that, burned-out and boarded-up buildings.

What you see before you is the product of millions of economic decisions made over hundreds of years. People at some point decided to spend time and money building those buildings and factories. Somebody cleared the land, laid the tracks, built the roads, and produced the cars and buses.

Industrial Revolution The period in England during the late eighteenth and early nineteenth centuries in which new manufacturing technologies and improved transportation gave rise to the modern factory system and a massive movement of the population from the countryside to the cities.

Economic decisions not only have shaped the physical environment but also have determined the character of society. At no time has the impact of economic change on a society been more evident than in England during the late eighteenth and early nineteenth centuries, a period that we now call the **Industrial Revolution**. Increases in the productivity of agriculture, new manufacturing technologies, and development of more efficient forms of transportation led to a massive movement of the British population from the countryside to the city. At the beginning of the eighteenth century, approximately 2 out of 3 people in Great Britain worked in agriculture. By 1812, only 1 in 3 remained in agriculture; by 1900, the figure was fewer than 1 in 10. People jammed into overcrowded cities and worked long hours in factories. England had changed completely in two centuries—a period that in the run of history was nothing more than the blink of an eye.

It is not surprising that the discipline of economics began to take shape during this period. Social critics and philosophers looked around and knew that their philosophies must expand to accommodate the changes. Adam Smith's *Wealth of Nations* appeared in 1776. It was followed by the writings of David Ricardo, Karl Marx, Thomas Malthus, and others. Each tried to make sense out of what was happening. Who was building the factories? Why? What determined the level of wages paid to workers or the price of food? What would happen in the future, and what *should* happen? The people who asked these questions were the first economists.

Similar changes continue to affect the character of life in more recent times. In fact, many argue that the late 1990s marked the beginning of a new Industrial Revolution. As we turned the corner into the new millennium, the "e" revolution was clearly having an impact on virtually every aspect of our lives: the way we buy and sell products, the way we get news, the way we plan vacations, the way we communicate with each other, the way we teach and take classes, and on and on. These changes have had and will clearly continue to have profound impacts on societies across the globe, from Beijing to Calcutta to New York.

These changes have been driven by economics. Although the government was involved in the early years of the World Wide Web, private firms that exist to make a profit (such as Facebook, YouTube, Yahoo!, Microsoft, Google, Monster.com, Amazon.com, and E-Trade) created almost all the new innovations and products. How does one make sense of all this? What will the effects of these innovations be on the number of jobs, the character of those jobs, the family incomes, the structure of our cities, and the political process both in the United States and in other countries?

During the last days of August 2005, Hurricane Katrina slammed into the coasts of Louisiana and Mississippi, causing widespread devastation, killing thousands, and leaving hundreds of thousands homeless. The economic impact of this catastrophic storm was huge. Thinking about various markets involved helps frame the problem.

For example, the labor market was massively affected. By some estimates, over 400,000 jobs were lost as the storm hit. Hotels, restaurants, small businesses, and oil refineries, to name just a few, were destroyed. All the people who worked in those establishments instantaneously lost their jobs and their incomes. The cleanup and rebuilding process took time to organize, and it eventually created a great deal of employment.

The storm created a major disruption in world oil markets. Loss of refinery capacity sent gasoline prices up immediately, nearly 40 percent to over $4 per gallon in some locations. The price per gallon of crude oil rose to over $70 per barrel. Local governments found their tax bases destroyed, with no resources to pay teachers and local officials. Hundreds of hospitals were destroyed, and colleges and universities were forced to close their doors, causing tens of thousands of students to change their plans.

While the horror of the storm hit all kinds of people, the worst hit were the very poor, who could not get out of the way because they had no cars or other means of escape. The storm raised fundamental issues of fairness, which we will be discussing for years to come.

The study of economics is an essential part of the study of society.

To Understand Global Affairs

A third reason for studying economics is to understand global affairs. News headlines are filled with economic stories. The environmental disaster associated with BP's oil spill has the potential to affect the future price of oil if deep sea drilling is banned, the price of fish, the extent of tourism, and tourist-related employment in the Gulf and numerous other markets. The discovery in 2010 of major new diamond deposits in Zimbabwe has implications for the future stability of Mugabe's government, with implications for developments in the rest of the region. China's new position as a major trading partner of both the United States and Europe clearly has implications for political interactions among these nations. Greece's economic struggles in 2010 over its large debt is affecting the enthusiasm of the rest of Europe's citizens for the European Union.

In a relatively open, market-oriented world, it is impossible to understand political affairs without a grounding in economics. While there is much debate about whether or not economic considerations dominate international relations, it is clear that they play a role as political leaders seek the economic well-being of their citizenry.

An understanding of economics is essential to an understanding of global affairs.

To Be an Informed Citizen

A knowledge of economics is essential to being an informed citizen. In 2009, most of the world suffered from a major recession, with diminished economic growth and high unemployment. Millions of people around the world lost their jobs. Governments from China to the United Kingdom to the United States all struggled to figure out policies to help their economies recover. Understanding what happens in a recession and what the government can and cannot do to help in a recovery is an essential part of being an informed citizen.

Economics is also essential in understanding a range of other everyday government decisions at the local and federal levels. Why do governments pay for public schools and roads, but not cell phones? In 2010, the federal government under President Obama moved toward universal health care for U.S. citizens. How do you understand the debate of whether this is or is not a good idea? In some states, scalping tickets to a ball game is illegal. Is this a good policy or not? Some governments control the prices that firms can charge for some goods, especially essentials like milk and bread. Is this a good idea? Every day, across the globe, people engage in political decision making around questions like these, questions that depend on an understanding of economics.

To be an informed citizen requires a basic understanding of economics.

ECONOMICS IN PRACTICE

iPod and the World

It is impossible to understand the workings of an economy without first understanding the ways in which economies are connected across borders. The United States was importing goods and services at a rate of over $2 trillion per year in 2007 and was exporting at a rate of over $1.5 trillion per year.

For literally hundreds of years, the virtues of free trade have been the subject of heated debate. Opponents have argued that buying foreign-produced goods costs Americans jobs and hurts American producers. Proponents argue that there are gains from trade—that all countries can gain from specializing in the production of the goods and services they produce best.

In the modern world, it is not always easy to track where products are made. A sticker that says "Made in China" can often be misleading. Recent studies of two iconic U.S. products, the iPod and the Barbie doll, make this complexity clear.

The Barbie doll is one of Mattel's best and longest selling products. The Barbie was designed in the United States. It is made of plastic fashioned in Taiwan, which came originally from the Mideast in the form of petroleum. Barbie's hair comes from Japan, while the cloth for her clothes mostly comes from China. Most of the assembly of the Barbie also is done in China, using, as we see, pieces from across the globe. A doll that sells for $10 in the United States carries an export value when leaving Hong Kong of $2, of which only 35 cents is for Chinese labor, with most of the rest covering transportation and raw materials. Because the Barbie comes to the United States from assembly in China and transport from Hong Kong, some would count it as being produced in China. Yet, for this Barbie, $8 of its retail value of $10 is captured by the United States![1]

The iPod is similar. A recent study by three economists, Greg Linden, Kenneth Kraemer, and Jason Dedrick, found that once one

includes Apple's payment for its intellectual property, distribution costs, and production costs for some components, almost 80% of the retail price of the iPod is captured by the United States.[2] Moreover, for some of the other parts of the iPod, it is not easy to tell exactly where they are produced. The hard drive, a relatively expensive component, was produced in Japan by Toshiba, but some of the components of that hard drive were actually produced elsewhere in Asia. Indeed, for the iPod, which is composed of many small parts, it is almost impossible to accurately tell exactly where each piece was produced without pulling it apart.

So, next time you see a label saying "Made in China" keep in mind that from an economics point of view one often has to dig a little deeper to see what is really going on.

[1] For a discussion of the Barbie see Robert Feenstra, "Integration of Trade and Disintegration of Production in the Global Economy," *Journal of Economic Perspectives*, Fall 1998, 31–50.
[2] Greg Linden, Kenneth Kraemer, and Jason Dedrick, "Who Profits from Innovation in Global Value Chains?" *Industrial and Corporate Change*, 2010: 19(1), 81–116.

The Scope of Economics

Most students taking economics for the first time are surprised by the breadth of what they study. Some think that economics will teach them about the stock market or what to do with their money. Others think that economics deals exclusively with problems such as inflation and unemployment. In fact, it deals with all those subjects, but they are pieces of a much larger puzzle.

Economics has deep roots in and close ties to social philosophy. An issue of great importance to philosophers, for example, is distributional justice. Why are some people rich and others poor? And whatever the answer, is this fair? A number of nineteenth-century social philosophers wrestled with these questions, and out of their musings, economics as a separate discipline was born.

The easiest way to get a feel for the breadth and depth of what you will be studying is to explore briefly the way economics is organized. First of all, there are two major divisions of economics: microeconomics and macroeconomics.

Microeconomics and Macroeconomics

microeconomics The branch of economics that examines the functioning of individual industries and the behavior of individual decision-making units—that is, firms and households.

Microeconomics deals with the functioning of individual industries and the behavior of individual economic decision-making units: firms and households. Firms' choices about what to produce and how much to charge and households' choices about what and how much to buy help to explain why the economy produces the goods and services it does.

Another big question addressed by microeconomics is who gets the goods and services that are produced. Wealthy households get more than poor households, and the forces that determine this distribution of output are the province of microeconomics. Why does poverty exist? Who is poor? Why do some jobs pay more than others?

Think again about what you consume in a day, and then think back to that view over a big city. Somebody decided to build those factories. Somebody decided to construct the roads, build the housing, produce the cars, and smoke the bacon. Why? What is going on in all those buildings? It is easy to see that understanding individual microdecisions is very important to any understanding of society.

Macroeconomics looks at the economy as a whole. Instead of trying to understand what determines the output of a single firm or industry or what the consumption patterns are of a single household or group of households, macroeconomics examines the factors that determine national output, or national product. Microeconomics is concerned with *household* income; macroeconomics deals with *national* income.

Whereas microeconomics focuses on individual product prices and relative prices, macroeconomics looks at the overall price level and how quickly (or slowly) it is rising (or falling). Microeconomics questions how many people will be hired (or fired) this year in a particular industry or in a certain geographic area and focuses on the factors that determine how much labor a firm or an industry will hire. Macroeconomics deals with *aggregate* employment and unemployment: how many jobs exist in the economy as a whole and how many people who are willing to work are not able to find work.

To summarize:

macroeconomics The branch of economics that examines the economic behavior of aggregates—income, employment, output, and so on—on a national scale.

> Microeconomics looks at the individual unit—the household, the firm, the industry. It sees and examines the "trees." Macroeconomics looks at the whole, the aggregate. It sees and analyzes the "forest."

Table 1.1 summarizes these divisions of economics and some of the subjects with which they are concerned.

TABLE 1.1 Examples of Microeconomic and Macroeconomic Concerns

Division of Economics	Production	Prices	Income	Employment
Microeconomics	*Production/output in individual industries and businesses* How much steel How much office space How many cars	*Prices of individual goods and services* Price of medical care Price of gasoline Food prices Apartment rents	*Distribution of income and wealth* Wages in the auto industry Minimum wage Executive salaries Poverty	*Employment by individual businesses and industries* Jobs in the steel industry Number of employees in a firm Number of accountants
Macroeconomics	*National production/output* Total industrial output Gross domestic product Growth of output	*Aggregate price level* Consumer prices Producer prices Rate of inflation	*National income* Total wages and salaries Total corporate profits	*Employment and unemployment in the economy* Total number of jobs Unemployment rate

The Diverse Fields of Economics

Individual economists focus their research and study in many diverse areas. Many of these specialized fields are reflected in the advanced courses offered at most colleges and universities. Some are concerned with economic history or the history of economic thought. Others focus on international economics or growth in less developed countries. Still others study the economics of cities (urban economics) or the relationship between economics and law. These fields are summarized in Table 1.2.

TABLE 1.2 The Fields of Economics

Behavioral economics	uses psychological theories relating to emotions and social context to help understand economic decision making and policy. Much of the work in behavioral economics focuses on the biases that individuals have that affect the decisions they make.
Comparative economic systems	examines the ways alternative economic systems function. What are the advantages and disadvantages of different systems?
Econometrics	applies statistical techniques and data to economic problems in an effort to test hypotheses and theories. Most schools require economics majors to take at least one course in statistics or econometrics.
Economic development	focuses on the problems of low-income countries. What can be done to promote development in these nations? Important concerns of development for economists include population growth and control, provision for basic needs, and strategies for international trade.
Economic history	traces the development of the modern economy. What economic and political events and scientific advances caused the Industrial Revolution? What explains the tremendous growth and progress of post–World War II Japan? What caused the Great Depression of the 1930s?
Environmental economics	studies the potential failure of the market system to account fully for the impacts of production and consumption on the environment and on natural resource depletion. Have alternative public policies and new economic institutions been effective in correcting these potential failures?
Finance	examines the ways in which households and firms actually pay for, or finance, their purchases. It involves the study of capital markets (including the stock and bond markets), futures and options, capital budgeting, and asset valuation.
Health economics	analyzes the health care system and its players: government, insurers, health care providers, and patients. It provides insight into the demand for medical care, health insurance markets, cost-controlling insurance plans (HMOs, PPOs, IPAs), government health care programs (Medicare and Medicaid), variations in medical practice, medical malpractice, competition versus regulation, and national health care reform.
The history of economic thought,	which is grounded in philosophy, studies the development of economic ideas and theories over time, from Adam Smith in the eighteenth century to the works of economists such as Thomas Malthus, Karl Marx, and John Maynard Keynes. Because economic theory is constantly developing and changing, studying the history of ideas helps give meaning to modern theory and puts it in perspective.
Industrial organization	looks carefully at the structure and performance of industries and firms within an economy. How do businesses compete? Who gains and who loses?
International economics	studies trade flows among countries and international financial institutions. What are the advantages and disadvantages for a country that allows its citizens to buy and sell freely in world markets? Why is the dollar strong or weak?
Labor economics	deals with the factors that determine wage rates, employment, and unemployment. How do people decide whether to work, how much to work, and at what kind of job? How have the roles of unions and management changed in recent years?
Law and economics	analyzes the economic function of legal rules and institutions. How does the law change the behavior of individuals and businesses? Do different liability rules make accidents and injuries more or less likely? What are the economic costs of crime?
Public economics	examines the role of government in the economy. What are the economic functions of government, and what should they be? How should the government finance the services that it provides? What kinds of government programs should confront the problems of poverty, unemployment, and pollution? What problems does government involvement create?
Urban and regional economics	studies the spatial arrangement of economic activity. Why do we have cities? Why are manufacturing firms locating farther and farther from the center of urban areas?

ECONOMICS IN PRACTICE

Trust and Gender

As you study economics, you will see that economists study quite a large range of topics. In the experimental area, this seems to be especially true. An interesting recent example is a paper on gender and trust by Nancy Buchan, Rachel Croson, and Sara Solnick.[1]

While many transactions happen in anonymous markets in which buyers and sellers don't know one another, there are many other occasions in which markets operate more effectively if individuals develop some trust in one another. Trust in the goodwill of your employer or of the staff of your local day care can make a big difference in the ways in which you transact business. What can economists say about who is or is not trustworthy?

To answer this question, Buchan et al. used a game economists call the Investment Game to explore the behavior of people when they are not being observed. In this game, there are two players, a responder and a sender, and the game begins with each person receiving $10 from the experimenter. The sender and responder are not known to each other and are put in separate rooms. Sender begins and is told he or she can send any or all of the $10 to the responder. Whatever is sent will be tripled by the experimenter. The responder then can send any or all of the money back.

Clearly the sender–responder pair stand to gain the most if the sender sends all $10 and has it tripled by the experimenter. In this way the pair could turn a starting sum of $20 ($10 each) to $40 (the tripled $10 plus the responder's original $10). As you will see in Chapter 14, economists who work on game theory expect no money to be sent in either direction: Because the sender doesn't trust the responder to share, he or she sends nothing in the first place.

What do Buchan et al. find? In experiments run at the University of Wisconsin and the University of Miami, the experimenters found that almost all subjects sent some money. Perhaps more interestingly, men sent significantly more than women did, but women returned significantly more than men. As the researchers conclude, "We find that men trust more than women, and women are more trustworthy than men."

[1] Nancy Buchan, Rachel Croson, and Sara Solnick. "Trust and Gender: An Examination of Behavior, Biases, and Beliefs in the Investment Game." *Journal of Economic Behavior and Organization*, 2008: 68(3), 466–476.

Economists also differ in the emphasis they place on theory. Some economists specialize in developing new theories, whereas other economists spend their time testing the theories of others. Some economists hope to expand the frontiers of knowledge, whereas other economists are more interested in applying what is already known to the formulation of public policies.

As you begin your study of economics, look through your school's course catalog and talk to the faculty about their interests. You will discover that economics encompasses a broad range of inquiry and is linked to many other disciplines.

The Method of Economics

Economics asks and attempts to answer two kinds of questions: positive and normative. **Positive economics** attempts to understand behavior and the operation of economic systems *without making judgments* about whether the outcomes are good or bad. It strives to describe what exists and how it works. What determines the wage rate for unskilled workers? What would happen if we abolished the corporate income tax? The answers to such questions are the subject of positive economics.

In contrast, **normative economics** looks at the outcomes of economic behavior and asks whether they are good or bad and whether they can be made better. Normative economics involves judgments and prescriptions for courses of action. Should the government subsidize or regulate the cost of higher education? Should medical benefits to the elderly under Medicare be available only to those with incomes below some threshold? Should the

positive economics An approach to economics that seeks to understand behavior and the operation of systems without making judgments. It describes what exists and how it works.

normative economics An approach to economics that analyzes outcomes of economic behavior, evaluates them as good or bad, and may prescribe courses of action. Also called *policy economics*.

United States allow importers to sell foreign-produced goods that compete with U.S.-made products? Should we reduce or eliminate inheritance taxes? Normative economics is often called *policy economics.*

Of course, most normative questions involve positive questions. To know whether the government *should* take a particular action, we must know first if it *can* and second what the consequences are likely to be. (For example, if we lower import fees, will there be more competition and lower prices?)

Some claim that positive, value-free economic analysis is impossible. They argue that analysts come to problems with biases that cannot help but influence their work. Furthermore, even in choosing what questions to ask or what problems to analyze, economists are influenced by political, ideological, and moral views.

Although this argument has some merit, it is nevertheless important to distinguish between analyses that attempt to be positive and those that are intentionally and explicitly normative. Economists who ask explicitly normative questions should be required to specify their grounds for judging one outcome superior to another.

Descriptive Economics and Economic Theory

descriptive economics The compilation of data that describe phenomena and facts.

Positive economics is often divided into descriptive economics and economic theory. **Descriptive economics** is simply the compilation of data that describe phenomena and facts. Examples of such data appear in the *Statistical Abstract of the United States*, a large volume of data published by the Department of Commerce every year that describes many features of the U.S. economy. Massive volumes of data can now be found on the World Wide Web. As an example, look at www.bls.gov (Bureau of Labor Statistics).

Where do these data come from? The Census Bureau collects an enormous amount of raw data every year, as do the Bureau of Labor Statistics, the Bureau of Economic Analysis, and nongovernment agencies such as the University of Michigan Survey Research Center. One important study now published annually is the *Survey of Consumer Expenditure*, which asks individuals to keep careful records of all their expenditures over a long period of time. Another is the *National Longitudinal Survey of Labor Force Behavior*, conducted over many years by the Center for Human Resource Development at the Ohio State University.

economic theory A statement or set of related statements about cause and effect, action and reaction.

Economic theory attempts to generalize about data and interpret them. An **economic theory** is a statement or set of related statements about cause and effect, action and reaction. One of the first theories you will encounter in this text is the *law of demand*, which was most clearly stated by Alfred Marshall in 1890: When the price of a product rises, people tend to buy less of it; when the price of a product falls, people tend to buy more.

Theories do not always arise out of formal numerical data. All of us have been observing people's behavior and their responses to economic stimuli for most of our lives. We may have observed our parents' reaction to a sudden increase—or decrease—in income or to the loss of a job or the acquisition of a new one. We all have seen people standing in line waiting for a bargain. Of course, our own actions and reactions are another important source of data.

Theories and Models

model A formal statement of a theory, usually a mathematical statement of a presumed relationship between two or more variables.

In many disciplines, including physics, chemistry, meteorology, political science, and economics, theorists build formal models of behavior. A **model** is a formal statement of a theory. It is usually a mathematical statement of a presumed relationship between two or more variables.

A **variable** is a measure that can change from time to time or from observation to observation. Income is a variable—it has different values for different people and different values for the same person at different times. The rental price of a movie on a DVD is a variable; it has different values at different stores and at different times. There are countless other examples.

variable A measure that can change from time to time or from observation to observation.

Because all models simplify reality by stripping part of it away, they are abstractions. Critics of economics often point to abstraction as a weakness. Most economists, however, see abstraction as a real strength.

The easiest way to see how abstraction can be helpful is to think of a map. A map is a representation of reality that is simplified and abstract. A city or state appears on a piece of paper as a series of lines and colors. The amount of reality that the mapmaker can strip away before the map loses something essential depends on what the map will be used for. If you want to drive from St. Louis to Phoenix, you need to know only the major interstate highways and roads. You lose absolutely nothing and gain clarity by cutting out the local streets and roads. However, if you need to get around Phoenix, you may need to see every street and alley.

Most maps are two-dimensional representations of a three-dimensional world; they show where roads and highways go but do not show hills and valleys along the way. Trail maps for hikers, however, have "contour lines" that represent changes in elevation. When you are in a car, changes in elevation matter very little; they would make a map needlessly complex and more difficult to read. However, if you are on foot carrying a 50-pound pack, a knowledge of elevation is crucial.

Like maps, economic models are abstractions that strip away detail to expose only those aspects of behavior that are important to the question being asked. The principle that irrelevant detail should be cut away is called the principle of **Ockham's razor** after the fourteenth-century philosopher William of Ockham.

Ockham's razor The principle that irrelevant detail should be cut away.

Be careful—although abstraction is a powerful tool for exposing and analyzing specific aspects of behavior, it is possible to oversimplify. Economic models often strip away a good deal of social and political reality to get at underlying concepts. When an economic theory is used to help formulate actual government or institutional policy, political and social reality must often be reintroduced if the policy is to have a chance of working.

The key here is that the appropriate amount of simplification and abstraction depends on the use to which the model will be put. To return to the map example: You do not want to walk around San Francisco with a map made for drivers—there are too many very steep hills.

All Else Equal: *Ceteris Paribus* It is usually true that whatever you want to explain with a model depends on more than one factor. Suppose, for example, that you want to explain the total number of miles driven by automobile owners in the United States. The number of miles driven will change from year to year or month to month; it is a variable. The issue, if we want to understand and explain changes that occur, is what factors cause those changes.

Obviously, many things might affect total miles driven. First, more or fewer people may be driving. This number, in turn, can be affected by changes in the driving age, by population growth, or by changes in state laws. Other factors might include the price of gasoline, the household's income, the number and age of children in the household, the distance from home to work, the location of shopping facilities, and the availability and quality of public transport. When any of these variables change, the members of the household may drive more or less. If changes in any of these variables affect large numbers of households across the country, the total number of miles driven will change.

Very often we need to isolate or separate these effects. For example, suppose we want to know the impact on driving of a higher tax on gasoline. This change would raise the price of gasoline at the pump but would not (at least in the short run) affect income, workplace location, number of children, and so on.

To isolate the impact of one single factor, we use the device of *ceteris paribus*, or **all else equal**. We ask, "What is the impact of a change in gasoline price on driving behavior, *ceteris paribus*, or assuming that nothing else changes?" If gasoline prices rise by 10 percent, how much less driving will there be, assuming no simultaneous change in anything else—that is, assuming that income, number of children, population, laws, and so on, all remain constant? Using the device of *ceteris paribus* is one part of the process of abstraction. In formulating economic theory, the concept helps us simplify reality to focus on the relationships that interest us.

***ceteris paribus,* or all else equal** A device used to analyze the relationship between two variables while the values of other variables are held unchanged.

Expressing Models in Words, Graphs, and Equations Consider the following statements: Lower airline ticket prices cause people to fly more frequently. Higher interest rates slow the rate of home sales. When firms produce more output, employment increases. Higher gasoline prices cause people to drive less and to buy more fuel-efficient cars.

Each of those statements expresses a relationship between two variables that can be quantified. In each case, there is a stimulus and a response, a cause and an effect. Quantitative relationships can be expressed in a variety of ways. Sometimes words are sufficient to express the essence of a theory, but often it is necessary to be more specific about the nature of a relationship or about the size of a response. The most common method of expressing the quantitative relationship between two variables is *graphing* that relationship on a two-dimensional plane. In fact, we will use graphic analysis extensively in Chapter 2 and beyond. Because it is essential that you be familiar with the basics of graphing, the appendix to this chapter presents a careful review of graphing techniques.

Quantitative relationships between variables can also be presented through *equations*. For example, suppose we discovered that over time, U.S. households collectively spend, or consume, 90 percent of their income and save 10 percent of their income. We could then write:

$$C = .90\,Y \text{ and } S = .10Y$$

where C is consumption spending, Y is income, and S is saving. Writing explicit algebraic expressions like these helps us understand the nature of the underlying process of decision making. Understanding this process is what economics is all about.

Cautions and Pitfalls In formulating theories and models, it is especially important to avoid two pitfalls: the *post hoc* fallacy and the fallacy of composition.

The **Post Hoc** *Fallacy* Theories often make statements or sets of statements about cause and effect. It can be quite tempting to look at two events that happen in sequence and assume that the first caused the second to happen. This is not always the case. This common error is called the ***post hoc, ergo propter hoc*** (or "after this, therefore because of this") fallacy.

post hoc, ergo propter hoc
Literally, "after this (in time), therefore because of this." A common error made in thinking about causation: If Event A happens before Event B, it is not necessarily true that A caused B.

There are thousands of examples. The Colorado Rockies have won seven games in a row. Last night you went to the game and they lost. You must have jinxed them. They lost *because* you went to the game.

Stock market analysts indulge in what is perhaps the most striking example of the *post hoc* fallacy in action. Every day the stock market goes up or down, and every day some analyst on some national news program singles out one or two of the day's events as *the* cause of some change in the market: "Today the Dow Jones industrial average rose 5 points on heavy trading; analysts say that the increase was due to progress in talks between Israel and Syria." Research has shown that daily changes in stock market averages are very largely random. Although major news events clearly have a direct influence on certain stock prices, most daily changes cannot be linked directly to specific news stories.

Very closely related to the *post hoc* fallacy is the often erroneous link between correlation and causation. Two variables are said to be *correlated* if one variable changes when the other variable changes. However, correlation does not imply causation. Cities that have high crime rates also have many automobiles, so there is a very high degree of correlation between number of cars and crime rates. Can we argue, then, that cars *cause* crime? No. The reason for the correlation may have nothing to do with cause and effect. Big cities have many people, many people have many cars; therefore, big cities have many cars. Big cities also have high crime rates for many reasons—crowding, poverty, anonymity, unequal distribution of wealth, and readily available drugs, to mention only a few. However, the presence of cars is probably not one of them.

This caution must also be viewed in reverse. Sometimes events that seem entirely unconnected actually *are* connected. In 1978, Governor Michael Dukakis of Massachusetts ran for reelection. Still quite popular, Dukakis was nevertheless defeated in the Democratic primary that year by a razor-thin margin. The weekend before, the Boston Red Sox, in the thick of the division championship race, had been badly beaten by the New York Yankees in four straight games. Some very respectable political analysts believe that hundreds of thousands of Boston sports fans vented their anger on the incumbent governor the following Tuesday.

The Fallacy of Composition   To conclude that what is true for a part is necessarily true for the whole is to fall into the **fallacy of composition**. Suppose that a large group of cattle ranchers graze their cattle on the same range. To an individual rancher, more cattle and more grazing mean a higher income. However, because its capacity is limited, the land can support only so many cattle. If every cattle rancher increased the number of cattle sent out to graze, the land would become overgrazed and barren; as a result, everyone's income would fall. In short, theories that seem to work well when applied to individuals or households often break down when they are applied to the whole.

fallacy of composition   The erroneous belief that what is true for a part is necessarily true for the whole.

Testing Theories and Models: Empirical Economics   In science, a theory is rejected when it fails to explain what is observed or when another theory better explains what is observed. The collection and use of data to test economic theories is called **empirical economics.**

Numerous large data sets are available to facilitate economic research. For example, economists studying the labor market can now test behavioral theories against the actual working experiences of thousands of randomly selected people who have been surveyed continuously since the 1960s. Macroeconomists continuously monitoring and studying the behavior of the national economy at the National Bureau of Economic Research (NBER) pass thousands of items of data, collected by both government agencies and private companies, over the Internet.

In the natural sciences, controlled experiments, typically done in the lab, are a standard way of testing theories. In recent years, economics has seen an increase in the use of experiments, both in the field and in the lab, as a tool to test its theories. One economist, John List of Chicago, tested the effect of changing the way an auction was run on bid prices for rare baseball cards with the help of the sports memorabilia dealers in trade show. (The experiment used a standard Cal Ripkin Jr. card.) Another economist, Keith Chen of Yale, has used experiments with monkeys to investigate the deeper biological roots of human decision making. The *Economics in Practice* on p. 9 describes another experiment on trust and gender.

empirical economics   The collection and use of data to test economic theories.

Economic Policy

Economic theory helps us understand how the world works, but the formulation of *economic policy* requires a second step. We must have objectives. What do we want to change? Why? What is good and what is bad about the way the system is operating? Can we make it better?

Such questions force us to be specific about the grounds for judging one outcome superior to another. What does it mean to be better? Four criteria are frequently applied in judging economic outcomes:

1. Efficiency
2. Equity
3. Growth
4. Stability

Efficiency   In physics, "efficiency" refers to the ratio of useful energy delivered by a system to the energy supplied to it. An efficient automobile engine, for example, is one that uses a small amount of fuel per mile for a given level of power.

In economics, **efficiency** means *allocative efficiency*. An efficient economy is one that produces what people want at the least possible cost. If the system allocates resources to the production of goods and services that nobody wants, it is inefficient. If all members of a particular society were vegetarians and somehow half of all that society's resources were used to produce meat, the result would be inefficient. It is inefficient when steel beams lie in the rain and rust because somebody fouled up a shipping schedule. If a firm could produce its product using 25 percent less labor and energy without sacrificing quality, it too is inefficient.

The clearest example of an efficient change is a voluntary exchange. If you and I each want something that the other has and we agree to exchange, we are both better off and no

efficiency   In economics, allocative efficiency. An efficient economy is one that produces what people want at the least possible cost.

one loses. When a company reorganizes its production or adopts a new technology that enables it to produce more of its product with fewer resources, without sacrificing quality, it has made an efficient change. At least potentially, the resources saved could be used to produce more of something.

Inefficiencies can arise in numerous ways. Sometimes they are caused by government regulations or tax laws that distort otherwise sound economic decisions. Suppose that land in Ohio is best suited for corn production and that land in Kansas is best suited for wheat production. A law that requires Kansas to produce only corn and Ohio to produce only wheat would be inefficient. If firms that cause environmental damage are not held accountable for their actions, the incentive to minimize those damages is lost and the result is inefficient.

equity Fairness.

Equity While efficiency has a fairly precise definition that can be applied with some degree of rigor, **equity** (fairness) lies in the eye of the beholder. To many, fairness implies a more equal distribution of income and wealth. Fairness may imply alleviating poverty, but the extent to which the poor should receive cash benefits from the government is the subject of enormous disagreement. For thousands of years, philosophers have wrestled with the principles of justice that should guide social decisions. They will probably wrestle with such questions for thousands of years to come.

Despite the impossibility of defining equity or fairness universally, public policy makers judge the fairness of economic outcomes all the time. Rent control laws were passed because some legislators thought that landlords treated low-income tenants unfairly. Certainly, most social welfare programs are created in the name of equity.

Growth As the result of technological change, the building of machinery, and the acquisition of knowledge, societies learn to produce new goods and services and to produce old ones better. In the early days of the U.S. economy, it took nearly half the population to produce the required food supply. Today less than 2.0 percent of the country's population works in agriculture.

economic growth An increase in the total output of an economy.

When we devise new and better ways of producing the goods and services we use now and when we develop new goods and services, the total amount of production in the economy increases. **Economic growth** is an increase in the total output of an economy. If output grows faster than the population, output per capita rises and standards of living increase. Presumably, when an economy grows, it produces more of what people want. Rural and agrarian societies become modern industrial societies as a result of economic growth and rising per capita output.

Some policies discourage economic growth, and others encourage it. Tax laws, for example, can be designed to encourage the development and application of new production techniques. Research and development in some societies are subsidized by the government. Building roads, highways, bridges, and transport systems in developing countries may speed up the process of economic growth. If businesses and wealthy people invest their wealth outside their country rather than in their country's industries, growth in their home country may be slowed.

stability A condition in which national output is growing steadily, with low inflation and full employment of resources.

Stability Economic **stability** refers to the condition in which national output is growing steadily, with low inflation and full employment of resources. During the 1950s and 1960s, the U.S. economy experienced a long period of relatively steady growth, stable prices, and low unemployment. Between 1951 and 1969, consumer prices never rose more than 5 percent in a single year, and in only 2 years did the number of unemployed exceed 6 percent of the labor force. From the end of the Gulf War in 1991 to the beginning of 2001, the U.S. economy enjoyed price stability and strong economic growth with rising employment. It was the longest expansion in American history.

The decades of the 1970s and 1980s, however, were not as stable. The United States experienced two periods of rapid price inflation (over 10 percent) and two periods of severe unemployment. In 1982, for example, 12 million people (10.8 percent of the workforce) were looking for work. The beginning of the 1990s was another period of instability, with a recession occurring in 1990–1991. In 2008–2009 much of the world, including the United States, experienced a large contraction in output and rise in unemployment. This was clearly an unstable period.

The causes of instability and the ways in which governments have attempted to stabilize the economy are the subject matter of macroeconomics.

An Invitation

This chapter has prepared you for your study of economics. The first part of the chapter invited you into an exciting discipline that deals with important issues and questions. You cannot begin to understand how a society functions without knowing something about its economic history and its economic system.

The second part of the chapter introduced the method of reasoning that economics requires and some of the tools that economics uses. We believe that learning to think in this very powerful way will help you better understand the world.

As you proceed, it is important that you keep track of what you have learned in earlier chapters. This book has a plan; it proceeds step-by-step, each section building on the last. It would be a good idea to read each chapter's table of contents at the start of each chapter and scan each chapter before you read it to make sure you understand where it fits in the big picture.

SUMMARY

1. *Economics* is the study of how individuals and societies choose to use the scarce resources that nature and previous generations have provided.

WHY STUDY ECONOMICS? *p. 2*

2. There are many reasons to study economics, including (a) to learn a way of thinking, (b) to understand society, (c) to understand global affairs, and (d) to be an informed citizen.

3. The best alternative that we forgo when we make a choice or a decision is the *opportunity cost* of that decision.

THE SCOPE OF ECONOMICS *p. 6*

4. *Microeconomics* deals with the functioning of individual markets and industries and with the behavior of individual decision-making units: business firms and households.

5. *Macroeconomics* looks at the economy as a whole. It deals with the economic behavior of aggregates—national output, national income, the overall price level, and the general rate of inflation.

6. Economics is a broad and diverse discipline with many special fields of inquiry. These include economic history, international economics, and urban economics.

THE METHOD OF ECONOMICS *p. 9*

7. Economics asks and attempts to answer two kinds of questions: positive and normative. *Positive economics* attempts to understand behavior and the operation of economies without making judgments about whether the outcomes are good or bad. *Normative economics* looks at the results of economic behavior and asks whether they are good or bad and whether they can be improved.

8. Positive economics is often divided into two parts. *Descriptive economics* involves the compilation of data that accurately describe economic facts and events. *Economic theory* attempts to generalize and explain what is observed. It involves statements of cause and effect—of action and reaction.

9. An economic *model* is a formal statement of an economic theory. Models simplify and abstract from reality.

10. It is often useful to isolate the effects of one variable on another while holding "all else constant." This is the device of *ceteris paribus*.

11. Models and theories can be expressed in many ways. The most common ways are in words, in graphs, and in equations.

12. Because one event happens before another, the second event does not necessarily happen as a result of the first. To assume that "after" implies "because" is to commit the fallacy of *post hoc, ergo propter hoc*. The erroneous belief that what is true for a part is necessarily true for the whole is the *fallacy of composition*.

13. *Empirical economics* involves the collection and use of data to test economic theories. In principle, the best model is the one that yields the most accurate predictions.

14. To make policy, one must be careful to specify criteria for making judgments. Four specific criteria are used most often in economics: *efficiency, equity, growth*, and *stability*.

REVIEW TERMS AND CONCEPTS

ceteris paribus, or all else equal, *p. 11*

descriptive economics, *p. 10*

economic growth, *p. 14*

economic theory, *p. 10*

economics, *p. 2*

efficiency, *p. 13*

efficient market, *p. 3*

empirical economics, *p. 13*

equity, *p. 14*

fallacy of composition, *p. 13*

Industrial Revolution, *p. 4*

macroeconomics, *p. 7*

marginalism, *p. 3*

microeconomics, *p. 6*

model, *p. 10*

normative economics, *p. 9*

Ockham's razor, *p. 11*

opportunity cost, *p. 2*

positive economics, *p. 9*

post hoc, ergo propter hoc, p. 12

scarce, *p. 2*

stability, *p. 14*

sunk costs, *p. 3*

variable, *p. 10*

PROBLEMS

All problems are available on www.myeconlab.com

1. One of the scarce resources that constrain our behavior is time. Each of us has only 24 hours in a day. How do you go about allocating your time in a given day among competing alternatives? How do you go about weighing the alternatives? Once you choose a most important use of time, why do you not spend all your time on it? Use the notion of opportunity cost in your answer.

2. In the summer of 2007, the housing market and the mortgage market were both in decline. Housing prices in most U.S. cities began to decline in mid-2006. With prices falling and the inventory of unsold houses rising, the production of new homes fell to around 1.5 million in 2007 from 2.3 million in 2005. With new construction falling dramatically, it was expected that construction *employment* would fall and that this would have the potential of slowing the national economy and increasing the general unemployment rate. Go to www.bls.gov and check out the recent data on total employment and construction employment. Have they gone up or down from their levels in August 2007? What has happened to the unemployment rate? Go to www.fhfa.gov and look at the housing price index. Have home prices risen or fallen since August 2007? Finally, look at the latest GDP release at www.bea.gov. Look at residential and nonresidential investment (Table 1.1.5) during the last 2 years. Do you see a pattern? Does it explain the employment numbers? Explain your answer.

3. Which of the following statements are examples of positive economic analysis? Which are examples of normative analysis?
   a. The inheritance tax should be repealed because it is unfair.
   b. Allowing Chile to join NAFTA would cause wine prices in the United States to drop.
   c. The first priorities of the new regime in the Democratic Republic of Congo (DRC, formerly Zaire) should be to rebuild schools and highways and to provide basic health care.

4. Sarita signed up with Netflix for a fixed fee of $16.99 per month. For this fee, she can receive up to 3 DVDs at a time in the mail and exchange each DVD as often as she likes. She also receives unlimited instant access to movies being streamed from Netflix to her computer or TV. During the average month in 2010, Sarita received and watched 6 movies sent to her through the mail and she watched an additional 13 movies which were streamed to her computer. What is the average cost of a movie to Sarita? What is the marginal cost of an additional movie?

5. A question facing many U.S. states is whether to allow casino gambling. States with casino gambling have seen a substantial increase in tax revenue flowing to state government. This revenue can be used to finance schools, repair roads, maintain social programs, or reduce other taxes.
   a. Recall that efficiency means producing what people want at the least cost. Can you make an efficiency argument in favor of allowing casinos to operate?
   b. What nonmonetary costs might be associated with gambling? Would these costs have an impact on the efficiency argument you presented in part **a**?
   c. Using the concept of equity, argue for or against the legalization of casino gambling.

6. For each of the following situations, identify the full cost (opportunity cost) involved:
   a. A worker earning an hourly wage of $8.50 decides to cut back to part-time to attend Houston Community College.
   b. Sue decides to drive to Los Angeles from San Francisco to visit her son, who attends UCLA.
   c. Tom decides to go to a wild fraternity party and stays out all night before his physics exam.
   d. Annie spends $200 on a new dress.
   e. The Confab Company spends $1 million to build a new branch plant that will probably be in operation for at least 10 years.
   f. Alex's father owns a small grocery store in town. Alex works 40 hours a week in the store but receives no compensation.

7. [**Related to the *Economics in Practice* on p. 6**] Log onto www.census.gov. Click on "Foreign Trade," then on "Statistics," and finally on "State Export Data." There you will find a list of the products produced in your state and exported to countries around the world. In looking over that list, are you surprised by anything? Do you know of any firms that produce these items? Search the Web to find a company that does. Do some research and write a paragraph about your company: what it produces, how many people it employs, and whatever else you can learn about the firm. You might even call the company to obtain the information.

8. Explain the pitfalls in the following statements.
   a. Whenever Jeremy decides to wash his car, the next day it usually rain. Since Jeremy's town is suffering from a severe drought, he decided to wash his car and, just as he expected, the next day the thunderstorms rolled in. Obviously it rained because Jeremy washed his car.

b. The principal of Hamilton High School found that requiring those students who were failing algebra to attend an after-school tutoring program resulted in a 30 percent average increase in their algebra grades. Based on this success, the principal decided to hire more tutors and require that all students must attend after-school tutoring, so everyone's algebra grades would improve.

c. People who drive hybrid automobiles recycle their trash more than people who do not drive hybrids. Therefore, recycling trash causes people to drive hybrid automobiles.

9. Explain whether each of the following is an example of a macro-economic concern or a microeconomic concern.
    a. Ford Motor Company is contemplating increasing the production of full-size SUVs based on projected future consumer demand.

b. Congress is debating the option of implementing a value-added tax as a means to cut the federal deficit.

c. The Federal Reserve announces it is increasing the discount rate in an attempt to slow the rate of inflation.

d. The Bureau of Labor Statistics projects a 22.5 percent increase in the number or workers in the healthcare industry from 2008 to 2018.

10. On the *Forbes* 2010 list of the World's Billionaires, Mexico's Carlos Slim Helu ranks at the top with a net worth of U.S. $53.5 billion. Does this "richest man in the world" face scarcity, or does scarcity only affect those with more limited incomes and lower net worth?

Source: "The World's Billionaires," *Forbes*, March 10, 2010.

CHAPTER 1 APPENDIX

How to Read and Understand Graphs

Economics is the most quantitative of the social sciences. If you flip through the pages of this or any other economics text, you will see countless tables and graphs. These serve a number of purposes. First, they illustrate important economic relationships. Second, they make difficult problems easier to understand and analyze. Finally, they can show patterns and regularities that may not be discernible in simple lists of numbers.

A **graph** is a two-dimensional representation of a set of numbers, or data. There are many ways that numbers can be illustrated by a graph.

Time Series Graphs

It is often useful to see how a single measure or variable changes over time. One way to present this information is to plot the values of the variable on a graph, with each value corresponding to a different time period. A graph of this kind is called a **time series graph**. On a time series graph, time is measured along the horizontal scale and the variable being graphed is measured along the vertical scale. Figure 1A.1 is a time series graph that presents the total disposable personal

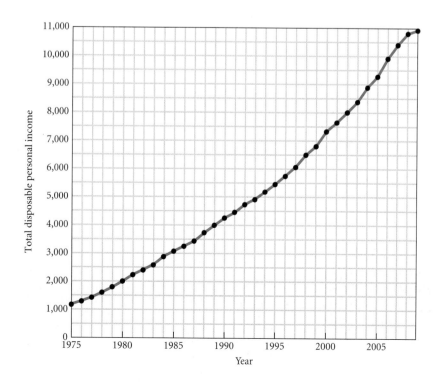

◀ **FIGURE 1A.1 Total Disposable Personal Income in the United States: 1975–2009 (in billions of dollars)**

Source: See Table 1A.1.

income in the U.S. economy for each year between 1975 and 2009.[1] This graph is based on the data found in Table 1A.1. By displaying these data graphically, we can see that (1) total disposable personal income has increased steadily since 1975 and (2) during certain periods, income has increased at a faster rate than during other periods.

TABLE 1A.1	Total Disposable Personal Income in the United States, 1975–2009 (in billions of dollars)		
Year	Total Disposable Personal Income	Year	Total Disposable Personal Income
1975	1,187.3	1993	4,921.6
1976	1,302.3	1994	5,184.3
1977	1,435.0	1995	5,457.0
1978	1,607.3	1996	5,759.6
1979	1,790.8	1997	6,074.6
1980	2,002.7	1998	6,498.9
1981	2,237.1	1999	6,803.3
1982	2,412.7	2000	7,327.2
1983	2,599.8	2001	7,648.5
1984	2,891.5	2002	8,009.7
1985	3,079.3	2003	8,377.8
1986	3,258.8	2004	8,889.4
1987	3,435.3	2005	9,277.3
1988	3,726.3	2006	9,915.7
1989	3,991.4	2007	10,403.1
1990	4,254.0	2008	10,806.4
1991	4,444.9	2009	10,923.6
1992	4,736.7		

Source: U.S. Department of Commerce, Bureau of Economic Analysis.

Graphing Two Variables on a Cartesian Coordinate System

More important than simple graphs of one variable are graphs that contain information on two variables at the same time. The most common method of graphing two variables is the **Cartesian coordinate system**. This system is constructed by drawing two perpendicular lines: a horizontal line, or **X-axis**, and a vertical line, or **Y-axis**. The axes contain measurement scales that intersect at 0 (zero). This point is called the **origin**. On the vertical scale, positive numbers lie above the horizontal axis (that is, above the origin) and negative numbers lie below it. On the horizontal scale, positive numbers lie to the right of the vertical axis (to the right of the origin) and negative numbers lie to the left of it. The point at which the graph intersects the **Y-axis** is called the **Y-intercept**. The point at which the graph intersects the **X-axis** is called the **X-intercept**.

When two variables are plotted on a single graph, each point represents a pair of numbers. The first number is measured on the *X*-axis, and the second number is measured on the *Y*-axis. For example, the following points (X, Y) are plotted on the set of axes

drawn in Figure 1A.2: (4, 2), (2, −1), (−3, 4), (−3, −2). Most, but not all, of the graphs in this book are plots of two variables where both values are positive numbers [such as (4, 2) in Figure 1A.2]. On these graphs, only the upper-right quadrant of the coordinate system (that is, the quadrant in which all *X* and *Y* values are positive) will be drawn.

Plotting Income and Consumption Data For Households

Table 1A.2 presents data collected by the Bureau of Labor Statistics (BLS). In a recent survey, 5,000 households were asked to keep track of all their expenditures. This table shows average income and average spending for those households,

TABLE 1A.2	Consumption Expenditures and Income, 2008	
	Average Income Before Taxes	Average Consumption Expenditures
Bottom fifth	$ 10,263	$22,304
2nd fifth	27,442	31,751
3rd fifth	47,196	42,659
4th fifth	74,090	58,632
Top fifth	158,652	97,003

Source: Consumer Expenditures in 2008, U.S. Bureau of Labor Statistics.

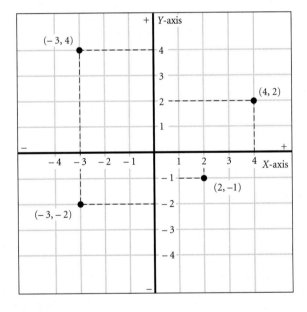

▲ **FIGURE 1A.2** **A Cartesian Coordinate System**
A Cartesian coordinate system is constructed by drawing two perpendicular lines: a vertical axis (the *Y*-axis) and a horizontal axis (the *X*-axis). Each axis is a measuring scale.

---

[1] The measure of income presented in Table 1A.1 and in Figure 1A.1 is disposable personal income in billions of dollars. It is the total personal income received by all households in the United States minus the taxes that they pay.

ranked by income. For example, the average income for the top fifth (20 percent) of the households was $158,652. The average spending for the top 20 percent was $97,003.

Figure 1A.3 presents the numbers from Table 1A.2 graphically using the Cartesian coordinate system. Along the horizontal scale, the X-axis, we measure average income. Along the vertical scale, the Y-axis, we measure average consumption spending. Each of the five pairs of numbers from the table is represented by a point on the graph. Because all numbers are positive numbers, we need to show only the upper right quadrant of the coordinate system.

To help you read this graph, we have drawn a dotted line connecting all the points where consumption and income would be equal. *This 45° line does not represent any data.* Instead, it represents the line along which all variables on the X-axis correspond exactly to the variables on the Y-axis, for example, (10,000, 10,000), (20,000, 20,000), and (37,000, 37,000). The heavy blue line traces the data; the purpose of the dotted line is to help you read the graph.

There are several things to look for when reading a graph. The first thing you should notice is whether the line slopes upward or downward as you move from left to right. The blue line in Figure 1A.3 slopes upward, indicating that there seems to be a **positive relationship** between income and spending: The higher a household's income, the more a household tends to consume. If we had graphed the percentage of each group receiving welfare payments along the Y-axis, the line would presumably slope downward, indicating that welfare payments are lower at higher income levels. The income level/welfare payment relationship is thus a **negative relationship**.

Slope

The **slope** of a line or curve is a measure that indicates whether the relationship between the variables is positive or negative and how much of a response there is in Y (the variable on the vertical axis) when X (the variable on the horizontal axis) changes. The slope of a line between two points is the change in the quantity measured on the Y-axis divided by the change in the quantity measured on the X-axis. We will normally use Δ (the Greek letter *delta*) to refer to a change in a variable. In Figure 1A.4, the slope of the line between points A and B is ΔY divided by ΔX. Sometimes it is easy to remember slope as "the rise over the run," indicating the vertical change over the horizontal change.

To be precise, ΔX between two points on a graph is simply X_2 minus X_1, where X_2 is the X value for the second point and X_1 is the X value for the first point. Similarly, ΔY is defined as Y_2 minus Y_1, where Y_2 is the Y value for the second point and Y_1 is the Y value for the first point. Slope is equal to

$$\frac{\Delta Y}{\Delta X} = \frac{Y_2 - Y_1}{X_2 - X_1}$$

As we move from A to B in Figure 1A.4(a), both X and Y increase; the slope is thus a positive number. However, as we move from A to B in Figure 1A.4(b), X increases [$(X_2 - X_1)$ is a positive number], but Y decreases [$(Y_2 - Y_1)$ is a negative number]. The slope in Figure 1A.4(b) is thus a negative number because a negative number divided by a positive number results in a negative quotient.

To calculate the numerical value of the slope between points A and B in Figure 1A.3, we need to calculate ΔY and ΔX. Because consumption is measured on the Y-axis, ΔY is 9,447 [$(Y_2 - Y_1) = (31,751 - 22,304)$]. Because income is measured along the X-axis, ΔX is 17,179 [$(X_2 - X_1) = (27,442 - 10,263)$]. The slope between A and B is ΔY/ΔX = 9,447/17,179 = + 0.55.

▶ **FIGURE 1A.3**
Household Consumption and Income

A graph is a simple two-dimensional geometric representation of data. This graph displays the data from Table 1A.2. Along the horizontal scale (X-axis), we measure household income. Along the vertical scale (Y-axis), we measure household consumption.
Note: At point A, consumption equals $22,304 and income equals $10,263. At point B, consumption equals $31,751 and income equals $27,442.

Source: See Table 1A.2.

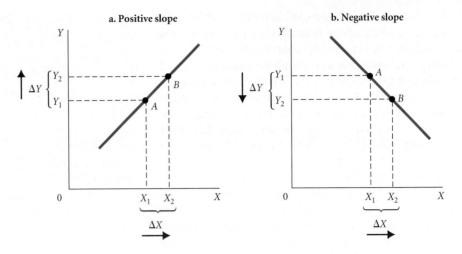

▲ **FIGURE 1A.4 A Curve with (a) Positive Slope and (b) Negative Slope**
A *positive* slope indicates that increases in *X* are associated with increases in *Y* and that decreases in *X* are associated with decreases in *Y*. A *negative* slope indicates the opposite—when *X* increases, *Y* decreases; and when *X* decreases, *Y* increases.

Another interesting thing to note about the data graphed in Figure 1A.3 is that all the points lie roughly along a straight line. (If you look very closely, however, you can see that the slope declines as you move from left to right; the line becomes slightly less steep.) A straight line has a constant slope. That is, if you pick any two points along it and calculate the slope, you will always get the same number. A horizontal line has a zero slope (ΔY is zero); a vertical line has an "infinite" slope because ΔY is too big to be measured.

Unlike the slope of a straight line, the slope of a *curve* is continually changing. Consider, for example, the curves in Figure 1A.5. Figure 1A.5(a) shows a curve with a positive slope that decreases as you move from left to right. The easiest way to think about the concept of increasing or decreasing

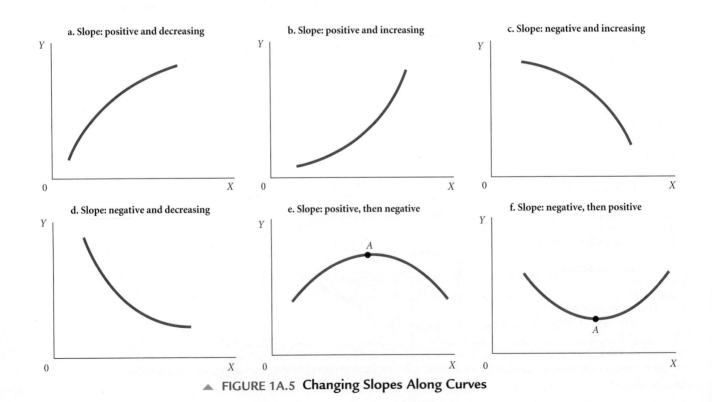

▲ **FIGURE 1A.5 Changing Slopes Along Curves**

slope is to imagine what it is like walking up a hill from left to right. If the hill is steep, as it is in the first part of Figure 1A.5(a), you are moving more in the Y direction for each step you take in the X direction. If the hill is less steep, as it is further along in Figure 1A.5(a), you are moving less in the Y direction for every step you take in the X direction. Thus, when the hill is steep, slope ($\Delta Y/\Delta X$) is a larger number than it is when the hill is flatter. The curve in Figure 1A.5(b) has a positive slope, but its slope *increases* as you move from left to right.

The same analogy holds for curves that have a negative slope. Figure 1A.5(c) shows a curve with a negative slope that increases (in absolute value) as you move from left to right. This time think about skiing down a hill. At first, the descent in Figure 1A.5(c) is gradual (low slope), but as you proceed down the hill (to the right), you descend more quickly (high slope). Figure 1A.5(d) shows a curve with a negative slope that *decreases* (in absolute value) as you move from left to right.

In Figure 1A.5(e), the slope goes from positive to negative as X increases. In Figure 1A.5(f), the slope goes from negative to positive. At point A in both, the slope is zero. [Remember, slope is defined as $\Delta Y/\Delta X$. At point A, Y is not changing ($\Delta Y = 0$). Therefore, the slope at point A is zero.]

Some Precautions

When you read a graph, it is important to think carefully about what the points in the space defined by the axes represent. Table 1A.3 and Figure 1A.6 present a graph of consumption and income that is very different from the one

TABLE 1A.3	Aggregate National Income and Consumption for the United States, 1930–2009 (in billions of dollars)

	Aggregate National Income	Aggregate Consumption
1930	82.9	70.1
1940	90.9	71.3
1950	263.9	192.2
1960	473.9	331.8
1970	929.5	648.3
1980	2,433.0	1,755.8
1990	5,059.8	3,835.5
2000	8,938.9	6,830.4
2005	11,273.8	8,819.0
2006	12,031.2	9,322.7
2007	12,448.2	9,826.4
2008	12,635.2	10,129.9
2009	12,280.0	10,089.1

Source: U.S. Department of Commerce, Bureau of Economic Analysis.

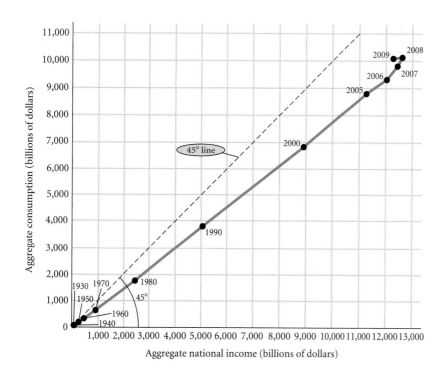

▲ **FIGURE 1A.6 National Income and Consumption**

It is important to think carefully about what is represented by points in the space defined by the axes of a graph. In this graph, we have graphed income with consumption, as in Figure 1A.3, but here each observation point is national income and aggregate consumption in *different years*, measured in billions of dollars.

Source: See Table 1A.3.

in Table 1A.2 and Figure 1A.3. First, each point in Figure 1A.6 represents a different year; in Figure 1A.3, each point represented a different group of households at the *same* point in time (2008). Second, the points in Figure 1A.6 represent *aggregate* consumption and income for the whole nation measured in *billions* of dollars; in Figure 1A.3, the points represented average *household* income and consumption measured in dollars.

It is interesting to compare these two graphs. All points on the aggregate consumption curve in Figure 1A.6 lie below the 45° line, which means that aggregate consumption is always less than aggregate income. However, the graph of average household income and consumption in Figure 1A.3 crosses the 45° line, implying that for some households, consumption is larger than income.

APPENDIX SUMMARY

1. A *graph* is a two-dimensional representation of a set of numbers, or data. A *time series graph* illustrates how a single variable changes over time.
2. The most common method of graphing two variables on one graph is the *Cartesian coordinate system*, which includes an *X* (horizontal)-*axis* and a *Y* (vertical)-*axis*. The points at which the two axes intersect is called the *origin*. The point at which a graph intersects the *Y*-axis is called the *Y-intercept*. The point at which a graph intersects the *X*-axis is called the *X-intercept*.

3. The *slope* of a line or curve indicates whether the relationship between the two variables graphed on a Cartesian coordinate system is positive or negative and how much of a response there is in *Y* (the variable on the vertical axis) when *X* (the variable on the horizontal axis) changes. The slope of a line between two points is the change in the quantity measured on the *Y*-axis divided by the change in the quantity measured on the *X*-axis.

APPENDIX REVIEW TERMS AND CONCEPTS

Cartesian coordinate system A common method of graphing two variables that makes use of two perpendicular lines against which the variables are plotted. *p. 18*

graph A two-dimensional representation of a set of numbers or data. *p. 17*

negative relationship A relationship between two variables, *X* and *Y*, in which a decrease in *X* is associated with an increase in *Y* and an increase in *X* is associated with a decrease in *Y*. *p. 19*

origin On a Cartesian coordinate system, the point at which the horizontal and vertical axes intersect. *p. 18*

positive relationship A relationship between two variables, *X* and *Y*, in which a decrease in *X* is associated with a decrease in *Y*, and an increase in *X* is associated with an increase in *Y*. *p. 19*

slope A measurement that indicates whether the relationship between variables is positive or negative and how much of a response there is in *Y* (the variable on the vertical axis) when *X* (the variable on the horizontal axis) changes. *p. 19*

time series graph A graph illustrating how a variable changes over time. *p. 17*

X-axis On a Cartesian coordinate system, the horizontal line against which a variable is plotted. *p. 18*

X-intercept The point at which a graph intersects the *X*-axis. *p. 18*

Y-axis On a Cartesian coordinate system, the vertical line against which a variable is plotted. *p. 18*

Y-intercept The point at which a graph intersects the *Y*-axis. *p. 18*

APPENDIX PROBLEMS

1. Graph each of the following sets of numbers. Draw a line through the points and calculate the slope of each line.

1		2		3		4		5		6	
X	Y	X	Y	X	Y	X	Y	X	Y	X	Y
1	5	1	25	0	0	0	40	0	0	0.1	100
2	10	2	20	10	10	10	30	10	10	0.2	75
3	15	3	15	20	20	20	20	20	20	0.3	50
4	20	4	10	30	30	30	10	30	10	0.4	25
5	25	5	5	40	40	40	0	40	0	0.5	0

2. For each of the graphs in Figure 1, determine whether the curve has a positive or negative slope. Give an intuitive explanation for what is happening with the slope of each curve.

3. For each of the following equations, graph the line and calculate its slope.
   a. $P = 10 - 2q_D$ (Put q_D on the *X*-axis.)
   b. $P = 100 - 4q_D$ (Put q_D on the *X*-axis.)
   c. $P = 50 + 6q_S$ (Put q_S on the *X*-axis.)
   d. $I = 10{,}000 - 500r$ (Put I on the *X*-axis.)

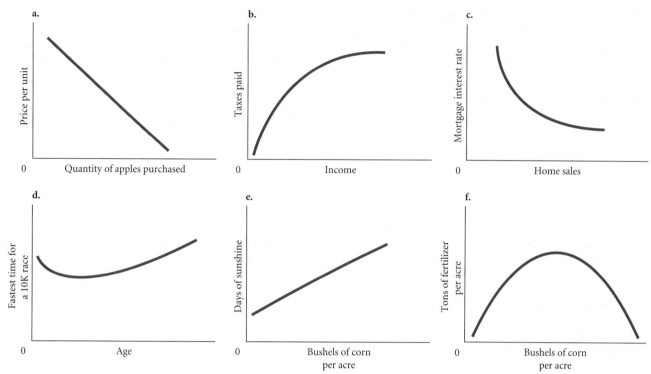

▲ **FIGURE 1**

4. The following table shows the relationship between the price of a dozen roses and the number of roses sold by Fiona's Flowers.
   a. Is the relationship between the price of roses and the number of roses sold by Fiona's Flowers a positive relationship or a negative relationship? Explain.
   b. Plot the data from the table on a graph, draw a line through the points, and calculate the slope of the line.

PRICE PER DOZEN	QUANTITY OF ROSES (DOZENS)	MONTH
$20	30	January
50	90	February
25	40	March
30	50	April
40	70	May

5. Calculate the slope of the demand curve at point *A* and at point *B* in the following figure.

The Economic Problem: Scarcity and Choice

2

Chapter 1 began with a very broad definition of economics. Every society, no matter how small or large, no matter how simple or complex, has a system or process that works to transform the resources that nature and previous generations provide into useful form. Economics is the study of that process and its outcomes.

Figure 2.1 illustrates three basic questions that must be answered to understand the functioning of the economic system:

- What gets produced?
- How is it produced?
- Who gets what is produced?

This chapter explores these questions in detail. In a sense, this entire chapter *is* the definition of economics. It lays out the central problems addressed by the discipline and presents a framework that will guide you through the rest of the book. The starting point is the presumption that *human wants are unlimited but resources are not*. Limited or scarce resources force individuals and societies to choose among competing uses of resources—alternative combinations of produced goods and services—and among alternative final distributions of what is produced among households.

These questions are *positive* or *descriptive*. That is, they ask how the system functions without passing judgment about whether the result is good or bad. They must be answered first before we ask more normative questions such as these:

- Is the outcome good or bad?
- Can it be improved?

The term *resources* is very broad. The sketch on the left side of Figure 2.1 shows several categories of resources. Some resources are the products of nature: land, wildlife, fertile soil, minerals, timber, energy, and even the rain and wind. In addition, the resources available to an economy include things such as buildings and equipment that have been produced in the past but are now being used to produce other things. And perhaps the most important resource of a society is its human workforce with people's talents, skills, and knowledge.

Things that are produced and then used in the production of other goods and services are called capital resources, or simply **capital**. Buildings, equipment, desks, chairs, software, roads, bridges, and highways are a part of the nation's stock of capital.

The basic resources available to a society are often referred to as **factors of production**, or simply **factors**. The three key factors of production are land, labor, and capital. The process that transforms scarce resources into useful goods and services is called **production**. In many societies, most of the production of goods and services is done by private firms.

capital Things that are produced and then used in the production of other goods and services.

factors of production (or factors) The inputs into the process of production. Another term for resources.

production The process that transforms scarce resources into useful goods and services.

The three basic questions:

1. What gets produced?   **2. How is it produced?**   **3. Who gets what is produced?**

Mix of output

Resources

Allocation of resources

Producers

Distribution of output

Households

▲ FIGURE 2.1 **The Three Basic Questions**
Every society has some system or process that transforms its scarce resources into useful goods and services. In doing so, it must decide what gets produced, how it is produced, and to whom it is distributed. The primary resources that must be allocated are land, labor, and capital.

Private airlines in the United States use land (runways), labor (pilots and mechanics), and capital (airplanes) to produce transportation services. But in all societies, some production is done by the public sector, or government. Examples of government-produced or government-provided goods and services include national defense, public education, police protection, and fire protection.

Resources or factors of production are the **inputs** into the process of production; goods and services of value to households are the **outputs** of the process of production.

inputs *or* **resources**
Anything provided by nature or previous generations that can be used directly or indirectly to satisfy human wants.

outputs Goods and services of value to households.

Scarcity, Choice, and Opportunity Cost

In the second half of this chapter we discuss the global economic landscape. Before you can understand the different types of economic systems, it is important to master the basic economic concepts of scarcity, choice, and opportunity cost.

Scarcity and Choice in a One-Person Economy

The simplest economy is one in which a single person lives alone on an island. Consider Bill, the survivor of a plane crash, who finds himself cast ashore in such a place. Here individual and society are one; there is no distinction between social and private. *Nonetheless, nearly all the same basic decisions that characterize complex economies must also be made in a simple economy.* That is, although Bill will get whatever he produces, he still must decide how to allocate the island's resources, what to produce, and how and when to produce it.

First, Bill must decide *what* he wants to produce. Notice that the word *needs* does not appear here. Needs are absolute requirements; but beyond just enough water, basic nutrition, and shelter to survive, needs are very difficult to define. What is an "absolute necessity" for one person may not be for another person. In any case, Bill must put his wants in some order of priority and make some choices.

Next, he must look at the *possibilities*. What can he do to satisfy his wants given the limits of the island? In every society, no matter how simple or complex, people are constrained in what they can do. In this society of one, Bill is constrained by time, his physical condition, his knowledge, his skills, and the resources and climate of the island.

Given that resources are limited, Bill must decide *how* to best use them to satisfy his hierarchy of wants. Food would probably come close to the top of his list. Should he spend his time gathering fruits and berries? Should he hunt for game? Should he clear a field and plant seeds?

The answers to those questions depend on the character of the island, its climate, its flora and fauna (*are* there any fruits and berries?), the extent of his skills and knowledge (does he know anything about farming?), and his preferences (he may be a vegetarian).

Opportunity Cost The concepts of *constrained choice* and *scarcity* are central to the discipline of economics. They can be applied when discussing the behavior of individuals such as Bill and when analyzing the behavior of large groups of people in complex societies.

Given the scarcity of time and resources, if Bill decides to hunt, he will have less time to gather fruits and berries. He faces a trade-off between meat and fruit. There is a trade-off between food and shelter too. If Bill likes to be comfortable, he may work on building a nice place to live, but that may require giving up the food he might have produced. As we noted in Chapter 1, the best alternative that we give up, or forgo, when we make a choice is the **opportunity cost** of that choice.

Bill may occasionally decide to rest, to lie on the beach, and to enjoy the sun. In one sense, that benefit is free—he does not have to buy a ticket to lie on the beach. In reality, however, relaxing does have an opportunity cost. The true cost of that leisure is the value of the other things Bill could have produced, but did not, during the time he spent on the beach.

During 2010, more than a dozen cities, including Minneapolis, Los Angeles, and Houston, were actively considering public funding for new football, soccer, and basketball arenas. An important part of that debate was the opportunity cost of the taxpayers' dollars: What else could tax dollars be spent on, and how much value would the alternatives bring to the local taxpayers? Perhaps without the new arena, taxes could be lower. Here the opportunity cost would include the value taxpayers receive from goods and services they would consume with the earnings that are no longer taxed. Most discussions of public expenditures at all levels of government include active considerations of opportunity costs.

In making everyday decisions, it is often helpful to think about opportunity costs. Should you go to the dorm party or not? First, it costs $4 to attend. When you pay money for anything, you give up the other things you could have bought with that money. Second, it costs 2 or 3 hours. Time is a valuable commodity for a college student. You have exams next week, and you need to study. You could go to a movie instead of the party. You could go to another party. You could sleep. Just as Bill must weigh the value of sunning on the beach against more food or better housing, so you must weigh the value of the fun you may have at the party against everything else you might otherwise do with the time and money.

opportunity cost The best alternative that we give up, or forgo, when we make a choice or decision.

Scarcity and Choice in an Economy of Two or More

Now suppose that another survivor of the crash, Colleen, appears on the island. Now that Bill is not alone, things are more complex and some new decisions must be made. Bill's and Colleen's preferences about what things to produce are likely to be different. They will probably not have the same knowledge or skills. Perhaps Colleen is very good at tracking animals and Bill has a knack for building things. How should they split the work that needs to be done? Once things are produced, the two castaways must decide how to divide them. How should their products be distributed?

The mechanism for answering these fundamental questions is clear when Bill is alone on the island. The "central plan" is his; he simply decides what he wants and what to do about it. The minute someone else appears, however, a number of decision-making arrangements immediately become possible. One or the other may take charge, in which case that person will decide for both of them. The two may agree to cooperate, with each having an equal say, and come up with a joint plan; or they may agree to split the planning as well as the production duties. Finally, they may go off to live alone at opposite ends of the island. Even if they live apart, however, they may take advantage of each other's presence by specializing and trading.

Modern industrial societies must answer the same questions that Colleen and Bill must answer, but the mechanics of larger economies are more complex. Instead of two people living together, the United States has over 300 million people. Still, decisions must be made about what to produce, how to produce it, and who gets it.

ECONOMICS IN PRACTICE

Frozen Foods and Opportunity Costs

In 2007, $27 billion of frozen foods were sold in U.S. grocery stores, one quarter of it in the form of frozen dinners and entrees. In the mid-1950s, sales of frozen foods amounted to only $1 billion, a tiny fraction of the overall grocery store sales. One industry observer attributes this growth to the fact that frozen food tastes much better than it did in the past. Can you think of anything else that might be occurring?

The growth of the frozen dinner entrée market in the last 50 years is a good example of the role of opportunity costs in our lives. One of the most significant social changes in the U.S. economy in this period has been the increased participation of women in the labor force. In 1950, only 24 percent of married women worked; by 2000, that fraction had risen to 61 percent. Producing a meal takes two basic ingredients: food and time. When both husbands and wives work, the opportunity cost of time for housework—including making meals—goes up. This tells us that making a home-cooked meal became more expensive in the last 50 years. A natural result is to shift people toward labor-saving ways to make meals. Frozen foods are an obvious solution to the problem of increased opportunity costs.

Another, somewhat more subtle, opportunity cost story is at work encouraging the consumption of frozen foods. In 1960, the first microwave oven was introduced. The spread of this device into America's kitchens was rapid. The microwave turned out to be a quick way to defrost and cook those frozen entrées. So this technology lowered the opportunity cost of making frozen dinners, reinforcing the

advantage these meals had over home-cooked meals. Microwaves made cooking with frozen foods cheaper once opportunity cost was considered while home-cooked meals were becoming more expensive.

The entrepreneurs among you also might recognize that the rise we described in the opportunity cost of the home-cooked meal *contributed* in part to the spread of the microwave, creating a reinforcing cycle. In fact, many entrepreneurs find that the simple tools of economics—like the idea of opportunity costs—help them anticipate what products will be profitable for them to produce in the future. The growth of the two-worker family has stimulated many entrepreneurs to search for labor-saving solutions to family tasks.

The public policy students among you might be interested to know that some researchers attribute part of the growth in obesity in the United States to the lower opportunity costs of making meals associated with the growth of the markets for frozen foods and the microwave. (See David M. Cutler, Edward L. Glaeser, and Jesse M. Shapiro, "Why Have Americans Become More Obese?" *Journal of Economic Perspectives*, Summer 2003, 93–118.)

---

theory of comparative advantage Ricardo's theory that specialization and free trade will benefit all trading parties, even those that may be "absolutely" more efficient producers.

Specialization, Exchange, and Comparative Advantage The idea that members of society benefit by specializing in what they do best has a long history and is one of the most important and powerful ideas in all of economics. David Ricardo, a major nineteenth-century British economist, formalized the point precisely. According to Ricardo's **theory of comparative advantage**, specialization and free trade will benefit all trading parties, even when some are "absolutely" more efficient producers than others. Ricardo's basic point applies just as much to Colleen and Bill as it does to different nations.

To keep things simple, suppose that Colleen and Bill have only two tasks to accomplish each week: gathering food to eat and cutting logs to burn. If Colleen could cut more logs than Bill in 1 day and Bill could gather more nuts and berries than Colleen could, specialization would clearly lead to more total production. Both would benefit if Colleen only cuts logs and Bill only gathers nuts and berries, as long as they can trade.

Suppose that Bill is slow and somewhat clumsy in his nut gathering and that Colleen is better at cutting logs *and* gathering food. At first, it might seem that since Colleen is better at everything, she should do everything. But that cannot be right. Colleen's time is limited after all, and even though Bill is clumsy and not very clever, he must be able to contribute something.

One of Ricardo's lasting contributions to economics has been his analysis of exactly this situation. His analysis, which is illustrated in Figure 2.2, shows both how Colleen and Bill should divide the work of the island and how much they will gain from specializing and exchanging even if, as in this example, one party is absolutely better at everything than the other party.

absolute advantage A producer has an absolute advantage over another in the production of a good or service if he or she can produce that product using fewer resources.

Suppose Colleen can cut 10 logs per day and Bill can cut only 4. Also suppose Colleen can gather 10 bushels of food per day and Bill can gather only 8. A producer has an **absolute advantage** over another in the production of a good or service if he or she can produce the good or service using fewer resources, including time. Since Colleen can cut more logs per day than Bill, we say that she has an absolute advantage in the production of logs. Similarly, Colleen has an absolute advantage over Bill in the production of food.

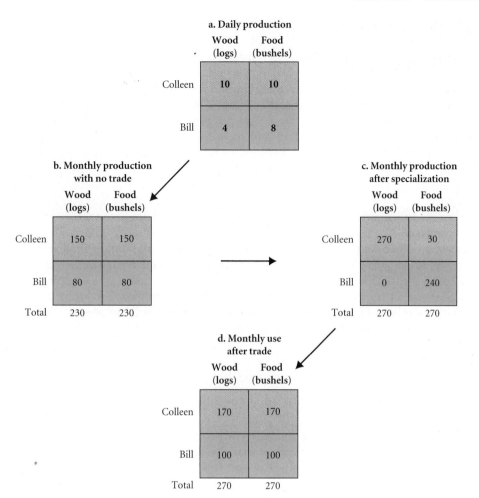

a. Daily production

	Wood (logs)	Food (bushels)
Colleen	10	10
Bill	4	8

b. Monthly production with no trade

	Wood (logs)	Food (bushels)
Colleen	150	150
Bill	80	80
Total	230	230

c. Monthly production after specialization

	Wood (logs)	Food (bushels)
Colleen	270	30
Bill	0	240
Total	270	270

d. Monthly use after trade

	Wood (logs)	Food (bushels)
Colleen	170	170
Bill	100	100
Total	270	270

◀ **FIGURE 2.2**
Comparative Advantage and the Gains from Trade
In this figure, (a) shows the number of logs and bushels of food that Colleen and Bill can produce for every day spent at the task and (b) shows how much output they could produce in a month, assuming they wanted an equal number of logs and bushels. Colleen would split her time 50/50, devoting 15 days to each task and achieving total output of 150 logs and 150 bushels of food. Bill would spend 20 days cutting wood and 10 days gathering food. As shown in (c) and (d), by specializing and trading, both Colleen and Bill will be better off. Going from (c) to (d), Colleen trades 100 logs to Bill in exchange for 140 bushels of food.

Thinking just about productivity and the output of food and logs, you might conclude that it would benefit Colleen to move to the other side of the island and be by herself. Since she is more productive in cutting logs and gathering food, would she not be better off on her own? How could she benefit by hanging out with Bill and sharing what they produce?

To answer that question we must remember that Colleen's time is limited: This limit creates opportunity cost. A producer has a **comparative advantage** over another in the production of a good or service if he or she can produce the good or service at a lower opportunity cost. First, think about Bill. He can produce 8 bushels of food per day, or he can cut 4 logs. To get 8 additional bushels of food, he must give up cutting 4 logs. Thus, *for Bill, the opportunity cost of 8 bushels of food is 4 logs*. Think next about Colleen. She can produce 10 bushels of food per day, or she can cut 10 logs. She thus gives up 1 log for each additional bushel; so *for Colleen, the opportunity cost of 8 bushels of food is 8 logs*. Bill has a comparative advantage over Colleen in the production of food because he gives up only 4 logs for an additional 8 bushels, whereas Colleen gives up 8 logs.

Think now about what Colleen must give up in terms of food to get 10 logs. To produce 10 logs she must work a whole day. If she spends a day cutting 10 logs, she gives up a day of gathering 10 bushels of food. Thus, *for Colleen, the opportunity cost of 10 logs is 10 bushels of food*. What must Bill give up to get 10 logs? To produce 4 logs, he must work 1 day. For each day he cuts logs, he gives up 8 bushels of food. He thus gives up 2 bushels of food for each log; so *for Bill, the opportunity cost of 10 logs is 20 bushels of food*. Colleen has a comparative advantage over Bill in the production of logs since she gives up only 10 bushels of food for an additional 10 logs, whereas Bill gives up 20 bushels.

Ricardo argues that two parties can benefit from specialization and trade even if one party has an absolute advantage in the production of both goods. Suppose Colleen and Bill both want

comparative advantage A producer has a comparative advantage over another in the production of a good or service if he or she can produce that product at a lower *opportunity cost.*

equal numbers of logs and bushels of food. If Colleen goes off on her own, in a 30-day month she can produce 150 logs and 150 bushels, devoting 15 days to each task. For Bill to produce equal numbers of logs and bushels on his own requires that he spend 10 days on food and 20 days on logs. This yields 80 bushels of food (10 days × 8 bushels per day) and 80 logs (20 days × 4 logs per day). Between the two, they produce 230 logs and 230 bushels of food.

Let's see if specialization and trade can work. If Bill spends all his time on food, he produces 240 bushels in a month (30 days × 8 bushels per day). If Colleen spends 3 days on food and 27 days on logs, she produces 30 bushels of food (3 days × 10 bushels per day) and 270 logs (27 days × 10 logs per day). Between the two, they produce 270 logs and 270 bushels of food, which is more than the 230 logs and 230 bushels they produced when not specializing. Thus, by specializing in the production of the good in which they enjoyed a comparative advantage, there are more of both goods. We see in this example how the fundamental concept of opportunity cost covered earlier in this chapter relates to the theory of comparative advantage.

Even if Colleen were to live at another place on the island, she could specialize, producing 30 bushels of food and 270 logs, then trading 100 of her logs to Bill for 140 bushels of food. This would leave her with 170 logs and 170 bushels of food, which is more than the 150 of each she could produce on her own. Bill would specialize completely in food, producing 240 bushels. Trading 140 bushels of food to Colleen for 100 logs leaves him with 100 of each, which is more than the 80 of each he could produce on his own.

The simple example of Bill and Colleen should begin to give you some insight into why most economists see value in free trade. Even if one country is absolutely better than another country at producing everything, our example has shown that there are gains to specializing and trading.

A Graphical Presentation of Comparative Advantage and Gains from Trade

Graphs can also be used to show the benefits from specialization and trade in the example of Colleen and Bill. To construct a graph reflecting Colleen's production choices (Figure 2.3 [a]), we start with the end points. If she were to devote an entire month (30 days) to log production, she could cut 300 logs—10 logs per day × 30 days. Similarly, if she were to devote an entire month to food gathering, she could produce 300 bushels. If she chose to split her time evenly (15 days to logs and 15 days to food), she would have 150 bushels and 150 logs. Her production possibilities are illustrated by the straight line between A and B and illustrate the trade-off that she faces between logs and food: By reducing her time spent in food gathering, Colleen is able to devote more time to logs; and for every 10 bushels of food that she gives up, she gets 10 logs.

In Figure 2.3(b), we construct a graph of Bill's production possibilities. Recall that Bill can produce 8 bushels of food per day, but he can cut only 4 logs. Again, starting with the end points, if Bill devoted all his time to food production, he could produce 240 bushels— 8 bushels of food per day × 30 days. Similarly, if he were to devote the entire 30 days to log cutting, he could cut 120 logs—4 logs per day × 30 days. By splitting his time, with 20 days spent on log cutting and 10 days spent gathering food, Bill could produce 80 logs and 80 bushels of food. His production possibilities are illustrated by the straight line between D and E. By shifting his resources and time from logs to food, he gets 2 bushels for every log.

Figures 2.3(a) and 2.3(b) illustrate the maximum amounts of food and logs that Bill and Colleen can produce acting independently with no specialization or trade, which is 230 logs and 230 bushels. Now let us have each specialize in producing the good in which he or she has a comparative advantage. Back in Figure 2.2 on p. 29, we showed that if Bill devoted all his time to food production, producing 240 bushels (30 days × 8 bushels per day), and Colleen devoted the vast majority of her time to cutting logs (27 days) and just a few days to gathering food (3 days), their combined total would be 270 logs and 270 bushels of food. Colleen would produce 270 logs and 30 bushels of food to go with Bill's 240 bushels of food.

Finally, we arrange a trade, and the result is shown in Figures 2.4(a) and 2.4(b). Bill trades 140 bushels of food to Colleen for 100 logs, and he ends up with 100 logs and 100 bushels of food, 20 more of each than he would have had before the specialization and trade.

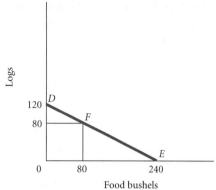

▲ **FIGURE 2.3 Production Possibilities with No Trade**

The figure in (a) shows all of the combinations of logs and bushels of food that Colleen can produce by herself. If she spends all 30 days each month on logs, she produces 300 logs and no food (point A). If she spends all 30 days on food, she produces 300 bushels of food and no logs (point B). If she spends 15 days on logs and 15 days on food, she produces 150 of each (point C).

The figure in (b) shows all of the combinations of logs and bushels of food that Bill can produce by himself. If he spends all 30 days each month on logs, he produces 120 logs and no food (point D). If he spends all 30 days on food, he produces 240 bushels of food and no logs (point E). If he spends 20 days on logs and 10 days on food, he produces 80 of each (point F).

▲ **FIGURE 2.4 Colleen and Bill Gain from Trade**

By specializing and engaging in trade, Colleen and Bill can move beyond their own production possibilities. If Bill spends all his time producing food, he will produce 240 bushels of food and no logs. If he can trade 140 of his bushels of food to Colleen for 100 logs, he will end up with 100 logs and 100 bushels of food. The figure in (b) shows that he can move from point F to point F'.

If Colleen spends 27 days cutting logs and 3 days producing food, she will produce 270 logs and 30 bushels of food. If she can trade 100 of her logs to Bill for 140 bushels of food, she will end up with 170 logs and 170 bushels of food. The figure in (a) shows that she can move from point C to point C'.

Colleen ends up with 170 logs and 170 bushels, again 20 more of each than she would have had before the specialization and trade. Both are better off. Both move beyond their individual production possibilities.

Weighing Present and Expected Future Costs and Benefits Very often we find ourselves weighing benefits available today against benefits available tomorrow. Here, too, the notion of opportunity cost is helpful.

While alone on the island, Bill had to choose between cultivating a field and just gathering wild nuts and berries. Gathering nuts and berries provides food now; gathering seeds and clearing a field for planting will yield food tomorrow if all goes well. Using today's time to farm may well be worth the effort if doing so will yield more food than Bill would otherwise have in the future. By planting, Bill is trading present value for future value.

The simplest example of trading present for future benefits is the act of saving. When you put income aside today for use in the future, you give up some things that you could have had today in exchange for something tomorrow. Because nothing is certain, some judgment about future events and expected values must be made. What will your income be in 10 years? How long are you likely to live?

We trade off present and future benefits in small ways all the time. If you decide to study instead of going to the dorm party, you are trading present fun for the expected future benefits of higher grades. If you decide to go outside on a very cold day and run 5 miles, you are trading discomfort in the present for being in better shape later.

Capital Goods and Consumer Goods A society trades present for expected future benefits when it devotes a portion of its resources to research and development or to investment in capital. As we said earlier in this chapter, *capital* in its broadest definition is anything that has already been produced that will be used to produce other valuable goods or services over time.

Building capital means trading present benefits for future ones. Bill and Colleen might trade gathering berries or lying in the sun for cutting logs to build a nicer house in the future. In a modern society, resources used to produce capital goods could have been used to produce **consumer goods**—that is, goods for present consumption. Heavy industrial machinery does not directly satisfy the wants of anyone, but producing it requires resources that could instead have gone into producing things that do satisfy wants directly—for example, food, clothing, toys, or golf clubs.

> **consumer goods** Goods produced for present consumption.

Capital is everywhere. A road is capital. Once a road is built, we can drive on it or transport goods and services over it for many years to come. A house is also capital. Before a new manufacturing firm can start up, it must put some capital in place. The buildings, equipment, and inventories that it uses comprise its capital. As it contributes to the production process, this capital yields valuable services over time.

In Chapter 1, we talked about the enormous amount of capital—buildings, factories, housing, cars, trucks, telephone lines, and so on—that you might see from a window high in a skyscraper. Much of that capital was put in place by previous generations, yet it continues to provide valuable services today; it is part of this generation's endowment of resources. To build every building, every road, every factory, every house, and every car or truck, society must forgo using resources to produce consumer goods today. To get an education, you pay tuition and put off joining the workforce for a while.

Capital does not need to be tangible. When you spend time and resources developing skills or getting an education, you are investing in human capital—your own human capital. This capital will continue to exist and yield benefits to you for years to come. A computer program produced by a software company and available online may cost nothing to distribute, but its true intangible value comes from the ideas embodied in the program itself. It too is capital.

> **investment** The process of using resources to produce new capital.

The process of using resources to produce new capital is called **investment**. (In everyday language, the term *investment* often refers to the act of buying a share of stock or a bond, as in "I invested in some Treasury bonds." In economics, however, investment *always* refers to the creation of capital: the purchase or putting in place of buildings, equipment, roads, houses, and the like.) A wise investment in capital is one that yields future benefits that are more valuable than the present cost. When you spend money for a house, for example, presumably you value its future benefits. That is, you expect to gain more from living in it than you would from the things you could buy today with the same money. Capital can also be intangible. Consider education that builds skills or knowledge in workers. Clearly education can yield decades of future "benefits" including higher wages. Because resources are scarce, the opportunity cost of every investment in capital is forgone present consumption.

The Production Possibility Frontier

A simple graphic device called the **production possibility frontier (ppf)** illustrates the principles of constrained choice, opportunity cost, and scarcity. The ppf is a graph that shows all the combinations of goods and services that can be produced if all of a society's resources are used efficiently. Figure 2.5 shows a ppf for a hypothetical economy.

On the Y-axis, we measure the quantity of capital goods produced. On the X-axis, we measure the quantity of consumer goods. All points below and to the left of the curve (the shaded area) represent combinations of capital and consumer goods that are possible for the society given the resources available and existing technology. Points above and to the right of the curve, such as point *G*, represent combinations that cannot be reached. If an economy were to end up at point *A* on the graph, it would be producing no consumer goods at all; all resources would be used for the production of capital. If an economy were to end up at point *B*, it would be devoting all its resources to the production of consumer goods and none of its resources to the formation of capital.

While all economies produce some of each kind of good, different economies emphasize different things. About 17.1 percent of gross output in the United States in 2005 was new capital. In Japan, capital historically accounted for a much higher percent of gross output, while in the Congo, the figure was 7 percent. Japan is closer to point *A* on its ppf, the Congo is closer to *B*, and the United States is somewhere in between.

Points that are actually on the ppf are points of both full resource employment and production efficiency. (Recall from Chapter 1 that an efficient economy is one that produces the things that people want at the least cost. *Production efficiency* is a state in which a given mix of outputs is produced at the least cost.) Resources are not going unused, and there is no waste. Points that lie within the shaded area but that are not on the frontier represent either unemployment of resources or production inefficiency. An economy producing at point *D* in Figure 2.5 can produce more capital goods and more consumer goods, for example, by moving to point *E*. This is possible because resources are not fully employed at point *D* or are not being used efficiently.

production possibility frontier (ppf) A graph that shows all the combinations of goods and services that can be produced if all of society's resources are used efficiently.

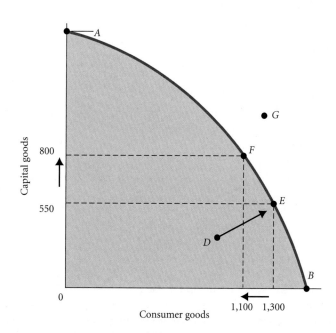

▲ **FIGURE 2.5 Production Possibility Frontier**
The ppf illustrates a number of economic concepts. One of the most important is *opportunity cost*. The opportunity cost of producing more capital goods is fewer consumer goods. Moving from *E* to *F*, the number of capital goods increases from 550 to 800, but the number of consumer goods decreases from 1,300 to 1,100.

Unemployment During the Great Depression of the 1930s, the U.S. economy experienced prolonged unemployment. Millions of workers found themselves without jobs. In 1933, 25 percent of the civilian labor force was unemployed. This figure stayed above 14 percent until 1940. More recently, between the end of 2007 and 2010, the United States lost over 8 million payroll jobs and unemployment rose to over 15 million.

In addition to the hardship that falls on the unemployed, unemployment of labor means unemployment of capital. During economic downturns or recessions, industrial plants run at less than their total capacity. When there is unemployment of labor and capital, we are not producing all that we can.

Periods of unemployment correspond to points inside the ppf, points such as *D* in Figure 2.5. Moving onto the frontier from a point such as *D* means achieving full employment of resources.

Inefficiency Although an economy may be operating with full employment of its land, labor, and capital resources, it may still be operating inside its ppf (at a point such as *D* in Figure 2.5). It could be using those resources *inefficiently.*

Waste and mismanagement are the results of a firm operating below its potential. If you are the owner of a bakery and you forget to order flour, your workers and ovens stand idle while you figure out what to do.

Sometimes inefficiency results from mismanagement of the economy instead of mismanagement of individual private firms. Suppose, for example, that the land and climate in Ohio are best suited for corn production and that the land and climate in Kansas are best suited for wheat production. If Congress passes a law forcing Ohio farmers to plant 50 percent of their acreage with wheat and Kansas farmers to plant 50 percent with corn, neither corn nor wheat production will be up to potential. The economy will be at a point such as *A* in Figure 2.6—inside the ppf. Allowing each state to specialize in producing the crop that it produces best increases the production of both crops and moves the economy to a point such as *B* in Figure 2.6.

The Efficient Mix of Output To be efficient, an economy must produce what people want. This means that in addition to operating *on* the ppf, the economy must be operating at the *right point* on the ppf. This is referred to as *output efficiency*, in contrast to production efficiency. Suppose that an economy devotes 100 percent of its resources to beef production and that the beef industry runs efficiently using the most modern techniques. Also suppose that everyone in the society is a vegetarian. The result is a total waste of resources (assuming that the society cannot trade its beef for vegetables produced in another country).

Points *B* and *C* in Figure 2.6 are points of production efficiency and full employment. Whether *B* is more or less efficient than *C*, however, depends on the preferences of members of society and is not shown in the ppf graph.

▶ **FIGURE 2.6**
Inefficiency from Misallocation of Land in Farming

Society can end up inside its ppf at a point such as *A* by using its resources inefficiently. If, for example, Ohio's climate and soil were best suited for corn production and those of Kansas were best suited for wheat production, a law forcing Kansas farmers to produce corn and Ohio farmers to produce wheat would result in less of both. In such a case, society might be at point *A* instead of point *B*.

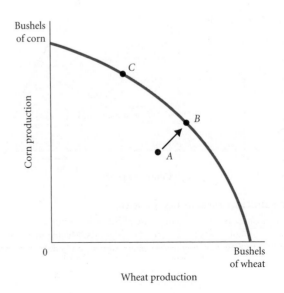

Negative Slope and Opportunity Cost As we have seen, points that lie on the ppf represent points of full resource employment and production efficiency. Society can choose only one point on the curve. Because a society's choices are constrained by available resources and existing technology, when those resources are fully and efficiently employed, it can produce more capital goods only by reducing production of consumer goods. The opportunity cost of the additional capital is the forgone production of consumer goods.

The fact that scarcity exists is illustrated by the negative slope of the ppf. (If you need a review of slope, see the Appendix to Chapter 1.) In moving from point *E* to point *F* in Figure 2.5, capital production *increases* by 800 − 550 = 250 units (a positive change), but that increase in capital can be achieved only by shifting resources out of the production of consumer goods. Thus, in moving from point *E* to point *F* in Figure 2.5, consumer goods production *decreases* by 1,300 − 1,100 = 200 units (a negative change). The slope of the curve, the ratio of the change in capital goods to the change in consumer goods, is negative.

The value of the slope of a society's ppf is called the **marginal rate of transformation (MRT)**. In Figure 2.5, the MRT between points *E* and *F* is simply the ratio of the change in capital goods (a positive number) to the change in consumer goods (a negative number).

> **marginal rate of transformation (MRT)** The slope of the production possibility frontier (ppf).

The Law of Increasing Opportunity Cost The negative slope of the ppf indicates the trade-off that a society faces between two goods. We can learn something further about the shape of the frontier and the terms of this trade-off. Let's look at the trade-off between corn and wheat production in Ohio and Kansas. In a recent year, Ohio and Kansas together produced 510 million bushels of corn and 380 million bushels of wheat. Table 2.1 presents these two numbers, plus some hypothetical combinations of corn and wheat production that might exist for Ohio and Kansas together. Figure 2.7 graphs the data from Table 2.1.

TABLE 2.1 Production Possibility Schedule for Total Corn and Wheat Production in Ohio and Kansas

Point on ppf	Total Corn Production (Millions of Bushels per Year)	Total Wheat Production (Millions of Bushels per Year)
A	700	100
B	650	200
C	510	380
D	400	500
E	300	550

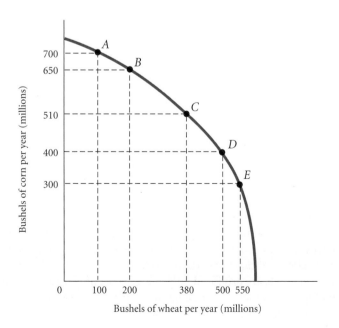

◀ **FIGURE 2.7 Corn and Wheat Production in Ohio and Kansas**

The ppf illustrates that the opportunity cost of corn production increases as we shift resources from wheat production to corn production. Moving from point *E* to *D*, we get an additional 100 million bushels of corn at a cost of 50 million bushels of wheat. Moving from point *B* to *A*, we get only 50 million bushels of corn at a cost of 100 million bushels of wheat. The *cost per bushel* of corn—measured in lost wheat—has increased.

Suppose that society's demand for corn dramatically increases. If this happens, farmers would probably shift some of their acreage from wheat production to corn production. Such a shift is represented by a move from point C (where corn = 510 and wheat = 380) up and to the left along the ppf toward points A and B in Figure 2.7. As this happens, it becomes more difficult to produce additional corn. The best land for corn production was presumably already in corn, and the best land for wheat production was already in wheat. As we try to produce more corn, the land is less well suited to that crop. As we take more land out of wheat production, we are taking increasingly better wheat-producing land. In other words, the opportunity cost of more corn, measured in terms of wheat, increases.

Moving from point E to D, Table 2.1 shows that we can get 100 million bushels of corn (400 − 300) by sacrificing only 50 million bushels of wheat (550 − 500)—that is, we get 2 bushels of corn for every bushel of wheat. However, when we are already stretching the ability of the land to produce corn, it becomes harder to produce more and the opportunity cost increases. Moving from point B to A, we can get only 50 million bushels of corn (700 − 650) by sacrificing 100 million bushels of wheat (200 − 100). For every bushel of wheat, we now get only half a bushel of corn. However, if the demand for *wheat* were to increase substantially and we were to move down and to the right along the ppf, it would become increasingly difficult to produce wheat and the opportunity cost of wheat, in terms of corn, would increase. This is the *law of increasing opportunity cost*.

If you think about the example we discussed earlier of Colleen and Bill producing logs and food on an island, you will recognize that the production possibilities described were highly simplified. In that example, we drew a downward slope, *straight line ppf*; to make the problem easier, we assumed constant opportunity costs. In a real economy, ppf's would be expected to look like Figure 2.5.

Although it exists only as an abstraction, the ppf illustrates a number of very important concepts that we will use throughout the rest of this book: scarcity, unemployment, inefficiency, opportunity cost, the law of increasing opportunity cost, economic growth, and the gains from trade.

It is important to remember that the ppf represents choices available within the constraints imposed by the current state of agricultural technology. In the long run, technology may improve, and when that happens, we have *growth*.

economic growth An increase in the total output of an economy. It occurs when a society acquires new resources or when it learns to produce more using existing resources.

Economic Growth **Economic growth** is characterized by an increase in the total output of an economy. It occurs when a society acquires new resources or learns to produce more with existing resources. New resources may mean a larger labor force or an increased capital stock. The production and use of new machinery and equipment (capital) increase workers' productivity. (Give a man a shovel, and he can dig a bigger hole; give him a steam shovel, and wow!) Improved productivity also comes from technological change and *innovation*, the discovery and application of new, more efficient production techniques.

In the past few decades, the productivity of U.S. agriculture has increased dramatically. Based on data compiled by the Department of Agriculture, Table 2.2 shows that yield per acre in corn production has increased fivefold since the late 1930s, while the labor required to produce it has dropped significantly. Productivity in wheat production has also increased, at only a slightly less remarkable rate: Output per acre has more than tripled, while labor requirements are down nearly 90 percent. These increases are the result of more efficient farming techniques, more and better capital (tractors, combines, and other equipment), and advances in scientific knowledge and technological change (hybrid seeds, fertilizers, and so on). As you can see in Figure 2.8, increases such as these shift the ppf up and to the right.

Sources of Growth and the Dilemma of Poor Countries Economic growth arises from many sources, the two most important over the years having been the accumulation of capital and technological advances. For poor countries, capital is essential; they must build the communication networks and transportation systems necessary to develop industries that function efficiently. They also need capital goods to develop their agricultural sectors.

Recall that capital goods are produced only at a sacrifice of consumer goods. The same can be said for technological advances. Technological advances come from research and development that use resources; thus, they too must be paid for. The resources used to produce capital

TABLE 2.2 Increasing Productivity in Corn and Wheat Production in the United States, 1935–2009

	Corn		Wheat	
	Yield per Acre (Bushels)	Labor Hours per 100 Bushels	Yield per Acre (Bushels)	Labor Hours per 100 Bushels
1935–1939	26.1	108	13.2	67
1945–1949	36.1	53	16.9	34
1955–1959	48.7	20	22.3	17
1965–1969	78.5	7	27.5	11
1975–1979	95.3	4	31.3	9
1981–1985	107.2	3	36.9	7
1985–1990	112.8	NA[a]	38.0	NA[a]
1990–1995	120.6	NA[a]	38.1	NA[a]
1998	134.4	NA[a]	43.2	NA[a]
2001	138.2	NA[a]	43.5	NA[a]
2006	145.6	NA[a]	42.3	NA[a]
2007	152.8	NA[a]	40.6	NA[a]
2008	153.9	NA[a]	44.9	NA[a]
2009	164.9	NA[a]	44.3	NA[a]

[a]Data not available.

Source: U.S. Department of Agriculture, Economic Research Service, Agricultural Statistics, Crop Summary.

goods—to build a road, a tractor, or a manufacturing plant—*and* to develop new technologies could have been used to produce consumer goods.

When a large part of a country's population is very poor, taking resources out of the production of consumer goods (such as food and clothing) is very difficult. In addition, in some countries, people wealthy enough to invest in domestic industries choose instead to invest abroad because of political turmoil at home. As a result, it often falls to the governments of poor countries to generate revenues for capital production and research out of tax collections.

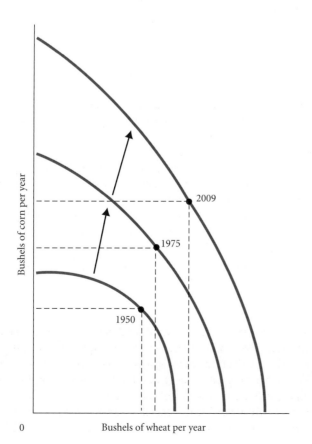

◀ **FIGURE 2.8 Economic Growth Shifts the PPF Up and to the Right**

Productivity increases have enhanced the ability of the United States to produce both corn and wheat. As Table 2.2 shows, productivity increases were more dramatic for corn than for wheat. Thus, the shifts in the ppf were not parallel.

Note: The ppf also shifts if the amount of land or labor in corn and wheat production changes. Although we emphasize productivity increases here, the actual shifts between years were due in part to land and labor changes.

All these factors have contributed to the growing gap between some poor and rich nations. Figure 2.9 shows the result using ppf's. On the left, the rich country devotes a larger portion of its production to capital while the poor country produces mostly consumer goods. On the right, you see the results: The ppf of the rich country shifts up and out farther and faster.

The importance of capital goods and technological developments to the position of workers in less developed countries is well illustrated by Robert Jensen's study of South India's industry. Conventional telephones require huge investments in wires and towers and, as a result, many less developed areas are without landlines. Mobile phones, on the other hand, require a less expensive investment; thus, in many areas, people upgraded from no phones directly to cell phones. Jensen found that in small fishing villages, the advent of cell phones allowed fishermen to determine on any given day where to take their catch to sell, resulting in a large decrease in fish wasted and an increase in fishing profits. The ability of newer communication technology to aid development is one of the exciting features of our times. (See Robert Jensen, "The Digital Provide: Information Technology, Market Performance, and Welfare in the South Indian Fisheries Sector," *Quarterly Journal of Economics*, August 2007, 879–924.)

The Economic Problem

Recall the three basic questions facing all economic systems: (1) What gets produced? (2) How is it produced? and (3) Who gets it?

When Bill was alone on the island, the mechanism for answering those questions was simple: He thought about his own wants and preferences, looked at the constraints imposed by the resources of the island and his own skills and time, and made his decisions. As Bill set about his work, he allocated available resources quite simply, more or less by dividing up his available time. Distribution of the output was irrelevant. Because Bill was the society, he got it all.

▶ FIGURE 2.9 **Capital Goods and Growth in Poor and Rich Countries**

Rich countries find it easier than poor countries to devote resources to the production of capital, and the more resources that flow into capital production, the faster the rate of economic growth. Thus, the gap between poor and rich countries has grown over time.

a. Poor country

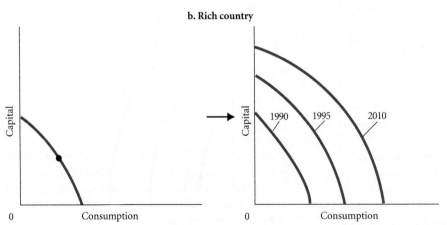

b. Rich country

ECONOMICS IN PRACTICE

Trade-Offs among the Rich and Poor

In all societies, for all people, resources are limited relative to people's demands. There are, however, quite large differences in the kinds of trade-offs individuals face in rich versus poor countries.

In 1990, the World Bank defined the extremely poor people of the world as those earning less than $1 a day. Among development economists and policy makers, this figure continues to be used as a rough rule of thumb. In a recent survey, Esther Duflo and Abhijit Banerjee, two MIT economists, surveyed individuals living at this level in 13 countries across the world.[1] What did they learn about the consumption trade-offs faced by these individuals versus consumers in the United States?

It should not surprise you to learn that for the extremely poor, food is a much larger component of the budget. On average over the 13 countries, between 56 percent and 78 percent of consumption was spent on food. In the United States just under 10 percent of the average budget goes to food. Even for the poorest consumers, however, biological need is not all determining. The Banerjee and Duflo study finds that in Udaipur, India, almost 10 percent of the typical food budget goes to sugar and processed foods rather than more nutritionally valuable grains. So even at these very low levels of income, some choice remains. Perhaps more interestingly, almost 10 percent of the budget of those surveyed goes to weddings, funerals, and other festivals. In societies with very few entertainment

outlets, Banerjee and Duflo suggest we may see more demand for festivals, indicating that even in extremely poor societies, household choice plays a role.

[1] Abhijit Banerjee and Esther Duflo, "The Economic Lives of the Poor," *Journal of Economic Perspective*, Winter 2007, 21(1), 141–167.

Introducing even one more person into the economy—in this case, Colleen—changed all that. With Colleen on the island, resource allocation involves deciding not only how each person spends his or her time but also who does what; now there are two sets of wants and preferences. If Bill and Colleen go off on their own and form two separate self-sufficient economies, there will be lost potential. Two people can do more things together than each person can do alone. They may use their comparative advantages in different skills to specialize. Cooperation and coordination may give rise to gains that would otherwise not be possible.

When a society consists of millions of people, the problem of coordination and cooperation becomes enormous, but so does the potential for gain. In large, complex economies, specialization can go wild, with people working in jobs as different in their detail as an impressionist painting is from a blank page. The range of products available in a modern industrial society is beyond anything that could have been imagined a hundred years ago, and so is the range of jobs.

The amount of coordination and cooperation in a modern industrial society is almost impossible to imagine. Yet something seems to drive economic systems, if sometimes clumsily and inefficiently, toward producing the goods and services that people want. Given scarce resources, how do large, complex societies go about answering the three basic economic questions? This is the economic problem, which is what this text is about.

Economic Systems and the Role of Government

Thus far we have described the questions that the economic system must answer. Now we turn to the mechanics of the system. Here the basic debate concerns the role of government.

On the one hand, many favor leaving the economy alone and keeping the government at bay while others believe that there are many circumstances in which the government may be able to improve the functioning of the market.

In November 2008, President Barack Obama was elected during a period of turmoil in the world economy. In the United States during the month of the election over 700,000 jobs were lost. A year later the unemployment rate was over 10 percent, and even into 2010, more than 15 million were unemployed. At the same time, the banking system nearly collapsed when massive home mortgage defaults led to bankruptcy filings by giants Bear Sterns and Lehmann Brothers. The Federal Reserve System and the Treasury in response took action to save some big banks and big auto companies with the Troubled Asset Relief Program (TARP). While some called it a "bail out," much of the federal expenditure on these troubled institutions was paid back with interest.

In addition, during his first year, President Obama pushed hard for major reform of the health care system, for much stronger government regulation of the financial markets, and for a system designed to more effectively regulate energy consumption and protect the environment.

All of a sudden, the debate is all about the nature of the system. What should the government be doing, and which decisions should be left to the free, private markets? Is it true that the government should save companies or banks in trouble on the grounds that they are "too big to fail"?

Command Economies

During the long struggle between the United States and the Soviet Union it was an all or nothing proposition. The Soviet Union had a planned economy run by the government. In a pure **command economy**, the basic economic questions are answered by a central government. Through a combination of government ownership of state enterprises and central planning, the government, either directly or indirectly, sets output targets, incomes, and prices.

command economy An economy in which a central government either directly or indirectly sets output targets, incomes, and prices.

While the extremes of central planning have been rejected, so too has the idea that "markets solve all problems." The real debate is not about whether we have government at all, it is about the extent and the character of a limited government role in the economy. One of the major themes of this book is that government involvement, in theory, may improve the efficiency and fairness of the allocation of a nation's resources. At the same time, a poorly functioning government can destroy incentives, lead to corruption, and result in the waste of a society's resources.

Laissez-Faire Economies: The Free Market

laissez-faire economy Literally from the French: "allow [them] to do." An economy in which individual people and firms pursue their own self-interest without any central direction or regulation.

market The institution through which buyers and sellers interact and engage in exchange.

At the opposite end of the spectrum from the command economy is the **laissez-faire economy**. The term *laissez-faire*, which translated literally from French means "allow [them] to do," implies a complete lack of government involvement in the economy. In this type of economy, individuals and firms pursue their own self-interest without any central direction or regulation; the sum total of millions of individual decisions ultimately determines all basic economic outcomes. The central institution through which a laissez-faire system answers the basic questions is the **market**, a term that is used in economics to mean an institution through which buyers and sellers interact and engage in exchange.

The interactions between buyers and sellers in any market range from simple to complex. Early explorers of the North American Midwest who wanted to exchange with Native Americans did so simply by bringing their goods to a central place and trading them. Today the Internet is revolutionizing exchange. A jewelry maker in upstate Maine can exhibit wares through digital photographs on the Web. Buyers can enter orders or make bids and pay by credit card. Companies such as eBay facilitate the worldwide interaction of tens of thousands of buyers and sellers sitting at their computers.

In short:

Some markets are simple and others are complex, but they all involve buyers and sellers engaging in exchange. The behavior of buyers and sellers in a laissez-faire economy determines what gets produced, how it is produced, and who gets it.

The following chapters explore market systems in great depth. A quick preview is worthwhile here, however.

Consumer Sovereignty   In a free, unregulated market, goods and services are produced and sold only if the supplier can make a profit. In simple terms, making a *profit* means selling goods or services for more than it costs to produce them. You cannot make a profit unless someone wants the product that you are selling. This logic leads to the notion of **consumer sovereignty**: The mix of output found in any free market system is dictated ultimately by the tastes and preferences of consumers who "vote" by buying or not buying. Businesses rise and fall in response to consumer demands. No central directive or plan is necessary.

consumer sovereignty   The idea that consumers ultimately dictate what will be produced (or not produced) by choosing what to purchase (and what not to purchase).

Individual Production Decisions: Free Enterprise   Under a free market system, individual producers must also determine how to organize and coordinate the actual production of their products or services. The owner of a small shoe repair shop must alone buy the needed equipment and tools, hang signs, and set prices. In a big corporation, so many people are involved in planning the production process that in many ways, corporate planning resembles the planning in a command economy. In a free market economy, producers may be small or large. One person who hand-paints eggshells may start to sell them as a business; a person good with computers may start a business designing Web sites. On a larger scale, a group of furniture designers may put together a large portfolio of sketches, raise several million dollars, and start a bigger business. At the extreme are huge corporations such as Microsoft, Mitsubishi, and Intel, each of which sells tens of billions of dollars' worth of products every year. Whether the firms are large or small, however, production decisions in a market economy are made by separate private organizations acting in what they perceive to be their own interests.

Often the market system is called a free enterprise system. **Free enterprise** means the freedom of individuals to start private businesses in search of profits. Because new businesses require capital investment before they can begin operation, starting a new business involves risk. A well-run business that produces a product for which demand exists is likely to succeed; a poorly run business or one that produces a product for which little demand exists now or in the future is likely to fail. It is through free enterprise that new products and new production techniques find their way into use.

free enterprise   The freedom of individuals to start and operate private businesses in search of profits.

Proponents of free market systems argue that free enterprise leads to more efficient production and better response to diverse and changing consumer preferences. If a producer produces inefficiently, competitors will come along, fight for the business, and eventually take it away. Thus, in a free market economy, competition forces producers to use efficient techniques of production. It is competition, then, that ultimately dictates how output is produced.

Distribution of Output   In a free market system, the distribution of output—who gets what—is also determined in a decentralized way. The amount that any one household gets depends on its income and wealth. *Income* is the amount that a household earns each year. It comes in a number of forms: wages, salaries, interest, and the like. *Wealth* is the amount that households have accumulated out of past income through saving or inheritance.

To the extent that income comes from working for a wage, it is at least in part determined by individual choice. You will work for the wages available in the market only if these wages (and the products and services they can buy) are sufficient to compensate you for what you give up by working. Your leisure certainly has a value also. You may discover that you can increase your income by getting more education or training. You *cannot* increase your income, however, if you acquire a skill that no one wants.

Price Theory   The basic coordinating mechanism in a free market system is price. A price is the amount that a product sells for per unit, and it reflects what society is willing to pay. Prices of inputs—labor, land, and capital—determine how much it costs to produce a product. Prices of various kinds of labor, or *wage rates*, determine the rewards for working in different jobs and professions. Many of the independent decisions made in a market economy involve the weighing of prices and costs, so it is not surprising that much of economic theory focuses on the factors that influence and determine prices. This is why microeconomic theory is often simply called *price theory*.

In sum:

> In a free market system, the basic economic questions are answered without the help of a central government plan or directives. This is what the "free" in free market means—the system is left to operate on its own with no outside interference. Individuals pursuing their own self-interest will go into business and produce the products and services that people want. Other individuals will decide whether to acquire skills; whether to work; and whether to buy, sell, invest, or save the income that they earn. The basic coordinating mechanism is price.

Mixed Systems, Markets, and Governments

The differences between command economies and laissez-faire economies in their pure forms are enormous. In fact, these pure forms do not exist in the world; all real systems are in some sense "mixed." That is, individual enterprise exists and independent choice is exercised even in economies in which the government plays a major role.

Conversely, no market economies exist without government involvement and government regulation. The United States has basically a free market economy, but government purchases accounted for just over 20 percent of the country's total production in 2010. Governments in the United States (local, state, and federal) directly employ about 14 percent of all workers (15 percent including active duty military). They also redistribute income by means of taxation and social welfare expenditures, and they regulate many economic activities.

One of the major themes in this book, and indeed in economics, is the tension between the advantages of free, unregulated markets and the desire for government involvement. Advocates of free markets argue that such markets work best when left to themselves. They produce only what people want; without buyers, sellers go out of business. Competition forces firms to adopt efficient production techniques. Wage differentials lead people to acquire needed skills. Competition also leads to innovation in both production techniques and products. The result is quality and variety, but market systems have problems too. Even staunch defenders of the free enterprise system recognize that market systems are not perfect. First, they do not always produce what people want at the lowest cost—there are inefficiencies. Second, rewards (income) may be unfairly distributed and some groups may be left out. Third, periods of unemployment and inflation recur with some regularity.

Many people point to these problems as reasons for government involvement. Indeed, for some problems, government involvement may be the only solution. However, government decisions are made by people who presumably, like the rest of us, act in their own self-interest. While governments may be called on to improve the functioning of the economy, there is no guarantee that they will do so. Just as markets may fail to produce an allocation of resources that is perfectly efficient and fair, governments may fail to improve matters. We return to this debate many times throughout this text.

Looking Ahead

This chapter described the economic problem in broad terms. We outlined the questions that all economic systems must answer. We also discussed very broadly the two kinds of economic systems. In the next chapter, we analyze the way market systems work.

SUMMARY

1. Every society has some system or process for transforming into useful form what nature and previous generations have provided. Economics is the study of that process and its outcomes.

2. *Producers* are those who take resources and transform them into usable products, or *outputs*. Private firms, households, and governments all produce something.

SCARCITY, CHOICE, AND OPPORTUNITY COST *p. 26*

3. All societies must answer *three basic questions*: What gets produced? How is it produced? Who gets what is produced? These three questions make up the *economic problem*.

4. One person alone on an island must make the same basic decisions that complex societies make. When a society consists of more than one person, questions of distribution, cooperation, and specialization arise.

5. Because resources are scarce relative to human wants in all societies, using resources to produce one good or service implies *not* using them to produce something else. This concept of *opportunity cost* is central to an understanding of economics.

6. Using resources to produce *capital* that will in turn produce benefits in the future implies *not* using those resources to produce consumer goods in the present.

7. Even if one individual or nation is absolutely more efficient at producing goods than another, all parties will gain if they specialize in producing goods in which they have a *comparative advantage*.

8. A *production possibility frontier* (ppf) is a graph that shows all the combinations of goods and services that can be produced if all of society's resources are used efficiently. The ppf illustrates a number of important economic concepts: scarcity, unemployment, inefficiency, increasing opportunity cost, and economic growth.

9. *Economic growth* occurs when society produces more, either by acquiring more resources or by learning to produce more with existing resources. Improved productivity may come from additional capital or from the discovery and application of new, more efficient techniques of production.

ECONOMIC SYSTEMS AND THE ROLE OF GOVERNMENT *p. 39*

10. In some modern societies, government plays a big role in answering the three basic questions. In pure *command economies*, a central authority directly or indirectly sets output targets, incomes, and prices.

11. A *laissez-faire economy* is one in which individuals independently pursue their own self-interest, without any central direction or regulation, and ultimately determine all basic economic outcomes.

12. A *market* is an institution through which buyers and sellers interact and engage in exchange. Some markets involve simple face-to-face exchange; others involve a complex series of transactions, often over great distances or through electronic means.

13. There are no purely planned economies and no pure laissez-faire economies; all economies are mixed. Individual enterprise, independent choice, and relatively free markets exist in centrally planned economies; there is significant government involvement in market economies such as that of the United States.

14. One of the great debates in economics revolves around the tension between the advantages of free, unregulated markets and the desire for government involvement in the economy. Free markets produce what people want, and competition forces firms to adopt efficient production techniques. The need for government intervention arises because free markets are characterized by inefficiencies and an unequal distribution of income, and experience regular periods of inflation and unemployment.

REVIEW TERMS AND CONCEPTS

absolute advantage, *p. 28*

capital, *p. 25*

command economy, *p. 40*

comparative advantage, *p. 29*

consumer goods, *p. 32*

consumer sovereignty, *p. 41*

economic growth, *p. 36*

factors of production (*or* factors), *p. 25*

free enterprise, *p. 41*

inputs *or* resources, *p. 26*

investment, *p. 32*

laissez-faire economy, *p. 40*

marginal rate of transformation (MRT), *p. 35*

market, *p. 40*

opportunity cost, *p. 27*

outputs, *p. 26*

production, *p. 25*

production possibility frontier (ppf), *p. 33*

theory of comparative advantage, *p. 28*

PROBLEMS

All problems are available on www.myeconlab.com

1. For each of the following, describe some of the potential opportunity costs:
   a. Studying for your economics test
   b. Spending 2 hours playing computer games
   c. Buying a new car instead of keeping the old one
   d. A local community voting to raise property taxes to increase school expenditures and to reduce class size
   e. A number of countries working together to build a space station
   f. Going to graduate school

2. "As long as all resources are fully employed and every firm in the economy is producing its output using the best available technology, the result will be efficient." Do you agree or disagree with this statement? Explain your answer.

3. You are an intern to the editor of a small-town newspaper in Mallsburg, Pennsylvania. Your boss, the editor, asks you to write the first draft of an editorial for this week's paper. Your assignment is to describe the costs and the benefits of building a new bridge across the railroad tracks in the center of town. Currently, most people who live in this town must drive 2 miles through thickly congested traffic to the existing bridge to get to the main shopping and employment center. The bridge will cost the citizens of Mallsburg $25 million, which will be paid for with a tax on their incomes over the next 20 years. What are the opportunity costs of building this bridge? What are the benefits that citizens will likely receive if the bridge is built? What other factors might you consider in writing this editorial?

4. Kristen and Anna live in the beach town of Santa Monica. They own a small business in which they make wristbands and pot holders and sell them to people on the beach. As shown in the table on the following page, Kristen can make 15 wristbands per hour but only 3 pot holders. Anna is a bit slower and can make only 12 wristbands or 2 pot holders in an hour.

	OUTPUT PER HOUR	
	WRISTBANDS	POT HOLDERS
Kristen	15	3
Anna	12	2

   a. For Kristen and for Anna, what is the opportunity cost of a pot holder? Who has a comparative advantage in the production of pot holders? Explain your answer.
   b. Who has a comparative advantage in the production of wristbands? Explain your answer.
   c. Assume that Kristen works 20 hours per week in the business. Assuming Kristen is in business on her own, graph the

possible combinations of pot holders and wristbands that she could produce in a week. Do the same for Anna.
   d. If Kristen devoted half of her time (10 out of 20 hours) to wristbands and half of her time to pot holders, how many of each would she produce in a week? If Anna did the same, how many of each would she produce? How many wristbands and pot holders would be produced in total?
   e. Suppose that Anna spent all 20 hours of her time on wristbands and Kristen spent 17 hours on pot holders and 3 hours on wristbands. How many of each item would be produced?
   f. Suppose that Kristen and Anna can sell all their wristbands for $1 each and all their pot holders for $5.50 each. If each of them worked 20 hours per week, how should they split their time between wristbands and pot holders? What is their maximum joint revenue?

5. Briefly describe the trade-offs involved in each of the following decisions. Specifically, list some of the opportunity costs associated with each decision, paying particular attention to the trade-offs between present and future consumption.
   a. After a stressful senior year in high school, Sherice decides to take the summer off instead of working before going to college.
   b. Frank is overweight and decides to work out every day and to go on a diet.
   c. Mei is diligent about taking her car in for routine maintenance even though it takes 2 hours of her time and costs $100 four times each year.
   d. Jim is in a hurry. He runs a red light on the way to work.

*6. The countries of Figistan and Blah are small island countries in the South Pacific. Both produce fruit and timber. Each island has a labor force of 1,200. The following table gives production per month for each worker in each country.

	BASKETS OF FRUIT	BOARD FEET OF TIMBER
Figistan workers	10	5
Blah workers	30	10

Productivity of one worker for one month

   a. Which country has an absolute advantage in the production of fruit? Which country has an absolute advantage in the production of timber?
   b. Which country has a comparative advantage in the production of fruit? of timber?
   c. Sketch the ppf's for both countries.
   d. Assuming no trading between the two, if both countries wanted to have equal numbers of feet of timber and baskets of fruit, how would they allocate workers to the two sectors?
   e. Show that specialization and trade can move both countries beyond their ppf's.

7. Suppose that a simple society has an economy with only one resource, labor. Labor can be used to produce only two commodities—X, a necessity good (food), and Y, a luxury good (music and merriment). Suppose that the labor force consists of 100 workers. One laborer can produce either 5 units of necessity per month (by hunting and gathering) or 10 units of luxury per month (by writing songs, playing the guitar, dancing, and so on).

   a. On a graph, draw the economy's ppf. Where does the ppf intersect the Y-axis? Where does it intersect the X-axis? What meaning do those points have?

   b. Suppose the economy produced at a point *inside* the ppf. Give at least two reasons why this could occur. What could be done to move the economy to a point *on* the ppf?

   c. Suppose you succeeded in lifting your economy to a point on its ppf. What point would you choose? How might your small society decide the point at which it wanted to be?

   d. Once you have chosen a point on the ppf, you still need to decide how your society's production will be divided. If you were a dictator, how would you decide? What would happen if you left product distribution to the free market?

*8. Match each diagram in Figure 1 with its description here. Assume that the economy is producing or attempting to produce at point A and that most members of society like meat and not fish. Some descriptions apply to more than one diagram, and some diagrams have more than one description.

   a. Inefficient production of meat and fish

   b. Productive efficiency

   c. An inefficient mix of output

   d. Technological advances in the production of meat and fish

   e. The law of increasing opportunity cost

   f. An impossible combination of meat and fish

9. A nation with fixed quantities of resources is able to produce any of the following combinations of bread and ovens:

LOAVES OF BREAD (MILLIONS)	OVENS (THOUSANDS)
75	0
60	12
45	22
30	30
15	36
0	40

These figures assume that a certain number of previously produced ovens are available in the current period for baking bread.

   a. Using the data in the table, graph the ppf (with ovens on the vertical axis).

   b. Does the principle of "increasing opportunity cost" hold in this nation? Explain briefly. (*Hint:* What happens to the opportunity cost of bread—measured in number of ovens—as bread production increases?)

   c. If this country chooses to produce both ovens and bread, what will happen to the ppf over time? Why?

*Note: Problems marked with an asterisk are more challenging.

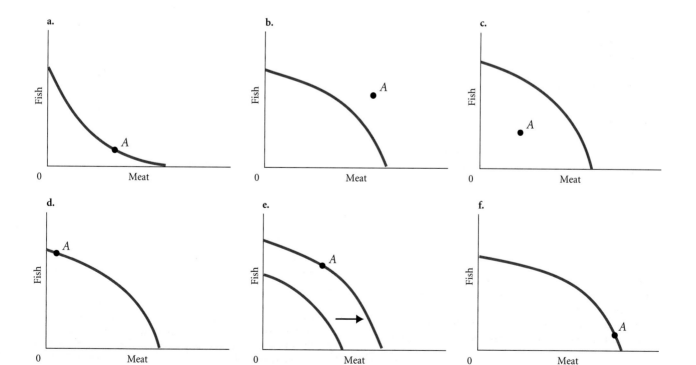

▲ FIGURE 1

Now suppose that a new technology is discovered that allows twice as many loaves of bread to be baked in each existing oven.

  d. Illustrate (on your original graph) the effect of this new technology on the ppf.

  e. Suppose that before the new technology is introduced, the nation produces 22 ovens. After the new technology is introduced, the nation produces 30 ovens. What is the effect of the new technology on the production of bread? (Give the number of loaves before and after the change.)

10. [Related to the *Economics in Practice* on *p. 28*] An analysis of a large-scale survey of consumer food purchases by Mark Aguiar and Erik Hurst indicates that retired people spend less for the same market basket of food than working people do. Use the concept of opportunity cost to explain this fact.

*11. Dr. Falk is a dentist who performs two basic procedures: filling cavities and whitening teeth. Falk charges $50 per cavity filled, a process that takes him 15 minutes per tooth and requires no help or materials. For tooth whitening, a process requiring 30 minutes, Falk charges $150 net of materials. Again, no help is required. Is anything puzzling about Falk's pricing pattern? Explain your answer.

12. In 2010, the Texas Lottery Commission began selling $5 Dallas Cowboys scratch-off game tickets. Prizes for winning tickets included cash, team merchandise, and Cowboys' season tickets for the 2010 season at their new $1.15 billion stadium. Suppose you received one of these Cowboys' scratch-off games as a birthday present and you won free season tickets for the 2010 season. Would there be a cost to you to attend the Cowboys' games during the 2010 season?

13. Describe a command economy and a laissez-faire economy. Do any economic systems in the world reflect the purest forms of command or laissez-faire economies? Explain.

14. The nation of Rougarou is able to produce turnips and potatoes in combinations represented by the data in the following table. Each number represents thousands of bushels.

	A	B	C	D	E
Turnips	100	90	70	40	0
Potatoes	0	10	20	30	40

Plot this data on a production possibilities graph and explain why the data shows that Rougarou experiences increasing opportunity costs.

15. Explain how each of the following situations would affect a nation's production possibilities curve.

  a. A technological innovation allows the nation to more efficiently convert solar energy into electricity.

  b. A prolonged recession increases the number of unemployed workers in the nation.

  c. A category 5 hurricane destroys over 40 percent of the nation's productive capacity.

  d. The quality of education in the nation's colleges and universities improves greatly.

  e. The nation passes a law requiring all employers to give their employees 16 weeks of paid vacation each year. Prior to this law, employers were not legally required to give employees any paid vacation time.

Demand, Supply, and Market Equilibrium

3

Chapters 1 and 2 introduced the discipline, methodology, and subject matter of economics. We now begin the task of analyzing how a market economy actually works. This chapter and the next present an overview of the way individual markets work. They introduce some of the concepts needed to understand both microeconomics and macroeconomics.

As we proceed to define terms and make assumptions, it is important to keep in mind what we are doing. In Chapter 1 we explained what economic theory attempts to do. Theories are abstract representations of reality, like a map that represents a city. We believe that the models presented here will help you understand the workings of the economy just as a map helps you find your way around a city. Just as a map presents one view of the world, so too does any given theory of the economy. Alternatives exist to the theory that we present. We believe, however, that the basic model presented here, while sometimes abstract, is useful in gaining an understanding of how the economy works.

In the simple island society discussed in Chapter 2, Bill and Colleen solved the economic problem directly. They allocated their time and used the island's resources to satisfy their wants. Bill might be a farmer, Colleen a hunter and carpenter. He might be a civil engineer, she a doctor. Exchange occurred, but complex markets were not necessary.

In societies of many people, however, production must satisfy wide-ranging tastes and preferences. Producers therefore specialize. Farmers produce more food than they can eat so that they can sell it to buy manufactured goods. Physicians are paid for specialized services, as are attorneys, construction workers, and editors. When there is specialization, there must be exchange, and *markets* are the institutions through which exchange takes place.

This chapter begins to explore the basic forces at work in market systems. The purpose of our discussion is to explain how the individual decisions of households and firms together, without any central planning or direction, answer the three basic questions: What gets produced? How is it produced? Who gets what is produced? We begin with some definitions.

Firms and Households: The Basic Decision-Making Units

Throughout this book, we discuss and analyze the behavior of two fundamental decision-making units: *firms*—the primary producing units in an economy—and *households*—the consuming units in an economy. Both are made up of people performing different functions and playing different roles. In essence, what we are developing is a theory of human behavior.

47

firm An organization that transforms resources (inputs) into products (outputs). Firms are the primary producing units in a market economy.

A **firm** exists when a person or a group of people decides to produce a product or products by transforming *inputs*—that is, resources in the broadest sense—into *outputs*, the products that are sold in the market. Some firms produce goods; others produce services. Some are large, many are small, and some are in between. All firms exist to transform resources into goods and services that people want. The Colorado Symphony Orchestra takes labor, land, a building, musically talented people, instruments, and other inputs and combines them to produce concerts. The production process can be extremely complicated. For example, the first flautist in the orchestra uses training, talent, previous performance experience, score, instrument, conductor's interpretation, and personal feelings about the music to produce just one contribution to an overall performance.

Most firms exist to make a profit for their owners, but some do not. Columbia University, for example, fits the description of a firm: It takes inputs in the form of labor, land, skills, books, and buildings and produces a service that we call education. Although the university sells that service for a price, it does not exist to make a profit; instead, it exists to provide education of the highest quality possible.

Still, most firms exist to make a profit. They engage in production because they can sell their product for more than it costs to produce it. The analysis of a firm's behavior that follows rests on the assumption that *firms make decisions in order to maximize profits*. Sometimes firms suffer losses instead of earning profits. In recent years this has occurred frequently. When firms suffer losses, we will assume that they act to minimize those losses.

entrepreneur A person who organizes, manages, and assumes the risks of a firm, taking a new idea or a new product and turning it into a successful business.

An **entrepreneur** is someone who organizes, manages, and assumes the risks of a firm. When a new firm is created, someone must organize the new firm, arrange financing, hire employees, and take risks. That person is an entrepreneur. Sometimes existing firms introduce new products, and sometimes new firms develop or improve on an old idea, but at the root of it all is entrepreneurship, which some see as the core of the free enterprise system.

households The consuming units in an economy.

The consuming units in an economy are **households**. A household may consist of any number of people: a single person living alone, a married couple with four children, or 15 unrelated people sharing a house. Household decisions are presumably based on individual tastes and preferences. The household buys what it wants and can afford. In a large, heterogeneous, and open society such as the United States, wildly different tastes find expression in the marketplace. A six-block walk in any direction on any street in Manhattan or a drive from the Chicago Loop south into rural Illinois should be enough to convince anyone that it is difficult to generalize about what people do and do not like.

Even though households have wide-ranging preferences, they also have some things in common. All—even the very rich—have ultimately limited incomes, and all must pay in some way for the goods and services they consume. Although households may have some control over their incomes—they can work more hours or fewer hours—they are also constrained by the availability of jobs, current wages, their own abilities, and their accumulated and inherited wealth (or lack thereof).

Input Markets and Output Markets: The Circular Flow

Households and firms interact in two basic kinds of markets: product (or output) markets and input (or factor) markets. Goods and services that are intended for use by households are exchanged in **product** or **output markets**. In output markets, firms *supply* and households *demand*.

product or **output markets** The markets in which goods and services are exchanged.

To produce goods and services, firms must buy resources in **input** or **factor markets**. Firms buy inputs from households, which supply these inputs. When a firm decides how much to produce (supply) in output markets, it must simultaneously decide how much of each input it needs to produce the desired level of output. To produce automobiles, Ford Motor Company must use many inputs, including tires, steel, complicated machinery, and many different kinds of labor.

input or **factor markets** The markets in which the resources used to produce goods and services are exchanged.

Figure 3.1 shows the *circular flow* of economic activity through a simple market economy. Note that the flow reflects the direction in which goods and services flow through input and output markets. For example, real goods and services flow from firms to households through output—or product—markets. Labor services flow from households to firms through input markets. Payment (most often in money form) for goods and services flows in the opposite direction.

In input markets, households *supply* resources. Most households earn their incomes by working—they supply their labor in the **labor market** to firms that demand labor and pay workers for their time and skills. Households may also loan their accumulated or inherited savings to firms for interest or exchange those savings for claims to future profits, as when a household buys shares of stock in a corporation. In the **capital market**, households supply the funds that firms use to buy capital goods. Households may also supply land or other real property in exchange for rent in the **land market**.

Inputs into the production process are also called **factors of production**. Land, labor, and capital are the three key factors of production. Throughout this text, we use the terms *input* and *factor of production* interchangeably. Thus, input markets and factor markets mean the same thing.

Early economics texts included entrepreneurship as a type of input, just like land, labor, and capital. Treating entrepreneurship as a separate factor of production has fallen out of favor, however, partially because it is unmeasurable. Most economists today implicitly assume that

labor market The input/factor market in which households supply work for wages to firms that demand labor.

capital market The input/factor market in which households supply their savings, for interest or for claims to future profits, to firms that demand funds to buy capital goods.

land market The input/factor market in which households supply land or other real property in exchange for rent.

factors of production The inputs into the production process. Land, labor, and capital are the three key factors of production.

▲ **FIGURE 3.1 The Circular Flow of Economic Activity**
Diagrams like this one show the circular flow of economic activity, hence the name *circular flow diagram*. Here goods and services flow clockwise: Labor services supplied by households flow to firms, and goods and services produced by firms flow to households. Payment (usually money) flows in the opposite (counterclockwise) direction: Payment for goods and services flows from households to firms, and payment for labor services flows from firms to households.

Note: Color Guide—In Figure 3.1 households are depicted in *blue* and firms are depicted in *red*. From now on all diagrams relating to the behavior of households will be blue or shades of blue and all diagrams relating to the behavior of firms will be red or shades of red.

entrepreneurship is in plentiful supply. That is, if profit opportunities exist, it is likely that entrepreneurs will crop up to take advantage of them. This assumption has turned out to be a good predictor of actual economic behavior and performance.

The supply of inputs and their prices ultimately determine household income. Thus, the amount of income a household earns depends on the decisions it makes concerning what types of inputs it chooses to supply. Whether to stay in school, how much and what kind of training to get, whether to start a business, how many hours to work, whether to work at all, and how to invest savings are all household decisions that affect income.

As you can see:

> Input and output markets are connected through the behavior of both firms and households. Firms determine the quantities and character of outputs produced and the types and quantities of inputs demanded. Households determine the types and quantities of products demanded and the quantities and types of inputs supplied.[1]

The following analysis of demand and supply will lead up to a theory of how market prices are determined. Prices are determined by the interaction between demanders and suppliers. To understand this interaction, we first need to know how product prices influence the behavior of demanders and suppliers *separately*. Therefore, we discuss output markets by focusing first on demanders, then on suppliers, and finally on their interaction.

Demand in Product/Output Markets

In real life, households make many decisions at the same time. To see how the forces of demand and supply work, however, let us focus first on the amount of a *single* product that an *individual* household decides to consume within some given period of time, such as a month or a year.

A household's decision about what quantity of a particular output, or product, to demand depends on a number of factors, including:

- The *price of the product* in question.
- The *income available* to the household.
- The household's *amount of accumulated wealth*.
- The *prices of other products* available to the household.
- The household's *tastes and preferences*.
- The household's *expectations* about future income, wealth, and prices.

quantity demanded The amount (number of units) of a product that a household would buy in a given period if it could buy all it wanted at the current market price.

Quantity demanded is the amount (number of units) of a product that a household would buy in a given period *if it could buy all it wanted at the current market price.* Of course, the amount of a product that households finally purchase depends on the amount of product actually available in the market. The expression *if it could buy all it wanted* is critical to the definition of quantity demanded because it allows for the possibility that quantity supplied and quantity demanded are unequal.

---

[1] Our description of markets begins with the behavior of firms and households. Modern orthodox economic theory essentially combines two distinct but closely related theories of behavior. The "theory of household behavior," or "consumer behavior," has its roots in the works of nineteenth-century utilitarians such as Jeremy Bentham, William Jevons, Carl Menger, Leon Walras, Vilfredo Parcto, and F. Y. Edgeworth. The "theory of the firm" developed out of the earlier classical political economy of Adam Smith, David Ricardo, and Thomas Malthus. In 1890, Alfred Marshall published the first of many editions of his *Principles of Economics.* That volume pulled together the main themes of both the classical economists and the utilitarians into what is now called *neoclassical economics.* While there have been many changes over the years, the basic structure of the model that we build can be found in Marshall's work.

Changes in Quantity Demanded versus Changes in Demand

The most important relationship in individual markets is that between market price and quantity demanded. For this reason, we need to begin our discussion by analyzing the likely response of households to changes in price using the device of *ceteris paribus*, or "all else equal." That is, we will attempt to derive a relationship between the quantity demanded of a good per time period and the price of that good, holding income, wealth, other prices, tastes, and expectations constant.

It is very important to distinguish between price changes, which affect the quantity of a good demanded, and changes in other factors (such as income), which change the entire relationship between price and quantity. For example, if a family begins earning a higher income, it might buy more of a good at every possible price. To be sure that we distinguish between changes in price and other changes that affect demand, throughout the rest of the text, we will be very precise about terminology. Specifically:

> Changes in the price of a product affect the *quantity demanded* per period. Changes in any other factor, such as income or preferences, affect *demand*. Thus, we say that an increase in the price of Coca-Cola is likely to cause a decrease in the *quantity of Coca-Cola demanded*. However, we say that an increase in income is likely to cause an increase in the *demand* for most goods.

Price and Quantity Demanded: The Law of Demand

A **demand schedule** shows how much of a product a person or household is willing to purchase per time period (each week or each month) at different prices. Clearly that decision is based on numerous interacting factors. Consider Alex who just graduated from college with an entry-level job at a local bank. During her senior year, Alex got a car loan and bought a used Mini Cooper. The Mini gets 25 miles per gallon of gasoline. Alex lives with several friends in a house 10 miles from her workplace and enjoys visiting her parents 50 miles away.

How often Alex will decide to drive herself to work and parties, visit her family, or even go joy riding depends on many things, including her income and whether she likes to drive. But the price of gasoline also plays an important role, and it is this relationship between price and quantity demanded that we focus on in the law of demand. With a gasoline price of $3.00 a gallon, Alex might decide to drive herself to work every day, visit her parents once a week, and drive another 50 miles a week for other activities. This driving pattern would add up to 250 miles a week, which would use 10 gallons of gasoline in her Mini. The demand schedule in Table 3.1 thus shows that at a price of $3.00 per gallon, Alex is willing to buy 10 gallons of gasoline. We can see that this demand schedule reflects a lot of information about Alex including where she lives and works and what she likes to do in her spare time.

Now suppose an international crisis in the Middle East causes the price of gasoline at the pump to rise to $5.00 per gallon. How does this affect Alex's demand for gasoline, assuming that everything else remains the same? Driving is now more expensive, and we would not be surprised if Alex decided to take the bus some mornings or share a ride with friends. She might visit her parents less frequently as well. On the demand schedule given in Table 3.1, Alex cuts her desired consumption of gasoline by half to 5 gallons when the price goes to $5.00. If, instead, the price of gasoline fell substantially, Alex might well spend more time driving, and that is in fact the pattern we see in the table. This same information presented graphically is called a **demand curve**. Alex's demand curve is presented in Figure 3.2. You will note in Figure 3.2 that *quantity* (*q*) is measured along the horizontal axis and *price* (*P*) is measured along the vertical axis. This is the convention we follow throughout this book.

demand schedule   A table showing how much of a given product a household would be willing to buy at different prices.

demand curve   A graph illustrating how much of a given product a household would be willing to buy at different prices.

TABLE 3.1	Alex's Demand Schedule for Gasoline
Price (per Gallon)	Quantity Demanded (Gallons per Week)
$8.00	0
7.00	2
6.00	3
5.00	5
4.00	7
3.00	10
2.00	14
1.00	20
0.00	26

Demand Curves Slope Downward   The data in Table 3.1 show that at lower prices, Alex buys more gasoline; at higher prices, she buys less. Thus, there is a *negative, or inverse, relationship between quantity demanded and price.* When price rises, quantity demanded falls, and when price falls, quantity demanded rises. Thus, demand curves always slope downward. This negative relationship between price and quantity demanded is often referred to as the **law of demand**, a term first used by economist Alfred Marshall in his 1890 textbook.

law of demand   The negative relationship between price and quantity demanded: As price rises, quantity demanded decreases; as price falls, quantity demanded increases.

Some people are put off by the abstraction of demand curves. Of course, we do not actually draw our own demand curves for products. When we want to make a purchase, we usually face only a single price and how much we would buy at other prices is irrelevant. However, demand curves help analysts understand the kind of behavior that households are *likely* to exhibit if they are actually faced with a higher or lower price. We know, for example, that if the price of a good rises enough, the quantity demanded must ultimately drop to zero. The demand curve is thus a tool that helps us explain economic behavior and predict reactions to possible price changes.

▲ **FIGURE 3.2 Alex's Demand Curve**

The relationship between price (*P*) and quantity demanded (*q*) presented graphically is called a demand curve. Demand curves have a negative slope, indicating that lower prices cause quantity demanded to increase. Note that Alex's demand curve is blue; demand in product markets is determined by household choice.

Marshall's definition of a social "law" captures the idea:

The term "law" means nothing more than a general proposition or statement of tendencies, more or less certain, more or less definite . . . a *social law* is a statement of social tendencies; that is, that a certain course of action may be expected from the members of a social group under certain conditions.[2]

It seems reasonable to expect that consumers will demand more of a product at a lower price and less of it at a higher price. Households must divide their incomes over a wide range of goods and services. At $3.00 per gallon and 25 miles to a gallon, driving the 20 miles round trip to work costs Alex $2.40. At $5.00 per gallon, the trip now costs $4.00. With the higher prices, Alex may have to give up her morning latte if she drives, and that may turn out to be too big a sacrifice for her. As the price of gasoline rises, the opportunity cost of driving in terms of other types of consumption also rises and that is why Alex ends up driving less as the price of gasoline rises. Goods compete with one another for our spending.

Economists use the concept of *utility* to explain the slope of the demand curve. Presumably, we consume goods and services because they give us utility or satisfaction. As we consume more of a product within a given period of time, it is likely that each additional unit consumed will yield successively less satisfaction. The utility you gain from a second ice cream cone is likely to be less than the utility you gained from the first, the third is worth even less, and so on. This *law of diminishing marginal utility* is an important concept in economics. If each successive unit of a good is worth less to you, you are not going to be willing to pay as much for it. Thus, it is reasonable to expect a downward slope in the demand curve for that good.

Thinking about the ways that people are affected by price changes also helps us see what is behind the law of demand. Consider this example: Luis lives and works in Mexico City. His elderly mother lives in Santiago, Chile. Last year the airlines servicing South America got into a price war, and the price of flying between Mexico City and Santiago dropped from 20,000 pesos to 10,000 pesos. How might Luis's behavior change?

First, he is better off. Last year he flew home to Chile three times at a total cost of 60,000 pesos. This year he can fly to Chile the same number of times, buy exactly the same combination of other goods and services that he bought last year, and have 30,000 pesos left over. Because he is better off—his income can buy more—he may fly home more frequently. Second, the opportunity cost of flying home has changed. Before the price war, Luis had to sacrifice 20,000 pesos worth of other goods and services each time he flew to Chile. After the price war, he must sacrifice only 10,000 pesos worth of other goods and services for each trip. The trade-off has changed. Both of these effects are likely to lead to a higher quantity demanded in response to the lower price.

In sum:

> It is reasonable to expect quantity demanded to fall when price rises, *ceteris paribus*, and to expect quantity demanded to rise when price falls, *ceteris paribus*. Demand curves have a negative slope.

Other Properties of Demand Curves   Two additional things are notable about Alex's demand curve. First, it intersects the *Y*, or price, axis. This means that there is a price above which she buys no gasoline. In this case, Alex simply stops driving when the price reaches $8 per gallon. As long as households have limited incomes and wealth, all demand curves will intersect the price axis. For any commodity, there is always a price above which a household will not or cannot pay. Even if the good or service is very important, all households are ultimately constrained, or limited, by income and wealth.

---

[2] Alfred Marshall, *Principles of Economics*, 8th ed. (New York: Macmillan, 1948), p. 33. (The first edition was published in 1890.)

Second, Alex's demand curve intersects the *X*, or quantity, axis. Even at a zero price, there is a limit to how much she will drive. If gasoline were free, she would use 26 gallons, but not more. That demand curves intersect the quantity axis is a matter of common sense. Demand in a given period of time is limited, if only by time, even at a zero price.

To summarize what we know about the shape of demand curves:

1. They have a negative slope. An increase in price is likely to lead to a decrease in quantity demanded, and a decrease in price is likely to lead to an increase in quantity demanded.
2. They intersect the quantity (*X*-) axis, a result of time limitations and diminishing marginal utility.
3. They intersect the price (*Y*-) axis, a result of limited income and wealth.

That is all we can say; it is not possible to generalize further. The actual shape of an individual household demand curve—whether it is steep or flat, whether it is bowed in or bowed out—depends on the unique tastes and preferences of the household and other factors. Some households may be very sensitive to price changes; other households may respond little to a change in price. In some cases, plentiful substitutes are available; in other cases, they are not. Thus, to fully understand the shape and position of demand curves, we must turn to the other determinants of household demand.

Other Determinants of Household Demand

Of the many factors likely to influence a household's demand for a specific product, we have considered only the price of the product. Other determining factors include household income and wealth, the prices of other goods and services, tastes and preferences, and expectations.

income The sum of all a household's wages, salaries, profits, interest payments, rents, and other forms of earnings in a given period of time. It is a flow measure.

Income and Wealth Before we proceed, we need to define two terms that are often confused, *income* and *wealth*. A household's **income** is the sum of all the wages, salaries, profits, interest payments, rents, and other forms of earnings received by the household *in a given period of time*. Income is thus a *flow* measure: We must specify a time period for it—income *per month* or *per year*. You can spend or consume more or less than your income in any given period. If you consume less than your income, you save. To consume more than your income in a period, you must either borrow or draw on savings accumulated from previous periods.

wealth *or* **net worth** The total value of what a household owns minus what it owes. It is a stock measure.

Wealth is the total value of what a household owns minus what it owes. Another word for wealth is **net worth**—the amount a household would have left if it sold all of its possessions and paid all of its debts. Wealth is a *stock* measure: It is measured at a given point in time. If, in a given period, you spend less than your income, you save; the amount that you save is added to your wealth. Saving is the flow that affects the stock of wealth. When you spend more than your income, you *dissave*—you reduce your wealth.

Households with higher incomes and higher accumulated savings or inherited wealth can afford to buy more goods and services. In general, we would expect higher demand at higher levels of income/wealth and lower demand at lower levels of income/wealth. Goods for which demand goes up when income is higher and for which demand goes down when income is lower are called **normal goods**. Movie tickets, restaurant meals, telephone calls, and shirts are all normal goods.

normal goods Goods for which demand goes up when income is higher and for which demand goes down when income is lower.

However, generalization in economics can be hazardous. Sometimes demand for a good falls when household income rises. Consider, for example, the various qualities of meat available. When a household's income rises, it is likely to buy higher-quality meats—its demand for filet mignon is likely to rise—but its demand for lower-quality meats—chuck steak, for example—is likely to fall. Transportation is another example. At higher incomes, people can afford to fly. People who can afford to fly are less likely to take the bus long distances. Thus, higher income may *reduce* the number of times someone takes a bus. Goods for which demand tends to fall when income rises are called **inferior goods**.

inferior goods Goods for which demand tends to fall when income rises.

Prices of Other Goods and Services No consumer decides in isolation on the amount of any one commodity to buy. Instead, each decision is part of a larger set of decisions that are made simultaneously. Households must apportion their incomes over many different goods and services. As a result, the price of any one good can and does affect the demand for other goods. This is most obviously the case when goods are substitutes for one another. For Alex the bus is an alternative that she uses when gasoline gets expensive.

ECONOMICS IN PRACTICE

Kindle in the College Market?

Most of you are likely quite aware of the high price of textbooks. For some students, high prices lead to sharing texts or using library copies. Jeff Bezos, who runs Amazon, the producer of the Kindle, thinks the high prices of printed text books provides an opportunity for his company to increase the demand for the Kindle.

People buy Kindles so that they can read books on them. Books are thus a complement to the Kindle. The cheaper the electronic books you can buy are, the higher your demand for the Kindle device. As the article here suggests, Amazon is working with several universities and textbook publishers to make textbooks available—for a much lower price—on the Kindle. As the last line of the article tells us, this move is clearly intended to build demand for the Kindle itself. The president of Amazon is well aware of the role of complements in his business.

information officer. The university plans to compare the experiences of students who get the Kindles and those who use traditional textbooks, he said.

Amazon has worked out a deal with several textbook publishers to make their materials available for the device. Five other universities are involved in the Kindle project, according to people briefed on the matter. They are Pace, Princeton, Reed, Darden School at the University of Virginia, and Arizona State. The moves are the latest by Amazon to promote the Kindle, which is the company's first consumer-electronics device.

Amazon to Launch Kindle for Textbooks

The Wall Street Journal

Beginning this fall, some students at Case Western Reserve University in Cleveland will be given large-screen Kindles with textbooks for chemistry, computer science, and a freshman seminar already installed, said Lev Gonick, the school's chief

Source: The Wall Street Journal, excerpted from "Amazon to Launch Kindle for Textbooks" by Geoffrey A. Fowler and Ben Worthen. Copyright 2009 by *Dow Jones & Company, Inc.* Reproduced with permission of *Dow Jones & Company, Inc.* via Copyright Clearance Center.

When an *increase* in the price of one good causes demand for another good to *increase* (a positive relationship), we say that the goods are **substitutes**. A *fall* in the price of a good causes a *decline* in demand for its substitutes. Substitutes are goods that can serve as replacements for one another.

To be substitutes, two products do not need to be identical. Identical products are called **perfect substitutes**. Japanese cars are not identical to American cars. Nonetheless, all have four wheels, are capable of carrying people, and run on gasoline. Thus, significant changes in the price of one country's cars can be expected to influence demand for the other country's cars. Restaurant meals are substitutes for meals eaten at home, and flying from New York to Washington, D.C., is a substitute for taking the train.

Often two products "go together"—that is, they complement each other. Bacon and eggs are **complementary goods**, as are cars and gasoline, and cameras and film. When two goods are **complements**, a *decrease* in the price of one results in an *increase* in demand for the other and vice versa. The makers of Guitar Hero and Rock Band, two popular and competitive video games, understand that there is a strong connection between how many songs can be played on their operating platforms and how strong the demand is for their games. For iPods and Kindles as well, the availability of content at low prices stimulates demand for the devices. The *Economics in Practice* above talks about the complementarity between the Kindle and e-books.

Tastes and Preferences Income, wealth, and prices of goods available are the three factors that determine the combinations of goods and services that a household is *able* to buy. You know that you cannot afford to rent an apartment at $1,200 per month if your monthly income is only $400, but within these constraints, you are more or less free to choose what to buy. Your final choice depends on your individual tastes and preferences.

substitutes Goods that can serve as replacements for one another; when the price of one increases, demand for the other increases.

perfect substitutes Identical products.

complements, complementary goods Goods that "go together"; a decrease in the price of one results in an increase in demand for the other and vice versa.

Changes in preferences can and do manifest themselves in market behavior. Thirty years ago the major big-city marathons drew only a few hundred runners. Now tens of thousands enter and run. The demand for running shoes, running suits, stopwatches, and other running items has greatly increased. For many years, people drank soda for refreshment. Today convenience stores are filled with a dizzying array of iced teas, fruit juices, natural beverages, and mineral waters.

Within the constraints of prices and incomes, preference shapes the demand curve, but it is difficult to generalize about tastes and preferences. First, they are volatile: Five years ago more people smoked cigarettes and fewer people had computers. Second, tastes are idiosyncratic: Some people like to text, whereas others still prefer to use e-mail; some people prefer dogs, whereas others are crazy about cats. Some eat fried cockroaches. The diversity of individual demands is almost infinite.

One of the interesting questions in economics is why, in some markets, diverse consumer tastes give rise to a variety of styles, while in other markets, despite a seeming diversity in tastes, we find only one or two varieties. All sidewalks in the United States are a similar gray color, yet houses are painted a rainbow of colors. Yet it is not obvious on the face of it that people would not prefer as much variety in their sidewalks as in their houses. To answer this type of question, we need to move beyond the demand curve. We will revisit this question in a later chapter.

Expectations What you decide to buy today certainly depends on today's prices and your current income and wealth. You also have expectations about what your position will be in the future. You may have expectations about future changes in prices too, and these may affect your decisions today.

There are many examples of the ways expectations affect demand. When people buy a house or a car, they often must borrow part of the purchase price and repay it over a number of years. In deciding what kind of house or car to buy, they presumably must think about their income today, as well as what their income is likely to be in the future.

As another example, consider a student in the final year of medical school living on a scholarship of $12,000. Compare that student with another person earning $6 an hour at a full-time job, with no expectation of a significant change in income in the future. The two have virtually identical incomes because there are about 2,000 working hours in a year (40 hours per week × 50 work weeks per year). But even if they have the same tastes, the medical student is likely to demand different goods and services, simply because of the expectation of a major increase in income later on.

Increasingly, economic theory has come to recognize the importance of expectations. We will devote a good deal of time to discussing how expectations affect more than just demand. For the time being, however, it is important to understand that demand depends on more than just *current* incomes, prices, and tastes.

Shift of Demand versus Movement Along a Demand Curve

Recall that a demand curve shows the relationship between quantity demanded and the price of a good. Demand curves are derived while holding income, tastes, and other prices constant. If income, tastes, or other prices change, we would have to derive an entirely new relationship between price and quantity.

Let us return once again to Alex. (See Table 3.1 and Figure 3.2 on p. 52.) Suppose that when we derived the demand curve in Figure 3.1 Alex was receiving a salary of $500 per week after taxes. If Alex faces a price of $3.00 per gallon and chooses to drive 250 miles per week, her total weekly expenditure works out to be $3.00 per gallon times 10 gallons of $30 per week. That amounts to 6.0 percent of her income.

Suppose now she were to receive a raise to $700 per week after taxes. Then if she continued to buy only 10 gallons of gasoline a week it would absorb a smaller percentage of her income. The higher income may well raise the amount of gasoline being used by Alex *regardless* of what she was using before. Notice in Figure 3.3 that the entire curve has shifted to the right—at $3.00 a gallon the curve shows an increase in the quantity demanded from 10 to 15 gallons. At $5.00, the quantity demanded by Alex increases from 5 gallons to 10 gallons.

The fact that demand *increased* when income increased implies that gasoline is a *normal good* to Alex.

TABLE 3.2   Shift of Alex's Demand Schedule Due to an Increase in Income

Price (per Gallon)	Schedule D_0 Quantity Demanded (Gallons per Week at an Income of $500 per Week)	Schedule D_1 Quantity Demanded (Gallons per Week at an Income of $700 per Week)
$8.00	0	3
7.00	2	5
6.00	3	7
5.00	5	10
4.00	7	12
3.00	10	15
2.00	14	19
1.00	20	24
0.00	26	30

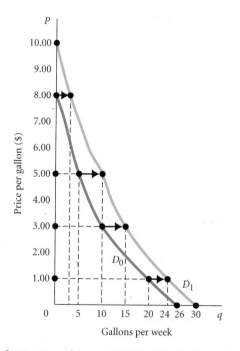

▲ **FIGURE 3.3 Shift of a Demand Curve Following a Rise in Income**
When the price of a good changes, we move *along* the demand curve for that good. When any other factor that influences demand changes (income, tastes, and so on), the relationship between price and quantity is different; there is a *shift* of the demand curve, in this case from D_0 to D_1. Gasoline is a normal good.

shift of a demand curve
The change that takes place in a demand curve corresponding to a new relationship between quantity demanded of a good and price of that good. The shift is brought about by a change in the original conditions.

movement along a demand curve The change in quantity demanded brought about by a change in price.

The conditions that were in place at the time we drew the original demand curve have now changed. In other words, a factor that affects Alex's demand for gasoline (in this case, her income) has changed, and there is now a new relationship between price and quantity demanded. Such a change is referred to as a **shift of a demand curve**.

It is very important to distinguish between a change in quantity demanded—that is, some movement *along* a demand curve—and a shift of demand. Demand schedules and demand curves show the relationship between the price of a good or service and the quantity demanded per period, *ceteris paribus*. If price changes, quantity demanded will change—this is a **movement along a demand curve**. When any of the *other* factors that influence demand change, however, a new relationship between price and quantity demanded is established—this is a *shift of a demand curve*. The result, then, is a *new* demand curve. Changes in income, preferences, or prices of other goods cause a demand curve to shift:

Change in price of a good or service leads to
└──➤ Change in *quantity demanded* (**movement along a demand curve**).

Change in income, preferences, or prices of other goods or services leads to
└──➤ Change in *demand* (**shift of a demand curve**).

Figure 3.4 on the next page illustrates the differences between movement along a demand curve and shifting demand curves. In Figure 3.4(a), an increase in household income causes demand for hamburger (an inferior good) to decline, or shift to the left from D_0 to D_1. (Because quantity is measured on the horizontal axis, a decrease means a *shift to the left*.) In contrast, demand for steak (a normal good) increases, or *shifts to the right*, when income rises.

In Figure 3.4(b), an increase in the price of hamburger from $1.49 to $3.09 a pound causes a household to buy less hamburger each month. In other words, the higher price causes the *quantity demanded* to decline from 10 pounds to 5 pounds per month. This change represents a movement *along* the demand curve for hamburger. In place of hamburger, the household buys more chicken. The household's demand for chicken (a substitute for hamburger) rises—the demand curve shifts to the right. At the same time, the demand for ketchup (a good that complements hamburger) declines—its demand curve shifts to the left.

From Household Demand to Market Demand

market demand The sum of all the quantities of a good or service demanded per period by all the households buying in the market for that good or service.

Market demand is simply the sum of all the quantities of a good or service demanded per period by all the households buying in the market for that good or service. Figure 3.5 shows the derivation of a market demand curve from three individual demand curves. (Although this market demand curve is derived from the behavior of only three people, most markets have thousands, or even millions, of demanders.) As the table in Figure 3.5 shows, when the price of a pound of coffee is $3.50, both household A and household C would purchase 4 pounds per month, while household B would buy none. At that price, presumably, B drinks tea. Market demand at $3.50 would thus be a total of 4 + 4, or 8 pounds. At a price of $1.50 per pound, however, A would purchase 8 pounds per month; B, 3 pounds; and C, 9 pounds. Thus, at $1.50 per pound, market demand would be 8 + 3 + 9, or 20 pounds of coffee per month.

The total quantity demanded in the marketplace at a given price is simply the sum of all the quantities demanded by all the individual households shopping in the market *at that price*. A market demand curve shows the total amount of a product that would be sold at each price if households could buy all they wanted at that price. As Figure 3.5 shows, the market demand curve is the sum of all the individual demand curves—that is, the sum of all the individual quantities demanded at each price. Thus, the market demand curve takes its shape and position from the shapes, positions, and number of individual demand curves. If more people decide to shop in

a. Income rises

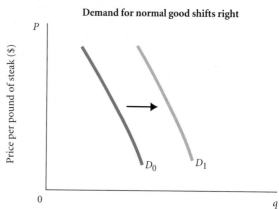

b. Price of hamburger rises

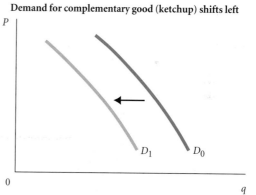

▲ FIGURE 3.4 **Shifts versus Movement Along a Demand Curve**
a. When income increases, the demand for inferior goods *shifts to the left* and the demand for normal goods
shifts to the right. **b.** If the price of hamburger rises, the quantity of hamburger demanded declines—this is a
movement along the demand curve. The same price rise for hamburger would shift the demand for chicken
(a substitute for hamburger) to the right and the demand for ketchup (a complement to hamburger) to
the left.

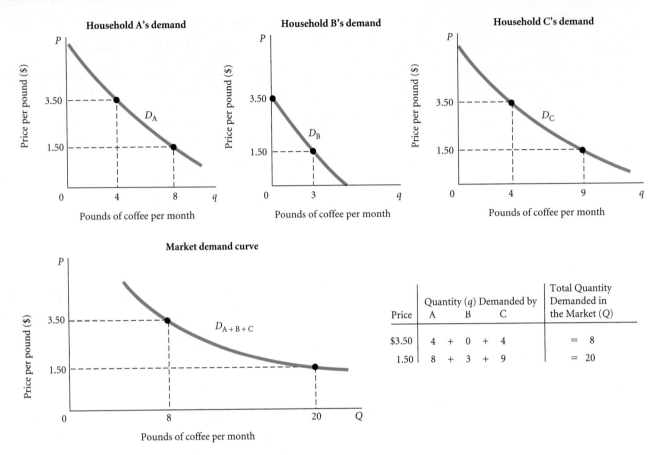

▲ FIGURE 3.5 Deriving Market Demand from Individual Demand Curves
Total demand in the marketplace is simply the sum of the demands of all the households shopping in a particular market. It is the sum of all the individual demand curves—that is, the sum of all the individual quantities demanded at each price.

a market, more demand curves must be added and the market demand curve will shift to the right. Market demand curves may also shift as a result of preference changes, income changes, or changes in the number of demanders.

An interesting fact about the market demand curve in Figure 3.5 is that at different prices, not only the number of people demanding the product may change but also the *type* of people demanding the product. When Apple halved the price of its iPhone in fall 2007, it announced that it wanted to make the iPhone available to a broader group of people. When prices fall, people like those in household B in Figure 3.5 move into markets that are otherwise out of their reach.

As a general rule throughout this book, capital letters refer to the entire market and lowercase letters refer to individual households or firms. Thus, in Figure 3.5, Q refers to total quantity demanded in the market, while q refers to the quantity demanded by individual households.

Supply in Product/Output Markets

We turn now to explore the other half of markets, the firms that supply the goods and services consumers want to purchase. What determines their willingness to produce and distribute the goods and services that people want? How do we understand the supply part of the market?

Firms build factories, hire workers, and buy raw materials because they believe they can sell the products they make for more than it costs to produce them. In other words, firms supply goods and services because they believe it will be profitable to do so. Supply decisions thus depend on profit potential. Because **profit** is the difference between revenues and costs, supply is likely to react to changes in revenues and changes in production costs. The amount of revenue that a firm earns depends on what the price of its product in the market is and on how much it sells. Costs of production depend on many factors, the most important of which are (1) the kinds of inputs needed to produce the product, (2) the amount of each input required, and (3) the prices of inputs.

profit The difference between revenues and costs.

In later chapters, we will focus on how firms decide *how* to produce their goods and services and explore the cost side of the picture more formally. For now, we will begin our examination of firm behavior by focusing on the output supply decision and the relationship between quantity supplied and output price, *ceteris paribus*.

Price and Quantity Supplied: The Law of Supply

Quantity supplied is the amount of a particular product that firms would be willing and able to offer for sale at a particular price during a given time period. A **supply schedule** shows how much of a product firms will sell at alternative prices.

quantity supplied The amount of a particular product that a firm would be willing and able to offer for sale at a particular price during a given time period.

Let us look at an agricultural market as an example. Table 3.3 itemizes the quantities of soybeans that an individual representative farmer such as Clarence Brown might sell at various prices. If the market paid $1.50 or less for a bushel for soybeans, Brown would not supply any soybeans: When Farmer Brown looks at the costs of growing soybeans, including the opportunity cost of his time and land, $1.50 per bushel will not compensate him for those costs. At $1.75 per bushel, however, at least some soybean production takes place on Brown's farm, and a price increase from $1.75 to $2.25 per bushel causes the quantity supplied by Brown to increase from 10,000 to 20,000 bushels per year. The higher price may justify shifting land from wheat to soybean production or putting previously fallow land into soybeans, or it may lead to more intensive farming of land already in soybeans, using expensive fertilizer or equipment that was not cost-justified at the lower price.

supply schedule A table showing how much of a product firms will sell at alternative prices.

TABLE 3.3 Clarence Brown's Supply Schedule for Soybeans	
Price (per Bushel)	Quantity Supplied (Bushels per Year)
$1.50	0
1.75	10,000
2.25	20,000
3.00	30,000
4.00	45,000
5.00	45,000

Generalizing from Farmer Brown's experience, we can reasonably expect an increase in market price, *ceteris paribus*, to lead to an increase in quantity supplied for Brown and farmers like him. In other words, there is a positive relationship between the quantity of a good supplied and price. This statement sums up the **law of supply**: An increase in market price will lead to an increase in quantity supplied, and a decrease in market price will lead to a decrease in quantity supplied.

law of supply The positive relationship between price and quantity of a good supplied: An increase in market price will lead to an increase in quantity supplied, and a decrease in market price will lead to a decrease in quantity supplied.

supply curve A graph illustrating how much of a product a firm will sell at different prices.

The information in a supply schedule may be presented graphically in a **supply curve**. Supply curves slope upward. The upward, or positive, slope of Brown's curve in Figure 3.6 reflects this positive relationship between price and quantity supplied.

Note in Brown's supply schedule, however, that when price rises from $4 to $5, quantity supplied no longer increases. Often an individual firm's ability to respond to an increase in price is constrained by its existing scale of operations, or capacity, in the short run. For example, Brown's ability to produce more soybeans depends on the size of his farm, the fertility of his soil, and the types of equipment he has. The fact that output stays constant at 45,000 bushels per year suggests that he is running up against the limits imposed by the size of his farm, the quality of his soil, and his existing technology.

In the longer run, however, Brown may acquire more land or technology may change, allowing for more soybean production. The terms *short run* and *long run* have very precise meanings in economics; we will discuss them in detail later. Here it is important only to understand that time plays a critical role in supply decisions. When prices change, firms' immediate response may be different from what they are able to do after a month or a year. Short-run and long-run supply curves are often different.

Other Determinants of Supply

Of the factors we have listed that are likely to affect the quantity of output supplied by a given firm, we have thus far discussed only the price of output. Other factors that affect supply include the cost of producing the product and the prices of related products.

The Cost of Production For a firm to make a profit, its revenue must exceed its costs. As an individual producer, like Farmer Brown, thinks about how much to supply at a particular price, the producer will be looking at his or her costs. Brown's supply decision is likely to change in response to changes in the cost of production. Cost of production depends on a

▶ **FIGURE 3.6 Clarence Brown's Individual Supply Curve**
A producer will supply more when the price of output is higher. The slope of a supply curve is positive. Note that the supply curve is red: Supply is determined by choices made by firms.

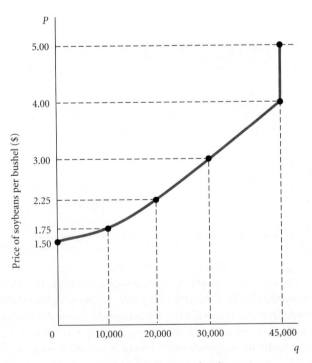

Bushels of soybeans produced per year

number of factors, including the available technologies and the prices and quantities of the inputs needed by the firm (labor, land, capital, energy, and so on).

Technological change can have an enormous impact on the cost of production over time. Consider agriculture. The introduction of fertilizers, the development of complex farm machinery, and the use of bioengineering to increase the yield of individual crops have all powerfully affected the cost of producing agricultural products. Farm productivity in the United States has been increasing dramatically for decades. Yield per acre of corn production has increased fivefold since the late 1930s, and the amount of labor required to produce 100 bushels of corn has fallen from 108 hours in the late 1930s to 20 hours in the late 1950s to less than 2 hours today. (See Table 2.2 on p. 37.)

When a technological advance lowers the cost of production, output is likely to increase. When yield per acre increases, individual farmers can and do produce more. The output of the Ford Motor Company increased substantially after the introduction of assembly-line techniques. The production of electronic calculators, and later personal computers, boomed with the development of inexpensive techniques to produce microprocessors.

Cost of production is also directly affected by the price of the factors of production. In the spring of 2008, the world price of oil rose to more than $100 per barrel from below $20 in 2002. As a result, cab drivers faced higher gasoline prices, airlines faced higher fuel costs, and manufacturing firms faced higher heating bills. The result: Cab drivers probably spent less time driving around looking for customers, airlines cut a few low-profit routes, and some manufacturing plants stopped running extra shifts. The moral of this story: Increases in input prices raise costs of production and are likely to reduce supply. The reverse occurred in 2009–2010 when oil prices fell back to $75 per barrel.

The Prices of Related Products Firms often react to changes in the prices of related products. For example, if land can be used for either corn or soybean production, an increase in soybean prices may cause individual farmers to shift acreage out of corn production into soybeans. Thus, an increase in soybean prices actually affects the amount of corn supplied.

Similarly, if beef prices rise, producers may respond by raising more cattle. However, leather comes from cowhide. Thus, an increase in beef prices may actually increase the supply of leather.

To summarize:

> Assuming that its objective is to maximize profits, a firm's decision about what quantity of output, or product, to supply depends on:
>
> 1. The price of the good or service.
> 2. The cost of producing the product, which in turn depends on:
>   - the price of required inputs (labor, capital, and land), and
>   - the technologies that can be used to produce the product.
> 3. The prices of related products.

Shift of Supply versus Movement Along a Supply Curve

A supply curve shows the relationship between the quantity of a good or service supplied by a firm and the price that good or service brings in the market. Higher prices are likely to lead to an increase in quantity supplied, *ceteris paribus*. Remember: The supply curve is derived holding everything constant except price. When the price of a product changes *ceteris paribus*, a change in the quantity supplied follows—that is, a **movement along a supply curve** takes place. As you have seen, supply decisions are also influenced by factors other than price. New relationships between price and quantity supplied come about when factors other than price change, and the

movement along a supply curve The change in quantity supplied brought about by a change in price.

shift of a supply curve
The change that takes place in a supply curve corresponding to a new relationship between quantity supplied of a good and the price of that good. The shift is brought about by a change in the original conditions.

result is a **shift of a supply curve**. When factors other than price cause supply curves to shift, we say that there has been a *change in supply*.

Recall that the cost of production depends on the price of inputs and the technologies of production available. Now suppose that a major breakthrough in the production of soybeans has occurred: Genetic engineering has produced a superstrain of disease- and pest-resistant seed. Such a technological change would enable individual farmers to supply more soybeans at *any* market price. Table 3.4 and Figure 3.7 describe this change. At $3 a bushel, farmers would have produced 30,000 bushels from the old seed (schedule S_0 in Table 3.4); with the lower cost of production and higher yield resulting from the new seed, they produce 40,000 bushels (schedule S_1 in Table 3.4). At $1.75 per bushel, they would have produced 10,000 bushels from the old seed; but with the lower costs and higher yields, output rises to 23,000 bushels.

Increases in input prices may also cause supply curves to shift. If Farmer Brown faces higher fuel costs, for example, his supply curve will shift to the left—that is, he will produce less at any

TABLE 3.4	Shift of Supply Schedule for Soybeans Following Development of a New Disease-Resistant Seed Strain	
	Schedule S_0	Schedule S_1
Price (per Bushel)	Quantity Supplied (Bushels per Year Using Old Seed)	Quantity Supplied (Bushels per Year Using New Seed)
$1.50	0	5,000
1.75	10,000	23,000
2.25	20,000	33,000
3.00	30,000	40,000
4.00	45,000	54,000
5.00	45,000	54,000

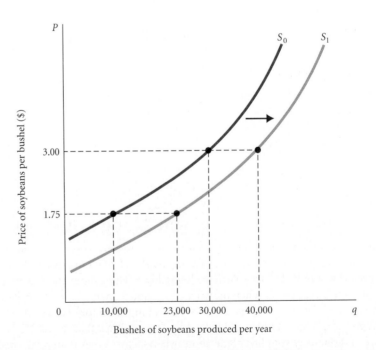

▲ FIGURE 3.7 **Shift of the Supply Curve for Soybeans Following Development of a New Seed Strain**

When the price of a product changes, we move *along* the supply curve for that product; the quantity supplied rises or falls. When any other factor affecting supply changes, the supply curve *shifts*.

given market price. If Brown's soybean supply curve shifted far enough to the left, it would intersect the price axis at a higher point, meaning that it would take a higher market price to induce Brown to produce any soybeans at all.

As with demand, it is very important to distinguish between *movements along* supply curves (changes in quantity supplied) and *shifts in* supply curves (changes in supply):

Change in price of a good or service leads to
→ Change in *quantity supplied* (**movement along a supply curve**).

Change in costs, input prices, technology, or prices of related goods and services leads to
→ Change in *supply* (**shift of a supply curve**).

From Individual Supply to Market Supply

Market supply is determined in the same fashion as market demand. It is simply the sum of all that is supplied each period by all producers of a single product. Figure 3.8 derives a market supply curve from the supply curves of three individual firms. (In a market with more firms, total market supply would be the sum of the amounts produced by each of the firms in that market.) As the table in Figure 3.8 shows, at a price of $3, farm A supplies 30,000 bushels of soybeans,

market supply The sum of all that is supplied each period by all producers of a single product.

Price	Quantity (q) Supplied by			Total Quantity Supplied in the Market (Q)
	A	B	C	
$3.00	30,000 +	10,000 +	25,000	= 65,000
1.75	10,000 +	5,000 +	10,000	= 25,000

▲ **FIGURE 3.8 Deriving Market Supply from Individual Firm Supply Curves**
Total supply in the marketplace is the sum of all the amounts supplied by all the firms selling in the market. It is the sum of all the individual quantities supplied at each price.

farm B supplies 10,000 bushels, and farm C supplies 25,000 bushels. At this price, the total amount supplied in the market is 30,000 + 10,000 + 25,000, or 65,000 bushels. At a price of $1.75, however, the total amount supplied is only 25,000 bushels (10,000 + 5,000 + 10,000). Thus, the market supply curve is the simple addition of the individual supply curves of all the firms in a particular market—that is, the sum of all the individual quantities supplied at each price.

The position and shape of the market supply curve depends on the positions and shapes of the individual firms' supply curves from which it is derived. The market supply curve also depends on the number of firms that produce in that market. If firms that produce for a particular market are earning high profits, other firms may be tempted to go into that line of business. When the technology to produce computers for home use became available, literally hundreds of new firms got into the act. The popularity and profitability of professional football has, three times, led to the formation of new leagues. When new firms enter an industry, the supply curve shifts to the right. When firms go out of business, or "exit" the market, the supply curve shifts to the left.

Market Equilibrium

So far, we have identified a number of factors that influence the amount that households demand and the amount that firms supply in product (output) markets. The discussion has emphasized the role of market price as a determinant of both quantity demanded and quantity supplied. We are now ready to see how supply and demand in the market interact to determine the final market price.

We have been very careful in our discussions thus far to separate household decisions about how much to demand from firm decisions about how much to supply. The operation of the market, however, clearly depends on the interaction between suppliers and demanders. At any moment, one of three conditions prevails in every market: (1) The quantity demanded exceeds the quantity supplied at the current price, a situation called *excess demand*; (2) the quantity supplied exceeds the quantity demanded at the current price, a situation called *excess supply*; or (3) the quantity supplied equals the quantity demanded at the current price, a situation called **equilibrium**. At equilibrium, no tendency for price to change exists.

equilibrium The condition that exists when quantity supplied and quantity demanded are equal. At equilibrium, there is no tendency for price to change.

excess demand *or* **shortage** The condition that exists when quantity demanded exceeds quantity supplied at the current price.

Excess Demand

Excess demand, or a **shortage**, exists when quantity demanded is greater than quantity supplied at the current price. Figure 3.9, which plots both a supply curve and a demand curve on the same graph, illustrates such a situation. As you can see, market demand at $1.75 per bushel (50,000 bushels) exceeds the amount that farmers are currently supplying (25,000 bushels).

When excess demand occurs in an unregulated market, there is a tendency for price to rise as demanders compete against each other for the limited supply. The adjustment mechanisms may differ, but the outcome is always the same. For example, consider the mechanism of an auction. In an auction, items are sold directly to the highest bidder. When the auctioneer starts the bidding at a low price, many people bid for the item. At first, there is a shortage: Quantity demanded exceeds quantity supplied. As would-be buyers offer higher and higher prices, bidders drop out until the one who offers the most ends up with the item being auctioned. Price rises until quantity demanded and quantity supplied are equal.

At a price of $1.75 (see Figure 3.9 again), farmers produce soybeans at a rate of 25,000 bushels per year, but at that price, the demand is for 50,000 bushels. Most farm products are sold to local dealers who in turn sell large quantities in major market centers, where bidding would push prices up if quantity demanded exceeded quantity supplied. As price rises above $1.75, two things happen: (1) The quantity demanded falls as buyers drop out of the market and perhaps choose a

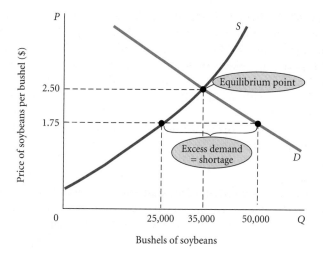

▲ FIGURE 3.9 Excess Demand, or Shortage

At a price of $1.75 per bushel, quantity demanded exceeds quantity supplied. When excess *demand* exists, there is a tendency for price to rise. When quantity demanded equals quantity supplied, excess demand is eliminated and the market is in equilibrium. Here the equilibrium price is $2.50 and the equilibrium quantity is 35,000 bushels.

substitute, and (2) the quantity supplied increases as farmers find themselves receiving a higher price for their product and shift additional acres into soybean production.[3]

This process continues until the shortage is eliminated. In Figure 3.9, this occurs at $2.50, where quantity demanded has fallen from 50,000 to 35,000 bushels per year and quantity supplied has increased from 25,000 to 35,000 bushels per year. When quantity demanded and quantity supplied are equal and there is no further bidding, the process has achieved an equilibrium, a situation in which *there is no natural tendency for further adjustment.* Graphically, the point of equilibrium is the point at which the supply curve and the demand curve intersect.

Increasingly, items are auctioned over the Internet. Companies such as eBay connect buyers and sellers of everything from automobiles to wine and from computers to airline tickets. Auctions are occurring simultaneously with participants located across the globe. The principles through which prices are determined in these auctions are the same: When excess demand exists, prices rise.

While the principles are the same, the process through which excess demand leads to higher prices is different in different markets. Consider the market for houses in the hypothetical town of Boomville with a population of 25,000 people, most of whom live in single-family homes. Normally, about 75 homes are sold in the Boomville market each year. However, last year a major business opened a plant in town, creating 1,500 new jobs that pay good wages. This attracted new residents to the area, and real estate agents now have more buyers than there are properties for sale. Quantity demanded now exceeds quantity supplied. In other words, there is a shortage.

Properties are sold very quickly, and housing prices begin to rise. Boomville sellers soon learn that there are more buyers than usual, and they begin to hold out for higher offers. As

---

[3] Once farmers have produced in any given season, they cannot change their minds and produce more, of course. When we derived Clarence Brown's supply schedule in Table 3.3, we imagined him reacting to prices that existed at the time he decided how much land to plant in soybeans. In Figure 3.9, the upward slope shows that higher prices justify shifting land from other crops. Final price may not be determined until final production figures are in. For our purposes here, however, we have ignored this timing problem. The best way to think about it is that demand and supply are *flows*, or *rates*, of production—that is, we are talking about the number of bushels produced *per production period*. Adjustments in the rate of production may take place over a number of production periods.

prices for Boomville houses rise, quantity demanded eventually drops off and quantity supplied increases: (1) Encouraged by the high prices, builders begin constructing new houses, and (2) some people, attracted by the higher prices their homes will fetch, put their houses on the market. Discouraged by higher prices, however, some potential buyers (demanders) may begin to look for housing in neighboring towns and settle on commuting. Eventually, equilibrium will be reestablished, with the quantity of houses demanded just equal to the quantity of houses supplied.

Although the mechanics of price adjustment in the housing market differ from the mechanics of an auction, the outcome is the same:

> When quantity demanded exceeds quantity supplied, price tends to rise. When the price in a market rises, quantity demanded falls and quantity supplied rises until an equilibrium is reached at which quantity demanded and quantity supplied are equal.

This process is called *price rationing*. When a shortage exists, some people will be satisfied and some will not. When the market operates without interference, price increases will distribute what is available to those who are willing and able to pay the most. As long as there is a way for buyers and sellers to interact, those who are willing to pay more will make that fact known somehow. (We discuss the nature of the price system as a rationing device in detail in Chapter 4.)

Excess Supply

excess supply *or* surplus
The condition that exists when quantity supplied exceeds quantity demanded at the current price.

Excess supply, or a **surplus**, exists when the quantity supplied exceeds the quantity demanded at the current price. As with a shortage, the mechanics of price adjustment in the face of a surplus can differ from market to market. For example, if automobile dealers find themselves with unsold cars in the fall when the new models are coming in, you can expect to see price cuts. Sometimes dealers offer discounts to encourage buyers; sometimes buyers themselves simply offer less than the price initially asked. In any event, products do no one any good sitting in dealers' lots or on warehouse shelves. The auction metaphor introduced earlier can also be applied here: If the initial asking price is too high, no one bids and the auctioneer tries a lower price. It is almost always true that certain items do not sell as well as anticipated during the Christmas holidays. After Christmas, most stores have big sales during which they lower the prices of overstocked items. Quantities supplied exceeded quantities demanded at the current prices, so stores cut prices.

Figure 3.10 illustrates another excess supply/surplus situation. At a price of $3 per bushel, suppose farmers are supplying soybeans at a rate of 40,000 bushels per year, but buyers are demanding only 20,000. With 20,000 (40,000 minus 20,000) bushels of soybeans going unsold, the market price falls. As price falls from $3.00 to $2.50, quantity supplied decreases from 40,000 bushels per year to 35,000. The lower price causes quantity demanded to rise from 20,000 to 35,000. At $2.50, quantity demanded and quantity supplied are equal. For the data shown here, $2.50 and 35,000 bushels are the equilibrium price and quantity, respectively.

Although oil prices rose to record levels in 2008, back in 2001, crude oil production worldwide exceeded the quantity demanded and prices fell significantly as competing producer countries tried to maintain their share of world markets. Although the mechanism by which price is adjusted is different for automobiles, housing, soybeans, and crude oil, the outcome is the same:

> When quantity supplied exceeds quantity demanded at the current price, the price tends to fall. When price falls, quantity supplied is likely to decrease and quantity demanded is likely to increase until an equilibrium price is reached where quantity supplied and quantity demanded are equal.

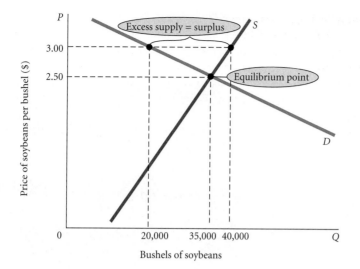

◀ **FIGURE 3.10 Excess Supply, or Surplus**
At a price of $3.00, quantity supplied exceeds quantity demanded by 20,000 bushels. This excess supply will cause the price to fall.

Changes in Equilibrium

When supply and demand curves shift, the equilibrium price and quantity change. The following example will help to illustrate this point.

South America is a major producer of coffee beans. A cold snap there can reduce the coffee harvest enough to affect the world price of coffee beans. In the mid-1990s, a major freeze hit Brazil and Colombia and drove up the price of coffee on world markets to a record $2.40 per pound. Severe hurricanes in the Caribbean caused a similar shift of supply in 2005.

Figure 3.11 illustrates how the freeze pushed up coffee prices. Initially, the market was in equilibrium at a price of $1.20. At that price, the quantity demanded was equal to quantity supplied (13.2 billion pounds). At a price of $1.20 and a quantity of 13.2 billion pounds, the demand curve (labeled D) intersected the initial supply curve (labeled S_0). (Remember that equilibrium exists when quantity demanded equals quantity supplied—the point at which the supply and demand curves intersect.)

The freeze caused a decrease in the supply of coffee beans. That is, the freeze caused the supply curve to shift to the left. In Figure 3.11, the new supply curve (the supply curve that shows the relationship between price and quantity supplied after the freeze) is labeled S_1.

At the initial equilibrium price, $1.20, there is now a shortage of coffee. If the price were to remain at $1.20, quantity demanded would not change; it would remain at 13.2 billion pounds.

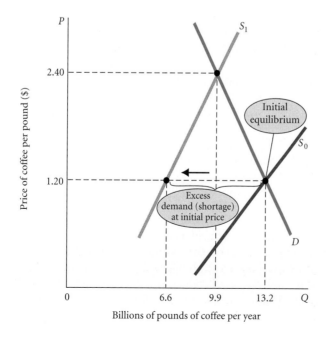

◀ **FIGURE 3.11**
**The Coffee Market:
A Shift of Supply
and Subsequent
Price Adjustment**
Before the freeze, the coffee market was in equilibrium at a price of $1.20 per pound. At that price, quantity demanded equaled quantity supplied. The freeze shifted the supply curve to the left (from S_0 to S_1), increasing the equilibrium price to $2.40.

ECONOMICS IN PRACTICE

High Prices for Tomatoes

The winter of 2010 was a very cold one for Florida, where much of the U.S. fresh fruit and vegetable supply is produced. The article below describes the effect on the price of fresh tomatoes resulting from the freeze. With fewer tomatoes around (the supply curve shifted left due to the freeze), the price of tomatoes increased fivefold. What the reporter calls a shortage, we economists simply note as a shift in the supply curve!

Note the interesting comment by Mr. Brown, the executive vice president of the Florida Tomato Growers Exchange, when people complained to him about the high price of tomatoes. "Doesn't matter," he opined, "because there isn't anything to sell." It is precisely *because* there is less to sell that the price has in fact risen!

Tomatoes Get Sliced From Menus

The Wall Street Journal

A shortage of tomatoes from weather-battered Florida is forcing restaurants and supermarkets to ration supplies amid soaring prices for America's most popular fresh vegetable.

Fast-food restaurant chains such as Wendy's have stopped automatically including tomatoes in sandwiches; now customers have to know to ask.

Even then, consumers might not get what they usually do. At Lloyd's, a white-table cloth restaurant across the street from the Chicago Mercantile Exchange, signs went up this week warning that only plum tomatoes are available.

"People love having tomatoes in their salad and in sandwiches, but we want people to know ahead of time that the quality just isn't what they are used to," said Sam Berngard, president of Taste America Restaurant Group LLC, which operates Lloyd's and two Chicago seafood restaurants.

Subway is continuing to offer tomatoes on its sandwiches, but the chain is using different varieties to ensure that it has enough on hand.

Fresh tomatoes are in short supply because of the unusual spell of freezing temperatures that hugged Florida in January. The cold temperatures that dented citrus production also destroyed roughly 70% of the tomato crop in Florida, which is the largest source of U.S.-grown fresh tomatoes this time of year.

Reggie Brown, executive vice president of Florida Tomato Growers Exchange, a Maitland, Florida, trade group, said Tuesday that a 25-pound box of tomatoes is trading for $30, compared with $6.45 a year ago.

Some restaurants have been told they would have to spend up to $45 for a box of tomatoes in recent days. "Doesn't matter though, because there isn't anything to sell," said Mr. Brown, who calculates the state's shipments are running at about 30% of normal.

Source: The Wall Street Journal, excerpted from "Tomatoes Get Sliced from Menus" by Scott Kilman and Julie Jargon. Copyright 2010 by Dow Jones & Company, Inc. Reproduced with permission of Dow Jones & Company, Inc. via Copyright Clearance Center.

However, at that price, quantity supplied would drop to 6.6 billion pounds. At a price of $1.20, quantity demanded is greater than quantity supplied.

When excess demand exists in a market, price can be expected to rise, and rise it did. As the figure shows, price rose to a new equilibrium at $2.40. At $2.40, quantity demanded is again equal to quantity supplied, this time at 9.9 billion pounds—the point at which the new supply curve (S_1) intersects the demand curve.

Notice that as the price of coffee rose from $1.20 to $2.40, two things happened. First, the quantity demanded declined (a movement along the demand curve) as people shifted to substitutes such as tea and hot cocoa. Second, the quantity supplied began to rise, but within the limits imposed by the damage from the freeze. (It might also be that some countries or areas with high costs of production, previously unprofitable, came into production and shipped to the world market at the higher price.) That is, the quantity supplied increased in response to the higher price *along* the new supply curve, which lies to the left of the old supply curve. The final result was a higher price ($2.40), a smaller quantity finally exchanged in the market (9.9 billion pounds), and coffee bought only by those willing to pay $2.40 per pound.

Since many market prices are driven by the interaction of millions of buyers and sellers, it is often difficult to predict how they will change. A series of events in the mid-1990s led to the left-ward shift in supply, thus driving up the price of coffee, but the opposite occurred more recently. Today coffee beans are exported by over 50 countries, with Brazil being the largest producer with about 30 percent of the market. Large increases in production have kept prices low. In July 2007, the average price per pound was $1.06.

Figure 3.12 summarizes the possible supply and demand shifts that have been discussed and the resulting changes in equilibrium price and quantity. Study the graphs carefully to ensure that you understand them.

a. Demand shifts

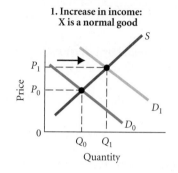

1. Increase in income:
X is a normal good

2. Increase in income:
X is an inferior good

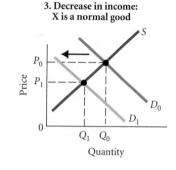

3. Decrease in income:
X is a normal good

4. Decrease in income:
X is an inferior good

5. Increase in the price
of a substitute for X

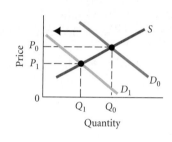

6. Increase in the price
of a complement for X

7. Decrease in the price
of a substitute for X

8. Decrease in the price
of a complement for X

b. Supply shifts

9. Increase in the cost
of production of X

10. Decrease in the cost
of production of X

▲ **FIGURE 3.12 Examples of Supply and Demand Shifts for Product X**

Demand and Supply in Product Markets: A Review

As you continue your study of economics, you will discover that it is a discipline full of controversy and debate. There is, however, little disagreement about the basic way that the forces of supply and demand operate in free markets. If you hear that a freeze in Florida has destroyed a good portion of the citrus crop, you can bet that the price of oranges will rise. If you read that the weather in the Midwest has been good and a record corn crop is expected, you can bet that corn prices will fall. When fishermen in Massachusetts go on strike and stop bringing in the daily catch, you can bet that the price of local fish will go up.

Here are some important points to remember about the mechanics of supply and demand in product markets:

1. A demand curve shows how much of a product a household would buy if it could buy all it wanted at the given price. A supply curve shows how much of a product a firm would supply if it could sell all it wanted at the given price.
2. Quantity demanded and quantity supplied are always per time period—that is, per day, per month, or per year.
3. The demand for a good is determined by price, household income and wealth, prices of other goods and services, tastes and preferences, and expectations.
4. The supply of a good is determined by price, costs of production, and prices of related products. Costs of production are determined by available technologies of production and input prices.
5. Be careful to distinguish between movements along supply and demand curves and shifts of these curves. When the price of a good changes, the quantity of that good demanded or supplied changes—that is, a movement occurs along the curve. When any other factor changes, the curve shifts, or changes position.
6. Market equilibrium exists only when quantity supplied equals quantity demanded at the current price.

Looking Ahead: Markets and the Allocation of Resources

You can already begin to see how markets answer the basic economic questions of what is produced, how it is produced, and who gets what is produced. A firm will produce what is profitable to produce. If the firm can sell a product at a price that is sufficient to ensure a profit after production costs are paid, it will in all likelihood produce that product. Resources will flow in the direction of profit opportunities.

■ Demand curves reflect what people are willing and able to pay for products; demand curves are influenced by incomes, wealth, preferences, prices of other goods, and expectations. Because product prices are determined by the interaction of supply and demand, prices reflect what people are willing to pay. If people's preferences or incomes change, resources will be allocated differently. Consider, for example, an increase in demand—a shift in the market demand curve. Beginning at an equilibrium, households simply begin buying more. At the equilibrium price, quantity demanded becomes greater than quantity supplied. When there is excess demand, prices will rise, and higher prices mean higher profits for firms in the industry. Higher profits, in turn,

ECONOMICS IN PRACTICE

Why Do the Prices of Newspapers Rise?

In 2006, the average price for a daily edition of a Baltimore newspaper was $0.50. In 2007, the average price had risen to $0.75. Three different analysts have three different explanations for the higher equilibrium price.

Analyst 1: The higher price for Baltimore newspapers is good news because it means the population is better informed about public issues. These data clearly show that the citizens of Baltimore have a new, increased regard for newspapers.

Analyst 2: The higher price for Baltimore newspapers is bad news for the citizens of Baltimore. The higher cost of paper, ink, and distribution reflected in these higher prices will further diminish the population's awareness of public issues.

Analyst 3: The higher price for Baltimore newspapers is an unfortunate result of newspapers trying to make money as many consumers have turned to the Internet to access news coverage for free.

As economists, we are faced with two tasks in looking at these explanations: Do they make sense based on what we know about economic principles? And if they do make sense, can we figure out which explanation applies to the case of rising newspaper prices in Baltmore?

What is Analyst 1 saying? Her observation about consumers' new increased regard for newspapers tells us something about the demand curve. Analyst 1 seems to be arguing that tastes have changed in favor of newspapers, which would mean a shift in the demand curve to the right. With upward-sloping supply, such a shift would produce a price increase. So Analyst 1's story is plausible.

Analyst 2 refers to an increased cost of newsprint. This would cause production costs of newspapers to rise, shifting the supply curve to the left. A downward-sloping demand curve also results in increased prices. So Analyst 2 also has a plausible story.

Since Analyst 1 and Analyst 2 have plausible stories based on economic principles, we can look at evidence to see who is in fact right. If you go back to the graphs in Figure 3.12 on p. 71, you will find a clue. When demand shifts to the right (as in Analyst 1's story) the price rises, but so does the quantity as shown in Figure (a). When supply shifts to the left (as in Analyst 2's story) the price rises, but the quantity falls as shown in Figure (b). So we would look at what happened to newspaper circulation during this period to see whether the price increase is from the demand side or the supply side. In fact, in most markets, including Baltimore, quantities of newspapers bought have been falling, so Analyst 2 is most likely correct.

But be careful. Both analysts may be correct. If demand shifts to the right and supply shifts to the left by a greater amount, the price will rise and the quantity sold will fall.

What about Analyst 3? Analyst 3 clearly never had an economics course! Free Internet access to news is a substitute for print media. A decrease in the price of this substitute should shift the demand for newspapers to the left. The result should be a lower price, not a price increase. The fact that the newspaper publishers are "trying to make money" faced with this new competition does not change the laws of supply and demand.

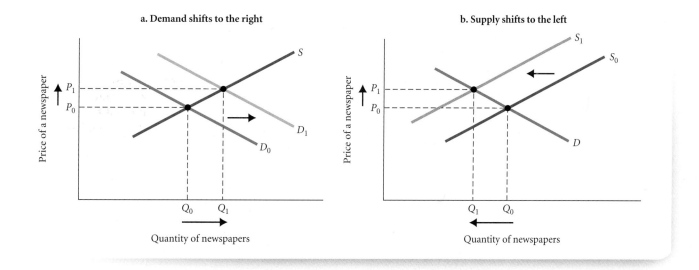

provide existing firms with an incentive to expand and new firms with an incentive to enter the industry. Thus, the decisions of independent private firms responding to prices and profit opportunities determine *what* will be produced. No central direction is necessary.

Adam Smith saw this self-regulating feature of markets more than 200 years ago:

> Every individual . . . by pursuing his own interest . . . promotes that of society. He is led . . . by an invisible hand to promote an end which was no part of his intention.[4]

The term Smith coined, the *invisible hand*, has passed into common parlance and is still used by economists to refer to the self-regulation of markets.

- Firms in business to make a profit have a good reason to choose the best available technology—lower costs mean higher profits. Thus, individual firms determine *how* to produce their products, again with no central direction.

- So far, we have barely touched on the question of distribution—*who* gets what is produced? You can see part of the answer in the simple supply and demand diagrams. When a good is in short supply, price rises. As they do, those who are willing and able to continue buying do so; others stop buying.

The next chapter begins with a more detailed discussion of these topics. How, exactly, is the final allocation of resources (the mix of output and the distribution of output) determined in a market system?

SUMMARY

1. In societies with many people, production must satisfy wide-ranging tastes and preferences, and producers must therefore specialize.

FIRMS AND HOUSEHOLDS: THE BASIC DECISION-MAKING UNITS *p. 47*

2. A *firm* exists when a person or a group of people decides to produce a product or products by transforming resources, or *inputs*, into *outputs*—the products that are sold in the market. Firms are the primary producing units in a market economy. We assume that firms make decisions to try to maximize profits.

3. *Households* are the primary consuming units in an economy. All households' incomes are subject to constraints.

INPUT MARKETS AND OUTPUT MARKETS: THE CIRCULAR FLOW *p. 48*

4. Households and firms interact in two basic kinds of markets: *product* or *output markets* and *input* or *factor markets*. Goods and services intended for use by households are exchanged in output markets. In output markets, competing firms supply and competing households demand. In input markets, competing firms demand and competing households supply.

5. Ultimately, firms choose the quantities and character of outputs produced, the types and quantities of inputs demanded, and the technologies used in production. Households choose the types and quantities of products demanded and the types and quantities of inputs supplied.

DEMAND IN PRODUCT/OUTPUT MARKETS *p. 50*

6. The quantity demanded of an individual product by an individual household depends on (1) price, (2) income, (3) wealth, (4) prices of other products, (5) tastes and preferences, and (6) expectations about the future.

7. *Quantity demanded* is the amount of a product that an individual household would buy in a given period if it could buy all that it wanted at the current price.

8. A *demand schedule* shows the quantities of a product that a household would buy at different prices. The same information can be presented graphically in a *demand curve*.

---

[4] Adam Smith, *The Wealth of Nations*, Modern Library Edition (New York: Random House, 1937), p. 456 (1st ed., 1776).

9. The *law of demand* states that there is a negative relationship between price and quantity demanded: As price rises, quantity demanded decreases and vice versa. Demand curves slope downward.

10. All demand curves eventually intersect the price axis because there is always a price above which a household cannot or will not pay. Also, all demand curves eventually intersect the quantity axis because demand for most goods is limited, if only by time, even at a zero price.

11. When an increase in income causes demand for a good to rise, that good is a *normal good*. When an increase in income causes demand for a good to fall, that good is an *inferior good*.

12. If a rise in the price of good X causes demand for good Y to increase, the goods are *substitutes*. If a rise in the price of X causes demand for Y to fall, the goods are *complements*.

13. *Market demand* is simply the sum of all the quantities of a good or service demanded per period by all the households buying in the market for that good or service. It is the sum of all the individual quantities demanded at each price.

SUPPLY IN PRODUCT/OUTPUT MARKETS *p. 60*

14. *Quantity supplied* by a firm depends on (1) the price of the good or service; (2) the cost of producing the product, which includes the prices of required inputs and the technologies that can be used to produce the product; and (3) the prices of related products.

15. *Market supply* is the sum of all that is supplied in each period by all producers of a single product. It is the sum of all the individual quantities supplied at each price.

16. It is very important to distinguish between *movements* along demand and supply curves and *shifts* of demand and supply curves. The demand curve shows the relationship between price and quantity demanded. The supply curve shows the relationship between price and quantity supplied. A change in price is a movement along the curve. Changes in tastes, income, wealth, expectations, or prices of other goods and services cause demand curves to shift; changes in costs, input prices, technology, or prices of related goods and services cause supply curves to shift.

MARKET EQUILIBRIUM *p. 66*

17. When quantity demanded exceeds quantity supplied at the current price, *excess demand* (or a *shortage*) exists and the price tends to rise. When prices in a market rise, quantity demanded falls and quantity supplied rises until an equilibrium is reached at which quantity supplied and quantity demanded are equal. At *equilibrium*, there is no further tendency for price to change.

18. When quantity supplied exceeds quantity demanded at the current price, *excess supply* (or a *surplus*) exists and the price tends to fall. When price falls, quantity supplied decreases and quantity demanded increases until an equilibrium price is reached where quantity supplied and quantity demanded are equal.

—————————— R E V I E W   T E R M S   A N D   C O N C E P T S ——————————

capital market, *p. 49*

complements, complementary goods, *p. 55*

demand curve, *p. 51*

demand schedule, *p. 51*

entrepreneur, *p. 48*

equilibrium, *p. 66*

excess demand *or* shortage, *p. 66*

excess supply *or* surplus, *p. 68*

factors of production, *p. 49*

firm, *p. 48*

households, *p. 48*

income, *p. 54*

inferior goods, *p. 54*

input *or* factor markets, *p. 48*

labor market, *p. 49*

land market, *p. 49*

law of demand, *p. 52*

law of supply, *p. 61*

market demand, *p. 58*

market supply, *p. 65*

movement along a demand curve, *p. 58*

movement along a supply curve, *p. 63*

normal goods, *p. 54*

perfect substitutes, *p. 55*

product *or* output markets, *p. 48*

profit, *p. 61*

quantity demanded, *p. 50*

quantity supplied, *p. 61*

shift of a demand curve, *p. 58*

shift of a supply curve, *p. 64*

substitutes, *p. 55*

supply curve, *p. 62*

supply schedule, *p. 61*

wealth *or* net worth, *p. 54*

PROBLEMS

All problems are available on www.myeconlab.com

1. Illustrate the following with supply and demand curves:
   a. With increased access to wireless technology and lighter weight, the demand for laptop computers has increased substantially. Laptops have also become easier and cheaper to produce as new technology has come online. Despite the shift of demand, prices have fallen.
   b. Cranberry production in Massachusetts totaled 2.37 million barrels in 2008, a 56 percent increase from the 1.52 million barrels produced in 2007. Demand increased by even more than supply, pushing 2008 prices to $56.70 per barrel from $49.80 in 2007.
   c. During the high-tech boom in the late 1990s, San Jose office space was in very high demand and rents were very high. With the national recession that began in March 2001, however, the market for office space in San Jose (Silicon Valley) was hit very hard, with rents per square foot falling. In 2005, the employment numbers from San Jose were rising slowly and rents began to rise again. Assume for simplicity that no new office space was built during the period.
   d. Before economic reforms were implemented in the countries of Eastern Europe, regulation held the price of bread substantially below equilibrium. When reforms were implemented, prices were deregulated and the price of bread rose dramatically. As a result, the quantity of bread demanded fell and the quantity of bread supplied rose sharply.
   e. The steel industry has been lobbying for high taxes on imported steel. Russia, Brazil, and Japan have been producing and selling steel on world markets at $610 per metric ton, well below what equilibrium would be in the United States with no imports. If no imported steel was permitted into the country, the equilibrium price would be $970 per metric ton. Show supply and demand curves for the United States, assuming no imports; then show what the graph would look like if U.S. buyers could purchase all the steel that they wanted from world markets at $610 per metric ton; show the quantity of imported steel.

2. On Sunday, August 19, the Detroit Tigers and the New York Yankees played baseball at Yankee Stadium. Both teams were in pursuit of league championships. Tickets to the game were sold out, and many more fans would have attended if additional tickets had been available. On that same day, the Cleveland Indians and the Tampa Bay Rays played each other and sold tickets to only 22,500 people in Tampa.

   The Rays stadium, Tropicana Field, holds 43,772. Yankee Stadium holds 57,478. Assume for simplicity that tickets to all regular-season games are priced at $40.
   a. Draw supply and demand curves for the tickets to each of the two games. (*Hint:* Supply is fixed. It does not change with price.) Draw one graph for each game.
   b. Is there a pricing policy that would have filled the ballpark for the Tampa game? If the Rays adopted such a strategy, would it bring in more or less revenue?
   c. The price system was not allowed to work to ration the New York tickets when they were initially sold to the public. How do you know? How do you suppose the tickets were rationed?

3. During the last 10 years, Orlando, Florida, grew rapidly, with new jobs luring young people into the area. Despite increases in population and income growth that expanded demand for housing, the price of existing houses barely increased. Why? Illustrate your answer with supply and demand curves.

4. Do you agree or disagree with each of the following statements? Briefly explain your answers and illustrate each with supply and demand curves.
   a. The price of a good rises, causing the demand for another good to fall. Therefore, the two goods are substitutes.
   b. A shift in supply causes the price of a good to fall. The shift must have been an increase in supply.
   c. During 2009, incomes fell sharply for many Americans. This change would likely lead to a decrease in the prices of both normal and inferior goods.
   d. Two normal goods cannot be substitutes for each other.
   e. If demand increases and supply increases at the same time, price will clearly rise.
   f. The price of good A falls. This causes an increase in the price of good B. Therefore, goods A and B are complements.

5. The U.S. government administers two programs that affect the market for cigarettes. Media campaigns and labeling requirements are aimed at making the public aware of the health dangers of cigarettes. At the same time, the Department of Agriculture maintains price supports for tobacco. Under this program, the supported price is above the market equilibrium price and the government limits the amount of land that can be devoted to tobacco production. Are these two programs at odds with the goal of reducing cigarette consumption? As part of your answer, illustrate graphically the effects of both policies on the market for cigarettes.

6. During the period 2006 through 2010, housing production in the United States fell from a rate of over 2.27 million housing starts per year to a rate of under 500,000, a decrease of over 80 percent. At the same time, the number of new households slowed to a trickle. Students without a job moved in with their parents, fewer immigrants came to the United States, and more of those already here went home. If there are fewer households, it is a decline in demand. If fewer new units are built, it is a decline in supply.
   a. Draw a standard supply and demand diagram which shows the demand for new housing units that are purchased each month, and the supply of new units built and put on the market each month. Assume that the quantity supplied and quantity demanded are equal at 45,000 units and at a price of $200,000.
   b. On the same diagram show a decline in demand. What would happen if this market behaved like most markets?
   c. Now suppose that prices did not change immediately. Sellers decided not to adjust price even though demand is below supply. What would happen to the number of homes for sale (the inventory of unsold new homes) if prices stayed the same following the drop in demand?

d. Now supposed that the supply of new homes put on the market dropped, but price still stayed the same at $200,000. Can you tell a story that brings the market back to equilibrium without a drop in price?

e. Go to www.census.gov/newhomesales. Look at the current press release, which contains data for the most recent month and the past year. What trends can you observe?

7. The following sets of statements contain common errors. Identify and explain each error:

a. Demand increases, causing prices to rise. Higher prices cause demand to fall. Therefore, prices fall back to their original levels.

b. The supply of meat in Russia increases, causing meat prices to fall. Lower prices always mean that Russian households spend more on meat.

8. For each of the following statements, draw a diagram that illustrates the likely effect on the market for eggs. Indicate in each case the impact on equilibrium price and equilibrium quantity.

a. A surgeon general warns that high-cholesterol foods cause heart attacks.

b. The price of bacon, a complementary product, decreases.

c. An increase in the price of chicken feed occurs.

d. Caesar salads become trendy at dinner parties. (The dressing is made with raw eggs.)

e. A technological innovation reduces egg breakage during packing.

*9. Suppose the demand and supply curves for eggs in the United States are given by the following equations:

$$Q_d = 100 - 20P$$
$$Q_s = 10 + 40P$$

where Q_d = millions of dozens of eggs Americans would like to buy each year; Q_s = millions of dozens of eggs U.S. farms would like to sell each year; and P = price per dozen of eggs.

a. Fill in the following table:

PRICE (PER DOZEN)	QUANTITY DEMANDED (Q_d)	QUANTITY SUPPLIED (Q_s)
$ .50	_____	_____
$1.00	_____	_____
$1.50	_____	_____
$2.00	_____	_____
$2.50	_____	_____

b. Use the information in the table to find the equilibrium price and quantity.

c. Graph the demand and supply curves and identify the equilibrium price and quantity.

10. Housing policy analysts debate the best way to increase the number of housing units available to low-income households. One strategy—the demand-side strategy—is to provide people with housing vouchers, paid for by the government, that can be used to rent housing supplied by the private market. Another—a supply-side strategy—is to have the government subsidize housing suppliers or to build public housing.

a. Illustrate supply- and demand-side strategies using supply and demand curves. Which results in higher rents?

b. Critics of housing vouchers (the demand-side strategy) argue that because the supply of housing to low-income households is limited and does not respond to higher rents, demand vouchers will serve only to drive up rents and make landlords better off. Illustrate their point with supply and demand curves.

*11. Suppose the market demand for pizza is given by $Q_d = 300 - 20P$ and the market supply for pizza is given by $Q_s = 20P - 100$, where P = price (per pizza).

a. Graph the supply and demand schedules for pizza using $5 through $15 as the value of P.

b. In equilibrium, how many pizzas would be sold and at what price?

c. What would happen if suppliers set the price of pizza at $15? Explain the market adjustment process.

d. Suppose the price of hamburgers, a substitute for pizza, doubles. This leads to a doubling of the demand for pizza. (At each price, consumers demand twice as much pizza as before.) Write the equation for the new market demand for pizza.

e. Find the new equilibrium price and quantity of pizza.

12. [Related to the *Economics in Practice* on p. 70] In the winter, which is the peak season for coats, the price of coats is typically higher than it is in the summer. In the case of strawberries, however, the reverse is true: The price of strawberries is lower in the peak season than it is in the winter season. How do we explain this seeming contradiction?

13. [Related to the *Economics in Practice* on p. 73] Analyst 1 suggested that the demand curve for newspapers in Baltimore might have shifted to the right because people were becoming more literate. Think of two other plausible stories that would result in this demand curve shifting to the right.

14. Explain whether each of the following statements describes a change in demand or a change in quantity demanded, and specify whether each change represents an increase or a decrease.

a. Baby Steps Footwear experiences a 40 percent increase in sales of baby shoes during a 3-day, half-price sale.

b. Tabitha gets a promotion and 15 percent increase in her salary and decides to reward herself by purchasing a new 3-D television.

c. When the price of peaches unexpectedly rises, many consumers choose to purchase plums instead.

d. Due to potential problems with its breaking system, Asteriod Motors has experienced a decline in sales of its Galactica automobile.

e. Antonio, an accountant working for the city of Santa Cristina, decides to forego his annual vacation to Hawaii when word leaks out that the city may be cutting all employees' salaries by 10 percent at the end of the year.

15. For each of the five statements (a–e) in the previous question, draw a demand graph representing the appropriate change in quantity demanded or change in demand.

16. Until 2008, General Motors held the title of the world's largest automobile manufacturer for 78 years. The recession of 2007–2009 and its accompanying financial crisis saw GM declare bankruptcy, receive over $50 billion in government bailout funds, and experience a significant decrease in demand

* Note: Problems marked with an asterisk are more challenging.

for its products. One area where GM saw huge declines in demand was its highly profitable large truck and SUV sector. In response to the fall in demand, GM drastically reduced the production of large trucks and SUVs, including discontinuing its Hummer brand. Explain what determinants of household demand contributed to the decision by GM to significantly reduce production of its large trucks and SUVs.

17. The market for manicures is made up of five firms, and the data in the following table represents each firm's quantity supplied at various prices. Fill in the column for the quantity supplied in the market, and draw a supply graph showing the market data.

Quantity supplied by:

PRICE	FIRM A	FIRM B	FIRM C	FIRM D	FIRM E	MARKET
$10	3	2	0	2	4	
20	4	4	2	3	5	
30	5	6	3	4	7	
40	6	8	5	5	8	

18. The following table represents the market for disposable digital cameras. Plot this data on a supply and demand graph and identify the equilibrium price and quantity. Explain what would happen if the market price is set at $30, and show this on the graph. Explain what would happen if the market price is set at $15, and show this on the graph.

PRICE	QUANTITY DEMANDED	QUANTITY SUPPLIED
$ 5.00	15	0
10.00	13	3
15.00	11	6
20.00	9	9
25.00	7	12
30.00	5	15
35.00	3	18

Demand and Supply Applications

4

Every society has a system of institutions that determines what is produced, how it is produced, and who gets what is produced. In some societies, these decisions are made centrally, through planning agencies or by government directive. However, in every society, many decisions are made in a *decentralized* way, through the operation of markets.

Markets exist in all societies, and Chapter 3 provided a bare-bones description of how markets operate. In this chapter, we continue our examination of demand, supply, and the price system.

The Price System: Rationing and Allocating Resources

The market system, also called the *price system*, performs two important and closely related functions. First, it provides an automatic mechanism for distributing scarce goods and services. That is, it serves as a **price rationing** device for allocating goods and services to consumers when the quantity demanded exceeds the quantity supplied. Second, the price system ultimately determines both the allocation of resources among producers and the final mix of outputs.

Price Rationing

Consider the simple process by which the price system eliminates a shortage. Figure 4.1 shows hypothetical supply and demand curves for wheat. Wheat is produced around the world, with large supplies coming from Russia and from the United States. Wheat is sold in a world market and used to produce a range of food products, from cereals and breads to processed foods, which line the kitchens of the average consumer. Wheat is thus demanded by large food companies as they produce breads, cereals, and cake for households.

As Figure 4.1 shows, the equilibrium price of wheat was $160 per millions of metric tons in the spring of 2010. At this price, farmers from around the world were expected to bring 61.7 million metric tons to market. Supply and demand were equal. Market equilibrium existed at a price of $160 per millions of metric tons because at that price, quantity demanded was equal to quantity supplied. (Remember that equilibrium occurs at the point where the supply and demand curves intersect. In Figure 4.1, this occurs at point C.)

In the summer of 2010, Russia experienced its warmest summer on record. Fires swept through Russia, destroying a substantial portion of the Russia wheat crop. With almost a third of the world wheat normally produced in Russia, the effect of this environmental disaster on world

price rationing The process by which the market system allocates goods and services to consumers when quantity demanded exceeds quantity supplied.

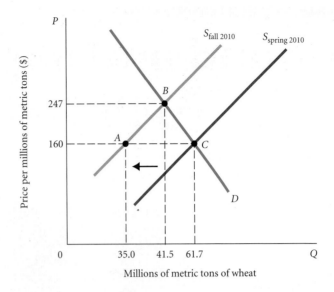

▲ **FIGURE 4.1 The Market for Wheat**

Fires in Russia in the summer of 2010 caused a shift in the world's supply of wheat to the left, causing the price to increase from $160 per millions of metric tons to $247. The equilibrium moved from C to B.

wheat supply was substantial. In the figure, the supply curve for wheat, which had been drawn in expectation of harvesting all the wheat planted in Russia along with the rest of the world, now shifted to the left, from $S_{spring\ 2010}$ to $S_{fall\ 2010}$. This shift in the supply curve created a situation of excess demand at the old price of $160. At that price, the quantity demanded is 61.7 million metric tons but the burning of much of the Russia supply left the world with only 35 millions of metric tons expected to be supplied. Quantity demanded exceeded quantity supplied at the original price by 26.7 million metric tons.

The reduced supply caused the price of wheat to rise sharply. As the price rises, the available supply is "rationed." Those who are willing and able to pay the most get it. You can see the market's rationing function clearly in Figure 4.1. As the price rises from $160, the quantity demanded declines along the demand curve, moving from point C (61.7 million tons) toward point B (41.5 million tons). The higher prices mean that prices for products like Pepperidge Farm bread and Shredded Wheat cereal, which use wheat as an essential ingredient, also rise. People bake fewer cakes, and begin to eat more rye bread and switch from Shredded Wheat to Corn Flakes in response to the price changes.

As prices rise, wheat farmers also change their behavior, though supply responsiveness is limited in the short term. Farmers outside of Russia, seeing the price rise, harvest their crops more carefully, getting more precious grains from each stalk. Perhaps some wheat is taken out of storage and brought to market. Quantity supplied increases from 35 million metric tons (point A) to 41.5 million tons (point B). The price increase has encouraged farmers who can to make up for part of the Russia wheat loss.

A new equilibrium is established at a price of $247 per millions of metric tons, with 41.5 million tons transacted. The market has determined who gets the wheat: *The lower total supply is rationed to those who are willing and able to pay the higher price.*

This idea of "willingness to pay" is central to the distribution of available supply, and willingness depends on both desire (preferences) and income/wealth. Willingness to pay does not necessarily mean that only the very rich will continue to buy wheat when the price increases. For anyone to continue to buy wheat at a higher price, his or her enjoyment comes at a higher cost in terms of other goods and services.

In sum:

The adjustment of price is the rationing mechanism in free markets. Price rationing means that whenever there is a need to ration a good—that is, when a shortage exists—in a free market, the price of the good will rise until quantity supplied equals quantity demanded— that is, until the market clears.

Prices and Total Expenditure: A Lesson From the Lobster Industry in 2008–2009

It is very important to distinguish between the *price* of a product and *total expenditure* from that product. A recent report on the lobster market in New England shows how it can be confusing. See if you can figure out what happened to the price and quantity of lobsters trapped in Maine between 2008 and 2009.

The following short passage was taken from an Associated Press article dated March 1, 2010.

Lobster Prices Plummet As Maine Fisherman Catch Way Too Many

Business Insider

PORTLAND, Maine (AP)—Officials say Maine lobstermen had a record harvest in 2009, but the value of the catch continued to plunge amid the sour global economy.

The Department of Marine Resources announced Monday that lobstermen caught 75.6 million pounds last year, up 8 percent from 2008. But the value of the catch fell $23 million, to $221.7 million.

Total revenue or expenditure in a market is simply the number of units sold multiplied by the price. The author of this article seems surprised that the total revenue in the lobster business (or *value* as he calls it) has fallen despite an increase in the catch. But of course, when supply curves shift right, as has happened here, prices typically fall, unless something has simultaneously happened to shift the demand curve. With an increase in volume and a decrease in price, total revenue could go up or down. In 2009, in the lobster market, revenue apparently fell.

Incidentally, the data given in the article allows you to find prices for 2008 and 2009 as well as quantities. (The price in 2008 was $3.50 and in 2009, $2.93.) Make sure you see how these numbers are derived.

There is some price that will clear any market you can think of. Consider the market for a famous painting such as Jackson Pollock's *No. 5, 1948*, illustrated in Figure 4.2. At a low price, there would be an enormous excess demand for such an important painting. The price would be bid up until there was only one remaining demander. Presumably, that price would be very high. In fact, the Pollock painting sold for a record $140 million in 2006. If the product is in strictly scarce supply, as a single painting is, its price is said to be *demand-determined*. That is,

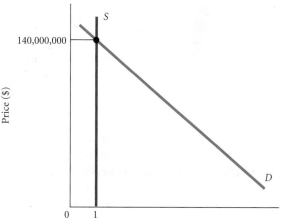

Quantity of Jackson Pollock's *"No. 5, 1948"*

◀ **FIGURE 4.2 Market for a Rare Painting**
There is some price that will clear any market, even if supply is strictly limited. In an auction for a unique painting, the price (bid) will rise to eliminate excess demand until there is only one bidder willing to purchase the single available painting. Some estimate that the *Mona Lisa* would sell for $600 million if auctioned.

its price is determined solely and exclusively by the amount that the highest bidder or highest bidders are willing to pay.

One might interpret the statement that "there is some price that will clear any market" to mean "everything has its price," but that is not exactly what it means. Suppose you own a small silver bracelet that has been in your family for generations. It is quite possible that you would not sell it for *any* amount of money. Does this mean that the market is not working, or that quantity supplied and quantity demanded are not equal? Not at all. It simply means that *you* are the highest bidder. By turning down all bids, you must be willing to forgo what anybody offers for it.

Constraints on the Market and Alternative Rationing Mechanisms

On occasion, both governments and private firms decide to use some mechanism other than the market system to ration an item for which there is excess demand at the current price. Policies designed to stop price rationing are commonly justified in a number of ways.

The rationale most often used is fairness. It is not "fair" to let landlords charge high rents, not fair for oil companies to run up the price of gasoline, not fair for insurance companies to charge enormous premiums, and so on. After all, the argument goes, we have no choice but to pay— housing and insurance are necessary, and one needs gasoline to get to work. Although it is not precisely true that price rationing allocates goods and services solely on the basis of income and wealth, income and wealth do constrain our wants. Why should all the gasoline or all the tickets to the World Series go just to the rich?

Various schemes to keep price from rising to equilibrium are based on several percep- tions of injustice, among them (1) that price-gouging is bad, (2) that income is unfairly distributed, and (3) that some items are necessities and everyone should be able to buy them at a "reasonable" price. Regardless of the rationale, the following examples will make two things clear:

1. Attempts to bypass price rationing in the market and to use alternative rationing devices are more difficult and more costly than they would seem at first glance.
2. Very often such attempts distribute costs and benefits among households in unintended ways.

Oil, Gasoline, and OPEC One of the most important prices in the world is the price of crude oil. Millions of barrels of oil are traded every day. It is a major input into virtually every product pro- duced. It heats our homes, and it is used to produce the gasoline that runs our cars. Its production has led to massive environmental disasters as well as wars. Its price has fluctuated wildly, leading to major macroeconomic problems. But oil is like other commodities in that its price is determined by the basic forces of supply and demand. Oil provides a good example of how markets work and how markets sometimes fail.

The Organization of the Petroleum Exporting Countries (OPEC) is an organization of twelve countries (Algeria, Angola, Ecuador, Iran, Iraq, Kuwait, Libya, Nigeria, Qatar, Saudi Arabia, the United Arab Emirates, and Venezuela) that together controlled about one-third of the known supply of oil in the year 2010. In 1973 and 1974, OPEC imposed an embargo on shipments of crude oil to the United States. What followed was a drastic reduction in the quantity of gasoline available at local gas pumps.

Had the market system been allowed to operate, refined gasoline prices would have increased dramatically until quantity supplied was equal to quantity demanded. However, the government decided that rationing gasoline only to those who were willing and able to pay the most was unfair, and Congress imposed a **price ceiling**, or maximum price, of $0.57 per gallon of leaded regular gasoline. That price ceiling was intended to keep gasoline "affordable," but it also perpetuated the shortage. At the restricted price, quantity demanded remained greater

price ceiling A maximum price that sellers may charge for a good, usually set by government.

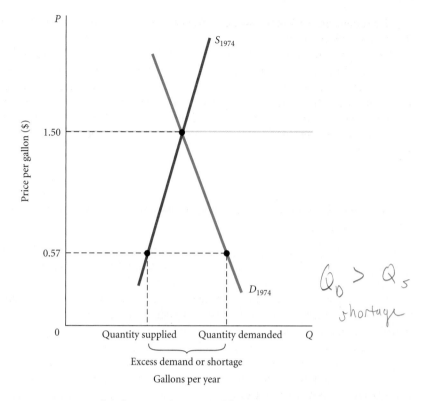

▲ **FIGURE 4.3 Excess Demand (Shortage) Created by a Price Ceiling**
In 1974, a ceiling price of $0.57 cents per gallon of leaded regular gasoline was imposed. If the price had been set by the interaction of supply and demand instead, it would have increased to approximately $1.50 per gallon. At $0.57 per gallon, the quantity demanded exceeded the quantity supplied. Because the price system was not allowed to function, an alternative rationing system had to be found to distribute the available supply of gasoline.

than quantity supplied, and the available gasoline had to be divided up somehow among all potential demanders.

You can see the effects of the price ceiling by looking carefully at Figure 4.3. If the price had been set by the interaction of supply and demand, it would have increased to approximately $1.50 per gallon. Instead, Congress made it illegal to sell gasoline for more than $0.57 per gallon. At that price, quantity demanded exceeded quantity supplied and a shortage existed. Because the price system was not allowed to function, an alternative rationing system had to be found to distribute the available supply of gasoline.

Several devices were tried. The most common of all nonprice rationing systems is **queuing**, a term that means waiting in line. During 1974, very long lines formed daily at gas stations, starting as early as 5 A.M. Under this system, gasoline went to those people who were willing to pay the most, but the sacrifice was measured in hours and aggravation instead of dollars.[1]

queuing Waiting in line as a means of distributing goods and services: a nonprice rationing mechanism.

---

[1] You can also show formally that the result is inefficient—that there is a resulting net loss of total value to society. First, there is the cost of waiting in line. Time has a value. With price rationing, no one has to wait in line and the value of that time is saved. Second, there may be additional lost value if the gasoline ends up in the hands of someone who places a lower value on it than someone else who gets no gas. Suppose, for example, that the market price of gasoline if unconstrained would rise to $2 but that the government has it fixed at $1. There will be long lines to get gas. Imagine that to motorist A, 10 gallons of gas is worth $35 but that she fails to get gas because her time is too valuable to wait in line. To motorist B, 10 gallons is worth only $15, but his time is worth much less, so he gets the gas. In the end, A could pay B for the gas and both would be better off. If A pays B $30 for the gas, A is $5 better off and B is $15 better off. In addition, A does not have to wait in line. Thus, the allocation that results from nonprice rationing involves a net loss of value. Such losses are called *deadweight losses*. See p. 92 of this chapter.

favored customers Those who receive special treatment from dealers during situations of excess demand.

A second nonprice rationing device used during the gasoline crisis was that of **favored customers**. Many gas station owners decided not to sell gasoline to the general public, but to reserve their scarce supplies for friends and favored customers. Not surprisingly, many customers tried to become "favored" by offering side payments to gas station owners. Owners also charged high prices for service. By doing so, they increased the real price of gasoline but hid it in service overcharges to get around the ceiling.

ration coupons Tickets or coupons that entitle individuals to purchase a certain amount of a given product per month.

Yet another method of dividing up available supply is the use of **ration coupons**. It was suggested in both 1974 and 1979 that families be given ration tickets or coupons that would entitle them to purchase a certain number of gallons of gasoline each month. That way, everyone would get the same amount regardless of income. Such a system had been employed in the United States during the 1940s when wartime price ceilings on meat, sugar, butter, tires, nylon stockings, and many other items were imposed.

When ration coupons are used with no prohibition against trading them, however, the result is almost identical to a system of price rationing. Those who are willing and able to pay the most buy up the coupons and use them to purchase gasoline, chocolate, fresh eggs, or anything else that is sold at a restricted price.[2] This means that the price of the restricted good will effectively rise to the market-clearing price. For instance, suppose that you decide not to sell your ration coupon. You are then forgoing what you would have received by selling the coupon. Thus, the "real" price of the good you purchase will be higher (if only in opportunity cost) than the restricted price. Even when trading coupons is declared illegal, it is virtually impossible to stop black markets from developing. In a **black market**, illegal trading takes place at market-determined prices.

black market A market in which illegal trading takes place at market-determined prices.

Rationing Mechanisms for Concert and Sports Tickets

Tickets for sporting events such as the World Series, the Super Bowl, and the World Cup command huge prices in the open market. In many cases, the prices are substantially above the original issue price. One of the hottest basketball tickets ever was one to the Boston Celtics and Los Angeles Lakers' NBA final series in 2010 that LA won in seven games. The online price for a courtside seat to one of the games in Los Angeles was $19,000. On September 16, 2007, Justin Timberlake performed at the Staples Center in Los Angeles. The day before the concert, you could buy a front row ticket for $16,000 on the StubHub Web site.

You might ask why a profit-maximizing enterprise would not charge the highest price it could? The answer depends on the event. If the Chicago Cubs got into the World Series, the people of Chicago would buy all the tickets available for thousands of dollars each. But if the Cubs actually *charged* $2,000 a ticket, the hard-working fans would be furious: "Greedy Cubs Gouge Fans" the headlines would scream. Ordinary loyal fans earning reasonable salaries would not be able to afford those prices. Next season, perhaps some of those irate fans would change loyalties, supporting the White Sox over the Cubs. In part to keep from alienating loyal fans, prices for championship games are held down. But not every concert promoter or sports team behaves this way. In 2000, Barbra Streisand gave a concert in Sydney, Australia. Tickets were issued with a *face value* of $1,530, a record for a concert that still stands today.

Let's consider a concert at the Staples Center, which has 20,000 seats. The supply of tickets is thus fixed at 20,000. Of course, there are good seats and bad seats, but to keep things simple, let's assume that all seats are the same and that the promoters charge $50 per ticket for all tickets. This is illustrated in Figure 4.4. Supply is represented by a vertical line at

---

[2] Of course, if you are assigned a number of tickets and you sell them, you are better off than you would be with price rationing. Ration coupons thus serve as a way of redistributing income.

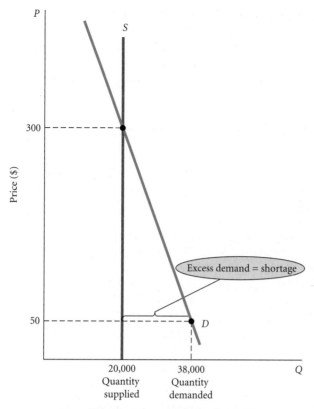

Tickets to a concert at the Staples Center

▲ FIGURE 4.4 **Supply of and Demand for a Concert at the Staples Center**
At the face-value price of $50, there is excess demand for seats to the concert. At $50 the quantity demanded is greater than the quantity supplied, which is fixed at 20,000 seats. The diagram shows that the quantity demanded would equal the quantity supplied at a price of $300 per ticket.

20,000. Changing the price does not change the supply of seats. In the figure the quantity demanded at the price of $50 is 38,000, so at this price there is excess demand of 18,000.

Who would get to buy the $50 tickets? As in the case of gasoline, a variety of rationing mechanisms might be used. The most common is queuing, waiting in line. The tickets would go on sale at a particular time, and people would show up and wait. Now ticket sellers have virtual waiting rooms online. Tickets for the World Series go on sale at a particular time in September, and the people who log on to team Web sites at the right moment get into an electronic queue and can buy tickets. Often tickets are sold out in a matter of minutes.

There are also, of course, favored customers. Those who get tickets without queuing are local politicians, sponsors, and friends of the artist or friends of the players.

But "once the dust settles," the power of technology and the concept of *opportunity cost* take over. Even if you get the ticket for the (relatively) low price of $50, that is not the true cost. The true cost is what you give up to sit in the seat. If people on eBay, StubHub, or Ticketmaster are willing to pay $300 for your ticket, that's what you must pay, or sacrifice, to go to the concert. Many people—even strong fans—will choose to sell that ticket. Once again, it is difficult to stop the market from rationing the tickets to those people who are willing and able to pay the most.

No matter how good the intentions of private organizations and governments, it is very difficult to prevent the price system from operating and to stop people's willingness to pay from asserting itself. Every time an alternative is tried, the price system seems to sneak in the back door. With favored customers and black markets, the final distribution may be even more unfair than what would result from simple price rationing.

Prices and the Allocation of Resources

Thinking of the market system as a mechanism for allocating scarce goods and services among competing demanders is very revealing, but the market determines more than just the distribution of final outputs. It also determines what gets produced and how resources are allocated among competing uses.

Consider a change in consumer preferences that leads to an increase in demand for a specific good or service. During the 1980s, for example, people began going to restaurants more frequently than before. Researchers think that this trend, which continues today, is partially the result of social changes (such as a dramatic rise in the number of two-earner families) and partially the result of rising incomes. The market responded to this change in demand by shifting resources, both capital and labor, into more and better restaurants.

With the increase in demand for restaurant meals, the price of eating out rose and the restaurant business became more profitable. The higher profits attracted new businesses and provided old restaurants with an incentive to expand. As new capital, seeking profits, flowed into the restaurant business, so did labor. New restaurants need chefs. Chefs need training, and the higher wages that came with increased demand provided an incentive for them to get it. In response to the increase in demand for training, new cooking schools opened and existing schools began to offer courses in the culinary arts. This story could go on and on, but the point is clear:

Price changes resulting from shifts of demand in output markets cause profits to rise or fall. Profits attract capital; losses lead to disinvestment. Higher wages attract labor and encourage workers to acquire skills. At the core of the system, supply, demand, and prices in input and output markets determine the allocation of resources and the ultimate combinations of goods and services produced.

Price Floor

price floor A minimum price below which exchange is not permitted.

minimum wage A price floor set for the price of labor.

As we have seen, price ceilings, often imposed because price rationing is viewed as unfair, result in alternative rationing mechanisms that are inefficient and may be equally unfair. Some of the same arguments can be made for price floors. A **price floor** is a minimum price below which exchange is not permitted. If a price floor is set above the equilibrium price, the result will be excess supply; quantity supplied will be greater than quantity demanded.

The most common example of a price floor is the **minimum wage**, which is a floor set for the price of labor. Employers (who demand labor) are not permitted under federal law to pay a wage less than $7.25 per hour (in 2010) to workers (who supply labor). Critics argue that since the minimum wage is above equilibrium, the result will be wasteful unemployment. At the wage of $7.25, the quantity of labor demanded is less than the quantity of labor supplied. Whenever a price floor is set above equilibrium, there will be an excess supply.

Supply and Demand Analysis: An Oil Import Fee

Delete to end of chapter

The basic logic of supply and demand is a powerful tool of analysis. As an extended example of the power of this logic, we will consider a proposal to impose a tax on imported oil. The idea of taxing imported oil is hotly debated, and the tools we have learned thus far will show us the effects of such a tax.

The Price Mechanism at Work for Shakespeare

Every summer, New York City puts on free performances of Shakespeare in the Park. Tickets are distributed on a first-come-first-serve basis at the Delacorte Theatre in the park beginning at 1 P.M. on the day of the show. People usually begin lining up at 6 A.M. when the park opens; by 10 A.M. the line has typically reached a length sufficient to give away all available tickets.

When you examine the people standing in line for these tickets, most of them seem to be fairly young. Many carry book bags identifying them as students in one of New York's many colleges. Of course, all college students may be fervent Shakespeare fans, but can you think of another reason for the composition of the line? Further, when you attend one of the plays and look around, the audience appears much older and much sleeker than the people who were standing in line. What is going on?

While the tickets are "free" in terms of financial costs, their true price includes the value of the time spent standing in line. Thus, the tickets are cheaper for people (for example, students) whose time value is lower than they are for high-wage earners, like an investment banker from Goldman Sachs. The true cost of a ticket is $0 plus the opportunity cost of the time spent in line. If the average person spends 4 hours in line, as is done in the Central Park case, for someone with a high wage, the true cost of the ticket might be very high. For example, a lawyer who earns $300 an hour would be giving up $1,200 to wait in line. It should not surprise you to see more people waiting in line for whom the tickets are inexpensive.

What about the people who are at the performance? Think about our discussion of the power of entrepreneurs. In this case, the students who stand in line as consumers of the tickets also can play a

role as producers. In fact, the students can produce tickets relatively cheaply by waiting in line. They can then turn around and sell those tickets to the high-wage Shakespeare lovers. These days eBay is a great source of tickets to free events, sold by individuals with low opportunity costs of their time who queued up. Craigslist even provides listings for people who are willing to wait in line for you.

Of course, now and again we do encounter a busy businessperson in one of the Central Park lines. Recently, one of the authors encountered one and asked him why he was waiting in line rather than using eBay, and he replied that it reminded him of when he was young, waiting in line for rock concerts.

Consider the facts. Between 1985 and 1989, the United States increased its dependence on oil imports dramatically. In 1989, total U.S. demand for crude oil was 13.6 million barrels per day. Of that amount, only 7.7 million barrels per day (57 percent) were supplied by U.S. producers, with the remaining 5.9 million barrels per day (43 percent) imported. The price of oil on world markets that year averaged about $18. This heavy dependence on foreign oil left the United States vulnerable to the price shock that followed the Iraqi invasion of Kuwait in August 1990. In the months following the invasion, the price of crude oil on world markets shot up to $40 per barrel.

Even before the invasion, many economists and some politicians had recommended a stiff oil import fee (or tax) that would, it was argued, reduce the U.S. dependence on foreign oil by (1) reducing overall consumption and (2) providing an incentive for increased domestic production. An added bonus would be improved air quality from the reduction in driving.

Supply and demand analysis makes the arguments of the import fee proponents easier to understand. Figure 4.5(a) shows the U.S. market for oil. The world price of oil is assumed to be $18, and the United States is assumed to be able to buy *all the oil that it wants* at this price. This means that domestic producers cannot charge any more than $18 per barrel. The curve labeled *Supply*$_{US}$ shows the amount that domestic suppliers will produce at each price level. At a price of $18, domestic production is 7.7 million barrels. U.S. producers will produce at point *A* on the supply curve. The total quantity of oil demanded in the United States in 1989 was 13.6 million barrels per day. At a price of $18, the quantity demanded in the United States is point *B* on the demand curve.

▶ **FIGURE 4.5 The U.S. Market for Crude Oil, 1989**

At a world price of $18, domestic production is 7.7 million barrels per day and the total quantity of oil demanded in the United States is 13.6 million barrels per day. The difference is total imports (5.9 million barrels per day).

If the government levies a 33 1/3 percent tax on imports, the price of a barrel of oil rises to $24. The quantity demanded falls to 12.2 million barrels per day. At the same time, the quantity supplied by domestic producers increases to 9.0 million barrels per day and the quantity imported falls to 3.2 million barrels per day.

a. U.S. market, 1989

b. Effects of an oil import fee in the United States

The difference between the total quantity demanded (13.6 million barrels per day) and domestic production (7.7 million barrels per day) is total imports (5.9 million barrels per day).

Now suppose that the government levies a tax of 33 1/3 percent on imported oil. Because the import price is $18, a tax of $6 (or .3333 × $18) per barrel means that importers of oil in the United States will pay a total of $24 per barrel ($18 + $6). This new, higher price means that U.S. producers can also charge up to $24 for a barrel of crude. Note, however, that the tax is paid only on imported oil. Thus, the entire $24 paid for domestic crude goes to domestic producers.

Figure 4.5(b) shows the result of the tax. First, because of a higher price, the quantity demanded drops to 12.2 million barrels per day. This is a movement *along* the demand curve from point *B* to point *D*. At the same time, the quantity supplied by domestic producers increased to 9.0 million barrels per day. This is a movement *along* the supply curve from point *A* to point *C*.

With an increase in domestic quantity supplied and a decrease in domestic quantity demanded, imports decrease to 3.2 million barrels per day (12.2 – 9.0).[3]

The tax also generates revenues for the federal government. The total tax revenue collected is equal to the tax per barrel ($6) times the number of imported barrels. When the quantity imported is 3.2 million barrels per day, total revenue is $6 × 3.2 million, or $19.2 million *per day* (about $7 billion per year).

What does all of this mean? In the final analysis, an oil import fee would (1) increase domestic production and (2) reduce overall consumption. To the extent that one believes that Americans are consuming too much oil, the reduced consumption may be a good thing.

Supply and Demand and Market Efficiency

Clearly, supply and demand curves help explain the way that markets and market prices work to allocate scarce resources. Recall that when we try to understand "how the system works," we are doing "positive economics."

Supply and demand curves can also be used to illustrate the idea of market efficiency, an important aspect of "normative economics." To understand the ideas, you first must understand the concepts of consumer and producer surplus.

Consumer Surplus

The argument, made several times already, that the market forces us to reveal a great deal about our personal preferences is an extremely important one, and it bears repeating at least once more here. If you are free to choose within the constraints imposed by prices and your income and you decide to buy, for example, a hamburger for $2.50, you have "revealed" that a hamburger is worth at least $2.50 to you.

A simple market demand curve such as the one in Figure 4.6(a) illustrates this point quite clearly. At the current market price of $2.50, consumers will purchase 7 million hamburgers per month. There is only one price in the market, and the demand curve tells us how many hamburgers households would buy if they could purchase all they wanted at the posted price of $2.50. Anyone who values a hamburger at $2.50 or more will buy it. Anyone who does not value a hamburger that highly will not buy it.

Some people, however, value hamburgers at more than $2.50. As Figure 4.6(a) shows, even if the price were $5.00, consumers would still buy 1 million hamburgers. If these people were able to buy the good at a price of $2.50, they would earn a **consumer surplus**. Consumer surplus is the difference between the maximum amount a person is willing to pay for a good and its current market price. The consumer surplus earned by the people willing to pay $5.00 for a hamburger is approximately equal to the shaded area between point *A* and the price, $2.50.

consumer surplus The difference between the maximum amount a person is willing to pay for a good and its current market price.

The second million hamburgers in Figure 4.6(a) are valued at more than the market price as well, although the consumer surplus gained is slightly less. Point *B* on the market demand curve shows the maximum amount that consumers would be willing to pay for the second million hamburgers. The consumer surplus earned by these people is equal to the shaded area between *B* and the price, $2.50. Similarly, for the third million hamburgers, maximum willingness to pay is given by point *C*; consumer surplus is a bit lower than it is at points *A* and *B*, but it is still significant.

The total value of the consumer surplus suggested by the data in Figure 4.6(a) is roughly equal to the area of the shaded triangle in Figure 4.6(b). To understand why this is so, think about offering hamburgers to consumers at successively lower prices. If the good were actually sold for $2.50, those near point *A* on the demand curve would get a large surplus; those at point *B* would get a smaller surplus. Those at point *E* would get no surplus.

---

[3] These figures were not chosen randomly. It is interesting to note that in 1985, the world price of crude oil averaged about $24 a barrel. Domestic production was 9.0 million barrels per day and domestic consumption was 12.2 million barrels per day, with imports of only 3.2 million. The drop in the world price between 1985 and 1989 increased imports to 5.9 million, an 84 percent increase.

a. A simple market demand curve for hamburgers

b. Consumer surplus

▲ FIGURE 4.6 **Market Demand and Consumer Surplus**
As illustrated in Figure 4.6(a), some consumers (see point A) are willing to pay as much as $5.00 each for hamburgers. Since the market price is just $2.50, they receive a consumer surplus of $2.50 for each hamburger that they consume. Others (see point B) are willing to pay something less than $5.00 and receive a slightly smaller surplus. Since the market price of hamburgers is just $2.50, the area of the shaded triangle in Figure 4.6(b) is equal to total consumer surplus.

Producer Surplus

Similarly, the supply curve in a market shows the amount that firms willingly produce and supply to the market at various prices. Presumably it is because the price is sufficient to cover the costs or the opportunity costs of production and give producers enough profit to keep them in business. When speaking of cost of production, we include everything that a producer must give up in order to produce a good.

A simple market supply curve like the one in Figure 4.7(a) illustrates this point quite clearly. At the current market price of $2.50, producers will produce and sell 7 million hamburgers. There is only one price in the market, and the supply curve tells us the quantity supplied at each price.

Notice, however, that if the price were just $0.75 (75 cents), although production would be much lower—most producers would be out of business at that price—a few producers would actually be supplying burgers. In fact, producers would supply about 1 million burgers to the market. These firms must have lower costs: They are more efficient or they have access to raw beef at a lower price or perhaps they can hire low-wage labor.

If these efficient, low-cost producers are able to charge $2.50 for each hamburger, they are earning what is called a **producer surplus**. Producer surplus is the difference between the current market price and the full cost of production for the firm. The first million hamburgers would generate a producer surplus of $2.50 minus $0.75, or $1.75 per hamburger: a total of $1.75 million. The second million hamburgers would also generate a producer surplus because the price of $2.50 exceeds the producers' total cost of producing these hamburgers, which is above $0.75 but much less than $2.50.

The total value of the producer surplus received by producers of hamburgers at a price of $2.50 per burger is roughly equal to the shaded triangle in Figure 4.7(b). Those producers just able to make a profit producing burgers will be near point E on the supply curve and will earn very little in the way of surplus.

producer surplus The difference between the current market price and the full cost of production for the firm.

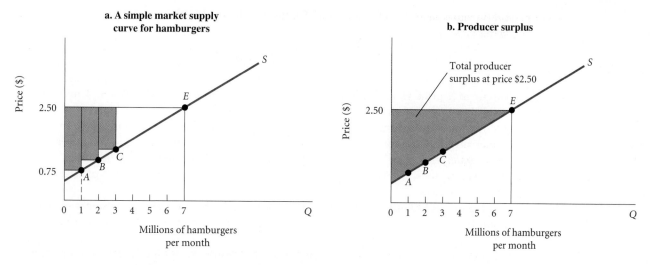

▲ **FIGURE 4.7 Market Supply and Producer Surplus**

As illustrated in Figure 4.7(a), some producers are willing to produce hamburgers for a price of $0.75 each. Since they are paid $2.50, they earn a producer surplus equal to $1.75. Other producers are willing to supply hamburgers at a price of $1.00; they receive a producer surplus equal to $1.50. Since the market price of hamburgers is $2.50, the area of the shaded triangle in Figure 4.7(b) is equal to total producer surplus.

Competitive Markets Maximize the Sum of Producer and Consumer Surplus

In the preceding example, the quantity of hamburgers supplied and the quantity of hamburgers demanded are equal at $2.50. Figure 4.8 shows the total net benefits to consumers and producers resulting from the production of 7 million hamburgers. Consumers receive benefits in excess of the price they pay and equal to the blue shaded area between the demand curve and the price line at $2.50; the area is equal to the amount of consumer surplus being earned. Producers receive compensation in excess of costs and equal to the red shaded area between the

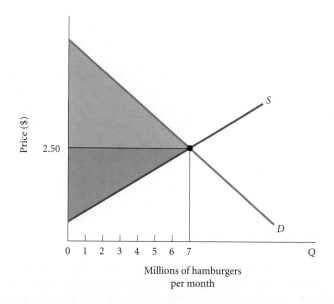

▲ **FIGURE 4.8 Total Producer and Consumer Surplus**

Total producer and consumer surplus is greatest where supply and demand curves intersect at equilibrium.

supply curve and the price line at $2.50; the area is equal to the amount of producer surplus being earned.

Now consider the result to consumers and producers if production were to be reduced to 4 million burgers. Look carefully at Figure 4.9(a). At 4 million burgers, consumers are willing to pay $3.75 for hamburgers and there are firms whose costs make it worthwhile to supply at a price as low as $1.50, yet something is stopping production at 4 million. The result is a loss of both consumer and producer surplus. You can see in Figure 4.9(a) that if production were expanded from 4 million to 7 million, the market would yield more consumer surplus and more producer surplus. The total loss of producer and consumer surplus from *underproduction* and, as we will see shortly, from overproduction is referred to as a **deadweight loss**. In Figure 4.9(a) the deadweight loss is equal to the area of triangle *ABC* shaded in yellow.

deadweight loss The total loss of producer and consumer surplus from underproduction or overproduction.

Figure 4.9(b) illustrates how a deadweight loss of both producer and consumer surplus can result from *overproduction* as well. For every hamburger produced above 7 million, consumers are willing to pay less than the cost of production. The cost of the resources needed to produce hamburgers above 7 million exceeds the benefits to consumers, resulting in a net loss of producer and consumer surplus equal to the yellow shaded area *ABC*.

Potential Causes of Deadweight Loss From Under- and Overproduction

Most of the next few chapters will discuss perfectly competitive markets in which prices are determined by the free interaction of supply and demand. As you will see, when supply and demand interact freely, competitive markets produce what people want at the least cost, that

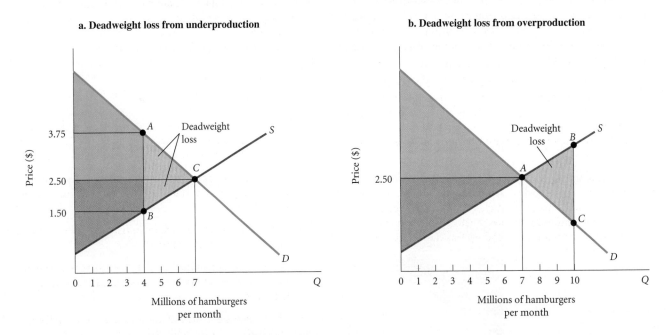

a. Deadweight loss from underproduction

b. Deadweight loss from overproduction

▲ **FIGURE 4.9 Deadweight Loss**

Figure 4.9(a) shows the consequences of producing 4 million hamburgers per month instead of 7 million hamburgers per month. Total producer and consumer surplus is reduced by the area of triangle *ABC* shaded in yellow. This is called the deadweight loss from underproduction. Figure 4.9(b) shows the consequences of producing 10 million hamburgers per month instead of 7 million hamburgers per month. As production increases from 7 million to 10 million hamburgers, the full cost of production rises above consumers' willingness to pay, resulting in a deadweight loss equal to the area of triangle *ABC*.

is, they are efficient. Beginning in Chapter 13, however, we will begin to relax assumptions and will discover a number of naturally occurring sources of market failure. Monopoly power gives firms the incentive to underproduce and overprice, taxes and subsidies may distort consumer choices, external costs such as pollution and congestion may lead to over- or underproduction of some goods, and artificial price floors and price ceilings may have the same effects.

Looking Ahead

We have now examined the basic forces of supply and demand and discussed the market/price system. These fundamental concepts will serve as building blocks for what comes next. Whether you are studying microeconomics or macroeconomics, you will be studying the functions of markets and the behavior of market participants in more detail in the following chapters.

Because the concepts presented in the first four chapters are so important to your understanding of what is to come, this might be a good time for you to review this material.

SUMMARY

THE PRICE SYSTEM: RATIONING AND ALLOCATING RESOURCES *p. 79*

1. In a market economy, the market system (or price system) serves two functions. It determines the allocation of resources among producers and the final mix of outputs. It also distributes goods and services on the basis of willingness and ability to pay. In this sense, it serves as a *price rationing* device.

2. Governments as well as private firms sometimes decide not to use the market system to ration an item for which there is excess demand. Examples of nonprice rationing systems include *queuing*, *favored customers*, and *ration coupons*. The most common rationale for such policies is "fairness."

3. Attempts to bypass the market and use alternative nonprice rationing devices are more difficult and costly than it would seem at first glance. Schemes that open up opportunities for favored customers, black markets, and side payments often end up less "fair" than the free market.

SUPPLY AND DEMAND ANALYSIS: AN OIL IMPORT FEE *p. 86*

4. The basic logic of supply and demand is a powerful tool for analysis. For example, supply and demand analysis shows that an oil import tax will reduce quantity of oil demanded, increase domestic production, and generate revenues for the government.

SUPPLY AND DEMAND AND MARKET EFFICIENCY *p. 89*

5. Supply and demand curves can also be used to illustrate the idea of market efficiency, an important aspect of normative economics.

6. *Consumer surplus* is the difference between the maximum amount a person is willing to pay for a good and the current market price.

7. *Producer surplus* is the difference between the current market price and the full cost of production for the firm.

8. At free market equilibrium with competitive markets, the sum of consumer surplus and producer surplus is maximized.

9. The total loss of producer and consumer surplus from underproduction or overproduction is referred to as a *deadweight loss*.

REVIEW TERMS AND CONCEPTS

black market, *p. 84*

consumer surplus, *p. 89*

deadweight loss, *p. 92*

favored customers, *p. 84*

minimum wage, *p. 86*

price ceiling, *p. 82*

price floor, *p. 86*

price rationing, *p. 79*

producer surplus, *p. 90*

queuing, *p. 83*

ration coupons, *p. 84*

PROBLEMS

All problems are available on www.myeconlab.com

1. Illustrate the following with supply and demand curves:
   a. In the summer of 2010, Spanish artist Pablo Picasso's *Portrait d'Angel Fernández de Soto* was sold in London for $51.6 million.
   b. In 2010, hogs in the United States were selling for 81 cents per pound, up from 58 cents per pound a year before. This was due primarily to the fact that supply had decreased during the period.
   c. Early in 2009, a survey of greenhouses indicated that the demand for houseplants was rising sharply. At the same time, large numbers of low-cost producers started growing plants for sale. The overall result was a drop in the average price of houseplants and an increase in the number of plants sold.

2. Every demand curve must eventually hit the quantity axis because with limited incomes, there is always a price so high that there is no demand for the good. Do you agree or disagree? Why?

3. When excess demand exists for tickets to a major sporting event or a concert, profit opportunities exist for scalpers. Explain briefly using supply and demand curves to illustrate. Some argue that scalpers work to the advantage of everyone and are "efficient." Do you agree or disagree? Explain briefly.

4. In an effort to "support" the price of some agricultural goods, the Department of Agriculture pays farmers a subsidy in cash for every acre that they leave *unplanted*. The Agriculture Department argues that the subsidy increases the "cost" of planting and that it will reduce supply and increase the price of competitively produced agricultural goods. Critics argue that because the subsidy is a payment to farmers, it will reduce costs and lead to lower prices. Which argument is correct? Explain.

5. The rent for apartments in New York City has been rising sharply. Demand for apartments in New York City has been rising sharply as well. This is hard to explain because the law of demand says that higher prices should lead to lower demand. Do you agree or disagree? Explain your answer.

6. Illustrate the following with supply and/or demand curves:
   a. The federal government "supports" the price of wheat by paying farmers not to plant wheat on some of their land.
   b. An increase in the price of chicken has an impact on the price of hamburger.
   c. Incomes rise, shifting the demand for gasoline. Crude oil prices rise, shifting the supply of gasoline. At the new equilibrium, the quantity of gasoline sold is less than it was before. (Crude oil is used to produce gasoline.)

7. Illustrate the following with supply and/or demand curves:
   a. A situation of excess labor supply (unemployment) caused by a "minimum wage" law.
   b. The effect of a sharp increase in heating oil prices on the demand for insulation material.

8. Suppose that the world price of oil is $70 per barrel and that the United States can buy all the oil it wants at this price. Suppose also that the demand and supply schedules for oil in the United States are as follows:

PRICE ($ PER BARREL)	U.S. QUANTITY DEMANDED	U.S. QUANTITY SUPPLIED
68	16	4
70	15	6
72	14	8
74	13	10
76	12	12

   a. On graph paper, draw the supply and demand curves for the United States.
   b. With free trade in oil, what price will Americans pay for their oil? What quantity will Americans buy? How much of this will be supplied by American producers? How much will be imported? Illustrate total imports on your graph of the U.S. oil market.
   c. Suppose the United States imposes a tax of $4 per barrel on imported oil. What quantity would Americans buy? How much of this would be supplied by American producers? How much would be imported? How much tax would the government collect?
   d. Briefly summarize the impact of an oil import tax by explaining who is helped and who is hurt among the following groups: domestic oil consumers, domestic oil producers, foreign oil producers, and the U.S. government.

9. Use the data in the preceding problem to answer the following questions. Now suppose that the United States allows no oil imports.
   a. What are the equilibrium price and quantity for oil in the United States?
   b. If the United States imposed a price ceiling of $74 per barrel on the oil market and prohibited imports, would there be an excess supply or an excess demand for oil? If so, how much?
   c. Under the price ceiling, quantity supplied and quantity demanded differ. Which of the two will determine how much oil is purchased? Briefly explain why.

10. Use the following diagram to calculate total consumer surplus at a price of $8 and production of 6 million meals per day. For the same equilibrium, calculate total producer surplus. Assuming price remained at $8 but production was cut to 3 million meals per day, calculate producer surplus and consumer surplus. Calculate the deadweight loss from underproduction.

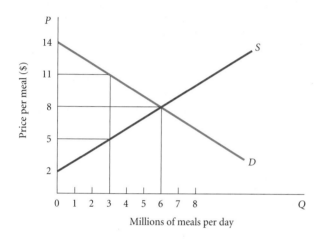

Millions of meals per day

11. In early 2008, many predicted that in a relatively short period of time, unleaded regular gasoline at the pump would be selling for over $4. Do some research on the price of gasoline. Have those dire predictions materialized? What is the price of unleaded regular today in your city or town? If it is below $4 per gallon, what are the reasons? Similarly, if it is higher than $4, what has happened to drive up the price? Illustrate with supply and demand curves.

12. [Related to the *Economics in Practice* on p. 87] Many cruise lines offer 5-day trips. A disproportionate number of these trips leave port on Thursday and return late Monday. Why might this be true?

13. [Related to the *Economics in Practice* on p. 87] Lines for free tickets to see Shakespeare in Central Park are often long. A local politician has suggested that it would be a great service if the park provided music to entertain those who are waiting in line. What do you think of this suggestion?

14. Suppose the market demand for burritos is given by $Q_d = 40 - 5P$ and the market supply for burritos is given by $Q_s = 10P - 20$, where P = price (per burrito).
   a. Graph the supply and demand schedules for burritos.
   b. What is the equilibrium price and equilibrium quantity?
   c. Calculate consumer surplus and producer surplus, and identify these on the graph.

15. On April 20, 2010, an oil-drilling platform owned by British Petroleum exploded in the Gulf of Mexico, causing oil to leak into the gulf at estimates of 1.5 to 2.5 million gallons per day for well over two months. Due to the oil spill, the government closed over 25 percent of federal waters, which has devastated the commercial fishing industry in the area. Explain how the reduction in supply from the reduced fishing waters will either increase or decrease consumer surplus and producer surplus, and show these changes graphically.

16. The following graph represents the market for DVDs.

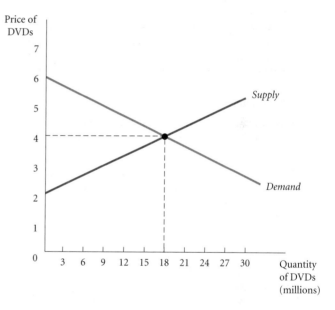

a. Find the values of consumer surplus and producer surplus when the market is in equilibrium, and identify these areas on the graph.
b. If underproduction occurs in this market, and only 9 million DVDs are produced, what happens to the amounts of consumer surplus and producer surplus? What is the value of the deadweight loss? Identify these areas on the graph.
c. If overproduction occurs in this market, and 27 million DVDs are produced, what happens to the amounts of consumer surplus and producer surplus? Is there a deadweight loss with overproduction? If so, what is its value? Identify these areas on the graph.

17. The following graph represents the market for wheat. The equilibrium price is $20 per bushel and the equilibrium quantity is 14 million bushels.

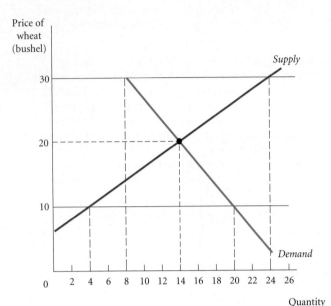

a. Explain what will happen if the government establishes a price ceiling of $10 per bushel of wheat in this market? What if the price ceiling was set at $30?

b. Explain what will happen if the government establishes a price floor of $30 per bushel of wheat in this market. What if the price floor was set at $10?

18. [Related to the *Economics in Practice* on *p. 81*] Go back to the *Economics in Practice* on page 81. Using the numbers in the newspaper article, find the total revenue, total catch, and market prices for lobsters in the years 2008 and 2009.

Elasticity

5

In economics, simple logic often tells us how a change in one variable, such as the price of a good or an interest rate, is likely to affect behavior. It is a safe bet, for example, that when Barnes & Noble and Amazon.com both lowered the price of their e-Readers in the summer of 2010, sales increased. When many universities lowered the price of football tickets to students (many to a price of zero), the schools did so in an attempt to increase the number of student fans in their stadiums. If the government helps to raise the price of cigarettes by increasing cigarette taxes, it is likely that tobacco sales will suffer.

The work we did in earlier chapters tells us the direction of the changes we would expect to see from price changes in markets. But in each of the preceding examples and in most other situations, knowing the direction of a change is not enough. What we really need to know to help us make the right decisions is how big the reactions are. How many more fans would come to a football game if the price were lowered? Is the added team spirit worth the lost ticket revenue? Would the university get more fans by charging students but giving them free hot dogs at the game? For profit-making firms, knowing the quantity that would be sold at a lowered price is key. If sales increases following a price cut are large enough, revenues may rise. To answer these questions, we must know more than just direction; we must know something about market responsiveness.

Understanding the responsiveness of consumers and producers in markets to price changes is key to answering a wide range of economic problems. Should McDonald's lower the price of its Big Mac? For McDonald's, the answer depends on whether that price cut increases or decreases its profits. The answer to that, in turn, depends on how its customers are likely to respond to the price cut. How many more Big Macs will be sold, and will the new sales come at the expense of the sandwiches sold at Subway or be a substitution of McDonald's Chicken McNuggets for Big Macs? How many potential new smokers will be deterred from smoking by higher cigarette prices the government has induced? Questions such as these lie at the core of economics. To answer these questions, we need to measure the magnitude of market responses.

The importance of actual measurement cannot be overstated. Much of the research being done in economics today involves the collection and analysis of quantitative data that measure behavior. The ability to analyze large amounts of data increased enormously with the advent of modern computers.

Economists commonly measure responsiveness using the concept of **elasticity**. Elasticity is a general concept that can be used to quantify the response in one variable when another variable

elasticity A general concept used to quantify the response in one variable when another variable changes.

changes. If some variable A changes in response to changes in another variable B, the elasticity of A with respect to B is equal to the percentage change in A divided by the percentage change in B:

$$\text{elasticity of } A \text{ with respect to } B = \frac{\%\Delta A}{\%\Delta B}$$

In the examples discussed previously, we often consider responsiveness or elasticity by looking at prices: How does demand for a product respond when its price changes? This is known as the price elasticity of demand. How does supply respond when prices change? This is the price elasticity of supply. As in the McDonald's example, sometimes it is important to know how the price of one good—for example, the Big Mac—affects the demand for another good—Chicken McNuggets. This is called the cross-price elasticity of demand.

But the concept of elasticity goes well beyond responsiveness to price changes. As we will see, we can look at elasticities as a way to understand responses to changes in income and almost any other major determinant of supply and demand in a market. We begin with a discussion of price elasticity of demand.

Price Elasticity of Demand

You have already seen the law of demand at work. Recall that *ceteris paribus*, when prices rise, quantity demanded can be expected to decline. When prices fall, quantity demanded can be expected to rise. The normal negative relationship between price and quantity demanded is reflected in the downward slope of demand curves.

Slope and Elasticity

The slope of a demand curve may in a rough way reveal the responsiveness of the quantity demanded to price changes, but slope can be quite misleading. In fact, it is not a good formal measure of responsiveness.

Consider the two identical demand curves in Figure 5.1. The only difference between the two is that quantity demanded is measured in pounds in the graph on the left and in ounces in the graph on the right. When we calculate the numerical value of each slope, however, we get very different

▶ **FIGURE 5.1 Slope Is Not a Useful Measure of Responsiveness**

Changing the unit of measure from pounds to ounces changes the numerical value of the demand slope dramatically, but the behavior of buyers in the two diagrams is identical.

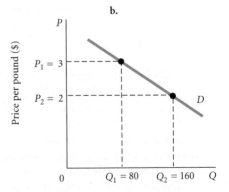

answers. The curve on the left has a slope of −1/5, and the curve on the right has a slope of −1/80; yet the two curves represent the *exact same behavior*. If we had changed dollars to cents on the *Y*-axis, the two slopes would be −20 and −1.25, respectively. (Review the Appendix to Chapter 1 if you do not understand how these numbers are calculated.)

The problem is that the numerical value of slope depends on the units used to measure the variables on the axes. To correct this problem, we must convert the changes in price and quantity to *percentages*. By looking at by how much the *percent* quantity demanded changes for a given *percent* price change, we have a measure of responsiveness that does not change with the unit of measurement. The price increase in Figure 5.1 leads to a decline of 5 pounds, or 80 ounces, in the quantity of steak demanded—a decline of 50 percent from the initial 10 pounds, or 160 ounces, whether we measure the steak in pounds or ounces.

We define **price elasticity of demand** simply as the ratio of the percentage of change in quantity demanded to the percentage change in price.

$$\text{price elasticity of demand} = \frac{\%\ \text{change in quantity demanded}}{\%\ \text{change in price}}$$

Percentage changes should always carry the sign (plus or minus) of the change. Positive changes, or increases, take a (+). Negative changes, or decreases, take a (−). The law of demand implies that price elasticity of demand is nearly always a negative number: Price increases (+) will lead to decreases in quantity demanded (−), and vice versa. Thus, the numerator and denominator should have opposite signs, resulting in a negative ratio.

price elasticity of demand The ratio of the percentage of change in quantity demanded to the percentage of change in price; measures the responsiveness of quantity demanded to changes in price.

Types of Elasticity

The elasticity of demand can vary between 0 and minus infinity. An elasticity of 0 indicates that the quantity demanded does not respond *at all* to a price change. A demand curve with an elasticity of 0 is called **perfectly inelastic** and is illustrated in Figure 5.2(a). A demand curve in which even the smallest price increase reduces quantity demanded to zero is known as a **perfectly elastic** demand curve and is illustrated in Figure 5.2(b). A good way to remember the difference between the two perfect elasticities is

perfectly inelastic demand Demand in which quantity demanded does not respond at all to a change in price.

perfectly elastic demand Demand in which quantity drops to zero at the slightest increase in price.

Perfectly **E**lastic
and Perfectly **I**nelastic

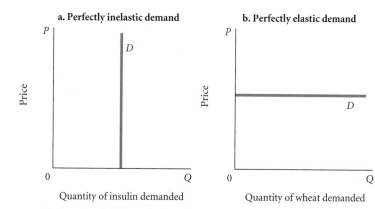

a. Perfectly inelastic demand

P

D

Price

0   *Q*

Quantity of insulin demanded

b. Perfectly elastic demand

P

D

Price

0   *Q*

Quantity of wheat demanded

▲ **FIGURE 5.2 Perfectly Inelastic and Perfectly Elastic Demand Curves**
Figure 5.2(a) shows a perfectly inelastic demand curve for insulin. Price elasticity of demand is zero. Quantity demanded is fixed; it does not change at all when price changes. Figure 5.2(b) shows a perfectly elastic demand curve facing a wheat farmer. A tiny price increase drives the quantity demanded to zero. In essence, perfectly elastic demand implies that individual producers can sell all they want at the going market price but cannot charge a higher price.

What type of good might have a perfectly elastic demand curve? Suppose there are two identical vendors selling Good Humor bars on a beach. If one vendor increased his price, all the buyers would flock to the second vendor. In this case, a small price increase costs the first vendor all his business; the demand he faces is perfectly elastic. Products with perfectly inelastic demand are harder to find, but some life-saving medical products like insulin may be close, in that very high price increases may elicit no response in terms of quantity demanded.

Of course, a lot of products have elasticities between the two extremes. When an elasticity is over −1.0 in absolute value,[1] we refer to the demand as **elastic**. In this case, the percentage change in quantity is larger in absolute value than the percentage change in price. Here consumers are responding a lot to a price change. When an elasticity is less than 1 in absolute value, it is referred to as **inelastic**. In these markets, consumers respond much less to price changes. The demand for oil is inelastic, for example, because even with a price increase, it is hard to substitute oil for other products. The demand for a Nestlé Crunch bar is much more elastic, in part because there are so many more substitutes.

A special case is one in which the elasticity of demand is minus one. Here, we say demand has **unitary elasticity**. In this case, the percentage change in price is exactly equal to the percentage change in quantity demanded, in absolute value terms. As you will see when we look at the relationship between revenue and elasticities later in this chapter, unitary elastic demand curves have some very interesting properties.

A warning: You must be very careful about signs. Because it is generally understood that demand elasticities are negative (demand curves have a negative slope), they are often reported and discussed without the negative sign. For example, a technical paper might report that the demand for housing "appears to be inelastic with respect to price, or less than 1 (.6)." What the writer means is that the estimated elasticity is −.6, which is between zero and −1. Its absolute value is less than 1.

elastic demand A demand relationship in which the percentage change in quantity demanded is larger than the percentage change in price in absolute value (a demand elasticity with an absolute value greater than 1).

inelastic demand Demand that responds somewhat, but not a great deal, to changes in price. Inelastic demand always has a numerical value between zero and −1.

unitary elasticity A demand relationship in which the percentage change in quantity of a product demanded is the same as the percentage change in price in absolute value (a demand elasticity of −1).

Calculating Elasticities

Elasticities must be calculated cautiously. Return for a moment to the demand curves in Figure 5.1 on p. 98. The fact that these two identical demand curves have dramatically different slopes should be enough to convince you that slope is a poor measure of responsiveness. As we will see shortly, a given straight line, which has the same slope all along it, will show different elasticities at various points.

The concept of elasticity circumvents the measurement problem posed by the graphs in Figure 5.1 by converting the changes in price and quantity to percentage changes. Recall that elasticity of demand is the *percentage* change in quantity demanded divided by the *percentage* change in price.

Calculating Percentage Changes

Because we need to know percentage changes to calculate elasticity, let us begin our example by calculating the percentage change in quantity demanded. Figure 5.1(a) shows that the quantity of steak demanded increases from 5 pounds (Q_1) to 10 pounds (Q_2) when price drops from \$3 to \$2 per pound. Thus, the change in quantity demanded is equal to $Q_2 - Q_1$, or 5 pounds.

To convert this change into a percentage change, we must decide on a *base* against which to calculate the percentage. It is often convenient to use the initial value of quantity demanded (Q_1) as the base.

To calculate percentage change in quantity demanded using the initial value as the base, the following formula is used:

$$\% \text{ change in quantity demanded} = \frac{\text{change in quantity demanded}}{Q_1} \times 100\%$$

$$= \frac{Q_2 - Q_1}{Q_1} \times 100\%$$

---

[1] *Absolute value* or *absolute size* means ignoring the sign. The absolute value of −4 is 4.

In Figure 5.1, $Q_2 = 10$ and $Q_1 = 5$. Thus,

$$\% \text{ change in quantity demanded} = \frac{10 - 5}{5} \times 100\% = \frac{5}{5} \times 100\% = 100\%$$

Expressing this equation verbally, we can say that an increase in quantity demanded from 5 pounds to 10 pounds is a 100 percent increase from 5 pounds. Note that you arrive at exactly the same result if you use the diagram in Figure 5.1(b), in which quantity demanded is measured in ounces. An increase from Q_1 (80 ounces) to Q_2 (160 ounces) is a 100 percent increase.

We can calculate the percentage change in price in a similar way. Once again, let us use the initial value of P—that is, P_1—as the base for calculating the percentage. By using P_1 as the base, the formula for calculating the percentage of change in P is

$$\% \text{ change in price} = \frac{\text{change in price}}{P_1} \times 100\%$$

$$= \frac{P_2 - P_1}{P_1} \times 100\%$$

In Figure 5.1(a), P_2 equals 2 and P_1 equals 3. Thus, the change in P, or ΔP, is a negative number: $P_2 - P_1 = 2 - 3 = -1$. This is true because the change is a decrease in price. Plugging the values of P_1 and P_2 into the preceding equation, we get

$$\% \text{ change in price} = \frac{2 - 3}{3} \times 100\% = \frac{-1}{3} \times 100\% = -33.3\%$$

In other words, decreasing the price from \$3 to \$2 is a 33.3 percent decline.

Elasticity Is a Ratio of Percentages

Once the changes in quantity demanded and price have been converted to percentages, calculating elasticity is a matter of simple division. Recall the formal definition of elasticity:

$$\text{price elasticity of demand} = \frac{\% \text{ change in quantity demanded}}{\% \text{ change in price}}$$

If demand is elastic, the ratio of percentage change in quantity demanded to percentage change in price will have an absolute value greater than 1. If demand is inelastic, the ratio will have an absolute value between 0 and 1. If the two percentages are equal, so that a given percentage change in price causes an equal percentage change in quantity demanded, elasticity is equal to -1; this is unitary elasticity.

Substituting the preceding percentages, we see that a 33.3 percent decrease in price leads to a 100 percent increase in quantity demanded; thus,

$$\text{price elasticity of demand} = \frac{+100\%}{-33.3\%} = -3.0$$

According to these calculations, the demand for steak is elastic when we look at the range between \$2 and \$3.

The Midpoint Formula

Although simple, the use of the initial values of P and Q as the bases for calculating percentage changes can be misleading. Let us return to the example of demand for steak in Figure 5.1(a), where we have a change in quantity demanded of 5 pounds. Using the initial value Q_1 as the base, we calculated that this change represents a 100 percent increase over the base. Now suppose that the price of steak rises to \$3 again, causing the quantity demanded to drop back to 5 pounds. How much of a percentage decrease in quantity demanded is this? We now have $Q_1 = 10$ and $Q_2 = 5$. With the same formula we used earlier, we get

$$\% \text{ change in quantity demanded} = \frac{\text{change in quantity demanded}}{Q_1} \times 100\%$$

$$= \frac{Q_2 - Q_1}{Q_1} \times 100\%$$

$$= \frac{5 - 10}{10} \times 100\% = -50\%$$

Thus, an increase from 5 pounds to 10 pounds is a 100 percent increase (because the initial value used for the base is 5), but a decrease from 10 pounds to 5 pounds is only a 50 percent decrease (because the initial value used for the base is 10). This does not make much sense because in both cases, we are calculating elasticity on the same interval on the demand curve. Changing the "direction" of the calculation should not change the elasticity.

To describe percentage changes more accurately, a simple convention has been adopted. Instead of using the initial values of Q and P as the bases for calculating percentages, we use the *midpoints* of these variables as the bases. That is, we use the value halfway between P_1 and P_2 for the base in calculating the percentage change in price and the value halfway between Q_1 and Q_2 as the base for calculating percentage change in quantity demanded.

Thus, the **midpoint formula** for calculating the percentage change in quantity demanded becomes

midpoint formula A more precise way of calculating percentages using the value halfway between P_1 and P_2 for the base in calculating the percentage change in price and the value halfway between Q_1 and Q_2 as the base for calculating the percentage change in quantity demanded.

$$\% \text{ change in quantity demanded} = \frac{\text{change in quantity demanded}}{(Q_1 + Q_2)/2} \times 100\%$$

$$= \frac{Q_2 - Q_1}{(Q_1 + Q_2)/2} \times 100\%$$

Substituting the numbers from the original Figure 5.1(a), we get

$$\% \text{ change in quantity demanded} = \frac{10 - 5}{(5 + 10)/2} \times 100\% = \frac{5}{7.5} \times 100\% = 66.7\%$$

Using the point halfway between P_1 and P_2 as the base for calculating the percentage change in price, we get

$$\% \text{ change in price} = \frac{\text{change in price}}{(P_1 + P_2)/2} \times 100\%$$

$$= \frac{P_2 - P_1}{(P_1 + P_2)/2} \times 100\%$$

Substituting the numbers from the original Figure 5.1(a) yields

$$\% \text{ change in price} = \frac{2 - 3}{(3 + 2)/2} \times 100\% = \frac{-1}{2.5} \times 100\% = -40.0\%$$

We can thus say that a change from a quantity of 5 to a quantity of 10 is a +66.7 percent change using the midpoint formula and that a change in price from \$3 to \$2 is a −40 percent change using the midpoint formula.

Using these percentages to calculate elasticity yields

$$\text{price elasticity of demand} = \frac{\% \text{ change in quantity demanded}}{\% \text{ change in price}} = \frac{66.7\%}{-40.0\%} = -1.67$$

Using the midpoint formula in this case gives a lower demand elasticity, but the demand remains elastic because the percentage change in quantity demanded is still greater than the percentage change in price in absolute size.

The calculations based on the midpoint approach are summarized in Table 5.1.

TABLE 5.1   Calculating Price Elasticity with the Midpoint Formula

First, Calculate Percentage Change in Quantity Demanded (%ΔQ_D):

$$\frac{\text{\% change in}}{\text{quantity demanded}} = \frac{\text{change in quantity demanded}}{(Q_1 + Q_2)/2} \times 100\% = \frac{Q_2 - Q_1}{(Q_1 + Q_2)/2} \times 100\%$$

Price elasticity compares the percentage change in quantity demanded and the percentage change in price.

By substituting the numbers from Figure 5.1(a):

$$\text{\% change in quantity demanded} = \frac{10 - 5}{(5 + 10)/2} \times 100\% = \frac{5}{7.5} \times 100\% = 66.7\%$$

$$\frac{\%\Delta Q_D}{\%\Delta P} = \frac{66.7\%}{-40.0\%}$$

$$= -1.67$$

$$= \textbf{Price elasticity of demand}$$

Next, Calculate Percentage Change in Price (%ΔP):

$$\text{\% change in price} = \frac{\text{change in price}}{(P_1 + P_2)/2} \times 100\% = \frac{P_2 - P_1}{(P_1 + P_2)/2} \times 100\%$$

Demand is elastic.

By substituting the numbers from Figure 5.1(a):

$$\text{\% change in price} = \frac{2 - 3}{(3 + 2)/2} \times 100\% = \frac{-1}{2.5} \times 100\% = -40.0\%$$

Elasticity Changes Along a Straight-Line Demand Curve

An interesting and important point is that elasticity changes from point to point along a demand curve even when the slope of that demand curve does not change—that is, even along a straight-line demand curve. Indeed, the differences in elasticity along a demand curve can be quite large.

Before we go through the calculations to show how elasticity changes along a demand curve, it is useful to think *why* elasticity might change as we vary price. Consider again McDonald's decision to reduce the price of a Big Mac. Suppose McDonald's found that at the current price of $3, a small price cut would generate a large number of new customers who wanted burgers. Demand, in short, was relatively elastic. What happens as McDonald's continues to cut its price? As the price moves from $2.50 to $2.00, for example, new customers lured in by the price cuts are likely to decrease; in some sense, McDonald's will be running out of customers who are interested in its burgers at any price. It should come as no surprise that as we move down a typical straight-line demand curve, price elasticity falls. Demand becomes less elastic as price is reduced. This lesson has important implications for price-setting strategies of firms.

Consider the demand schedule shown in Table 5.2 and the demand curve in Figure 5.3. Herb works about 22 days per month in a downtown San Francisco office tower. On the top floor

---

TABLE 5.2   Demand Schedule for Office Dining Room Lunches

Price (per Lunch)	Quantity Demanded (Lunches per Month)
$11	0
10	2
9	4
8	6
7	8
6	10
5	12
4	14
3	16
2	18
1	20
0	22

(handwritten note: TR / 0 / 20 / 36)

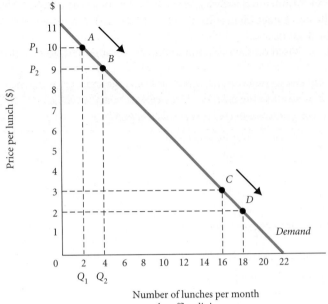

of the building is a nice dining room. If lunch in the dining room were $10, Herb would eat there only twice a month. If the price of lunch fell to $9, he would eat there 4 times a month. (Herb would bring his lunch to work on other days.) If lunch were only a dollar, he would eat there 20 times a month.

Let us calculate price elasticity of demand between points *A* and *B* on the demand curve in Figure 5.3. Moving from *A* to *B*, the price of a lunch drops from $10 to $9 (a decrease of $1) and the number of dining room lunches that Herb eats per month increases from two to four (an increase of two). We will use the midpoint approach.

First, we calculate the percentage change in quantity demanded:

$$\% \text{ change in quantity demanded} = \frac{Q_2 - Q_1}{(Q_1 + Q_2)/2} \times 100\%$$

Substituting the numbers from Figure 5.3, we get

$$\% \text{ change in quantity demanded} = \frac{4 - 2}{(2 + 4)/2} \times 100\% = \frac{2}{3} \times 100\% = 66.7\%$$

Next, we calculate the percentage change in price:

$$\% \text{ change in price} = \frac{P_2 - P_1}{(P_1 + P_2)/2} \times 100\%$$

Substituting the numbers from Figure 5.3, we get

$$\% \text{ change in price} = \frac{9 - 10}{(10 + 9)/2} \times 100\% = \frac{-1}{9.5} \times 100\% = -10.5\%$$

Finally, we calculate elasticity by dividing

$$\text{elasticity of demand} = \frac{\% \text{ change in quantity demanded}}{\% \text{ change in price}}$$

$$= \frac{66.7\%}{-10.5\%} = -6.4$$

The percentage change in quantity demanded is 6.4 times larger than the percentage change in price. In other words, Herb's demand between points *A* and *B* is quite responsive; his demand between points *A* and *B* is elastic.

Now consider a different movement along the *same* demand curve in Figure 5.3. Moving from point *C* to point *D*, the graph indicates that at a price of $3, Herb eats in the office dining room 16 times per month. If the price drops to $2, he will eat there 18 times per month. These changes expressed in numerical terms are exactly the same as the price and quantity changes between points *A* and *B* in the figure—price falls $1, and quantity demanded increases by two meals. Expressed in *percentage* terms, however, these changes are very different.

By using the midpoints as the base, the $1 price decline is only a 10.5 percent reduction when price is around $9.50, between points *A* and *B*. The same $1 price decline is a 40 percent reduction when price is around $2.50, between points *C* and *D*. The two-meal increase in quantity demanded is a 66.7 percent increase when Herb averages only 3 meals per month, but it is only an 11.76 percent increase when he averages 17 meals per month. The elasticity of demand between points *C* and *D* is thus 11.76 percent divided by −40 percent, or −0.294. (Work these numbers out for yourself by using the midpoint formula.)

The percentage changes between *A* and *B* are very different from those between *C* and *D*, and so are the elasticities. Herb's demand is quite elastic (−6.4) between points *A* and *B*; a 10.5 percent reduction in price caused a 66.7 percent increase in quantity demanded. However, his demand is inelastic (−0.294) between points *C* and *D*; a 40 percent decrease in price caused only an 11.76 percent increase in quantity demanded.

Again, it is useful to keep in mind the underlying economics as well as the mathematics. At high prices, there is a great deal of potential demand for the dining room to capture. Hence, quantity is likely to respond well to price cuts. At low prices, everyone who is likely to come to the dining room already has.

Elasticity and Total Revenue

As we saw in Chapter 4, the oil-producing countries have had some success keeping oil prices high by controlling supply. To some extent, reducing supply and driving up prices has increased the total oil revenues to the producing countries. We would not, however, expect this strategy to work for everyone. If the organization of banana-exporting countries (OBEC) had done the same thing, the strategy would not have worked.

Why? Suppose OBEC decides to cut production by 30 percent to drive up the world price of bananas. At first, when the quantity of bananas supplied declines, the quantity demanded is greater than the quantity supplied and the world price rises. The issue for OBEC, however, is *how much* the world price will rise. That is, how much will people be willing to pay to continue consuming bananas? Unless the percentage *increase* in price is greater than the percentage *decrease* in output, the OBEC countries will lose revenues.

A little research shows us that the prospects are not good for OBEC. There are many reasonable substitutes for bananas. As the price of bananas rises, people simply eat fewer bananas as they switch to eating more pineapples or oranges. Many people are simply not willing to pay a higher price for bananas. The quantity of bananas demanded declines 30 percent—to the new quantity supplied—after only a modest price rise, and OBEC fails in its mission; its revenues decrease instead of increase.

We have seen that oil-producing countries often can increase their revenues by restricting supply and pushing up the market price of crude oil. We also argued that a similar strategy by banana-producing countries would probably fail. Why? The quantity of oil demanded is not as responsive to a change in price as is the quantity of bananas demanded. In other words, the demand for oil is more inelastic than is the demand for bananas. One of the very useful features of elasticity is that knowing the value of price elasticity allows us to quickly see what happens to a firm's revenue as it raises and cuts its prices. When demand is inelastic, raising prices will raise revenues; when (as in the banana case) demand is elastic, price increases reduce revenues.

We can now use the more formal definition of elasticity to make more precise our argument of why oil producers would succeed and banana producers would fail as they raise prices. In any market, $P \times Q$ is total revenue (*TR*) received by producers:

$$TR = P \times Q$$
$$\text{total revenue} = \text{price} \times \text{quantity}$$

The oil producers' total revenue is the price per barrel of oil (P) times the number of barrels its participant countries sell (Q). To banana producers, total revenue is the price per bunch times the number of bunches sold.

When price increases in a market, quantity demanded declines. As we have seen, when price (P) declines, quantity demanded (Q_D) increases. This is true in all markets. The two factors, P and Q_D, move in opposite directions:

$$\text{effects of price changes on quantity demanded:} \qquad \begin{array}{c} P \uparrow \; \rightarrow \; Q_D \downarrow \\ \text{and} \\ P \downarrow \; \rightarrow \; Q_D \uparrow \end{array}$$

Because total revenue is the product of P and Q, whether TR rises or falls in response to a price increase depends on which is bigger: the percentage increase in price or the percentage decrease in quantity demanded. If the percentage decrease in quantity demanded is smaller than the percentage increase in price, total revenue will rise. This occurs when demand is *inelastic*. In this case, the percentage price rise simply outweighs the percentage quantity decline and $P \times Q = (TR)$ rises:

$$\text{effect of price increase on a product with inelastic demand:} \qquad \uparrow P \times Q_D \downarrow = TR \uparrow$$

If, however, the percentage decline in quantity demanded following a price increase is larger than the percentage increase in price, total revenue will fall. This occurs when demand is *elastic*. The percentage price increase is outweighed by the percentage quantity decline:

$$\text{effect of price increase on a product with elastic demand:} \qquad \uparrow P \times Q_D \downarrow = TR \downarrow$$

The opposite is true for a price cut. When demand is elastic, a cut in price increases total revenues:

$$\text{effect of price cut on a product with elastic demand:} \qquad \downarrow P \times Q_D \uparrow = TR \uparrow$$

When demand is inelastic, a cut in price reduces total revenues:

$$\text{effect of price cut on a product with inelastic demand:} \qquad \downarrow P \times Q_D \uparrow = TR \downarrow$$

Review the logic of these equations to make sure you thoroughly understand the reasoning. Having a responsive (or elastic) market is good when we are lowering price because it means that we are dramatically increasing our units sold. But that same responsiveness is unattractive as we contemplate raising prices because now it means that we are losing customers. And, of course, the reverse logic works in the inelastic market. Note that if there is unitary elasticity, total revenue is unchanged if the price changes.

With this knowledge, we can now see why reducing supply by the oil-producing countries was so effective. The demand for oil is inelastic. Restricting the quantity of oil available led to a huge increase in the price of oil—the percentage increase was larger in absolute value than the percentage decrease in the quantity of oil demanded. Hence, oil producers' total revenues went up. In contrast, a banana cartel would not be effective because the demand for bananas is elastic. A small increase in the price of bananas results in a large decrease in the quantity of bananas demanded and thus causes total revenues to fall.

The Determinants of Demand Elasticity

Elasticity of demand is a way of measuring the responsiveness of consumers' demand to changes in price. As a measure of behavior, it can be applied to individual households or to market demand as a whole. You love peaches, and you would hate to give them up. Your demand for peaches is therefore inelastic. However, not everyone is crazy about peaches; in fact, the market demand for peaches is relatively elastic. Because no two people have exactly the same preferences, reactions to price changes will be different for different people, which makes generalizations risky. Nonetheless, a few principles do seem to hold.

Availability of Substitutes

Perhaps the most obvious factor affecting demand elasticity is the availability of substitutes. Consider a number of farm stands lined up along a country road. If every stand sells fresh corn of roughly the same quality, Mom's Green Thumb will find it very difficult to charge a price much higher than the competition charges because a nearly perfect substitute is available just down the road. The demand for Mom's corn is thus likely to be very elastic: An increase in price will lead to a rapid decline in the quantity demanded of Mom's corn.

In the oil versus banana example, the demand for oil is inelastic in large measure due to the lack of substitutes. When the price of crude oil went up in the early 1970s, 130 million motor vehicles, getting an average of 12 miles per gallon and consuming over 100 billion gallons of gasoline each year, were on the road in the United States. Millions of homes were heated with oil, and industry ran on equipment that used petroleum products. When the oil-producing countries (OPEC) cut production, the price of oil rose sharply. Quantity demanded fell somewhat, but price increased over 400 percent. What makes the cases of OPEC and OBEC different is the *magnitude* of the response in the quantity demanded to a change of price.

The Importance of Being Unimportant

When an item represents a relatively small part of our total budget, we tend to pay little attention to its price. For example, if you pick up a pack of mints once in a while, you might not notice an increase in price from 25 cents to 35 cents. Yet this is a 40 percent increase in price (33.3 percent using the midpoint formula). In cases such as these, we are not likely to respond very much to changes in price and demand is likely to be inelastic.

ECONOMICS IN PRACTICE

Who Are the Elastic Smokers?

In the United States, taxes are imposed on cigarettes at the state level. As a result, there are large differences among states. As of July 1, 2010, three states had cigarette taxes in excess of $3.00 per pack: Rhode Island, Connecticut, and Washington. Seven more had rates between $2.00 and $3.00 (including the District of Columbia). Missouri had the lowest rate among the 50 states at $0.17 a pack. The following article describes a proposal to raise taxes by $1.00 per pack in the state of Washington.

We would expect an increase in the tax on cigarettes to increase their price to consumers. An interesting question from the point of view of health and tax revenue is how much a price increase lowers demand. One of the commentators in the article claims that increasing cigarette prices by 10 percent reduces youth smokers by 6–7 percent; this is an implied demand elasticity of –0.6 (6%/10%). How do you think this compares to what we would expect from adult smokers? Many people would argue that because more young people are new smokers and because they have less money than adults, their demand for cigarettes would be more elastic. On the other hand, if peer pressure favors smoking, this could lower demand elasticity for youths.

One problem that states face as they increase their cigarette taxes is that people will seek cigarette substitutes from cheaper areas. In Washington, the state pressured Indian tribes to raise the tribal tax rate on cigarettes to the overall state level. By making these substitutes to state-taxed cigarettes more expensive, the loss of customers in response to the state tax increase would be less.

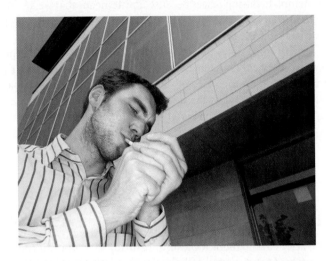

The proposed tax would raise the current $1.425 a pack by more than a dollar. The additional revenue would generate an estimated $300 million in two years for the state's health-care fund, according to bill sponsors. Proponents also say the substantial tax would deter people from smoking, saving nearly $1 billion in future health-care costs.

Eric Lindblom, manager for policy research at Campaign for Tobacco-Free Kids, said "raising cigarette prices is one of the quickest, most effective ways to reduce youth smoking."

Every time a state increases cigarette taxes by 10 percent, there is a 6 to 7 percent decrease in youth smokers, he said.

Bill Aims to Raise Tax on Cigarettes

Seattle Times

OLYMPIA—If lawmakers pass a House bill raising the state cigarette tax to $2.50 a pack, Washington would be the second most expensive place in the country to buy cigarettes.

Source: Copyright 2005, Seattle Times Company. Used with permission.

The Time Dimension

When the oil-producing nations first cut output and succeeded in pushing up the price of crude oil, few substitutes were immediately available. Demand was relatively inelastic, and prices rose substantially. During the last 30 years, however, there has been some adjustment to higher oil prices. Automobiles manufactured today get on average more miles per gallon, and some drivers have cut down on their driving. Millions of home owners have insulated their homes, most people have turned down their thermostats, and some people have explored alternative energy sources.

Oil prices again rose dramatically during the weeks following Hurricane Katrina in 2005 because of the disruption to oil refineries and oil rigs. Once again, the response of demand to the resulting higher gasoline prices took place slowly over time. This time many former SUV drivers switched to hybrids.

All of this illustrates a very important point: The elasticity of demand in the short run may be very different from the elasticity of demand in the long run. In the longer run, demand is likely to become more elastic, or responsive, simply because households make adjustments over time and producers develop substitute goods.

ECONOMICS IN PRACTICE

Elasticities at a Delicatessen in the Short Run and Long Run

Frank runs a corner delicatessen and decides one Monday morning to raise the prices of his sandwiches by 10 percent. Because Frank knows a little economics, he expects that this price increase will cause him to lose some business, since demand curves slope down, but he decides to try it anyway. At the end of the day, Frank discovers that his revenue has, in fact, gone up in the sandwich department. Feeling pleased with himself, Frank hires someone to create signs showing the new prices for the sandwich department. At the end of the month, however, he discovers that sandwich revenue is way down. What is going on?

The first thing to notice about this situation is that it poses a puzzle about what happens to revenue following a price increase. Seeing a linkage between price increases (or cuts) and revenue immediately leads an economist to think about *elasticity*. We remember from earlier in the chapter that *when demand is elastic*, (that is, an *absolute value* greater than 1), *price increases reduce revenue* because a small price increase will bring a large quantity decrease, thus depressing revenue. Conversely, when demand is inelastic (that is, an absolute value less than 1), price increases do little to curb demand and revenues rise. In this case, Monday's price increase brings increases in revenue; therefore, this pattern tells us that the demand from Frank's customers appears to be inelastic. In the longer term, however, demand appears to be more elastic (revenue is down after a month). Another way to pose this puzzle is to ask why the monthly demand curve might have a different elasticity than the daily demand.

To answer that question, you need to think about what determines elasticity. The most fundamental determinant of demand elasticity is the availability of substitutes. In this case, the product we are looking at is sandwiches. At first, you might think that the substitutes for Monday's sandwich would be the same as the substitutes for the sandwiches for the rest of the month. But this is not correct. Once you are in Frank's store, planning to buy a sandwich, your demand tends to be relatively inelastic because your ability to substitute by going elsewhere or choosing a different lunch item is relatively limited. You have already come to the part of town where Frank's Delicatessen is located, and you may already have chosen chips and a beverage to go along with your sandwich. Once you know that Frank's sandwiches are expensive, you can make different plans, and this broadening of your substitute choices increases your elasticity. In general, longer-term demand curves tend to be more elastic than shorter-term curves because customers have more choices.

The graph below shows the expected relationship between long-run and short-run demand for Frank's sandwiches. Notice if you raise prices above the current level, the expected quantity change read off the short-run curve is less than that from the long-run curve.

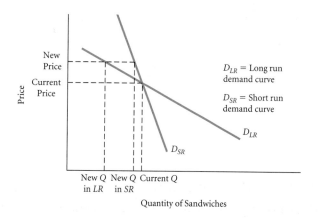

Other Important Elasticities

So far, we have been discussing price elasticity of demand, which measures the responsiveness of quantity demanded to changes in price. However, as we noted earlier, elasticity is a general concept. If *B* causes a change in *A* and we can measure the change in both, we can calculate the elasticity of *A* with respect to *B*. Let us look briefly at three other important types of elasticity.

Income Elasticity of Demand

income elasticity of demand A measure of the responsiveness of demand to changes in income.

Income elasticity of demand, which measures the responsiveness of demand to changes in income, is defined as

$$\text{income elasticity of demand} = \frac{\%\ \text{change in quantity demanded}}{\%\ \text{change in income}}$$

Measuring income elasticity is important for many reasons. Government policy makers spend a great deal of time and money weighing the relative merits of different policies. During the 1970s, for example, the Department of Housing and Urban Development (HUD) conducted a huge experiment in four cities to estimate the income elasticity of housing demand. In this "housing allowance demand experiment," low-income families received housing vouchers over an extended period of time and researchers watched their housing consumption for several years. Most estimates, including the ones from the HUD study, put the income elasticity of housing demand between 0.5 and 0.8. That is, a 10 percent increase in income can be expected to raise the quantity of housing demanded by a household by 5 percent to 8 percent.

Income elasticities can be positive or negative. During periods of rising income, people increase their spending on some goods (positive income elasticity) but reduce their spending on other goods (negative income elasticity). The income elasticity of demand for jewelry is positive, while the income elasticity of demand for low-quality beef is negative. As incomes rise in many low-income countries, the birth rate falls, implying a negative income elasticity of demand for children. Also, as incomes rise in most countries, the demand for education and health care rises, a positive income elasticity.

Cross-Price Elasticity of Demand

cross-price elasticity of demand A measure of the response of the quantity of one good demanded to a change in the price of another good.

Cross-price elasticity of demand, which measures the response of quantity of one good demanded to a change in the price of another good, is defined as

$$\text{cross-price elasticity of demand} = \frac{\%\ \text{change in quantity of } Y \text{ demanded}}{\%\ \text{change in price of } X}$$

Like income elasticity, cross-price elasticity can be either positive or negative. A *positive* cross-price elasticity indicates that an increase in the price of X causes the demand for Y to rise. This implies that the goods are substitutes. For McDonald's, Big Macs and Chicken McNuggets are substitutes with a positive cross-price elasticity. In our earlier example, as McDonald's lowered the price of Big Macs, it saw a decline in the quantity of McNuggets sold as consumers substituted between the two meals. If cross-price elasticity turns out to be *negative*, an increase in the price of X causes a decrease in the demand for Y. This implies that the goods are complements. Hot dogs and football games are complements with a negative cross-price elasticity.

As we have already seen, knowing the cross-price elasticity can be a very important part of a company's business strategy. Sony and Toshiba recently competed in the market for high-definition DVD players: Sony's Blu-ray versus Toshiba's HD DVD. Both firms recognized that an important driver of a customer's choice of a DVD player is movie price and availability. No one wants a new high-definition player if there is nothing to watch on it or if the price of movies is expensive. Inexpensive and available movies are a key complement to new DVD players. The cross-price elasticity of movies and high-definition DVD players is strong and negative. Sony won, and some observers think that Sony's ownership of a movie studio gave it an important advantage.

Elasticity of Supply

So far, we have focused on the consumer part of the market. But elasticity also matters on the producer's side.

Elasticity of supply, which measures the response of quantity of a good supplied to a change in price of that good, is defined as

elasticity of supply A measure of the response of quantity of a good supplied to a change in price of that good. Likely to be positive in output markets.

$$\text{elasticity of supply} = \frac{\text{\% change in quantity supplied}}{\text{\% change in price}}$$

In output markets, the elasticity of supply is likely to be a positive number—that is, a higher price leads to an increase in the quantity supplied, *ceteris paribus*. (Recall our discussion of upward-sloping supply curves in the preceding two chapters.)

The elasticity of supply is a measure of how easily producers can adapt to a price increase and bring increased quantities to market. In some industries, it is relatively easy for firms to increase their output. Ballpoint pens fall into this category, as does most software that has already been developed. For these products, the elasticity of supply is very high. In the oil industry, supply is inelastic, much like demand.

In input markets, however, some interesting problems arise in looking at elasticity. Perhaps the most studied elasticity of all is the **elasticity of labor supply**, which measures the response of labor supplied to a change in the price of labor. Economists have examined household labor supply responses to government programs such as welfare, Social Security, the income tax system, need-based student aid, and unemployment insurance.

elasticity of labor supply A measure of the response of labor supplied to a change in the price of labor.

In simple terms, the elasticity of labor supply is defined as

$$\text{elasticity of labor supply} = \frac{\text{\% change in quantity of labor supplied}}{\text{\% change in the wage rate}}$$

It seems reasonable at first glance to assume that an increase in wages increases the quantity of labor supplied. That would imply an upward-sloping supply curve and a positive labor supply elasticity, but this is not necessarily so. An increase in wages makes workers better off: They can work the same number of hours and have higher incomes. One of the things workers might like to "buy" with that higher income is more leisure time. "Buying" leisure simply means working fewer hours, and the "price" of leisure is the lost wages. Thus, it is quite possible that to some groups, an increase in wages above some level will lead to a reduction in the quantity of labor supplied.

Looking Ahead

The purpose of this chapter was to convince you that measurement is important. If all we can say is that a change in one economic factor causes another to change, we cannot say whether the change is important or whether a particular policy is likely to work. The most commonly used tool of measurement is elasticity, and the term will recur as we explore economics in more depth.

We now return to the study of basic economics by looking in detail at household behavior. Recall that households *demand* goods and services in product markets but *supply* labor and savings in input or factor markets.

— S U M M A R Y —

1. *Elasticity* is a general measure of responsiveness that can be used to quantify many different relationships. If one variable *A* changes in response to changes in another variable *B*, the elasticity of *A* with respect to *B* is equal to the percentage change in *A* divided by the percentage change in *B*.

2. The slope of a demand curve is an inadequate measure of responsiveness because its value depends on the units of measurement used. For this reason, elasticities are calculated using percentages.

PRICE ELASTICITY OF DEMAND *p. 98*

3. *Price elasticity of demand* is the ratio of the percentage change in quantity demanded of a good to the percentage change in price of that good.

4. *Perfectly inelastic* demand is demand whose quantity demanded does not respond at all to changes in price; its numerical value is zero.

5. *Inelastic* demand is demand whose quantity demanded responds somewhat, but not a great deal, to changes in price; its numerical value is between zero and −1.

6. *Elastic* demand is demand in which the percentage change in quantity demanded is larger in absolute value than the percentage change in price. Its numerical value is less than −1.

7. *Unitary elasticity* of demand describes a relationship in which the percentage change in the quantity of a product demanded is the same as the percentage change in price; unitary elasticity has a numerical value of −1.

8. *Perfectly elastic* demand describes a relationship in which a small increase in the price of a product causes the quantity demanded for that product to drop to zero.

CALCULATING ELASTICITIES *p. 100*

9. If demand is elastic, a price increase will reduce the quantity demanded by a larger percentage than the percentage increase in price and total revenue ($P \times Q$) will fall. If demand is inelastic, a price increase will increase total revenue.

10. If demand is elastic, a price cut will cause quantity demanded to increase by a greater percentage than the percentage decrease in price and total revenue will rise. If demand is inelastic, a price cut will cause quantity demanded to increase by a smaller percentage than the percentage decrease in price and total revenue will fall.

THE DETERMINANTS OF DEMAND ELASTICITY *p. 107*

11. The elasticity of demand depends on (1) the availability of substitutes, (2) the importance of the item in individual budgets, and (3) the time frame in question.

OTHER IMPORTANT ELASTICITIES *p. 109*

12. There are several important elasticities. *Income elasticity of demand* measures the responsiveness of the quantity demanded with respect to changes in income. *Cross-price elasticity of demand* measures the response of the quantity of one good demanded to a change in the price of another good. *Elasticity of supply* measures the response of the quantity of a good supplied to a change in the price of that good. The *elasticity of labor supply* measures the response of the quantity of labor supplied to a change in the price of labor.

— R E V I E W   T E R M S   A N D   C O N C E P T S —

cross-price elasticity of demand, *p. 110*

elastic demand, *p. 100*

elasticity, *p. 97*

elasticity of labor supply, *p. 111*

elasticity of supply, *p. 111*

income elasticity of demand, *p. 110*

inelastic demand, *p. 100*

midpoint formula, *p. 102*

perfectly elastic demand, *p. 99*

perfectly inelastic demand, *p. 99*

price elasticity of demand, *p. 99*

unitary elasticity, *p. 100*

PROBLEMS

All problems are available on www.myeconlab.com

1. Fill in the missing amounts in the following table:

	% CHANGE IN PRICE	% CHANGE IN QUANTITY	ELASTICITY
Demand for Ben & Jerry's Ice Cream	+10%	−12%	**a.**
Demand for beer at San Francisco 49ers football games	−20%	**b.**	−.5
Demand for Broadway theater tickets in New York	**c.**	−15%	−1.0
Supply of chickens	+10%	**d.**	+1.2
Supply of beef cattle	−15%	−10%	**e.**

2. Use the table in the preceding problem to defend your answers to the following questions:
   a. Would you recommend that Ben & Jerry's move forward with a plan to raise prices if the company's only goal is to increase revenues?
   b. Would you recommend that beer stands cut prices to increase revenues at 49ers football games next year?

3. Using the midpoint formula, calculate elasticity for each of the following changes in demand by a household.

	P_1	P_2	Q_1	Q_2
Demand for:				
a. Long-distance telephone service	$0.25 per min.	$0.15 per min.	300 min. per month	400 min. per month
b. Orange juice	1.49 per qt	1.89 per qt	14 qt per month	12 qt per month
c. Big Macs	2.89	1.00	3 per week	6 per week
d. Cooked shrimp	$9 per lb	$12 per lb	2 lb per month	1.5 lb per month

4. A sporting goods store has estimated the demand curve for a popular brand of running shoes as a function of price. Use the diagram to answer the questions that follow.

Shoe sales per week

   a. Calculate demand elasticity using the midpoint formula between points *A* and *B*, between points *C* and *D*, and between points *E* and *F*.

b. If the store currently charges a price of $50, then increases that price to $60, what happens to total revenue from shoe sales (calculate $P \times Q$ before and after the price change)? Repeat the exercise for initial prices being decreased to $40 and $20, respectively.
   c. Explain why the answers to a. can be used to predict the answers to b.

5. For each of the following scenarios, decide whether you agree or disagree and explain your answer.
   a. If the elasticity of demand for cocaine is −.2 and the Drug Enforcement Administration succeeds in reducing supply substantially, causing the street price of the drug to rise by 50%, buyers will spend less on cocaine.
   b. Every year Christmas tree vendors bring tens of thousands of trees from the forests of New England to New York City and Boston. During the last two years, the market has been very competitive; as a result, price has fallen by 10 percent. If the price elasticity of demand was −1.3, vendors would lose revenues altogether as a result of the price decline.
   c. If the demand for a good has unitary elasticity, or elasticity is −1, it is always true that an increase in its price will lead to more revenues for sellers taken as a whole.

6. For the following statements, decide whether you agree or disagree and explain your answer.
   a. The demand curve pictured here is elastic.

   b. If supply were to increase slightly in the following diagram, prices would fall and firms would earn less revenue.

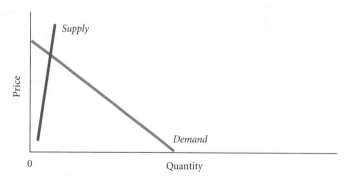

7. Taxicab fares in most cities are regulated. Several years ago taxicab drivers in Boston obtained permission to raise their fares 10 percent, and they anticipated that revenues would increase by about 10 percent as a result. They were disappointed, however. When the commissioner granted the 10 percent increase, revenues increased by only about 5 percent. What can you infer

about the elasticity of demand for taxicab rides? What were taxicab drivers assuming about the elasticity of demand?

*8. Studies have fixed the short-run price elasticity of demand for gasoline at the pump at −0.20. Suppose that international hostilities lead to a sudden cutoff of crude oil supplies. As a result, U.S. supplies of refined gasoline drop 10 percent.

   a. If gasoline were selling for $2.60 per gallon before the cutoff, how much of a price increase would you expect to see in the coming months?

   b. Suppose that the government imposes a price ceiling on gas at $2.60 per gallon. How would the relationship between consumers and gas station owners change?

9. Prior to 2005, it seemed like house prices always rose and never fell. When the demand for housing increases, prices in the housing market rise but not always by very much. For prices to rise substantially, the supply of housing must be relatively inelastic. That is, if the quantity supplied increases rapidly whenever house prices rise, price increases will remain small. Many have suggested government policies to increase the elasticity of supply. What specific policies might hold prices down when demand increases? Explain.

10. For each of the following statements, state the relevant elasticity and state what its value should be (negative, positive, greater than one, zero, and so on).

   a. The supply of labor is inelastic but slightly backward-bending.

   b. The demand for BMWs in an area increases during times of rising incomes just slightly faster than income rises.

   c. The demand for lobsters falls when lobster prices rise (*ceteris paribus*), but the revenue received by restaurants from the sale of lobsters stays the same.

   d. Demand for many goods rise when the price of substitutes rise.

   e. Land for housing development near Youngstown, Ohio, is in plentiful supply. At the current price, there is essentially an infinite supply.

11. [Related to the *Economics in Practice* on p. 108] A number of towns in the United States have begun charging their residents for garbage pickup based on the number of garbage cans filled per week. The town of Chase decided to increase its per-can price from 10 cents to 20 cents per week. In the first week, Chase found that the number of cans that were brought to the curb fell from 550 to 525 (although the city workers complained that the cans were heavier). The town economist ran the numbers, informed the mayor that the demand for disposal was inelastic, and recommended that the city raise the price more to maximize town revenue from the program. Six months later, at a price of 30 cents per can, the number of cans has fallen to 125 and town revenues are down. What might have happened?

12. [Related to the *Economics in Practice* on p. 109] At Frank's Delicatessen, Frank noticed that the elasticity of customers differed in the short and longer term. Frank also noticed that his increase in the price of sandwiches had other effects on his store. In particular, the number of sodas sold declined while the number of yogurts sold went up. How might you explain this pattern?

13. Describe what will happen to total revenue in the following situations.

   a. Price decreases and demand is elastic.

   b. Price decreases and demand is inelastic.

   c. Price increases and demand is elastic.

   d. Price increases and demand is inelastic.

   e. Price increases and demand is unitary elastic.

   f. Price decreases and demand is perfectly inelastic.

   g. Price increases and demand is perfectly elastic.

14. The cross-price elasticity values for three sets of products are listed in the table below. What can you conclude about the relationships between each of these sets of products?

	PRODUCTS A AND B	PRODUCTS C AND D	PRODUCTS E AND F
Cross-price elasticity	−8.7	+5.5	0.0

15. Income elasticity of demand measures the responsiveness of demand to changes in income. Explain what is happening to demand and what kind of good is being represented in the following situations.

   a. Income is rising, and income elasticity of demand is positive.

   b. Income is rising, and income elasticity of demand is negative.

16. Using the midpoint formula and the following graph, calculate the price elasticity of demand and the price elasticity of supply when the price changes from $4 to $9 and when the price changes from $9 to $15.

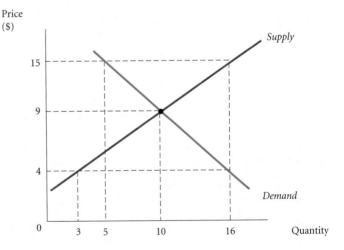

*Note: Problems marked with an asterisk are more challenging.

17. Use the following total revenue graph to identify which sections of the total revenue curve reflect elastic demand, inelastic demand, and unitary elastic demand. Explain your answers.

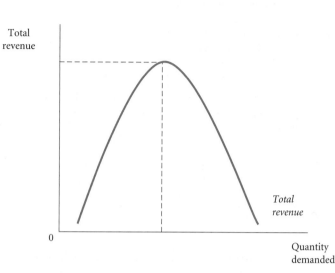

18. For each of the following products, explain whether demand is likely to be elastic or inelastic.
    a. Cigarettes
    b. Tacos
    c. Gasoline
    d. Milk
    e. Honda Accord automobiles
    f. Newspapers

CHAPTER 5 APPENDIX

Point Elasticity (Optional)

Two different elasticities were calculated along the demand curve in Figure 5.3 on p. 104. Between points *A* and *B*, we discovered that Herb's demand for lunches in the fancy dining room was very elastic: A price decline of only 10.5 percent resulted in his eating 66.7 percent more lunches in the dining room (elasticity = −6.4). Between points *C* and *D*, however, on the same demand curve, we discovered that his demand for meals was very inelastic: A price decline of 40 percent resulted in only a modest increase in lunches consumed of 11.76 percent (elasticity = −0.294).

Now consider the straight-line demand curve in Figure 5A.1. We can write an expression for elasticity at point *C* as follows:

$$\text{elasticity} = \frac{\%\Delta Q}{\%\Delta P} = \frac{\dfrac{\Delta Q}{Q} \cdot 100}{\dfrac{\Delta P}{P} \cdot 100} = \frac{\dfrac{\Delta Q}{Q_1}}{\dfrac{\Delta P}{P_1}} = \boxed{\frac{\Delta Q}{\Delta P} \cdot \frac{P_1}{Q_1}}$$

$\Delta Q/\Delta P$ is the *reciprocal* of the slope of the curve. Slope in the diagram is constant along the curve, and it is negative. To calculate the reciprocal of the slope to plug into the previous elasticity equation, we take Q_1B, or M_1, and divide by *minus* the length of line segment CQ_1. Thus,

$$\frac{\Delta Q}{\Delta P} = \frac{M_1}{CQ_1}$$

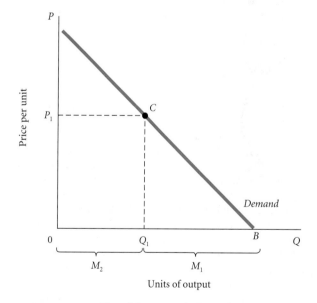

▲ **FIGURE 5A.1 Elasticity at a Point Along a Demand Curve**

Because the length of CQ_1 is equal to P_1, we can write

$$\frac{\Delta Q}{\Delta P} = \frac{M_1}{P_1}$$

By substituting, we get

$$\text{elasticity} = \frac{M_1}{P_1} \cdot \frac{P_1}{Q_1} = \frac{M_1}{P_1} \cdot \frac{P_1}{M_2} = \boxed{\frac{M_1}{M_2}}$$

(The second equal sign uses the fact that Q_1 equals M_2 in Figure 5A.1.)

Elasticity at point C is simply the ratio of line segment M_1 to line segment M_2. It is easy to see that if we had chosen a point to the left of Q_1, M_1 would have been larger and M_2 would have been smaller, indicating a higher elasticity. If we had chosen a point to the right of Q_1, M_1 would have been smaller and M_2 would have been larger, indicating a lower elasticity.

In Figure 5A.2, you can see that elasticity is unitary (equal to -1) at the midpoint of the demand curve, Q_3. At points to the right, such as Q_2, segment Q_2C (M_1 from Figure 5A.1) is smaller than segment $0Q_1$ (M_2 from Figure 5A.1). This means that the absolute size of the ratio is *less than 1* and that demand is *inelastic* at point A. At points to the left, such as Q_1, segment Q_1C (M_1) is larger than segment $0Q_1$ (M_2). This means that the absolute size of the ratio is *greater than 1* and that demand is elastic at point B.

Compare the results here with the results using the mid-point formula for elasticity for Herb.

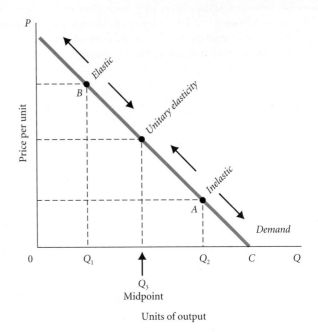

▲ **FIGURE 5A.2** **Point Elasticity Changes Along a Demand Curve**

The Market System

Choices Made by Households and Firms

Now that we have discussed the basic forces of supply and demand, we can explore the underlying behavior of the two fundamental decision-making units in the economy: households and firms.

Figure II.1 presents a diagram of a simple competitive economy. The figure is an expanded version of the circular flow diagram first presented in Figure 3.1 on p. 49. It is designed to guide you through Part II (Chapters 6 through 12) of this book. You will see the

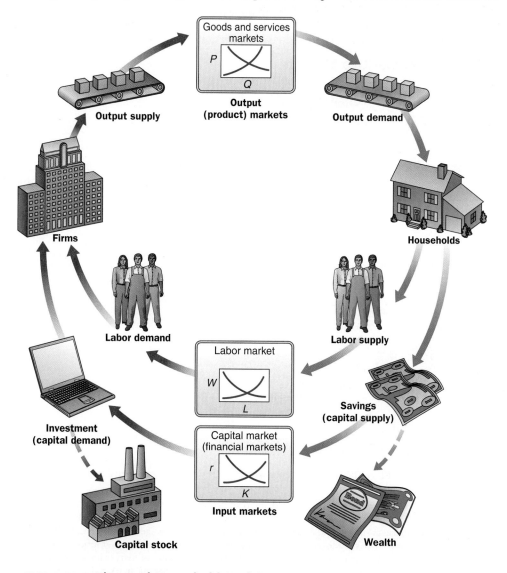

▲ **FIGURE II.1 Firm and Household Decisions**

Households demand in output markets and supply labor and capital in input markets. To simplify our analysis, we have not included the government and international sectors in this circular flow diagram. These topics will be discussed in detail later.

big picture more clearly if you follow this diagram closely as you work your way through this part of the book.

Recall that households and firms interact in two kinds of markets: output (product) markets, shown at the top of Figure II.1, and input (factor) markets, shown at the bottom. Households *demand* outputs and *supply* inputs. In contrast, firms *supply* outputs and *demand* inputs. Chapter 6 explores the behavior of households, focusing first on household demand for outputs and then on household supply in labor and capital markets.

The remaining chapters in Part II focus on firms and the interaction between firms and households. Chapters 7 through 9 analyze the behavior of firms in output markets in both the short run and the long run. Chapter 10 focuses on the behavior of firms in input markets in general, especially the labor and land markets. Chapter 11 discusses the capital market in more detail. Chapter 12 puts all the pieces together and analyzes the functioning of a complete market system. Following Chapter 12, Part III of the book relaxes many assumptions and analyzes market imperfections as well as the potential for and pitfalls of government involvement in the economy. The plan for Chapters 6 through 19 is outlined in Figure II.2.

Recall that throughout this book, all diagrams that describe the behavior of households are drawn or highlighted in *blue*. All diagrams that describe the behavior of firms are drawn or highlighted in *red*. Look carefully at the supply and demand diagrams in Figure II.1; notice that in both the labor and capital markets, the supply curves are blue. The reason is that labor and capital are supplied by households. The demand curves for labor and capital are red because firms demand these inputs for production.

▲ FIGURE II.2 **Understanding the Microeconomy and the Role of Government**
To understand how the economy works, it helps to build from the ground up. We start in Chapters 6–8 with an overview of **household** and **firm** decision making in simple perfectly competitive markets. In Chapters 9–11, we see how firms and households interact in **output markets** (product markets) and **input markets** (labor/land and capital) to determine prices, wages, and profits. Once we have a picture of how a simple perfectly competitive economy works, we begin to relax assumptions. Chapter 12 is a pivotal chapter that links perfectly competitive markets with a discussion of market imperfections and the role of government. In Chapters 13–19, we cover the three noncompetitive market structures (monopoly, monopolistic competition, and oligopoly), externalities, public goods, uncertainty and asymmetric information, and income distribution as well as taxation and government finance.

In Figure II.1, much of the detail of the real world is stripped away just as it is on a highway map. A map is a highly simplified version of reality, but it is a very useful tool when you need to know where you are. Figure II.1 is intended to serve as a map to help you understand basic market forces before we add more complicated market structures and government.

Before we proceed with our discussion of household choice, we need to make a few basic assumptions. These assumptions pertain to Chapters 6 through 12.

We first assume that households and firms possess all the information they need to make market choices. Specifically, we assume that households possess knowledge of the qualities and prices of everything available in the market. Firms know all that there is to know about wage rates, capital costs, and output prices. This assumption is often called the assumption of **perfect knowledge**.

The next assumption is **perfect competition**. Perfect competition is a precisely defined form of industry structure. (The word *perfect* here does not refer to virtue. It simply means "total" or "complete.") In a perfectly competitive industry, no single firm has control over prices. That is, no single firm is large enough to affect the market price of its product or the prices of the inputs that it buys. This follows from two characteristics of competitive industries. First, a competitive industry is composed of many firms, each one small relative to the size of the industry. Second, every firm in a perfectly competitive industry produces exactly the same product; the output of one firm cannot be distinguished from the output of the others. Products in a perfectly competitive industry are said to be **homogeneous**.

These characteristics limit the decisions open to competitive firms and simplify the analysis of competitive behavior. Because all firms in a perfectly competitive industry produce virtually identical products and because each firm is small relative to the market, perfectly competitive firms have no control over the prices at which they sell their output. By taking prices as a given, each firm can decide only how much output to produce and how to produce it.

Consider agriculture, the classic example of a perfectly competitive industry. A wheat farmer in South Dakota has absolutely no control over the price of wheat. Prices are determined not by the individual farmers, but by the interaction of many suppliers and many demanders. The only decisions left to the wheat farmer are how much wheat to plant and when and how to produce the crop.

We finally assume that each household is small relative to the size of the market. Households face a set of product prices that they individually cannot control. Prices again are set by the interaction of many suppliers and many demanders.

By the end of Chapter 10, we will have a complete picture of an economy, but it will be based on this set of fairly restrictive assumptions. At first, this may seem unrealistic to you, but keep the following in mind. Much of the economic analysis in the chapters that follow applies to all forms of market structure. Indeed, much of the power of economic reasoning is that it is quite general. As we continue in microeconomics, in Chapters 13 and 14, we will define and explore several different kinds of market organization and structure, including monopoly, oligopoly, and monopolistic competition. Because monopolists, oligopolists, monopolistic competitors, and perfect competitors share the objective of maximizing profits, it should not be surprising that their behavior is in many ways similar. We focus here on perfect competition because many of these basic principles are easier to learn using the simplest of cases.

---

perfect knowledge The assumption that households possess a knowledge of the qualities and prices of everything available in the market and that firms have all available information concerning wage rates, capital costs, and output prices.

perfect competition An industry structure in which there are many firms, each being small relative to the industry and producing virtually identical products, and in which no firm is large enough to have any control over prices.

homogeneous products Undifferentiated outputs; products that are identical to or indistinguishable from one another.

Household Behavior and Consumer Choice

6

Every day people in a market economy make decisions. Some of those decisions involve the products they plan to buy: Should you buy a Coke for lunch, a bottle of tea, or just drink water? Should you purchase a laptop computer or stick with your old desktop? Some decisions are about the labor market: Should you continue your schooling or go to work instead? If you do start working, how much should you work? Should you work more when you get a raise or just take it easy? Many decisions involve a time element. If you decide to buy a laptop, you may have to use your savings or borrow money. That will leave you with fewer choices about what you can buy in the future. On the other hand, the laptop itself is an investment.

To many people, the decisions listed in the previous paragraph seem very different from one another. As you will see in this chapter, however, from an economics perspective, these decisions have a great deal in common. In this chapter, we will develop a set of principles that can be used to understand decisions in the product market and the labor market—decisions for today and for the future.

As you read this chapter, you might want to think about some of the following questions, questions that you will be able to answer by chapter's end. Baseball, even when it was more popular than it is today, was never played year-round. Indeed, no professional sport has a year-round season. Is this break necessary to give the athletes a rest, or is there something about household choice that helps explain this pattern? When the price of gasoline rises, people drive less, but one study suggests that they also switch from brand name products to generics or store brands.[1] Why might this be? Studying household choice will help you understand many decisions that underpin our market economy.

A constant theme that will run through the analysis is the idea of *constrained choice*. That is, the decisions that we make we make under constraints that exist in the marketplace. Household consumption choices are constrained by income, wealth, and existing prices. Household decisions about labor supply and job choice are clearly constrained by the availability of jobs. This was on everyone's minds when the number of unemployed reached 15 million and the unemployment rate hovered at about 10 percent during the 2009–2010 period. In addition, the choices we make in the workforce are constrained by the existing structure of market wages.

Household Choice in Output Markets

Every household must make three basic decisions:

1. How much of each product, or output, to demand
2. How much labor to supply
3. How much to spend today and how much to save for the future

[1] Dora Gicheva, Justine Hastings, and Sofia Villas-Boas, "Revisiting the Income Effect: Gasoline Prices and Grocery Purchases," NBER Working Paper No. 13614, October 2007.

As we begin our look at demand in output markets, you must keep in mind that the choices underlying the demand curve are only part of the larger household choice problem. Closely related decisions about how much to work and how much to save are equally important and must be made simultaneously with output–demand decisions.

The Determinants of Household Demand

As we saw in Chapter 3, several factors influence the quantity of a given good or service demanded by a single household:

- The price of the product
- The income available to the household
- The household's amount of accumulated wealth
- The prices of other products available to the household
- The household's tastes and preferences
- The household's expectations about future income, wealth, and prices

Recall that demand schedules and demand curves express the relationship between quantity demanded and price, *ceteris paribus*. A change in price leads to a movement along a demand curve. Changes in income, in other prices, or in preferences shift demand curves to the left or right. We refer to these shifts as "changes in demand." However, the interrelationship among these variables is more complex than the simple exposition in Chapter 3 might lead you to believe.

The Budget Constraint

Before we examine the household choice process, we need to discuss what choices are open and not open to households. If you look carefully at the list of items that influence household demand, you will see that the first four actually define the set of options available. Information on household income and wealth, together with information on product prices, makes it possible to distinguish those combinations of goods and services that are affordable from those that are not.[2]

budget constraint   The limits imposed on household choices by income, wealth, and product prices.

Income, wealth, and prices thus define what we call household **budget constraint**. The budget constraint facing any household results primarily from limits imposed externally by one or more markets. In competitive markets, for example, households cannot control prices; they must buy goods and services at market-determined prices. A household has some control over its income: Its members can choose whether to work, and they can sometimes decide how many hours to work and how many jobs to hold. However, constraints exist in the labor market too. The amount that household members are paid is limited by current market wage rates. Whether they can get a job is determined by the availability of jobs.

Although income does depend, at least in part, on the choices that households make, we will treat it as a given for now. Later in this chapter, we will relax this assumption and explore labor supply choices in more detail.

The income, wealth, and price constraints that surround choice are best illustrated with an example. Consider Barbara, a recent graduate of a midwestern university who takes a job as an account manager at a public relations firm. Let us assume that she receives a salary of $1,000 per month (after taxes) and that she has no wealth and no credit. Barbara's monthly expenditures are limited to her flow of income. Table 6.1 summarizes some of the choices open to her.

TABLE 6.1 Possible Budget Choices of a Person Earning $1,000 per Month after Taxes					
Option	Monthly Rent	Food	Other Expenses	Total	Available?
A	$ 400	$250	$350	$1,000	Yes
B	600	200	200	1,000	Yes
C	700	150	150	1,000	Yes
D	1,000	100	100	1,200	No

[2] Remember that we drew the distinction between income and wealth in Chapter 3. *Income* is the sum of household earnings within a given period; it is a flow variable. In contrast, *wealth* is a stock variable; it is what a household owns minus what it owes at a given point in time.

A careful search of the housing market reveals four vacant apartments. The least expensive is a one-room studio with a small kitchenette that rents for $400 per month, including utilities (option A). If she lived there, Barbara could afford to spend $250 per month on food and still have $350 left over for other things.

About four blocks away is a one-bedroom apartment with wall-to-wall carpeting and a larger kitchen. It has more space, but the rent is $600, including utilities. If Barbara took this apartment, she might cut her food expenditures by $50 per month and have only $200 per month left for everything else.

In the same building as the one-bedroom apartment is an identical unit on the top floor of the building with a balcony facing west toward the sunset. The balcony and view add $100 to the monthly rent. To live there, Barbara would be left with only $300 to split between food and other expenses.

Just because she was curious, Barbara looked at a town house in the suburbs that was renting for $1,000 per month. Obviously, unless she could get along without eating or doing anything else that cost money, she could not afford it. The combination of the town house and any amount of food is outside her budget constraint.

Notice that we have used the information that we have on income and prices to identify different combinations of housing, food, and other items that are available to a single-person household with an income of $1,000 per month. We have said nothing about the process of choosing. Instead, we have carved out what is called a **choice set** or **opportunity set**, the set of options that is defined and limited by Barbara's budget constraint.

choice set *or* **opportunity set** The set of options that is defined and limited by a budget constraint.

Preferences, Tastes, Trade-Offs, and Opportunity Cost

So far, we have identified only the combinations of goods and services that are and are not available to Barbara. Within the constraints imposed by limited incomes and fixed prices, however, households are free to choose what they will and will not buy. Their ultimate choices are governed by their individual preferences and tastes.

It will help you to think of the household choice process as a process of allocating income over a large number of available goods and services. Final demand of a household for any single product is just one of many outcomes that result from the decision-making process. Think, for example, of a demand curve that shows a household's reaction to a drop in the price of air travel. During certain periods when people travel less frequently, special fares flood the market and many people decide to take trips that they otherwise would not have taken. However, if you live in Florida and decide to spend $400 to visit your mother in Nashville, you cannot spend that $400 on new clothes, dinners at restaurants, or a new set of tires.

A change in the price of a single good changes the constraints within which households choose, and this may change the entire allocation of income. Demand for some goods and services may rise while demand for others falls. A complicated set of trade-offs lies behind the shape and position of a household demand curve for a single good. Whenever a household makes a choice, it is weighing the good or service that it chooses against all the other things that the same money could buy.

Consider again our young account manager and her options listed in Table 6.1. If she hates to cook, likes to eat at restaurants, and goes out three nights a week, she will probably trade off some housing for dinners out and money to spend on clothes and other things. She will probably rent the studio for $400. She may, however, love to spend long evenings at home reading, listening to classical music, and sipping tea while watching the sunset. In that case, she will probably trade off some restaurant meals, evenings out, and travel expenses for the added comfort of the larger apartment with the balcony and the view. As long as a household faces a limited budget—and all households ultimately do—the real cost of any good or service is the value of the other goods and services that could have been purchased with the same amount of money. The real cost of a good or service is its opportunity cost, and opportunity cost is determined by relative prices.

The Budget Constraint More Formally

Ann and Tom are struggling graduate students in economics at the University of Virginia. Their tuition is paid by graduate fellowships. They live as resident advisers in a first-year dormitory, in return for which they receive an apartment and meals. Their fellowships also give them $200 each month to cover all their other expenses. To simplify things, let us assume that Ann and Tom spend their money on only two things: meals at a local Thai restaurant and nights at a local jazz club, The Hungry Ear. Thai meals go for a fixed price of $20 per couple. Two tickets to the jazz club, including espresso, are $10.

As Figure 6.1 shows, we can graphically depict the choices that are available to our dynamic duo. The axes measure the *quantities* of the two goods that Ann and Tom buy. The horizontal axis

▶ **FIGURE 6.1 Budget Constraint and Opportunity Set for Ann and Tom**

A budget constraint separates those combinations of goods and services that are available, given limited income, from those that are not. The available combinations make up the opportunity set.

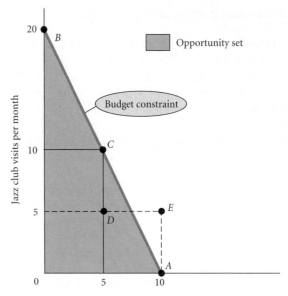

measures the number of Thai meals consumed per month, and the vertical axis measures the number of trips to The Hungry Ear. (Note that price is not on the vertical axis here.) Every point in the space between the axes represents some combination of Thai meals and nights at the jazz club. The question is this: Which of these points can Ann and Tom purchase with a fixed budget of $200 per month? That is, which points are in the opportunity set and which are not?

One possibility is that the students in the dorm are driving Ann and Tom crazy. The two grad students want to avoid the dining hall at all costs. Thus, they might decide to spend all their money on Thai food and none of it on jazz. This decision would be represented by a point *on* the horizontal axis because all the points on that axis are points at which Ann and Tom make no jazz club visits. How many meals can Ann and Tom afford? The answer is simple: When income is $200 and the price of Thai meals is $20, they can afford $200 ÷ $20 = 10 meals. This point is labeled *A* on the budget constraint in Figure 6.1.

Another possibility is that general exams are coming up and Ann and Tom decide to relax at The Hungry Ear to relieve stress. Suppose they choose to spend all their money on jazz and none of it on Thai food. This decision would be represented by a point *on* the vertical axis because all the points on this axis are points at which Ann and Tom eat no Thai meals. How many jazz club visits can they afford? Again, the answer is simple: With an income of $200 and with the price of jazz/espresso at $10, they can go to The Hungry Ear $200 ÷ $10 = 20 times. This is the point labeled *B* in Figure 6.1. The line connecting points *A* and *B* is Ann and Tom's budget constraint.

What about all the points between *A* and *B* on the budget constraint? Starting from point *B*, suppose Ann and Tom give up trips to the jazz club to buy more Thai meals. Each additional Thai meal "costs" two trips to The Hungry Ear. The opportunity cost of a Thai meal is two jazz club trips.

Point *C* on the budget constraint represents a compromise. Here Ann and Tom go to the club 10 times and eat at the Thai restaurant 5 times. To verify that point *C* is on the budget constraint, price it out: 10 jazz club trips cost a total of $10 × 10 = $100, and 5 Thai meals cost a total of $20 × 5 = $100. The total is $100 + $100 = $200.

The budget constraint divides all the points between the axes into two groups: those that can be purchased for $200 or less (the opportunity set) and those that are unavailable. Point *D* on the diagram costs less than $200; point *E* costs more than $200. (Verify that this is true.) The opportunity set is the shaded area in Figure 6.1.

Clearly, both prices and incomes affect the size of a household's opportunity set. If a price or a set of prices falls but income stays the same, the opportunity set gets bigger and the household is better off. If we define **real income** as the set of opportunities to purchase real goods and services, "real income" will have gone up in this case even if the household's money income has not. A consumer's opportunity set expands as the result of a price decrease. On the other hand, when money income increases and prices go up even more, we say that the household's "real income" has fallen.

The concept of real income is very important in macroeconomics, which is concerned with measuring real output and the price level.

real income The set of opportunities to purchase real goods and services available to a household as determined by prices and money income.

The Equation of the Budget Constraint

Yet another way to look at the budget constraint is to write the consumer's problem as an equation. In the previous example, the constraint is that total expenditure on Thai meals plus total expenditure on jazz club visits must be less than or equal to Ann and Tom's income. Total expenditure on Thai meals is equal to the *price* of Thai meals times the number, or *quantity*, of meals consumed. Total expenditure on jazz club visits is equal to the *price* of a visit times the number, or *quantity*, of visits. That is,

$$\$20 \times \text{Thai meals} + \$10 \times \text{jazz visits} \leq \$200$$

If we let *X* represent the number of Thai meals and we let *Y* represent the number of jazz club visits and we assume that Ann and Tom spend their entire income on either *X* or *Y*, this can be written as follows:

$$20X + 10Y = \$200$$

This is the equation of the budget constraint—the line connecting points *A* and *B* in Figure 6.1. Notice that when Ann and Tom spend nothing at the jazz club, $Y = 0$. When you plug $Y = 0$ into the equation of the budget constraint, $20X = 200$ and $X = 10$. Since *X* is the number of Thai meals, Ann and Tom eat Thai food 10 times. Similarly, when $X = 0$, you can solve for *Y*, which equals 20. When Ann and Tom eat no Thai food, they can go to the jazz club 20 times.

In general, the budget constraint can be written

$$P_X X + P_Y Y = I,$$

where P_X = the price of *X*, *X* = the quantity of *X* consumed, P_Y = the price of *Y*, *Y* = the quantity of *Y* consumed, and *I* = household income.[3]

Budget Constraints Change When Prices Rise or Fall   Now suppose the Thai restaurant is offering two-for-one certificates good during the month of November. In effect, this means that the price of Thai meals drops to $10 for Ann and Tom. How would the budget constraint in Figure 6.1 change?

First, point *B* would not change. If Ann and Tom spend all their money on jazz, the price of Thai meals is irrelevant. Ann and Tom can still afford only 20 trips to the jazz club. What has changed is point *A*, which moves to point *A'* in Figure 6.2. At the new lower price of $10, if Ann and Tom spent all their money on Thai meals, they could buy twice as many, $200 ÷ $10 = 20. The budget constraint *swivels*, as shown in Figure 6.2.

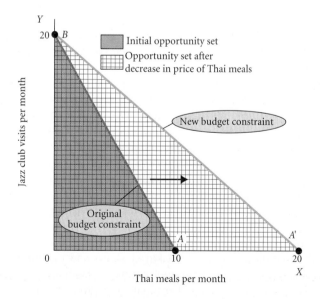

◀ **FIGURE 6.2 The Effect of a Decrease in Price on Ann and Tom's Budget Constraint**

When the price of a good decreases, the budget constraint swivels to the right, increasing the opportunities available and expanding choice.

---

[3] You can calculate the slope of the budget constraint as $-P_X/P_Y$, the ratio of the price of *X* to the price of *Y*. This gives the trade-off that consumers face. In the example, $-P_X/P_Y = -2$, meaning to get another Thai meal, Ann and Tom must give up two trips to the jazz club.

The new, flatter budget constraint reflects the new trade-off between Thai meals and Hungry Ear visits. Now after the price of Thai meals drops to $10, the opportunity cost of a Thai meal is only one jazz club visit. The opportunity set has expanded because at the lower price, more combinations of Thai meals and jazz are available.

Figure 6.2 thus illustrates a very important point. When the price of a single good changes, more than just the quantity demanded of that good may be affected. The household now faces an entirely different problem with regard to choice—the opportunity set has expanded. At the same income of $200, the new lower price means that Ann and Tom might choose more Thai meals, more jazz club visits, or more of both. They are clearly better off. The budget constraint is defined by income, wealth, and prices. Within those limits, households are free to choose, and the household's ultimate choice depends on its own likes and dislikes.

Notice that when the price of meals falls to $10, the equation of the budget constraint changes to $10X + 10Y = 200$, which is the equation of the line connecting points A' and B in Figure 6.2.

The range of goods and services available in a modern society is as vast as consumer tastes are variable, and this makes any generalization about the household choice process risky. Nonetheless, the theory of household behavior that follows is an attempt to derive some logical propositions about the way households make choices.

The Basis of Choice: Utility

Somehow, from the millions of things that are available, each of us manages to sort out a set of goods and services to buy. When we make our choices, we make specific judgments about the relative worth of things that are very different.

During the nineteenth century, the weighing of values was formalized into a concept called utility. Whether one item is preferable to another depends on how much **utility**, or satisfaction, it yields relative to its alternatives. How do we decide on the relative worth of a new puppy or a stereo? a trip to the mountains or a weekend in New York City? working or not working? As we make our choices, we are effectively weighing the utilities we would receive from all the possible available goods.

Certain problems are implicit in the concept of utility. First, it is impossible to measure utility. Second, it is impossible to compare the utilities of different people—that is, we cannot say whether person A or person B has a higher level of utility. Despite these problems, however, the idea of utility helps us better understand the process of choice.

Diminishing Marginal Utility

In making their choices, most people spread their incomes over many different kinds of goods. One reason people prefer variety is that consuming more and more of any one good reduces the marginal, or extra, satisfaction they get from further consumption of the same good. Formally, **marginal utility (MU)** is the additional satisfaction gained by the consumption or use of *one more* unit of a good or service.

It is important to distinguish marginal utility from total utility. **Total utility** is the total amount of satisfaction obtained from consumption of a good or service. Marginal utility comes only from the *last unit* consumed; total utility comes from *all* units consumed.

Suppose you live next to a store that sells homemade ice cream that you are crazy about. Even though you get a great deal of pleasure from eating ice cream, you do not spend your entire income on it. The first cone of the day tastes heavenly. The second is merely delicious. The third is still very good, but it is clear that the glow is fading. Why? The answer is because the more of any one good we consume in a given period, the less satisfaction, or utility, we get from each additional, or marginal, unit. In 1890, Alfred Marshall called this "familiar and fundamental tendency of human nature" the **law of diminishing marginal utility**.

Consider this simple example. Frank loves country music, and a country band is playing seven nights a week at a club near his house. Table 6.2 shows how the utility he derives from the band might change as he goes to the club more frequently. The first visit generates 12 "utils," or units of utility. When Frank goes back another night, he enjoys it, but not quite as much as the first night. The second night by itself yields 10 additional utils. *Marginal utility* is 10, while the *total utility* derived from two nights at the club is 22. Three nights per week at the club provide 28 total utils; the marginal utility of the third night is 6 because total utility rose from 22 to 28. Figure 6.3 graphs total and marginal utility using the data in Table 6.2. Total utility increases up

utility The satisfaction a product yields.

marginal utility (MU) The additional satisfaction gained by the consumption or use of *one more* unit of a good or service.

total utility The total amount of satisfaction obtained from consumption of a good or service.

law of diminishing marginal utility The more of any one good consumed in a given period, the less satisfaction (utility) generated by consuming each additional (marginal) unit of the same good.

TABLE 6.2	Total Utility and Marginal Utility of Trips to the Club Per Week	
Trips to Club	Total Utility	Marginal Utility
1	12	12
2	22	10
3	28	6
4	32	4
5	34	2
6	34	0

through Frank's fifth trip to the club but levels off on the sixth night. Marginal utility, which has declined from the beginning, is now at zero.

Diminishing marginal utility helps explain the reason most sports have limited seasons. Even rabid fans have had enough baseball by late October. Given this fact, it would be hard to sell out ball games for a year-round season. While diminishing marginal utility is a simple and intuitive idea, it has great power in helping us understand the economic world.

Allocating Income to Maximize Utility

How many times in one week would Frank go to the club to hear his favorite band? The answer depends on three things: Frank's income, the price of admission to the club, and the alternatives available. If the price of admission was zero and no alternatives existed, he would probably go to

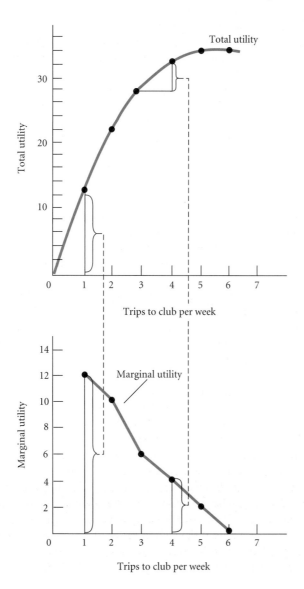

◀ FIGURE 6.3 **Graphs of Frank's Total and Marginal Utility**

Marginal utility is the additional utility gained by consuming one additional unit of a commodity—in this case, trips to the club. When marginal utility is zero, total utility stops rising.

the club five nights a week. (Remember, the sixth night does not increase his utility, so why should he bother to go?) However, Frank is also a basketball fan. His city has many good high school and college teams, and he can go to games six nights a week if he so chooses.

Let us say for now that admission to both the country music club and the basketball games is free—that is, there is no price/income constraint. There is a time constraint, however, because there are only seven nights in a week. Table 6.3 lists Frank's total and marginal utilities from attending basketball games and going to country music clubs. From column 3 of the table, we can conclude that on the first night, Frank will go to a basketball game. The game is worth far more to him (21 utils) than a trip to the club (12 utils).

On the second night, Frank's decision is not so easy. Because he has been to one basketball game this week, the second game is worth less (12 utils as compared to 21 for the first basketball game). In fact, because it is worth the same as a first trip to the club, he is indifferent as to whether he goes to the game or the club. So he splits the next two nights: One night he sees ball game number two (12 utils); the other night he spends at the club (12 utils). At this point, Frank has been to two ball games and has spent one night at the club. Where will Frank go on evening four? He will go to the club again because the marginal utility from a second trip to the club (10 utils) is greater than the marginal utility from attending a third basketball game (9 utils).

Frank is splitting his time between the two activities to maximize total utility. At each successive step, he chooses the activity that yields the most marginal utility. Continuing with this logic, you can see that spending three nights at the club and four nights watching basketball produces total utility of 76 utils each week (28 plus 48). No other combination of games and club trips can produce as much utility.

So far, the only cost of a night of listening to country music is a forgone basketball game and the only cost of a basketball game is a forgone night of country music. Now let us suppose that it costs $3 to get into the club and $6 to go to a basketball game. Suppose further that after paying rent and taking care of other expenses, Frank has only $21 left to spend on entertainment. Typically, consumers allocate limited incomes, or budgets, over a large set of goods and services. Here we have a limited income ($21) being allocated between only two goods, but the principle is the same. Income ($21) and prices ($3 and $6) define Frank's budget constraint. Within that constraint, Frank chooses to maximize utility.

Because the two activities now cost different amounts, we need to find the *marginal utility per dollar* spent on each activity. If Frank is to spend his money on the combination of activities lying within his budget constraint that gives him the most total utility, each night he must choose the activity that gives him the *most utility per dollar spent*. As you can see from column 5 in Table 6.3, Frank gets 4 utils per dollar on the first night he goes to the club (12 utils ÷ $3 = 4 utils per dollar). On night two, he goes to a game and gets 3.5 utils per dollar (21 utils ÷ $6 = 3.5 utils per dollar). On night three, it is back to the club. Then what happens? When all is said and done—work this out for yourself—Frank ends up going to two games and spending three nights at the club. No other combination of activities that $21 will buy yields more utility.

TABLE 6.3 Allocation of Fixed Expenditure per Week Between Two Alternatives

(1) Trips to Club per Week	(2) Total Utility	(3) Marginal Utility (*MU*)	(4) Price (*P*)	(5) Marginal Utility per Dollar (*MU/P*)
1	12	12	$3.00	4.0
2	22	10	3.00	3.3
3	28	6	3.00	2.0
4	32	4	3.00	1.3
5	34	2	3.00	0.7
6	34	0	3.00	0

(1) Basketball Games per Week	(2) Total Utility	(3) Marginal Utility (*MU*)	(4) Price (*P*)	(5) Marginal Utility per Dollar (*MU/P*)
1	21	21	$6.00	3.5
2	33	12	6.00	2.0
3	42	9	6.00	1.5
4	48	6	6.00	1.0
5	51	3	6.00	0.5
6	51	0	6.00	0

The Utility-Maximizing Rule

In general, utility-maximizing consumers spread out their expenditures until the following condition holds:

$$\text{utility-maximizing rule:} \quad \frac{MU_X}{P_X} = \frac{MU_Y}{P_Y} \text{ for all goods,}$$

where MU_X is the marginal utility derived from the last unit of X consumed, MU_Y is the marginal utility derived from the last unit of Y consumed, P_X is the price per unit of X, and P_Y is the price per unit of Y.

To see why this **utility-maximizing rule** is true, think for a moment about what would happen if it were *not* true. For example, suppose MU_X/P_X was greater than MU_Y/P_Y; that is, suppose a consumer purchased a bundle of goods so that the marginal utility from the last dollar spent on X was greater than the marginal utility from the last dollar spent on Y. This would mean that the consumer could increase his or her utility by spending a dollar less on Y and a dollar more on X. As the consumer shifts to buying more X and less Y, he or she runs into diminishing marginal utility. Buying more units of X *decreases* the marginal utility derived from consuming additional units of X. As a result, the marginal utility of another dollar spent on X falls. Now *less* is being spent on Y, and that means its marginal utility *increases*. This process continues until $MU_X/P_X = MU_Y/P_Y$. When this condition holds, there is no way for the consumer to increase his or her utility by changing the bundle of goods purchased.

You can see how the utility-maximizing rule works in Frank's choice between country music and basketball. At each stage, Frank chooses the activity that gives him the most utility per dollar. If he goes to a game, the utility he will derive from the next game—marginal utility—falls. If he goes to the club, the utility he will derive from his next visit falls, and so on.

The principles we have been describing help us understand an old puzzle dating from the time of Plato and familiar to economists beginning with Adam Smith. Adam Smith wrote about it in 1776:

> The things which have the greatest value in use have frequently little or no value in exchange; and on the contrary, those which have the greatest value in exchange have frequently little or no value in use. Nothing is more useful than water: but it will purchase scarce anything; scarce anything can be had in exchange for it. A diamond, on the contrary, has scarce any value in use; but a very great quantity of other goods may frequently be had in exchange for it.[4]

Although diamonds have arguably more than "scarce any value in use" today (for example, they are used to cut glass), Smith's **diamond/water paradox** is still instructive, at least where water is concerned.

The low price of water owes much to the fact that it is in plentiful supply. Even at a price of zero, we do not consume an infinite amount of water. We consume up to the point where *marginal* utility drops to zero. The *marginal* value of water is zero. Each of us enjoys an enormous consumer surplus when we consume nearly free water. At a price of zero, consumer surplus is the entire area under the demand curve. We tend to take water for granted, but imagine what would happen to its price if there were not enough for everyone. It would command a high price indeed.

Diminishing Marginal Utility and Downward-Sloping Demand

The concept of diminishing marginal utility offers one reason people spread their incomes over a variety of goods and services instead of spending all income on one or two items. It also leads us to conclude that demand curves slope downward.

To see why this is so, let us return to our friends Ann and Tom, the struggling graduate students. Recall that they chose between meals at a Thai restaurant and trips to a jazz club. Now think about their demand curve for Thai meals, shown in Figure 6.4. When the price of a meal is $40, they decide not to buy any Thai meals. What they are really deciding is that the utility gained

utility-maximizing rule
Equating the ratio of the marginal utility of a good to its price for all goods.

diamond/water paradox A paradox stating that (1) the things with the greatest value in use frequently have little or no value in exchange and (2) the things with the greatest value in exchange frequently have little or no value in use.

---

[4] Adam Smith, *The Wealth of Nations*, Modern Library Edition (New York: Random House, 1937), p. 28 (1st ed. 1776). The cheapness of water is referred to by Plato in *Euthydemus*, 304 B.C.

▶ **FIGURE 6.4**
Diminishing Marginal Utility and Downward-Sloping Demand
At a price of $40, the utility gained from even the first Thai meal is not worth the price. However, a lower price of $25 lures Ann and Tom into the Thai restaurant 5 times a month. (The utility from the sixth meal is not worth $25.) If the price is $15, Ann and Tom will eat Thai meals 10 times a month—until the marginal utility of a Thai meal drops below the utility they could gain from spending $15 on other goods. At 25 meals a month, they cannot tolerate the thought of another Thai meal even if it is free.

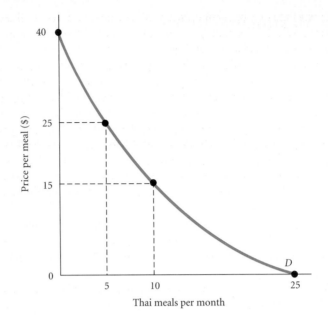

from even that first scrumptious meal each month is not worth the utility that would come from the other things that $40 can buy.

Now consider a price of $25. At this price, Ann and Tom buy five Thai meals. The first, second, third, fourth, and fifth meals each generate enough utility to justify the price. Tom and Ann "reveal" this by buying five meals. After the fifth meal, the utility gained from the next meal is not worth $25.

Ultimately, every demand curve hits the quantity (horizontal) axis as a result of diminishing marginal utility—in other words, demand curves slope downward. How many times will Ann and Tom go to the Thai restaurant if meals are free? Twenty-five times is the answer; and after 25 times a month, they are so sick of Thai food that they will not eat any more even if it is free. That is, marginal utility—the utility gained from the last meal—has dropped to zero. If you think this is unrealistic, ask yourself how much water you drank today.

Income and Substitution Effects

Although the idea of utility is a helpful way of thinking about the choice process, there is an explanation for downward-sloping demand curves that does not rely on the concept of utility or the assumption of diminishing marginal utility. This explanation centers on income and substitution effects.

Keeping in mind that consumers face constrained choices, consider the probable response of a household to a decline in the price of some heavily used product, *ceteris paribus*. How might a household currently consuming many goods be likely to respond to a fall in the price of one of those goods if the household's income, its preferences, and all other prices remained unchanged? The household would face a new budget constraint, and its final choice of all goods and services might change. A decline in the price of gasoline, for example, may affect not only how much gasoline you purchase but also what kind of car you buy, when and how much you travel, where you go, and (not so directly) how many movies you see this month and how many projects around the house you get done.

The Income Effect

Price changes affect households in two ways. First, if we assume that households confine their choices to products that improve their well-being, then a decline in the price of any product, *ceteris paribus*, will make the household unequivocally better off. In other words, if a household continues to buy the same amount of every good and service after the price decrease, it will have income left over. That extra income may be spent on the product whose price has declined, hereafter called good *X*, or on other products. The change in consumption of *X* due to this improvement in well-being is called the *income effect of a price change*.

Suppose you live in Florida and four times a year you fly to Nashville to visit your mother. Suppose further that last year a round-trip ticket to Nashville cost $400. Thus, you spend a total of $1,600 per year on trips to visit Mom. This year, however, increased competition among the airlines has led one airline to offer round-trip tickets to Nashville for $200. Assuming the price remains $200 all year, you can now fly home the same number of times and you will have spent $800 less for airline tickets than you did last year. Now that you are better off, you have additional opportunities. You can fly home a fifth time this year, leaving $600 ($800 − $200) to spend on other things, or you can fly home the same number of times (four) and spend the extra $800 on other things. When the price of something we buy falls, we are *better off*. When the price of something we buy rises, we are *worse off*.

Look back at Figure 6.2 on p. 125. When the price of Thai meals fell, the opportunity set facing Tom and Ann expanded—they were able to afford more Thai meals, more jazz club trips, or more of both. They were unequivocally better off because of the price decline. In a sense, their "real" income was higher.

Now recall from Chapter 3 the definition of a *normal good*. When income rises, demand for normal goods increases. Most goods are normal goods. Because of the price decline, Tom and Ann can afford to buy more. If Thai food is a normal good, a decline in the price of Thai food should lead to an increase in the quantity demanded of Thai food.

The Substitution Effect

The fact that a price decline leaves households better off is only part of the story. When the price of a product falls, that product also becomes *relatively* cheaper. That is, it becomes more attractive relative to potential substitutes. A fall in the price of product *X* might cause a household to shift its purchasing pattern away from substitutes toward *X*. This shift is called the *substitution effect of a price change*.

Earlier we made the point that the "real" cost or price of a good is what one must sacrifice to consume it. This opportunity cost is determined by relative prices. To see why this is so, consider again the choice that you face when a round-trip ticket to Nashville costs $400. Each trip that you take requires a sacrifice of $400 worth of other goods and services. When the price drops to $200, the opportunity cost of a ticket has dropped by $200. In other words, after the price decline, you have to sacrifice only $200 (instead of $400) worth of other goods and services to visit Mom.

To clarify the distinction between the income and substitution, imagine how you would be affected if two things happened to you at the same time. First, the price of round-trip air travel between Florida and Nashville drops from $400 to $200. Second, your income is reduced by $800. You are now faced with new relative prices, but—assuming you flew home four times last year—you are no better off now than you were before the price of a ticket declined. The decrease in the price of air travel has offset your decrease in income.

You are still likely to take more trips home. Why? The opportunity cost of a trip home is now lower, *ceteris paribus*, assuming no change in the prices of other goods and services. A trip to Nashville now requires a sacrifice of only $200 worth of other goods and services, not the $400 worth that it did before. Thus, you will substitute away from other goods toward trips to see your mother.

Everything works in the opposite direction when a price rises, *ceteris paribus*. A price increase makes households worse off. If income and other prices do not change, spending the same amount of money buys less and households will be forced to buy less. This is the income effect. In addition, when the price of a product rises, that item becomes more expensive relative to potential substitutes and the household is likely to substitute other goods for it. This is the substitution effect.

What do the income and substitution effects tell us about the demand curve? Both the income and the substitution effects imply a negative relationship between price and quantity demanded—in other words, downward-sloping demand. When the price of something falls, *ceteris paribus*, we are better off and we are likely to buy more of that good and other goods (income effect). Because lower price also means "less expensive relative to substitutes," we are likely to buy more of the good (substitution effect). When the price of something rises, we are worse off and we will buy less of it (income effect). Higher price also means "more expensive relative to substitutes," and we are likely to buy less of it and more of other goods (substitution effect).[5]

Figure 6.5 summarizes the income and substitution effects of a price change of gasoline prices.

If you recall the example of gasoline prices from early in the chapter, income and substitution effects help us answer the question posed. When gas prices rise, the income effects can cause a fall in the demand for other goods. Since gas is a big part of many budgets, these income effects can be very large. It is the income effect from gasoline price increases that some argue causes consumers to switch away from high-priced brand name products.

▶ **FIGURE 6.5 Income and Substitution Effects of a Price Change**

For normal goods, the income and substitution effects work in the same direction. Higher prices lead to a lower quantity demanded, and lower prices lead to a higher quantity demanded.

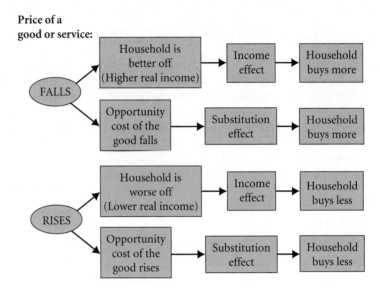

Price of a good or service:

Household Choice in Input Markets

So far, we have focused on the decision-making process that lies behind output demand curves. Households with limited incomes allocate those incomes across various combinations of goods and services that are available and affordable. In looking at the factors affecting choices in the output market, we assumed that income was fixed, or given. We noted at the outset, however, that income is in fact partially determined by choices that households make in input markets. (Look back at Figure II.1 on p. 117.) We now turn to a brief discussion of the two decisions that households make in input markets: the labor supply decision and the saving decision.

The Labor Supply Decision

Most income in the United States is wage and salary income paid as compensation for labor. Household members supply labor in exchange for wages or salaries. As in output markets, households face constrained choices in input markets. They must decide

1. Whether to work
2. How much to work
3. What kind of a job to work at

---

[5] For some goods, the income and substitution effects work in opposite directions. When our income rises, we may buy less of some goods. In Chapter 3, we called such goods *inferior goods*. When the price of an inferior good rises, it is, like any other good, more expensive relative to substitutes and we are likely to replace it with lower-priced substitutes. However, when we are worse off, we increase our demand for inferior goods. Thus, the income effect could lead us to buy more of the good, partially offsetting the substitution effect.

Even if a good is "very inferior," demand curves will slope downward as long as the substitution effect is larger than the income effect. It is possible, at least in theory, for the income effect to be larger. In such a case, a price increase would actually lead to an increase in quantity demanded. This possibility was pointed out by Alfred Marshall in *Principles of Economics*. Marshall attributes the notion of an upward-sloping demand curve to Sir Robert Giffen; for this reason, the notion is often referred to as *Giffen's paradox*. Fortunately or unfortunately, no one has ever demonstrated that a Giffen good has existed.

Substitution and Market Baskets

In driving to work one day, one of the authors of this text heard the following advertisement for a local grocery store, which we will call Harry's Food.

"Harry's has the best prices in town, and we can prove it! Yesterday we chose Mr. Smith out of our checkout line for a comparison test. Mr. Smith is an average consumer, much like you and me. In doing his weekly grocery shopping yesterday at Harry's, he spent $125. We then sent Mr. Smith to the neighboring competitor with instructions to buy the same market basket of food. When he returned with his food, he saw that his grocery total was $134. You too will see that Harry's can save you money!"

Advertisements like this one are commonplace. As you evaluate the claims in the ad, several things may come to mind. Perhaps Mr. Smith is not representative of consumers or is not much like you. That might make Harry's a good deal for him but not for you. (So your demand curve looks different from Mr. Smith's demand curve.) Or perhaps yesterday was a sale day, meaning yesterday was not typical of Harrys' prices. But there is something more fundamentally wrong with the claims in this ad even if you are just like Mr. Smith and Harry's offers the same prices every day. The fundamental error in this ad is revealed by the work you have done in this chapter.

When Mr. Smith shopped, he presumably looked at the prices of the various food choices offered at the market and tried to do the best he could for his family given those prices and his family's tastes. If we go back to the utility-maximizing rule that you learned in this chapter, we see that Mr. Smith was comparing the marginal utility of each product he consumes relative to its price

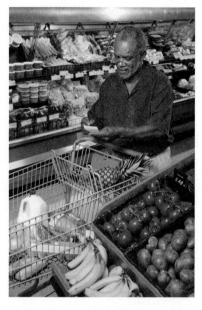

in deciding what bundle to buy. In pragmatic terms, if Mr. Smith likes apples and pears about the same, while he was shopping in Harry's, he would have bought the cheaper of the two. When he was sent to the neighboring store, however, he was constrained to buy the same goods that he bought at Harry's. (So he was forced to buy pears even if they were more expensive just to duplicate the bundle.) When we artificially restrict Mr. Smith's ability to substitute goods, we almost inevitably give him a more expensive bundle. The real question is this: Would Mr. Smith have been more happy or less happy with his market basket after spending $125 at Harry's or at its rival? Without knowing more about the shape of Mr. Smith's utility curve and the prices he faces, we cannot answer that question. The dollar comparison in the ad doesn't tell the whole story!

In essence, household members must decide how much labor to supply. The choices they make are affected by:

1. Availability of jobs
2. Market wage rates
3. Skills they possess

As with decisions in output markets, the labor supply decision involves a set of trade-offs. There are basically two alternatives to working for a wage: (1) not working and (2) doing unpaid work. If you do not work, you sacrifice income for the benefits of staying home and reading, watching TV, swimming, or sleeping. Another option is to work, but not for a money wage. In this case, you sacrifice money income for the benefits of growing your own food, raising your children, or taking care of your house.

As with the trade-offs in output markets, your final choice depends on how you value the alternatives available. If you work, you earn a wage that you can use to buy things. Thus, the trade-off is between the value of the goods and services you can buy with the wages you earn versus the value of things you can produce at home—home-grown food, manageable children, clean clothes, and so on—or the value you place on leisure. This choice is illustrated in Figure 6.6. In general, the wage rate can be thought of as the price—or the opportunity cost—of the benefits of either unpaid work or leisure. Just as you choose among different goods by comparing the marginal utility of each relative to its price, you also choose between leisure and other goods by comparing the marginal utility of leisure relative to its price (the wage rate) with the marginal utility of other goods relative to their prices.

▶ FIGURE 6.6 **The Trade-Off Facing Households**

The decision to enter the workforce involves a trade-off between wages (and the goods and services that wages will buy) on the one hand and leisure and the value of nonmarket production on the other hand.

The Price of Leisure

In our analysis in the early part of this chapter, households had to allocate a limited budget across a set of goods and services. Now they must choose among goods, services, and *leisure*.

When we add leisure to the picture, we do so with one important distinction. Trading one good for another involves buying less of one and more of another, so households simply reallocate *money* from one good to the other. "Buying" more leisure, however, means reallocating time between work and nonwork activities. For each hour of leisure that you decide to consume, you give up one hour's wages. Thus, the wage rate is the *price of leisure*.

Conditions in the labor market determine the budget constraints and final opportunity sets that households face. The availability of jobs and these job wage rates determine the final combinations of goods and services that a household can afford. The final choice within these constraints depends on the unique tastes and preferences of each household. Different people place more or less value on leisure—but everyone needs to put food on the table.

Income and Substitution Effects of a Wage Change

labor supply curve A curve that shows the quantity of labor supplied at different wage rates. Its shape depends on how households react to changes in the wage rate.

A **labor supply curve** shows the quantity of labor supplied at different wage rates. The shape of the labor supply curve depends on how households react to changes in the wage rate.

Consider an increase in wages. First, an increase in wages makes households better off. If they work the same number of hours—that is, if they supply the same amount of labor—they will earn higher incomes and be able to buy more goods and services. They can also buy more leisure. If leisure is a normal good—that is, a good for which demand increases as income increases—an increase in income will lead to a higher demand for leisure and a lower labor supply. This is the *income effect of a wage increase*.

However, there is also a potential *substitution effect of a wage increase*. A higher wage rate means that leisure is more expensive. If you think of the wage rate as the price of leisure, each individual hour of leisure consumed at a higher wage costs more in forgone wages. As a result, we would expect households to substitute other goods for leisure. This means working more, or a lower quantity demanded of leisure and a higher quantity supplied of labor.

Note that in the labor market, the income and substitution effects work in *opposite* directions when leisure is a normal good. The income effect of a wage increase implies buying more leisure and working less; the substitution effect implies buying less leisure and working more. Whether households will supply more labor overall or less labor overall when wages rise depends on the relative strength of both the income and the substitution effects.

If the substitution effect is greater than the income effect, the wage increase will increase labor supply. This suggests that the labor supply curve slopes upward, or has a positive slope, like the one in Figure 6.7(a). If the income effect outweighs the substitution effect, however, a higher wage will lead to added consumption of leisure and labor supply will decrease. This implies that the labor supply curve "bends back," as the one in Figure 6.7(b) does.

During the early years of the Industrial Revolution in late eighteenth-century Great Britain, the textile industry operated under what was called the "putting-out" system. Spinning and weaving were done in small cottages to supplement the family farm income—hence the term *cottage industry*. During that period, wages and household incomes rose considerably. Some economic historians claim that this higher income actually led many households to take more leisure and work fewer hours; the empirical evidence suggests a backward-bending labor supply curve.

Just as income and substitution effects helped us understand household choices in output markets, they now help us understand household choices in input markets. The point here is simple: When leisure is added to the choice set, the line between input and output market decisions becomes blurred. In fact, households decide simultaneously how much of each good to consume and how much leisure to consume.

Saving and Borrowing: Present versus Future Consumption

We began this chapter by examining the way households allocate a fixed income over a large number of goods and services. We then pointed out that, at least in part, choices made by households determine income levels. Within the constraints imposed by the market, households decide whether to work and how much to work.

So far, however, we have talked about only the current period—the allocation of current income among alternative uses and the work/leisure choice *today*. Households can also (1) use present income to finance future spending—they can *save*—or (2) use future income to finance present spending—they can *borrow*.

When a household decides to save, it is using current income to finance future consumption. That future consumption may come in 3 years, when you use your savings to buy a car; in 10 years, when you sell stock to put a deposit on a house; or in 45 years, when you retire and begin to receive money from your pension plan. Most people cannot finance large purchases—a house or condominium, for example—out of current income and savings. They almost always borrow money and sign a mortgage. When a household borrows, it is in essence financing a current purchase with future income. It pays back the loan out of future income.

Even in simple economies such as the two-person desert-island economy of Colleen and Bill (see Chapter 2), people must make decisions about *present versus future consumption*. Colleen and Bill could (1) produce goods for today's consumption by hunting and gathering, (2) consume leisure by sleeping on the beach, or (3) work on projects to enhance future consumption opportunities. Building a house or a boat over a 5-year period is trading present

a. Substitution effect dominates

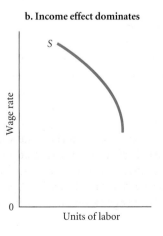

b. Income effect dominates

◀ FIGURE 6.7 **Two Labor Supply Curves**

When the substitution effect outweighs the income effect, the labor supply curve slopes upward (a). When the income effect outweighs the substitution effect, the result is a "backward-bending" labor supply curve: The labor supply curve slopes downward (b).

ECONOMICS IN PRACTICE

What Happens When the Cost of Self-Discovery Falls?

College graduates in 2009 and 2010 entered a difficult job market, with fewer opportunities than their counterparts a few years earlier. As the article below suggests, many ended up taking unpaid internships. Why take an unpaid internship rather than continue to look for paid work?

Many new graduates are quite uncertain about what career to pursue. A first job provides more than a paycheck. It provides an opportunity to learn more about what a career in a particular area looks like and whether it appeals to you. First jobs, in other words, provide a chance to learn about both the world and oneself. When jobs are plentiful, pursuing an unpaid internship in an area you are interested in has a big opportunity cost: the lost wages associated with a full-time job in what might be a less attractive industry. In a world of few paying jobs, the opportunity cost of following your heart in career terms is much lower.

New Experience: Interns Pay to Work For-Profits Finding Flood of Candidates in Poor Job Market

The Boston Globe

Throughout her senior year at Boston College, Brynn Merritt worked part time at Entercom Boston, which owns four radio stations, including WEEI and WRKO. She blogged, called businesses to solicit merchandise for WEEI's Web site, produced ad displays, and sent newsletter e-mail blasts.

For all of this, she was paid nothing.

"I did the same amount of work as a lot of people getting paid did," says Merritt, 22, who graduated this spring. But she's not complaining; in fact, she feels lucky. "I learned a ton," says Merritt, who received a course credit for the internship. "I feel I could go into the business right now."

Unpaid internships have long been offered by nonprofits, but for-profit businesses are increasingly taking advantage of the number of students who, in a tight job market, are willing to forgo a paycheck for practical experience.

Source: The Boston Globe by Bella English. Copyright 2010 by *Globe Newspaper Company - MA.* Reproduced with permission of *Globe Newspaper Company - MA* via Copyright Clearance Center.

consumption for future consumption. As with all of the other choices we have examined in this chapter, the broad principle will be to look at marginal utilities and prices. How much do Colleen and Bill value having something now versus waiting for the future? How much do they gain by waiting?

When a household saves, it usually puts the money into something that will generate income. There is no sense in putting money under your mattress when you can make it work in so many ways: savings accounts, money market funds, stocks, corporate bonds, and so on—many of which are virtually risk-free. When you put your money in any of these places, you are actually lending it out and the borrower pays you a fee for its use. This fee usually takes the form of *interest*. The interest paid is the possible benefit Colleen and Bill get from forgoing current consumption.

Just as changes in wage rates affect household behavior in the labor market, changes in interest rates affect household behavior in capital markets. Higher interest rates mean that borrowing is more expensive—required monthly payments on a newly purchased house or car will be higher. Higher interest rates also mean that saving will earn a higher return: $1,000 invested in a 5 percent savings account or bond yields $50 per year. If rates rise to 10 percent, the annual interest will rise to $100.

What impact do interest rates have on saving behavior? As with the effect of wage changes on labor supply, the effect of changes in interest rates on saving can best be understood in terms of income and substitution effects. Suppose, for example, that I have been saving for a number of years for retirement. Will an increase in interest rates lead to an increase or a decrease in my saving? The answer is not obvious. First, because each dollar saved will earn a higher rate of return, the "price" of spending today in terms of forgone future spending is higher. That is, each dollar that I spend today (instead of saving) costs me more in terms of future consumption because my saving will now earn a higher return. On this score, I will be led to save *more*, which is the substitution effect at work.

However, higher interest rates mean more than that. Higher interest rates mean that it will take less saving today to reach a specific target amount of savings tomorrow. I will not need to save as much for retirement or future consumption as I did before. One hundred dollars put into a savings account with 5 percent compound interest will double in 14 years. If interest was paid at a rate of 10 percent, I would have my $200 in just 7 years. Consequently, I may be led to save less, which is the income effect at work. Higher interest rates mean savers are better off; so higher interest rates may lead to less saving. The final impact of a change in interest rates on saving depends on the relative size of the income and substitution effects. Most empirical evidence indicates that saving tends to increase as the interest rate rises. In other words, the substitution effect is larger than the income effect.

Saving and investment decisions involve a huge and complex set of institutions, the **financial capital market**, in which the suppliers of capital (households that save) and the demand for capital (firms that want to invest) interact. The amount of capital investment in an economy is constrained in the long run by that economy's saving rate. You can think of household *saving* as the economy's supply of capital. When a firm borrows to finance a capital acquisition, it is almost as if households have supplied the capital in exchange for the fee we call interest. We treat capital markets in detail in Chapter 11.[6]

financial capital market
The complex set of institutions in which suppliers of capital (households that save) and the demand for capital (firms wanting to invest) interact.

A Review: Households in Output and Input Markets

In probing the behavior of households in both input and output markets and examining the nature of constrained choice, we went behind the household demand curve using the simplifying assumption that income was fixed and given. Income, wealth, and prices set the limits, or *constraints*, within which households make their choices in output markets. Within those limits, households make their choices on the basis of personal tastes and preferences.

The notion of *utility* helps explain the process of choice. The law of *diminishing marginal utility* partly explains why people seem to spread their incomes over many different goods and services and why demand curves have a negative slope. Another important explanation behind the negative relationship between price and quantity demanded lies in *income effects* and *substitution effects*.

As we turned to input markets, we relaxed the assumption that income was fixed and given. In the labor market, households are forced to weigh the value of leisure against the value of goods and services that can be bought with wage income. Once again, we found household preferences for goods and leisure operating within a set of constraints imposed by the market. Households also face the problem of allocating income and consumption over more than one period of time. They can finance spending in the future with today's income by saving and earning interest, or they can spend tomorrow's income today by borrowing.

We now have a rough sketch of the factors that determine output demand and input supply. (You can review these in Figure II.1 on p. 117.) In the next three chapters, we turn to firm behavior and explore in detail the factors that affect output supply and input demand.

---

[6] Here in Chapter 6, we are looking at a country as if it were isolated from the rest of the world. Very often, however, capital investment is financed by funds loaned or provided by foreign citizens or governments. For example, in recent years, a substantial amount of foreign savings has found its way into the United States for the purchase of stocks, bonds, and other financial instruments. In part, these flows finance capital investment. Also, the United States and other countries that contribute funds to the World Bank and the International Monetary Fund have provided billions in outright grants and loans to help developing countries produce capital. For more information on these institutions, see Chapter 21.

SUMMARY

HOUSEHOLD CHOICE IN OUTPUT MARKETS *p. 121*

1. Every household must make three basic decisions: (1) how much of each product, or output, to demand; (2) how much labor to supply; and (3) how much to spend today and how much to save for the future.

2. Income, wealth, and prices define household *budget constraint*. The budget constraint separates those combinations of goods and services that are available from those that are not. All the points below and to the left of a graph of a household budget constraint make up the *choice set*, or *opportunity set*.

3. It is best to think of the household choice problem as one of allocating income over a large number of goods and services. A change in the price of one good may change the entire allocation. Demand for some goods may rise, while demand for others may fall.

4. As long as a household faces a limited income, the real cost of any single good or service is the value of the next pre-ferred *other* goods and services that could have been pur-chased with the same amount of money.

5. Within the constraints of prices, income, and wealth, household decisions ultimately depend on preferences—likes, dislikes, and tastes.

THE BASIS OF CHOICE: UTILITY *p. 126*

6. Whether one item is preferable to another depends on how much *utility*, or satisfaction, it yields relative to its alternatives.

7. The *law of diminishing marginal utility* says that the more of any good we consume in a given period of time, the less sat-isfaction, or utility, we get out of each additional (or mar-ginal) unit of that good.

8. Households allocate income among goods and services to maximize utility. This implies choosing activities that yield the highest marginal utility per dollar. In a two-good world, households will choose to equate the marginal utility per dollar spent on *X* with the marginal utility per dollar spent on *Y*. This is the *utility-maximizing rule*.

INCOME AND SUBSTITUTION EFFECTS *p. 130*

9. The fact that demand curves have a negative slope can be explained in two ways: (1) Marginal utility for all goods diminishes. (2) For most normal goods, both the *income and the substitution effects* of a price decline lead to more con-sumption of the good.

HOUSEHOLD CHOICE IN INPUT MARKETS *p. 132*

10. In the labor market, a trade-off exists between the value of the goods and services that can be bought in the market or produced at home and the value that one places on leisure. The opportunity cost of paid work is leisure and unpaid work. The wage rate is the price, or opportunity cost, of the benefits of unpaid work or leisure.

11. The income and substitution effects of a change in the wage rate work in opposite directions. Higher wages mean that (1) leisure is more expensive (likely response: people work *more*—substitution effect) and (2) more income is earned in a given number of hours, so some time may be spent on leisure (likely response: people work *less*—income effect).

12. In addition to deciding how to allocate its present income among goods and services, a household may also decide to save or borrow. When a household decides to save part of its current income, it is using current income to finance future spending. When a household borrows, it finances current purchases with future income.

13. An increase in interest rates has a positive effect on saving if the substitution effect dominates the income effect and a negative effect if the income effect dominates the substitu-tion effect. Most empirical evidence shows that the substitu-tion effect dominates here.

REVIEW TERMS AND CONCEPTS

budget constraint, *p. 122*

choice set *or* opportunity set, *p. 123*

diamond/water paradox, *p. 129*

financial capital market, *p. 137*

homogeneous products, *p. 119*

labor supply curve, *p. 134*

law of diminishing marginal utility, *p. 126*

marginal utility (*MU*), *p. 126*

perfect competition, *p. 119*

perfect knowledge, *p. 119*

real income, *p. 124*

total utility, *p. 126*

utility, *p. 126*

utility-maximizing rule, *p. 129*

PROBLEMS

All problems are available on www.myeconlab.com

1. For each of the following events, consider how you might react. What things might you consume more or less of? Would you work more or less? Would you increase or decrease your saving? Are your responses consistent with the discussion of household behavior in this chapter?

   a. You have a very close friend who lives in another city, a 3-hour bus ride away. The price of a round-trip ticket rises from $20 to $45.

   b. Tuition at your college is cut 25 percent.

   c. You receive an award that pays you $300 per month for the next 5 years.

   d. Interest rates rise dramatically, and savings accounts are now paying 10% interest annually.

   e. The price of food doubles. (If you are on a meal plan, assume that your board charges double.)

   f. A new business opens up nearby offering part-time jobs at $20 per hour.

2. The following table gives a hypothetical total utility schedule for the Cookie Monster (CM):

# OF COOKIES PER DAY	TOTAL UTILITY PER DAY
0	0
1	100
2	200
3	275
4	325
5	350
6	360
7	360

Calculate the CM's marginal utility schedule. Draw a graph of total and marginal utility. If cookies cost the CM 5 cents each and CM had a good income, what is the maximum number of cookies he would most likely eat in a day?

3. Kamika lives in Chicago but goes to school in Tucson, Arizona. For the last 2 years, she has made four trips home each year. During 2010, the price of a round-trip ticket from Chicago to Tucson increased from $350 to $600. As a result, Kamika decided not to buy a new outfit that year and decided not to drive to Phoenix with friends for an expensive rock concert.
   a. Explain how Kamika's demand for clothing and concert tickets can be affected by an increase in air travel prices.
   b. By using this example, explain why both income and substitution effects might be expected to reduce Kamika's number of trips home.

4. Sketch the following budget constraints:

	P_X	P_Y	INCOME
a.	$20	$50	$1,000
b.	40	50	1,000
c.	20	100	1,000
d.	20	50	2,000
e.	0.25	0.25	7.00
f.	0.25	0.50	7.00
g.	0.50	0.25	7.00

5. On January 1, Professor Smith made a resolution to lose some weight and save some money. He decided that he would strictly budget $100 for lunches each month. For lunch, he has only two choices: the faculty club, where the price of a lunch is $5, and Alice's Restaurant, where the price of a lunch is $10. Every day that he does not eat lunch, he runs 5 miles.
   a. Assuming that Professor Smith spends the $100 each month at either Alice's or the club, sketch his budget constraint. Show actual numbers on the axes.
   b. Last month Professor Smith chose to eat at the club 10 times and at Alice's 5 times. Does this choice fit within his budget constraint? Explain your answer.
   c. Last month Alice ran a half-price lunch special all month. All lunches were reduced to $5. Show the effect on Professor Smith's budget constraint.

6. During 2010, Congress debated the advisability of retaining some or all of the tax cuts signed into law by former President George W. Bush in 2001 and 2003 and set to expire at the end of 2010. By reducing tax rates across the board, take-home pay for all taxpaying workers would increase. The purpose, in part, was to encourage work and increase the supply of labor. Households would respond the way the president hoped, but only if income

effects were stronger than substitution effects. Do you agree or disagree? Explain your answer.

7. Assume that Mei has $100 per month to divide between dinners at a Chinese restaurant and evenings at Zanzibar, a local pub. Assume that going to Zanzibar costs $20 and eating at the Chinese restaurant costs $10. Suppose Mei spends two evenings at Zanzibar and eats six times at the Chinese restaurant.
   a. Draw Mei's budget constraint and show that she can afford six dinners and two evenings at Zanzibar.
   b. Assume that Mei comes into some money and can now spend $200 per month. Draw her new budget constraint.
   c. As a result of the increase in income, Mei decides to spend eight evenings at Zanzibar and eat at the Chinese restaurant four times. What kind of a good is Chinese food? What kind of a good is a night at Zanzibar?
   d. What part of the increase in Zanzibar trips is due to the income effect, and what part is due to the substitution effect? Explain your answer.

8. Decide whether you agree or disagree with each of the following statements and explain your reason:
   a. If the income effect of a wage change dominates the substitution effect for a given household and the household works longer hours following a wage change, wages must have risen.
   b. In product markets, when a price falls, the substitution effect leads to more consumption; but for normal goods, the income effect leads to less consumption.

9. Suppose the price of X is $5 and the price of Y is $10 and a hypothetical household has $500 to spend per month on goods X and Y.
   a. Sketch the household budget constraint.
   b. Assume that the household splits its income equally between X and Y. Show where the household ends up on the budget constraint.
   c. Suppose the household income doubles to $1,000. Sketch the new budget constraint facing the household.
   d. Suppose after the change the household spends $200 on Y and $800 on X. Does this imply that X is a normal or an inferior good? What about Y?

10. For this problem, assume that Joe has $80 to spend on books and movies each month and that both goods must be purchased whole (no fractional units). Movies cost $8 each, and books cost $20 each. Joe's preferences for movies and books are summarized by the following information:

	MOVIES				BOOKS		
NO. PER MONTH	TU	MU	MU/$	NO. PER MONTH	TU	MU	MU/$
1	50	—	—	1	22	—	—
2	80	—	—	2	42	—	—
3	100	—	—	3	52	—	—
4	110	—	—	4	57	—	—
5	116	—	—	5	60	—	—
6	121	—	—	6	62	—	—
7	123	—	—	7	63	—	—

   a. Fill in the figures for marginal utility and marginal utility per dollar for both movies and books.
   b. Are these preferences consistent with the law of diminishing marginal utility? Explain briefly.
   c. Given the budget of $80, what quantity of books and what quantity of movies will maximize Joe's level of satisfaction? Explain briefly.

d. Draw the budget constraint (with books on the horizontal axis) and identify the optimal combination of books and movies as point *A*.

e. Now suppose the price of books falls to $10. Which of the columns in the table must be recalculated? Do the required recalculations.

f. After the price change, how many movies and how many books will Joe purchase?

g. Draw the new budget constraint and identify the new optimal combination of books and movies as point *B*.

h. If you calculated correctly, you found that a decrease in the price of books caused Joe to buy more movies as well as more books. How can this be?

11. [Related to the *Economics in Practice* on *p. 133*] John's New York–based firm has sent him to work in its Paris office. Recognizing that the cost of living differs between Paris and New York, the company wants to adjust John's salary so that John is as well off (or happy) in Paris as he was in New York. John suggests that he submit a list of the things he bought in New York in a typical month. The firm can use the list to determine John's salary by figuring out how much the same items cost in Paris. Is this a good idea? Explain your answer.

12. [Related to the *Economics in Practice* on *p. 136*] Using graphs, show what you would expect to see happen to the labor supply curve facing companies offering unpaid internships as the job market starts to improve.

13. Thomas has allocated $48 per month for entertainment expenses, which he uses either to go bowling or to play billiards. One night of bowling costs Thomas $8, and one night of billiards costs Thomas $4. Use the information in the following graphs to determine how many nights Thomas should spend bowling and how many nights he should play billiards in order to maximize his utility. Explain your answer.

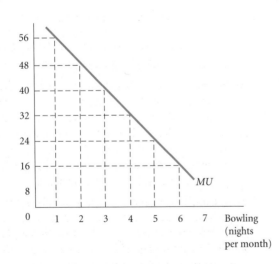

14. For most normal goods, the income effect and the substitution effect work in the same direction; so when the price of a good falls, both the income and substitution effects lead to a higher quantity demanded. How would this change if the good is an inferior good?

15. Explain why in product markets the substitution and income effects work in the same direction for normal goods, but in the labor market, the income and substitution effects work in opposite directions when leisure is considered a normal good.

16. Samantha has $7 to spend on apples and bananas and wants to maximize her utility on her purchase. Based on the data in the table, how many apples and bananas should Samantha purchase, and what is her total utility from the purchase? Does the utility-maximizing rule hold true for her purchase? Explain.

APPLES $1.00			BANANAS $0.50		
QUANTITY	MU	TU	QUANTITY	MU	TU
1	28	28	1	12	12
2	24	52	2	10	22
3	20	72	3	8	30
4	16	88	4	6	36
5	12	100	5	4	40
6	8	108	6	2	42
7	4	112	7	0	42
8	0	112	8	-2	40

17. The table shows Regina's marginal utility numbers for hamburgers and pizzas. Regina is trying to decide which item to purchase first, a hamburger or a pizza, knowing that she wants to receive the most utility for each dollar she spends. Assuming she has enough money in her budget to purchase either item, which item should she purchase first?

HAMBURGERS $4		PIZZAS $6	
QUANTITY	MU	QUANTITY	MU
1	12	1	18
2	8	2	14
3	4	3	8

18. Jake and Gonzalo are roommates and have saved a total of $360 to spend on summer entertainment. They have decided to use this money on tickets to baseball games and on tickets to their local amusement park. Their original budget constraint is shown in the graph below. Let X represent amusement park tickets and Y represent baseball tickets.

a. What is the equation of the original budget constraint?
b. What is the price of an amusement park ticket? a baseball ticket?
c. Assume a price change occurs and Jake and Gonzalo now face the new budget constraint. What is the equation of the new budget constraint?
d. With the new budget constraint, what is the price of an amusement park ticket? a baseball ticket?

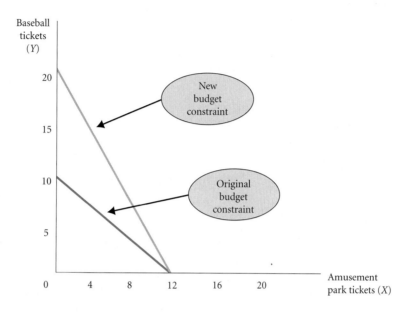

CHAPTER 6 APPENDIX

Indifference Curves

Early in this chapter, we saw how a consumer choosing between two goods is constrained by the prices of those goods and by his or her income. This Appendix returns to that example and analyzes the process of choice more formally. (Before we proceed, carefully review the text under the heading "The Budget Constraint More Formally," p. 123)

Assumptions

We base the following analysis on four assumptions:

1. We assume that this analysis is restricted to goods that yield positive marginal utility, or, more simply, that "more is better." One way to justify this assumption is to say that when more of something makes you worse off, you can simply throw it away at no cost. This is the assumption of free disposal.

2. The **marginal rate of substitution** is defined as MU_X/MU_Y, or the ratio at which a household is willing to substitute X for Y. When MU_X/MU_Y is equal to 4, for example, I would be willing to trade 4 units of Y for 1 additional unit of X.

   We assume a diminishing marginal rate of substitution. That is, as more of X and less of Y are consumed, MU_X/MU_Y

declines. As you consume more of X and less of Y, X becomes less valuable in terms of units of Y, or Y becomes more valuable in terms of X. This is almost but not precisely equivalent to assuming diminishing marginal utility.

3. We assume that consumers have the ability to choose among the combinations of goods and services available. Confronted with the choice between two alternative combinations of goods and services, A and B, a consumer responds in one of three ways: (1) She prefers A over B, (2) she prefers B over A, or (3) she is indifferent between A and B—that is, she likes A and B equally.

4. We assume that consumer choices are consistent with a simple assumption of rationality. If a consumer shows that he prefers A to B and subsequently shows that he prefers B to a third alternative, C, he should prefer A to C when confronted with a choice between the two.

Deriving Indifference Curves

If we accept these four assumptions, we can construct a "map" of a consumer's preferences. These preference maps are made up of indifference curves. An **indifference curve** is a set of points, each point representing a combination of goods X and Y, all of which yield the same total utility.

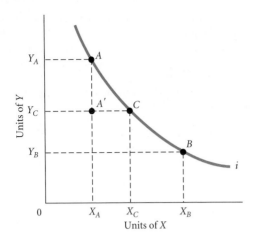

▲ **FIGURE 6A.1 An Indifference Curve**

An indifference curve is a set of points, each representing a combination of some amount of good X and some amount of good Y, that all yield the same amount of total utility. The consumer depicted here is indifferent between bundles A and B, B and C, and A and C.

Figure 6A.1 shows how we might go about deriving an indifference curve for a hypothetical consumer. Each point in the diagram represents some amount of X and some amount of Y. Point A in the diagram, for example, represents X_A units of X and Y_A units of Y. Now suppose we take some amount of Y away from our hypothetical consumer, moving him or her to A'. At A', the consumer has the same amount of X—that is, X_A units—but less Y and now has only Y_C units of Y. Because "more is better," our consumer is unequivocally worse off at A' than at A.

To compensate for the loss of Y, we begin giving our consumer some more X. If we give the individual just a little, he or she will still be worse off than at A. If we give this individual a great deal of X, he or she will be better off. There must be some quantity of X that will just compensate for the loss of Y. By giving the consumer that amount, we will have put together a bundle, Y_C and X_C, that yields the same total utility as bundle A. This is bundle C in Figure 6A.1. If confronted with a choice between bundles A and C, our consumer will say, "Either one; I do not care." In other words, the consumer is *indifferent* between A and C. When confronted with a choice between bundles C and B (which represent X_B and Y_B units of X and Y), this person is also indifferent. The points along the curve labeled i in Figure 6A.1 represent all the combinations of X and Y that yield the same total utility to our consumer. That curve is thus an indifference curve.

Each consumer has a whole set of indifference curves. Return for a moment to Figure 6A.1. Starting at point A again, imagine that we give the consumer a tiny bit more X *and* a tiny bit more Y. Because more is better, we know that the new bundle will yield a higher level of total utility and the consumer will be better off. Now just as we constructed the first indifference curve, we can construct a second one. What we get is an indifference curve that is *higher* and to the *right* of the first curve. Because utility along an indifference curve is constant at all points, every point along the new curve represents a higher level of total utility than every point along the first.

Figure 6A.2 shows a set of four indifference curves. The curve labeled i_4 represents the combinations of X and Y that

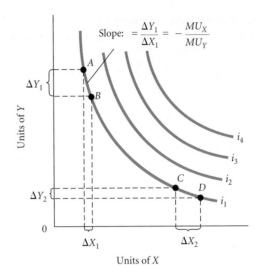

▲ **FIGURE 6A.2 A Preference Map: A Family of Indifference Curves**

Each consumer has a unique family of indifference curves called a preference map. Higher indifference curves represent higher levels of total utility.

yield the highest level of total utility among the four. Many other indifference curves exist between those shown on the diagram; in fact, their number is infinite. Notice that as you move up and to the right, utility increases.

The shapes of the indifference curves depend on the preferences of the consumer, and the whole set of indifference curves is called a **preference map**. Each consumer has a unique preference map.

Properties of Indifference Curves

The indifference curves shown in Figure 6A.2 are drawn bowing in toward the origin, or zero point, on the axes. In other words, the absolute value of the slope of the indifference curves decreases, or the curves get flatter, as we move to the right. Thus, we say that indifference curves are convex toward the origin. This shape follows directly from the assumption of diminishing marginal rate of substitution and makes sense if you remember the law of diminishing marginal utility.

To understand the convex shape, compare the segment of curve i_1 between A and B with the segment of the same curve between C and D. Moving from A to B, the consumer is willing to give up a substantial amount of Y to get a small amount of X. (Remember that total utility is constant along an indifference curve; the consumer is therefore indifferent between A and B.) Moving from C and D, however, the consumer is willing to give up only a small amount of Y to get more X.

This changing trade-off makes complete sense when you remember the law of diminishing marginal utility. Notice that between A and B, a great deal of Y is consumed and the marginal utility derived from a unit of Y is likely to be small. At the same time, though, only a little of X is being consumed; so the marginal utility derived from consuming a unit of X is likely to be high.

Suppose, for example, that X is pizza and Y is soda. Near A and B, a thirsty, hungry football player who has 10 sodas in front of him but only one slice of pizza will trade several sodas for another slice. Down around C and D, however, he has 20 slices of pizza and a single soda. Now he will trade several slices of pizza to get an additional soda.

We can show how the trade-off changes more formally by deriving an expression for the slope of an indifference curve. Let us look at the arc (that is, the section of the curve) between A and B. We know that in moving from A to B, total utility remains constant. That means that the utility lost as a result of consuming less Y must be matched by the utility gained from consuming more X. We can approximate the loss of utility by multiplying the marginal utility of Y (MU_Y) by the number of units by which consumption of Y is curtailed (ΔY). Similarly, we can approximate the utility gained from consuming more X by multiplying the marginal utility of X (MU_X) by the number of additional units of X consumed (ΔX). Remember: Because the consumer is indifferent between points A and B, total utility is the same at both points. Thus, these two must be equal in magnitude—that is, the gain in utility from consuming more X must equal the loss in utility from consuming less Y. Because ΔY is a negative number (because consumption of Y decreases from A to B), it follows that

$$MU_X \cdot \Delta X = -(MU_Y \cdot \Delta Y)$$

When we divide both sides by MU_Y and by ΔX, we obtain

$$\frac{\Delta Y}{\Delta X} = -\left(\frac{MU_X}{MU_Y}\right)$$

Recall that the slope of any line is calculated by dividing the change in Y—that is, ΔY—by the change in X—that is, ΔX. Thus, the slope of an indifference curve is the ratio of the marginal utility of X to the marginal utility of Y, and it is negative.

Now let us return to our pizza (X) and soda (Y) example. As we move down from the A:B area to the C:D area, our football player is consuming less soda and more pizza. The marginal utility of pizza (MU_X) is falling, and the marginal utility of soda (MU_Y) is rising. That means that MU_X/MU_Y (the marginal rate of substitution) is falling and the absolute value of the slope of the indifference curve is declining. Indeed, it does get flatter.

Consumer Choice

As you recall, demand depends on income, the prices of goods and services, and preferences or tastes. We are now ready to see how preferences as embodied in indifference curves interact with budget constraints to determine how the final quantities of X and Y will be chosen.

In Figure 6A.3, a set of indifference curves is superimposed on a consumer's budget constraint. Recall that the budget constraint separates those combinations of X and Y that are available from those that are not. The constraint simply shows those combinations that can be purchased with an income of I at prices P_X and P_Y. The budget constraint crosses the X-axis at I/P_X, or the number of units of X that can be purchased with I if nothing is spent on Y. Similarly, the budget constraint crosses the Y-axis at I/P_Y, or the number of units of Y that can be purchased with an income of I if nothing is spent on X. The

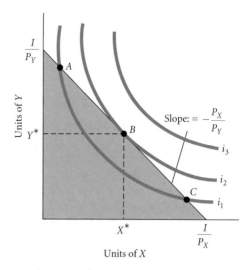

▲ **FIGURE 6A.3 Consumer Utility-Maximizing Equilibrium**

Consumers will choose the combination of X and Y that maximizes total utility. Graphically, the consumer will move along the budget constraint until the highest possible indifference curve is reached. At that point, the budget constraint and the indifference curve are tangent. This point of tangency occurs at X^* and Y^* (point B).

shaded area is the consumer's opportunity set. The slope of a budget constraint is $-P_X/P_Y$.

Consumers will choose from among available combinations of X and Y the one that maximizes utility. In graphic terms, a consumer will move along the budget constraint until he or she is on the highest possible indifference curve. Utility rises by moving from points such as A or C (which lie on i_1) toward B (which lies on i_2). Any movement away from point B moves the consumer to a lower indifference curve—a lower level of utility. In this case, utility is maximized when our consumer buys X^* units of X and Y^* units of Y. At point B, the budget constraint is just tangent to—that is, just touches—indifference curve i_2. As long as indifference curves are convex to the origin, utility maximization will take place at that point at which the indifference curve is just tangent to the budget constraint.

The tangency condition has important implications. Where two curves are tangent, they have the same slope, which implies that the slope of the indifference curve is equal to the slope of the budget constraint at the point of tangency:

$$\underbrace{-\frac{MU_X}{MU_Y}}_{\text{slope of indifference curve}} = \underbrace{-\frac{P_X}{P_Y}}_{\text{slope of budget constraint}}$$

slope of indifference curve = slope of budget constraint

By multiplying both sides of this equation by MU_Y and dividing both sides by P_X, we can rewrite this utility-maximizing rule as

$$\frac{MU_X}{P_X} = \frac{MU_Y}{P_Y}$$

This is the same rule derived in our earlier discussion without using indifference curves. We can describe this rule intuitively by saying that consumers maximize their total utility by equating the marginal utility per dollar spent on X with the marginal utility per dollar spent on Y. If this rule did not hold, utility could be increased by shifting money from one good to the other.

Deriving a Demand Curve from Indifference Curves and Budget Constraints

We now turn to the task of deriving a simple demand curve from indifference curves and budget constraints. A demand curve shows the quantity of a single good, X in this case, that a consumer will demand at various prices. To derive the demand curve, we need to confront our consumer with several alternative prices for X while keeping other prices, income, and preferences constant.

Figure 6A.4 shows the derivation. We begin with price P_X^1. At that price, the utility-maximizing point is A, where the consumer demands X_1 units of X. Therefore, in the right-hand diagram, we plot P_X^1 against X_1. This is the first point on our demand curve.

Now we lower the price of X to P_X^2. Lowering the price expands the opportunity set, and the budget constraint swivels to the right. Because the price of X has fallen, when our consumer spends all of the income on X, he or she can buy more of it. Our consumer is also better off because of being able to move to a higher indifference curve. The new utility-maximizing point is B, where the consumer demands X_2 units of X. Because the consumer demands X_2 units of X at a price of P_X^2, we plot P_X^2 against X_2 in the right-hand diagram. A second price cut to P_X^3 moves our consumer to point C, with a demand of X_3 units of X, and so on. Thus, we see how the demand curve can be derived from a consumer's preference map and budget constraint.

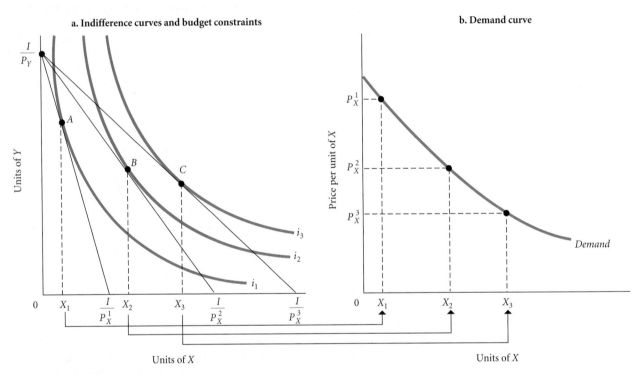

▲ **FIGURE 6A.4 Deriving a Demand Curve from Indifference Curves and Budget Constraint**

Indifference curves are labeled i_1, i_2, and i_3; budget constraints are shown by the three diagonal lines from I/P_Y to I/P_X^1, I/P_X^2, and I/P_X^3. Lowering the price of X from P_X^1 to P_X^2 and then to P_X^3 swivels the budget constraint to the right. At each price, there is a different utility-maximizing combination of X and Y. Utility is maximized at point A on i_1, point B on i_2, and point C on i_3. Plotting the three prices against the quantities of X chosen results in a standard downward-sloping demand curve.

APPENDIX SUMMARY

1. An *indifference curve* is a set of points, each point representing a combination of goods X and Y, all of which yield the same total utility. A particular consumer's set of indifference curves is called a *preference map*.

2. The slope of an indifference curve is the ratio of the marginal utility of X to the marginal utility of Y, and it is negative.

3. As long as indifference curves are convex to the origin, utility maximization will take place at that point at which the indifference curve is just tangent to—that is, just touches—the budget constraint. The utility-maximizing rule can also be written as $MU_X/P_X = MU_Y/P_Y$.

─── APPENDIX REVIEW TERMS AND CONCEPTS ───

Indifference curve A set of points, each point representing a combination of goods X and Y, all of which yield the same total utility. *p. 141*

Marginal rate of substitution MU_X/MU_Y; the ratio at which a household is willing to substitute good Y for good X. *p. 141*

Preference map A consumer's set of indifference curves. *p. 142*

──── APPENDIX PROBLEMS ────

1. Which of the four assumptions made at the beginning of the Appendix are violated by the indifference curves in Figure 1? Explain.

2. Assume that a household receives a weekly income of $100. If Figure 2 represents the choices of that household as the price of X changes, plot three points on the household demand curve.

3. If Ann's marginal rate of substitution of X for Y is 5—that is, $MU_X/MU_Y = 5$—the price of X is $9, and the price of Y is $2, she is spending too much of her income on Y. Do you agree or disagree? Explain your answer using a graph.

*4. Assume that Jim is a rational consumer who consumes only two goods, apples (A) and nuts (N). Assume that his marginal rate of substitution of apples for nuts is given by the following formula:

$$MRS = MU_N/MU_A = A/N$$

That is, Jim's MRS is equal to the ratio of the number of apples consumed to the number of nuts consumed.
   a. Assume that Jim's income is $100, the price of nuts is $5, and the price of apples is $10. What quantities of apples and nuts will he consume?
   b. Find two additional points on his demand curve for nuts $(P_N = \$10$ and $P_N = \$2)$.
   c. Sketch one of the equilibrium points on an indifference curve graph.

*Note: Problems marked with an asterisk are more challenging.

▲ FIGURE 1

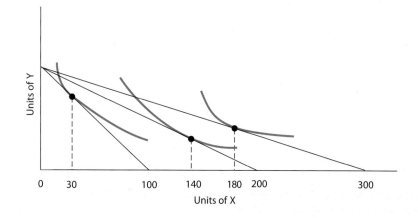

▲ FIGURE 2

5. Yolanda has $48 to spend on soft-shell crabs and chocolate truffles, and the data in the following table represent an indifference curve for these two products. If soft-shell crabs are $3 each and chocolate truffles are $4 each, draw a graph showing Yolanda's indifference curve and her budget constraint, putting soft-shell crabs on the vertical axis and chocolate truffles on the horizontal axis. What combination of soft-shell crabs and chocolate truffles will Yolanda purchase? Will this combination maximize Yolanda's total utility? Explain.

SOFT-SHELL CRABS	CHOCOLATE TRUFFLES
14	4
8	6
6	8
4	12

6. The following graph shows three indifference curves and the accompanying budget constraints for products X and Y. The graph represents the price of product X falling from P_{1x} to P_{2x} and then to P_{3x}. Explain how a demand curve for product X can be derived from this graph and draw a graph showing the demand curve for product X.

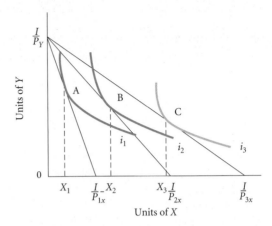

The Production Process: The Behavior of Profit-Maximizing Firms

production The process by which inputs are combined, transformed, and turned into outputs.

In Chapter 6, we took a brief look at the household decisions that lie behind supply and demand curves. We spent some time discussing household choices: how much to work and how to choose among the wide range of goods and services available within the constraints of prices and income. We also identified some of the influences on household demand in output markets, as well as some of the influences on household supply behavior in input markets.

We now turn to the other side of the system and examine the behavior of firms. Firms purchase inputs to produce and sell outputs that range from computers to string quartet performances. In other words, they *demand* factors of production in input markets and *supply* goods and services in output markets. In this chapter, we look inside the firm at the production process that transforms inputs into outputs. Although Chapters 7 through 12 describe the behavior of perfectly competitive firms, much of what we say in these chapters also applies to firms that are not perfectly competitive. For example, when we turn to monopoly in Chapter 13, we will be describing firms that are similar to competitive firms in many ways. All firms, whether competitive or not, demand inputs, engage in production, and produce outputs. All firms have an incentive to maximize profits and thus to minimize costs.

Central to our analysis is **production**, the process by which inputs are combined, transformed, and turned into outputs. Firms vary in size and internal organization, but they all take inputs and transform them into goods and services for which there is some demand. For example, an independent accountant combines labor, paper, telephone and e-mail service, time, learning, and a Web site to provide help to confused taxpayers. An automobile plant uses steel, labor, plastic, electricity, machines, and countless other inputs to produce cars. If we want to understand a firm's costs, we first need to understand how it efficiently combines inputs to produce goods and services. Before we begin our discussion of the production process, however, we need to clarify some of the assumptions on which our analysis is based.

Although our discussions in the next several chapters focus on profit-making business firms, it is important to understand that production and productive activity are not confined to private business firms. Households also engage in transforming factors of production (labor, capital, energy, natural resources, and so on) into useful things. When you work in your garden, you are combining land, labor, fertilizer, seeds, and tools (capital) into the vegetables you eat and the flowers you enjoy. The government also combines land, labor, and capital to produce public services for which demand exists: national defense, homeland security, police and fire protection, and education, to name a few.

firm   An organization that comes into being when a person or a group of people decides to produce a good or service to meet a perceived demand.

Private business firms are set apart from other producers, such as households and government, by their purpose. A **firm** exists when a person or a group of people decides to produce a good or service to meet a perceived demand. Firms engage in production—that is, they transform inputs into outputs—because they can sell their products for more than it costs to produce them.

The Behavior of Profit-Maximizing Firms

All firms must make several basic decisions to achieve what we assume to be their primary objective—maximum profits.

As Figure 7.1 states, the three decisions that all firms must make include:

1. How much output to supply (quantity of product)
2. How to produce that output (which production technique/technology to use)
3. How much of each input to demand

▶ FIGURE 7.1 **The Three Decisions That All Firms Must Make**

1. How much output to supply	2. Which production technology to use	3. How much of each input to demand

The first and last choices are linked by the second choice. Once a firm has decided how much to produce, the choice of a production method determines the firm's input requirements. If a sweater company decides to produce 5,000 sweaters this month, it knows how many production workers it will need, how much electricity it will use, how much raw yarn to purchase, and how many sewing machines to run.

Similarly, given a technique of production, any set of input quantities determines the amount of output that can be produced. Certainly, the number of machines and workers employed in a sweater mill determines how many sweaters can be produced.

Changing the *technology* of production will change the relationship between input and output quantities. An apple orchard that uses expensive equipment to raise pickers up into the trees will harvest more fruit with fewer workers in a given period of time than an orchard in which pickers use simple ladders. It is also possible that two different technologies can produce the same quantity of output. For example, a fully computerized textile mill with only a few workers running the machines may produce the same number of sweaters as a mill with no sophisticated machines but many workers. A profit-maximizing firm chooses the technology that minimizes its costs for a given level of output.

In this chapter, all firms in a given industry produce the same exact product and we are concerned solely with production. In later chapters, these three basic decisions will be expanded to include the setting of prices and the determination of product quality.

Profits and Economic Costs

profit (economic profit)   The difference between total revenue and total cost.

total revenue   The amount received from the sale of the product ($q \times P$).

total cost (total economic cost)   The total of (1) out-of-pocket costs and (2) opportunity cost of all factors of production.

We assume that firms are in business to make a profit and that a firm's behavior is guided by the goal of maximizing profits. What is profit? **Profit** is the difference between total revenue and total cost:

$$\text{profit} = \text{total revenue} - \text{total cost}$$

Total revenue is the amount received from the sale of the product; it is equal to the number of units sold (q) times the price received per unit (P). **Total cost** is less straightforward to define. We define total cost here to include (1) out-of-pocket costs and (2) opportunity cost of all inputs or factors of production. *Out-of-pocket costs* are sometimes referred to as *explicit costs* or *accounting costs*. These refer to costs as an accountant would calculate them. *Economic costs* include the opportunity cost of every input. These opportunity costs are often referred to as *implicit costs*. The term *profit* will from here on refer to *economic profit*. So whenever we say profit = total revenue − total cost, what we really mean is

$$\text{economic profit} = \text{total revenue} - \text{total economic cost}$$

The reason we take opportunity costs into account is that we are interested in analyzing the behavior of firms from the standpoint of a potential investor or a potential new competitor. If I am thinking about buying a firm or shares in a firm or entering an industry as a new firm, I need to consider the *full* costs of production. For example, if a family business employs three family members but pays them no wage, there is still a cost: the opportunity cost of their labor. In evaluating the business from the outside, these costs must be added if we want to figure out whether the business is successful.

The most important opportunity cost that is included in economic cost is the opportunity cost of capital. The way we treat the opportunity cost of capital is to add a *normal rate of return* to capital as part of economic cost.

Normal Rate of Return   When someone decides to start a firm, that person must commit resources. To operate a manufacturing firm, you need a plant and some equipment. To start a restaurant, you need to buy grills, ovens, tables, chairs, and so on. In other words, you must invest in capital. To start an e-business, you need a host site, some computer equipment, some software, and a Web-site design. Such investment requires resources that stay tied up in the firm as long as it operates. Even firms that have been around a long time must continue to invest. Plant and equipment wear out and must be replaced. Firms that decide to expand must put new capital in place. This is as true of proprietorships, where the resources come directly from the proprietor, as it is of corporations, where the resources needed to make investments come from shareholders.

Whenever resources are used to invest in a business, there is an opportunity cost. Instead of opening a candy store, you could put your funds into an alternative use such as a certificate of deposit or a government bond, both of which earn interest. Instead of using its retained earnings to build a new plant, a firm could earn interest on those funds or pay them out to shareholders.

Rate of return is the annual flow of net income generated by an investment expressed as a percentage of the total investment. For example, if someone makes a $100,000 investment in capital to start a small restaurant and the restaurant produces a flow of profit of $15,000 every year, we say the project has a "rate of return" of 15 percent. Sometimes we refer to the rate of return as the *yield* of the investment.

A **normal rate of return** is the rate that is just sufficient to keep owners and investors satisfied. If the rate of return were to fall below normal, it would be difficult or impossible for managers to raise resources needed to purchase new capital. Owners of the firm would be receiving a rate of return that was lower than what they could receive elsewhere in the economy, and they would have no incentive to invest in the firm.

If the firm has fairly steady revenues and the future looks secure, the normal rate of return should be very close to the interest rate on risk-free government bonds. A firm certainly will not keep investors interested in it if it does not pay them a rate of return at least as high as they can get from a risk-free government or corporate bond. If a firm is rock solid and the economy is steady, it may not have to pay a much higher rate. However, if a firm is in a very speculative industry and the future of the economy is shaky, it may have to pay substantially more to keep its shareholders happy. In exchange for a risk that the business may falter or even fail, the shareholders will expect a higher return.

A normal rate of return is considered a part of the total cost of a business. Adding a normal rate of return to total cost has an important implication: When a firm earns a normal rate of return, it is earning a zero profit as we have defined profit. If the level of profit is positive, the firm is earning an above-normal rate of return on capital.

A simple example will illustrate the concepts of a normal rate of return being part of total cost. Suppose that Sue and Ann decide to start a small business selling turquoise belts in the Denver airport. To get into the business, they need to invest in a fancy pushcart. The price of the pushcart is $20,000 with all the displays and attachments included. Suppose that Sue and Ann estimate that they will sell 3,000 belts each year for $10 each. Further assume that each belt costs $5 from the supplier. Finally, the cart must be staffed by one clerk, who works for an annual wage of $14,000. Is this business going to make a profit?

To answer this question, we must determine total revenue and total cost. First, annual revenue is $30,000 (3,000 belts × $10). Total cost includes the cost of the belts—$15,000 (3,000 belts × $5)—plus the labor cost of $14,000, for a total of $29,000. Thus, on the basis of the annual revenue and cost flows, the firm *seems* to be making a profit of $1,000 ($30,000 − $29,000).

normal rate of return   A rate of return on capital that is just sufficient to keep owners and investors satisfied. For relatively risk-free firms, it should be nearly the same as the interest rate on risk-free government bonds.

What about the $20,000 initial investment in the pushcart? This investment is *not* a direct part of the cost of Sue and Ann's firm. If we assume that the cart maintains its value over time, *the only thing that Sue and Ann are giving up is the interest they might have earned had they not tied up their funds in the pushcart.* That is, the only real cost is the opportunity cost of the investment, which is the forgone interest on the $20,000.

Now suppose that Sue and Ann want a minimum return equal to 10 percent—which is, say, the rate of interest that they could have gotten by purchasing corporate bonds. This implies a normal return of 10 percent, or $2,000 annually (= $20,000 × 0.10) on the $20,000 investment. As we determined earlier, Sue and Ann will earn only $1,000 annually. This is only a 5 percent return on their investment. Thus, they are really earning a below-normal return. Recall that the opportunity cost of capital must be added to total cost in calculating profit. Thus, the total cost in this case is $31,000 ($29,000 + $2,000 in forgone interest on the investment). The level of profit is negative: $30,000 minus $31,000 equals −$1,000. These calculations are summarized in Table 7.1. Because the level of profit is negative, Sue and Ann are actually suffering a loss on their belt business.

TABLE 7.1 Calculating Total Revenue, Total Cost, and Profit	
Initial Investment:	$20,000
Market Interest Rate Available:	0.10, or 10%
Total revenue (3,000 belts × $10 each)	**$30,000**
Costs	
Belts from supplier	$15,000
Labor cost	14,000
Normal return/opportunity cost of capital ($20,000 × 0.10)	2,000
Total Cost	**$31,000**
Profit = total revenue − total cost	**−$1,000**[a]

[a]There is a loss of $1,000.

When a firm earns a *positive* level of profit, it is earning more than is sufficient to retain the interest of investors. In fact, positive profits are likely to attract new firms into an industry and cause existing firms to expand.

When a firm suffers a *negative* level of profit—that is, when it incurs a loss—it is earning at a rate below that required to keep investors happy. Such a loss may or may not be a loss as an accountant would measure it. Even if a firm is earning a rate of return of 10 percent, it is earning a below-normal rate of return, or a loss, if a normal return for its industry is 15 percent. Losses may cause some firms to exit the industry; others will contract in size. Certainly, new investment will not flow into such an industry.

Short-Run versus Long-Run Decisions

The decisions made by a firm—how much to produce, how to produce it, and what inputs to demand—all take time into account. If a firm decides that it wants to double or triple its output, it may need time to arrange financing, hire architects and contractors, and build a new plant. Planning for a major expansion can take years. In the meantime, the firm must decide how much to produce within the constraint of its existing plant. If a firm decides to get out of a particular business, it may take time to arrange an orderly exit. There may be contract obligations to fulfill, equipment to sell, and so on. Once again, the firm must decide what to do in the meantime.

A firm's immediate response to a change in the economic environment may differ from its response over time. Consider, for example, a small restaurant with 20 tables that becomes very popular. The immediate problem for the owners is getting the most profit within the constraint of the existing restaurant. The owner might consider adding a few tables or speeding up service to squeeze in a few more customers. Some popular restaurants do not take reservations, forcing people to wait at the bar. This practice increases drink revenues and keeps tables full at all times. At the same time, the owner may be thinking of expanding the current facility, moving to a larger facility, or opening a second restaurant. In the future, the owner might buy the store next door and double the capacity. Such decisions might require negotiating a lease, buying new equipment, and hiring more staff. It takes time to make and implement these decisions.

Because the character of immediate response differs from long-run adjustment, it is useful to define two time periods: the short run and the long run. Two assumptions define the **short run**: (1) a fixed scale (or a fixed factor of production) and (2) no entry into or exit from the industry. First, the short run is defined as that period during which existing firms have some *fixed factor of production*—that is, during which time some factor locks them into their current scale of operations. Second, new firms cannot enter and existing firms cannot exit an industry in the short run. Firms may curtail operations, but they are still locked into some costs even though they may be in the process of going out of business.

Which factor or factors of production are fixed in the short run differs from industry to industry. For a manufacturing firm, the size of the physical plant is often the greatest limitation. A factory is built with a given production rate in mind. Although that rate can be increased, output cannot increase beyond a certain limit in the short run. For a private physician, the limit may be the capacity to see patients; the day has only so many hours. In the long run, the doctor may invite others to join the practice and expand; but for now, in the short run, this sole physician *is* the firm, with a capacity that is the firm's only capacity. For a farmer, the fixed factor may be land. The capacity of a small farm is limited by the number of acres being cultivated.

In the **long run**, there are no fixed factors of production. Firms can plan for any output level they find desirable. They can double or triple output, for example. In addition, new firms can start up operations (enter the industry) and existing firms can go out of business (exit the industry).

No hard-and-fast rule specifies how long the short run is. The point is that firms make two basic kinds of decisions: those that govern the day-to-day operations of the firm and those that involve longer-term strategic planning. Sometimes major decisions can be implemented in weeks. Often, however, the process takes years. In many large firms, different people often make the short- and long-run decisions. A production manager might well be charged with trying to do the best she can with the plant and equipment that she has, while her boss, the division head, figures out whether expansion of the plant is a good idea. In a single proprietorship, one person may wear both hats, thinking simultaneously about how to make the most out of the present while taking steps to improve the future of the business.

short run The period of time for which two conditions hold: The firm is operating under a fixed scale (fixed factor) of production, and firms can neither enter nor exit an industry.

long run That period of time for which there are no fixed factors of production: Firms can increase or decrease the scale of operation, and new firms can enter and existing firms can exit the industry.

The Bases of Decisions: Market Price of Outputs, Available Technology, and Input Prices

As we said earlier, a firm's three fundamental decisions are made with the objective of maximizing profits. Because profits equal total revenues minus total costs, each firm needs to know how much it costs to produce its product and how much its product can be sold for.

To know how much it costs to produce a good or service, a firm needs to know something about the production techniques that are available and about the prices of the inputs required. To estimate how much it will cost to operate a gas station, for instance, a firm needs to know equipment needs, number of workers, kind of building, and so on. The firm also needs to know the going wage rates for mechanics and unskilled laborers, the cost of gas pumps, interest rates, the rents per square foot of land on high-traffic corners, and the wholesale price of gasoline. Of course, the firm also needs to know how much it can sell gasoline and repair services for.

In the language of economics, a firm needs to know three things:

1. The market price of output
2. The techniques of production that are available
3. The prices of inputs

Output price determines potential revenues. The techniques available tell me how much of each input I need, and input prices tell me how much they will cost. Together the available production techniques and the prices of inputs determine costs.

The rest of this chapter and the next chapter focus on costs of production. We begin at the heart of the firm, with the production process. Faced with a set of input prices, firms must decide on the best, or optimal, method of production (Figure 7.2). The **optimal method of production** is the one that minimizes cost. With cost determined and the market price of output known, a firm will make a final judgment about the quantity of product to produce and the quantity of each input to demand.

optimal method of production The production method that minimizes cost.

▶ **FIGURE 7.2**
Determining the Optimal Method of Production

The Production Process

production technology
The quantitative relationship between inputs and outputs.

Production is the process through which inputs are combined and transformed into outputs. **Production technology** relates inputs to outputs. Specific quantities of inputs are needed to produce any given service or good. A loaf of bread requires certain amounts of water, flour, and yeast; some kneading and patting; and an oven and gas or electricity. A trip from downtown New York to Newark, New Jersey, can be produced with a taxicab, 45 minutes of a driver's labor, some gasoline, and so on.

Most outputs can be produced by a number of different techniques. You can tear down an old building and clear a lot to create a park in several ways, for example. Five hundred men and women could descend on the park with sledgehammers and carry the pieces away by hand; this would be a **labor-intensive technology**. The same park could be produced by two people with a wrecking crane, a steam shovel, a backhoe, and a dump truck; this would be a **capital-intensive technology**. Similarly, different inputs can be combined to transport people from Oakland to San Francisco. The Bay Area Rapid Transit carries thousands of people simultaneously under San Francisco Bay and uses a massive amount of capital relative to labor. Cab rides to San Francisco require more labor relative to capital; a driver is needed for every few passengers.

labor-intensive technology Technology that relies heavily on human labor instead of capital.

capital-intensive technology Technology that relies heavily on capital instead of human labor.

In choosing the most appropriate technology, firms choose the one that minimizes the cost of production. For a firm in an economy with a plentiful supply of inexpensive labor but not much capital, the optimal method of production will involve labor-intensive techniques. For example, assembly of items such as running shoes is done most efficiently by hand. That is why Nike produces virtually all its shoes in developing countries where labor costs are very low. In contrast, firms in an economy with high wages and high labor costs have an incentive to substitute away from labor and to use more capital-intensive, or labor-saving, techniques. Suburban office parks use more land and have more open space in part because land in the suburbs is more plentiful and less expensive than land in the middle of a big city.

Production Functions: Total Product, Marginal Product, and Average Product

production function *or* **total product function** A numerical or mathematical expression of a relationship between inputs and outputs. It shows units of total product as a function of units of inputs.

The relationship between inputs and outputs—that is, the production technology—expressed numerically or mathematically is called a **production function** (or **total product function**). A production function shows units of total product as a function of units of inputs.

Imagine, for example, a small sandwich shop. All the sandwiches made in the shop are grilled, and the shop owns only one grill, which can accommodate only two workers comfortably. As columns 1 and 2 of the production function in Table 7.2 show, one person working alone can produce only 10 sandwiches per hour in addition to answering the phone, waiting on customers, keeping the tables clean, and so on. The second worker can stay at the grill full-time and not worry about anything except making sandwiches. Because the two workers together can produce 25 sandwiches, the second worker can produce $25 - 10 = 15$ sandwiches per hour. A third person trying to use the grill produces crowding, but with careful use of space, more sandwiches can be

TABLE 7.2   Production Function

(1) Labor Units (Employees)	(2) Total Product (Sandwiches per Hour)	(3) Marginal Product of Labor	(4) Average Product of Labor (Total Product ÷ Labor Units)
0	0	—	—
1	10	10	10.0
2	25	15	12.5
3	35	10	11.7
4	40	5	10.0
5	42	2	8.4
6	42	0	7.0

[handwritten annotations: "marginal product" pointing to Total Product column; beside values 10, 25, 35, 40, 42, 42: "15", "10", "5", "2", "0"; bracket around (4) heading; "Law of Diminishing Marginal Return"]

produced. The third worker adds 10 sandwiches per hour. Note that the added output from hiring a third worker is less because of the capital constraint, *not* because the third worker is somehow less efficient or hardworking. We assume that all workers are equally capable.

The fourth and fifth workers can work at the grill only while the first three are putting the pickles, onions, and wrapping on the sandwiches they have made. Then the first three must wait to get back to the grill. Worker four adds five sandwiches per hour to the total, and worker five adds just two. Adding a sixth worker adds no output at all: The current maximum capacity of the shop is 42 sandwiches per hour.

Figure 7.3(a) graphs the total product data from Table 7.2. As you look at Table 7.2 and think about marginal product, you should begin to see how important the nature of the production function is to a firm. We see that the sandwich firm that hires a fourth worker will be expanding its sandwich production by five. Is it worth it? That will in turn depend on how much the worker costs and for how much the shop can sell the sandwich. As we proceed to analyze the firm's decision in the next few chapters, we will explore this further.

Marginal Product and the Law of Diminishing Returns
Marginal product is the additional output that can be produced by hiring one more unit of a specific input, holding all other inputs constant. As column 3 of Table 7.2 shows, the marginal product of the first unit of labor in the sandwich shop is 10 sandwiches; the marginal product of the second is 15; the third, 10; and so on. The marginal product of the sixth worker is zero. Figure 7.3(b) graphs the marginal product of labor curve from the data in Table 7.2.

marginal product   The additional output that can be produced by adding one more unit of a specific input, *ceteris paribus.*

a. Production function (Total product)

b. Marginal product of labor

[handwritten annotations on graph b: "increasing M returns", "diminishing marginal return", "negative marginal return"]

▲ **FIGURE 7.3 Production Function for Sandwiches**
A *production function* is a numerical representation of the relationship between inputs and outputs. In Figure 7.3(a), total product (sandwiches) is graphed as a function of labor inputs. The *marginal product* of labor is the additional output that one additional unit of labor produces. Figure 7.3(b) shows that the marginal product of the second unit of labor at the sandwich shop is 15 units of output; the marginal product of the fourth unit of labor is 5 units of output.

law of diminishing returns When additional units of a variable input are added to fixed inputs, after a certain point, the marginal product of the variable input declines.

The **law of diminishing returns** states that *after a certain point, when additional units of a variable input are added to fixed inputs* (in this case, the building and grill), *the marginal product of the variable input* (in this case, labor) *declines*. The British economist David Ricardo first formulated the law of diminishing returns on the basis of his observations of agriculture in nineteenth-century England. Within a given area of land, he noted, successive "doses" of labor and capital yielded smaller and smaller increases in crop output. The law of diminishing returns is true in agriculture because only so much more can be produced by farming the same land more intensely. In manufacturing, diminishing returns set in when a firm begins to strain the capacity of its existing plant.

At our sandwich shop, diminishing returns set in when the third worker is added. The marginal product of the second worker is actually higher than the first [Figure 7.3(b)]. The first worker takes care of the phone and the tables, thus freeing the second worker to concentrate exclusively on sandwich making. From that point on, the grill gets crowded. It is important to note here that diminishing returns are setting in, not because the third worker is worse than workers one or two (we assume they are identical), but because as we add staff, each has a smaller amount of capital (here a grill) to work with.

Diminishing returns, or *diminishing marginal product*, begin to show up when more and more units of a variable input are added to a fixed input, such as the scale of the plant. Recall that we defined the short run as that period in which some fixed factor of production constrains the firm. It then follows that diminishing returns always apply in the short run and that in the short run, every firm will face diminishing returns. This means that every firm finds it progressively more difficult to increase its output as it approaches capacity production.

average product The average amount produced by each unit of a variable factor of production.

Marginal Product versus Average Product

Average product is the average amount produced by each unit of a variable factor of production. At our sandwich shop with one grill, that variable factor is labor. In Table 7.2, you saw that the first two workers together produce 25 sandwiches per hour. Their average product is therefore 12.5 (25 ÷ 2). The third worker adds only 10 sandwiches per hour to the total. These 10 sandwiches are the *marginal* product of labor. The *average* product of the first three units of labor, however, is 11.7 (the average of 10, 15, and 10). Stated in equation form, the average product of labor is the *total* product divided by total units of labor:

$$\text{average product of labor} = \frac{\text{total product}}{\text{total units of labor}}$$

Average product "follows" marginal product, but it does not change as quickly. If marginal product is above average product, the average rises; if marginal product is below average product, the average falls. Suppose, for example, that you have had six exams and that your average is 86. If you score 75 on the next exam, your average score will fall, but not all the way to 75. In fact, it will fall only to 84.4. If you score a 95 instead, your average will rise to 87.3. As columns 3 and 4 of Table 7.2 show, marginal product at the sandwich shop declines continuously after the third worker is hired. Average product also decreases, but more slowly.

Figure 7.4 shows a typical production function and the marginal and average product curves derived from it. The marginal product curve is a graph of the slope of the total product curve—that is, of the production function. Average product and marginal product start out equal, as they do in Table 7.2. As marginal product climbs, the graph of average product follows it, but more slowly, up to L_1 (point A).

Notice that marginal product starts out increasing. (It did so in the sandwich shop as well.) Most production processes are designed to be run well by more than one worker. Take an assembly line, for example. To work efficiently, an assembly line needs a worker at every station; it's a cooperative process. The marginal product of the first workers is low or zero. As workers are added, the process starts to run and marginal product rises.

At point A (L_1 units of labor), marginal product begins to fall. Because every plant has a finite capacity, efforts to increase production will always run into the limits of that capacity. At point B (L_2 units of labor), marginal product has fallen to equal the average product, which has been increasing. Between point B and point C (between L_2 and L_3 units of labor), marginal product falls below average product and average product begins to follow it *down*. Average product is at its maximum at point B, where it is equal to marginal product. At L_3, more labor yields no more output and marginal product is zero—the assembly line has no more positions, the grill is jammed.

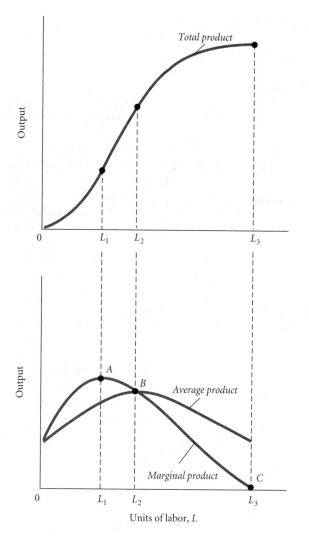

◀ **FIGURE 7.4 Total Average and Marginal Product**

Marginal and average product curves can be derived from total product curves. Average product is at its maximum at the point of intersection with marginal product.

Production Functions with Two Variable Factors of Production

So far, we have considered production functions with only one variable factor of production. However, inputs work together in production. In general, additional capital increases the productivity of labor. Because capital—buildings, machines, and so on—is of no use without people to operate it, we say that capital and labor are *complementary inputs*.

A simple example will clarify this point. Consider again the sandwich shop. If the demand for sandwiches began to exceed the capacity of the shop to produce them, the shop's owner might decide to expand capacity. This would mean purchasing more capital in the form of a new grill.

A second grill would essentially double the shop's productive capacity. The new higher capacity would mean that the sandwich shop would not run into diminishing returns as quickly. With only one grill, the third and fourth workers are less productive because the single grill gets crowded. With two grills, however, the third and fourth workers could produce 15 sandwiches per hour using the second grill. In essence, the added capital raises the *productivity* of labor—that is, the amount of output produced per worker per hour.

Just as the new grill enhances the productivity of workers in the sandwich shop, new businesses and the capital they put in place raise the productivity of workers in countries such as Malaysia, India, and Kenya.

This simple relationship lies at the heart of worries about productivity at the national and international levels. Building new, modern plants and equipment enhances a nation's productivity. In the last decade, China has accumulated capital (that is, built plants and equipment) at a very high rate. The result is growth in the average quantity of output per worker in China.

ECONOMICS IN PRACTICE

Learning about Growing Pineapples in Ghana

In this chapter we have focused on the way in which labor, capital, and other inputs are used to produce outputs of various sorts. We have described a somewhat abstract production function, linking specific combinations of inputs and output levels. In reading this chapter, you might have wondered where real people interested in producing something learn about production functions. How does an entrepreneur know what the ideal combination of inputs is to produce a given output?

In a recent interesting article, Timothy Conley from Chicago and Christopher Udry from Yale asked precisely this question in thinking about the production of pineapples in Ghana. What they learned helps us think about the production process more generally.

In farming, as in manufacturing, we need a given combination of labor and capital to produce output, here a crop. The capital doesn't come in the form of a grill, as in the sandwich shop, but tractors, or plows, or shovels. Raw materials include seeds and fertilizer. There are clearly substitution possibilities among these inputs; farmers can weed more and fertilize or water less, for example. How does a farmer know what the right mix of inputs is, given input prices?

Ghana proved to be an interesting place to ask this question. In the 1990s, an area of Ghana changed from an exclusive reliance on maize as the agricultural crop to the development of pineapple

farms. This transformation happened slowly over time to various neighborhoods. Conley and Udry found that social learning was key in the process of technology adoption. For farmers in Ghana, the choice of how much fertilizer to use was highly dependent on how much fertilizer their more successful neighbor farmers used. Social learning was especially important for novice pineapple farmers located near more veteran producers.[1]

Social learning obviously plays a role in the diffusion of manufacturing technology as well. It is no accident that many high-tech entrepreneurs began their careers in other high-tech firms where they learned much about the right production techniques.

[1] Timothy Conley and Christopher Udry, "Learning About a New Technology: Pineapples in Ghana," *American Economic Review*, March 2010, 35–69.

Choice of Technology

As our sandwich shop example shows, inputs (factors of production) are complementary. Capital enhances the productivity of labor. Workers in the sandwich shop are more productive when they are not crowded at a single grill. Similarly, labor enhances the productivity of capital. When more workers are hired at a plant that is operating at 50 percent of capacity, previously idle machines suddenly become productive.

However, inputs can also be substituted for one another. If labor becomes expensive, firms can adopt labor-saving technologies; that is, they can substitute capital for labor. Assembly lines can be automated by replacing human beings with machines, and capital can be substituted for land when land is scarce. If capital becomes relatively expensive, firms can substitute labor for capital. In short, most goods and services can be produced in a number of ways through the use of alternative technologies. One of the key decisions that all firms must make is which technology to use.

Consider the choices available to the diaper manufacturer in Table 7.3. Five different techniques of producing 100 diapers are available. Technology *A* is the most labor-intensive, requiring 10 hours of labor and 2 units of capital to produce 100 diapers. (You can think of units of capital as machine hours.) Technology *E* is the most capital-intensive, requiring only 2 hours of labor but 10 hours of machine time.

TABLE 7.3	Inputs Required to Produce 100 Diapers Using Alternative Technologies	
Technology	Units of Capital (*K*)	Units of Labor (*L*)
A	2	10
B	3	6
C	4	4
D	6	3
E	10	2

ECONOMICS IN PRACTICE

How Fast Should a Truck Driver Go?

The trucking business gives us an opportunity to think about choice among technologies in a concrete way.

Suppose you own a truck and use it to haul merchandise for retailers such as Target and Sears. Your typical run is 200 miles, and you hire one person to drive the truck at a cost of $20 per hour. How fast should you instruct him to drive the truck? Consider the cost per trip.

Notice that even with fixed inputs of one truck and one driver, you still have some choices to make. In the language of this chapter, you can think of the choice as one of slow-drive technology (let's say 50 mph) versus fast-drive technology (say, 60 mph).

If the driver's time were the only input, the problem would be simple: Labor costs are minimized if you tell him to drive fast. At 60 mph, a trip takes the driver only 3.33 hours (200 miles divided by 60 mph) and costs you $66.67 given his $20 wage rate. However, at a speed of 50 mph, it takes four hours and costs you $80. With one variable input, the best technology is the one that uses that input most efficiently. In fact, with only one variable input, you would tell the driver to speed regardless of his wage rate.

But, of course, trucks require not only drivers but also fuel, which is where the question gets more interesting. As it turns out, the fuel mileage that a truck gets diminishes with speed beyond about 50 mph. Let's say in this case that the truck gets 15 miles per gallon at 50 mph but only 12 miles per gallon at 60 mph. Now we have a trade-off. When you tell the driver to go fast, your labor costs are lower but your fuel costs are higher.

So what instructions do you give? It should be clear that your instructions depend on the price of fuel. First suppose that fuel costs $3.50 per gallon. If the trucker drives fast, he will get 12 miles per gallon. Since the trucker has to drive 200 miles per trip, he burns 16.66 gallons (200 divided by 12) and total fuel cost is $58.31. Driving fast, the trucker goes 60 miles per hour. You have to pay him for 3.33 hours (200 divided by 60), which at $20 per hour, is a total of $66.67. The total for the trip is $124.98.

On the other hand, if your trucker drives slowly, he will get 15 miles per gallon, which means you need only 13.33 gallons, which costs $46.67. But now it takes more time. He takes four hours, and you must pay him 4 × $20, or $80 per trip. Total cost is now $126.67. Thus, the cost-minimizing solution is to have him drive fast.

Now try a price of $4.50 per gallon. Doing the same calculations, you should be able to show that when driving slowly, the total cost is

$139.99; when driving fast, the cost is $141.63. Thus, the higher fuel price means that you tell the driver to slow down.

Going one step further, you should be able to show that at a fuel price of $4, the trip costs the same whether your trucker drives fast or slowly.

In fact, you should be able to see that at fuel prices in excess of $4 per gallon, you tell your driver to slow down, while at cheaper prices, you tell him to speed up. With more than one input, the choice of technologies often depends on the unit cost of those inputs.

The observation that the optimal "technology" to use in trucking depends on fuel prices is one reason we might expect accident rates to fall with rises in fuel prices (in addition to the fact that everyone drives less when fuel is expensive). Modern technology, in the form of on-board computers, allows a modern trucking firm to monitor driving speed and instruct drivers.

Here is a summary of the cost per trip.

Fuel Price	$3.50	$4.00	$4.50
Drive Fast	$124.97	$133.33	$141.63
Drive Slowly	$126.66	$133.33	$139.99

To choose a production technique, the firm must look to input markets to learn the current market prices of labor and capital. What is the wage rate (P_L), and what is the cost per hour of capital (P_K)? The right choice among inputs depends on how productive an input is and what its price is.

Suppose that labor and capital are both available at a price of $1 per unit. Column 4 of Table 7.4 presents the calculations required to determine which technology is best. The winner is technology C. Assuming that the firm's objective is to maximize profits, it will choose the least-cost technology. Using technology C, the firm can produce 100 diapers for $8. All four of the other technologies produce 100 diapers at a higher cost.

Now suppose that the wage rate (P_L) were to rise sharply, from $1 to $5. You might guess that this increase would lead the firm to substitute labor-saving capital for workers, and you would be right. As column 5 of Table 7.4 shows, the increase in the wage rate means that technology E is now the cost-minimizing choice for the firm. Using 10 units of capital and only 2 units of labor,

TABLE 7.4 Cost-Minimizing Choice Among Alternative Technologies (100 Diapers)

(1) Technology	(2) Units of Capital (K)	(3) Units of Labor (L)	Cost = $(L \times P_L) + (K \times P_K)$	
			(4) $P_L = \$1$ $P_K = \$1$	(5) $P_L = \$5$ $P_K = \$1$
A	2	10	$12	52
B	3	6	9	33
C	4	4	8	24
D	6	3	9	21
E	10	2	12	20

the firm can produce 100 diapers for $20. All other technologies are now more costly. Notice too from the table that the firm's ability to shift its technique of production softened the impact of the wage increase on its costs. The flexibility of a firm's techniques of production is an important determinant of its costs. Two things determine the cost of production: (1) technologies that are available and (2) input prices. Profit-maximizing firms will choose the technology that minimizes the cost of production given current market input prices.

Looking Ahead: Cost and Supply

So far, we have looked only at a *single* level of output. That is, we have determined how much it will cost to produce 100 diapers using the best available technology when $P_K = \$1$ and $P_L = \$1$ or $5. The best technique for producing 1,000 diapers or 10,000 diapers may be entirely different. The next chapter explores the relationship between cost and the level of output in some detail. One of our main objectives in that chapter is to determine the amount that a competitive firm will choose to *supply* during a given time period.

--- SUMMARY ---

1. Firms vary in size and internal organization, but they all take inputs and transform them into outputs through a process called *production*.

2. In perfect competition, no single firm has any control over prices. This follows from two assumptions: (1) Perfectly competitive industries are composed of many firms, each small relative to the size of the industry, and (2) each firm in a perfectly competitive industry produces *homogeneous products*.

3. The demand curve facing a competitive firm is perfectly elastic. If a single firm raises its price above the market price, it will sell nothing. Because it can sell all it produces at the market price, a firm has no incentive to reduce price.

THE BEHAVIOR OF PROFIT-MAXIMIZING FIRMS p. 148

4. Profit-maximizing firms in all industries must make three choices: (1) how much output to supply, (2) how to produce that output, and (3) how much of each input to demand.

5. *Profit* equals total revenue minus total cost. Total cost (economic cost) includes (1) out-of-pocket costs and (2) the opportunity cost of each factor of production, including a normal rate of return on capital.

6. A *normal rate of return* on capital is included in total cost because tying up resources in a firm's capital stock has an opportunity cost. If you start a business or buy a share of

stock in a corporation, you do so because you expect to make a normal rate of return. Investors will not invest their money in a business unless they expect to make a normal rate of return.

7. A positive profit level occurs when a firm is earning an above-normal rate of return on capital.

8. Two assumptions define the *short run*: (1) a fixed scale or fixed factor of production and (2) no entry to or exit from the industry. In the *long run*, firms can choose any scale of operations they want and firms can enter and leave the industry.

9. To make decisions, firms need to know three things: (1) the market price of their output, (2) the production techniques that are available, and (3) the prices of inputs.

THE PRODUCTION PROCESS p. 152

10. The relationship between inputs and outputs (the *production technology*) expressed numerically or mathematically is called a *production function* or *total product function*.

11. The *marginal product* of a variable input is the additional output that an added unit of that input will produce if all other inputs are held constant. According to the *law of diminishing returns*, when additional units of a variable input are added to fixed inputs, after a certain point, the marginal product of the variable input will decline.

12. *Average product* is the average amount of product produced by each unit of a variable factor of production. If marginal product is above average product, the average product rises; if marginal product is below average product, the average product falls.

13. Capital and labor are at the same time complementary and substitutable inputs. Capital enhances the productivity of labor, but it can also be substituted for labor.

CHOICE OF TECHNOLOGY p. 156

14. One of the key decisions that all firms must make is which technology to use. Profit-maximizing firms will choose the combination of inputs that minimizes costs and therefore maximizes profits.

REVIEW TERMS AND CONCEPTS

average product, *p. 154*

capital-intensive technology, *p. 152*

firm, *p. 148*

labor-intensive technology, *p. 152*

law of diminishing returns, *p. 154*

long run, *p. 151*

marginal product, *p. 153*

normal rate of return, *p. 149*

optimal method of production, *p. 151*

production, *p. 147*

production function *or* total product function, *p. 152*

production technology, *p. 152*

profit (economic profit), *p. 148*

short run, *p. 151*

total cost (total economic cost), *p. 148*

total revenue, *p. 148*

$Profit = total\ revenue - total\ cost$

$Average\ product\ of\ labor = \dfrac{total\ product}{total\ units\ of\ labor}$

PROBLEMS

All problems are available on www.myeconlab.com

1. Consider a firm that uses capital and labor as inputs and sells 5,000 units of output per year at the going market price of $10. Also assume that total labor costs to the firm are $45,000 annually. Assume further that the total capital stock of the firm is currently worth $100,000, that the return available to investors with comparable risks is 10 percent annually, and that there is no depreciation. Is this a profitable firm? Explain your answer.

2. Two former Northwestern University students worked in an investment bank at a salary of $60,000 each for 2 years after they graduated. Together they saved $50,000. After 2 years, they decided to quit their jobs and start a business designing Web sites. They used the $50,000 to buy computer equipment, desks, and chairs. For the next 2 years, they took in $40,000 in revenue each year, paid themselves $10,000 annually each, and rented an office for $18,000 per year. Prior to the investment, their $50,000 was in bonds earning interest at a rate of 10 percent. Are they now earning economic profits? Explain your answer.

3. Suppose that in 2010, you became president of a small non-profit theater company. Your playhouse has 120 seats and a small stage. The actors have national reputations, and demand for tickets is enormous relative to the number of seats available; every performance is sold out months in advance. You are elected because you have demonstrated an ability to raise funds successfully. Describe some of the decisions that you must make in the short run. What might you consider to be your "fixed factor"? What alternative decisions might you be able to make in the long run? Explain.

4. The following table gives total output or total product as a function of labor units used.

LABOR	TOTAL OUTPUT
0	0
1	5
2	9
3	12
4	14
5	15

a. Define diminishing returns.

b. Does the table indicate a situation of diminishing returns? Explain your answer.

5. Suppose that widgets can be produced using two different production techniques, *A* and *B*. The following table provides the total input requirements for each of five different total output levels.

	Q = 1		Q = 2		Q = 3		Q = 4		Q = 5	
Tech.	K	L	K	L	K	L	K	L	K	L
A	2	5	1	10	5	14	6	18	8	20
B	5	2	8	3	11	4	14	5	16	6

a. Assuming that the price of labor (P_L) is $1 and the price of capital (P_K) is $2, calculate the total cost of production for each of the five levels of output using the optimal (least-cost) technology at each level.

b. How many labor hours (units of labor) would be employed at each level of output? How many machine hours (units of capital)?

c. Graph total cost of production as a function of output. (Put cost on the *Y*-axis and output, *q*, on the *X*-axis.) Again assume that the optimal technology is used.

d. Repeat a. through c. under the assumption that the price of labor (P_L) rises from $1 to $3 while the price of capital (P_K) remains at $2.

6. A female student who lives on the fourth floor of Bates Hall is assigned to a new room on the seventh floor during her junior year. She has 11 heavy boxes of books and "stuff" to move. Discuss the alternative combinations of capital and labor that might be used to make the move. How would your answer differ if the move were to a new dorm 3 miles across campus and to a new college 400 miles away?

7. The following is a production function.

a. Draw a graph of marginal product as a function of output. (*Hint:* Marginal product is the additional number of units of output per unit of labor at each level of output.)

b. Does this graph exhibit diminishing returns? Explain your answer.

8. [Related to the *Economics in Practice* on *p. 156*] Identical sweaters can be made in one of two ways. With a machine that can be rented for $50 per hour and a person to run the machine who can be hired at $25 per hour, five sweaters can be produced in an hour using $10 worth of wool. Alternatively, I can run the machine with a less skilled worker, producing only four sweaters in an hour with the same $10 worth of wool. (The less skilled worker is slower and wastes material.) At what wage rate would I choose the less skilled worker?

9. [Related to the *Economics in Practice* on *p. 157*] When the price of fuel rises, we typically observe fewer accidents. Offer two reasons this might be true.

10. A firm earning zero economic profits is probably suffering losses from the standpoint of general accounting principles. Do you agree or disagree with this argument? Explain why.

11. During the early phases of industrialization, the number of people engaged in agriculture usually drops sharply, even as agricultural output is growing. Given what you know about production technology and production functions, explain this seeming inconsistency.

12. The number of repairs produced by a computer repair shop depends on the number of workers as follows:

NUMBER OF WORKERS	NUMBER OF REPAIRS (PER WEEK)
0	0
1	8
2	20
3	35
4	45
5	52
6	57
7	60

Assume that all inputs (office space, telephone, and utilities) other than labor are fixed in the short run.

a. Add two additional columns to the table and enter the marginal product and average product for each number of workers.

b. Over what range of labor input are there increasing returns to labor? diminishing returns to labor? negative returns to labor?

c. Over what range of labor input is marginal product greater than average product? What is happening to average product as employment increases over this range?

d. Over what range of labor input is marginal product smaller than average product? What is happening to average product as employment increases over this range?

13. Since the end of World War II, manufacturing firms in the United States and in Europe have been moving farther and farther outside of central cities. At the same time, firms in finance, insurance, and other parts of the service sector have been locating near downtown areas in tall buildings. One major reason seems to be that manufacturing firms find it difficult to substitute capital for land, while service-sector firms that use office space do not.

a. What kinds of buildings represent substitution of capital for land?

b. Why do you think that manufacturing firms might find it difficult to substitute capital for land?

c. Why is it relatively easier for a law firm or an insurance company to substitute capital for land?

d. Why is the demand for land likely to be very high near the center of a city?

*e. One of the reasons for substituting capital for land near the center of a city is that land is more expensive near the center. What is true about the relative supply of land near the center of a city? (*Hint:* What is the formula for the area of a circle?)

14. Ted Baxter runs a small, very stable newspaper company in southern Oregon. The paper has been in business for 25 years. The total value of the firm's capital stock is $1 million, which Ted owns outright. This year the firm earned a total of $250,000 after out-of-pocket expenses. Without taking the opportunity cost of capital into account, this means that Ted is earning a 25 percent return on his capital. Suppose that risk-free bonds are currently paying a rate of 10 percent to those who buy them.

a. What is meant by the "opportunity cost of capital"?

b. Explain why opportunity costs are "real" costs even though they do not necessarily involve out-of-pocket expenses.

*Note: Problems marked with an asterisk are more challenging.

c. What is the opportunity cost of Ted's capital?

d. How much excess profit is Ted earning?

15. A firm can use three different production technologies, with capital and labor requirements at each level of output as follows:

Daily Output	TECHNOLOGY 1		TECHNOLOGY 2		TECHNOLOGY 3	
	K	L	K	L	K	L
100	3	7	4	5	5	4
150	3	10	4	7	5	5
200	4	11	5	8	6	6
250	5	13	6	10	7	8

a. Suppose the firm is operating in a high-wage country, where capital cost is $100 per unit per day and labor cost is $80 per worker per day. For each level of output, which technology is cheapest?

b. Now suppose the firm is operating in a low-wage country, where capital cost is $100 per unit per day but labor cost is only $40 per unit per day. For each level of output, which technology is cheapest?

c. Suppose the firm moves from a high-wage to a low-wage country but its level of output remains constant at 200 units per day. How will its total employment change?

16. An article on Techspot.com reported on the findings of the marketing research firm iSuppli in its investigation of the cost of the components used to produce the Amazon Kindle 2: "After performing a "teardown," the firm concluded that each Kindle 2 runs approximately $185.49 to produce in-total, or 52% less than its [retail price] of $359." Does this mean that Amazon is making a profit of approximately $173 per Kindle 2?

Source: Matthew DeCarlo, "Teardown reveals production cost of Amazon's Kindle 2," *Techspot.com*, April 22, 2009.

17. The following table represents data for Samantha's Smoothies. Draw a graph showing the total product, marginal product of labor, and average product of labor. Identify where increasing returns, diminishing returns and negative returns set in on the total product curve.

LABOR UNITS (EMPLOYEES)	TOTAL PRODUCT (SMOOTHIES PER HOUR)	MARGINAL PRODUCT OF LABOR	AVERAGE PRODUCT OF LABOR
0	0	—	—
1	50	50	50.0
2	120	70	60.0
3	200	80	66.7
4	250	50	62.5
5	270	20	54.0
6	280	10	46.7
7	260	-20	37.1

18. Which of the following are short-run decisions and which are long-run decisions?

a. General Motors decides to add a second shift to its Arlington, Texas production plant.

b. Gotham Foods International chooses to exit the restaurant industry to concentrate on its wholesale grocery supply business.

c. The Sahara Hotel and Casino in Las Vegas closes two of its three hotel towers in response to low demand.

d. Tony Andretti, owner of Tony the Taxman, hires five new CPAs to work at his tax preparation business.

e. German tool and appliance manufacturer Bosch enters the electric bicycle industry in 2010.

f. General Electric builds a new offshore wind manufacturing plant in the United Kingdom.

19. The data in the table represents annual costs and revenue for Aurora's Orchid Emporium. Aurora works 60 hours a week at the Orchid Emporium, and if she closed the shop, she could rent out the building for $40,000 per year and go to work for Acme Flowers and earn a salary of $30,000 per year. Calculate the economic profit and economic cost for Aurora's Orchid Emporium. Are these figures the same as the accounting cost and accounting profit? Explain.

Wages Paid	$ 22,000
Interest Paid on Loans	8,000
Other Expenditures for Factors of Production	26,000
Total Revenue	115,000

20. Assume that we have a production process that exhibits increasing and then decreasing marginal productivity. That is, as we increase output, the marginal product of labor starts at some level above zero, rises to a maximum, and then eventually falls to zero. Which of the following statements is true? Briefly explain.

a. Total product reaches its highest level where marginal product is equal to average product.

b. Marginal product and average product are equal when marginal product is at its maximum.

c. When marginal product is equal to zero, average product is rising.

d. When marginal product is above average product, average product is rising.

e. When marginal product is equal to average product, output is maximized.

21. Following is information on the production levels of three different firms.

Firm A is currently producing at a quantity where it is experiencing increasing returns.

Firm B is currently producing at a quantity where it is experiencing diminishing returns.

Firm C is currently producing at a quantity where it is experiencing negative returns.

a. If each of the firms cut back on its labor force, what will happen to its marginal product of labor? Why?

b. If each of the firms adds to its labor force, what will happen to its marginal product of labor? Why?

CHAPTER 7 APPENDIX

Isoquants and Isocosts

This chapter has shown that the cost structure facing a firm depends on two key pieces of information: (1) input (factor) prices and (2) technology. This Appendix presents a more formal analysis of technology and factor prices and their relationship to cost.

New Look at Technology: Isoquants

Table 7A.1 is expanded from Table 7.3 to show the various combinations of capital (K) and labor (L) that can be used to produce three different levels of output (q). For example, 100 units of X can be produced with 2 units of capital and 10 units of labor, with 3 units of K and 6 units of L, or with 4 units of K and 4 units of L, and so on. Similarly, 150 units of X can be produced with 3 units of K and 10 units of L, with 4 units of K and 7 units of L, and so on.

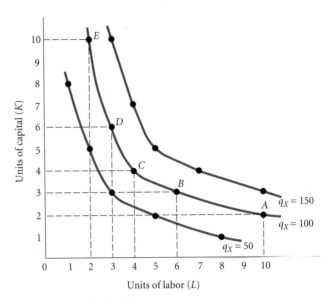

▲ **FIGURE 7A.1 Isoquants Showing All Combinations of Capital and Labor That Can Be Used to Produce 50, 100, and 150 Units of Output**

TABLE 7A.1 Alternative Combinations of Capital (K) and Labor (L) Required to Produce 50, 100, and 150 Units of Output

	$Q_X = 50$		$Q_X = 100$		$Q_X = 150$	
	K	L	K	L	K	L
A	1	8	2	10	3	10
B	2	5	3	6	4	7
C	3	3	4	4	5	5
D	5	2	6	3	7	4
E	8	1	10	2	10	3

A graph that shows all the combinations of capital and labor that can be used to produce a given amount of output is called an **isoquant**. Figure 7A.1 graphs three isoquants, one each for $q_X = 50$, $q_X = 100$, and $q_X = 150$ based on the data in Table 7A.1. Notice that all the points on the graph have been connected, indicating that there are an infinite number of combinations of labor and capital that can produce each level of output. For example, 100 units of output can also be produced with 3.50 units of labor and 4.75 units of capital. (Verify that this point is on the isoquant labeled $q_X = 100$.)

Figure 7A.1 shows only three isoquants, but many more are not shown. For example, there are separate isoquants for $q_X = 101$, $q_X = 102$, and so on. If we assume that producing fractions of a unit of output is possible, there must be an isoquant for $q_X = 134.57$, for $q_X = 124.82$, and so on. One could imagine an infinite number of isoquants in Figure 7A.1. The higher the level of output, the farther up and to the right the isoquant will lie.

Figure 7A.2 derives the slope of an isoquant. Because points F and G are both on the $q_X = 100$ isoquant, the two points represent two different combinations of K and L that can be used to produce 100 units of output. In moving from

point F to point G along the curve, less capital is employed but more labor is used. An approximation of the amount of output lost by using less capital is ΔK times the marginal product of capital (MP_K). The *marginal product of capital* is the number of units of output produced by a single marginal unit of capital. Thus, $\Delta K \cdot MP_K$ is the total output lost by using less capital.

For output to remain constant (as it must because F and G are on the same isoquant), the loss of output from using less capital must be matched by the added output produced by using more labor. This amount can be approximated by ΔL times the marginal product of labor (MP_L). Because the two must be equal, it follows that

$$\Delta K \cdot MP_K = -\Delta L \cdot MP_L{}^1$$

If we then divide both sides of this equation by ΔL and then by MP_K, we arrive at the following expression for the slope of the isoquant:

$$\text{slope of isoquant:} \quad \frac{\Delta K}{\Delta L} = -\frac{MP_L}{MP_K}$$

The ratio of MP_L to MP_K is called the **marginal rate of technical substitution**. It is the rate at which a firm can substitute capital for labor and hold output constant.

---

[1] We need to add the negative sign to ΔL because in moving from point F to point G, ΔK is a negative number and ΔL is a positive number. The minus sign is needed to balance the equation.

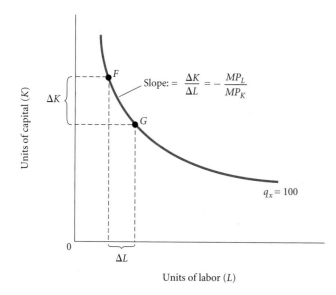

▲ **FIGURE 7A.2 The Slope of an Isoquant Is Equal to the Ratio of MP_L to MP_K**

Factor Prices and Input Combinations: Isocosts

A graph that shows all the combinations of capital and labor that are available for a given total cost is called an **isocost line**. (Recall that total cost includes opportunity costs and normal rate of return.) Just as there are an infinite number of isoquants (one for every possible level of output), there are an infinite number of isocost lines, one for every possible level of total cost.

Figure 7A.3 shows three simple isocost lines assuming that the price of labor (P_L) is $1 per unit and the price of capital (P_K) is $1 per unit. The lowest isocost line shows all the combinations of K and L that can be purchased for $5. For example, $5 will buy 5 units of labor and no capital (point A), 3 units of labor and 2 units of capital (point B), or no units of labor and 5 units of capital (point C). All these points lie along a straight line. The equation of that straight line is

$$(P_K \cdot K) + (P_L \cdot L) = TC$$

Substituting our data for the lowest isocost line into this general equation, we get

$$(\$1 \cdot K) + (\$1 \cdot L) = \$5, \text{ or } K + L = 5$$

Remember that the X- and Y-scales are units of labor and units of capital, not dollars.

On the same graph are two additional isocosts showing the various combinations of K and L available for a total cost of $6 and $7. These are only three of an infinite number of isocosts. At any total cost, there is an isocost that shows all the combinations of K and L available for that amount.

Figure 7A.4 shows another isocost line. This isocost assumes a different set of factor prices, $P_L = \$5$ and $P_K = \$1$. The diagram shows all the combinations of K and L that can be bought for $25. One way to draw the line is to determine the endpoints. For example, if the entire $25 were spent on labor, how much labor could be purchased? The answer is, of course, 5 units ($25 divided by $5 per

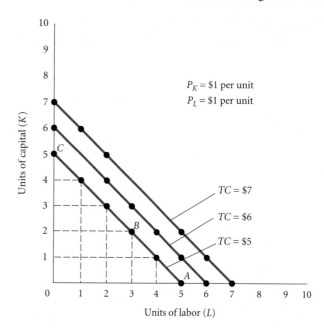

▲ **FIGURE 7A.3 Isocost Lines Showing the Combinations of Capital and Labor Available for $5, $6, and $7**

An isocost line shows all the combinations of capital and labor that are available for a given total cost.

unit). Thus, point A, which represents 5 units of labor and no capital, is on the isocost line. Similarly, if all of the $25 were spent on capital, how much capital could be purchased? The answer is 25 units ($25 divided by $1 per unit). Thus, point B, which represents 25 units of capital and no labor, is also on the isocost line. Another point on this particular isocost is 3 units of labor and 10 units of capital, point C.

The slope of an isocost line can be calculated easily if you first find the endpoints of the line. In Figure 7A.4, we can calculate the slope of the isocost line by taking $\Delta K / \Delta L$ between points B and A. Thus,

$$\text{slope of isocost line: } \frac{\Delta K}{\Delta L} = -\frac{TC/P_K}{TC/P_L} = -\frac{P_L}{P_K}$$

Plugging in the endpoints from our example, we get

$$\text{slope of line } AB = -\frac{\$5}{\$1} = -5$$

Finding the Least-Cost Technology with Isoquants and Isocosts

Figure 7A.5 superimposes the isoquant for $q_X = 50$ on the isocost lines in Figure 7A.3, which assume that $P_K = \$1$ and $P_L = \$1$. The question now becomes one of choosing among the combinations of K and L that can be used to produce 50 units of output. Recall that each point on the isoquant (labeled $q_X = 50$ in Figure 7A.5) represents a different technology—a different combination of K and L.

We assume that our firm is a perfectly competitive, profit-maximizing firm that will choose the combination that minimizes

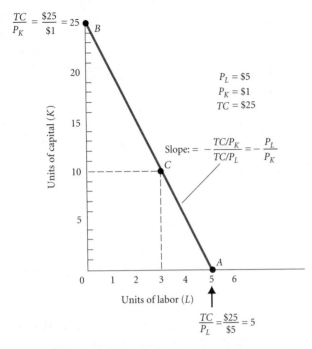

▲ **FIGURE 7A.4 Isocost Line Showing All Combinations of Capital and Labor Available for $25**

One way to draw an isocost line is to determine the endpoints of that line and draw a line connecting them.

▲ **FIGURE 7A.5 Finding the Least-Cost Combination of Capital and Labor to Produce 50 Units of Output**

Profit-maximizing firms will minimize costs by producing their chosen level of output with the technology represented by the point at which the isoquant is tangent to an isocost line. Here the cost-minimizing technology—3 units of capital and 3 units of labor—is represented by point C.

cost. Because every point on the isoquant lies on some particular isocost line, we can determine the total cost for each combination along the isoquant. For example, point D (5 units of capital and 2 units of labor) lies along the isocost for a total cost of $7. Notice that 5 units of capital and 2 units of labor cost a total of $7. (Remember, $P_K = \$1$ and $P_L = \$1$.) The same amount of output (50 units) can be produced at lower cost. Specifically, by using 3 units of labor and 3 units of capital (point C), total cost is reduced to $6. *No other combination of K and L along isoquant* $q_X = 50$ *is on a lower isocost line.* In seeking to maximize profits, the firm will choose the combination of inputs that is least costly. The least costly way to produce any given level of output is indicated by the point of tangency between an isocost line and the isoquant corresponding to that level of output.[2]

In Figure 7A.5, the least-cost technology of producing 50 units of output is represented by point C, the point at which the $q_X = 50$ isoquant is just tangent to—that is, just touches—the isocost line.

Figure 7A.6 adds the other two isoquants from Figure 7A.1 to Figure 7A.5. Assuming that $P_K = \$1$ and $P_L = \$1$, the firm will move along each of the three isoquants until it finds the least-cost combination of K and L that can be used to produce that particular level of output. The result is plotted in

Figure 7A.7. The minimum cost of producing 50 units of X is $6, the minimum cost of producing 100 units of X is $8, and the minimum cost of producing 150 units of X is $10.

The Cost-Minimizing Equilibrium Condition

At the point where a line is just tangent to a curve, the two have the same slope. (We have already derived expressions for the slope of an isocost and the slope of an isoquant.) At each point of tangency (such as at points A, B, and C in Figure 7A.6), the following must be true:

$$\text{slope of isoquant} = -\frac{MP_L}{MP_K} = \text{slope of isocost} = -\frac{P_L}{P_K}$$

Thus,

$$\frac{MP_L}{MP_K} = \frac{P_L}{P_K}$$

Dividing both sides by P_L and multiplying both sides by MP_K, we get

$$\frac{MP_L}{P_L} = \frac{MP_K}{P_K}$$

This is the firm's cost-minimizing equilibrium condition.

This expression makes sense if you think about what it says. The left side of the equation is the marginal product of labor

---

[2] This assumes that the isoquants are continuous and convex (bowed) toward the origin.

▲ **FIGURE 7A.6 Minimizing Cost of Production for** q_X = 50, q_X = 100, and q_X = 150

Plotting a series of cost-minimizing combinations of inputs—shown in this graph as points A, B, and C—on a separate graph results in a *cost curve* like the one shown in Figure 7A.7.

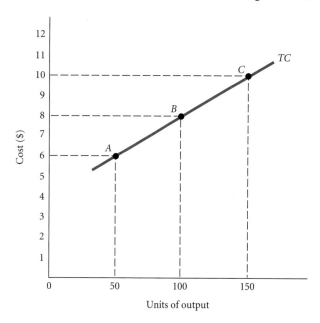

▲ **FIGURE 7A.7 A Cost Curve Shows the** *Minimum* **Cost of Producing Each Level of Output**

divided by the price of a unit of labor. Thus, it is the product derived from the last dollar spent on labor. The right-hand side of the equation is the product derived from the last dollar spent on capital. If the product derived from the last dollar

spent on labor was not equal to the product derived from the last dollar spent on capital, the firm could decrease costs by using more labor and less capital or by using more capital and less labor.

Look back to Chapter 6 and see if you can find a similar expression and some similar logic in our discussion of household behavior. In fact, there is great symmetry between the theory of the firm and the theory of household behavior.

─────────────── **APPENDIX SUMMARY** ───────────────

1. An *isoquant* is a graph that shows all the combinations of capital and labor that can be used to produce a given amount of output. The slope of an isoquant is equal to $-MP_L/MP_K$. The ratio of MP_L to MP_K is the *marginal rate of technical substitution*. It is the rate at which a firm can substitute capital for labor and hold output constant.

2. An *isocost line* is a graph that shows all the combinations of capital and labor that are available for a given total cost. The slope of an isocost line is equal to $-P_L/P_K$.

3. The least-cost method of producing a given amount of output is found graphically at the point at which an isocost line is just tangent to—that is, just touches—the isoquant corresponding to that level of production. The firm's cost-minimizing equilibrium condition is $MP_L/P_L = MP_K/P_K$.

──────── **APPENDIX REVIEW TERMS AND CONCEPTS** ────────

isocost line   A graph that shows all the combinations of capital and labor available for a given total cost. *p. 163*

isoquant   A graph that shows all the combinations of capital and labor that can be used to produce a given amount of output. *p. 162*

marginal rate of technical substitution The rate at which a firm can substitute capital for labor and hold output constant. *p. 162*

1. Slope of isoquant:

$$\frac{\Delta K}{\Delta L} = -\frac{MP_L}{MP_K}$$

2. Slope of isocost line:

$$\frac{\Delta K}{\Delta L} = -\frac{TC/P_K}{TC/P_L} = -\frac{P_L}{P_K}$$

APPENDIX PROBLEMS

1. Assume that $MP_L = 5$ and $MP_K = 10$. Assume also that $P_L = \$2$ and $P_K = \$5$. This implies that the firm should substitute labor for capital. Explain why.

2. In the isoquant/isocost diagram (Figure 1) suppose the firm is producing 1,000 units of output at point A using 100 units of labor and 200 units of capital. As an outside consultant, what actions would you suggest to management to improve profits? What would you recommend if the firm were operating at point B, using 100 units of capital and 200 units of labor?

TABLE 1			
OUTPUT UNITS	TOTAL COST OF OUTPUT	UNITS OF LABOR DEMANDED	UNITS OF CAPITAL DEMANDED
100			
200			
300			

4. Each month a company can rent capital for $5,000 per unit and can hire workers for $2,000 each. Currently, the company is using 2 units of capital and 5 workers to produce 10,000 units of output. This combination of capital and labor represents a cost-minimizing equilibrium. Draw an isoquant/isocost diagram to illustrate this situation.

5. The Red Racer Company and the Blue Bomber Company are each capable of minimizing cost and producing 4,000 bicycles per month. Red Racer's factory is located in an area where the cost of labor is significantly less and the cost of capital is significantly more than the costs of labor and capital for Blue Bomber. Assume that each company has access to the same technology to produce bicycles and draw an isoquant/isocost diagram to illustrate why the cost-minimizing combinations of inputs for these companies are different. Be sure to identify the isocost line, amount of capital, amount of labor, and cost-minimizing combination of inputs for each company.

▲ **FIGURE 1**

3. Using the information from the isoquant/isocost diagram (Figure 2) and assuming that $P_L = P_K = \$2$, complete Table 1.

▲ **FIGURE 2**

Short-Run Costs and Output Decisions

This chapter continues our examination of the decisions that firms make in their quest for profits. You have seen that firms make three specific decisions (Figure 8.1) involving their production. These decisions are:

1. How much output to supply
2. How to produce that output —that is, which production technique/technology to use
3. What quantity of each input to demand

We have assumed so far that firms are in business to earn profits and that they make choices to maximize those profits. (Remember that *profit* refers to economic profit, the difference between revenues and costs—full economic costs.)

In the last chapter, we focused on the production process. This chapter focuses on the *costs* of production. To calculate costs, a firm must know two things: what quantity and combination of inputs it needs to produce its product and how much those inputs cost. (Do not forget that economic costs include a normal return to capital—the opportunity cost of capital.)

Take a moment and look back at the circular flow diagram, Figure II.1 on p. 117. There you can see where we are in our study of the competitive market system. The goal of this chapter is to look behind the supply curve in output markets. It is important to understand, however, that producing output implies demanding inputs at the same time. You can also see in Figure II.1 two of the information sources that firms use in their output supply and input demand decisions: Firms look to *output markets* for the price of output and to *input markets* for the prices of capital and labor.

DECISIONS	are based on	INFORMATION
1. The quantity of output to *supply*		1. The price of output
2. How to produce that output (which technique to use)		2. Techniques of production available*
3. The quantity of each input to *demand*		3. The price of inputs*
		*Determines production costs

◀ **FIGURE 8.1 Decisions Facing Firms**

Costs in the Short Run

Our emphasis in this chapter is on costs *in the short run only*. Recall that the short run is that period during which two conditions hold: (1) existing firms face limits imposed by some fixed factor of production, and (2) new firms cannot enter and existing firms cannot exit an industry.

In the short run, all firms (competitive and noncompetitive) have costs that they must bear regardless of their output. In fact, some costs must be paid even if the firm stops producing—that is, even if output is zero. These costs are called **fixed costs**, and firms can do nothing in the short run to avoid them or to change them. In the long run, a firm has no fixed costs because it can expand, contract, or exit the industry.

Firms also have certain costs in the short run that depend on the level of output they have chosen. These kinds of costs are called **variable costs**. Total fixed costs and total variable costs together make up **total costs**:

$$TC = TFC + TVC$$

where *TC* denotes total costs, *TFC* denotes total fixed costs, and *TVC* denotes total variable costs. We will return to this equation after discussing fixed costs and variable costs in detail.

Fixed Costs

In discussing fixed costs, we must distinguish between total fixed costs and average fixed costs.

Total Fixed Cost (*TFC*)   Total fixed cost is sometimes called *overhead*. If you operate a factory, you must heat the building to keep the pipes from freezing in the winter. Even if no production is taking place, you may have to keep the roof from leaking, pay a guard to protect the building from vandals, and make payments on a long-term lease. There may also be insurance premiums, taxes, and city fees to pay, as well as contract obligations to workers.

Fixed costs represent a larger portion of total costs for some firms than for others. Electric companies, for instance, maintain generating plants, thousands of miles of distribution wires, poles, transformers, and so on. Usually, such plants are financed by issuing bonds to the public—that is, by borrowing. The interest that must be paid on these bonds represents a substantial part of the utilities' operating cost and is a fixed cost in the short run, no matter how much (if any) electricity they are producing.

For the purposes of our discussion in this chapter, we will assume that firms use only two inputs: labor and capital. Although this may seem unrealistic, virtually everything that we will say about firms using these two factors can easily be generalized to firms that use many factors of production. Recall that capital yields services over time in the production of other goods and services. It is the plant and equipment of a manufacturing firm and the computers, desks, chairs, doors, and walls of a law office; it is the software of a Web-based firm and the boat that Bill and Colleen built on their desert island. It is sometimes assumed that capital is a fixed input in the short run and that labor is the only variable input. To be more realistic, however, we will assume that capital has both a fixed *and* a variable component. After all, some capital can be purchased in the short run.

Consider a small consulting firm that employs several economists, research assistants, and secretaries. It rents space in an office building and has a 5-year lease. The rent on the office space can be thought of as a fixed cost in the short run. The monthly electric and heating bills are also essentially fixed (although the amounts may vary slightly from month to month). So are the salaries of the basic administrative staff. Payments on some capital equipment—a large copying machine and the main word-processing system, for instance—can also be thought of as fixed.

The same firm also has costs that vary with output. When there is a great deal of work, the firm hires more employees at both the professional and research assistant levels. The capital used by the consulting firm may also vary, even in the short run. Payments on the computer system do not change, but the firm may rent additional computer time when necessary. The firm can buy additional personal computers, network terminals, or databases quickly if needed. It must pay for the copy machine, but the machine costs more when it is running than when it is not.

Total fixed costs (*TFC*) or overhead are those costs that do not change with output even if output is zero. Column 2 of Table 8.1 presents data on the fixed costs of a hypothetical firm. Fixed costs are $1,000 at all levels of output (*q*). Figure 8.2(a) shows total fixed costs as a function of

---

fixed cost   Any cost that does not depend on the firms' level of output. These costs are incurred even if the firm is producing nothing. There are no fixed costs in the long run.

variable cost   A cost that depends on the level of production chosen.

total cost (*TC*)   Total fixed costs plus total variable costs.

total fixed costs (*TFC*) or overhead   The total of all costs that do not change with output even if output is zero.

output. Because *TFC* does not change with output, the graph is simply a straight horizontal line at $1,000. The important thing to remember here is that firms have no control over fixed costs in the short run.

TABLE 8.1	Short-Run Fixed Cost (Total and Average) of a Hypothetical Firm	
(1) q	(2) TFC	(3) AFC (TFC/q)
0	$1,000	$ –
1	1,000	1,000
2	1,000	500
3	1,000	333
4	1,000	250
5	1,000	200

Average Fixed Cost (AFC)   **Average fixed cost (AFC)** is total fixed cost (*TFC*) divided by the number of units of output (*q*):

$$AFC = \frac{TFC}{q}$$

For example, if the firm in Figure 8.2 produced 3 units of output, average fixed costs would be $333 ($1,000 ÷ 3). If the same firm produced 5 units of output, average fixed cost would be $200 ($1,000 ÷ 5). *Average fixed cost falls as output rises* because the same total is being spread over, or divided by, a larger number of units (see column 3 of Table 8.1). This phenomenon is sometimes called **spreading overhead**.

Graphs of average fixed cost, like that in Figure 8.2(b) (which presents the average fixed cost data from Table 8.1), are downward-sloping curves. Notice that *AFC* approaches zero as the quantity of output increases. If output were 100,000 units, average fixed cost would equal only 1 cent per unit in our example ($1,000 ÷ 100,000 = $0.01). *AFC* never actually reaches zero.

average fixed cost (AFC) Total fixed cost divided by the number of units of output; a per-unit measure of fixed costs.

spreading overhead The process of dividing total fixed costs by more units of output. Average fixed cost declines as quantity rises.

Variable Costs

Total Variable Cost (TVC)   **Total variable cost (TVC)** is the sum of those costs that vary with the level of output in the short run. To produce more output, a firm uses more inputs. The cost of additional output depends directly on what additional inputs are required and how much they cost.

total variable cost (TVC) The total of all costs that vary with output in the short run.

▲ **FIGURE 8.2 Short-Run Fixed Cost (Total and Average) of a Hypothetical Firm**
Average fixed cost is simply total fixed cost divided by the quantity of output. As output increases, average fixed cost declines because we are dividing a fixed number ($1,000) by a larger and larger quantity.

As you saw in Chapter 7, input requirements are determined by technology. Firms generally have a number of production techniques available to them, and the option they choose is assumed to be the one that produces the desired level of output at the least cost. To find out which technology involves the least cost, a firm must compare the total variable costs of producing that level of output using different production techniques.

This is as true of small businesses as it is of large manufacturing firms. Suppose, for example, that you own a small farm. A certain amount of work has to be done to plant and harvest your 120 acres. You might hire four farmhands and divide up the tasks, or you might buy several pieces of complex farm machinery (capital) and do the work single-handedly. Your final choice depends on a number of things. What machinery is available? What does it do? Will it work on small fields such as yours? How much will it cost to buy each piece of equipment? What wage will you have to pay farmhands? How many will you need to hire to get the job done? If machinery is expensive and labor is cheap, you will probably choose the labor-intensive technology. If farm labor is expensive and the local farm equipment dealer is going out of business, you might get a good deal on some machinery and choose the capital-intensive method.

Having compared the costs of alternative production techniques, the firm may be influenced in its choice by the current scale of its operation. Remember, in the short run, a firm is locked into a *fixed* scale of operations. A firm currently producing on a small scale may find that a labor-intensive technique is least costly whether or not labor is comparatively expensive. The same firm producing on a larger scale might find a capital-intensive technique to be less costly.

total variable cost curve A graph that shows the relationship between total variable cost and the level of a firm's output.

The **total variable cost curve** is a graph that shows the relationship between total variable cost and the level of a firm's output (q). At any given level of output, total variable cost depends on (1) the techniques of production that are available and (2) the prices of the inputs required by each technology. To examine this relationship in more detail, let us look at some hypothetical production figures.

Table 8.2 presents an analysis that might lie behind three points on a typical firm's total variable cost curve. In this case, there are two production techniques available, A and B, one somewhat more capital-intensive than the other. We will assume that the price of labor is $1 per unit and the price of capital is $2 per unit. For the purposes of this example, we focus on *variable capital*—that is, on capital that can be changed in the short run. In practice, some capital (such as buildings and large, specialized machines) is fixed in the short run. In our example, we will use K to denote variable capital. Remember, however, that the firm has other capital, capital that is fixed in the short run.

Analysis reveals that to produce 1 unit of output, the labor-intensive technique is least costly. Technique A requires 4 units of both capital and labor, which would cost a total of $12. Technique B requires 6 units of labor but only 2 units of capital for a total cost of only $10. To maximize profits, the firm would use technique B to produce 1 unit. The total variable cost of producing 1 unit of output would thus be $10.

The relatively labor-intensive technique B is also the best method of production for 2 units of output. By using B, the firm can produce 2 units for $18. If the firm decides to produce 3 units of output, however, technique A is cheaper. By using the least-cost technology (A), the total variable cost of production is $24. The firm will use 9 units of capital at $2 each and 6 units of labor at $1 each.

Figure 8.3 graphs the relationship between total variable cost and output based on the data in Table 8.2, assuming the firm chooses the least-cost technology for each output. The total

TABLE 8.2 Derivation of Total Variable Cost Schedule from Technology and Factor Prices

Produce	Using Technique	Units of Input Required (Production Function) K	L	Total Variable Cost Assuming $P_K = \$2, P_L = \$1$ $TVC = (K \times P_K) + (L \times P_L)$
1 unit of output	A	4	4	$(4 \times \$2) + (4 \times \$1) = \$12$
	B	2	6	$(2 \times \$2) + (6 \times \$1) = \boxed{\$10}$
2 units of output	A	7	6	$(7 \times \$2) + (6 \times \$1) = \$20$
	B	4	10	$(4 \times \$2) + (10 \times \$1) = \boxed{\$18}$
3 units of output	A	9	6	$(9 \times \$2) + (6 \times \$1) = \boxed{\$24}$
	B	6	14	$(6 \times \$2) + (14 \times \$1) = \$26$

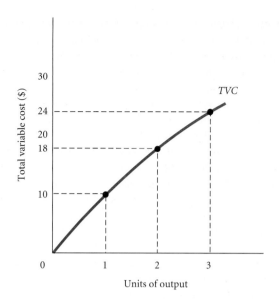

◀ **FIGURE 8.3** **Total Variable Cost Curve**
In Table 8.2, total variable cost is derived from production requirements and input prices. A total variable cost curve expresses the relationship between *TVC* and total output.

variable cost curve embodies information about both factor, or input, prices and technology. It shows the cost of production using the best available technique at each output level given current factor prices.

Marginal Cost (*MC*)   The most important of all cost concepts is that of **marginal cost (*MC*)**, the increase in total cost that results from the production of 1 more unit of output. Let us say, for example, that a firm is producing 1,000 units of output per period and decides to raise its rate of output to 1,001. Producing the extra unit raises costs, and the increase—that is, the cost of producing the 1,001st unit—is the marginal cost. Focusing on the "margin" is one way of looking at variable costs: marginal costs reflect changes in variable costs because they vary when output changes. Fixed costs do not change when output changes.

> **marginal cost (*MC*)**   The increase in total cost that results from producing 1 more unit of output. Marginal costs reflect changes in variable costs.

Table 8.3 shows how marginal cost is derived from total variable cost by simple subtraction. The total variable cost of producing the first unit of output is $10. Raising production from 1 unit to 2 units increases total variable cost from $10 to $18; the difference is the marginal cost of the second unit, or $8. Raising output from 2 to 3 units increases total variable cost from $18 to $24. The marginal cost of the third unit, therefore, is $6.

TABLE 8.3 Derivation of Marginal Cost from Total Variable Cost		
Units of Output	Total Variable Costs ($)	Marginal Costs ($)
0	0	
1	10	10
2	18	8
3	24	6

It is important to think for a moment about the nature of marginal cost. Specifically, marginal cost is the cost of the added inputs, or resources, needed to produce 1 additional unit of output. Look back at Table 8.2 and think about the additional capital and labor needed to go from 1 unit to 2 units. Producing 1 unit of output with technique *B* requires 2 units of capital and 6 units of labor; producing 2 units of output using the same technique requires 4 units of capital and 10 units of labor. Thus, the second unit requires 2 *additional* units of capital and 4 *additional* units of labor. What, then, is the added, or marginal, cost of the second unit? Two units of capital cost $2 each ($4 total) and 4 units of labor cost $1 each (another $4), for a total marginal cost of $8, which is the number we derived in Table 8.3. Although the easiest way to derive marginal cost is to look at total variable cost and subtract, do not lose sight of the fact that when a firm increases its output level, it hires or demands more inputs. *Marginal cost* measures the *additional* cost of inputs required to produce each successive unit of output.

The Shape of the Marginal Cost Curve in the Short Run   The assumption of a fixed factor of production in the short run means that a firm is stuck at its current scale of operation (in our example, the size of the plant). As a firm tries to increase its output, it will eventually find itself trapped by that scale. Thus, our definition of the short run also implies that *marginal cost eventually rises with output*. The firm can hire more labor and use more materials—that is, it can add variable inputs—but diminishing returns eventually set in.

Recall from Chapter 7 the sandwich shop with one grill and too many workers trying to prepare sandwiches on it. With a fixed grill capacity, more laborers could make more sandwiches, but the marginal product of each successive cook declined as more people tried to use the grill. If each additional unit of labor adds less and less to total output, *it follows that more labor is needed to produce each additional unit of output*. Thus, each additional unit of output costs more to produce. In other words, *diminishing returns, or decreasing marginal product, imply increasing marginal cost* as illustrated in Figure 8.4.

To reiterate:

> In the short run, every firm is constrained by some fixed input that (1) leads to diminishing returns to variable inputs and (2) limits its capacity to produce. As a firm approaches that capacity, it becomes increasingly costly to produce successively higher levels of output. Marginal costs ultimately increase with output in the short run.

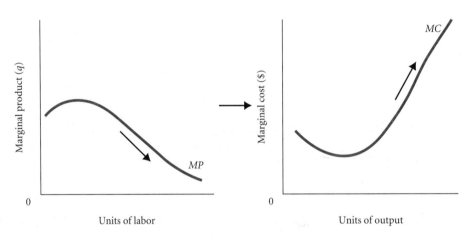

▲ **FIGURE 8.4 Declining Marginal Product Implies That Marginal Cost Will Eventually Rise with Output**

In the short run, every firm is constrained by some fixed factor of production. A fixed factor implies diminishing returns (declining marginal product) and a limited capacity to produce. As that limit is approached, marginal costs rise.

Graphing Total Variable Costs and Marginal Costs   Figure 8.5 shows the total variable cost curve and the marginal cost curve of a typical firm. Notice first that the shape of the marginal cost curve is consistent with short-run diminishing returns. At first, *MC* declines, but eventually the fixed factor of production begins to constrain the firm and marginal cost rises. Up to 100 units of output, producing each successive unit of output costs slightly less than producing the one before. Beyond 100 units, however, the cost of each successive unit is greater than the one before. (Remember the sandwich shop.)

More output costs more than less output. Total variable costs (*TVC*), therefore, *always increase* when output increases. Even though the cost of each additional unit changes, *total* variable cost rises when output rises. Thus, the *total* variable cost curve always has a positive slope.

You might think of the total variable cost curve as a staircase. Each step takes you out along the quantity axis by a single unit, and the height of each step is the increase in total variable cost.

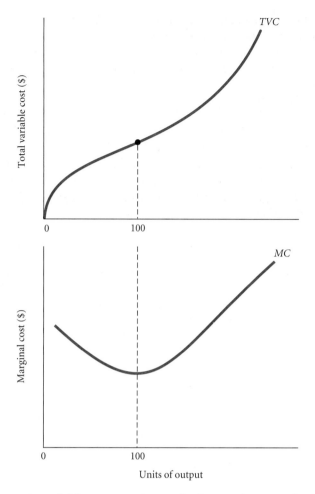

▲ **FIGURE 8.5 Total Variable Cost and Marginal Cost for a Typical Firm**
Total variable costs always increase with output. Marginal cost is the cost of producing each additional unit.
Thus, the marginal cost curve shows how total variable cost changes with single-unit increases in total output.

As you climb the stairs, you are always going up, but the steps have different heights. At first, the stairway is steep, but as you climb, the steps get smaller (marginal cost declines). The 100th stair is the smallest. As you continue to walk out beyond 100 units, the steps begin to get larger; the staircase gets steeper (marginal cost increases).

Remember that the slope of a line is equal to the change in the units measured on the *Y*-axis divided by the change in the units measured on the *X*-axis. The slope of a total variable cost curve is thus the change in total variable cost divided by the change in output ($\Delta TVC/\Delta q$). Because marginal cost is by definition the change in total variable cost resulting from an increase in output of one unit ($\Delta q = 1$), *marginal cost actually is the slope of the total variable cost curve*:

$$\text{slope of } TVC = \frac{\Delta TVC}{\Delta q} = \frac{\Delta TVC}{1} = \Delta TVC = MC$$

Notice that up to 100 units, marginal cost decreases and the variable cost curve becomes flatter. The slope of the total variable cost curve is declining—that is, total variable cost increases, but at a *decreasing rate*. Beyond 100 units of output, marginal cost increases and the total variable cost curve gets steeper—total variable costs continue to increase, but at an *increasing rate*.

A more complete picture of the costs of a hypothetical firm appears in Table 8.4. Column 2 shows total variable costs derived from information on input prices and technology. Column 3 derives marginal cost by simple subtraction. For example, raising output from 3 units to 4 units increases variable costs from $24 to $32, making the marginal cost of the fourth unit $8 ($32 − $24). The marginal cost of the fifth unit is $10, the difference between $32 (*TVC*) for 4 units and $42 (*TVC*) for 5 units.

average variable cost (AVC)
Total variable cost divided by the number of units of output.

Average Variable Cost (AVC)

Average variable cost (AVC) is total variable cost divided by the number of units of output (q):

$$AVC = \frac{TVC}{q}$$

In Table 8.4, we calculate *AVC* in column 4 by dividing the numbers in column 2 (*TVC*) by the numbers in column 1 (*q*). For example, if the total variable cost of producing 5 units of output is $42, then the average variable cost is $42 ÷ 5, or $8.40. Marginal cost is the cost of 1 *additional unit*. Average variable cost is the total variable cost divided by the total number of units produced.

		(3)	(4)		(6)	(7)	(8)
(1)	(2)	MC	AVC	(5)	TC	AFC	ATC
q	TVC	(Δ TVC)	(TVC/q)	TFC	(TVC + TFC)	(TFC/q)	(TC/q or AFC + AVC)
0	$ 0	$ –	$ –	$1,000	$1,000	$ –	$ –
1	10	10	10	1,000	1,010	1,000	1,010
2	18	8	9	1,000	1,018	500	509
3	24	6	8	1,000	1,024	333	341
4	32	8	8	1,000	1,032	250	258
5	42	10	8.4	1,000	1,042	200	208.4
—	—	—	—	—	—	—	—
—	—	—	—	—	—	—	—
—	—	—	—	—	—	—	—
500	8,000	20	16	1,000	9,000	2	18

TABLE 8.4 Short-Run Costs of a Hypothetical Firm

Graphing Average Variable Costs and Marginal Costs The relationship between average variable cost and marginal cost can be illustrated graphically. When marginal cost is *below* average variable cost, average variable cost declines toward it. When marginal cost is *above* average variable cost, average variable cost increases toward it.

Figure 8.6 duplicates the bottom graph for a typical firm in Figure 8.5 but adds average variable cost. As the graph shows, average variable cost *follows* marginal cost but lags behind. As we move from left to right, we are looking at higher and higher levels of output per period. As we increase production, marginal cost—which at low levels of production is above $3.50 per unit—falls as coordination and cooperation begin to play a role. At 100 units of output, marginal cost has fallen to $2.50. Notice that average variable cost falls as well, but not as rapidly as marginal cost.

After 100 units of output, we begin to see diminishing returns. Marginal cost begins to increase as higher and higher levels of output are produced. However, notice that average cost is still falling until 200 units because marginal cost remains below it. At 100 units of output, marginal cost is $2.50 per unit but the *average* variable cost of production is $3.50. Thus, even though marginal cost is rising after 100 units, it is still pulling the average of $3.50 downward.

▶ **FIGURE 8.6 More Short-Run Costs**

When marginal cost is *below* average cost, average cost is declining. When marginal cost is *above* average cost, average cost is increasing. Rising marginal cost intersects average variable cost at the minimum point of *AVC*.

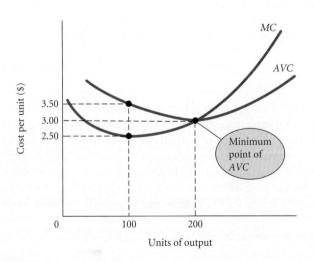

At 200 units, however, marginal cost has risen to $3 and average cost has fallen to $3; marginal and average costs are equal. At this point, marginal cost continues to rise with higher output. From 200 units upward, *MC* is *above AVC* and thus exerts an upward pull on the average variable cost curve. At levels of output below 200 units, marginal cost is below average variable cost and average variable cost decreases as output increases. At levels of output above 200 units, *MC* is above *AVC* and *AVC* increases as output increases. If you follow this logic, you will see that marginal cost intersects average variable cost at the lowest, or minimum, point of *AVC*.

An example using test scores should help you understand the relationship between *MC* and *AVC*. Consider the following sequence of test scores: 95, 85, 92, 88. The average of these four scores is 90. Suppose you get an 80 on your fifth test. This score will drag down your average to 88. Now suppose you get an 85 on your sixth test. This score is higher than 80, but its still *below* your 88 average. As a result, your average continues to fall (from 88 to 87.5) even though your marginal test score rose. If instead of an 85 you get an 89—just one point over your average—you have turned your average around; it is now rising.

Total Costs

We are now ready to complete the cost picture by adding total fixed costs to total variable costs. Recall that

$$TC = TFC + TVC$$

Total cost is graphed in Figure 8.7, where the same vertical distance (equal to *TFC*, which is constant) is simply added to *TVC* at every level of output. In Table 8.4, column 6 adds the total fixed cost of $1,000 to total variable cost to arrive at total cost.

Average Total Cost (*ATC*)   Average total cost (*ATC*) is total cost divided by the number of units of output (*q*):

average total cost (*ATC*) Total cost divided by the number of units of output.

$$ATC = \frac{TC}{q}$$

Column 8 in Table 8.4 shows the result of dividing the costs in column 6 by the quantities in column 1. For example, at 5 units of output, *total* cost is $1,042; *average* total cost is $1,042 ÷ 5, or $208.40. The average total cost of producing 500 units of output is only $18—that is, $9,000 ÷ 500.

Another, more revealing, way of deriving average total cost is to add average fixed cost and average variable cost together:

$$ATC = AFC + AVC$$

For example, column 8 in Table 8.4 is the sum of column 4 (*AVC*) and column 7 (*AFC*).

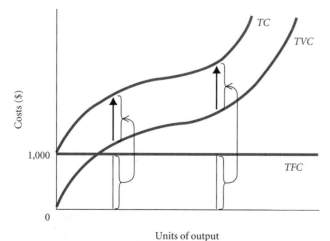

▲ **FIGURE 8.7 Total Cost = Total Fixed Cost + Total Variable Cost**
Adding *TFC* to *TVC* means adding the same amount of total fixed cost to every level of total variable cost. Thus, the total cost curve has the same shape as the total variable cost curve; it is simply higher by an amount equal to *TFC*.

Figure 8.8 derives average total cost graphically for a typical firm. The bottom part of the figure graphs average fixed cost. At 100 units of output, average fixed cost is $TFC/q = \$1,000 \div 100 = \$10$. At 400 units of output, $AFC = \$1,000 \div 400 = \$2.50$. The top part of Figure 8.8 shows the declining AFC added to AVC at each level of output. Because AFC gets smaller and smaller, ATC gets closer and closer to AVC as output increases, but the two lines never meet.

The Relationship Between Average Total Cost and Marginal Cost The relationship between average *total* cost and marginal cost is exactly the same as the relationship between average *variable* cost and marginal cost. The average total cost curve follows the marginal cost curve but lags behind because it is an average over all units of output. The average total cost curve lags behind the marginal cost curve even more than the average variable cost curve does because the cost of each added unit of production is now averaged not only with the variable cost of all previous units produced but also with fixed costs.

Fixed costs equal $1,000 and are incurred even when the output level is zero. Thus, the first unit of output in the example in Table 8.4 costs $10 in variable cost to produce. The second unit costs only $8 in variable cost to produce. The total cost of 2 units is $1,018; average total cost of the two is ($1,010 + $8)/2, or $509. The marginal cost of the third unit is only $6. The total cost of 3 units is thus $1,024, or $1,018 + $6, and the average total cost of 3 units is ($1,010 + $8 + $6)/3, or $341.

As you saw with the test scores example, marginal cost is what drives changes in average total cost. If marginal cost is *below* average total cost, average total cost will *decline* toward marginal cost. If marginal cost is *above* average total cost, average total cost will *increase*. As a result, marginal cost

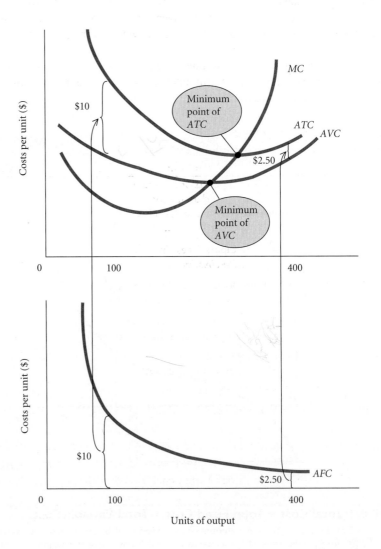

▶ **FIGURE 8.8 Average Total Cost = Average Variable Cost + Average Fixed Cost**

To get average total cost, we add average fixed and average variable costs at all levels of output. Because average fixed cost falls with output, an ever-declining amount is added to *AVC*. Thus, *AVC* and *ATC* get closer together as output increases, but the two lines never meet.

intersects average *total* cost at *ATC*'s minimum point for the same reason that it intersects the average *variable* cost curve at its minimum point.

Short-Run Costs: A Review

Let us now pause to review what we have learned about the behavior of firms. We know that firms make three basic choices: how much product or output to produce or supply, how to produce that output, and how much of each input to demand to produce what they intend to supply. We assume that these choices are made to maximize profits. Profits are equal to the difference between a firm's revenue from the sale of its product and the costs of producing that product: profit = total revenue − total cost.

So far, we have looked only at costs, but costs are just one part of the profit equation. To complete the picture, we must turn to the output market and see how these costs compare with the price that a product commands in the market. Before we do so, however, it is important to consolidate what we have said about costs.

Before a firm does anything else, it needs to know the different methods that it can use to produce its product. The technologies available determine the combinations of inputs that are needed to produce each level of output. Firms choose the technique that produces the desired level of output at the least cost. The cost curves that result from the analysis of all this information show the cost of producing each level of output using the best available technology.

Remember that so far, we have talked only about short-run costs. The curves we have drawn are therefore *short-run cost curves*. The shape of these curves is determined in large measure by the assumptions that we make about the short run, especially the assumption that some fixed factor of production leads to diminishing returns. Given this assumption, marginal costs eventually rise and average cost curves are likely to be U-shaped. Table 8.5 summarizes the cost concepts that we have discussed.

After gaining a complete knowledge of how to produce a product and how much it will cost to produce it at each level of output, the firm turns to the market to find out what it can sell its product for. We now turn our attention to the output market.

TABLE 8.5 A Summary of Cost Concepts

Term	Definition	Equation
Accounting costs	Out-of-pocket costs or costs as an accountant would define them. Sometimes referred to as *explicit costs*.	—
Economic costs	Costs that include the full opportunity costs of all inputs. These include what are often called *implicit costs*.	—
Total fixed costs (TFC)	Costs that do not depend on the quantity of output produced. These must be paid even if output is zero.	—
Total variable costs (TVC)	Costs that vary with the level of output.	—
Total cost (TC)	The total economic cost of all the inputs used by a firm in production.	$TC = TFC + TVC$
Average fixed costs (AFC)	Fixed costs per unit of output.	$AFC = TFC/q$
Average variable costs (AVC)	Variable costs per unit of output.	$AVC = TVC/q$
Average total costs (ATC)	Total costs per unit of output.	$ATC = TC/q \quad ATC = AFC + AVC$
Marginal costs (MC)	The increase in total cost that results from producing 1 additional unit of output.	$MC = \Delta TC/\Delta q$

Average and Marginal Costs at a College

Pomona College in California has an annual operating budget of $120 million. With this budget, the college educates and houses 1,500 students. So the average total cost of educating a Pomona student is $80,000 per year, some of which comes from the college endowment and gifts. Suppose college administrators are considering a small increase in the number of students it accepts and believe they could do so without sacrificing quality of teaching and research. Given that the level of tuition and room and board is considerably less than $80,000, can the administrators make a financial case to support such a move?

The key issue here is to recognize that for a college like Pomona—and indeed for most colleges—the average total cost of educating a student is higher than the marginal. For a very small increase in the number of students, the course-related expenses probably would not go up at all. These students could

likely be absorbed into existing courses with no added expense for faculty, buildings, or administrators. Housing might be more of a constraint, but even in that regard administrators might find some flexibility. Thus, from a financial perspective, the key question about expansion is not how the average total cost of education compares to the tuition, but how tuition compares to the marginal cost. For this reason, many colleges would, in fact, find it financially advantageous to expand student populations if they could do so without changing the quality and environment of the school.

Suppose that of Pomona's $120 million budget, $60 million was fixed costs: maintenance of the physical campus, basic salaries, and other fixed operating costs. Suppose further that the full marginal cost of providing the education was $40,000 per student and constant. Using these figures, one can easily create the following table and draw the cost curves.

| | | Costs in Dollars | | |
Students	Total Fixed Cost	Total Variable Cost	Total Cost	Average Total Cost
500	$60 million	$ 20 million	$ 80 million	$160,000
1,000	60 million	40 million	100 million	100,000
1,500	60 million	60 million	120 million	80,000
2,000	60 million	80 million	140 million	70,000
2,500	60 million	100 million	160 million	64,000

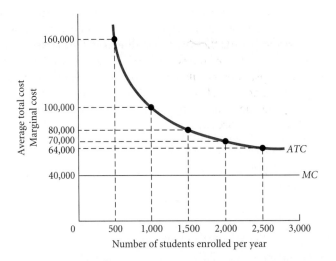

The cost curves also help us understand the downward spiral that can affect colleges as their populations fall. In 2005, Antioch College in Ohio announced that it would be phasing out its undergraduate program. The culprit? Declining attendance caused the average total cost of educating the remaining few students to skyrocket despite attempts to control costs. Given the

inevitability of some fixed costs of education (to educate even a modest student body requires facilities and a college president, for example), as the number of students falls, the average total cost—which is total cost divided by the number of students—rises. For organizations such as colleges and museums, the numbers game is very important to their survival.

Output Decisions: Revenues, Costs, and Profit Maximization

To calculate potential profits, firms must combine their cost analyses with information on potential revenues from sales. After all, if a firm cannot sell its product for more than the cost of production, it will not be in business long. In contrast, if the market gives the firm a price that is significantly greater than the cost it incurs to produce a unit of its product, the firm may have an incentive to expand output. Large profits might also attract new competitors to the market.

Let us now examine in detail how a firm goes about determining how much output to produce. We will begin by examining the decisions of a perfectly competitive firm.

Perfect Competition

Perfect competition exists in an industry that contains many relatively small firms producing identical products. In a perfectly competitive industry, no single firm has any control over prices. In other words, an individual firm cannot affect the market price of its product or the prices of the inputs that it buys. This important characteristic follows from two assumptions. First, a competitive industry is composed of many firms, each small relative to the size of the industry. Second, every firm in a perfectly competitive industry produces **homogeneous products**, which means that one firm's output cannot be distinguished from the output of the others.

These assumptions limit the decisions open to competitive firms and simplify the analysis of competitive behavior. Firms in perfectly competitive industries do not differentiate their products and do not make decisions about price. Instead, each firm takes prices as given—that is, as determined in the market by the laws of supply and demand—and decides only how much to produce and how to produce it.

The idea that competitive firms are "price-takers" is central to our discussion. Of course, we do not mean that firms cannot affix price tags to their merchandise; all firms have this ability. We mean that given the availability of perfect substitutes, any product priced over the market price will not be sold.

These assumptions also imply that the demand for the product of a competitive firm is perfectly elastic (Chapter 5). For example, consider the Ohio corn farmer whose situation is shown in Figure 8.9. The left side of the diagram represents the current conditions in the market. Corn is currently selling for $6.00 per bushel.[1] The right side of the diagram shows the demand for corn as the farmer sees it. If she were to raise her price, she would sell no corn at all; because there are perfect substitutes available, the quantity demanded of her corn would drop to zero. To lower her price would be silly because she can sell all she wants at the current price. (Remember, each farmer's production is very small relative to the entire corn market.)

perfect competition   An industry structure in which there are many firms, each small relative to the industry, producing identical products and in which no firm is large enough to have any control over prices. In perfectly competitive industries, new competitors can freely enter and exit the market.

homogenous products   Undifferentiated products; products that are identical to, or indistinguishable from, one another.

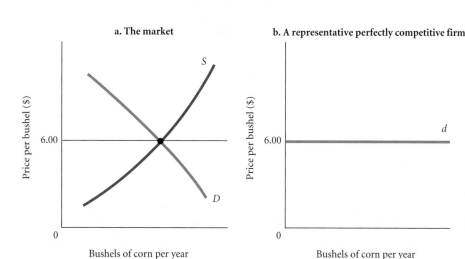

◀ **FIGURE 8.9 Demand Facing a Single Firm in a Perfectly Competitive Market**

If a representative firm in a perfectly competitive market raises the price of its output above $6.00, the quantity demanded of *that firm's* output will drop to zero. Each firm faces a perfectly elastic demand curve, *d*.

---

[1] Capital letters refer to the entire market, and lowercase letters refer to representative firms. For example, in Figure 8.9, the market demand curve is labeled *D* and the demand curve facing the firm is labeled *d*.

In perfect competition, we also assume easy entry—that firms can easily enter and exit the industry. If firms in an industry are earning high profits, new firms are likely to spring up. There are no barriers that prevent a new firm from competing. Fast-food restaurants are quick to spring up when a new shopping center opens, and new gas stations appear when a housing development or a new highway is built. When it became clear a number of years ago that many people would be buying products online, thousands of e-commerce start-ups flooded the Web with new online "shops."

We also assume *easy exit*. When a firm finds itself suffering losses or earning low profits, one option is to go out of business, or exit the industry. Everyone knows a favorite restaurant that went out of business. Changes in cost of production, falling prices from international or regional competition, and changing technology may turn business profits into losses and failure.

The best examples of perfect competition are probably found in agriculture. In that industry, products are absolutely homogeneous—it is impossible to distinguish one farmer's wheat from another's—and prices are set by the forces of supply and demand in a huge national market.

Total Revenue and Marginal Revenue

total revenue (*TR*) The total amount that a firm takes in from the sale of its product: the price per unit times the quantity of output the firm decides to produce ($P \times q$).

Profit is the difference between total revenue and total cost. **Total revenue (*TR*)** is the total amount that a firm takes in from the sale of its product. A perfectly competitive firm sells each unit of product for the same price, regardless of the output level it has chosen. Therefore, total revenue is simply the price per unit times the quantity of output that the firm decides to produce:

$$total\ revenue = price \times quantity$$

$$TR = P \times q$$

marginal revenue (*MR*) The additional revenue that a firm takes in when it increases output by one additional unit. In perfect competition, $P = MR$.

Marginal revenue (*MR*) is the added revenue that a firm takes in when it increases output by 1 additional unit. If a firm producing 10,521 units of output per month increases that output to 10,522 units per month, it will take in an additional amount of revenue each month. The revenue associated with the 10,522nd unit is the amount for which the firm sells that 1 unit. Thus, for a competitive firm, marginal revenue is equal to the current market price of each additional unit sold. In Figure 8.9, for example, the market price is $6.00. Thus, if the representative firm raises its output from 10,521 units to 10,522 units, its revenue will increase by $6.00.

A firm's *marginal revenue curve* shows how much revenue the firm will gain by raising output by 1 unit at every level of output. The *marginal revenue curve and the demand curve facing a competitive firm are identical*. The horizontal line in Figure 8.9(b) can be thought of as both the demand curve facing the firm and its marginal revenue curve:

$$P^* = d = MR$$

Comparing Costs and Revenues to Maximize Profit

The discussion in the next few paragraphs conveys one of the most important concepts in all of microeconomics. As we pursue our analysis, remember that we are working under two assumptions: (1) that the industry we are examining is perfectly competitive and (2) that firms choose the level of output that yields the maximum total profit.

The Profit-Maximizing Level of Output Look carefully at the graphs in Figure 8.10. Once again, we have the whole market, or industry, on the left and a single, typical small firm on the right. And again the current market price is P^*.

First, the firm observes the market price [Figure 8.10(a)] and knows that it can sell all that it wants for $P^* = \$5$ per unit. Next, the firm must decide how much to produce. It might seem reasonable for the firm to pick the output level where marginal cost is at its minimum point—in this case, at an output of 100 units. Here the difference between marginal revenue, $5.00, and marginal cost, $2.50, is the greatest. As it happens, 100 units is *not* the optimal production level.

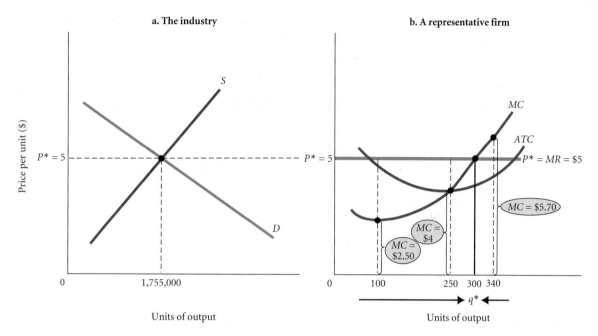

▲ **FIGURE 8.10 The Profit-Maximizing Level of Output for a Perfectly Competitive Firm**

If price is above marginal cost, as it is at 100 and 250 units of output, profits can be increased by raising output; each additional unit increases revenues by more than it costs to produce the additional output. Beyond $q^* = 300$, however, added output will reduce profits. At 340 units of output, an additional unit of output costs more to produce than it will bring in revenue when sold on the market. Profit-maximizing output is thus q^*, the point at which $P^* = MC$.

Remember that a firm wants to maximize the difference between *total* revenue and *total* cost, not the difference between *marginal* revenue and *marginal* cost. The fact that marginal revenue is greater than marginal cost at a level of 100 indicates that profit is *not* being maximized. Think about the 101st unit. Adding that single unit to production each period adds $5.00 to revenues but adds only about $2.50 to cost. Profits each period would be higher by about $2.50. Thus, the optimal (profit-maximizing) level of output is clearly higher than 100 units.

Now look at an output level of 250 units. Here, once again, raising output increases profit. The revenue gained from producing the 251st unit (marginal revenue) is still $5, and the cost of the 251st unit (marginal cost) is only about $4. As long as marginal revenue is greater than marginal cost, even though the difference between the two is getting smaller, added output means added profit. Whenever marginal revenue exceeds marginal cost, the revenue gained by increasing output by 1 unit per period exceeds the cost incurred by doing so. This logic leads us to 300 units of output. At 300 units, marginal cost has risen to $5. At 300 units of output, $P^* = MR = MC = \$5$.

Notice that if the firm were to produce *more* than 300 units, marginal cost would rise above marginal revenue. At 340 units of output, for example, the cost of the 341st unit is about $5.70 while that added unit of output still brings in only $5 in revenue, thus reducing profit. It simply does not pay to increase output above the point where marginal cost rises above marginal revenue because such increases will *reduce* profit. The profit-maximizing perfectly competitive firm will produce up to the point where the price of its output is just equal to short-run marginal cost—the level of output at which $P^* = MC$. Thus, in Figure 8.10, the profit-maximizing level of output, q^*, is 300 units.

Keep in mind, though, that all types of firms (not just those in perfectly competitive industries) are profit maximizers. The profit-maximizing output level for *all* firms is the output level where $MR = MC$. In perfect competition, however, $MR = P$, as shown earlier. Hence, for perfectly competitive firms, we can rewrite our profit-maximizing condition as $P = MC$.

Important note: The key idea here is that firms will produce as long as marginal revenue exceeds marginal cost. When marginal cost rises smoothly, as it does in Figure 8.10, the profit-maximizing condition is that *MR* (or *P*) *exactly equals MC*. If marginal cost moves up in increments—as it does in the following numerical example—marginal revenue or price may never exactly equal marginal cost. The key idea still holds.

ECONOMICS IN PRACTICE

Case Study in Marginal Analysis: An Ice Cream Parlor

The following is a description of the decisions made in 2000 by the owner of a small ice cream parlor in Ohio. After being in business for 1 year, this entrepreneur had to ask herself whether she should stay in business.

The cost figures on which she based her decisions are presented next. These numbers are real, but they do not include one important item: the managerial labor provided by the owner. In her calculations, the entrepreneur did not include a wage for herself, but we will assume an opportunity cost of $30,000 per year ($2,500 per month).

FIXED COSTS

The fixed components of the store's monthly costs include the following:

Rent (1,150 square feet)	$2,012.50
Electricity	.325.00
Interest on loan	.737.50
Maintenance	.295.00
Telephone	65.00
Total	$3,435.00

Not all the items on this list are strictly fixed, however. Electricity costs, for example, would be slightly higher if the store produced more ice cream and stayed open longer, but the added cost would be minimal.

VARIABLE COSTS

The ice cream store's variable costs include two components: (1) behind-the-counter labor costs and (2) cost of making ice cream. The store hires employees at a wage of $5.15 per hour. Including the employer's share of the Social Security tax, the gross cost of labor is $5.54 per hour. Two employees work in the store at all times. The full cost of producing ice cream is $3.27 per gallon. Each gallon contains approximately 12 servings. Customers can add toppings free of charge, and the average cost of the toppings taken by a customer is about $.05:

Gross labor costs	$5.54/hour
Costs of producing one gallon of ice cream (12 servings per gallon)	$3.27
Average cost of added toppings per serving	$.05

REVENUES

The store sells ice cream cones, sundaes, and floats. The average price of a purchase at the store is $1.45. The store is open 8 hours per day, 26 days a month, and serves an average of 240 customers per day:

Average purchase	$1.45
Days open per month	.26
Average number of customers per day	.240

From the preceding information, it is possible to calculate the store's average monthly profit. Total revenue is equal to 240 customers × $1.45 per customer × 26 days open in an average month: $TR = \$9,048$ per month.

PROFITS

The store sells 240 servings per day. Because there are 12 servings of ice cream per gallon, the store uses exactly 20 gallons per day (240 servings divided by 12). Total costs are $3.27 × 20, or $65.40, per day for ice cream and $12 per day for toppings (240 × $.05). The cost of variable labor is $5.54 × 8 hours × 2 workers, or $88.64 per day. Total variable costs are therefore $166.04 ($65.40 + $12.00 + $88.64) per day. The store is open 26 days a month, so the total variable cost per month is $4,317.04.

Adding fixed costs of $3,435.00 to variable costs of $4,317.04, we get a total cost of operation of $7,752.04 per month. Thus, the firm is averaging a profit of $1,295.96 per month ($9,048.00 − $7,752.04). *This is not an "economic profit" because we have not accounted for the opportunity cost of the owner's time and efforts.* In fact, when we factor in an implicit wage of $2,500 per month for the owner, we see that the store is suffering *losses* of $1,204.04 per month ($1,295.96 − $2,500.00).

Total revenue (TR)	$9,048.00
Total fixed cost (TFC)	.3,435.00
+ Total variable cost (TVC)	4,317.04
Total costs (TC)	.7,752.04
Total profit ($TR - TC$)	.1,295.96
Adjustment for implicit wage	2,500.00
Economic profit	−1,204.04

Should the entrepreneur stay in business? If she wants to make $2,500 per month and she thinks that nothing about her business will change, she must shut down in the long run. However, two things keep her going: (1) a decision to stay open longer and (2) the hope for more customers in the future.

OPENING LONGER HOURS: MARGINAL COSTS AND MARGINAL REVENUES

The store's normal hours of operation are noon until 8 P.M. On an experimental basis, the owner extends its hours until 11 P.M. for 1 month. The following table shows the average number of additional customers for each of the added hours:

Hours (P.M.)	Customers
8–9	41
9–10	20
10–11	8

Assuming that the late customers spend an average of $1.45, we can calculate the marginal revenue and the marginal cost of staying open longer. The marginal cost of one serving of ice cream is $3.27 divided by 12 = $0.27 + .05 (for topping) = $0.32. (See the table that follows.)

Marginal analysis tells us that the store should stay open for 2 additional hours. Each day that the store stays open from 8 P.M. to 9 P.M. it will make an added profit of $59.45 – $24.20, or $35.25. Staying open from 9 P.M. to 10 P.M. adds $29.00 – $17.48, or $11.52, to profit. Staying open the third hour, however, *decreases* profits because the marginal revenue generated by staying open from 10 P.M. to 11 P.M. is less than the marginal cost. The entrepreneur decides to stay open for 2 additional hours per day. This adds $46.77 ($35.25 + 11.52) to profits each day, a total of $1,216.02 per month.

By adding the 2 hours, the store turns an economic loss of $1,204.04 per month into a small ($11.98) profit after accounting for the owner's implicit wage of $2,500 per month.

The owner decided to stay in business. She now serves over 350 customers per day, and the price of a dish of ice cream has risen to $2.50 while costs have not changed very much. In 2001, she cleared a profit of nearly $10,000 per month.

Hour (P.M.)	Marginal Revenue (MR)	Marginal Cost (MC)	Added Profit per Hour (MR – MC)
8–9	$1.45 × 41 = $59.45	Ice cream: $0.32 × 41 = $13.12 Labor: 2 × $5.54 = 11.08 Total $24.20	$35.25
9–10	1.45 × 20 = $29.00	Ice cream: $0.32 × 20 = $6.40 Labor: 2 × $5.54 = 11.08 Total $17.48	$11.52
10–11	1.45 × 8 = $11.60	Ice cream: $0.32 × 8 = $2.56 Labor: 2 × $5.54 = 11.08 Total $13.64	–$2.04

A Numerical Example   Table 8.6 presents some data for another hypothetical firm. Let us assume that the market has set a $15 unit price for the firm's product. Total revenue in column 6 is the simple product of $P \times q$ (the numbers in column 1 times $15). The table derives total, marginal, and average costs exactly as Table 8.4 did. Here, however, we have included revenues, and we can calculate the profit, which is shown in column 8.

TABLE 8.6   Profit Analysis for a Simple Firm

(1)	(2)	(3)	(4)	(5)	(6)	(7)	(8)
					TR	TC	Profit
q	TFC	TVC	MC	P = MR	(P × q)	(TFC + TVC)	(TR – TC)
0	$10	$ 0	$–	$15	$ 0	$10	$–10
1	10	10	10	15	15	20	–5
2	10	15	5	15	30	25	5
3	10	20	5	15	45	30	15
4	10	30	10	15	60	40	20
5	10	50	20	15	75	60	15
6	10	80	30	15	90	90	0

Column 8 shows that a profit-maximizing firm would choose to produce 4 units of output. At this level, profits are $20. At all other output levels, they are lower. Now let us see if "marginal" reasoning leads us to the same conclusion.

First, should the firm produce at all? If it produces nothing, it suffers losses equal to $10. If it increases output to 1 unit, marginal revenue is $15 (remember that it sells each unit for $15) and marginal cost is $10. Thus, it gains $5, reducing its loss from $10 each period to $5.

Should the firm increase output to 2 units? The marginal revenue from the second unit is again $15, but the marginal cost is only $5. Thus, by producing the second unit, the firm gains $10 ($15 – $5) and turns a $5 loss into a $5 profit. The third unit adds $10 to profits. Again, marginal revenue is $15 and marginal cost is $5, an increase in profit of $10, for a total profit of $15.

The fourth unit offers still more profit. Price is still above marginal cost, which means that producing that fourth unit will increase profits. Price, or marginal revenue, is $15, and marginal cost is just $10. Thus, the fourth unit adds $5 to profit. At unit number five, however, diminishing returns push marginal cost above price. The marginal revenue from producing the fifth unit is $15, while marginal cost is now $20. As a result, profit per period drops by $5, to $15 per period. Clearly, the firm will not produce the fifth unit.

The profit-maximizing level of output is thus 4 units. The firm produces as long as price (marginal revenue) is greater than marginal cost. For an in-depth example of profit maximization, see "Case Study in Marginal Analysis: An Ice Cream Parlor" on p. 182.

The Short-Run Supply Curve

Consider how the typical firm shown in Figure 8.10 on p. 181 would behave in response to an increase in price. In Figure 8.11(a), assume that something causes demand to increase (shift to the right), driving price from $5 to $6 and finally to $7. When price is $5, a profit-maximizing firm will choose an output level of 300 in Figure 8.11(b). To produce any less, or to raise output above that level, would lead to a lower level of profit. At $6, the same firm would increase output to 350, but it would stop there. Similarly, at $7, the firm would raise output to 400 units of output.

The *MC* curve in Figure 8.11(b) relates price and quantity supplied. At any market price, the marginal cost curve shows the output level that maximizes profit. A curve that shows how much output a profit-maximizing firm will produce at every price also fits the definition of a supply curve. (Review Chapter 3 if this point is not clear to you.) Thus, the marginal cost curve of a competitive firm is the firm's short-run supply curve.

As you will see, one very important exception exists to this general rule: There is some price level below which the firm will shut down its operations and simply bear losses equal to fixed costs even if price is above marginal cost. This important point is discussed in Chapter 9.

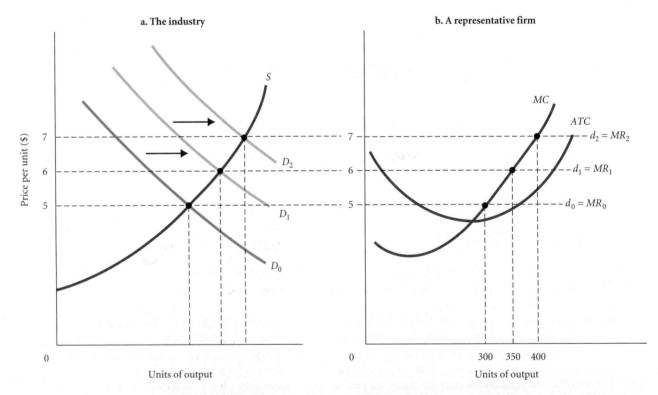

▲ FIGURE 8.11 **Marginal Cost Is the Supply Curve of a Perfectly Competitive Firm**
At any market price,[a] the marginal cost curve shows the output level that maximizes profit. Thus, the marginal cost curve of a perfectly competitive profit-maximizing firm is the firm's short-run supply curve.

[a] This is true except when price is so low that it pays a firm to shut down—a point that will be discussed in Chapter 9.

Looking Ahead

At the beginning of this chapter, we set out to combine information on technology, factor prices, and output prices to understand the supply curve of a competitive firm. We have now accomplished that goal.

Because marginal cost is such an important concept in microeconomics, you should carefully review any sections of this chapter that were unclear to you. Above all, keep in mind that the *marginal cost curve* carries information about both *input prices* and *technology*. The firm looks to output markets for information on potential revenues, and the current market price defines the firm's marginal revenue curve. The point where price (which is equal to marginal revenue in perfect competition) is just equal to marginal cost is the perfectly competitive firm's profit-maximizing level of output. Thus, with one important exception, the marginal cost curve *is* the perfectly competitive firm's supply curve in the short run.

In the next chapter, we turn to the long run. What happens when firms are free to choose their scale of operations without being limited by a fixed factor of production? Without diminishing returns that set in as a result of a fixed scale of production, what determines the shape of cost curves? What happens when new firms can enter industries in which profits are being earned? How do industries adjust when losses are being incurred? How does the structure of an industry evolve over time?

S U M M A R Y
---

1. Profit-maximizing firms make decisions to maximize profit (total revenue minus total cost).

2. To calculate production costs, firms must know two things: (1) the quantity and combination of inputs they need to produce their product and (2) the cost of those inputs.

COSTS IN THE SHORT RUN p. 168

3. *Fixed costs* are costs that do not change with a firm's output. In the short run, firms cannot avoid fixed costs or change them even if production is zero.

4. *Variable costs* are those costs that depend on the level of output chosen. Fixed costs plus variable costs equal *total costs* ($TC = TFC + TVC$).

5. *Average fixed cost* (AFC) is total fixed cost divided by the quantity of output. As output rises, average fixed cost declines steadily because the same total is being spread over a larger and larger quantity of output. This phenomenon is called *spreading overhead*.

6. Numerous combinations of inputs can be used to produce a given level of output. *Total variable cost* (TVC) is the sum of all costs that vary with output in the short run.

7. *Marginal cost* (MC) is the increase in total cost that results from the production of 1 more unit of output. If a firm is producing 1,000 units, the additional cost of increasing output to 1,001 units is marginal cost. Marginal cost measures the cost of the additional inputs required to produce each successive unit of output. Because fixed costs do not change when output changes, marginal costs reflect changes in variable costs.

8. In the short run, a firm is limited by a fixed factor of production or a fixed scale of a plant. As a firm increases output, it will eventually find itself trapped by that scale. Because of the fixed scale, marginal cost eventually rises with output.

9. Marginal cost is the slope of the total variable cost curve. The total variable cost curve always has a positive slope because total costs always rise with output. However, increasing marginal cost means that total costs ultimately rise at an increasing rate.

10. *Average variable cost* (AVC) is equal to total variable cost divided by the quantity of output.

11. When marginal cost is above average variable cost, average variable cost is *increasing*. When marginal cost is below average variable cost, average variable cost is *declining*. Marginal cost intersects average variable cost at AVC's minimum point.

12. *Average total cost* (ATC) is equal to total cost divided by the quantity of output. It is also equal to the sum of average fixed cost and average variable cost.

13. When marginal cost is below average total cost, average total cost is declining toward marginal cost. When marginal cost is above average total cost, average total cost is increasing. Marginal cost intersects average total cost at ATC's minimum point.

OUTPUT DECISIONS: REVENUES, COSTS, AND PROFIT MAXIMIZATION p. 179

14. A perfectly competitive firm faces a demand curve that is a horizontal line (in other words, perfectly elastic demand).

15. *Total revenue* (TR) is simply price times the quantity of output that a firm decides to produce and sell. *Marginal revenue* (MR) is the additional revenue that a firm takes in when it increases output by 1 unit.

16. For a perfectly competitive firm, marginal revenue is equal to the current market price of its product.

17. A profit-maximizing firm in a perfectly competitive industry will produce up to the point at which the price of its output is just equal to short-run marginal cost: $P = MC$. The more general profit-maximizing formula is $MR = MC$ ($P = MR$ in perfect competition). The marginal cost curve of a perfectly competitive firm is the firm's short-run supply curve, with one exception (discussed in Chapter 9).

REVIEW TERMS AND CONCEPTS

average fixed cost (AFC), *p. 169*

average total cost (ATC), *p. 175*

average variable cost (AVC), *p. 174*

fixed cost, *p. 168*

homogeneous product, *p. 179*

marginal cost (MC), *p. 171*

marginal revenue (MR), *p. 180*

perfect competition, *p. 179*

spreading overhead, *p. 169*

total cost (TC), *p. 168*

total fixed costs (TFC) *or* overhead, *p. 168*

total revenue (TR), *p. 180*

total variable cost (TVC), *p. 169*

total variable cost curve, *p. 170*

variable cost, *p. 168*

1. $TC = TFC + TVC$

2. $AFC = TFC/q$

3. Slope of $TVC = MC$

4. $AVC = TVC/q$

5. $ATC = TC/q = AFC + AVC$

6. $TR = P \times q$

7. Profit-maximizing level of output for all firms: $MR = M$

8. Profit-maximizing level of output for perfectly competitive firms: $P = MC$

PROBLEMS

All problems are available on www.myeconlab.com

MC=MR

1. Consider the following costs of owning and operating a car. A $25,000 Ford Taurus financed over 60 months at 7 percent interest means a monthly payment of $495.03. Insurance costs $100 a month regardless of how much you drive. The car gets 20 miles per gallon and uses unleaded regular gasoline that costs $3.50 per gallon. Finally, suppose that wear and tear on the car costs about 15 cents a mile. Which costs are fixed, and which are variable? What is the marginal cost of a mile driven? In deciding whether to drive from New York to Pittsburgh (about 1,000 miles round-trip) to visit a friend, which costs would you consider? Why?

2. July 23, 2007 LONDON (Reuters)—The final volume of the Harry Potter saga sold more than 11 million copies in the first 24 hours it went on sale in the United States and Britain to become the fastest-selling book in history, publishers said. In book publishing, fixed costs are very high and marginal costs are very low and fairly constant. Suppose that the fixed cost of producing the new Harry Potter volume is $30 million. What is the *average fixed cost* if the publisher produces 5 million copies? 10 million copies? 20 million copies?

    Now suppose that the marginal cost of a Harry Potter book is $1.50 per book and is the same for each book up to 40 million copies. Assume that this includes all variable costs. Explain why in this case marginal cost is a horizontal line, as is average variable cost. What is the *average total cost* of the book if the publisher produces 5 million copies? 10 million copies? 20 million copies?

    Sketch the average fixed cost curve and the average total cost curve facing the publisher.

3. Do you agree or disagree with this statement? Firms minimize costs; thus, a firm earning short-run economic profits will choose to produce at the minimum point on its average total cost function.

4. You are given the following cost data:

    Total fixed costs are 100.

q	TVC	*MC*
0	0	
1	5	5
2	10	5
3	20	10 ←
4	40	20
5	65	25
6	95	30

If the price of output is $15, how many units of output will this firm produce? What is total revenue? What is total cost? Briefly explain using the concept of marginal cost. What do you think the firm is likely to do in the short run? ~~In the long run?~~

5. [Related to the *Economics in Practice* on *p. 178*] While charging admission most days of the week, the Museum of Contemporary Art in Los Angeles offers free admission on Thursday evenings. Why do museums often price this way? Why do they choose Thursday rather than Saturday?

6. The following table gives capital and labor requirements for 10 different levels of production.

q	K	L
0	0	0
1	2	5
2	4	9
3	6	12
4	8	15
5	10	19
6	12	24
7	14	30
8	16	37
9	18	45
10	20	54

a. Assuming that the price of labor (P_L) is $5 per unit and the price of capital (P_K) is $10 per unit, compute and graph total cost, marginal cost, and average variable cost for the firm.

b. Do the graphs have the shapes that you might expect? Explain.

c. Using the numbers here, explain the relationship between marginal cost and average variable cost.

d. Using the numbers here, explain the meaning of "marginal cost" in terms of additional inputs needed to produce a marginal unit of output.

e. If the output price was $57, how many units of output would the firm produce? Explain.

7. Do you agree or disagree with each of the following statements? Explain your reasons.
   a. For a competitive firm facing a market price above average total cost, the existence of economic profits means that the firm should increase output in the short run even if price is below marginal cost.
   b. If marginal cost is rising with increasing output, average cost must also be rising.
   c. Fixed cost is constant at every level of output except zero. When a firm produces no output, fixed costs are zero in the short run.

8. A firm's cost curves are given in the following table.

q	TC	TFC	TVC	AVC	ATC	MC
0	$100	$100	—	—	—	—
1	130	100	—	—	—	—
2	150	100	—	—	—	—
3	160	100	—	—	—	—
4	172	100	—	—	—	—
5	185	100	—	—	—	—
6	210	100	—	—	—	—
7	240	100	—	—	—	—
8	280	100	—	—	—	—
9	330	100	—	—	—	—
10	390	100	—	—	—	—

   a. Complete the table.
   b. Graph AVC, ATC, and MC on the same graph. What is the relationship between the MC curve and the ATC and between MC and AVC?
   c. Suppose market price is $30. How much will the firm produce in the short run? How much are total profits?
   d. Suppose market price is $50. How much will the firm produce in the short run? What are total profits?

9. A 2010 Georgia Tech graduate inherited her mother's printing company. The capital stock of the firm consists of three machines of various vintages, all in excellent condition. All machines can be running at the same time.

	COST OF PRINTING AND BINDING PER BOOK	MAXIMUM TOTAL CAPACITY (BOOKS) PER MONTH
Machine 1	$1.00	100
Machine 2	2.00	200
Machine 3	3.00	500

   a. Assume that "cost of printing and binding per book" includes *all* labor and materials, including the owner's wages. Assume further that Mom signed a long-term contract (50 years) with a service company to keep the machines in good repair for a fixed fee of $100 per month.
      (1) Derive the firm's marginal cost curve.
      (2) Derive the firm's total cost curve.
   b. At a price of $2.50, how many books would the company produce? What would total revenues, total costs, and total profits be?

10. The following is a total cost curve. Sketch the corresponding marginal cost curve. If the price of output is $3 and there are no fixed costs, what is the profit-maximizing level of output?

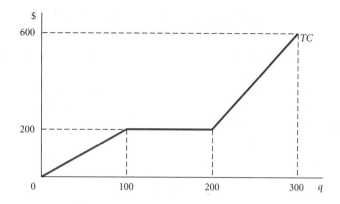

11. The following curve is a production function for a firm that uses just one variable factor of production, labor. It shows total output, or product, for every level of input.
    a. Derive and graph the marginal product curve.
    b. Suppose the wage rate is $4. Derive and graph the firm's marginal cost curve.
    c. If output sells for $6, what is the profit-maximizing level of output? How much labor will the firm hire?

12. [Related to the *Economics in Practice* on p. 182] Elena and Emmanuel live on the Black Sea in Bulgaria and own a small fishing boat. A crew of four is required to take the boat out fishing. The current wage paid to the four crew members is a total of 5,000 levs per day. (A lev is the Bulgarian unit of currency.) Assume that the cost of operating and maintaining the boat is 1,000 levs per day when fishing and zero otherwise. The following schedule gives the appropriate catch for each period during the year.

PERIOD	CATCH PER DAY (KILOGRAMS)
Prime fishing: 180 days	100
Month 7: 30 days	80
Month 8: 30 days	60
Rest of the year	40

   The price of fish in Bulgaria is no longer regulated by the government and is now determined in competitive markets. Suppose the price has been stable all year at 80 levs per kilogram.
   a. What is the marginal product of a day's worth of fishing during prime fishing season? during month 7? during month 8?
   b. What is the marginal cost of a kilogram of fish during prime fishing season? during month 7, during month 8, and during the rest of the year?
   c. If you were Elena and Emmanuel, how many months per year would you hire the crew and go out fishing? Explain your answer using marginal logic.

13. For each of the following businesses, what is the likely fixed factor of production that defines the short run?
    a. Potato farm of 160 acres
    b. Chinese restaurant
    c. Dentist in private practice
    d. Car dealership
    e. Bank

14. Explain which of the following is a fixed cost or a variable cost for Southwest Airlines.
    a. The cost of jet fuel used in its airplanes. V
    b. The monthly rent on its Dallas, Texas headquarters. F
    c. The yearly lease payments on its current inventory of Boeing 737 jets. F
    d. The cost of peanuts it serves to passengers. V
    e. The salary paid to Laura Wright, Southwest's Senior Vice President of Finance and Chief Financial Officer. F
    f. The gate rental fees it pays to McCarran International Airport in Las Vegas, Nevada. F or not enough info

15. Use the information in the graph to find the values for the following costs at an output level of 500.
    a. Total fixed cost 20 x 500
    b. Total variable cost 7500
    c. Total cost 17,500
    d. Marginal cost 5,000

16. Explain how the following events would affect the cost curves in the graph from the previous question.
    a. Hourly wages for employees increase.
    b. The company signs a new 3-year contract with its landlord which lowers its monthly rent by 10 percent.
    c. The company employs a new technology which lowers its utility costs.
    d. The company receives notice of a 5 percent increase in its property insurance rate.
    e. The company's primary supplier of resources implements a 3 percent price increase for all of its supplies.

17. Fill in the columns in the following table. What quantity should a profit-maximizing firm produce? Verify your answer with marginal reasoning.

q	TFC	TVC	MC	P = MR	TR	TC	Profit
0	$20	$0	0	$22	0	20	-20
1	20	10	10	22	22	30	-8
2	20	15	5	22	44	35	9
3	20	25	10	22	66	45	
4	20	40	15	22	88	60	
5	20	60	20	22	110	80	
6	20	90	30	22	132	110	

18. Use the information from your answer to the previous question to construct a rough plot showing marginal revenue, marginal cost, and average total cost. Also identify the profit-maximizing quantity of output on the graph. You will have to calculate average total cost from the information in the table.

19. Marginal cost represents the increase in total cost that results from producing one more unit of output. Marginal product represents the additional output that can be produced by adding one more unit of a specific input, holding all other inputs constant. What does this imply about the relationship between marginal cost and marginal product?

20. Evaluate the following statement. If the total variable cost of production is the sum of the marginal cost of each additional unit of output, we can calculate the marginal cost by taking the total variable cost of production and dividing it by the quantity of output produced.

35
+ 17500

Long-Run Costs and Output Decisions

The last two chapters discussed the behavior of profit-maximizing competitive firms in the short run. Recall that all firms must make three fundamental decisions: (1) how much output to produce or supply, (2) how to produce that output, and (3) how much of each input to demand.

Firms use information on input prices, output prices, and technology to make the decisions that will lead to the most profit. Because profits equal revenues minus costs, firms must know how much their products will sell for

and how much production will cost, using the most efficient technology.

In Chapter 8, we saw how cost curves can be derived from production functions and input prices. Once a firm has a clear picture of its short-run costs, the price at which it sells its output determines the quantity of output that will maximize profit. Specifically, a profit-maximizing perfectly competitive firm will supply output up to the point that price (marginal revenue) equals marginal cost. The marginal cost curve of such a firm is thus the same as its supply curve.

In this chapter, we turn from the short run to the long run. The condition in which firms find themselves in the short run (Are they making profits? Are they incurring losses?) determines what is likely to happen in the long run. Remember that output (supply) decisions in the long run are less constrained than in the short run, for two reasons. First, in the long run, the firm can increase any or all of its inputs and thus has no fixed factor of production that confines its production to a given scale. Second, firms are free to enter industries to seek profits and to leave industries to avoid losses.

In thinking about the relationship between the short run and long run, it is useful to put yourself in the position of a manager of a firm. At times, you will be making what we term *short-run* decisions: You are stuck with a particular factory and set of machines, and your decisions involve asking how best to use those assets to produce output. At the same time, you or another manager at the firm will be doing more strategic *long-run* thinking: Should you be in this business at all, or should you close up shop? In better times, you might consider expanding the operation. In thinking about the long run, you will also have to reckon with other firms entering and exiting the industry. Managers simultaneously make short- and long-run decisions, making the best of the current constraints while planning for the future.

In making decisions or understanding industry structure, the shape of the long-run cost curve is important. As we saw in the short run, a fixed factor of production eventually causes marginal cost to increase along with output. In the long run, all factors can be varied. In the earlier sandwich shop example, in the long run, we can add floor space and grills along with more people to make the sandwiches. Under these circumstances, it is no longer inevitable that increased volume comes with higher costs. In fact, as we will see, long-run cost curves need not slope up at all. You might have wondered why there are only a few automobile and steel companies in the United States but dozens of firms producing books and furniture. Differences in the shapes of the long-run cost curves in those industries do a good job of explaining these differences in the industry structures.

We begin our discussion of the long run by looking at firms in three short-run circumstances: (1) firms that earn economic profits, (2) firms that suffer economic losses but continue to operate to reduce or minimize those losses, and (3) firms that decide to shut down and bear losses just equal to fixed costs. We then examine how these firms make their long-run decisions in response to conditions in their markets.

Although we continue to focus on perfectly competitive firms, *all* firms are subject to the spectrum of short-run profit or loss situations regardless of *market structure*. Assuming perfect competition allows us to simplify our analysis and provides us with a strong background for understanding the discussions of imperfectly competitive behavior in later chapters.

Short-Run Conditions and Long-Run Directions

Before beginning our examination of firm behavior, let us review the concept of profit. Recall that a normal rate of return is included in the definition of total cost (Chapter 7). A *normal rate of return* is a rate that is just sufficient to keep current investors interested in the industry. Because we define *profit* as total revenue minus total cost and because total cost includes a normal rate of return, our concept of profit takes into account the opportunity cost of capital. When a firm is earning an above-normal rate of return, it has a positive profit level; otherwise, it does not. When there are positive profits in an industry, new investors are likely to be attracted to the industry.

When we say that a firm is suffering a *loss*, we mean that it is earning a rate of return that is below normal. Such a firm may be suffering a loss as an accountant would measure it, or it may be earning at a very low—that is, below normal—rate. Investors are not going to be attracted to an industry in which there are losses. A firm that is **breaking even**, or earning a zero level of profit, is one that is earning exactly a normal rate of return. New investors are not attracted, but current ones are not running away either.

breaking even   The situation in which a firm is earning exactly a normal rate of return.

With these distinctions in mind, we can say that for any firm, one of three conditions holds at any given moment: (1) The firm is making positive profits, (2) the firm is suffering losses, or (3) the firm is just breaking even. Profitable firms will want to maximize their profits in the short run, while firms suffering losses will want to minimize those losses in the short run.

Maximizing Profits

The best way to understand the behavior of a firm that is currently earning profits is by way of example.

Example: The Blue Velvet Car Wash   When a firm earns revenues in excess of costs (including a normal rate of return), we say it is earning positive or excess profits. Let us consider as an example the Blue Velvet Car Wash. Looking at a few numbers will help you see how the specifics of a business operation translate into economic graphs.

Car washes require a facility. In the case of Blue Velvet, suppose investors have put up $500,000 to construct a building and purchase all the equipment required to wash cars. If the car wash closes, the building and equipment can be sold for its original purchase price, but as long as the firm is in business, that capital is tied up. If the investors could get 10 percent return on their investment in another business, then for them to keep their money in this business, they will also expect 10 percent from Blue Velvet. Thus, the annual cost of the capital needed for the business is $50,000 (10 percent of $500,000).

The car wash is currently servicing 800 cars a week and can be open 50 weeks a year (2 weeks are needed for maintenance). The cost of the basic maintenance contract on the equipment is $50,000 per year, and Blue Velvet has a contract to pay for those services for a year whether it opens the car wash or not. The fixed costs then for the car wash are $100,000 per year: $50,000 for the capital costs and $50,000 for the equipment contract. On a weekly basis, these costs amount to $2,000 per week. If the car wash operates at the level of 800 cars per week, fixed costs are $2.50 per car ($2,000/800).

There are also variable costs associated with the business. To run a car wash, one needs workers and soap and water. Workers can be hired by the hour for $10.00 an hour, and at a customer level of 800 cars per week, each worker can wash 8 cars an hour. At this service level, then, Blue Velvet hires workers for 100 hours and has a wage bill of $1,000. The labor cost of each car wash, when Blue Velvet serves 800 customers, is $1.25 ($10/8).

The number of cars each worker can service depends on the number of cars being worked on. When there is too little business and few workers, no specialization is possible and cars washed per worker fall. With many cars to service, workers start getting in one another's way. We saw that at 800 cars per week, workers could wash 8 each per hour. Later when we graph the operation, we will assume that the number of cars washed per worker rises and then falls, reaching a maximum at a volume less than the current 800 cars.

Every car that is washed costs $0.75 in soap, adding $600 to the weekly bill if 800 car washes are done. Table 9.1 summarizes the costs of Blue Velvet at the 800 washes per week level.

TABLE 9.1   Blue Velvet Car Wash Weekly Costs

TFC Total Fixed Cost			*TVC* Total Variable Cost (800 Washes)		*TC* Total Cost (800 Washes)	*TR* Total Revenue (*P* = $5)
1. Normal return to investors	$1,000	1. Labor	$1,000		*TC = TFC + TVC* = $2,000 + $1,600 = **$3,600**	*TR* = $5 × 800 = **$4,000**
2. Other fixed costs (maintenance contract)		2. Soap	600	**$1,600**		*Profit = TR − TC* = **$400**
	1,000 **$2,000**					

This car wash business is quite competitive, and the market price for this service at the moment we are considering is $5. (Recall the perfectly elastic demand curve facing a competitive firm we discussed in Chapter 8.) At a service level of 800 cars, as you see from the table, Blue Velvet is making a positive profit of $400 per week. For each car washed, it receives $5 and spends $4.50 ($2.50 in fixed costs + $1.25 in labor costs + $0.75 in soap), for an excess profit of $0.50 per car.

Graphic Presentation   For Blue Velvet, we have seen a snapshot of the business as it operates with 800 cars serviced a week. We have also learned a little about the business, which we can use to construct a graphical representation of Blue Velvet to help us see why the firm chose to service 800 cars. Figure 9.1 graphs the performance of Blue Velvet in this first period in which it is making money.

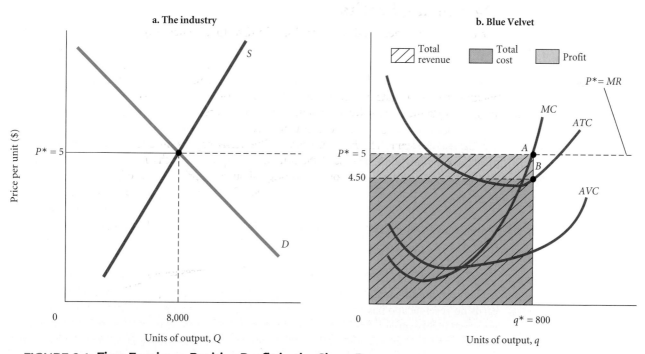

▲ **FIGURE 9.1 Firm Earning a Positive Profit in the Short Run**
A profit-maximizing perfectly competitive firm will produce up to the point where *P* * = *MC*. Profit is the difference between total revenue and total cost. At *q* * = 800, total revenue is $5 × 800 = $4,000, total cost is $4.50 × 800 = $3,600, and profit = $4,000 − $3,600 = $400.

The industry price is $5.00, and we have assumed that the total number of car washes done in the market area in a week is 8,000; so there are 10 firms like Blue Velvet in this competitive marketplace all earning economic profits. There are three key cost curves shown in the graph that represents Blue Velvet. The average variable cost (AVC) curve shows what happens to the per unit costs of workers and the other variable factor, soap, as we change output. Initially as output increases workers can service more cars per hour as they work together, thus causing the AVC to decline, but eventually diminishing returns set in and AVC begins to rise. Now look at the average total cost (ATC) curve. The average total cost curve falls at first in response to the spreading of the fixed costs over more and more units and eventually begins to rise as the inefficiencies in labor take their toll. At the output of 800 washes, the ATC has a value of $4.50. Look back at Table 9.1. The total cost of Blue Velvet at a service level of 800 cars is $3,600. The $4.50 comes from dividing this $3,600 by 800 cars. Finally, we see the marginal cost (MC) curve, which rises after a certain point because of the fixed factor of the building and equipment.

With a price of $5.00, Blue Velvet is producing 800 units and making a profit (the gray box). Blue Velvet is a perfectly competitive firm, and it maximizes profits by producing up to the point where price equals marginal cost, here 800 car washes. Any units produced beyond 800 would add more to cost than they would bring in revenue. Notice Blue Velvet is producing at a level that is larger than the output that minimizes average costs. The high price in the marketplace has induced Blue Velvet to increase its service level even though the result is slightly less labor productivity and thus higher per unit costs.

Both revenues and costs are shown graphically. *Total revenue (TR)* is simply the product of price and quantity: $P^* \times q^* = \$5 \times 800 = \$4,000$. On the diagram, total revenue is equal to the area of the rectangle P^*Aq^*0. (The area of a rectangle is equal to its length times its width.) At output q^*, average total cost is $4.50 (point B). Numerically, it is equal to the length of line segment q^*B. Because average total cost is derived by dividing total cost by q, we can get back to total cost by *multiplying* average total cost by q. That is,

$$ATC = \frac{TC}{q}$$

and so

$$TC = ATC \times q$$

Total cost (TC), then, is $4.50 \times 800 = \$3,600$, the area shaded blue in the diagram. *Profit* is simply the difference between total revenue (*TR*) and total cost (*TC*), or $400. This is the area that is shaded gray in the diagram. This firm is earning positive profits.

A firm, like Blue Velvet, that is earning a positive profit in the short run and expects to continue doing so has an incentive to expand its scale of operation in the long run. Managers in these firms will likely be planning to expand even as they concentrate on producing 800 units. We expect greater output to be produced in the long run as firms react to profits they are earning.

Minimizing Losses

A firm that is not earning a positive profit or breaking even is suffering a loss. Firms suffering losses fall into two categories: (1) those that find it advantageous to shut down operations immediately and bear losses equal to total fixed costs and (2) those that continue to operate in the short run to minimize their losses. The most important thing to remember here is that firms cannot exit the industry in the short run. The firm can shut down, but it cannot get rid of its fixed costs by going out of business. Fixed costs must be paid in the short run no matter what the firm does.

Whether a firm suffering losses decides to produce or not to produce in the short run depends on the advantages and disadvantages of continuing production. If a firm shuts down, it earns no revenue and has no variable costs to bear. If it continues to produce, it both earns revenue and incurs variable costs. Because a firm must bear fixed costs *whether or not* it shuts down, its decision depends *solely on whether total revenue from operating is sufficient to cover total variable cost.*

- If total revenue exceeds total variable cost, the excess revenue can be used to offset fixed costs and reduce losses, and it will pay the firm to keep operating.
- If total revenue is smaller than total variable cost, the firm that operates will suffer losses in excess of fixed costs. In this case, the firm can minimize its losses by shutting down.

Producing at a Loss to Offset Fixed Costs: Blue Velvet Revisited   Suppose consumers suddenly decide that car washing is a waste of money and demand falls. The price begins to fall, and Blue Velvet is no longer so profitable. We can see what Blue Velvet's management will decide to do by looking back at Figure 9.1. With an upward-sloping marginal cost curve, as price begins to fall, the Blue Velvet management team first will choose to reduce the number of cars it services. As long as the price is greater than ATC (which is minimized at about $4.35 on the graph), Blue Velvet continues to make a profit. What happens if the price falls below this level, say to $3 per car?

Now Blue Velvet has to decide not only how many cars to wash but whether to be open at all. If the car wash closes, there are no labor and soap costs. But Blue Velvet still has to pay for its unbreakable year-long contract, and it still owns its building, which will take some time to sell. So the fixed costs of $2,000 per week remain. For Blue Velvet, the key question is can it do better than losing $2,000? The answer depends on whether the market price is greater or less than average variable costs—the costs per unit for the variable factors. If the price is greater than the average variable cost, then Blue Velvet can pay for its workers and the soap and have something left for the investors. It will still lose money, but it will be less than $2,000. If price is less than average variable cost, the firm will not only lose its $2,000 but also have added losses on every car it washes. So the simple answer for Blue Velvet is that it should stay open and wash cars as long as it covers its variable costs. Economists call this the **shutdown point**. At all prices above this shutdown point, the marginal cost curve shows the profit-maximizing level of output. At all points below this point, optimal short-run output is zero.

We can now refine our earlier statement, from Chapter 8, that a perfectly competitive firm's marginal cost curve is its short-run supply curve. As we have just seen, a firm will shut down when the market price is less than the minimum point on the AVC curve. Also recall (or notice from the graph) that the marginal cost curve intersects the AVC at AVC's lowest point. It therefore follows that the short-run supply curve of a competitive firm is that portion of its marginal cost curve that lies above its average variable cost curve. For Blue Velvet, the firm will shut down at a price of about $1.50 (reading off the graph).

Figure 9.2 shows the short-run supply curve for the general case of a perfectly competitive firm like Blue Velvet.

shutdown point   The lowest point on the average variable cost curve. When price falls below the minimum point on AVC, total revenue is insufficient to cover variable costs and the firm will shut down and bear losses equal to fixed costs.

▲ **FIGURE 9.2 Short-Run Supply Curve of a Perfectly Competitive Firm**
At prices below average variable cost, it pays a firm to shutdown rather than continue operating. Thus, the short-run supply curve of a competitive firm is the part of its marginal cost curve that lies *above* its average variable cost curve.

The Short-Run Industry Supply Curve

short-run industry supply curve The sum of the marginal cost curves (above *AVC*) of all the firms in an industry.

Supply in a competitive industry is the sum of the quantity supplied by the individual firms in the industry at each price level. The **short-run industry supply curve** is the sum of the individual firm supply curves—that is, the marginal cost curves (above *AVC*) of all the firms in the industry. Because quantities are being added—that is, because we are finding the total quantity supplied in the industry at each price level—the curves are added horizontally.

Figure 9.3 shows the supply curve for an industry with three identical firms.[1] At a price of $6, each firm produces 150 units, which is the output where $P = MC$. The total amount supplied on the market at a price of $6 is thus 450. At a price of $5, each firm produces 120 units, for an industry supply of 360. Below $4.50, all firms shut down; P is less than *AVC*.

Two things can cause the industry supply curve to shift. In the short run, the industry supply curve shifts if something—a decrease in the price of some input, for instance—shifts the marginal cost curves of all the individual firms simultaneously. For example, when the cost of producing components of home computers decreased, the marginal cost curves of all computer manufacturers shifted downward. Such a shift amounted to the same thing as an outward shift in their supply curves. Each firm was willing to supply more computers at each price level because computers were now cheaper to produce.

In the long run, an increase or decrease in the number of firms—and, therefore, in the number of individual firm supply curves—shifts the total industry supply curve. If new firms enter the industry, the industry supply curve moves to the right; if firms exit the industry, the industry supply curve moves to the left.

We return to shifts in industry supply curves and discuss them further when we take up long-run adjustments later in this chapter.

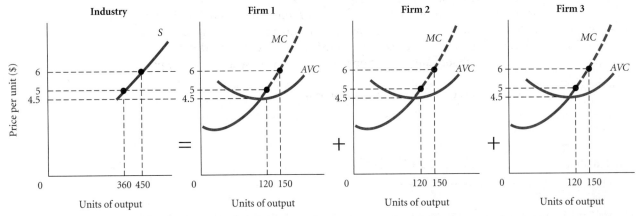

▲ **FIGURE 9.3 The Industry Supply Curve in the Short Run Is the Horizontal Sum of the Marginal Cost Curves (above *AVC*) of All the Firms in an Industry**

If there are only three firms in the industry, the industry supply curve is simply the sum of all the products supplied by the three firms at each price. For example, at $6 each firm supplies 150 units, for a total industry supply of 450.

Long-Run Directions: A Review

Table 9.2 summarizes the different circumstances that perfectly competitive firms may face as they plan for the long run. Profit-making firms will produce up to the point where price and marginal cost are equal in the short run. If there are positive profits, in the long run, there is an incentive for firms to expand their scales of plant and for new firms to enter the industry.

---

[1] Perfectly competitive industries are assumed to have many firms. Many is, of course, more than three. We use three firms here simply for purposes of illustration. The assumption that all firms are identical is often made when discussing a perfectly competitive industry.

TABLE 9.2	Profits, Losses, and Perfectly Competitive Firm Decisions in the Long and Short Run		
	Short-Run Condition	Short-Run Decision	Long-Run Decision
Profits	$TR > TC$	$P = MC$: operate	Expand: new firms enter
Losses	1. $TR \geq TVC$	$P = MC$: operate	Contract: firms exit
		(loss < total fixed cost)	
	2. $TR < TVC$	Shut down:	Contract: firms exit
		loss = total fixed cost	

A firm suffering losses will produce if and only if revenue is sufficient to cover total variable cost. Such firms, like profitable firms, will also produce up to the point where $P = MC$. If a firm suffering losses cannot cover total variable cost by operating, it will shut down and bear losses equal to total fixed cost. Whether a firm that is suffering losses decides to shut down in the short run or not, the losses create an incentive to contract in the long run. When firms are suffering losses, they generally exit the industry in the long run.

Thus, the short-run profits of firms cause them to expand or contract when opportunities exist to change their scale of plant. If expansion is desired because economic profits are positive, firms must consider what their costs are likely to be at different scales or operation. (When we use the term "scale of operation," you may find it helpful to picture factories of varying sizes.) Just as firms have to analyze different technologies to arrive at a cost structure in the short run, they must also compare their costs at different scales of plant to arrive at long-run costs. Perhaps a larger scale of operations will reduce average production costs and provide an even greater incentive for a profit-making firm to expand, or perhaps large firms will run into problems that constrain growth. The analysis of long-run possibilities is even more complex than the short-run analysis because more things are variable—scale of plant is not fixed, for example, and there are no fixed costs because firms can exit their industry in the long run. In theory, firms may choose *any* scale of operation; so they must analyze many possible options.

Now let us turn to an analysis of cost curves in the long run.

Long-Run Costs: Economies and Diseconomies of Scale

The shapes of short-run cost curves follow directly from the assumption of a fixed factor of production. As output increases beyond a certain point, the fixed factor (which we usually think of as fixed scale of plant) causes diminishing returns to other factors and thus increasing marginal costs. In the long run, however, there is no fixed factor of production. Firms can choose any scale of production. They can build small or large factories, double or triple output, or go out of business completely.

The shape of a firm's *long-run* average cost curve shows how costs vary with scale of operations. In some firms, production technology is such that increased scale, or size, reduces costs. For others, increased scale leads to higher per-unit costs. When an increase in a firm's scale of production leads to lower average costs, we say that there are **increasing returns to scale**, or **economies of scale**. When average costs do not change with the scale of production, we say that there are **constant returns to scale**. Finally, when an increase in a firm's scale of production leads to higher average costs, we say that there are **decreasing returns to scale,** or **diseconomies of scale**. Because these economies of scale are a property of production characteristics of the individual firm, they are considered *internal* economies of scale. In the Appendix to this chapter, we talk about *external* economies of scale, which describe economies or diseconomies of scale on an industry-wide basis.

increasing returns to scale, *or* economies of scale An increase in a firm's scale of production leads to lower costs per unit produced.

constant returns to scale An increase in a firm's scale of production has no effect on costs per unit produced.

decreasing returns to scale, *or* diseconomies of scale An increase in a firm's scale of production leads to higher costs per unit produced.

Increasing Returns to Scale

Technically, the phrase *increasing returns to scale* refers to the relationship between inputs and outputs. When we say that a production function exhibits increasing returns, we mean that a given percentage of increase in inputs leads to a *larger* percentage of increase in the production of output. For example, if a firm doubled or tripled inputs, it would more than double or triple output.

When firms can count on fixed input prices—that is, when the prices of inputs do not change with output levels—increasing returns to scale also means that as output rises, average cost of production falls. The term *economies of scale* refers directly to this reduction in cost per unit of output that follows from larger-scale production.

The Sources of Economies of Scale   Most of the economies of scale that immediately come to mind are technological in nature. Automobile production, for example, would be more costly per unit if a firm were to produce 100 cars per year by hand. In the early 1900s, Henry Ford introduced standardized production techniques that increased output volume, reduced costs per car, and made the automobile available to almost everyone. The new technology is not very cost-effective at small volumes of cars, but at larger volumes costs are greatly reduced. Ford's innovation provided a source of scale economics at the plant level of the auto firm.

Some economies of scale result not from technology but from firm-level efficiencies and bargaining power that can come with size. Very large companies, for instance, can buy inputs in volume at discounted prices. Large firms may also produce some of their own inputs at considerable savings, and they can certainly save in transport costs when they ship items in bulk. Wal-Mart has become the largest retailer in the United States in part because of scale economies of this type. Economics of scale have come from advantages of larger *firm* size rather than gains from plant size.

Economies of scale can be seen all around us. A bus that carries 50 people between Vancouver and Seattle uses less labor, capital, and gasoline than 50 people driving 50 different automobiles. The cost per passenger (average cost) is lower on the bus. Roommates who share an apartment are taking advantage of economies of scale. Costs per person for heat, electricity, and space are lower when an apartment is shared than if each person rents a separate apartment.

Example: Economies of Scale in Egg Production   Nowhere are economies of scale more visible than in agriculture. Consider the following example. A few years ago a major agribusiness moved to a small Ohio town and set up a huge egg-producing operation. The new firm, Chicken Little Egg Farms Inc., is completely mechanized. Complex machines feed the chickens and collect and box the eggs. Large refrigerated trucks transport the eggs all over the state daily. In the same town, some small farmers still own fewer than 200 chickens. These farmers collect the eggs, feed the chickens, clean the coops by hand, and deliver the eggs to county markets.

Table 9.3 presents some hypothetical cost data for Homer Jones's small operation and for Chicken Little Inc. Jones has his operation working well. He has several hundred chickens and

TABLE 9.3 Weekly Costs Showing Economies of Scale in Egg Production	
Jones Farm	**Total Weekly Costs**
15 hours of labor (implicit value $8 per hour)	$120
Feed, other variable costs	25
Transport costs	15
Land and capital costs attributable to egg production	17
	$177
Total output	2,400 eggs
Average cost	$0.074 per egg
Chicken Little Egg Farms Inc.	**Total Weekly Costs**
Labor	$ 5,128
Feed, other variable costs	4,115
Transport costs	2,431
Land and capital costs	19,230
	$30,904
Total output	1,600,000 eggs
Average cost	$0.019 per egg

ECONOMICS IN PRACTICE

Economies of Scale in the World Marketplace

In this chapter we describe a range of possible long-run cost curves. The form of the long-run production function and possible existence of economies of scale in production have much to say about industrial structure in ways we will explore further in a later chapter.

In a world economy in which trade occurs across geographical boundaries, if economies of scale exist, it is possible to exploit those economies across a very large output base. The 2009 World Development Report from the World Bank has an interesting chapter on scale economies with a few fascinating examples from around the world.

Dongguan is a major manufacturing city in Southeast China, lying between Guangzhou and Shenzhen. A single plant in Dongguan produces more than 30 percent of the world's magnetic recording heads used in hard disk drives. Another plant in the same city produces 60 percent of the electronic learning devices sold in the United States, while a third plant produces 30 million mobile

phones, again all in one plant. Clearly, the scale economies in these three sectors must be very large indeed. Notice in the case of all three examples that products are also light and easy to ship.

spends about 15 hours per week feeding, collecting, delivering, and so on. During the rest of his time, he raises soybeans. We can value Jones's time at $8 per hour because that is the wage he could earn working at a local manufacturing plant. When we add up all Jones's costs, including a rough estimate of the land and capital costs attributable to egg production, we arrive at $177 per week. Total production on the Jones farm runs about 200 dozen, or 2,400, eggs per week, which means that Jones's average cost comes out to $0.074 per egg.

The costs of Chicken Little Inc. are much higher in total; weekly costs run over $30,000. A much higher percentage of costs are capital costs—the firm uses a great many pieces of sophisticated machinery that cost millions to put in place. Total output is 1.6 million eggs per week, and the product is shipped all over the Midwest. The comparatively huge scale of plant has driven average production costs all the way down to $0.019 per egg.

Although these numbers are hypothetical, you can see why small farmers in the United States are finding it difficult to compete with large-scale agribusiness concerns that can realize significant economies of scale.

Many large firms have multiple plants or sites where they produce their goods and services. In our discussion in this chapter, we will distinguish between cost changes that come about because a firm decides to build a large versus a small plant and cost changes that result from firms adding volume to their production by building more plants. Coors originally produced its beer in Colorado in what was, at the time, one of the largest U.S. brewing plants; the firm believed that large size at the plant level brought cost savings. Most electronics companies, on the other hand, produce their output in multiple moderate-sized plants and hope to achieve cost savings through firm size. Both sources of scale economies are important in the economy.

Graphic Presentation A firm's **long-run average cost curve (*LRAC*)** shows the different scales at which it can choose to operate in the long run. A given point on the *LRAC* tells us the average cost of producing the associated level of output. At that point, the existing scale of plant determines the position and shape of the firm's short-run cost curves. The long-run average cost curve shows the positions of the different sets of short-run curves among which the firm must choose. In making the long-run strategic choice of plant scale, the firm then confronts an associated set of short-run cost curves. The long-run average cost curve is the "envelope" of a series of short-run curves; it "wraps around" the set of all possible short-run curves like an envelope.

When the firm experiences economies of scale, its *LRAC* will decline with output. Figure 9.4 shows short-run and long-run average cost curves for a firm that realizes economies of scale up to about 100,000 units of production and roughly constant returns to scale after that. The 100,000 unit output level in Figure 9.4 is sometimes called the **minimum efficient scale (MES)** of the firm. The

long-run average cost curve (*LRAC*) The "envelope" of a series of short-run cost curves.

minimum efficient scale (MES) The smallest size at which the long-run average cost curve is at its minimum.

Economies of Scale in Solar

Concerns about the environment and interest in sustainable energy have greatly increased the excitement by both consumers and investors in alternative energies such as wind and solar power. For both alternatives, the price of more conventional energy sources, like oil, is very important. As the price of oil rises, solar power, one of the substitutes for oil, becomes more viable. But there are also forces at work on the cost side. As the article below discusses, the process of producing solar panels is subject to scale economies, so that as the use of solar panels increases, the long-run average cost of producing them is likely to fall.

Utility Scale Solar Market Shares, Strategies, and Forecasts, Worldwide, 2010–2016

PR Newswire

Solar energy market driving forces relate to the opportunity to harness a cheap, long lasting, powerful energy source. Solar energy can be used to create electricity in huge quantity. Solar panels are mounted in a weatherproof frame and then mounted in areas with direct exposure to the sun to generate electricity from sunlight.

Solar power systems are composed of solar modules, related power electronics, and other components. Solar panels are used in residential, commercial, and industrial applications. Solar compositions of arrays that make up electric utility grids appear to be the wave of the future. Other solar systems are concentrating systems that leverage thermal transport of heated fluids and utilize traditional steam generators. The demand for solar energy is dependent on lower prices for solar and higher prices for petroleum. A combination of economies of scale being

realized in manufacturing along with increases in the current prices for petroleum will drive solar energy adoption.

Large solar farms are more popular initially, but solar is anticipated to be built out on commercial roof tops in increased quantity. The electricity generated will be fed to local substations and distributed to homes from there.

There is growing global demand for cost-effective and reliable solar power. Molten salt storage and solar electricity generation by use of steam turbines are poised to achieve significant growth. The economies of scale have not yet kicked in and will do so after 100 projects have been built out. The technology promises to be significant because the projects generate so much electricity.

Source: Excerpted from press release "Utility Scale Solar Market Shares, Strategies, and Forecasts, Worldwide, 2010–2016 Now Available at ReportsandReports.com," June 28, 2010.

MES is the smallest size at which the long-run average cost curve is at its minimum. Essentially, it is the answer to the question, how large does a firm have to be to have the best per-unit cost position possible? Consider a firm operating in an industry in which all of the firms in that industry face the long-run average cost curve shown in Figure 9.4. If you want your firm to be cost-competitive in that market, you need to produce at least 100,000 units. At smaller volumes, you will have higher costs than other firms in the industry, which makes it hard for you to stay in the industry. Policy makers are often interested in learning how large MES is relative to the total market for a product, since when MES is large relative to the total market size, we typically expect fewer firms to be in the industry. And, as we will see in the next chapter, competition may be reduced.

Figure 9.4 shows three potential scales of operation, each with its own set of short-run cost curves. Each point on the *LRAC* curve represents the minimum cost at which the associated output level can be produced. Once the firm chooses a scale on which to produce, it becomes locked into one set of cost curves in the short run. If the firm were to settle on scale 1, it would not realize the major cost advantages of producing on a larger scale. By roughly doubling its scale of operations from 50,000 to 100,000 units (scale 2), the firm reduces average costs per unit significantly.

Figure 9.4 shows that at every moment, firms face two different cost constraints. In the long run, firms can change their scale of operation, and costs may be different as a result.

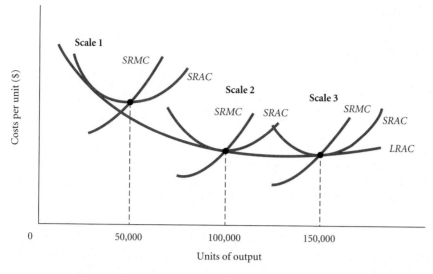

▲ **FIGURE 9.4 A Firm Exhibiting Economies of Scale**

The long-run average cost curve of a firm shows the different scales on which the firm can choose to operate in the long run. Each scale of operation defines a different short run. Here we see a firm exhibiting economies of scale; moving from scale 1 to scale 3 reduces average cost.

However, at any *given* moment, a particular scale of operation exists, constraining the firm's capacity to produce in the short run. That is why we see both short- and long-run curves in the same diagram.

Constant Returns to Scale

Technically, the term *constant returns* means that the quantitative relationship between input and output stays constant, or the same, when output is increased. If a firm doubles inputs, it doubles output; if it triples inputs, it triples output; and so on. Furthermore, if input prices are fixed, constant returns imply that average cost of production does not change with scale. In other words, constant returns to scale mean that the firm's long-run average cost curve remains flat.

The firm in Figure 9.4 exhibits roughly constant returns to scale between scale 2 and scale 3. The average cost of production is about the same in each. If the firm exhibited constant returns at levels above 150,000 units of output, the *LRAC* would continue as a flat, straight line.

Economists have studied cost data extensively over the years to estimate the extent to which economies of scale exist. Evidence suggests that in most industries, firms do not have to be gigantic to realize cost savings from scale economies. In other words, the MES is moderate relative to market size. Perhaps the best example of efficient production on a small scale is the manufacturing sector in Taiwan. Taiwan has enjoyed very rapid growth based on manufacturing firms that employ fewer than 100 workers.

One simple argument supports the empirical result that most industries seem to exhibit constant returns to scale (a flat *LRAC*) after some level of output at least at the level of the plant. Competition always pushes firms to adopt the least-cost technology and scale. If cost advantages result with larger-scale operations, the firms that shift to that scale will drive the smaller, less efficient firms out of business. A firm that wants to grow when it has reached its "optimal" size can do so by building another identical plant. It thus seems logical to conclude that most firms face constant returns to scale at the plant level *as long as* they can replicate their existing plants.

Decreasing Returns to Scale

When average cost increases with scale of production, a firm faces *decreasing returns to scale*, or *diseconomies of scale*. The most often cited example of a diseconomy of scale is bureaucratic inefficiency. As size increases beyond a certain point, operations tend to become more difficult to manage. Large size often entails increased bureaucracy, affecting both managerial incentives and control. The coordination function is more complex for larger firms than for smaller ones, and the chances that it will break down are greater. You can see that this diseconomy of scale is firm-level in type.

A large firm is also more likely than a small firm to find itself facing problems with organized labor. Unions can demand higher wages and more benefits, go on strike, force firms to incur legal expenses, and take other actions that increase production costs. (This does not mean that unions are "bad," but instead that their activities often increase costs.)

U-Shaped Long-Run Average Costs

As we have seen, the shape of a firm's long-run average cost curve depends on how costs react to changes in scale. Some firms do see economies of scale, and their long-run average cost curves slope downward. Most firms seem to have flat long-run average cost curves. Still others encounter diseconomies, and their long-run average cost curves slope upward.

Figure 9.5 describes a firm that exhibits both economies of scale and diseconomies of scale. Average costs decrease with scale of plant up to q^* and increase with scale after that. The *Economics in Practice* on p. 201 discusses the history of the U-shaped curve.

The U-shaped average cost curve looks very much like the short-run average cost curves we have examined in the last two chapters, but do not confuse the two. All short-run average cost curves are U-shaped because we assume a fixed scale of plant that constrains production and drives marginal cost upward as a result of diminishing returns. In the long run, we make no such assumption; instead, we assume that scale of plant can be changed and ask how costs change with scale.

It is important to note that economic efficiency requires taking advantage of economies of scale (if they exist) and avoiding diseconomies of scale. The **optimal scale of plant** is the scale of plant that minimizes average cost. In fact, as we will see next, competition forces firms to use the optimal scale. In Figure 9.5, q^* is the unique optimal scale.

optimal scale of plant The scale of plant that minimizes average cost.

▶ **FIGURE 9.5 A Firm Exhibiting Economies and Diseconomies of Scale**

Economies of scale push this firm's average costs down to q^*. Beyond q^*, the firm experiences diseconomies of scale; q^* is the level of production at lowest average cost, using optimal scale.

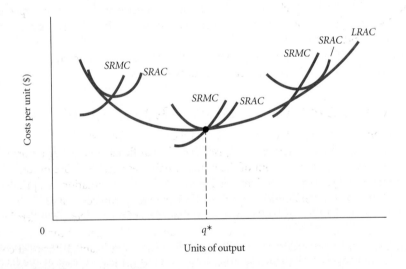

Long-Run Adjustments to Short-Run Conditions

We began this chapter by discussing the different short-run positions in which firms like Blue Velvet may find themselves. Firms can be operating at a profit or suffering economic losses; they can be shut down or producing. The industry is not in long-run equilibrium if firms have an incentive to

ECONOMICS IN PRACTICE

The Long-Run Average Cost Curve: Flat or U-Shaped?

The long-run average cost curve has been a source of controversy in economics for many years. A long-run average cost curve was first drawn as the "envelope" of a series of short-run curves in a classic article written by Jacob Viner in 1931.[1] In preparing that article, Viner gave his draftsman the task of drawing the long-run curve through the minimum points of all the short-run average cost curves.

In a supplementary note written in 1950, Viner commented:

... the error in Chart IV is left uncorrected so that future teachers and students may share the pleasure of many of their predecessors of pointing out that if I had known what an envelope was, I would not have given my excellent draftsman the technically impossible and economically inappropriate task of drawing an *AC* curve which would pass through the lowest cost points of all the *AC* curves yet not rise above any *AC* curve at any point....[2]

While this story is an interesting part of the lore of economics, a more recent debate concentrates on the economic content of this controversy. In 1986, Professor Herbert Simon of Carnegie-Mellon University stated bluntly in an interview for *Challenge* magazine that most textbooks are wrong to use the U-shaped long-run cost curve to predict the size of firms. Simon explained that studies show the firm's cost curves are not U-shaped but instead slope down to the right and then level off.[3]

What difference does it make if the long-run average cost curve has a long flat section with no upturn? In this case, there is no single point on the long-run curve that is the best. Once a firm achieves some scale, it has the same costs no matter how much larger it gets. As Simon tells us, this means we can't predict firm size. But we can still predict industry size: In this situation, we still have forces of profit seeking causing firms to enter and exit until excess profits are zero. The unique industry output is the one that corresponds to a price equal to long-run average cost that also equates supply and demand. Simon is right that this type of cost curve means the economic theory doesn't explain everything, but it still tells us a good deal.

[1] Jacob Viner, "Cost Curves and Supply Curves," *Zeitschrift fur Nationalokonomie*, Vol. 3 (1–1931), 23–46. [2] George J. Stigler and Kenneth E. Boulding, eds., *AEA Readings in Price Theory*, Vol. 6 (Chicago: Richard D. Irwin, 1952), p. 227. [3] Based on interview with Herbert A. Simon, "The Failure of Armchair Economics," *Challenge*, November–December, 1986, 23–24.

enter or exit in the long run. Thus, when firms are earning economic profits (profits above normal, or positive) or are suffering economic losses (profits below normal, or negative), the industry is not at an equilibrium and firms will change their behavior. What firms are likely to do depends in part on costs in the long run. This is why we have spent a good deal of time discussing economies and diseconomies of scale.

We can now put these two ideas together and discuss the actual long-run adjustments that are likely to take place in response to short-run profits and losses.

Short-Run Profits: Moves In and Out of Equilibrium

Consider a competitive market in which demand and costs have been stable for some period and the industry is in equilibrium. The market price is such that firms are earning a normal rate of return and the flow of firms in and out of the industry balances out. Firms are producing as efficiently as possible, and supply equals demand. Figure 9.6 shows this situation at a price of $6 and an output of 200,000 units for an industry with a U-shaped long-run cost curve.

Now suppose demand increases. Perhaps this is the market for green tea, and there has been a news report on the health benefits of the tea. What happens? Managers at the firms notice the demand increase—they too read the paper! But each firm has a fixed capital stock—it owns a set tea plantation, for example. Entry also is impossible in the short run. But existing firms can do something to meet the new demand, even within the constraints of their existing plant. They can hire overtime workers, for example, to increase yield. But this increases average costs. In Figure 9.7, firms will move up their *SRMC* curves as they produce output beyond the level of 2,000. Why do firms do this? Because the increased demand has increased the price. The new higher price makes it worthwhile for the firms to increase their output even though in the short run it is expensive to do so. In fact, the firms increase output as long as the new price is greater than the short-run marginal cost curve. We have noted the new short-run equilibrium in Figure 9.7.

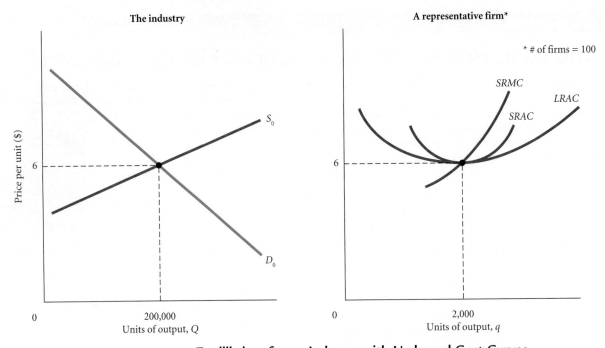

▲ **FIGURE 9.6 Equilibrium for an Industry with U-shaped Cost Curves**
The individual firm on the right is producing 2,000 units, and so we also know that the industry consists of 100 firms. All firms are identical, and all are producing at the uniquely best output level of 2,000 units.

Again supply equals demand. But there are two important differences. First, and most important, firms are making profits. The profits are noted in the gray-shaded rectangle in Figure 9.8 and are the difference between the new higher price and the new higher average cost. Second, firms are also operating at too large an output level for minimum average cost. Managers in these firms are scrambling to get increased output from a plant designed for a smaller output level.

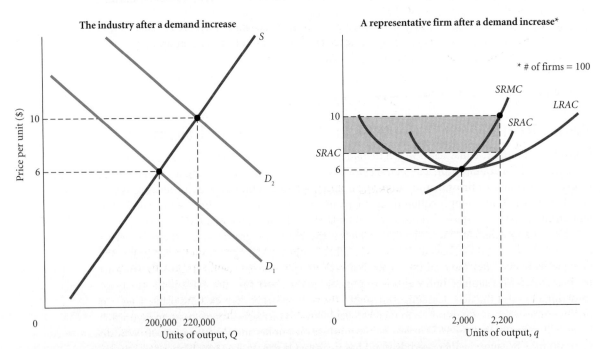

▲ **FIGURE 9.7 Industry Response to an Increase in Demand**

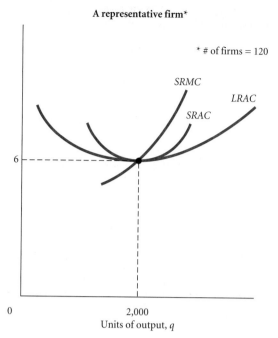

▲ **FIGURE 9.8 New Equilibrium with Higher Demand**

What happens next? Other entrepreneurs observing the industry see the excess profits and enter. Each one enters at a scale of 2,000 because that is the optimal scale in this industry. Perhaps existing firms also build new plants. With each new entry, the industry supply curve (which is just the sum of all the individual firms' supply curves) shifts to the right. More supply is available because there are more firms. Price begins to fall. As long as the price is above $6, each of the firms, both old and new, is making excess profits and more entry will occur. Once price is back to $6, there are no longer excess profits and thus no further entry. Figure 9.8 shows this new equilibrium where supply has shifted sufficiently to return the industry to the original price of $6 at a new quantity level.

Again, notice the characteristics of the final equilibrium: Each individual firm chooses a scale of operations that minimizes its long-run average cost. It operates this plant at an output level that minimizes short-run average cost. In equilibrium, each firm has

$$SRMC = SRAC = LRAC$$

Firms make no excess profits so that

$$P = SRMC = SRAC = LRAC$$

and there are enough firms so that supply equals demand.

Suppose instead of a positive demand shock, the industry experiences an unexpected cut in demand. Precisely the same economic logic holds. When demand falls (shifts to the left), the price falls. In the short run, firms cannot shrink plants, nor can they exit. But with the lower price, firms begin to produce less in their plants than before. In fact, firms cut back production so long as the price they receive is less than their short-run marginal cost. At this point, firms earn losses and are producing at too small a level and thus have higher average cost than before. Some firms drop out, and when they do so, the supply curve shifts to the left. How many firms leave? Enough so that the equilibrium is restored with the price again at $6 and the industry output has fallen reduced to reflect the reduced demand for the product.

The Fortunes of the Auto Industry

In 2010 the majority shareholder in General Motors, once counted among the top Fortune 500 firms, was the U.S. government. The government bought its interest in General Motors as a "reluctant shareholder" to help the firm move out of the bankruptcy that it entered in 2009.

The article below describes the return of the firm to profitability in mid-2010. We can use the tools of this chapter to dig into the lessons of the article.

GM Reports First Quarterly Profit Since 2007

The Wall Street Journal

Ten months after emerging from a government-orchestrated bankruptcy, General Motors Co. on Monday reported its first quarterly profit in three years, driven by dramatic cost reductions and improved global sales.

GM made $863 million in the first three months of 2010, compared with a $6 billion loss a year earlier, a performance that surprised analysts who expected more modest results. Revenue grew 40 percent to $31.5 billion, and the company generated $1 billion in cash.

GM has managed to drive up prices by building fewer vehicles and turning out cars and trucks more desirable to U.S. consumers, such as GM's revamped Chevrolet Equinox crossover, while tighter supply means the company doesn't have to rely on deals to clear out inventory.

Another factor: In North America, GM's factories are operating at 84 percent of capacity, up from less than 40 percent a year ago. Underutilized factories are a major cost drain for auto makers.

The company, meantime, has increased global sales by 24 percent amid rapid growth in emerging markets, including China.

Cost reductions made possible by last year's bankruptcy were a major factor in GM's profit.

Source: The Wall Street Journal, excerpted from "GM Reports First Quarterly Profits Since 2007" by Sharon Terlep. Copyright 2010 by *Dow Jones & Company, Inc.* Reproduced with permission of *Dow Jones & Company, Inc.* via Copyright Clearance Center.

How has GM improved profits? First, demand for autos shifted right as the recession eased and GM built vehicles "more desirable to U.S. consumers," as the article tells us. The demand shift allowed GM to raise prices and allowed it to sell more vehicles. Improved sales also helped on the cost side. The auto industry exhibits large economies of scale due in part to the large capital investment of the assembly lines. In the 2008–2009 recession, the auto industry found itself with excess capacity (the article tells us GM was operating at 40 percent capacity in the trough) and the per unit costs of cars rocketed up. By using more of its capacity, average costs fell, making for better profitability.

The demand shift is only part of the story, however. GM had also taken other actions, both in terms of union wage negotiations and restructuring, to reduce its costs. This had the effect *of shifting down* the long-run average cost curve, further increasing profits. A hard question now being asked is whether these cost reductions will be long lived.

The Long-Run Adjustment Mechanism: Investment Flows Toward Profit Opportunities

The central idea in our discussion of entry, exit, expansion, and contraction is this: In efficient markets, investment capital flows toward profit opportunities. The actual process is complex and varies from industry to industry.

We talked about efficient markets in Chapter 1. In efficient markets, profit opportunities are quickly eliminated as they develop. To illustrate this point, we described driving up to a toll booth and suggested that shorter-than-average lines are quickly eliminated as cars shift into those lines. Profits in competitive industries also are eliminated as new competing firms move into open slots, or perceived opportunities, in the industry.

In practice, the entry and exit of firms in response to profit opportunities usually involve the financial capital market. In capital markets, people are constantly looking for profits. When firms in an industry do well, capital is likely to flow into that industry in a variety of forms. Entrepreneurs start new firms, and firms producing entirely different products may join the competition to break into new markets. It happens all around us. The tremendous success of premium ice cream makers Ben and Jerry's and Häagen-Dazs spawned dozens of competitors. In

ECONOMICS IN PRACTICE

Why Are Hot Dogs So Expensive in Central Park?

Recently, one of the authors of this textbook was walking in Central Park in New York City. Since it was lunchtime and she was hungry, she decided to indulge her secret passion for good old-fashioned hot dogs. Because she did this frequently, she was well aware that the standard price for a hot dog in New York City was $1.50. So she was surprised when she handed the vendor $2 that she received no change back. As it turned out, the price of a hot dog inside the park was $2.00, not the $1.50 vendors charged elsewhere in the city. Since she was trained as an economist, she wanted to know what caused the difference in price.

First, she looked to the demand side of the market. If hot dogs are selling for $2.00 in the park but only $1.50 outside the park, people must be willing and able to pay more for them in the park. Why? Perhaps hot dogs are more enjoyable to people when eaten while walking through Central Park. Hot dogs and "walking through the park" may be complementary goods. Or maybe people who walk in the park at noon are richer.

You might ask, if hot dogs are available outside the park for $1.50, why don't people buy them there and bring them to the park? The fact is that hot dogs are good only when they are hot, and they get cold very quickly. A hot dog purchased 5 minutes away from Central Park will be stone cold by the time someone reaches the park.

But looking at the demand side is not enough to understand a market. We also have to explain the behavior of the hot dog vendors who comprise the supply side of the market. On the supply side, the author knew that the market for hot dogs was virtually perfectly competitive outside the park. First, the product is homogeneous. Essentially all vendors supply the same product: a standard quality-certified hot dog and two varieties of mustard. Second, there is free entry. Since most vendors have wheels on their carts, if the price of hot dogs rises above $1.50 in one part of town, we would expect vendors to move there. The added supply would then push prices back to Price (P) = short-run marginal cost $(SRAC)$ = long-run average cost $(LRAC)$. At P = $1.50, individual vendors around the city must be earning enough to cover average costs including a normal rate of

return (see the discussion in the text on p. 190). If the market price produces excess profits, new vendors will show up to compete those excess profits away.

All of this would suggest that the price of hot dogs should be the same everywhere in New York City. If a vendor is able to charge $2 in the park and has the same costs as a vendor outside the park, he must be earning above-normal profits. After all, the vendor makes $.50 more on each hot dog. Something must be preventing the outside vendors from rolling their carts into the park, which would increase the supply of hot dogs and drive the price back to $1.50.

That something is a more expensive license. In New York, you need a license to operate a hot dog cart, and a license to operate in the park costs more. Since hot dogs are $0.50 more in the park, the added cost of a license each year must be roughly $0.50 per hot dog sold. In fact, in New York City, licenses to sell hot dogs in the park are auctioned off for many thousands of dollars, while licenses to operate in more remote parts of the city cost only about $1,000.

one Massachusetts town of 35,000, a small ice cream store opened to rave reviews, long lines, and high prices and positive profits. Within a year, there were four new ice cream/frozen yogurt stores, no lines, and lower prices. Magic? No, just the natural functioning of competition.

A powerful example of an industry expanding with higher prices and higher economic profits is the housing sector prior to 2007. From the late 1990s until early 2006, the housing market was booming nationally. Demand was shifting to the right for a number of reasons. As it did, housing prices rose substantially and with them the profits being made by builders. As builders responded with higher output, the number of new units started (housing starts) increased to a near record level of over 2.2 million per year in 2005. Construction employment grew to over 7.5 million.

Starting in 2006, housing demand shifted to the left. The inventory of unsold property began to build, and prices started to fall. That turned profits into losses. Home builders cut their production, and many went out of business. These moves had major ramifications for the performance of the whole economy. Go back and look at Figure 9.7 and Figure 9.8. Make sure you understand how these diagrams explain both the expansion and contraction of the housing sector since 2000.

Many believe that part of the explosion of technology-based dot-com companies is due to the ease of entering the sector. All it takes to start a company is an idea, a terminal, and Web access. The number of new firms entering the industry is so large that statistical agencies cannot keep pace.

long-run competitive equilibrium When $P = SRMC = SRAC = LRAC$ and profits are zero.

When there is promise of positive profits, investments are made and output expands. When firms end up suffering losses, firms contract and some go out of business. It can take quite a while, however, for an industry to achieve **long-run competitive equilibrium**, the point at which $P = SRMC = SRAC = LRAC$ and profits are zero. In fact, because costs and tastes are in a constant state of flux, very few industries ever really get there. The economy is always changing. There are always some firms making profits and some firms suffering losses.

This, then, is a story about tendencies:

> Investment—in the form of new firms and expanding old firms—will over time tend to favor those industries in which profits are being made; and over time, industries in which firms are suffering losses will gradually contract from disinvestment.

Output Markets: A Final Word

In the last four chapters, we have been building a model of a simple market system under the assumption of perfect competition. Let us provide just one more example to review the actual response of a competitive system to a change in consumer preferences.

Over the past two decades, Americans have developed a taste for wine in general and for California wines in particular. We know that household demand is constrained by income, wealth, and prices and that income is (at least in part) determined by the choices that households make. Within these constraints, households increasingly choose—or demand—wine. The demand curve for wine has shifted to the right, causing excess demand followed by an increase in price.

With higher prices, wine producers find themselves earning positive profits. *This increase in price and consequent rise in profits is the basic signal that leads to a reallocation of society's resources.* In the short run, wine producers are constrained by their current scales of operation. California has only a limited number of vineyards and only a limited amount of vat capacity, for example.

In the long run, however, we would expect to see resources flow in to compete for these profits, and this is exactly what happens. New firms enter the wine-producing business. New vines are planted, and new vats and production equipment are purchased and put in place. Vineyard owners move into new states—Rhode Island, Texas, and Maryland—and established growers increase production. Overall, more wine is produced to meet the new consumer demand. At the same time, competition is forcing firms to operate using the most efficient technology available.

What starts as a shift in preferences thus ends up as a shift in resources. Land is reallocated, and labor moves into wine production. All this is accomplished without any central planning or direction.

You have now seen what lies behind the demand curves and supply curves in competitive output markets. The next two chapters take up competitive *input* markets and complete the picture.

SUMMARY

1. For any firm, one of three conditions holds at any given moment: (1) The firm is earning positive profits, (2) the firm is suffering losses, or (3) the firm is just breaking even—that is, earning a normal rate of return and thus zero profits.

SHORT-RUN CONDITIONS AND LONG-RUN DIRECTIONS *p. 190*

2. A firm that is earning positive profits in the short run and expects to continue doing so has an incentive to expand in the long run. Profits also provide an incentive for new firms to enter the industry.

3. In the short run, firms suffering losses are stuck in the industry. They can shut down operations ($q = 0$), but they must still bear fixed costs. In the long run, firms suffering losses can exit the industry.

4. A firm's decision about whether to shut down in the short run depends solely on whether its total revenue from operating is sufficient to cover its total variable cost. If total revenue exceeds total variable cost, the excess can be used to pay some fixed costs and thus reduce losses.

5. Anytime that price is below the minimum point on the average variable cost curve, total revenue will be less than total variable cost, and the firm will shut down. The minimum point on the average variable cost curve (which is also the point where marginal cost and average variable cost intersect) is called the *shutdown point*. At all prices above the shutdown point, the *MC* curve shows the profit-maximizing level of output. At all prices below it, optimal short-run output is zero.

6. The *short-run supply curve* of a firm in a perfectly competitive industry is the portion of its marginal cost curve that lies above its average variable cost curve.

7. Two things can cause the industry supply curve to shift: (1) in the short run, anything that causes marginal costs to change across the industry, such as an increase in the price of a particular input, and (2) in the long run, entry or exit of firms.

LONG-RUN COSTS: ECONOMIES AND DISECONOMIES OF SCALE *p. 195*

8. When an increase in a firm's scale of production leads to lower average costs, the firm exhibits *increasing returns to scale*, or *economies of scale*. When average costs do not change with the scale of production, the firm exhibits *constant returns to scale*. When an increase in a firm's scale of production leads to higher average costs, the firm exhibits *decreasing returns to scale*, or *diseconomies of scale*.

9. A firm's *long-run average cost curve (LRAC)* shows the costs associated with different scales on which it can choose to operate in the long run.

LONG-RUN ADJUSTMENTS TO SHORT-RUN CONDITIONS *p. 200*

10. When short-run profits exist in an industry, firms enter and existing firms expand. These events shift the industry supply curve to the right. When this happens, price falls and ultimately profits are eliminated.

11. When short-run losses are suffered in an industry, some firms exit and some firms reduce scale. These events shift the industry supply curve to the left, raising price and eliminating losses.

12. *Long-run competitive equilibrium* is reached when $P = SRMC = SRAC = LRAC$ and profits are zero.

13. In efficient markets, investment capital flows toward profit opportunities.

REVIEW TERMS AND CONCEPTS

breaking even, *p. 190*

constant returns to scale, *p. 195*

decreasing returns to scale *or diseconomies of scale, p. 195*

increasing returns to scale *or economies of scale, p. 195*

long-run average cost curve (*LRAC*), *p. 197*

long-run competitive equilibrium, *p. 206*

minimum efficient scale (MES), *p. 197*

optimal scale of plant, *p. 200*

short-run industry supply curve, *p. 194*

shutdown point, *p. 193*

long-run competitive equilibrium, $P = SRMC = SRAC = LRAC$

PROBLEMS

All problems are available on www.myeconlab.com

1. For each of the following, decide whether you agree or disagree and explain your answer:
   a. Firms that exhibit constant returns to scale have U-shaped long-run average cost curves.
   b. A firm suffering losses in the short run will continue to operate as long as total revenue at least covers fixed cost.

2. Ajax is a competitive firm operating under the following conditions: Price of output is $5, the profit-maximizing level of output is 20,000 units of output, and the total cost (full economic cost) of producing 20,000 units is $120,000. The firm's *only* fixed factor of production is a $300,000 stock of capital (a building). If the interest rate available on comparable risks is

10 percent, should this firm shut down immediately in the short run? Explain your answer.

3. Explain why it is possible that a firm with a production function that exhibits increasing returns to scale can run into diminishing returns at the same time.

4. Which of the following industries do you think are likely to exhibit large economies of scale? Explain why in each case.
   a. Home building
   b. Electric power generation
   c. Vegetable farming
   d. Software development
   e. Aircraft manufacturing

5. For cases *A* through *F* in the following table, would you (1) operate or shut down in the short run and (2) expand your plant or exit the industry in the long run?

	A	B	C	D	E	F
Total revenue	1,500	2,000	2,000	5,000	5,000	5,000
Total cost	1,500	1,500	2,500	6,000	7,000	4,000
Total fixed cost	500	500	200	1,500	1,500	1,500

6. [Related to the *Economics in Practice* on p. 201] Do you agree or disagree with the following statements? Explain in a sentence or two.
   a. A firm will never sell its product for less than it costs to produce it.
   b. If the short-run marginal cost curve is U-shaped, the long-run average cost curve is likely to be U-shaped as well.

7. The Smythe chicken farm outside Little Rock, Arkansas, produces 25,000 chickens per month. Total cost of production at Smythe Farm is $28,000. Down the road are two other farms. Faubus Farm produces 55,000 chickens a month, and total cost is $50,050. Mega Farm produces 100,000 chickens per month, at a total cost of $91,000. These data suggest that there are significant economies of scale in chicken production. Do you agree or disagree with this statement? Explain your answer.

8. Indicate whether you agree or disagree with the following statements. Briefly explain your answers.
   a. Increasing returns to scale refers to a situation where an increase in a firm's scale of production leads to higher costs per unit produced.
   b. Constant returns to scale refers to a situation where an increase in a firm's scale of production has no effect on costs per unit produced.
   c. Decreasing returns to scale refers to a situation where an increase in a firm's scale of production leads to lower costs per unit produced.

9. You are given the following cost data:

q	TFC	TVC
0	12	0
1	12	5
2	12	9
3	12	14
4	12	20
5	12	28
6	12	38

If the price of output is $7, how many units of output will this firm produce? What is the total revenue? What is the total cost? Will the firm operate or shut down in the short run? in the long run? Briefly explain your answers.

10. The concept of economies of scale refers to lower per-unit production costs at higher levels of output. The easiest way to understand this is to look at whether long-run average cost decreases with output (economies of scale) or whether long-run average cost increases with output (diseconomies of scale). If average cost is constant as output rises, there is constant returns to scale. But the concept of falling unit costs is all around us. Explain how the concept of economies of scale helps shed light on each of the following:
   a. car pooling

   b. doubling up to reduce rent
   c. farming
   d. a single-family car versus public transit
   e. a huge refinery

11. According to its Web site, Netflix is the world's largest online entertainment subscription service. It ships over 2 million DVDs daily to its more than 15 million members. On its Web site, Netflix indicates that its growth strategy is to "focus on subscription growth in order to realize economies of scale." In this business, where do you think scale economies come from?

12. From 2000 to 2005, the home building sector was expanding and new housing construction as measured by housing starts was approaching an all-time high. (At www.census.gov, click "Housing," then click "Construction data.") Big builders such as Lennar Corporation were making exceptional profits. The industry was expanding. Existing home building firms invested in more capacity and raised output. New home building firms entered the industry. From 2006 to 2009, demand for new and existing homes dropped. The inventory of unsold homes grew sharply. Home prices began to fall. Home builders suffered losses, and the industry contracted. Many firms went out of business, and many workers in the construction industry went bankrupt. Use the Internet to verify that all of these events happened. Access www.bls.gov for employment data and www.bea.gov for information on residential construction as part of gross domestic product. What has happened since the beginning of 2010? Has the housing market recovered? Have housing starts stopped falling? If so, at what level? Write a short essay about whether the housing sector is about to expand or contract.

13. [Related to the *Economics in Practice* on p. 205] St. Mark's Square is a beautiful plaza in Venice that is often frequented by both tourists and pigeons. Ringing the piazza are many small, privately owned cafes. In these cafes, a cappuccino costs 7 euros despite the fact that an equally good cappuccino costs only 3 euros a block a way. What is going on here?

14. The following problem traces the relationship between firm decisions, market supply, and market equilibrium in a perfectly competitive market.
   a. Complete the following table for a single firm in the short run.

OUTPUT	TFC	TVC	TC	AVC	ATC	MC
0	$300	$ 0	—	—	—	—
1	—	100	—	—	—	—
2	—	150	—	—	—	—
3	—	210	—	—	—	—
4	—	290	—	—	—	—
5	—	400	—	—	—	—
6	—	540	—	—	—	—
7	—	720	—	—	—	—
8	—	950	—	—	—	—
9	—	1,240	—	—	—	—
10	—	1,600	—	—	—	—

   b. Using the information in the table, fill in the following supply schedule for this individual firm under perfect competition and indicate profit (positive or negative) at each output level. (*Hint:* At each hypothetical price, what is the *MR* of producing 1 more unit of output? Combine this with the *MC* of another unit to figure out the quantity supplied.)

PRICE	QUANTITY SUPPLIED	PROFIT
$ 50	—	——
70	—	——
100	—	——
130	—	——
170	—	——
220	—	——
280	—	——
350	—	——

c. Now suppose there are 100 firms in this industry, all with identical cost schedules. Fill in the market quantity supplied at each price in this market.

PRICE	MARKET QUANTITY SUPPLIED	MARKET QUANTITY DEMANDED
$ 50	—	1,000
70	—	900
100	—	800
130	—	700
170	—	600
220	—	500
280	—	400
350	—	300

d. Fill in the blanks: From the market supply and demand schedules in c., the equilibrium market price for this good is _____ and the equilibrium market quantity is _____. Each firm will produce a quantity of _____ and earn a _____ (profit/loss) equal to _____.

e. In d., your answers characterize the short-run equilibrium in this market. Do they characterize the long-run equilibrium as well? If so, explain why. If not, explain why not (that is, what would happen in the long run to change the equilibrium and why?).

*15. Assume that you are hired as an analyst at a major New York consulting firm. Your first assignment is to do an industry analysis of the tribble industry. After extensive research and two all-nighters, you have obtained the following information:
■ *Long-run costs*:
Capital costs: $5 per unit of output
Labor costs: $2 per unit of output
■ No economies or diseconomies of scale
■ Industry currently earning a normal return to capital (profit of zero)
■ Industry perfectly competitive, with each of 100 firms producing the same amount of output
■ *Total industry output*: 1.2 million tribbles
Demand for tribbles is expected to grow rapidly over the next few years to a level twice as high as it is now, but (due to short-run diminishing returns) each of the 100 existing firms is likely to be producing only 50 percent more.

a. Sketch the long-run cost curve of a representative firm.

b. Show the current conditions by drawing two diagrams, one showing the industry and one showing a representative firm.

c. Sketch the increase in demand and show how the industry is likely to respond in the short run and in the long run.

16. The following graph shows the supply curve and three different demand curves for a perfectly competitive industry. The table represents cost data for a representative firm in the industry.

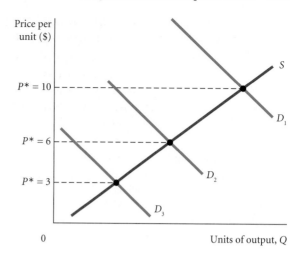

MARKET PRICE	q^* @ p^* = MC	ATC @ p^* = MC	AVC @ p^* = MC
$p^* = 10$	250	$8	$6
$p^* = 6$	175	8	4
$p^* = 3$	100	9	4

a. Use the data in the table and draw a graph for the representative firm in the industry when the industry demand curve is represented by D_1. What is the profit or loss for this firm? Shade in the profit or loss area on the graph.

b. Draw a graph for the representative firm when the industry demand curve falls to D_2. What is the profit or loss for this firm? Shade in the profit or loss area on the graph.

c. Draw a graph for the representative firm when the industry demand curve falls to D_3. What is the profit or loss for this firm? Shade in the profit or loss area on the graph.

17. For each of the three scenarios in the previous question ($p^* = 10$, $p^* = 6$, and $p^* = 3$), explain the long-run incentives for each representative firm in the industry. Also explain what should happen to the size of the industry as a whole.

18. Construct a graph with AVC, ATC, and MC curves. On this graph add a marginal revenue curve for a representative firm in a perfectly competitive industry which is maximizing profits at a price of p^*_1. Add a second marginal revenue curve for a firm which is minimizing losses but continues to produce when the price is p^*_2. Add a third marginal revenue curve for a firm which is shutting down when the price is p^*_3. Explain where you decided to place each of the marginal revenue curves and identify the shutdown point on the graph.

19. The shape of a firm's long-run average cost curve depends on how costs vary with scale of operation. Draw a long-run average cost curve for a firm which exhibits economies of scale, constant returns to scale, and diseconomies of scale. Identify each of these sections of the cost curve and explain why each section exemplifies its specific type of returns to scale.

20. [Related to the *Economics in Practice* on p. 198] A new innovation in computer technology is called "cloud computing." With cloud computing, information and software are provided to computers on an "as-needed" basis, much like utilities are provided to homes and businesses. In a statement advocating the advantages of large, public cloud providers like Amazon.com over smaller enterprise data centers, James Hamilton, a vice president at Amazon claimed that "server,

*Note: Problems marked with an asterisk are more challenging.

networking and administration costs the average enterprise five to seven times what it costs a large provider." What does Hamilton's statement imply about the returns to scale in the cloud computing industry?

Source: James Urquhart, "James Hamilton on cloud economies of scale," *cnet.com*, April 28, 2010.

21. The long-run average cost curve for an industry is represented in the following graph. Add short-run average cost curves and short-run marginal cost curves for three firms in this industry, with one firm producing an output of 10,000 units, one firm producing an output of 20,000, and one firm producing an output of 30,000. Label these as Scale 1, Scale 2, and Scale 3, respectively. What is likely to happen to the scale of each of these three firms in the long run?

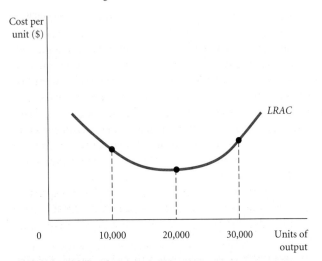

22. On the following graph for a purely competitive industry, Scale 1 represents the short-run production for a representative firm. Explain what is currently happening with firms in this industry in the short run and what will likely happen in the long run.

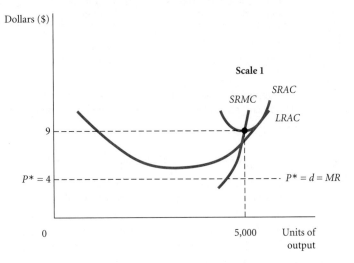

CHAPTER 9 APPENDIX

External Economies and Diseconomies and the Long-Run Industry Supply Curve

Sometimes average costs increase or decrease with the size of the industry, in addition to responding to changes in the size of the firm itself. When long-run average costs decrease as a result of industry growth, we say that there are **external economies**. When average costs increase as a result of industry growth, we say that there are **external diseconomies**. (Remember the distinction between internal and external economies: *Internal economies of scale are found within firms, whereas external economies occur on an industry-wide basis.*)

The expansion of the home building sector of the economy between 2000 and 2005 illustrates how external diseconomies of scale arise and how they imply a rising long-run average cost curve.

Beginning in 2000, the overall economy suffered a slowdown as the dot-com exuberance turned to a bursting stock market bubble, and the events of 9/11 raised the specter of international terrorism.

One sector, however, came alive between 2000 and 2005: housing. Very low interest rates lowered the monthly cost of

home ownership, immigration increased the number of households, millions of baby boomers traded up and bought second homes, and investors who had been burned by the stock market bust turned to housing as a "real" asset.

All of this increased the demand for single-family homes and condominiums around the country. Table 9A.1 shows what happened to house prices, output, and the costs of inputs during the first 5 years of the decade.

First, house prices began to rise faster than other prices while the cost of construction materials stayed flat. Profitability in the home building sector took off. Next, as existing builders expanded their operations, new firms started up. The number of new housing units "started" stood at just over 1.5 million annually in 2000 and then rose to over 2 million by 2005. All of this put pressure on the prices of construction materials such as lumber and wallboard. The table shows that construction materials costs rose more than 8 percent in 2004. These input prices increased the costs of home building. The expanding *industry* caused external diseconomies of scale.

The Long-Run Industry Supply Curve

Recall that long-run competitive equilibrium is achieved when entering firms responding to profits or exiting firms fleeing from losses drive price to a level that just covers long-run average

TABLE 9A.1 Construction of New Housing and Construction Materials Costs, 2000–2005

Year	House Prices % Over the Previous Year	Housing Starts (Thousands)	Housing Starts % Change Over the Previous Year	Construction Materials Prices % Change Over the Previous Year	Consumer Prices % Change Over the Previous Year
2000	—	1,573	—	—	—
2001	7.5	1,661	56%	0%	2.8%
2002	7.5	1,710	2.9%	1.5%	1.5%
2003	7.9	1,853	8.4%	1.6%	2.3%
2004	12.0	1,949	5.2%	8.3%	2.7%
2005	13.0	2,053	5.3%	5.4%	2.5%

Source: Economy.com and the Office of Federal Housing Enterprise Oversight (OFHEO).

costs. Profits are zero, and $P = LRAC = SRAC = SRMC$. At this point, individual firms are operating at the most efficient scale of plant—that is, at the minimum point on their $LRAC$ curve.

As we saw in the text, long-run equilibrium is not easily achieved. Even if a firm or an industry does achieve long-run equilibrium, it will not remain at that point indefinitely. Economies are dynamic. As population and the stock of capital grow and as preferences and technology change, some sectors will expand and some will contract. How do industries adjust to long-term changes? The answer depends on both internal and external factors.

The extent of *internal* economies (or diseconomies) determines the shape of a firm's long-run average cost curve ($LRAC$). If a firm changes its scale and either expands or contracts, its average costs will increase, decrease, or stay the same *along* the $LRAC$ curve. Recall that the $LRAC$ curve shows the relationship between a firm's output (q) and average total cost (ATC). A firm enjoying internal economies will see costs decreasing as it expands its scale; a firm facing internal diseconomies will see costs increasing as it expands its scale.

However, external economies and diseconomies have nothing to do with the size of *individual* firms in a competitive market. Because individual firms in perfectly competitive industries are very small relative to the market, other firms are affected only minimally when an individual firm changes its output or scale of operation. *External* economies and diseconomies arise from industry expansions; that is, they arise when many firms increase their output simultaneously or when new firms enter an industry. If industry expansion causes costs to increase (external diseconomies), the $LRAC$ curves facing individual firms shift upward; costs increase regardless of the level of output finally chosen by the firm. Similarly, if industry expansion causes costs to decrease (external economies), the $LRAC$ curves facing individual firms shift downward; costs decrease at all potential levels of output.

An example of an expanding industry facing external economies is illustrated in Figure 9A.1. Initially, the industry and the representative firm are in long-run competitive equilibrium at the price P_0 determined by the intersection of the initial demand curve D_0 and the initial supply curve S_0. P_0 is

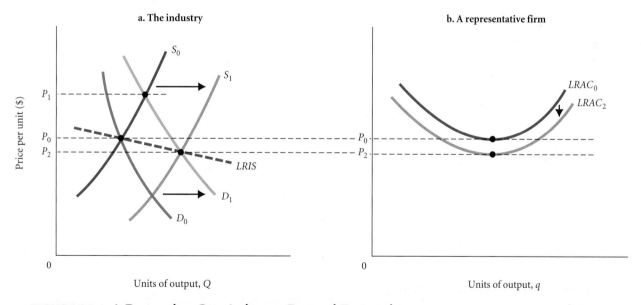

a. The industry

b. A representative firm

▲ **FIGURE 9A.1 A Decreasing-Cost Industry: External Economies**
In a decreasing-cost industry, average cost declines as the industry expands. As demand expands from D_0 to D_1, price rises from P_0 to P_1. As new firms enter and existing firms expand, supply shifts from S_0 to S_1, driving price down. If costs decline as a result of the expansion to $LRAC_2$, the final price will be below P_0 at P_2. The long-run industry supply curve ($LRIS$) slopes downward in a decreasing-cost industry.

the long-run equilibrium price; it intersects the initial long-run average cost curve ($LRAC_0$) at its minimum point. At this point, economic profits are zero.

Let us assume that as time passes, demand increases—that is, the demand curve shifts to the right from D_0 to D_1. This increase in demand will push price all the way to P_1. Without drawing the short-run cost curves, we know that economic profits now exist and that firms are likely to enter the industry to compete for them. In the absence of external economies or diseconomies, firms would enter the industry, shifting the supply curve to the right and driving price back to the bottom of the long-run average cost curve, where profits are zero. Nevertheless, the industry in Figure 9A.1 enjoys external economies. As firms enter and the industry expands, costs decrease; and as the supply curve shifts to the right from S_0 toward S_1, the long-run average cost curve shifts downward to $LRAC_2$. Thus, to reach the new long-run equilibrium level of price and output, the supply curve must shift all the way to S_1. Only when the supply curve reaches S_1 is price driven down to the new equilibrium price of P_2, the minimum point on the *new* long-run average cost curve.

Presumably, further expansion would lead to even greater savings because the industry encounters external economies.

The red dashed line in Figure 9A.1(a) that traces out price and total output over time as the industry expands is called the **long-run industry supply curve (LRIS)**. When an industry enjoys external economies, its long-run supply curve slopes down. Such an industry is called a **decreasing-cost industry**.

Figure 9A.2 shows the long-run industry supply curve for an industry that faces external *diseconomies*. (These were suffered in the construction industry, you will recall, when increased house building activity drove up lumber prices.) As demand expands from D_0 to D_1, price is driven up from P_0 to P_1. In response to the resulting higher profits, firms enter, shifting the short-run supply schedule to the right and driving price down. However, this time, as the industry expands, the long-run average cost curve shifts up to $LRAC_2$ as a result of external diseconomies. Now, price has to fall back only to P_2 (the minimum point on $LRAC_2$), not all the way to P_0, to eliminate economic profits. This type of industry, whose long-run industry supply curve slopes up to the right, is called an **increasing-cost industry**.

It should not surprise you to know that industries in which there are no external economies or diseconomies of scale have flat, or horizontal, long-run industry supply curves. These industries are called **constant-cost industries**.

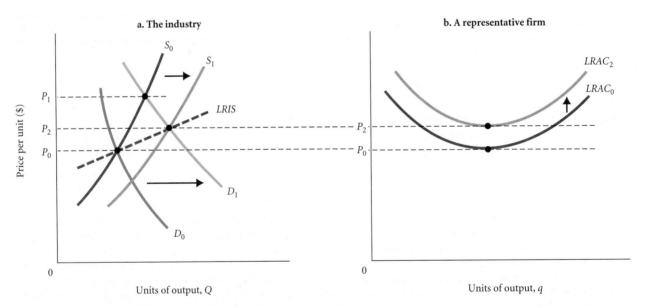

a. The industry **b. A representative firm**

▲ **FIGURE 9A.2 An Increasing-Cost Industry: External Diseconomies**

In an increasing-cost industry, average cost increases as the industry expands. As demand shifts from D_0 to D_1, price rises from P_0 to P_1. As new firms enter and existing firms expand output, supply shifts from S_0 to S_1, driving price down. If long-run average costs rise, as a result, to $LRAC_2$, the final price will be P_2. The long-run industry supply curve (*LRIS*) slopes up in an increasing-cost industry.

APPENDIX SUMMARY

EXTERNAL ECONOMIES AND DISECONOMIES *p. 210*

1. When long-run average costs decrease as a result of industry growth, we say that the industry exhibits *external economies*. When long-run average costs increase as a result of industry growth, we say that the industry exhibits *external diseconomies*.

THE LONG-RUN INDUSTRY SUPPLY CURVE *p. 210*

2. The *long-run industry supply curve* (*LRIS*) is a graph that traces out price and total output over time as an industry expands. A *decreasing-cost industry* is an industry in which

average costs fall as the industry expands. It exhibits external economies, and its long-run industry supply curve slopes downward. An *increasing-cost industry* is an industry in which average costs rise as the industry expands. It exhibits external diseconomies, and its long-run industry supply curve slopes upward. A *constant-cost industry* is an industry that shows no external economies or diseconomies as the industry grows. Its long-run industry supply curve is horizontal, or flat.

APPENDIX REVIEW TERMS AND CONCEPTS

constant-cost industry An industry that shows no economies or diseconomies of scale as the industry grows. Such industries have flat, or horizontal, long-run supply curves. *p. 212*

decreasing-cost industry An industry that realizes external economies—that is, average costs decrease as the industry grows. The long-run supply curve for such an industry has a negative slope. *p. 212*

external economies and diseconomies When industry growth results in a decrease of long-run average costs, there are *external economies*; when industry growth results in an increase of long-run average costs, there are *external diseconomies. p. 210*.

increasing-cost industry An industry that encounters external diseconomies—that is, average costs increase as the industry grows. The long-run supply curve for such an industry has a positive slope. *p. 212*

long-run industry supply curve (*LRIS*) A graph that traces out price and total output over time as an industry expands. *p. 212*

APPENDIX PROBLEMS

1. In deriving the short-run industry supply curve (the sum of firms' marginal cost curves), we assumed that input prices are constant because competitive firms are price-takers. This same assumption holds in the derivation of the long-run industry supply curve. Do you agree or disagree? Explain.

2. Consider an industry that exhibits external diseconomies of scale. Suppose that over the next 10 years, demand for that industry's product increases rapidly. Describe in detail the adjustments likely to follow. Use diagrams in your answer.

3. A representative firm producing cloth is earning a normal profit at a price of $10 per yard. Draw a supply and demand diagram showing equilibrium at this price. Assuming that the industry is a constant-cost industry, use the diagram to show the long-term adjustment of the industry as demand grows over time. Explain the adjustment m echanism.

4. Evaluate the following statement. It is impossible for a firm facing internal economies of scale to be in an industry which is experiencing external diseconomies.

5. Assume demand is decreasing in a contracting industry. Draw three supply and demand diagrams which reflect this, with the first representing an increasing-cost industry, the second representing a decreasing-cost industry, and the third representing a constant-cost industry. Assume that prior to the decrease in demand, the industry is in competitive long-run equilibrium. Include the long-run industry supply curve in each diagram and explain what is happening in each scenario. Specify whether each diagram represents external economies or external diseconomies.

Input Demand: The Labor and Land Markets

10

In 2009 the average yearly wage for a welder was $36,630, while the average yearly wage for a computer programmer was $74,690. What determines these wages? *Why* is the price for an acre of land in Toledo, Ohio, less than it is in San Francisco, California? It should not surprise you to learn that the same forces of supply and demand that determine the prices of the goods and services we consume can also be used to explain what happens in the markets for inputs like labor,

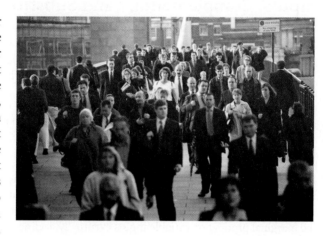

land, and capital. These input markets are the subject of our next two chapters. In this chapter we set out a basic framework and discuss labor and land, while in Chapter 11 we tackle the more complicated topic of capital and investment.

Input Markets: Basic Concepts

As we begin to discuss the market for labor and land, four concepts will be important to understand: derived demand, complementary and substitutable inputs, diminishing returns, and marginal revenue product. Once we outline these four concepts, we will be in a position to look at supply and demand in input markets.

Demand for Inputs: A *Derived* Demand

When we looked at the Blue Velvet Car Wash in Chapter 9, we saw that the number and price of car washes depended on, among other things, how much drivers liked getting their cars washed (the demand curve). If we want to explain the price of ice cream, knowing that most people have a sweet tooth would be helpful. Now think about the demand for a welder. Why might someone have a demand for a welder? In input markets, the reason we demand something is not because it is itself useful, but because it can be used to produce something else that we want. We demand a welder because he or she is needed to make a car and that car has value. The central difference between the demand for goods and services and the demand for an input is that input demand is a **derived demand**. The higher the demand for cars, the higher the demand for welders.

> Inputs are demanded by a firm if and only if households demand the good or service provided by that firm.

derived demand The demand for resources (inputs) that is dependent on the demand for the outputs those resources can be used to produce.

productivity of an input The amount of output produced per unit of that input.

Valuing an input requires us to look at the output that the input is used to produce. The **productivity of an input** is the amount of output produced per unit of that input. When a large amount of output is produced per unit of an input, the input is said to exhibit *high productivity*. When only a small amount of output is produced per unit of the input, the input is said to exhibit *low productivity*.

In the press, we often read about conflicts between labor unions and manufacturing firms. But understanding that labor demand is a derived demand shows us the common ground between labor and management: An increase in the demand for a product potentially improves the position not only of owners of the firm producing that good, but also the position of workers providing labor input.

Inputs: Complementary and Substitutable

Inputs can be *complementary* or *substitutable*. Two inputs used together may enhance, or complement, each other. For example, a new machine is often useless without someone to run it. Machines can also be substituted for labor, or—less often—labor can be substituted for machines.

All this means that a firm's input demands are tightly linked to one another. An increase or decrease in wages naturally causes the demand for labor to change, but it may also have an effect on the demand for capital or land. If we are to understand the demand for inputs, therefore, we must understand the connections among labor, capital, and land.

Diminishing Returns

Recall that the short run is the period during which some fixed factor of production limits a firm's capacity to expand. Under these conditions, the firm that decides to increase output will eventually encounter diminishing returns. Stated more formally, a fixed scale of plant means that the marginal product of variable inputs eventually declines.

marginal product of labor (MP_L) The additional output produced by 1 additional unit of labor.

Recall also that **marginal product of labor (MP_L)** is the additional output produced if a firm hires 1 additional unit of labor. For example, if a firm pays for 400 hours of labor per week—10 workers working 40 hours each—and asks one worker to stay an extra hour, the product of the 401st hour is the marginal product of labor for that firm.

In Chapter 7, we talked at some length about declining marginal product at a sandwich shop. The first two columns of Table 10.1 reproduce some of the production data from that shop. You may remember that the shop has only one grill, at which only two or three people can work comfortably. In this example, the grill is the fixed factor of production in the short run. Labor is the variable factor. The first worker can produce 10 sandwiches per hour, and the second worker can produce 15 (column 3 of Table 10.1). The second worker can produce more because the first worker is busy answering the phone and taking care of customers, as well as making sandwiches. After the second worker, however, marginal product declines. The third worker adds only 10 sandwiches per hour because the grill gets crowded. The fourth worker can squeeze in quickly while the others are serving or wrapping, but he or she adds only five additional sandwiches each hour, and so on.

TABLE 10.1 Marginal Revenue Product per Hour of Labor in Sandwich Production (One Grill)

(1) Total Labor Units (Employees)	(2) Total Product (Sandwiches per Hour)	(3) Marginal Product of Labor (MP_L) (Sandwiches per Hour)	(4) Price (P_X) (Value Added per Sandwich)[a]	(5) Marginal Revenue Product ($MP_L \times P_X$) (per Hour)
0	0	—	—	—
1	10	10	$0.50	$5.00
2	25	15	0.50	7.50
3	35	10	0.50	5.00
4	40	5	0.50	2.50
5	42	2	0.50	1.00
6	42	0	0.50	0.00

[a]The "price" is essentially profit per sandwich; see discussion in text.

Sometimes Workers Play Hooky!

In this chapter we have described the connection between firm demand for workers and the productivity of those workers. In practice, firms know that worker productivity is not always the same each day. Monday mornings and Friday afternoons are sometimes less productive than the mid week, and employers typically think of average productivity over a time period as they contemplate hiring workers.

The article below describes the way in which the World Cup matches, which occur every four years, tend to disrupt the usual worker productivity, especially in soccer-crazy countries like the United Kingdom. In the summer of 2010, the World Cup was held in South Africa. Spain won, but in many firms, productivity took a hit!

World Cup Challenges Bosses

To Minimize Productivity Drop, They Juggle Worker Schedules and Bring In TVs

The Wall Street Journal

The World Cup's winner won't be determined until July. But there are already clear losers: bosses.

On Friday, managers on both sides of the Atlantic braced for the quadrennial month-long productivity drain that soccer's global championship brings. The tournament lasts more than four weeks, with many games scheduled in the middle of the workday in the Americas and Europe.

In soccer-mad countries like the U.K., many companies don't even try to ban the matches. Some let employees watch games at work. At others, managers juggle staffers' schedules to accommodate game-watching.

In Paraguay, President Fernando Lugo issued a decree giving public workers Monday afternoon off to watch Paraguay's game against Italy.

In past years, the U.S. was mostly immune to the contagion. But this year, Americans' growing World Cup curiosity sparked scattered hooky outbreaks on Friday, the first day of play.

In the U.K., productivity losses tied to the World Cup could total just under £1 billion ($1.45 billion), according to a survey by the Chartered Management Institute. Just over half of working men and 21 percent of working women intend to watch the matches scheduled to take place during office hours as they happen, according to a PricewaterhouseCoopers LLP survey of 1,000 U.K. workers.

Source: The Wall Street Journal, excerpted from "World Cup Challenges Bosses" by Dana Mattioli and Javier Espinoza. Copyright 2010 by *Dow Jones & Company, Inc.* Reproduced with permission of *Dow Jones & Company, Inc.* via Copyright Clearance Center.

In this case, the grill's capacity ultimately limits output. To see how the firm might make a rational choice about how many workers to hire, we need to know more about the value of the firm's product and the cost of labor.

Marginal Revenue Product

The **marginal revenue product (MRP)** of a variable input is the additional revenue a firm earns by employing 1 additional unit of that input, *ceteris paribus*. If labor is the variable factor, for example, hiring an additional unit will lead to added output (the *marginal product* of labor). The sale of that added output will yield revenue. *Marginal revenue product* is the revenue produced by selling the good or service that is produced by the marginal unit of labor. In a competitive firm, marginal revenue product is the value of a factor's marginal product.

By using labor as our variable factor, we can state this proposition more formally by saying that if MP_L is the marginal product of labor and P_X is the price of output, then the marginal revenue product of labor is

$$MRP_L = MP_L \times P_X$$

When calculating marginal revenue product, we need to be precise about what is being produced. A sandwich shop sells sandwiches, but it does not produce the bread, meat, cheese, mustard,

marginal revenue product (MRP) The additional revenue a firm earns by employing 1 additional unit of input, *ceteris paribus*.

and mayonnaise that go into the sandwiches. What the shop is producing is "sandwich cooking and assembly services." The shop is "adding value" to the meat, bread, and other ingredients by preparing and putting them all together in ready-to-eat form. With this in mind, let us assume that each finished sandwich in our shop sells for $0.50 over and above the costs of its ingredients. Thus, the *price of the service* the shop is selling is $0.50 per sandwich, and the only variable cost of providing that service is that of the labor used to put the sandwiches together. Thus, if X is the product of our shop, $P_X = \$0.50$.

Table 10.1, column 5, calculates the marginal revenue product of each worker if the shop charges $0.50 per sandwich over and above the costs of its ingredients. The first worker produces 10 sandwiches per hour, which at $0.50 each, generates revenues of $5.00 per hour. The addition of a second worker yields $7.50 an hour in revenues. After the second worker, diminishing returns drive MRP_L down. The marginal revenue product of the third worker is $5.00 per hour, of the fourth worker is only $2.50, and so on.

Figure 10.1 graphs the data from Table 10.1. Notice that the marginal revenue product curve has the same downward slope as the marginal product curve but that MRP is measured in dollars, not units of output. The MRP curve shows the dollar value of labor's marginal product.

▲ FIGURE 10.1 **Deriving a Marginal Revenue Product Curve from Marginal Product**

The marginal revenue product of labor is the price of output, P_X, times the marginal product of labor, MP_L.

Labor Markets

Let us begin our discussion of input markets by discussing a firm that uses only one variable factor of production.

A Firm Using Only One Variable Factor of Production: Labor

Demand for an input depends on that input's marginal revenue product and its unit cost, or price. The price of labor, for example, is the wage determined in the labor market. (At this point, we are continuing to assume that the sandwich shop uses only one variable factor of production—labor. Remember that competitive firms are price-takers in both output and input markets. Such firms can hire all the labor they want to hire as long as they pay the market wage.) We can think of the hourly wage at the sandwich shop as the marginal cost of a unit of labor. A profit-maximizing firm will add inputs—in the case of labor, it will hire workers—as long as the marginal revenue product of that input exceeds the market price of that input—in the case of labor, the wage.

Look again at the figures for the sandwich shop in Table 10.1, column 5. Now suppose the going wage for sandwich makers is $4 per hour. A profit-maximizing firm would hire three workers. The first worker would yield $5 per hour in revenue, and the second would yield $7.50, but they each would cost only $4 per hour. The third worker would bring in $5 per hour, but still cost only $4 in marginal wages. The marginal product of the fourth worker, however, would not bring in enough revenue ($2.50) to pay this worker's salary. Total profit is thus maximized by hiring three workers.

Figure 10.2 presents this same concept graphically. The labor market appears in Figure 10.2(a); Figure 10.2(b) shows a single firm that employs workers. This firm, incidentally, does not represent just the firms in a single industry. Because firms in many different industries demand labor, the representative firm in Figure 10.2(b) represents any firm in any industry that uses labor.

The firm faces a market wage rate of $10. We can think of this as the marginal cost of a unit of labor. (Note that we are now discussing the margin in units of *labor*; in previous chapters, we talked about marginal units of *output*.) Given a wage of $10, how much labor would the firm demand?

You might think that the firm would hire 100 units, the point at which the difference between marginal revenue product and wage rate is greatest. However, the firm is interested in maximizing *total* profit, not *marginal* profit. Hiring the 101st unit of labor generates $20 in revenue at a cost of only $10. Because MRP_L is greater than the cost of the input required to produce it, hiring 1 more unit of labor adds to profit. This will continue to be true as long as MRP_L remains above $10, which is all the way to 210 units. At that point, the wage rate is equal to the marginal revenue product of labor, or $W^* = MRP_L = 10$. The firm will not demand labor beyond 210 units because the cost of hiring the 211th unit of labor would be greater than the value of what that unit produces. (Recall that the fourth sandwich maker, requiring a wage of $4 per hour, can produce only an extra $2.50 an hour in sandwiches.)

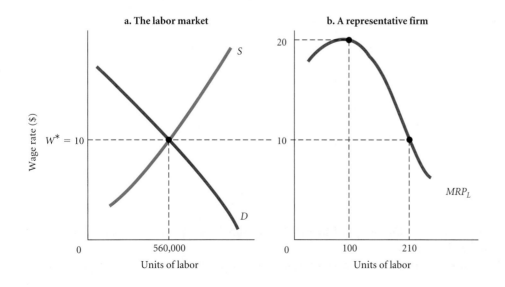

a. The labor market

b. A representative firm

◀ **FIGURE 10.2**

Marginal Revenue Product and Factor Demand for a Firm Using One Variable Input (Labor)

A competitive firm using only one variable factor of production will use that factor as long as its marginal revenue product exceeds its unit cost. A perfectly competitive firm will hire labor as long as MRP_L is greater than the going wage, W^*. The hypothetical firm will demand 210 units of labor.

Thus, the curve in Figure 10.2(b) tells us how much labor a firm that uses only one variable factor of production will hire at each potential market wage rate. If the market wage falls, the quantity of labor demanded will rise. If the market wage rises, the quantity of labor demanded will fall. This description should sound familiar to you—it is, in fact, the description of a demand curve. Therefore we can now say that when a firm uses only one variable factor of production, that factor's marginal revenue product curve is the firm's demand curve for that factor in the short run.

Comparing Marginal Revenue and Marginal Cost to Maximize Profits In Chapter 8, we saw that a competitive firm's marginal cost curve is the same as its supply curve. That is, at any output price, the marginal cost curve determines how much output a profit-maximizing firm will produce. We came to this conclusion by comparing the marginal revenue that a firm would earn by producing one more unit of output with the marginal cost of producing that unit of output.

There is no difference between the reasoning in Chapter 8 and the reasoning in this chapter. The only difference is that what is being measured at the margin has changed. In Chapter 8, the firm was comparing the marginal revenues and costs of producing *another unit of output*. Here the firm is comparing the marginal revenues and costs of employing *another unit of input*. To see this similarity, look at Figure 10.3. When the only variable factor of production is labor, the condition $W = MRP_L$ is the same condition as $P = MC$. The two statements say exactly the same thing.

In both cases, the firm is comparing the cost of production with potential revenues from the sale of product *at the margin*. In Chapter 8, the firm compared the price of output (P, which is equal to MR in perfect competition) directly with cost of production (MC), where cost was derived from information on factor prices and technology. (Review the derivation of cost curves in Chapter 8 if this is unclear.) Here information on output price and technology is contained in the marginal revenue product curve, which the firm compares with information on input price to determine the optimal level of input to demand.

The assumption of one variable factor of production makes the trade-off facing firms easy to see. Figure 10.4 shows that, in essence, firms weigh the value of labor as reflected in the market wage against the value of the product of labor as reflected in the price of output. Assuming that labor is the only variable input, if society values a good more than it costs firms to hire the workers to produce that good, the good will be produced. In general, the same logic also holds for more than one input. Firms weigh the value of outputs as reflected in output price against the value of inputs as reflected in marginal costs.

Deriving Input Demands For the small sandwich shop, calculating the marginal product of a variable input (labor) and marginal revenue product was easy. Although it may be more complex, the decision process is essentially the same for both big corporations and small proprietorships.

When an airline hires more flight attendants, for example, it increases the quality of its service to attract more passengers and thus to sell more of its product. In deciding how many flight attendants to hire, the airline must figure out how much new revenue the added attendants are likely to generate relative to their wages.

▶ **FIGURE 10.3**

The Two Profit-Maximizing Conditions Are Simply Two Views of the Same Choice Process

The Trade-Off Facing Firms

Firms weigh the cost of labor as reflected in wage rates against the value of labor's marginal product. Assume that labor is the only variable factor of production. Then, if society values a good more than it costs firms to hire the workers to produce that good, the good will be produced.

At the sandwich shop, diminishing returns set in at a certain point. The same holds true for an airplane. Once a sufficient number of attendants are on a plane, additional attendants add little to the quality of service, and beyond a certain level, they might even give rise to negative marginal product. The presence of too many attendants could bother the passengers and make it difficult to get to the restrooms.

In making your own decisions, you also compare marginal gains with input costs in the presence of diminishing returns. Suppose you grow vegetables in your yard. First, you save money at the supermarket. Second, you can plant what you like, and the vegetables taste better fresh from the garden. Third, you simply like to work in the garden.

Like the sandwich shop and the airline, you also face diminishing returns. You have only 625 square feet of garden to work with, and with land as a fixed factor in the short run, your marginal product will certainly decline. You can work all day every day, but your limited space will produce only so many string beans. The first few hours you spend each week watering, fertilizing, and dealing with major weed and bug infestations probably have a high marginal product. However, after 5 or 6 hours, there is little else you can do to increase yield. Diminishing returns also apply to your sense of satisfaction. The farmers' markets are now full of inexpensive fresh produce that tastes nearly as good as yours. Once you have been out in the garden for a few hours, the hot sun and hard work start to lose their charm. Although your gardening does not involve a salary (unlike the sandwich shop and the airline, which pay out wages), the labor you supply has a value that must be weighed. You must weigh the value of additional gardening time against leisure and the other options available to you.

Less labor is likely to be employed as the cost of labor rises. If the competitive labor market pushed the daily wage to $6 per hour, the sandwich shop would hire only two workers instead of three (Table 10.1). If you suddenly became very busy at school, the opportunity cost of your time would rise and you would probably devote fewer hours to gardening.

We have recently seen an example of what may seem to be an exception to the rule that workers will be hired only if the revenues they generate are equal to or greater than their wages. Many start-up companies pay salaries to workers before the companies begin to take in revenue. This has been particularly true for Internet start-ups in recent years. How does a company pay workers if it is not earning any revenue? The answer is that the entrepreneur (or the venture capital fund supporting the entrepreneur) is betting that the firm will earn substantial revenue in the future. Workers are hired because the entrepreneur expects that their current efforts will produce future revenue greater than their wage costs.

A Firm Employing Two Variable Factors of Production in the Short and Long Run

When a firm employs more than one variable factor of production, the analysis of input demand becomes more complicated, but the principles stay the same. We shall now consider a firm that employs variable capital (K) and labor (L) inputs and thus faces factor prices P_K and P_L.[1] (Recall that *capital* refers to plant, equipment, and inventory used in production. We assume that some portion of the firm's capital stock is fixed in the short run, but that some of it is variable—for example, some machinery and equipment can be installed quickly.) Our analysis can be applied to any two factors of production and can easily be generalized to three or more. It can also be applied to the long run, when all factors of production are variable.

You have seen that inputs can be complementary or substitutable. Land, labor, and capital are used *together* to produce outputs. The worker who uses a shovel digs a bigger hole than another worker with no shovel. Add a steam shovel and that worker becomes even more productive. When an expanding firm adds to its stock of capital, it raises the productivity of its labor, and vice versa. Thus, each factor complements the other. At the same time, though, land, labor, and capital can also be *substituted* for one another. If labor becomes expensive, some labor-saving technology—robotics, for example—may take its place.

In firms employing just one variable factor of production, a change in the price of that factor affects only the demand for the factor itself. When more than one factor can vary, however, we must consider the impact of a change in one factor price on the demand for other factors as well.

Substitution and Output Effects of a Change in Factor Price   Table 10.2 presents data on a hypothetical firm that employs variable capital and labor. Suppose that the firm faces a choice between two available technologies of production—technique *A*, which is capital intensive, and technique *B*, which is labor intensive. When the market price of labor is $1 per unit and the market price of capital is $1 per unit, the labor-intensive method of producing output is less costly. Each unit costs only $13 to produce using technique *B*, while the unit cost of production using technique *A* is $15. If the price of labor rises to $2, however, technique *B* is no longer less costly. Labor has become more expensive relative to capital. The unit cost rises to $23 for labor-intensive technique *B*, but to only $20 for capital-intensive technique *A*.

	Input Requirements per Unit of Output		**Unit Cost if** $P_L = \$1$ $P_K = \$1$ $(P_L \times L) + (P_K \times K)$	**Unit Cost if** $P_L = \$2$ $P_K = \$1$ $(P_L \times L) + (P_K \times K)$
TABLE 10.2 Response of a Firm to an Increasing Wage Rate				
Technology	K	L		
A (capital intensive)	10	5	$15	$20
B (labor intensive)	3	10	$13	$23

Table 10.3 shows the effect of such an increase in the price of labor on both capital and labor demand when a firm produces 100 units of output. When the price of labor is $1 and the price of capital is $1, the firm chooses technique *B* and demands 300 units of capital and 1,000 units of labor. Total variable cost is $1,300. An increase in the price of labor to $2 causes the firm to switch from technique *B* to technique *A*. In doing so, the firm *substitutes* capital for labor. The amount of labor demanded drops from 1,000 to 500 units. The amount of capital demanded increases from 300 to 1,000 units, while total variable cost increases to $2,000.

The tendency of firms to substitute away from a factor whose relative price has risen and toward a factor whose relative price has fallen is called the **factor substitution effect**. The factor substitution effect is part of the reason that *input demand curves slope downward*. When an input,

factor substitution effect   The tendency of firms to substitute away from a factor whose price has risen and toward a factor whose price has fallen.

---

[1] The price of labor, P_L, is the same as the wage rate, W. We will often use the term P_L instead of W to emphasize the symmetry between labor and capital.

ECONOMICS IN PRACTICE

What is Denzel Washington's Marginal Revenue Product in Broadway's *Fences*?

Denzel Washington is well known for his movie performances, where he has been paid as much as $20 million for a film. In the spring and summer of 2010, Washington starred in August Wilson's *Fences* at the Cort Theater on Broadway in New York. How would we go about estimating Washington's marginal revenue product in that job? What is the most the producers of *Fences* should be willing to pay Washington?

In the case of Broadway theater, revenues come principally from ticket revenues. The Cort Theater seats just over 1,000 people, and the average ticket price is $110. *Fences* has eight performances a week. So the total maximum weekly "gate," as it is called in the theater, is $880,000 assuming the theater is fully sold out. How much of this should the producers be willing to pay Washington to secure him in the role?

As with the sandwich workers, the key here is to figure out what Washington adds to the gate. Given that all revenues come from ticket sales, we really need to know how many more people Washington can attract to the Cort Theater than could another actor. Suppose the producer believed that Washington could increase demand for tickets by 10 percent, so that instead of selling half the theater's seats in a week, or 4,000 tickets, as is common for a Broadway show, the theater sold 4,400 seats per week. That would add $44,000 to the revenues over what would be achievable with another actor. Moreover, in contrast to the sandwich shop, Washington can add this revenue with no other added inputs; it costs nothing more to play to a house three-fourths full than to one half full. In this case, the producer should be willing to pay Washington as much as $44,000 per week over a lesser actor.

Notice this salary is considerably less than Washington makes for a movie. Movies take about 3 months of acting time. At $15 to $20 million for a movie, that amounts to well over $1 million per week. Why should Washington's acting have an *MRP* of $44,000 per week when on the stage and $1 million per week for a movie? We are back to the principle of derived demand. Washington's *MRP* is higher in movies than in the live theater because the earnings potential of the former is higher. Movie audiences are not limited to 1,000 per week; Washington's 2010 movie, *Book of Eli*, showed to more than 3 million people in its opening weekend, and most critics thought that Washington was the primary audience draw. With DVD sales in addition, it is easy to see how Washington's *MRP* in films might be quite high.

TABLE 10.3	The Substitution Effect of an Increase in Wages on a Firm Producing 100 Units of Output		
	To Produce 100 Units of Output		
	Total Capital Demanded	Total Labor Demanded	Total Variable Cost
When P_L = $1, P_K = $1, firm uses technology *B*	300	1,000	$1,300
When P_L = $2, P_K = $1, firm uses technology *A*	1,000	500	$2,000

or factor of production, becomes less expensive, firms tend to substitute it for other factors and thus buy *more* of it. When a particular input becomes more expensive, firms tend to substitute other factors and buy *less* of it.

The firm described in Table 10.2 and Table 10.3 continued to produce 100 units of output after the wage rate doubled. An *increase* in the price of a production factor, however, also means an increase in the costs of production. Notice that total variable cost increased from $1,300 to $2,000. When a firm faces higher costs, it is likely to produce less in the short run. When a firm decides to decrease output, its demand for all factors declines—including, of

output effect of a factor price increase (decrease) When a firm decreases (increases) its output in response to a factor price increase (decrease), this decreases (increases) its demand for all factors.

course, the factor whose price increased in the first place. This is called the **output effect of a factor price increase**.

A *decrease* in the price of a factor of production, in contrast, means lower costs of production. If their output price remains unchanged, firms will increase output. This, in turn, means that demand for all factors of production will increase. This is the **output effect of a factor price decrease**.

The output effect helps explain why input demand curves slope downward. Output effects and factor substitution effects work in the same direction. Consider, for example, a decline in the wage rate. Lower wages mean that a firm will substitute labor for capital and other inputs. Stated somewhat differently, the factor substitution effect leads to an increase in the quantity of labor demanded. Lower wages mean lower costs, and lower costs lead to more output. This increase in output means that the firm will hire more of all factors of production, including labor. This is the output effect of a factor price decrease. Notice that both effects lead to an increase in the quantity demanded for labor when the wage rate falls.

Many Labor Markets

Although Figure 10.1 depicts "*the* labor market," many labor markets exist. There is a market for baseball players, for carpenters, for chemists, for college professors, and for unskilled workers. Still other markets exist for taxi drivers, assembly-line workers, secretaries, and corporate executives. Each market has a set of skills associated with it and a supply of people with the requisite skills. If labor markets are competitive, the wages in those markets are determined by the interaction of supply and demand. As we have seen, firms will hire additional workers only as long as the value of their product exceeds the relevant market wage. This is true in all competitive labor markets.

Land Markets

Unlike labor and capital, land has a special feature that we have not yet considered: It is in strictly fixed (perfectly inelastic) supply in total. The only real questions about land thus center around how much it is worth and how it will be used.

demand-determined price The price of a good that is in fixed supply; it is determined exclusively by what households and firms are willing to pay for the good.

pure rent The return to any factor of production that is in fixed supply.

Because land is fixed in supply, we say that its price is **demand determined**. In other words, the price of land is determined exclusively by what households and firms are willing to pay for it. The return to any factor of production in fixed supply is called a **pure rent**.

Thinking of the price of land as demand determined can be confusing because all land is not the same. Some land is clearly more valuable than other land. What lies behind these differences? As with any other factor of production, land will presumably be sold or rented to the user who is willing to pay the most for it. The value of land to a potential user may depend on the characteristics of the land or on its location. For example, more fertile land should produce more farm products per acre and thus command a higher price than less fertile land. A piece of property located at the intersection of two highways may be of great value as a site for a gas station because of the volume of traffic that passes the intersection daily.

A numerical example may help to clarify our discussion. Consider the potential uses of a corner lot in a suburb of Kansas City. Alan wants to build a clothing store on the lot. He anticipates that he can earn economic profits of $10,000 per year because of the land's excellent location. Bella, another person interested in buying the corner lot, believes that she can earn $35,000 per year in economic profit if she builds a pharmacy there. Because of the higher profit that she expects to earn, Bella will be able to outbid Alan, and the landowner will sell (or rent) to the highest bidder.

Because location is often the key to profits, landowners are frequently able to "squeeze" their renters. One of the most popular locations in the Boston area, for example, is Harvard Square. There are dozens of restaurants in and around the square, and most of them are full a good deal of the time. Despite this seeming success, most Harvard Square restaurant owners are not getting rich. Why? Because they must pay very high rents on the location of their restaurants. A substantial portion of each restaurant's revenues goes to rent the land that (by virtue of its scarcity) is the key to unlocking those same revenues.

Although Figure 10.5 shows that the supply of land is perfectly inelastic (a vertical line), the supply of land in a *given use* may not be perfectly inelastic or fixed. Think, for example, about

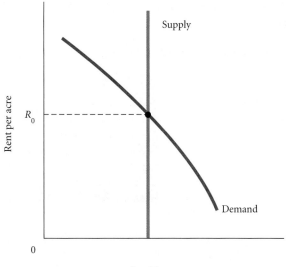

◀ **FIGURE 10.5**

The Rent on Land Is Demand Determined

Because land in general (and each parcel in particular) is in fixed supply, its price is demand determined. Graphically, a fixed supply is represented by a vertical, perfectly inelastic supply curve. Rent, R_0, depends exclusively on demand—what people are willing to pay.

farmland available for housing developments. As a city's population grows, housing developers find themselves willing to pay more for land. As land becomes more valuable for development, some farmers sell out, and the supply of land available for development increases. This analysis would lead us to draw an upward-sloping supply curve (not a perfectly inelastic supply curve) for land in the land-for-development category.

Nonetheless, our major point—that land earns a pure rent—is still valid. The supply of land of a *given quality* at a *given location* is truly fixed in supply. Its value is determined exclusively by the amount that the highest bidder is willing to pay for it. Because land cannot be reproduced, supply is perfectly inelastic.

Rent and the Value of Output Produced on Land

Because the price of land is demand determined, rent depends on what the potential users of the land are willing to pay for it. As we have seen, land will end up being used by whoever is willing to pay the most for it. What determines this willingness to pay? Let us now connect our discussion of land markets with our earlier discussions of factor markets in general.

As our example of two potential users bidding for a plot of land shows, the bids depend on the land's potential for profit. Alan's plan would generate $10,000 a year; Bella's would generate $35,000 a year. Nevertheless, these profits do not just materialize. Instead, they come from producing and selling an output that is valuable to households. Land in a popular downtown location is expensive because of what can be produced on it. Note that land is needed as an input into the production of nearly all goods and services. A restaurant located next to a popular theater can charge a premium price because it has a relatively captive clientele. The restaurant must produce a quality product to stay in business, but the location alone provides a substantial profit opportunity.

It should come as no surprise that the demand for land follows the same rules as the demand for inputs in general. A profit-maximizing firm will employ an additional factor of production as long as its marginal revenue product exceeds its market price. For example, a profit-maximizing firm will hire labor as long as the revenue earned from selling labor's product is sufficient to cover the cost of hiring additional labor—which for perfectly competitive firms, equals the wage rate. The same thing is true for land. A firm will pay for and use land as long as the revenue earned from selling the product produced on that land is sufficient to cover the price of the land. Stated in equation form, the firm will use land up to the point at which $MRP_A = P_A$, where A is land (acres).

Just as the demand curve for labor reflects the value of labor's product as determined in output markets, so the demand for land depends on the value of land's product in output markets. The profitability of the restaurant located next to the theater results from the fact that the meals produced there command a price in the marketplace.

ECONOMICS IN PRACTICE

Time Is Money: European High-Speed Trains

In the past few years, many parts of Europe have invested in high-speed trains. In the article that follows, we see the way in which these trains increase land value. The rise in land value following the introduction of high-speed trains is another example of the importance of the opportunity cost of time. As train speeds increase, the time cost of living far from one's workplace decreases; the natural result is an increased willingness to live far from one's workplace and thus an increase in outlying land values.

High-Speed Rail Give Short-Haul Air a Run for the Money in Europe, With More Flexible Travel, Greater Comfort, Lower Environmental Impact

Travel Industry News

While air travelers put up with longer delays, cancelled flights and tedious security procedures, and drivers face rising gas prices and ever-increasing congestion, life keeps getting easier for passengers on Europe's expanding network of high-speed trains. The latest developments and the far-reaching benefits of high-speed European train travel were the topics of a press conference, "High-speed trains: Changing the European Experience" held in New York today. Speakers included: CEO of the French National Railroads (SNCF), Guillaume Pepy; Commercial Director of the Eurostar train, Nicholas Mercer; and High-Speed Director of the Paris-based International Railway Association (UIC),

Inaki Barron. Rail Europe—North America's leading seller of European rail travel—was the host of the conference.

Traveling at speed of 150 mph or higher (compared to regular trains going 100 mph or less), high-speed trains currently run on 3,034 miles of track in 10 European countries. By 2010, another 1,711 miles are scheduled to be in operation, and there are plans beyond that to add on average 346 miles each year through 2020, according to the UIC's Barron.

High-speed trains not only benefit travelers and the environment, they also boost the economies of communities served. In France, they call it the "TGV effect"—increases in property values, rents/real estate prices and number of jobs/businesses in towns in or near high-speed rail lines.

Real estate prices in Avignon rose more than 30% in the first three years following the launch of TGV Mediterranean. In Vendome, near the TGV Atlantique line (Paris-Tours in the Loire region) real estate prices went up 50% in five years.

Source: Travel Industry Wire, March 24, 2008.

The allocation of a given plot of land among competing uses thus depends on the trade-off between competing products that can be produced there. Agricultural land becomes developed when its value in producing housing or manufactured goods (or providing space for a mini-mall) exceeds its value in producing crops. A corner lot in Kansas City becomes the site of a pharmacy instead of a clothing store because the people in that neighborhood have a greater need for a pharmacy.

One final word about land: Because land cannot be moved physically, the value of any one parcel depends to a large extent on the uses to which adjoining parcels are put. A factory belching acrid smoke will probably reduce the value of adjoining land, while a new highway that increases accessibility may enhance it.

The Firm's Profit-Maximizing Condition in Input Markets

Thus far, we have discussed the labor and land markets in some detail. Although we will put off a detailed discussion of capital until the next chapter, it is now possible to generalize about competitive demand for factors of production. Every firm has an incentive to use variable inputs as long as the revenue generated by those inputs covers the costs of those inputs at the margin. More formally, firms will employ each input up to the point that its price equals its marginal revenue product. This condition holds for all factors at all levels of output.

The profit-maximizing condition for the perfectly competitive firm is

$$P_L = MRP_L = (MP_L \times P_X)$$

$$P_K = MRP_K = (MP_K \times P_X)$$

$$P_A = MRP_A = (MP_A \times P_X)$$

where L is labor, K is capital, A is land (acres), X is output, and P_X is the price of that output.

When all these conditions are met, the firm will be using the optimal, or least costly, combination of inputs. If all the conditions hold at the same time, it is possible to rewrite them another way:

$$\frac{MP_L}{P_L} = \frac{MP_K}{P_K} = \frac{MP_A}{P_A} = \frac{1}{P_X}$$

Your intuition tells you much the same thing that these equations do: The marginal product of the last dollar spent on labor must be equal to the marginal product of the last dollar spent on capital, which must be equal to the marginal product of the last dollar spent on land, and so on. If this was not the case, the firm could produce more with less and reduce cost. Suppose, for example, that $MP_L/P_L > MP_K/P_K$. In this situation, the firm can produce more output by shifting dollars out of capital and into labor. Hiring more labor drives down the marginal product of labor, and using less capital increases the marginal product of capital. This means that the ratios come back to equality as the firm shifts out of capital and into labor.

So far, we have used very general terms to discuss the nature of input demand by firms in competitive markets, where input prices and output prices are taken as given. The most important point is that demand for a factor depends on the value that the market places on its marginal product.[2] The rest of this chapter explores the forces that determine the shapes and positions of input demand curves.

Input Demand Curves

In Chapter 5, we considered the factors that influence the responsiveness, or elasticity, of output demand curves. We have not yet talked about *input* demand curves in any detail, however, so we now need to say more about what lies behind them.

Shifts in Factor Demand Curves

Factor (input) demand curves are derived from information on technology—that is, production functions—and output price (see Figure 10.4 on p. 221). A change in the demand for outputs, a change in the quantity of complementary or substitutable inputs, changes in the prices of other inputs, and technological change all can cause factor demand curves to shift. These shifts in demand are important because they directly affect the allocation of resources among alternative uses as well as the level and distribution of income.

The Demand for Outputs   A firm will demand an input as long as its marginal revenue product exceeds its market price. Marginal revenue product, which in perfect competition is equal to a factor's marginal product times the price of output, is the value of the factor's marginal product:

$$MRP_L = MP_L \times P_X$$

The amount that a firm is willing to pay for a factor of production depends directly on the value of the things the firm produces. It follows that if product demand increases, product price will rise and marginal revenue product (factor demand) will increase—the *MRP* curve will shift to the right. If product demand declines, product price will fall and marginal revenue product (factor demand) will decrease—the *MRP* curve will shift to the left.

---

[2] If you worked through the Appendix to Chapter 7, you saw this same condition derived graphically from an isocost/isoquant diagram. *Note:* $MP_L/P_L = MP_K/P_K \rightarrow MP_L/MP_K = P_L/P_K$.

Go back and raise the price of sandwiches from $0.50 to $1.00 in the sandwich shop example examined in Table 10.1 on p. 216 to see that this is so.

To the extent that any input is used intensively in the production of some product, changes in the demand for that product cause factor demand curves to shift and the prices of those inputs to change. Land prices are a good example. Forty years ago, the area in Manhattan along the west side of Central Park from about 80th Street north was a run-down neighborhood full of abandoned houses. The value of land there was virtually zero. During the mid-1980s, increased demand for housing caused rents to hit record levels. Some single-room apartments, for example, rented for as much as $1,400 per month. With the higher price of output (rent), input prices increased substantially. By 2008, small one-bedroom apartments on 80th Street and Central Park West sold for well over $500,000, and the value of the land figures very importantly in these prices. In essence, a shift in demand for an output (housing in the area) pushed up the marginal revenue product of land from zero to very high levels.

The Quantity of Complementary and Substitutable Inputs

In our discussion thus far, we have kept coming back to the fact that factors of production complement one another. The productivity of, and thus the demand for, any one factor of production depends on the quality and quantity of the other factors with which it works.

The effect of capital accumulation on wages is one of the most important themes in all of economics. In general, the production and use of capital enhances the productivity of labor and normally increases the demand for labor and drives up wages. Consider as an example transportation. In a poor country such as Bangladesh, one person with an ox cart can move a small load over bad roads very slowly. By contrast, the stock of capital used by workers in the transportation industry in the United States is enormous. A truck driver in the United States works with a substantial amount of capital. The typical 18-wheel tractor trailer, for example, is a piece of capital worth over $100,000. The roads themselves are capital that was put in place by the government. The amount of material that a single driver can move between distant points in a short time is staggering relative to what it was just 50 years ago.

The Prices of Other Inputs

When a firm has a choice among alternative technologies, the choice it makes depends to some extent on relative input prices. You saw in Table 10.2 on p. 222 and Table 10.3 on p. 223 that an increase in the price of labor substantially increased the demand for capital as the firm switched to a more capital-intensive production technique.

During the 1970s, the large increase in energy prices relative to prices of other factors of production had a number of effects on the demand for those other inputs. Insulation of new buildings, installation of more efficient heating plants, and similar efforts substantially raised the demand for capital as capital was substituted for energy in production. It has also been argued that the energy crisis led to an increase in demand for labor. If capital and energy are complementary inputs—that is, if technologies that are capital-intensive are also energy-intensive—the argument goes, the higher energy prices tended to push firms away from capital-intensive techniques toward more labor-intensive techniques. A new highly automated technique, for example, might need fewer workers, but it would also require a vast amount of electricity to operate. High electricity prices could lead a firm to reject the new techniques and stick with an old, more labor-intensive method of production.

technological change
The introduction of new methods of production or new products intended to increase the productivity of existing inputs or to raise marginal products.

Technological Change

Closely related to the impact of capital accumulation on factor demand is the potential impact of **technological change**—that is, the introduction of new methods of production or new products. New technologies usually introduce ways to produce outputs with fewer inputs by increasing the productivity of existing inputs or by raising marginal products. Because marginal revenue product reflects productivity, increases in productivity directly shift input demand curves. If the marginal product of labor rises, for example, the demand for labor shifts to the right (increases). Technological change can and does have a powerful influence on factor demands. As new products and new techniques of production are born, so are demands for new inputs and new skills. As old products become obsolete, so do the labor skills and other inputs needed to produce them.

Looking Ahead

We now have a complete, but simplified picture of household and firm decision making. We have also examined some of the basic forces that determine the allocation of resources and the mix of output in perfectly competitive markets.

In this competitive environment, profit-maximizing firms make three fundamental decisions: (1) how much to produce and supply in output markets, (2) how to produce (which technology to use), and (3) how much of each input to demand. Chapters 7 through 9 looked at these three decisions from the perspective of the output market. We derived the supply curve of a competitive firm in the short run and discussed output market adjustment in the long run. Deriving cost curves, we learned, involves evaluating and choosing among alternative technologies. Finally, we saw how a firm's decision about how much product to supply in output markets implicitly determines input demands. Input demands, we argued, are also derived demands. That is, they are ultimately linked to the demand for output.

To show the connection between output and input markets, this chapter took these same three decisions and examined them from the perspective of input markets. Firms hire up to the point at which each input's marginal revenue product is equal to its price.

The next chapter takes up the complexity of what we have been loosely calling the "capital market." There we discuss the relationship between the market for physical capital and financial capital markets and look at some of the ways that firms make investment decisions. Once we examine the nature of overall competitive equilibrium in Chapter 12, we can finally begin relaxing some of the assumptions that have restricted the scope of our inquiry—most importantly, the assumption of perfect competition in input and output markets.

SUMMARY

1. The same set of decisions that lies behind output supply curves also lies behind input demand curves. Only the perspective is different.

INPUT MARKETS: BASIC CONCEPTS *p. 215*

2. Demand for inputs depends on demand for the outputs that they produce; input demand is thus a *derived demand*. *Productivity* is a measure of the amount of output produced per unit of input.

3. In general, firms will demand workers as long as the value of what those workers produce exceeds what they must be paid. Households will supply labor as long as the wage exceeds the value of leisure or the value that they derive from nonpaid work.

4. Inputs are at the same time *complementary* and *substitutable*.

5. In the short run, some factor of production is fixed. This means that all firms encounter diminishing returns in the short run. Stated somewhat differently, diminishing returns means that all firms encounter declining marginal product in the short run.

6. The *marginal revenue product* (MRP) of a variable input is the additional revenue a firm earns by employing one additional unit of the input, *ceteris paribus*. MRP is equal to the input's marginal product times the price of output.

LABOR MARKETS *p. 219*

7. Demand for an input depends on that input's marginal revenue product. Profit-maximizing perfectly competitive firms will buy an input (for example, hire labor) up to the point where the input's marginal revenue product equals its price. For a firm employing only one variable factor of production, the *MRP* curve is the firm's demand curve for that factor in the short run.

8. For a perfectly competitive firm employing one variable factor of production, labor, the condition $W = MRP_L$ is exactly the same as the condition $P = MC$. Firms weigh the value of outputs as reflected in output price against the value of inputs as reflected in marginal costs.

9. When a firm employs two variable factors of production, a change in factor price has both a *factor substitution effect* and an *output effect*.

10. A wage increase may lead a firm to substitute capital for labor and thus cause the quantity demanded of labor to decline. This is the *factor substitution effect of the wage increase*.

11. A wage increase increases cost, and higher cost may lead to lower output and less demand for all inputs, including labor. This is the *output effect of the wage increase*. The effect is the opposite for a wage decrease.

LAND MARKETS *p. 224*

12. Because land is in strictly fixed supply, its price is *demand determined*—that is, its price is determined exclusively by what households and firms are willing to pay for it. The return to any factor of production in fixed supply is called a *pure rent*. A firm will pay for and use land as long as the revenue earned from selling the product produced on that land is sufficient to cover the price of the land. The firm will use land up to the point at which $MRP_A = P_A$, where A is land (acres).

THE FIRM'S PROFIT-MAXIMIZING CONDITION IN INPUT MARKETS *p. 226*

13. Every firm has an incentive to use variable inputs as long as the revenue generated by those inputs covers the costs of those inputs at the margin. Therefore, firms will employ each input up to the point that its price equals its marginal revenue product. This profit-maximizing condition holds for all factors at all levels of output.

INPUT DEMAND CURVES *p. 227*

14. A shift in a firm's demand curve for a factor of production can be influenced by the demand for the firm's product, the quantity of complementary and substitutable inputs, the prices of other inputs, and changes in technology.

REVIEW TERMS AND CONCEPTS

demand-determined price, *p. 224*

derived demand, *p. 215*

factor substitution effect, *p. 222*

marginal product of labor (*MP_L*), *p. 216*

marginal revenue product (*MRP*), *p. 217*

output effect of a factor price increase (decrease), *p. 224*

productivity of an input, *p. 216*

pure rent, *p. 224*

technological change, *p. 228*

Equations:

$MRP_L = MP_L \times P_X$

PROBLEMS

All problems are available on www.myeconlab.com

1. According to the Bureau of Labor Statistics, the average weekly earnings of production and nonsupervisory employees in education and health services was $638 in January 2010, up from $440 in January 2000. All else equal, such an increase in wages would be expected to reduce the demand for labor and employment should fall. Instead, the quantity demanded for labor has increased dramatically with more than 4 million jobs being created between 2000 and 2010. How can you explain this seeming discrepancy?

2. Assume that a firm that manufactures widgets can produce them with one of three processes used alone or in combination. The following table indicates the amounts of capital and labor required by each of the three processes to produce one widget.

	UNITS OF LABOR	UNITS OF CAPITAL
Process 1	4	1
Process 2	2	2
Process 3	1	3

   a. Assuming capital costs $3 per unit and labor costs $1 per unit, which process will be employed?

   b. Plot the three points on the firm's *TVC* curve corresponding to *q* = 10, *q* = 30, and *q* = 50.

   c. At each of the three output levels, how much *K* and *L* will be demanded?

   d. Repeat parts a. through c. assuming the price of capital is $3 per unit and the price of labor has risen to $4 per unit.

3. During the two decades leading up to the new millennium, wage inequality in the United States increased substantially. That is, high-income workers saw their salaries increase substantially while wages of lower-income workers stagnated or even fell. Using the logic of marginal revenue product, give an explanation for this change in the distribution of income. In your explanation, you may want to consider the rise of the high-technology, high-skill sector and the decline of industries requiring low-skill labor.

4. The following schedule shows the technology of production at the Delicious Apple Orchard for 2010:

WORKERS	TOTAL BUSHELS OF APPLES PER DAY
0	0
1	40
2	70
3	90
4	100
5	105
6	102

   If apples sell for $2 per bushel and workers can be hired in a competitive labor market for $30 per day, how many workers should be hired? What if workers unionized and the wage rose to $50? (*Hint:* Create marginal product and marginal revenue product columns for the table.) Explain your answers clearly.

5. The following graph is the production function for a firm using only one variable factor of production, labor.

   a. Graph the marginal product of labor for the firm as a function of the number of labor units hired.

   b. Assuming the price of output, *P_X*, is equal to $6, graph the firm's marginal revenue product schedule as a function of the number of labor units hired.

   c. If the current equilibrium wage rate is $4 per hour, how many hours of labor will you hire? How much output will you produce?

6. Describe how each of the following events would affect (1) demand for construction workers and (2) construction wages in Portland, Oregon. Illustrate with supply and demand curves.
   a. A sharp increase in interest rates on new-home mortgages reduces the demand for new houses substantially.
   b. The economy of the area booms. Office rents rise, creating demand for new office space.
   c. A change in the tax laws in 2010 made real estate developments more profitable. As a result, three major developers start planning to build major shopping centers.

7. The demand for land is a derived demand. Think of a popular location near your school. What determines the demand for land in that area? What outputs are sold by businesses located there? Discuss the relationship between land prices and the prices of those products.

8. Many states provide firms with an "investment tax credit" that effectively reduces the price of capital. In theory, these credits are designed to stimulate new investment and thus create jobs. Critics have argued that if there are strong factor substitution effects, these subsidies could *reduce* employment in the state. Explain their arguments.

9. Doug's farm in Idaho has four major fields that he uses to grow potatoes. The productivity of each field follows:

ANNUAL YIELD, HUNDREDS OF POUNDS

Field 1	10,000
Field 2	8,000
Field 3	5,000
Field 4	3,000

Assume that each field is the same size and that the variable costs of farming are $25,000 per year per field. The variable costs cover labor and machinery time, which is rented. Doug must decide each year how many fields to plant. In 2009, potato farmers received $6.35 per 100 pounds. How many fields did Doug plant? Explain. By 2011, the price of potatoes had fallen to $4.50 per 100 pounds. How will this price decrease change Doug's decision? How will it affect his demand for labor? How will it affect the value of Doug's land?

10. Assume that you are living in a house with two other people and that the house has a big lawn that must be mowed. One of your roommates, who dislikes working outdoors, suggests hiring a neighbor's daughter to mow the grass for $40 per week instead of sharing the work and doing it yourselves. How would you go about deciding who will mow the lawn? What factors would you raise in deciding? What are the trade-offs here?

11. Consider the following information for a T-shirt manufacturing firm that can sell as many T-shirts as it wants for $3 per shirt.

NUMBER OF WORKERS	NUMBER OF SHIRTS PRODUCED PER DAY	MP_L	TR	MRP_L
0	0	—	—	—
1	30	—	—	—
2	80	—	—	—
3	110	—	—	—
4	135	—	—	—
5	—	20	—	—
6	170	—	—	—
7	—	—	—	30
8	—	—	—	15

a. Fill in all the blanks in the table.
b. Verify that MRP_L for this firm can be calculated in two ways: (1) change in TR from adding another worker and (2) MP_L times the price of output.
c. If this firm must pay a wage rate of $40 per worker per day, how many workers should it hire? Briefly explain why.
d. Suppose the wage rate rises to $50 per worker. How many workers should be hired now? Why?
e. Suppose the firm adopts a new technology that doubles output at each level of employment and the price of shirts remains at $3. What is the effect of this new technology on MP_L and on MRP_L? At a wage of $50, how many workers should the firm hire now?

12. [Related to *Economics in Practice* on p. 223] At some colleges, the highest paid member of the faculty is the football coach. How would you explain this?

13. [Related to *Economics in Practice* on p. 226] In Orlando, Florida, the land value went up dramatically when Disney built its theme park there. How do you explain this land price increase?

*14. For a given firm, $MRP_L = 50 and $MRP_K = 100 while $P_L = 10 and $P_K = 20.
   a. Is the firm maximizing profits? Why or why not?
   b. Identify a specific action that would increase this firm's profits.

15. In 2007, the CEO of Harley-Davidson, James L. Ziemer, earned $1,350,000 in total compensation (salary, bonuses, and other compensation) and Roy Williams, the chief executive with the non-profit Boy Scouts of America, earned $1,577,600. How can a non-profit organization like the Boy Scouts justify compensating its chief executive at a similar level to the CEO of a successful for-profit company like Harley-Davidson?

Sources: Scott DeCarlo "CEO Compensation," *Forbes*, April 30, 2008 and Teri Sforza, "National Boy Scouts explain $1.6 million salary for top exec," *Orange County Register*, August 7, 2009.

16. On April 20, 2010, the Deepwater Horizon oil drilling rig exploded in the Gulf of Mexico, causing one of the worst oil spills in history. The oil spill was devastating to many gulf coast industries, with one of the hardest-hit being the oyster-fishing industry. Explain the effect this oil spill will have on the following:
   a. Price of oysters
   b. Marginal product of oyster fishermen
   c. Demand for oyster fishermen

17. The price of land is said to be "demand-determined." Explain what this means and draw a graph to exemplify your explanation.

18. Houston, Texas, is the only major U.S. city with virtually no zoning laws. This means that single-family homes, apartment buildings, shopping centers, high-rise buildings, and industrial complexes can all be built in the same neighborhood. Of the major U.S. cities, Houston was also one of the least impacted by the housing market crisis of 2008. In 2009, Houston issued 42,697 building permits and was the top-ranked city in the list of healthiest housing markets. How might the lack of zoning laws have played a part in Houston's healthy housing and building markets?

Sources: La Familia, "Zoning in on Zoning Laws," *El Gato*, June 2, 2010.

19. The Sunshine Shirt Manufacturing Company uses both capital and labor as substitutable resources in the production of shirts, and the price of capital used by Sunshine has just decreased. What do the substitution and output effects suggest will happen to the demand for capital and the demand for labor at Sunshine?

20. For a perfectly competitive firm, the marginal cost curve determines how much output a profit-maximizing firm will produce. For input markets, the marginal revenue product curve determines how much labor a profit-maximizing firm will hire in a perfectly competitive labor market. Explain how the reasoning behind these two concepts is related.

21. [Related to the *Economics in Practice* on *p. 217*] Each year in New Orleans, Carnival season begins on January 6 and culminates with the city's biggest celebration of the year, Mardi Gras. This wildly popular celebration attracts people from around the world, and the city of New Orleans estimates that over half a million visitors attended the festivities in 2010. The Tuesday on which Mardi Gras falls each year has been declared a state holiday in Louisiana, with banks, post offices, and many private businesses closing for the day. On the basis of labor, explain why you think Mardi Gras has been declared a state holiday in Louisiana and why so many businesses in New Orleans are closed on that day.

*Note: Problems marked with an asterisk are more challenging.

Input Demand: The Capital Market and the Investment Decision

In Chapter 10 we explored the labor and land markets in some detail. In this chapter, we consider the capital market more fully. Transactions between households and firms in the labor and land markets are direct. In the labor market, households offer their labor directly to firms in exchange for wages. In the land market, landowners rent or sell their land directly to firms in exchange for rent or an agreed-to price. In the capital market, though, households often *indirectly* supply the financial resources necessary for firms to purchase capital. When households save and add

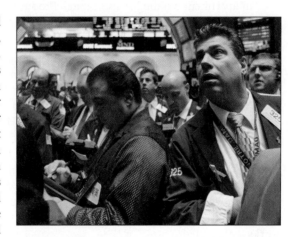

funds to their bank accounts, for example, firms can borrow those funds from the bank to finance their capital purchases.

The importance of the movement of capital from individuals to firms in a market economy cannot be overemphasized. For firms to enter new industries or produce new products, capital is required. In market capitalist systems, decisions about which enterprises to support via capital is made by private citizens seeking private gain. The *Economics in Practice* on p. 235 describes this process for one firm, Tesla, maker of electric cars. These decisions are risky—it is hard to know which new firms will succeed and which will fail. Understanding the institutions through which capital flows from households to firms is the subject of this chapter.

Capital, Investment, and Depreciation

Before we proceed with our analysis of the capital market, we need to review some basic economic principles and introduce some related concepts.

Capital

One of the most important concepts in all of economics is the concept of **capital**. Capital goods are those goods produced by the economic system that are used as inputs to produce other goods and services in the future. Capital goods thus yield valuable productive services over time. The value of capital is only as great as the value of the services it renders over time.

capital Those goods produced by the economic system that are used as inputs to produce other goods and services in the future.

Tangible Capital When we think of capital, we generally think of the physical, material capital employed by firms. The major categories of **physical,** or **tangible, capital** are (1) nonresidential structures (for example, office buildings, power plants, factories, shopping centers, warehouses, and docks) (2) durable equipment (for example, machines, trucks, sandwich grills, and automobiles), (3) residential structures, and (4) inventories of inputs and outputs that firms have in stock.

Most firms need tangible capital, along with labor and land, to produce their products. A restaurant's capital requirements include a kitchen, ovens and grills, tables and chairs, silverware, dishes, and light fixtures. These items must be purchased up front and maintained if the restaurant is to function properly. A manufacturing firm must have a plant, specialized machinery,

physical, *or* **tangible, capital** Material things used as inputs in the production of future goods and services. The major categories of physical capital are nonresidential structures, durable equipment, residential structures, and inventories.

233

trucks, and inventories of parts. A winery needs casks, vats, piping, temperature-control equipment, and cooking and bottling machinery.

The capital stock of a retail pharmacy is made up mostly of inventories. Pharmacies do not produce the aspirin, vitamins, and toothbrushes that they sell. Instead, they buy those items from manufacturers and put them on display. The product actually produced and sold by a pharmacy is convenience. Like any other product, convenience is produced with labor and capital in the form of a store with many products, or inventory, displayed on the sales floor and kept in storerooms. The inventories of inputs and outputs that manufacturing firms maintain are also capital. To function smoothly and meet the demands of buyers, for example, the Ford Motor Company maintains inventories of both auto parts (tires, windshields, and so on) and completed cars.

An apartment building is also capital. Produced by the economic system, it yields valuable services over time and it is used as an input to produce housing services, which are rented.

Social Capital: Infrastructure

social capital, *or* infrastructure Capital that provides services to the public. Most social capital takes the form of public works (roads and bridges) and public services (police and fire protection).

Some physical or tangible capital is owned by the public instead of by private firms. **Social capital,** sometimes called **infrastructure**, is capital that provides services to the public. Most social capital takes the form of public works such as highways, roads, bridges, mass transit systems, and sewer and water systems. Police stations, fire stations, city halls, courthouses, and police cars are all forms of social capital that are used as inputs to produce the services that government provides.

All firms use some forms of social capital in producing their outputs. Recent economic research has shown that a country's infrastructure plays a very important role in helping private firms produce their products efficiently. When public capital is not properly cared for—for example, when roads deteriorate or when airports are not modernized to accommodate increasing traffic—private firms that depend on efficient transportation networks suffer.

Intangible Capital

intangible capital Nonmaterial things that contribute to the output of future goods and services.

Not all capital is physical. Some things that are intangible (nonmaterial) satisfy every part of our definition of capital. When a firm invests in advertising to establish a brand name, it is producing a form of **intangible capital** called goodwill. This goodwill yields valuable services to the firm over time.

human capital A form of intangible capital that includes the skills and other knowledge that workers have or acquire through education and training and that yields valuable services to a firm over time.

When a firm establishes a training program for employees, it is investing in its workers' skills. We can think of such an investment as the production of an intangible form of capital called **human capital**. It is produced with labor (instructors) and capital (classrooms, computers, projectors, and books). Human capital in the form of new or augmented skills is an input—it will yield valuable productive services for the firm in the future.

When research produces valuable results, such as a new production process that reduces costs or a new formula that creates a new product, the new technology can be considered capital. Furthermore, even ideas can be patented and the rights to them can be sold.

A large number of "new economy" start-up technology companies have responded to the growth of the Internet. These dot-com and e-commerce companies generally start with limited capital, and most of that capital is in the skills and knowledge of their employees: human capital.

Measuring Capital

capital stock For a single firm, the current market value of the firm's plant, equipment, inventories, and intangible assets.

Labor is measured in hours, and land is measured in square feet or acres. Because capital comes in so many forms, it is virtually impossible to measure it directly in physical terms. The indirect measure generally used is *current market value*. The measure of a firm's **capital stock** is the current market value of its plant, equipment, inventories, and intangible assets. By using value as a measuring stick, business managers, accountants, and economists can, in a sense, add buildings, barges, and bulldozers into a measure of total capital.

Capital is measured as a *stock* value. That is, it is measured at a point in time: The capital stock of the XYZ Corporation on July 31, 2007, is $3,453,231. According to Department of Commerce estimates, the capital stock of the U.S. economy in 2008 (in 2005 dollars) was about $44.2 trillion. Of that amount, $17.1 trillion was residential structures; $8.1 trillion was owned by the federal, state, and local governments (for example, aircraft carriers and school buildings); and $6.3 trillion was equipment and software.

ECONOMICS IN PRACTICE

Investment Banking, IPOs, and Electric Cars

Automobile production is, as we noted in Chapter 9, subject to economies of scale. Becoming a new car manufacturer requires considerable capital, well beyond what most individuals can put together. In the summer of 2010 Tesla Motors, a new electric car manufacturer, turned to the public to seek capital.

How did Tesla do this? Tesla decided to become a *public company*, with shares offered to the public on a stock exchange. The process of doing this is called an IPO (initial public offering). As the article indicates, Tesla initially offered the public 13.3 million shares, each for a price of $17, for a total increase in capital for the firm of $226 million. In mounting its IPO Tesla, like most other firms, relied on investment banks to help figure out the right price and manage the sales. In Tesla's case a number of firms were involved, including Goldman Sachs, J.P. Morgan, and Morgan Stanley. Managing IPOs is one of the functions of investment banks, as they help move capital from households to entrepreneurs with new ideas.

TSLA: What Does Tesla's IPO Mean for the Future of Electric Cars?

The Wall Street Journal

Tesla Motors today became the first American car company to make an initial public offering since Ford did so in 1956. And one could argue the sleek, fast Tesla Roadster the company has been selling is in some ways a bit like Ford's old Model T, which revolutionized assembly-line manufacturing.

Tesla seems poised to be part of the redefinition of the way we drive. After all, the Palo Alto, California, electric-car maker has in many ways been showing the rest of the auto industry how electric cars are done. The sleek Tesla Roadster is an emblem of electric cars' potential in terms of power, speed, and range. Without it I doubt many of the larger car makers would

be pursuing electric cars as vigorously as they are. Still, I worry about Tesla's endurance. Building cars is a difficult, expensive endeavor that has broken many small manufacturers who have tried to bring innovation to the table, from John DeLorean to Preston Tucker.

For now the outlook is promising. Not only did the IPO take place but it included more shares at a higher price than expected. The company boosted the number of shares to as much as 13.3 million and the price to $17 per share, for a total value of $226 million. The company previously had said it could sell up to 11.1 million shares at a price of $14 to $16 per share, or a total of $178 million. The increase in part reflects interest in electric cars that is greater than expected and growing surprisingly fast. Tesla is trading on the Nasdaq stock market under the symbol TSLA.

Source: The Wall Street Journal Online, "TSLA: What Does Tesla's IPO Mean for the Future of Electric Cars?" by Jonathan Welsh. Copyright 2010 by Dow Jones & Company, Inc. Reproduced with permission of Dow Jones & Company, Inc. via Copyright Clearance Center.

Although it is measured in terms of money, or value, it is very important to think of the actual capital stock. When we speak of capital, we refer not to money or to financial assets such as bonds and stocks, but instead to the firm's physical plant, equipment, inventory, and intangible assets.

Investment and Depreciation

Recall the difference between stock and flow measures discussed in earlier chapters. *Stock measures* are valued at a particular point in time, whereas *flow measures* are valued over a period of time. The easiest way to think of the difference between a stock and a flow is to think about a tub of water. The volume of water in the tub is measured at a point in time and is a stock. The amount of water that flows into the tub *per hour* and the amount of water that evaporates out of the tub *per day* are flow measures. Flow measures have meaning only when the time dimension is added. Water flowing into the tub at a rate of 5 gallons per hour is very different from water flowing at a rate of 5 gallons per year.

Capital stocks are affected over time by two flows: investment and depreciation. When a firm produces or puts in place new capital—a new piece of equipment, for example—it has invested. **Investment** is a flow that increases the stock of capital. Because it has a time dimension, we speak of investment per period (by the month, quarter, or year).

As you proceed, keep in mind that the term *investing* is *not* used in economics to describe the act of buying a share of stock or a bond. Although people commonly use the term this way ("I invested in some Union Carbide stock" or "he invested in Treasury bonds"), the term *investment* when used correctly refers *only to an increase in capital*.

investment New capital additions to a firm's capital stock. Although capital is measured at a given point in time (a stock), investment is measured over a period of time (a flow). The flow of investment increases the capital stock.

Table 11.1 presents data on private investment in the U. S. economy in 2009. About half of the total was equipment and software. Almost all the rest was investment in structures, both residential (apartment buildings, condominiums, houses, and so on) and nonresidential (factories, shopping malls, and so on). Inventory investment was negative (sales exceeded production in 2009). Column 3 looks at private investment as a percent of gross domestic product (GDP), a measure of the total output of the economy.

TABLE 11.1 Private Investment in the U.S. Economy, 2009			
GDP = $14,256.3 billion			
	Billions of Current Dollars	As a Percentage of Total Gross Investment	As a Percentage of GDP
Nonresidential structures	480.0	29.5	3.4
Equipment and software	908.8	55.8	6.4
Change in private inventories	−120.9	−7.4	−0.8
Residential structures	361.0	22.2	2.5
Total gross private investment	1,628.9	100.0	11.4
− depreciation	−1,538.8	−94.5	−10.8
Net investment =			
gross investment − depreciation	90.1	5.5	0.6

Source: U.S. Department of Commerce, Bureau of Economic Analysis.

depreciation The decline in an asset's economic value over time.

Depreciation is the decline in an asset's (resource's) economic value over time. If you have ever owned a car, you are aware that its resale value falls with age. Suppose you bought a new Toyota Prius for $30,500 and you decide to sell it 2 years and 25,000 miles later. Checking the newspaper and talking to several dealers, you find out that, given its condition and mileage, you can expect to get $22,000 for it. It has depreciated $8,500 ($30,500 − $22,000). Table 11.1 shows that in 2009, private depreciation in the U.S. economy was $1,538.8 billion.

A capital asset can depreciate because it wears out physically or because it becomes obsolete. Take, for example, a computer control system in a factory. If a new, technologically superior system does the same job for half the price, the old system may be replaced even if it still functions well. The Prius depreciated because of wear and tear *and* because new models had become available.

The Capital Market

Where does capital come from? How and why is it produced? How much and what kinds of capital are produced? Who pays for it? These questions are answered in the complex set of institutions in which households supply their savings to firms that demand funds to buy capital goods. Collectively, these institutions are called the **capital market**.

capital market The market in which households supply their savings to firms that demand funds to buy capital goods.

Although governments and households make some capital investment decisions, most decisions to produce new capital goods—that is, to invest—are made by firms. However, a firm cannot invest unless it has the funds to do so. Although firms can invest in many ways, it is always the case that the funds that firms use to buy capital goods come, directly or indirectly, from households. When a household decides not to consume a portion of its income, it saves. Investment by firms is the *demand for capital*. Saving by households is the *supply of capital*. Various financial institutions facilitate the transfer of households' savings to firms that use them for capital investment.

Let us use a simple example to see how the system works. Suppose some firm wants to purchase a machine that costs $1,000 and some household decides at the same time to save $1,000 from its income. Figure 11.1 shows one way that the household's decision to save might connect with the firm's decision to invest.

bond A contract between a borrower and a lender, in which the borrower agrees to pay the loan at some time in the future, along with interest payments along the way.

Either directly or through a financial intermediary (such as a bank), the household agrees to loan its savings to the firm. In exchange, the firm contracts to pay the household interest at some agreed-to rate each period. Interest is the fee paid by a borrower to a lender or by a bank to a depositor for the use of funds. The interest rate is that fee paid annually, and it is expressed as a percentage of the loan or deposit. If the household lends directly to the firm, the firm gives the household a **bond**, which is nothing more than a contract promising to repay the loan at some specific time in the future. The bond also specifies the flow of interest to be paid in the meantime.

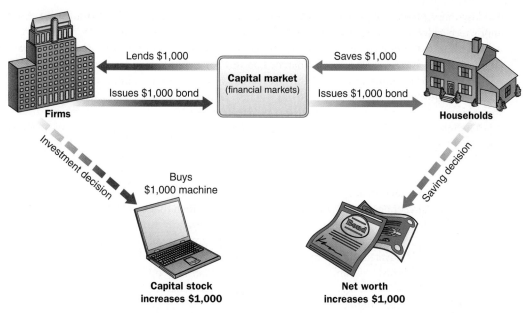

Lends $1,000

Issues $1,000 bond

Firms

Capital market
(financial markets)

Saves $1,000

Issues $1,000 bond

Households

Investment decision

Saving decision

**Buys
$1,000 machine**

**Capital stock
increases $1,000**

**Net worth
increases $1,000**

▲ FIGURE 11.1 **$1,000 in Savings Becomes $1,000 of Investment**

The new saving adds to the household's stock of wealth. The household's *net worth* has increased by the $1,000, which it holds in the form of a bond.[1] The bond represents the firm's promise to repay the $1,000 at some future date with interest. The firm uses the $1,000 to buy a new $1,000 machine, which it adds to its capital stock. In essence, the household has supplied the capital demanded by the firm. It is almost as if the household bought the machine and rented it to the firm for an annual fee. Presumably, this investment will generate added revenues that will facilitate the payment of interest to the household. In general, projects are undertaken as long as the revenues likely to be realized from the investment are sufficient to cover the interest payments to the household.

Sometimes the transfer of household savings through the capital market into investment occurs without a financial intermediary. An *entrepreneur* is one who organizes, manages, and assumes the risk of a new firm. When entrepreneurs start a new business by buying capital with their own savings, they are both demanding capital and supplying the resources (that is, their savings) needed to purchase that capital. No third party is involved in the transaction. Most investment, however, is accomplished with the help of financial intermediaries (third parties such as banks, insurance companies, and pension funds) that stand between the supplier (saver) and the demander (investing firm). The part of the capital market in which savers and investors interact through intermediaries is often called the **financial capital market**.

Capital Income: Interest and Profits

It should now be clear to you how capital markets fit into the circular flow: They facilitate the movement of household savings into the most productive investment projects. When households allow their savings to be used to purchase capital, they receive payments, and these payments (along with wages and salaries) are part of household incomes. Income that is earned on savings that have been put to use through financial capital markets is called **capital income**. Capital income is received by households in many forms, the two most important of which are *interest* and *profits*.

Interest The most common form of capital income received by households is interest. In simplest terms, **interest** is the payment made for the use of money. Banks pay interest to depositors, whose deposits are loaned out to businesses or individuals who want to make investments.[2] Banks also *charge* interest to those who borrow money. Corporations pay interest to households

financial capital market The part of the capital market in which savers and investors interact through intermediaries.

capital income Income earned on savings that have been put to use through financial capital markets.

interest The payments made for the use of money.

---

[1] Note that the *act of saving* increases the household's wealth, not the act of buying the bond. Buying the bond simply transforms one financial asset (money) into another (a bond). The household could simply have held on to the money.

[2] Although we are focusing on investment by businesses, households can and do make investments also. The most important form of household investment is the construction of a new house, usually financed by borrowing in the form of a mortgage. A household may also borrow to finance the purchase of an existing house, but when it does so, no new investment is taking place.

that buy their bonds. The government borrows money by issuing bonds, and the buyers of those bonds receive interest payments.

interest rate Interest payments expressed as a percentage of the loan.

The **interest rate** is almost always expressed as an annual rate. It is the annual interest payment expressed as a percentage of the loan or deposit. For example, a $1,000 bond (representing a $1,000 loan from a household to a firm) that carries a fixed 10 percent interest rate will pay the household $100 per year ($1,000 × .10) in interest. A savings account that carries a 5 percent annual interest rate will pay $50 annually on a balance of $1,000.

The interest rate is usually agreed to at the time a loan or deposit is made. Sometimes borrowers and lenders agree to periodically adjust the level of interest payments depending on market conditions. These types of loans are called *adjustable* or *floating-rate loans*. (*Fixed rate loans* are loans in which the interest rate never varies.) In recent years, there have even been adjustable rates of interest on savings accounts and certificates of deposit.

A loan's interest rate depends on a number of factors. A loan that involves more risk will generally pay a higher interest rate than a loan with less risk. Similarly, firms that are considered bad credit risks will pay higher interest rates than firms with good credit ratings. You have probably heard radio or TV advertisements by finance companies offering to loan money to borrowers "regardless of credit history." This means that they will loan to people or businesses that pose a relatively high risk of *defaulting*, or not paying off the loan. What they do not tell you is that the interest rate will be quite high.

It is generally agreed that the safest borrower is the U.S. government. With the "full faith and credit" of the U.S. government pledged to buyers of U.S. Treasury bonds and bills, most people believe that there is little risk that the government will not repay its loans. For this reason, the U.S. government can borrow money at a lower interest rate than any other borrower.

Profits *Profits* is another word for the net income of a firm: revenue minus costs of production. Some firms are owned by individuals or partners who sell their products for more than it costs to produce them. The profits of proprietors or partnerships generally go directly to the owner or owners who run the firm. Corporations are firms owned by shareholders who usually are not otherwise connected with the firms. Corporations are organized and chartered under state laws that grant limited liability status to their owners or shareholders. Essentially, that means that shareholders cannot lose more than they have invested if the company incurs liabilities it cannot pay.

stock A share of stock is an ownership claim on a firm, entitling its owner to a profit share.

A share of common **stock** is a certificate that represents the ownership of a share of a business, almost always a corporation. For example, Lincoln Electric is a Cleveland-based company that makes welding and cutting equipment. The company has 41 million shares of common stock that are owned by tens of thousands of shareholders, some of whom are private individuals, some of whom are institutions such as Carlton College, and some of whom may be employees of the firm. Shareholders are entitled to a share of the company's profit. When profits are paid directly to shareholders, the payment is called a dividend. Lincoln Electric made a profit of $54 million in a recent year, which was $1.31 per share, of which $0.43 was paid out to shareholders as dividends and the rest retained for investment. [3]

In discussing profit, it is important to distinguish between profit as defined by generally accepting *accounting* practices and *economic* profits as we defined them in Chapter 7. Recall that our definition of profit is total revenue minus total cost, where total cost includes the normal rate of return on capital. We defined profit this way because true economic cost includes the opportunity cost of capital.

Functions of Interest and Profit Capital income serves several functions. First, interest may function as an incentive to postpone gratification. When you save, you pass up the chance to buy things that you want right now. One view of interest holds that it is the reward for postponing consumption.

Second, profit serves as a reward for innovation and risk taking. Every year *Forbes* magazine publishes the names of the richest people in the United States, and virtually every major fortune

---

[3] Shares of common stock are traded openly on private stock exchanges or markets. Most of the billions of shares traded every day are one shareholder selling shares to another. When shares are first issued, the proceeds are used to buy capital or to "buy out" the entrepreneurs who started the firm.

listed there is traceable to the founding of some business enterprise that "made it big." In recent years, big winners have included retail stores (the Walton family of Wal-Mart), high-tech companies (Bill Gates of Microsoft and Eric Schmidt of Google), and a real estate empire (the Pritzker family).

Many argue that rewards for innovation and risk taking are the essence of the U.S. free enterprise system. Innovation is at the core of economic growth and progress. More efficient production techniques mean that the resources saved can be used to produce new things. There is another side to this story, however: Critics of the free enterprise system claim that such large rewards are not justified and that accumulations of great wealth and power are not in society's best interests.

Financial Markets in Action

When a firm issues a fixed-interest-rate bond, it borrows funds and pays interest at an agreed-to rate to the person or institution that buys the bond. Many other mechanisms, four of which are illustrated in Figure 11.2, also channel household savings into investment projects.

Case A: Business Loans As I look around my hometown, I see several ice cream stores doing very well; but I think that I can make better ice cream than they do. To go into the business, I need capital: ice cream-making equipment, tables, chairs, freezers, signs, and a store. Because I put up my house as collateral, I am not a big risk; so the bank grants me a loan at a fairly reasonable interest rate. Banks have these funds to lend only because households deposit their savings there.

Case B: Venture Capital A scientist at a leading university develops an inexpensive method of producing a very important family of virus-fighting drugs, using microorganisms created through gene splicing. The business could very well fail within 12 months, but if it succeeds, the potential for profit is huge.

Our scientist goes to a *venture capital fund* for financing. Such funds take household savings and put them into high-risk ventures in exchange for a share of the profits if the new businesses succeed. By investing in many different projects, the funds reduce the risk of going broke. Once

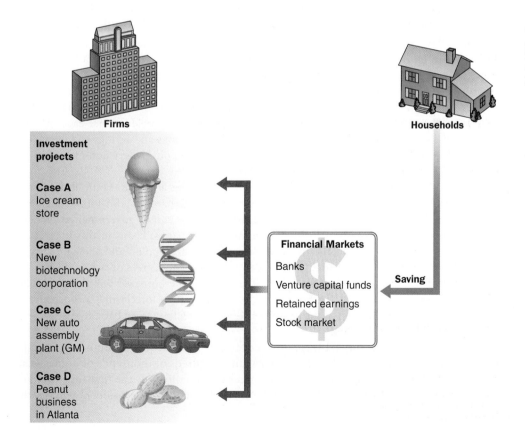

◀ FIGURE 11.2

Financial Markets Link Household Saving and Investment by Firms

again, household funds make it possible for firms to undertake investments. If a venture succeeds, those owning shares in the venture capital fund receive substantial profits.

Case C: Retained Earnings   IBM decides in 2009 to build a new plant in Dubuque, Iowa, and it discovers that it has enough funds to pay for the new facility. The new investment is thus paid for through internal funds, or *retained earnings*.

The result is the same as if the firm had gone to households via some financial intermediary and borrowed the funds. If IBM uses its profits to buy new capital, it does so only with the shareholders' implicit consent. When a firm takes its own profit and uses it to buy capital assets instead of paying it out to its shareholders, the total value of the firm goes up, as does the value of the shares held by stockholders. As in our other examples, IBM capital stock increases and so does the net worth of households.

When a household owns a share of stock that *appreciates*, or increases in value, the appreciation is part of the household's income. Unless the household sells the stock and consumes the gain, that gain is part of saving. In essence, when a firm retains earnings for investment purposes, it is actually saving on behalf of its shareholders.

Case D: The Stock Market   A former high-ranking government official decides to start a new peanut-processing business in Atlanta; he also decides to raise the funds needed by issuing shares of stock. Households buy the shares with income that they decide not to spend. In exchange, they are entitled to a share of the peanut firm's profits.

The shares of stock become part of households' net worth. The proceeds from stock sales are used to buy plant equipment and inventory. Savings flow into investment, and the firm's capital stock goes up by the same amount as household net worth. The *Economics in Practice* on p. 235 describes how Tesla raised funds in this way.

Mortgages and the Mortgage Market

Most real estate in the United States is financed by mortgages. A mortgage, like a bond, is a contract in which the borrower promises to repay the lender in the future. Mortgages are backed by real estate. When a household buys a home, it usually borrows most of the money by signing a mortgage in which it agrees to repay the money with interest often over as long as 30 years. While in recent years all kinds of exotic payment schemes have complicated the mortgage market, the most common form of mortgage is the 30-year fixed rate mortgage. Almost all mortgage loans require a monthly payment. As an example, a home financed with a 30-year fixed rate mortgage loan of $250,000 at 6.4 percent will face a monthly payment of $1,563.76. If the borrower pays that amount each month for 30 years, he or she will have paid off the loan while paying interest at a rate of 6.4 percent on the unpaid balance each month.

Until the last decade, most mortgage loans were made by banks and savings and loans. The lenders used depositors' money to make the loans, and the signed promissory notes were kept by the lenders who collected the payment every month.

Recently, the mortgage market changed dramatically and became more complicated. Most mortgages are now written by mortgage brokers or mortgage bankers who immediately sell the mortgages to a secondary market. The secondary market is run by governmental agencies such as Fannie Mae and Freddie Mac and large investment banks. Loans in this market are "securitized," which means that the mortgage documents are pooled and then mortgage-backed securities are sold to investors who want to take different degrees of risk.

The risk of owning mortgages is primarily the risk that the borrower will default on the obligation. When default occurs, the house may be taken through foreclosure, a procedure in which the lender takes possession of the borrower's house and sells it to get back at least some of the amount that the lender is owed.

In 2007, the mortgage market was hit by a dramatic increase in the number of defaults and foreclosures. Lenders lost billions of dollars, and hundreds of thousands of homes went into foreclosure. The reasons were that home prices began falling for the first time in many years and that a large number of loans were made to buyers who could not make the required payments.

ECONOMICS IN PRACTICE

Who Owns Stocks in the United States?

In the text we describe how households buy shares of stock as a way to invest in businesses and to generate hoped-for returns. In some cases households do this as individuals. There have always been individuals who have invested in stocks in specific companies through brokerage firms. As the number of low-cost brokerage firms has grown, many more people have begun trading this way. In the last decade, we have seen the growth of *day traders*, individuals who buy and sell shares of stock quickly in the hopes of making money. But, in terms of value, the bulk of the stock in the United States is held by households through institutions, pension funds, insurance companies, mutual

funds, and the like. For some companies, a large majority of their stock is held by households through institutions. In the two charts below, taken from Yahoo Finance on June 23, 2010, we see the extent of institutional holding in two companies: Microsoft and Activision, the producer of video games like Guitar Hero and World of Warcraft. You can see that a more mature company like Microsoft has a much higher rate of institutional holdings than does the newer Activision. You can also see that for both firms, insiders (people who work for the company) hold quite a lot of the firm's stock, and this is especially true for the newer Activision.

Microsoft Data Share Statistics		Activision Data Share Statistics	
Avg Vol (3 month):	69,351,300	Avg Vol (3 month):	14,813,700
Avg Vol (10 day):	55,999,100	Avg Vol (10 day):	14,016,300
Shares Outstanding:	8.76B	Shares Outstanding:	1.24B
% Held by Insiders:	12.25%	% Held by Insiders:	58.03%
% Held by Institutions:	64.60%	% Held by Institutions:	36.40%

Capital Accumulation and Allocation

You can see from the preceding examples that various, and sometimes complex, connections between households and firms facilitate the movement of savings into productive investment. The methods may differ, but the results are the same. Industrialized or agrarian, small or large, simple or complex, all societies exist through time and must allocate resources over time. In simple societies, investment and saving decisions are made by the same people. However:

In modern industrial societies, investment decisions (capital production decisions) are made primarily by firms. Households decide how much to save, and in the long run, savings limit or constrain the amount of investment that firms can undertake. The capital market exists to direct savings into profitable investment projects.

The Demand for New Capital and the Investment Decision

We saw in Chapter 9 that firms have an incentive to expand in industries that earn positive profits—that is, a rate of return above normal—and in industries in which economies of scale lead to lower average costs at higher levels of output. We also saw that positive profits in an industry stimulate the entry of new firms. The expansion of existing firms and the creation of new firms both involve investment in new capital.

Even when there are no profits in an industry, firms must still do some investing. First, equipment wears out and must be replaced if the firm is to stay in business. Second, firms are constantly changing. A new technology may become available, sales patterns may shift, or the firm may expand or contract its product line.

With these points in mind, we now turn to a discussion of the investment decision process within the individual firm. In the end, we will see (just as we did in Chapter 10) that a perfectly competitive firm invests in capital up to the point at which the marginal revenue product of capital is equal to the price of capital.

Forming Expectations

We have already said that the most important dimension of capital is time. Capital produces useful services over *some period of time*. In building an office tower, a developer makes an investment that will be around for decades. In deciding where to build a branch plant, a manufacturing firm commits a large amount of resources to purchase capital that will be in place for a long time.

It is important to remember, though, that capital goods do not begin to yield benefits until they are *used*. Often the decision to build a building or purchase a piece of equipment must be made years before the actual project is completed. Although the acquisition of a small business computer may take only days, the planning process for downtown development projects in big U.S. cities has been known to take decades.

The Expected Benefits of Investments   Decision makers must have expectations about what is going to happen in the future. A new plant will be very valuable—that is, it will produce much profit—if the market for a firm's product grows and the price of that product remains high. The same plant will be worth little if the economy goes into a slump or consumers grow tired of the firm's product. The Tesla's success will depend not only on consumer tastes for electric cars, but also on the government's energy policy. The investment process requires that the potential investor evaluate the expected flow of future productive services that an investment project will yield.

An official of the General Electric Corporation (GE) once described the difficulty involved in making such predictions. GE subscribes to a number of different economic forecasting services. In the early 1980s, those services provided the firm with 10-year predictions of new housing construction that ranged from a low of 400,000 new units per year to a high of 4 million new units per year. Because GE sells millions of household appliances to contractors building new houses, condominiums, and apartments, the forecast was critical. If GE decided that the high number was more accurate, it would need to spend billions of dollars on new plant and equipment to prepare for the extra demand. If GE decided that the low number was more accurate, it would need to begin closing several of its larger plants and disinvesting. In fact, GE took the middle road. It assumed that housing production would be between 1.5 and 2 million units—which, in fact, it was.

GE is not an exception. All firms must rely on forecasts to make sensible investment and production decisions, but forecasting is an inexact science because so much depends on events that cannot be foreseen.

The Expected Costs of Investments   The benefits of any investment project take the form of future profits. These profits must be forecast, but costs must also be evaluated. Like households, firms have access to financial markets, both as borrowers and as lenders. If a firm borrows, it must *pay* interest over time. If it lends, it will *earn* interest. If the firm borrows to finance a project, the interest on the loan is part of the cost of the project.

Even if a project is financed with the firm's own fund instead of through borrowing, an opportunity cost is involved. A thousand dollars put into a capital investment project will generate an expected flow of future profit; the same $1,000 put into the financial market (in essence, loaned to another firm) will yield a flow of interest payments. The project will not be undertaken unless it is expected to yield more than the market interest rate. The cost of an investment project may thus be direct or indirect because the ability to lend at the market rate of interest means that there is an *opportunity cost* associated with every investment project. The evaluation process thus involves not only estimating future benefits but also comparing them with the possible alternative uses of the funds required to undertake the project. At a minimum, those funds could earn interest in financial markets.

ECONOMICS IN PRACTICE

Chinese Wind Power

One of the most interesting investment phenomena in the last few years has been the strong interest by the Chinese in wind power. As the article below indicates, by 2009 China had become the world's largest wind power market. As we suggest in the text, investments—because they are long-lived—depend critically on future expectations. In the case of wind power investments, investors have to make judgments about government climate and energy policy, both in China and elsewhere, about tariff policy, about the future of substitute products like oil, and about economic growth more generally. The uncertainty of these complex factors makes wind investing in China a risky business.

Gone With The Wind: Capital for China's Turbine Makers

The Wall Street Journal

"A great wind is blowing, and that gives you either imagination or a headache." Catherine the Great surely was referring to capital raising for China's wind turbine makers. As Dow Jones Investment Banker reports, for them, a headache is more likely.

Last year was a good time for China when it became the largest wind market by annual installed capacity at 13 gigawatts, according to the Global Wind Energy Council.

Unfortunately that growth heralds overcapacity for Chinese turbine makers, suggesting a shake-out for some smaller names after 2009's aggressive build out. That should, of course, play to survivors' advantage in the long-term.

Favorable macro-tailwinds and preferential policy over the last five years have helped China's wind industry. For example, farm operators are aided by on-grid tariffs for wind being higher than fossil fuels', while local component-makers gain from rules ensuring at least 70 percent of turbine components by purchase value are made domestically.

Source: Wall Street Journal Online, excerpted from "Gone With The Wind: Capital for China's Turbine Makers" by Jamie Miyazaki. Copyright 2010 by *Dow Jones & Company, Inc.* Reproduced with permission of *Dow Jones & Company, Inc.* via Copyright Clearance Center.

Comparing Costs and Expected Return

Once expectations have been formed, firms must quantify them—that is, they must assign some dollars-and-cents value to them. One way to quantify expectations is to calculate an **expected rate of return** on the investment project. For example, if a new computer network that costs $400,000 is likely to save $100,000 per year in data-processing costs forever after, the expected rate of return on that investment is 25 percent per year. Each year the firm will save $100,000 as a result of the $400,000 investment. The expected rate of return will be less than 25 percent if the computer network wears out or becomes obsolete after a while and the cost saving ceases. The expected rate of return on an investment project depends on the price of the investment, the expected length of time the project provides additional cost savings or revenue, and the expected amount of revenue attributable each year to the project.

expected rate of return The annual rate of return that a firm expects to obtain through a capital investment.

Table 11.2 presents a menu of investment choices and expected rates of return that a hypothetical firm faces. Because expected rates of return are based on forecasts of future

TABLE 11.2	Potential Investment Projects and Expected Rates of Return for a Hypothetical Firm, Based on Forecasts of Future Profits Attributable to the Investment	
Project	(1) Total Investment (Dollars)	(2) Expected Rate of Return (Percent)
A. New computer network	400,000	25
B. New branch plant	2,600,000	20
C. Sales office in another state	1,500,000	15
D. New automated billing system	100,000	12
E. Ten new delivery trucks	400,000	10
F. Advertising campaign	1,000,000	7
G. Employee cafeteria	100,000	5

profits attributable to the investments, any change in expectations would change all the numbers in column 2.

Figure 11.3 graphs the total amount of investment in millions of dollars that the firm would undertake at various interest rates. If the interest rate were 24 percent, the firm would fund only project A, the new computer network. It can borrow at 24 percent and invest in a computer that is expected to yield 25 percent. At 24 percent, the firm's total investment is $400,000. The first vertical red line in Figure 11.3 shows that at any interest rate above 20 percent and below 25 percent, only $400,000 worth of investment (that is, project A) will be undertaken.

If the interest rate were 18 percent, the firm would fund projects A and B, and its total investment would rise to $3 million ($400,000 + $2,600,000). If the firm could borrow at 18 percent, the flow of additional profits generated by the new computer and the new plant would more than cover the costs of borrowing, but none of the other projects would be justified. The rates of return on projects A and B (25 percent and 20 percent, respectively) both exceed the 18 percent interest rate. Only if the interest rate fell below 5 percent would the firm fund all seven investment projects.

The investment schedule in Table 11.2 and its graphic depiction in Figure 11.3 describe the firm's demand for new capital, expressed as a function of the market interest rate. If we add the total investment undertaken by *all* firms at every interest rate, we arrive at the demand for new capital in the economy as a whole. In other words, the market demand curve for new capital is the sum of all the individual demand curves for new capital in the economy (Figure 11.4). In a sense, the investment demand schedule is a ranking of all the investment opportunities in the economy in order of expected yield. Only those investment projects in the economy that are expected to yield a rate of return higher than the market interest rate will be funded. At lower market interest rates, more investment projects are undertaken.

The most important thing to remember about the investment demand curve is that its shape and position depend critically on the *expectations* of those making the investment decisions. Because many influences affect these expectations, they are usually volatile and subject to frequent change. Thus, although lower interest rates tend to stimulate investment and higher interest rates tend to slow it, many other hard-to-measure and hard-to-predict factors also affect the level of investment spending.

The Expected Rate of Return and the Marginal Revenue Product of Capital
The concept of the expected rate of return on investment projects is analogous to the concept of the marginal revenue product of capital (MRP_K). Recall that we defined an input's marginal revenue product as the additional revenue a firm earns by employing one additional unit of that input, *ceteris paribus*.

▶ **FIGURE 11.3**

Total Investment as a Function of the Market Interest Rate

The demand for new capital depends on the interest rate. When the interest rate is low, firms are more likely to invest in new plant and equipment than when the interest rate is high. This is so because the interest rate determines the direct cost (interest on a loan) or the opportunity cost (alternative investment) of each project.

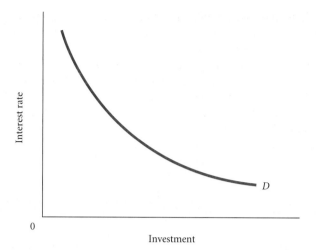

◀ FIGURE 11.4

Investment Demand

Lower interest rates are likely to stimulate investment in the economy as a whole, whereas higher interest rates are likely to slow investment.

Now think carefully about the return on an additional unit of new capital (the marginal revenue product of capital). Suppose that the rate of return on an investment in a new machine is 15 percent. This means that the investment project yields the same return as a bond yielding 15 percent. If the current interest rate is less than 15 percent, the investment project will be undertaken because a perfectly competitive profit-maximizing firm will keep investing in new capital up to the point at which the expected rate of return is equal to the interest rate. This is analogous to saying that the firm will continue investing up to the point at which the marginal revenue product of capital is equal to the price of capital, or $MRP_K = P_K$, which is what we learned in Chapter 10.

A Final Word on Capital

The concept of capital is one of the central ideas in economics. Capital is produced by the economic system itself. Capital generates services over time, and it is used as an input in the production of goods and services.

The enormous productivity of modern industrial societies is due in part to the tremendous amount of capital that they have accumulated over the years. It may surprise you to know that the average worker in the United States works with about $170,000 worth of capital. Recall that in the United States, total investment (new capital) was 11.4 percent of GDP in 2009 (Table 11.1). High rates of investment have had enormous impacts in countries such as China and Malaysia. According to recent World Bank figures, capital goods represent 40 percent of China's total output of goods and services, and in Malaysia the figure is 32 percent. In 2009, China had a growth rate of output of over 9 percent and Malaysia had over 7 percent.

Most of this chapter described the institutions and processes that determine the amount and types of capital produced in a market economy. Existing firms in search of increased profits, potential new entrants to the markets, and entrepreneurs with new ideas are continuously evaluating potential investment projects. At the same time, households are saving. Each year households save some portion of their after-tax incomes. These new savings become part of their net worth, and they want to earn a return on those savings. Each year a good portion of the savings finds its way into the hands of firms that use it to buy new capital goods.

Between households and firms is the financial capital market. Millions of people participate in financial markets every day. There are literally thousands of financial managers, pension funds, mutual funds, brokerage houses, options traders, and banks whose sole purpose is to earn the highest possible rate of return on people's savings.

Brokers, bankers, and financial managers are continuously scanning the financial horizons for profitable investments. What businesses are doing well? What businesses are doing poorly? Should we lend to an expanding firm? All the analysis done by financial managers seeking to earn a high yield for clients, by managers of firms seeking to earn high profits for their stockholders, and by entrepreneurs seeking profits from innovation serves to channel capital into its most productive uses. Within firms, the evaluation of individual investment projects involves forecasting costs and benefits and valuing streams of potential income that will be earned only in future years.

We have now completed our discussion of competitive input and output markets. We have looked at household and firm choices in output markets, labor markets, land markets, and capital markets.

We now turn to a discussion of the allocative process that we have described. How do all the parts of the economy fit together? Is the result good or bad? Can we improve on it? All of this is the subject of Chapter 12.

SUMMARY

CAPITAL, INVESTMENT, AND DEPRECIATION *p. 233*

1. In market capitalist systems, the decision to put capital to use in a particular enterprise is made by private citizens putting their savings at risk in search of private gain. The set of institutions through which such transactions occur is called the *capital market*.

2. *Capital goods* are those goods produced by the economic system that are used as inputs to produce other goods and services in the future. Capital goods thus yield valuable productive services over time.

3. The major categories of *physical*, or *tangible, capital* are nonresidential structures, durable equipment, residential structures, and inventories. *Social capital* (or *infrastructure*) is capital that provides services to the public. *Intangible (nonmaterial) capital* includes *human capital* and goodwill.

4. The most important dimension of capital is that it exists through time. Therefore, its value is only as great as the value of the services it will render over time.

5. The most common measure of a firm's *capital stock* is the current market value of its plant, equipment, inventories, and intangible assets. However, in thinking about capital, it is important to focus on the actual capital stock instead of its simple monetary value.

6. In economics, the term *investment* refers to the creation of new capital, not to the purchase of a share of stock or a bond. Investment is a flow that increases the capital stock.

7. *Depreciation* is the decline in an asset's economic value over time. A capital asset can depreciate because it wears out physically or because it becomes obsolete.

THE CAPITAL MARKET *p. 236*

8. Income that is earned on savings that have been put to use through *financial capital markets* is called *capital income*. The two most important forms of capital income are *interest* and *profits*. Interest is the fee paid by a borrower to a lender.

Interest rewards households for postponing gratification, and profit rewards entrepreneurs for innovation and risk taking.

9. In modern industrial societies, investment decisions (capital production decisions) are made primarily by firms. Households decide how much to save, and in the long run, saving limits the amount of investment that firms can undertake. The capital market exists to direct savings into profitable investment projects.

THE DEMAND FOR NEW CAPITAL AND THE INVESTMENT DECISION *p. 241*

10. Before investing, investors must evaluate the expected flow of future productive services that an investment project will yield.

11. The availability of interest to lenders means that there is an opportunity cost associated with every investment project. This cost must be weighed against the stream of earnings that a project is expected to yield.

12. A firm will decide whether to undertake an investment project by comparing costs with expected returns. The *expected rate of return* on an investment project depends on the price of the investment, the expected length of time the project provides additional cost savings or revenue, and the expected amount of revenue attributable each year to the project.

13. The investment demand curve shows the demand for capital in the economy as a function of the market interest rate. Only those investment projects that are expected to yield a rate of return higher than the market interest rate will be funded. Lower interest rates should stimulate investment.

14. A perfectly competitive profit-maximizing firm will keep investing in new capital up to the point at which the expected rate of return is equal to the interest rate. This is equivalent to saying that the firm will continue investing up to the point at which the marginal revenue product of capital is equal to the price of capital, or $MRP_K = P_K$.

REVIEW TERMS AND CONCEPTS

bond, *p. 236*

capital, *p. 233*

capital income, *p. 237*

capital market, *p. 236*

capital stock, *p. 234*

depreciation, *p. 236*

expected rate of return, *p. 243*

financial capital market, *p. 237*

human capital, *p. 234*

intangible capital, *p. 234*

interest, *p. 237*

interest rate, *p. 238*

investment, *p. 235*

physical, *or* tangible, capital, *p. 233*

social capital, *or* infrastructure, *p. 234*

stock, *p. 238*

PROBLEMS

All problems are available on www.myeconlab.com

1. Which of the following are capital, and which are not? Explain your answers.
   a. A video poker game machine at a local bar that takes quarters
   b. A $10 bill
   c. A college education
   d. The Golden Gate Bridge
   e. The shirts on the rack at Sears
   f. A government bond
   g. The Empire State Building
   h. A savings account
   i. The Washington Monument
   j. A Honda plant in Marysville, Ohio

2. For each of the following, decide whether you agree or disagree and explain your answer:
   a. *Savings* and *investment* are just two words for the same thing.
   b. When I buy a share of Microsoft stock, I have invested; when I buy a government bond, I have not.
   c. Higher interest rates lead to more investment because those investments pay a higher return.

3. You and 99 other partners are offered the chance to buy a gas station. Each partner would put up $10,000. The revenues from the operation of the station have been steady at $420,000 per year for several years and are projected to remain steady into the future. The costs (not including opportunity costs) of operating the station (including maintenance and repair, depreciation, and salaries) have also been steady at $360,000 per year. Currently, 5-year Treasury bills are yielding 7.5 percent interest. Would you go in on the deal? Explain your answer.

4. The board of directors of the Quando Company in Singapore was presented with the following list of investment projects for implementation in 2010:

PROJECT	TOTAL COST SINGAPORE DOLLARS	ESTIMATED RATE OF RETURN
Factory in Kuala Lumpur	$17,356,400	13%
Factory in Bangkok	15,964,200	15
A new company aircraft	10,000,000	12
A factory outlet store	3,500,000	18
A new computer network	2,000,000	20
A cafeteria for workers	1,534,000	7

Sketch total investment as a function of the interest rate (with the interest rate on the *Y*-axis). Currently, the interest rate in Singapore is 8 percent. How much investment would you recommend to Quando's board?

5. The Federal Reserve Board of Governors has the power to raise or lower short-term interest rates. Between 2005 and 2006, the Fed aggressively increased the benchmark federal funds interest rate from 2.5 percent in February 2005 to 5.25 percent in June 2006. Assuming that other interest rates also increased, what effects do you think that move had on investment spending in the economy? Explain your answer. What do you think the Fed's objective was?

6. Give at least three examples of how savings can be channeled into productive investment. Why is investment so important for an economy? What do you sacrifice when you save today?

7. From a newspaper such as *The Wall Street Journal*, from the business section of your local daily, or from the Internet, look up the prime interest rate, the corporate bond rate, and the interest rate on 10-year U.S. government bonds today. List some of the reasons these three rates are different.

8. Explain what we mean when we say that "households supply capital and firms demand capital."

9. [**Related to** *Economics in Practice* on *p. 243*] Venture capital funds have been very active in rapidly developing countries such as China and India. Explain why this is so.

10. Describe the capital stock of your college or university. How would you go about measuring its value? Has your school made any major investments in recent years? If so, describe them. What does your school hope to gain from these investments?

11. In March 2008, the General Motors building, a skyscraper in Manhattan, was up for bid. At the time, the skyscraper was expected to fetch more than $3 billion, a record for a single building. If you were a real estate investment company considering bidding on this building, what would you want to know first? What specific factors would you need to form expectations about? What information would you need to form those expectations?

12. On October 29, 2007, the Red Sox won the World Series. That same day the stock market rose. The S&P 500 index (an index of the stock prices of the 500 largest corporations in the United States) closed up at 1540.98. Ten-year Treasury notes were paying 4.38% on 10-year obligations of the government. The Fed was poised to announce a cut in the fed funds rate of a quarter of a percent to 4.75 percent.

    Look up today's S&P index, the 10-year treasury interest rate, and the fed funds rate. You can find them at http://money.cnn.com. Provide an explanation for what has happened to those three numbers since 2007.

13. Lending institutions charge different interest rates for different classifications of mortgages. Two of these mortgage types are Alt-A mortgages and subprime mortgages. Alt-A mortgages generally carry a higher interest rate than a typical "prime rate" mortgage, and subprime mortgage rates are generally even higher than Alt-A rates. What is the likely economic justification for the higher interest rates for these two types of mortgages?

14. Celia, an analyst with a venture capital firm, is approached by Wanda about financing her new business venture, a company which will build electricity-generating windmills for residential use. What information should Celia have before making a decision about financing Wanda's new company?

15. Draw a graph showing an investment demand curve and explain the slope of the curve.

16. Bailey, Kaylee, Haley, and Joyce are sorority sisters who have discovered an opportunity to purchase an Internet café. Each of the women would have to put up $80,000 to make the purchase. The revenue from the café is expected to remain constant at $225,000 per year for the next several years. The costs (not including the opportunity costs of the investment) of operating the café are expected to remain constant at $185,000 for the

next several years. The current market interest rate on enterprises with comparable risks is 9% per year. Should the four sorority sisters purchase the café? Explain.

17. **[Related to the Economics in Practice on *p. 241*]** The text states that in terms of value, the majority of stock in the United States is held by households through institutions and the percentage of institutional holding of stock (as well as the percentage of insider holding) often varies based on the maturity of the

company. Choose two publicly traded companies based in your local area; one relatively new and the other relatively mature. Go to www.finance.yahoo.com and enter each company in the "GET QUOTES" dialog box, then click on "Key Statistics" to find trading information. Look at the Share Statistics for each company. Describe the variation in the percentage of shares held by institutions and the percentage of shares held by insiders for the two companies.

CHAPTER 11 APPENDIX

Calculating Present Value

We have seen in this chapter that a firm's major goal in making investment decisions is to evaluate revenue streams that will not materialize until the future. One way for the firm to decide whether to undertake an investment project is to compare the expected rate of return from the investment with the current interest rate available (assuming comparable risk) in the financial market. We discussed this procedure in the text. The purpose of this Appendix is to present a more complete method of evaluating future revenue streams through present-value analysis.

Present Value

Consider the investment project described in Table 11A.1. We use the word *project* in this example to refer to buying a machine or a piece of capital for $1,200 and receiving the cash flow given in the right-hand column of the table. Would you do the project? At first glance, you might answer yes. After all, the total flow of cash that you will receive is $1,600, which is $400 greater than the amount that you have to pay. But be careful: The $1,600 comes to you over a 5-year period, and your $1,200 must be paid right now. You must consider the alternative uses and opportunity costs of the $1,200. At the same time, you must consider the risks that you are taking.

TABLE 11A.1	Expected Profits from a $1,200 Investment Project
Year 1	$100
Year 2	100
Year 3	400
Year 4	500
Year 5	500
All later years	0
Total	1,600

What are these alternatives? At a bare minimum, the same $1,200 could be put in a bank account, where it would earn interest. In addition, there are other things that you could do with the same money. You could buy Treasury bonds from the federal government that guarantee you interest of 4 percent for 5 years. Or you might find other projects with a similar degree of risk that produce more than $1,600.

Recall that the *interest rate* is the amount of money that a borrower agrees to pay a lender or a bank agrees to pay a depositor each year, expressed as a percentage of the deposit or the loan. For example, if I deposited $1,000 in an account paying 10 percent interest, I would receive $100 per year for the term of the deposit. Sometimes we use the term *rate of return* to refer to the amount of money that the lender receives from its investment each year, expressed as a percentage of the investment.

The idea is that in deciding to do any project, you must consider the opportunity costs: What are you giving up? If you did not do this project but put the money to use elsewhere, would you do better?

Almost all investments that you might consider involve risks: The project might not work out the way you anticipate, the economy may change, or market interest rates could go up or down. To assess the opportunity costs and to decide whether this project is worth it, you first have to think about those risks and decide on the rate of return that you require to compensate yourself for taking the risks involved.

If there were no risk, the opportunity cost of investing in a project would be the government-guaranteed or bank-guaranteed interest rate. But in considering a project that involves risk, you would want more profit in return for bearing that risk. For example, you might invest in a sure deal if you received a 3 percent annual return comparable to what you might earn with a bank account or certificate of deposit, whereas you might demand 15 percent or even 20 percent on a very risky investment.

Evaluating the opportunity costs of any investment project requires taking the following steps:

Step 1: The first step in evaluating the opportunity costs of an investment project is to look at the market. What are interest rates today? What rates of interest are people earning by putting their money in bank accounts? If there is risk that something could go wrong, what interest rate is the market paying to those who accept that risk? The *discount rate* used to evaluate an investment project is the interest rate that you could earn by investing a similar amount of money in an alternative investment *of comparable risk.*

Let's suppose that the investment project described in Table 11A.1 involved some risk. While you are quite certain that the expected flow of profits in years 1–5 ($100, $100, $400, and so on) is a very good estimate, the future is always uncertain. Let's further suppose that alternative investments of comparable risks are paying a 10 percent rate of interest (rate of return). So you will not do this project unless it earns at least 10 percent per year. We will thus use a 10 percent discount rate in evaluating the project.

Step 2: Now comes the trick. Is your investment worth it? By doing the project, you must consider the opportunity cost of the money. To do this, imagine a bank that will pay 10 percent on deposits. The question that you must answer is, how much would you have to put in a bank paying 10 percent interest on deposits in order to get the same flow of profits that you would get if you did the project?

If it turns out that you can replicate the flow of profits for *less* money up front than the project costs—$1,200—you will *not* do the project. The project would be paying you less than a 10 percent rate of return. On the other hand, if it turns out that you would have to put *more* than $1,200 in the bank to replicate the flow of profits from the project, the project would be earning more than 10 percent, and you would do it.

The amount of money that you would have to put in the imaginary bank to replicate the flow of profits from an investment project is called the **present discounted value (PDV)** or simply the **present value (PV)** of the expected flow of profits from the project. To determine that flow, we have to look at the flow *1 year at a time.*

At the end of a year, you will receive $100 if you do the project. To receive $100 a year from now from your hypothetical bank, how much would you have to deposit now? The answer is clearly less than $100 because you will earn interest. Let's call the interest rate r. In the example, $r = .10$ (10 percent). To get back $100 next year, you need to deposit X, where X plus a year's interest on X is equal to $100. That is,

$$X + rX = \$100 \text{ or } X(1 + r) = \$100$$

And if we solve for X, we get

$$X = \frac{\$100}{(1 + r)}$$

and that means if $r = .10$,

$$X = \frac{\$100}{1.1}$$

or

$$X = \$90.91$$

To convince yourself that this is right, think of putting $90.91 into your hypothetical bank and coming back in a year. You get back your $90.91 plus interest of 10 percent, which is $9.09. When you add the interest to

the initial deposit, you get $90.91 + 9.09, or exactly $100. *We say that the present value of $100 a year from now at a discount rate of 10 percent ($r = .10$) is $90.91.*

Notice that if you paid more than $90.91 for the $100 that you will receive from the project after a year, you would be receiving *less than a 10 percent return*. For example, suppose that you paid $95. If you put $95 in an account and came back after a year and found exactly $100, you would have received $5 in interest. Since $5 is just about .0526 (or 5.26 percent) of $95, the interest rate that the bank paid you is only 5.26 percent, not 10 percent.

What about the next year and the years after that? At the end of year 2, you get another $100. How much would you have to put in the bank today to be able to come back in *2* years and take away $100? Assume that you put amount X in the bank today. Then at the end of year 1, you have $X + rX$, which you keep in the account. At the end of year 2, you have $X + rX$ *plus* interest on $X + rX$; so at the end of year 2 you have

$$(X + rX) + r(X + rX)$$

which can be written

$$X(1 + r) + rX(1 + r) \text{ or } X(1 + r)(1 + r) \text{ or } X(1 + r)^2$$

Therefore,

$$X = \frac{\$100}{(1 + r)^2}$$

is the amount you must deposit today to get back $100 in 2 years.

If $r = .10$, then

$$X = \frac{\$100}{(1.1)^2} \quad \text{or} \quad X = \$82.65$$

To convince yourself that this calculation is right, if you put $82.65 in your hypothetical bank today and came back to check the balance after a year, you would have $82.65 plus interest of 10 percent, or $8.26, which is $90.91. But this time you leave it in the bank and receive 10 percent on the entire balance during the second year, which is $9.09. Adding the additional 10 percent, you get back to $100. Thus, if you deposit $82.65 in an account and come back in 2 years, you will have $100. The present value of $100 2 years from now is $82.65.

Now on to year 3. This time you receive a check for $400, but you don't get it until 3 years have passed. Again, how much would you have to put in your hypothetical bank to end up with $400? Without doing all the math, you can show that X, the amount that you must deposit to get back $400 in 3 years, is

$$X = \frac{\$400}{(1 + r)^3}$$

and if $r = .10$,

$$X = \frac{\$400}{(1.1)^3} \quad \text{or} \quad X = \$300.53$$

In general, the present value (PV), or present discounted value, of R dollars to be received in t years is

$$PV = \frac{R}{(1 + r)^t}$$

Step 3: Once you have looked at the project 1 year at a time, you must add up the total present value to see what the whole project is worth. In Table 11A.2, the right-hand column shows the present value of each year's return. If you add up the total, you have arrived at the amount that you would have to put in your hypothetical bank (that pays interest on deposits at 10 percent) today to receive the exact flow that is expected to come from the project. That total is $1,126.06.

So if you go to the bank today and put in $1,126.06, then come back in a year and withdraw $100, then come back after 2 years and withdraw another $100, then come back in 3 years and withdraw $400, and so on, until 5 years have passed, when you show up to close the account at the end of the fifth year, there will be exactly $500 left to withdraw. Lo and behold, you have figured out that you can receive the exact flow of profit that the project is expected to yield for $1,126.06. If you were looking for a 10 percent yield, you would *not* spend $1,200 for it. You would not do the project.

TABLE 11A.2	Calculation of Total Present Value of a Hypothetical Investment Project (Assuming $r = 10$ Percent)		
END OF...	(r)	DIVIDED BY $(1 + r)^t$ =	PRESENT VALUE ($)
Year 1	100	(1.1)	90.91
Year 2	100	$(1.1)^2$	82.64
Year 3	400	$(1.1)^3$	300.53
Year 4	500	$(1.1)^4$	341.51
Year 5	500	$(1.1)^5$	310.46
Total present value			1,126.05

What you have done is to convert an expected *flow* of dollars from an investment project that comes to you over some extended period of time to a *single number*: the present value of the flow.

We can restate the point this way: If the present value of the income stream associated with an investment is less than the full cost of the investment project, the investment should not be undertaken. This is illustrated in Figure 11A.1.

It is important to remember that we are discussing the *demand for new capital*. Business firms must evaluate potential investments to decide whether they are worth

▲ **FIGURE 11A.1 Investment Project: Go or No? A Thinking Map**

undertaking. This involves predicting the flow of potential future profits arising from each project and comparing those future profits with the return available in the financial market at the current interest rate. The present-value method allows firms to calculate how much it would *cost today* to purchase a contract for the same flow of earnings in the financial market.

Lower Interest Rates, Higher Present Values

Now consider what would happen if you used a lower interest rate in calculating the present value of a flow of earnings. You might use a lower rate in the analysis because interest rates in general have gone down in financial markets, making the opportunity cost of investment lower in general. You might also find out that the project is less risky than you believed earlier. For whatever reason, let's say that you would now do the project if it produced a return of 5 percent.

In evaluating the present value, the firm now looks at each year's flow of profit and asks how much it would cost to earn that amount if it were able to earn exactly 5 percent on its money in a hypothetical bank. With a lower interest rate, the firm will have to *pay more* now to purchase the same number of future dollars. Consider, for example, the present value of $100 in 2 years. We saw that if the firm puts aside $82.65 at 10 percent interest, it will have $100 in 2 years—at a

10 percent interest rate, the present discounted value (or current market price) of $100 in 2 years is $82.65. However, $82.65 put aside at a 5 percent interest rate would generate only $4.13 in interest in the first year and $4.34 in the second year, for a total balance of $91.11 after 2 years. To get $100 in 2 years, the firm needs to put aside more than $82.65 now. Solving for X as we did before,

$$X = \frac{\$100}{(1 + r)^2} = \frac{\$100}{(1.05)^2} = \$90.70$$

When the interest rate falls from 10 percent to 5 percent, the present value of $100 in 2 years rises by $8.05 ($90.70 − $82.65).

Table 11A.3 recalculates the present value of the full stream at the lower interest rate; it shows that a decrease in the interest rate from 10 percent to 5 percent causes the total present value to rise to $1,334.59. Because the investment project costs less than this (only $1,200), it should be undertaken. It is now a better deal than can be obtained in the financial market. Under these conditions, a profit-maximizing firm will make the investment. As discussed in the chapter, a lower interest rate leads to more investment.

TABLE 11A.3 Calculation of Total Present Value of a Hypothetical Investment Project (Assuming $r = 5$ Percent)

END OF...	$	DIVIDED BY $(1 + r)^t$ =	PRESENT VALUE ($)
Year 1	100	(1.05)	95.24
Year 2	100	$(1.05)^2$	90.70
Year 3	400	$(1.05)^3$	345.54
Year 4	500	$(1.05)^4$	411.35
Year 5	500	$(1.05)^5$	391.76
Total present value			1,334.59

The basic rule is as follows:

If the present value of an expected stream of earnings from an investment exceeds the cost of the investment necessary to undertake it, the investment should be undertaken. However, if the present value of an expected stream of earnings falls short of the cost of the investment, the financial market can generate the same stream of income for a smaller initial investment and the investment should not be undertaken.

─────────────── **APPENDIX SUMMARY** ───────────────

1. The present value (*PV*) of *R* dollars to be paid *t* years in the future is the amount you need to pay today, at current interest rates, to ensure that you end up with *R* dollars *t* years from now. It is the current market value of receiving *R* dollars in *t* years.

2. If the present value of the income stream associated with an investment is less than the full cost of the investment project, the investment project should not be undertaken. If the present value of an expected stream of income exceeds the cost of the investment necessary to undertake it, the investment should be undertaken.

─────── **APPENDIX REVIEW TERMS AND CONCEPTS** ───────

present discounted value (PDV) *or* **present value (PV)** The present discounted value of *R* dollars to be paid *t* years in the future is the amount you need

to pay today, at current interest rates, to ensure that you end up with *R* dollars *t* years from now. It is the current market value of receiving *R* dollars in *t* years. *p. 249*

$$PV = \frac{R}{(1 + r)^t}$$

─────────────── **APPENDIX PROBLEMS** ───────────────

1. Suppose you were offered $2,000 to be delivered in 1 year. Further suppose you had the alternative of putting money into a safe certificate of deposit paying annual interest at 10 percent. Would you pay $1,900 in exchange for the $2,000 after 1 year? What is the *maximum* amount you would pay for the offer of $2,000? Suppose the offer was $2,000, but delivery was to be in 2 years instead of 1 year. What is the maximum amount you would be willing to pay?

2. Your Uncle Joe just died and left $10,000 payable to you when you turn 30 years old. You are now 20. Currently, the annual rate

of interest that can be obtained by buying 10-year bonds is 6.5 percent. Your brother offers you $6,000 cash right now to sign over your inheritance. Should you do it? Explain your answer.

3. A special task force has determined that the present discounted value of the benefits from a bridge project comes to $23,786,000. The total construction cost of the bridge is $25 million. This implies that the bridge should be built. Do you agree with this conclusion? Explain your answer. What impact could a substantial decline in interest rates have on your answer?

4. Calculate the present value of the income streams *A* to *E* in Table 1 at an 8 percent interest rate and again at a 10 percent rate.

    Suppose the investment behind the flow of income in *E* is a machine that cost $1,235 at the beginning of year 1. Would you buy the machine if the interest rate were 8 percent? if the interest rate were 10 percent?

TABLE 1

END OF YEAR	A	B	C	D	E
1	$ 80	$ 80	$ 100	$ 100	$500
2	80	80	100	100	300
3	80	80	1,100	100	400
4	80	80	0	100	300
5	1,080	80	0	100	0
6	0	80	0	1,100	0
7	0	1,080	0	0	0

5. Determine what someone should be willing to pay for each of the following bonds when the market interest rate for borrowing and lending is 5 percent.
    a. A bond that promises to pay $3,000 in a lump-sum payment after 1 year.
    b. A bond that promises to pay $3,000 in a lump-sum payment after 2 years.
    c. A bond that promises to pay $1,000 per year for 3 years.

6. What should someone be willing to pay for each of the bonds in question 5 if the interest rate is 10 percent?

7. Based on your answers to questions 5 and 6, state whether each of the following is true or false:
    a. *Ceteris paribus*, the price of a bond increases when the interest rate increases.
    b. *Ceteris paribus*, the price of a bond increases when any given amount of money is received sooner rather than later.

8. Assume that the present discounted value of an investment project (commercial development) at a discount rate of 7 percent is $234,756,000. Assume that the building just sold for $254 million. Will the buyer earn a rate of return of more than 7 percent, exactly 7 percent, or less than 7 percent? Briefly explain.

9. Assume that I promise to pay you $100 at the end of each of the next 3 years. Using the following formula,

$$X = 100/(1 + r) + 100/(1 + r)^2 + 100/(1 + r)^3$$

   if $r = 0.075$, then $X = \$260.06$.

    Assuming that somebody of roughly comparable reliability offers to pay out 7.5 percent on anything you let him or her borrow from you, would you be willing to pay me $270 for my promise? Explain your answer.

10. Teresa won the Florida lottery and was given the option of receiving $22 million immediately or $1,250,000 per year for 30 years.
    a. If Teresa opts for the 30 annual payments, how much in total will she receive?
    b. What is the present value of the 30 annual payments if the interest rate is 4 percent? Based on this value, should Teresa opt for the up-front payment or the 30 installments?
    c. What is the present value of the 30 annual payments if the interest rate is 8 percent? Based on this value, should Teresa opt for the up-front payment or the 30 installments?

11. How would your answers to the previous question change if the annual payments changed to $2,000,000 per year for 15 years?

12. Explain what will happen to the present value of money one year from now if the market interest rate falls? What if the market interest rate rises?

General Equilibrium and the Efficiency of Perfect Competition

12

In the last nine chapters, we have built a model of a simple, perfectly competitive economy. Our discussion has revolved around the two fundamental decision-making units, *households* and *firms*, which interact in two basic market arenas, *input markets* and *output markets*. (Look again at the circular flow diagram, shown in Figure II.1 on p. 117.) By limiting our discussion to perfectly competitive firms, we have been able to examine how the basic decision-making units interact in the two basic market arenas.

Households make constrained choices in both input and output markets. Household income, for example, depends on choices made in input markets: whether to work, how much to work, what skills to acquire, and so on. Input market choices are constrained by such factors as current wage rates, availability of jobs, and interest rates.

Firms are the primary producing units in a market economy. Profit-maximizing firms, to which we have limited our discussion, earn their profits by selling products and services for more than it costs to produce them. With firms, as with households, output markets and input markets cannot be analyzed separately. All firms make three specific decisions simultaneously: (1) how much output to supply, (2) how to produce that output—that is, which technology to use, and (3) how much of each input to demand.

In Chapters 7 through 9, we explored these three decisions from the viewpoint of output markets. We saw that the portion of the marginal cost curve that lies above a firm's average variable cost curve is the supply curve of a perfectly competitive firm in the short run. Implicit in the marginal cost curve is a choice of technology and a set of input demands. In Chapters 10 and 11, we looked at the perfectly competitive firm's three basic decisions from the viewpoint of input markets.

Output and input markets are connected because firms and households make simultaneous choices in both arenas, but there are other connections among markets as well. Firms buy in both capital and labor markets, for example, and they can substitute capital for labor and vice versa. A change in the price of one factor can easily change the demand for other factors. Buying more *capital*, for instance, usually changes the marginal revenue product of *labor* and shifts the labor demand curve. Similarly, a change in the price of a single good or service usually affects household demand for other goods and services, as when a price decrease makes one good more attractive than other close substitutes. The same change also makes households better off when they find that the same amount of income will buy more. Such additional "real income" can be spent on any of the other goods and services that the household buys.

The point here is simple:

> Input and output markets cannot be considered as if they were separate entities or as if they operated independently. Although it is important to understand the decisions of individual firms and households and the functioning of individual markets, we now need to add it all up so we can look at the operation of the system as a whole.

You have seen the concept of equilibrium applied both to markets and to individual decision-making units. In individual markets, supply and demand determine an equilibrium price. Perfectly competitive firms are in short-run equilibrium when price and marginal cost are equal ($P = MC$). In the long run, however, equilibrium in a competitive market is achieved only when economic profits are eliminated. Households are in equilibrium when they have equated the marginal utility per dollar spent on each good to the marginal utility per dollar spent on all other goods. This process of examining the equilibrium conditions in individual markets and for individual households and firms separately is called **partial equilibrium analysis**.

partial equilibrium analysis The process of examining the equilibrium conditions in individual markets and for households and firms separately.

A **general equilibrium** exists when all markets in an economy are in simultaneous equilibrium. An event that disturbs the equilibrium in one market may disturb the equilibrium in many other markets as well. The ultimate impact of the event depends on the way *all* markets adjust to it. Thus, partial equilibrium analysis, which looks at adjustments in one isolated market, may be misleading.

general equilibrium The condition that exists when all markets in an economy are in simultaneous equilibrium.

Thinking in terms of a general equilibrium leads to some important questions. Is it possible for all households and firms and all markets to be in equilibrium simultaneously? Are the equilibrium conditions that we have discussed separately compatible with one another? Why is an event that disturbs an equilibrium in one market likely to disturb many other equilibriums simultaneously?

In talking about general equilibrium in the beginning of this chapter, we continue our exercise in *positive economics*—that is, we seek to understand how systems operate without making value judgments about outcomes. Later in the chapter, we turn from positive economics to *normative economics* as we begin to judge the economic system. Are its results good or bad? Can we make them better?

efficiency The condition in which the economy is producing what people want at least possible cost.

In judging the performance of any economic system, you will recall, it is essential first to establish specific criteria by which to judge. In this chapter, we use two such criteria: *efficiency* and *equity* (fairness). First, we demonstrate the **efficiency** of the allocation of resources—that is, the system produces what people want and does so at the least possible cost—if all the assumptions that we have made thus far hold. When we begin to relax some of our assumptions, however, it will become apparent that free markets may *not* be efficient. Several sources of inefficiency naturally occur within an unregulated market system. In the final part of this chapter, we introduce the potential role of government in correcting market inefficiencies and achieving fairness.

Market Adjustment to Changes in Demand

All economies, particularly market systems, are dynamic: Change occurs all the time. Markets experience shifts of demand, both up and down; costs and technology change; and prices and outputs change. We have spent a lot of time looking at how these changes affect individual markets. But markets are also connected to one another. If capital flows into one market, often that means it is flowing out of another market. If consumers ride trains, often that means they stay off the bus. How do we think about connections across markets?

As we look at the general case, you might find it helpful to keep an example in mind. In 2007, Amazon introduced the Kindle, a small machine that allows a person to read e-books. We could analyze this product introduction in a partial equilibrium setting, considering the responsiveness of potential buyers to price or quality changes in the Kindle. But the introduction of the Kindle and subsequent pricing decisions by Amazon affect other markets as well. E-books substitute in part for printed books. The introduction of the Kindle and subsequent price reductions in the device thus shift the demand for printed books to the left. When the demand for printed books falls, storefront booksellers like Barnes and Noble suffer profit losses. Likely their sales of other products in the stores—complements to their book sales—also decline. Many printed books are ordered over the Web, many in fact through Amazon itself. When demand for these books falls, shipping services like UPS lose business. Printed books are produced using paper. When the demand for books falls, so does the demand for paper, and through that channel the demand for forest products falls.

Nor is the story over there. When Amazon prices the Kindle, it must take into account what is going on in the marketplace for printed books. If Barnes and Noble responds to the shift in its demand by lowering prices of printed books, that move will influence the optimal price for the Kindle. If the fall in demand for paper reduces the cost of paper, the costs of printing books will fall, and that too will lead to a lower price for printed books. Amazon will need to respond to that as well. In a general equilibrium analysis one needs to work through all the feedback loops and connections across industries to get to a final answer.

Figure 12.1 begins our discussion of the more general case of market connections. In the figure we assume that there are two sectors in the economy, X and Y, and that both are currently in long-run equilibrium. Total output in sector X is Q_X^0, the product is selling for a price of P_X^0, and each firm in the industry produces up to where P_X^0 is equal to marginal cost—q_X^0. At that point,

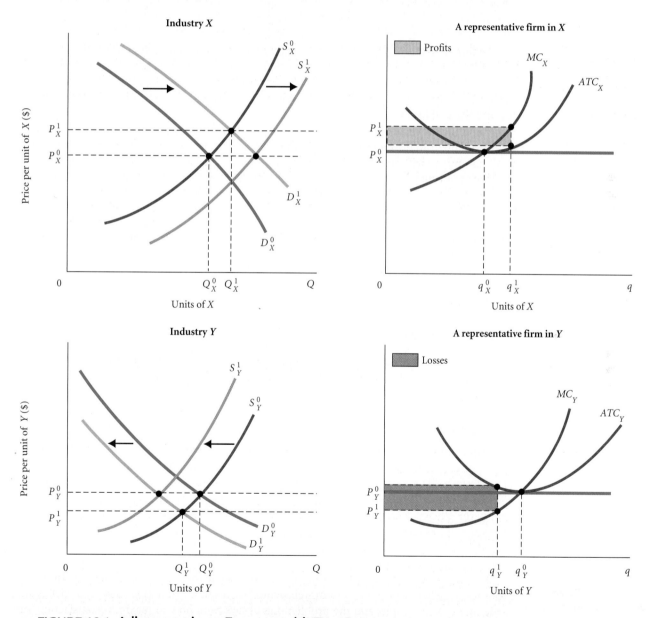

▲ FIGURE 12.1 Adjustment in an Economy with Two Sectors

Initially, demand for X shifts from D_X^0 to D_X^1. This shift pushes the price of X up to P_X^1, creating profits. Demand for Y shifts down from D_Y^0 to D_Y^1, pushing the price of Y down to P_Y^1 and creating losses. Firms have an incentive to leave sector Y and an incentive to enter sector X. Exiting sector Y shifts supply in that industry to S_Y^1, raising price and eliminating losses. Entry shifts supply in X to S_X^1, thus reducing and eliminating profits.

price is just equal to average cost and economic profits are zero. The same condition holds initially in sector Y. The market is in zero profit equilibrium at a price of P_Y^0.

Now assume that a change in consumer preferences (or in the age distribution of the population or in something else) shifts the demand for X out to the right from D_X^0 to D_X^1. That shift drives the price up to P_X^1. If households decide to buy more X, without an increase in income, they must buy *less* of something else. Because everything else is represented by Y in this example, the demand for Y must decline and the demand curve for Y shifts to the left, from D_Y^0 to D_Y^1.

With the shift in demand for X, price rises to P_X^1 and profit-maximizing firms immediately increase output to q_X^1 (the point where $P_X^1 = MC_X$). However, now there are positive profits in X. With the downward shift of demand in Y, price falls to P_Y^1. Firms in sector Y cut back to q_Y^1 (the point where $P_Y^1 = MC_Y$), and the lower price causes firms producing Y to suffer losses.

In the short run, adjustment is simple. Firms in both industries are constrained by their current scales of plant. Firms can neither enter nor exit their respective industries. Each firm in industry X raises output somewhat, from q_X^0 to q_X^1. Firms in industry Y cut back from q_Y^0 to q_Y^1.

In response to the existence of profit in sector X, the capital market begins to take notice. In Chapter 9, we saw that new firms are likely to enter an industry in which there are profits to be earned. Financial analysts see the profits as a signal of future healthy growth, and entrepreneurs may become interested in moving into the industry.

Adding all of this together, we would expect to see investment begin to favor sector X. This is indeed the case: Capital begins to flow into sector X. As new firms enter, the short-run supply curve in the industry shifts to the right and continues to do so until all profits are eliminated. In the top-left diagram in Figure 12.1, the supply curve shifts out from S_X^0 to S_X^1, a shift that drives the price back down to P_X^0.

We would also expect to see a movement out of sector Y because of losses. Some firms will exit the industry. In the bottom-left diagram in Figure 12.1, the supply curve shifts back from S_Y^0 to S_Y^1, a shift that drives the price back up to P_Y^0. At this point, all losses are eliminated.

Note that a new general equilibrium is not reached until equilibrium is reestablished in all markets. If costs of production remain unchanged, as they do in Figure 12.1, this equilibrium occurs at the initial product prices, but with more resources and production in X and fewer in Y. In contrast, if an expansion in X drives up the prices of resources used specifically in X, the cost curves in X will shift upward and the final postexpansion zero-profit equilibrium will occur at a higher price. Such an industry is called an *increasing-cost industry*.

Allocative Efficiency and Competitive Equilibrium

As we have gone through and built models of a competitive economic system, we have often referred to the efficiency of that system. How do we think about efficiency in a general equilibrium world, in which many markets are interconnected?

Pareto Efficiency

In Chapter 1, we introduced several specific criteria used by economists to judge the performance of economic systems and to evaluate alternative economic policies. These criteria are (1) efficiency, (2) equity, (3) growth, and (4) stability. In Chapter 1, you also learned that an *efficient* economy is one that produces the things that people want at the least cost. The idea behind the efficiency criterion is that the economic system exists to serve the wants and needs of people. If resources somehow can be reallocated to make people "better off," then they should be. We want to use the resources at our disposal to produce maximum well-being. The trick is defining *maximum well-being*.

For many years, social philosophers wrestled with the problem of "aggregation," or "adding up." When we say "maximum well-being," we mean maximum *for society*. Societies are made up of many people, and the problem has always been how to maximize satisfaction, or well-being, for all members of society. What has emerged is the now widely accepted concept of *allocative efficiency*, first developed by the Italian economist Vilfredo Pareto in the nineteenth century. Pareto's very precise definition of efficiency is often referred to as **Pareto efficiency** or **Pareto optimality**.

Pareto efficiency *or* **Pareto optimality** A condition in which no change is possible that will make some members of society better off without making some other members of society worse off.

ECONOMICS IN PRACTICE

Ethanol and Land Prices

The U.S. government provides large subsidies for ethanol, a fuel produced from corn. Proponents of the ethanol subsidies suggest that it is one piece of a policy that can help the United States reduce its dependence on foreign oil. In part, as a result of these subsidies, the midwestern United States has seen a large increase in corn production relative to other grains. The following article traces another of the general equilibrium consequences of the ethanol subsidies: an increase in the price of agricultural land.

Nebraska ethanol boom causing land prices to soar

TheIndependent.com

Ethanol is not only pumping up the price of corn in Nebraska, but also farm real estate market values and cash rent rates values have seen a 14-percent increase, according to the preliminary results of the University of Nebraska-Lincoln's annual Farm Real Estate Market Development Survey.

According to the survey, Nebraska farmland's average value for the year ending Feb. 1 was $1,155 per acre, compared to $1,013 per acre at this time last year, said Bruce Johnson, the UNL agricultural economist who conducts this annual survey.

He said preliminary findings show this was the largest all-land value increase in the past 19 years. It is also the fourth

straight year of what Johnson called "solid advances" in land values. He said the state's current all-land average value is more than 50 percent higher than the 2003 level.

Higher prices for corn because of ethanol demand are driving the sharp rise in land prices. By early 2008, Nebraska should have about 25 ethanol plants online, producing 1.2 billion gallons of ethanol and using more than 425 million bushels of corn.

"The demand from rapidly growing ethanol production has triggered the commodity market advances, and, in turn, worked into the agricultural land market dynamic, particularly in the major corn-producing areas of the state," Johnson said.

Source: Robert Pore, robert.pore@theindependent.com. Reprinted with permission.

As we see in the article, a number of markets are affected by the ethanol subsidies. The increase in the demand for ethanol drives up the demand for corn, which in turn increases the demand for land. Since the supply of land is finite, the price of land used to produce corn rises. But what about the rest of the agricultural economy? Increasing land prices increases the cost of other grains, such as wheat. As you learned in Chapter 2, land is a key factor of production. The increase in wheat costs shifts the supply curve to the left, as in the figure below. Wheat prices thus also rise.

Corn

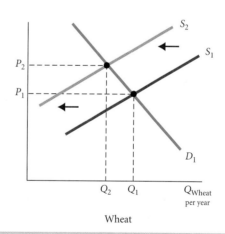

Wheat

Specifically, a change is said to be efficient when it makes some members of society better off without making other members of society worse off. An efficient, or *Pareto optimal*, system is one in which no such changes are possible. An example of a change that makes some people better off and nobody worse off is a simple voluntary exchange. I have apples and you have nuts. I like nuts and you like apples. We trade. We both gain, and no one loses.

For such a definition to have any real meaning, we must answer two questions: (1) What do we mean by "better off"? and (2) How do we account for changes that make some people better off and others worse off?

The answer to the first question is simple. People decide what "better off" and "worse off" mean. I am the only one who knows whether I am better off after a change. If you and I exchange one item for another because I like what you have and you like what I have, we both "reveal" that we are better off after the exchange because we agreed to it voluntarily. If everyone in the neighborhood wants a park and the residents all contribute to a fund to build one, they have consciously changed the allocation of resources and they all are better off for it.

The answer to the second question is more complex. Nearly every change that one can imagine leaves some people better off and some people worse off. If some gain and some lose as the result of a change, and it can be demonstrated that the value of the gains exceeds the value of the losses, then the change is said to be *potentially efficient*. In practice, however, the distinction between a *potentially* and an *actually* efficient change is often ignored and all such changes are simply called *efficient*.

Example: Budget Cuts in Massachusetts   Several years ago, in an effort to reduce state spending, the budget of the Massachusetts Registry of Motor Vehicles was cut substantially. Among other things, the state sharply reduced the number of clerks in each office. Almost immediately Massachusetts residents found themselves waiting in line for hours when they had to register their automobiles or get their driver's licenses.

Drivers and car owners began paying a price: standing in line, which used time and energy that could otherwise have been used more productively. However, before we can make sensible efficiency judgments, we must be able to measure, or at least approximate, the value of both the gains and the losses produced by the budget cut. To approximate the losses to car owners and drivers, we might ask how much people would be willing to pay to avoid standing in those long lines.

One office estimated that 500 people stood in line every day for about 1 hour each. If each person were willing to pay just $2 to avoid standing in line, the damage incurred would be $1,000 (500 × $2) per day. If the registry were open 250 days per year, the reduction in labor force at that office alone would create a cost to car owners, conservatively estimated, of $250,000 (250 × $1,000) per year.

Estimates also showed that taxpayers in Massachusetts saved about $80,000 per year by having fewer clerks at that office. If the clerks were reinstated, there would be some gains and some losses. Car owners and drivers would gain, and taxpayers would lose. However, because we can show that the value of the gains would substantially exceed the value of the losses, it can be argued that reinstating the clerks would be an efficient change. Note that the only *net* losers would be those taxpayers who do not own a car and do not hold driver's licenses.[1]

Revisiting Consumer and Producer Surplus

In Chapter 4 we introduced the concept of consumer and producer surplus. Consumer surplus was defined as the difference between the maximum amount that buyers are willing to pay for a good and its current market price. You can think of a demand curve as defining a boundary that shows maximum willingness to pay per unit at every quantity.

When you visit your favorite sandwich store, it will make you a sandwich and charge you a fixed price. Say that the sandwich is priced at $7. If you really crave sandwiches made at that place, you may be gaining consumer surplus. Indeed, if you were willing to pay $12 for a sandwich and it is selling for a price of $7, you earn a consumer surplus of $5 when you buy it.

Producer surplus is defined as the difference between the current market price of a good and the full cost of producing it. It is, in a way, a measure of profitability.

If you go back to pages 89–91 and review the argument, you will see that demand and supply curves, if left to their own natural adjustments, will lead the markets to an efficient equilibrium. Specifically, they will allocate demand across sectors in a way that maximizes the total surplus (consumer + producer) being generated by the exchange. Any change in quantity imposed on the market will shift the curves (or one of the curves) to the left or the right, and the result will be "deadweight losses."

---

[1] You might wonder whether there are other gainers and losers. What about the clerks? In analysis like this, it is usually assumed that the citizens who pay lower taxes spend their added income on other things. The producers of those other things need to expand to meet the new demand, and they hire more labor. Thus, a contraction of 100 jobs in the public sector will open up 100 jobs in the private sector. If the economy is fully employed, the transfer of labor to the private sector is assumed to create no net gains or losses to the workers.

To really understand the argument that a perfectly competitive economy is economically efficient and will lead to a Pareto efficient set of outcomes requires that we spend more time talking about some of the basic ideas.

The Efficiency of Perfect Competition

All societies answer these basic questions in the design of their economic systems:

1. *What gets produced?* What determines the final mix of output?
2. *How is it produced?* How do capital, labor, and land get divided up among firms? In other words, what is the allocation of resources among producers?
3. *Who gets what is produced?* What determines which households get how much? What is the distribution of output among consuming households?

The following discussion of efficiency uses these three questions and their answers to prove informally that perfect competition is efficient. To demonstrate that the perfectly competitive system leads to an efficient, or Pareto optimal, allocation of resources, we need to show that no changes are possible that will make some people better off without making others worse off. Specifically, we will show that under perfect competition, (1) resources are allocated among firms efficiently, (2) final products are distributed among households efficiently, and (3) the system produces the things that people want.

Efficient Allocation of Resources Among Firms   The simple definition of efficiency holds that firms must produce their products using the best available—that is, lowest-cost—technology. If more output could be produced with the same amount of inputs, it would be possible to make some people better off without making others worse off.

The perfectly competitive model we have been using rests on several assumptions that assure us that resources in such a system would indeed be efficiently allocated among firms. Most important of these is the assumption that individual firms maximize profits. To maximize profit, a firm must minimize the cost of producing its chosen level of output. With a full knowledge of existing technologies, firms will choose the technology that produces the output they want at the least cost.

There is more to this story than meets the eye, however. Inputs must be allocated *across* firms in the best possible way. If we find that it is possible, for example, to take capital from firm A and swap it for labor from firm B and produce more product in both firms, then the original allocation was inefficient. Recall our example from Chapter 2. Farmers in Ohio and Kansas both produce wheat and corn. The climate and soil in most of Kansas are best suited to wheat production, and the climate and soil in Ohio are best suited to corn production. Kansas should produce most of the wheat, and Ohio should produce most of the corn. A law that forces Kansas land into corn production and Ohio land into wheat production would result in less of both—an inefficient allocation of resources. However, if markets are free and open, Kansas farmers will naturally find a higher return by planting wheat and Ohio farmers will find a higher return in corn. The free market, then, should lead to an efficient allocation of resources among firms. As you think back on Chapter 2, you should now see that societies operating on the production possibility frontier are efficiently using their inputs.

The same argument can be made more general. Misallocation of resources among firms is unlikely as long as every single firm faces the same set of prices and trade-offs in input markets. Recall from Chapter 10 that perfectly competitive firms will hire additional factors of production as long as their marginal revenue product exceeds their market price. As long as all firms have access to the *same* factor markets and the *same* factor prices, the last unit of a factor hired will produce the same value in each firm. Certainly, firms will use different technologies and factor combinations, but at the margin, no single profit-maximizing firm can get more value out of a factor than that factor's current market price. For example, if workers can be hired in the labor market at a wage of $6.50, *all* firms will hire workers as long as the marginal revenue product (MRP_L) produced by the marginal worker (labor's MRP_L) remains above $6.50. *No* firms will hire labor beyond the point at which MRP_L falls below $6.50. Thus, at equilibrium, additional workers are not worth more than $6.50 to any firm, and switching labor from one firm to another will not produce output of any greater value to society. Each firm has hired the profit-maximizing amount of labor. In short:

> The assumptions that factor markets are competitive and open, that all firms pay the same prices for inputs, and that all firms maximize profits lead to the conclusion that the allocation of resources among firms is efficient.

You should now have a greater appreciation for the power of the price mechanism in a market economy. Each individual firm needs only to make decisions about which inputs to use by looking at its own labor, capital, and land productivity relative to their prices. But because all firms face identical input prices, the market economy achieves efficient input use among firms. Prices are the instrument of Adam Smith's "invisible hand," allowing for efficiency without explicit coordination or planning.

Efficient Distribution of Outputs Among Households

Even if the system is producing the right things and is doing so efficiently, these things still have to get to the right people. Just as open, competitive factor markets ensure that firms do not end up with the wrong inputs, open, competitive output markets ensure that households do not end up with the wrong goods and services.

Within the constraints imposed by income and wealth, households are free to choose among all the goods and services available in output markets. A household will buy a good as long as that good generates utility, or subjective value, greater than its market price. Utility value is revealed in market behavior. You do not go out and buy something unless you are willing to pay *at least* the market price.

Remember that the value you place on any one good depends on what you must give up to have that good. The trade-offs available to you depend on your budget constraint. The trade-offs that are desirable depend on your preferences. If you buy a $300 iPhone, you may be giving up a trip home. If I buy it, I may be giving up four new tires for my car. We have both revealed that the iPhone is worth at least as much to us as all the other things that $300 can buy. As long as we are free to choose among all the things that $300 can buy, we will not end up with the wrong things; it is not possible to find a trade that will make us both better off. Again, the price mechanism plays an important role. Each of us faces the same price for the goods that we choose, and that in turn leads us to make choices that ensure that goods are allocated efficiently among consumers.

> We all know that people have different tastes and preferences and that they will buy very different things in very different combinations. As long as everyone shops freely in the same markets, no redistribution of final outputs among people will make them better off. If you and I buy in the same markets and pay the same prices and I buy what I want and you buy what you want, we cannot possibly end up with the wrong combination of things. Free and open markets are essential to this result.

Producing What People Want: The Efficient Mix of Output

It does no good to produce things efficiently or to distribute them efficiently if the system produces the wrong things. Will competitive markets produce the things that people want?

If the system is producing the wrong mix of output, we should be able to show that producing more of one good and less of another will make people better off. To show that perfectly competitive markets are efficient, we must demonstrate that no such changes in the final mix of output are possible.

The condition that ensures that the right things are produced is $P = MC$. That is, in both the long run and the short run, a perfectly competitive firm will produce at the point where the price of its output is equal to the marginal cost of production. As long as price is above marginal cost, it pays for a firm to increase output. The logic is this: When a firm weighs price and marginal cost, it weighs the value of its product to society *at the margin* against the value of the things that could otherwise be produced with the same resources. Figure 12.2 summarizes this logic.

The argument is quite straightforward. *First, price reflects households' willingness to pay.* By purchasing a good, individual households reveal that it is worth at least as much as the other goods that the same money could buy. Thus, current price reflects the value that households place on a good.

Second, marginal cost reflects the opportunity cost of the resources needed to produce a good. If a firm producing X hires a worker, it must pay the market wage. That wage must be sufficient to

If $P_X > MC_X$, society gains value by producing *more* X.
If $P_X < MC_X$, society gains value by producing *less* X.

The value placed on good X by society through the market, or the social value of a marginal unit of X.	$$P_X = MC_X$$	Market-determined value of resources needed to produce a marginal unit of X. MC_X is equal to the opportunity cost of those resources: lost production of other goods or the value of the resources left unemployed (leisure, vacant land, and so on).

▲ FIGURE 12.2 **The Key Efficiency Condition: Price Equals Marginal Cost**

attract that worker out of leisure or away from firms producing other goods. The same argument holds for capital and land.

Thus, if the price of a good ends up greater than marginal cost, producing more of it will generate benefits to households in excess of opportunity costs, and society gains. Similarly, if the price of a good ends up below marginal cost, resources are being used to produce something that households value less than opportunity costs. Producing less of it creates gains to society.[2]

Society will produce the efficient mix of output if all firms equate price and marginal cost.

Figure 12.3 shows how a simple competitive market system leads individual households and firms to make efficient choices in input and output markets. For simplicity, the figure assumes only one factor of production, labor. Households weigh the market wage against the value of

▲ FIGURE 12.3 **Efficiency in Perfect Competition Follows from a Weighing of Values by Both Households and Firms**

---

[2] It is important to understand that firms do not act *consciously* to balance social costs and benefits. In fact, the usual assumption is that firms are self-interested private profit maximizers. It just works out that in perfectly competitive markets, when firms are weighing private benefits against private costs, they are actually (perhaps without knowing it) weighing the benefits and costs to society as well.

leisure and time spent in unpaid household production. However, the wage is a measure of labor's potential product because firms weigh labor cost (wages) against the value of the product produced and hire up to the point at which $W = MRP_L$. Households use wages to buy market-produced goods. Thus, households implicitly weigh the value of market-produced goods against the value of leisure and household production.

When a firm's scale is balanced, it is earning maximum profit; when a household's scale is balanced, it is maximizing utility. Under these conditions, no changes can improve social welfare.

Perfect Competition versus Real Markets

So far, we have built a model of a perfectly competitive market system that produces an efficient allocation of resources, an efficient mix of output, and an efficient distribution of output. The perfectly competitive model is built on a set of assumptions, all of which must hold for our conclusions to be fully valid. We have assumed that all firms and households are price-takers in input and output markets, that firms and households have perfect information, and that all firms maximize profits.

These assumptions do not always hold in real-world markets. When this is the case, the conclusion breaks down that free, unregulated markets will produce an efficient outcome. The remainder of this chapter discusses some inefficiencies that occur naturally in markets and some of the strengths, as well as the weaknesses, of the market mechanism. We also discuss the usefulness of the competitive model for understanding the real economy.

The Sources of Market Failure

In suggesting some of the problems encountered in real markets and some of the possible solutions to these problems, the rest of this chapter previews the next part of this book, which focuses on the economics of market failure and the potential role of government in the economy.

market failure Occurs when resources are misallocated, or allocated inefficiently. The result is waste or lost value.

Market failure occurs when resources are misallocated, or allocated inefficiently. The result is waste or lost value. In this section, we briefly describe four important sources of market failure: (1) *imperfect market structure*, or noncompetitive behavior; (2) the existence of *public goods*; (3) the presence of *external costs and benefits*; and (4) *imperfect information*. Each condition results from the failure of one of the assumptions basic to the perfectly competitive model, and each is discussed in more detail in later chapters. Each also points to a potential role for government in the economy. The desirability and the extent of actual government involvement in the economy are hotly debated subjects.

Imperfect Markets

One of the elements of the efficiency of a perfectly competitive market that we described is the efficient mix of outputs. Society produces the right mix of goods given their costs and the preferences of households in the economy. Efficient mix comes because products are sold at prices equal to their marginal costs.

Think back to two goods, nuts and apples. For efficiency, we would like, in equilibrium, to find that the relative prices of nuts and apples reflect their relative costs. If the marginal costs of apples is twice that of nuts, efficiency means that consumption should be adjusted so that the relative price of apples is twice that of nuts. Otherwise, society does better in using its resources differently. In a perfectly competitive market, this comes easily. If both goods are sold at prices equal to their marginal costs, then the ratio of the prices of the two goods will also equal the ratio of the marginal costs. Equilibrium in separate markets gives us efficiency in the general equilibrium setting. But suppose one of the two goods is priced for some reason at a level in excess of its marginal costs. Now relative prices will no longer reflect relative costs.

So we can see that efficiency of output mix comes from marginal cost pricing. As we will learn in the next few chapters, however, in imperfectly competitive markets, with fewer firms competing and limited entry by new firms, prices will not necessarily equal marginal costs. As a consequence, in a market with firms that have some market power, where firms do not behave as price-takers, we are not guaranteed an efficient mix of output.

Public Goods

A second major source of inefficiency lies in the fact that private producers may not find it in their best interest to produce everything that members of society want because for one reason or another they are unable to charge prices to reflect values people place on those goods. More specifically, there is a whole class of goods and services called **public goods** or **social goods**, that will be underproduced or not produced at all in a completely unregulated market economy.[3]

Public goods are goods and services that bestow collective benefits on society; they are, in a sense, collectively consumed. The classic example is national defense, but there are countless others—police protection, homeland security, preservation of wilderness lands, and public health, to name a few. These things are "produced" using land, labor, and capital just like any other good. Some public goods, such as national defense, benefit the whole nation. Others, such as clean air, may be limited to smaller areas—the air may be clean in a Kansas town but dirty in a Southern California city. Public goods are consumed by everyone, not just by those who pay for them. The inability to exclude nonpayers from consumption of a public good makes it, not surprisingly, hard to charge people a price for the good.

If the provision of public goods were left to private profit-seeking producers with no power to force payment, a serious problem would arise. Suppose, for example, you value some public good, X. If there were a functioning market for X, you would be willing to pay for X. Suppose you are asked to contribute voluntarily to the production of X. Should you contribute? Perhaps you should on moral grounds, but not on the basis of pure self-interest.

At least two problems can get in the way. First, because you cannot be excluded from using X for not paying, you get the good whether you pay or not. Why should you pay if you do not have to? Second, because public goods that provide collective benefits to large numbers of people are expensive to produce, any one person's contribution is not likely to make much difference to the amount of the good ultimately produced. Would the national defense suffer, for example, if you did not pay your share of the bill? Probably not. Thus, nothing happens if you do not pay. The output of the good does not change much, and you get it whether you pay or not. Private provision of public goods fails. A completely laissez-faire market system will not produce everything that all members of a society might want. Citizens must band together to ensure that desired public goods are produced, and this is generally accomplished through government spending financed by taxes. Public goods are the subject of Chapter 16.

public goods, *or* **social goods**   Goods and services that bestow collective benefits on members of society. Generally, no one can be excluded from enjoying their benefits. The classic example is national defense.

Externalities

A third major source of inefficiency is the existence of external costs and benefits. An **externality** is a cost or benefit imposed or bestowed on an individual or a group that is outside, or external to, the transaction—in other words, something that affects a third party. In a city, external costs are pervasive. The classic example is air or water pollution, but there are thousands of others, such as noise, congestion, and your house painted a color that the neighbors think is ugly. Global warming is an externality at the level of the world.

Not all externalities are negative, however. For example, housing investment may yield benefits for neighbors. A farm located near a city provides residents in the area with nice views and a less congested environment.

Externalities are a problem only if decision makers do not take them into account. The logic of efficiency presented earlier in this chapter required that firms weigh social benefits against social costs. If a firm in a competitive environment produces a good, it is because the value of that good to society exceeds the social cost of producing it—this is the logic of $P = MC$. If social costs or benefits are overlooked or left out of the calculations, inefficient decisions result. In essence, if the calculation of either MC or P in the equation is "wrong," equating the two will clearly not lead to an optimal result.

The effects of externalities can be enormous. For years, companies piled chemical wastes indiscriminately into dump sites near water supplies and residential areas. In some locations, those wastes seeped into the ground and contaminated the drinking water. In response to the evidence that smoking damages not only the smoker but also others, governments have increased prohibitions against smoking on airplanes and in public places.

externality   A cost or benefit imposed or bestowed on an individual or a group that is outside, or external to, the transaction.

---

[3] Although they are normally referred to as public *goods*, many of the things we are talking about are *services*.

Imperfect Information

imperfect information The absence of full knowledge concerning product characteristics, available prices, and so on.

The fourth major source of inefficiency is **imperfect information** on the part of buyers and sellers. The conclusion that markets work efficiently rests heavily on the assumption that consumers and producers have full knowledge of product characteristics, available prices, and so on. The absence of full information can lead to transactions that are ultimately disadvantageous.

Some products are so complex that consumers find it difficult to judge the potential benefits and costs of purchase. Buyers of life insurance have a very difficult time sorting out the terms of the more complex policies and determining the true "price" of the product. Consumers of almost any service that requires expertise, such as plumbing and medical care, have a hard time evaluating what is needed, much less how well it is done. With imperfect information, prices may no longer reflect individual preferences.

Some forms of misinformation can be corrected with simple rules such as truth-in-advertising regulations. In some cases, the government provides information to citizens; job banks and consumer information services exist for this purpose. In certain industries, such as medical care, there is no clear-cut solution to the problem of noninformation or misinformation. We discuss all these topics in detail in Chapter 16.

Evaluating the Market Mechanism

Is the market system good or bad? Should the government be involved in the economy, or should it leave the allocation of resources to the free market? So far, our information is mixed and incomplete. To the extent that the perfectly competitive model reflects the way markets really operate, there seem to be some clear advantages to the market system. When we relax the assumptions and expand our discussion to include noncompetitive behavior, public goods, externalities, and the possibility of imperfect information, we see at least a potential role for government.

The market system may not provide participants with the incentive to weigh costs and benefits and to operate efficiently. If there are no externalities or if such costs or benefits are properly internalized, firms *will* weigh social benefits and costs in their production decisions. Under these circumstances, the profit motive should provide competitive firms with an incentive to minimize cost and to produce their products using the most efficient technologies. Likewise, competitive input markets should provide households with the incentive to weigh the value of their time against the social value of what they can produce in the labor force.

However, markets are far from perfect. Freely functioning markets in the real world do not always produce an efficient allocation of resources, and this result provides a potential role for government in the economy. Many have called for government involvement in the economy to correct for market failure—that is, to help markets function more efficiently. As you will see, however, many believe that government involvement in the economy creates more inefficiency than it cures.

In addition, we have thus far discussed only the criterion of efficiency, but economic systems and economic policies must be judged by many other criteria, not the least of which is *equity*, or fairness. Indeed, some contend that the outcome of any free market is ultimately unfair because some become rich while others remain poor.

Part III, which follows, explores in greater depth the issue of market imperfections and government involvement in the economy.

SUMMARY

1. Both firms and households make simultaneous choices in input and output markets. For example, input prices determine output costs and affect firms' output supply decisions. Wages in the labor market affect labor supply decisions, income, and ultimately the amount of output households can and do purchase.

2. A *general equilibrium* exists when all markets in an economy are in simultaneous equilibrium. An event that disturbs the equilibrium in one market may disturb the equilibrium in many other markets as well. *Partial equilibrium* analysis can be misleading because it looks only at adjustments in one isolated market.

MARKET ADJUSTMENT TO CHANGES IN DEMAND *p. 254*

3. General equilibrium is reached when equilibrium is established in all markets.

ALLOCATIVE EFFICIENCY AND COMPETITIVE EQUILIBRIUM *p. 256*

4. An *efficient* economy is one that produces the goods and services that people want at the least possible cost. A change is said to be efficient if it makes some members of society better off without making others worse off. An efficient, or *Pareto optimal*, system is one in which no such changes are possible.

5. If a change makes some people better off and some people worse off but it can be shown that the value of the gains exceeds the value of the losses, the change is said to be *potentially efficient* or simply *efficient*.

6. If all the assumptions of perfect competition hold, the result is an efficient, or Pareto optimal, allocation of resources. To prove this statement, it is necessary to show that resources are allocated efficiently among firms, that final products are distributed efficiently among households, and that the system produces what people want.

7. The assumptions that factor markets are competitive and open, that all firms pay the same prices for inputs, and that all firms maximize profits lead to the conclusion that the allocation of resources among firms is efficient.

8. People have different tastes and preferences, and they buy very different things in very different combinations. As long as everyone shops freely in the same markets, no redistribution of outputs among people will make them better off. This leads to the conclusion that final products are distributed efficiently among households.

9. Because perfectly competitive firms will produce as long as the price of their product is greater than the marginal cost of production, they will continue to produce as long as a gain for society is possible. The market thus guarantees that the right things are produced. In other words, the perfectly competitive system produces what people want.

THE SOURCES OF MARKET FAILURE *p. 262*

10. When the assumptions of perfect competition do not hold, the conclusion breaks down that free, unregulated markets will produce an efficient allocation of resources.

11. An imperfectly competitive industry is one in which single firms have some control over price and competition. In all imperfectly competitive industries, output is lower and price is higher than they would be in perfect competition. Imperfect competition is a major source of market inefficiency.

12. *Public*, or *social*, *goods* bestow collective benefits on members of society. Because the benefits of social goods are collective, people cannot, in most cases, be excluded from enjoying them. Thus, private firms usually do not find it profitable to produce public goods. The need for public goods is thus another source of inefficiency.

13. An *externality* is a cost or benefit that is imposed or bestowed on an individual or a group that is outside, or external to, the transaction. If such social costs or benefits are overlooked, the decisions of households or firms are likely to be wrong or inefficient.

14. Market efficiency depends on the assumption that buyers have perfect information on product quality and price and that firms have perfect information on input quality and price. *Imperfect information* can lead to wrong choices and inefficiency.

EVALUATING THE MARKET MECHANISM *p. 264*

15. Sources of market failure—such as imperfect markets, public goods, externalities, and imperfect information—are considered by many to justify the existence of government and governmental policies that seek to redistribute costs and income on the basis of efficiency, equity, or both.

REVIEW TERMS AND CONCEPTS

efficiency, *p. 254*

externality, *p. 263*

general equilibrium, *p. 254*

imperfect information, *p. 264*

market failure, *p. 262*

Pareto efficiency *or* Pareto optimality, *p. 256*

partial equilibrium analysis, *p. 254*

public goods *or* social goods, *p. 263*

Key efficiency condition in perfect competition: $P_X = MC_X$

PROBLEMS

All problems are available on www.myeconlab.com

1. Numerous times in history, the courts have issued consent decrees requiring large companies to break up into smaller competing companies for violating the antitrust laws. The two best-known examples are American Telephone and Telegraph (AT&T) in the 1980s and Microsoft 20 years later. (AT&T was broken up into the "Baby Bells"; but the Microsoft breakup was successfully appealed, and the breakup never occurred.)

   Many argue that breaking up a monopoly is a Pareto-efficient change. This interpretation cannot be so because breaking up a monopoly makes its owners (or shareholders) worse off. Do you agree or disagree? Explain your answer.

2. [Related to the *Economics in Practice* on p. 257] The *Economics in Practice* in this chapter describes the adjustment of the corn and wheat markets to the massive U.S. subsidy given to ethanol production. The subsidy drives up the prices of other agricultural goods such as wheat and substantially raises the value of farmland. How would this story change if oil prices were to rise extensively at the same time? if oil prices were to fall? Trace these changes on the economy using supply and demand curves.

3. For each of the following, tell a story about what is likely to happen in labor and capital markets using the model of the whole economy that we developed over the first 11 chapters.
   a. A sharp drop in demand for automobiles raises the unemployment rate in Flint, Michigan, and cuts into the profits of local gas stations where my nephew lost his job.
   b. As the baby boomers age, many of them are moving back to the city. They are also buying smaller units. This will have a big effect on owners of suburban homes who find their home values falling.
   c. In 2007–2008, the mortgage markets crashed. This led to a serious decline in the availability of credit to buyers who, a couple of years ago, were able to borrow far more than they needed.

4. A medium-sized bakery has just opened in Slovakia. A loaf of bread is currently selling for 14 koruna (the Slovakian currency) over and above the cost of intermediate goods (flour, yeast, and so on). Assuming that labor is the only variable factor of production, the following table gives the production function for the bread.

WORKERS	LOAVES OF BREAD
0	0
1	15
2	30
3	42
4	52
5	60
6	66
7	70

   a. Suppose the current wage rate in Slovakia is 119 koruna per hour. How many workers will the bakery employ?
   b. Suppose the economy of Slovakia begins to grow, incomes rise, and the price of a loaf of bread is pushed up to 20 koruna. Assuming no increase in the price of labor, how many workers will the bakery hire?
   c. An increase in the demand for labor pushes up wages to 125 koruna per hour. What impact will this increase in cost have on employment and output in the bakery at the 20-koruna price of bread?
   d. If all firms behaved like our bakery, would the allocation of resources in Slovakia be efficient? Explain your answer.

5. Country A has soil that is suited to corn production and yields 135 bushels per acre. Country B has soil that is not suited for corn and yields only 45 bushels per acre. Country A has soil that is not suited for soybean production and yields 15 bushels per acre. Country B has soil that is suited for soybeans and yields 35 bushels per acre. In 2004, there was no trade between A and B because of high taxes and both countries together produced huge quantities of corn and soybeans. In 2005, taxes were eliminated because of a new trade agreement. What is likely to happen? Can you justify the trade agreement on the basis of Pareto efficiency? Why or why not?

6. Do you agree or disagree with each of the following statements? Explain your answer.
   a. Housing is a public good and should be produced by the public sector because private markets will fail to produce it efficiently.
   b. Monopoly power is inefficient because large firms will produce too much product, dumping it on the market at artificially low prices.
   c. Medical care is an example of a potentially inefficient market because consumers do not have perfect information about the product.

7. The point of scalping is to find someone who wants a ticket more than the person who presently has it. Whenever two different prices exist in a market, arbitrage opportunities (buy and then sell at a higher price) are there. Professional scalpers buy up tickets when they are first offered to the public, while some buy them on the street the night of the event. They can sell any ticket, even those in short supply, *at some price*. When many people want to go to an event that has a limited supply of tickets, the scalping price can be quite high. Go online and find scalping agencies like Stub-Hub and Ace Tickets. See if you can find an event for which the scalping price is much higher than the original price. What determines whether the event is worth the higher price?

   It is argued that scalping is efficient. Explain that argument. Others ask how could it be efficient "if only rich people can afford to go to most games?" Do you agree? Why or why not?

8. Which of the following are examples of Pareto-efficient changes? Explain your answers.
   a. Cindy trades her laptop computer to Bob for his old car.
   b. Competition is introduced into the electric industry, and electricity rates drop. A study shows that benefits to consumers are larger than the lost monopoly profits.
   c. A high tax on wool sweaters deters buyers. The tax is repealed.
   d. A federal government agency is reformed, and costs are cut 23 percent with no loss of service quality.

9. A major source of chicken feed in the United States is anchovies, small fish that can be scooped out of the ocean at low cost. Every 7 years, when the anchovies disappear to spawn, producers must turn to grain, which is more expensive, to feed their chickens. What is likely to happen to the cost of chicken when the anchovies disappear? What are substitutes for chicken? How are the markets for these substitutes affected? Name some complements to chicken. How are the markets for these complements affected? How might the allocation of farmland be changed as a result of the disappearance of anchovies?

10. Suppose two passengers end up with a reservation for the last seat on a train from San Francisco to Los Angeles. Two alternatives are proposed:
    a. Toss a coin
    b. Sell the ticket to the highest bidder

    Compare the two options from the standpoint of efficiency and equity.

11. Assume that there are two sectors in an economy: goods (*G*) and services (*S*). Both sectors are perfectly competitive, with large numbers of firms and constant returns to scale. As income rises, households spend a larger portion of their income on *S* and a smaller portion on *G*. Using supply and demand curves for both sectors and a diagram showing a representative firm in

each sector, explain what would happen to output and prices in the short run and the long run in response to an increase in income. (Assume that the increase in income causes demand for *G* to shift left and demand for *S* to shift right.) In the long run, what would happen to employment in the goods sector? in the service sector? (*Hint:* See Figure 12.2 on p. 261.)

12. Which of the following are actual Pareto-efficient changes? Explain briefly.
    a. You buy three oranges for $1 from a street vendor.
    b. You are near death from thirst in the desert and must pay a passing vagabond $10,000 for a glass of water.
    c. A mugger steals your wallet.
    d. You take a taxi ride in downtown Manhattan during rush hour.

13. Each instance that follows is an example of one of the four types of market failure discussed in this chapter. In each case, identify the type of market failure and defend your choice briefly.
    a. An auto repair shop convinces you that you need a $2,000 valve job when all you really need is an oil change.
    b. Everyone in a neighborhood would benefit if an empty lot were turned into a park, but no entrepreneur will come forward to finance the transformation.
    c. A bar opens next to your apartment building and plays loud music on its patio every night until 4 A.M.
    d. The only two airlines flying direct between St. Louis and Atlanta make an agreement to raise their prices.

14. Two factories in the same town hire workers with the same skills. Union agreements require factory A to pay its workers $10 per hour, while factory B must pay $6 per hour. Each factory hires the profit-maximizing number of workers. Is the allocation of labor between these two factories efficient? Explain why or why not.

15. Explain why resources are allocated efficiently among firms and why output is distributed efficiently among households in perfectly competitive markets.

16. Under what condition would society benefit from more of a good being produced, and under what condition would society benefit from less of a good being produced?

17. James lives on a cul-de-sac where he and all his neighbors park on the street. After his car was vandalized, James decided to install motion-sensitive lighting on the front of his house. Now any movement activates the lights, which shine across the entire parking area on the street. Explain why the installation of the lights might lead to an inefficient outcome.

18. Briefly explain whether each of the following represents a public good.
    a. A chef salad sold at the cafeteria in the county courthouse
    b. Palm trees planted along the median of the Pacific Coast Highway
    c. A Doppler radar station built at Chicago's O'Hare International Airport
    d. A new roller coaster at Cedar Point, an amusement park in Sandusky, Ohio
    e. A new fleet of police cars for the Oklahoma City Police Department
    f. The Vietnam Memorial in Washington, D.C.

19. Explain the difference between a positive externality and a negative externality. Can both types of externalities result in market failure? Why or why not?

Monopoly and Antitrust Policy

13

In 1911 the U.S. Supreme Court found that Standard Oil of New Jersey, the largest oil company in the United States, was a monopoly and ordered that it be divided up. In 1999 a U.S. court similarly found that Microsoft had exercised monopoly power and ordered it to change a series of its business practices. In 2010 the Federal Trade Commission—one of the government agencies empowered to protect consumers—argued that Google possessed monopoly power and should also be restrained by the gov-

ernment in its business practices. What do we mean by a monopoly, and why might the government and the courts try to control monopolists? Have our ideas on what constitutes a monopoly changed over time with new technology?

In earlier chapters, we described in some detail the workings and benefits of perfect competition. Market competition among firms producing undifferentiated or homogeneous products limits the choices of firms. Firms decide how much to produce and how to produce, but in setting prices, they look to the market. Moreover, because of entry and competition, firms do no better than earn the opportunity cost of capital in the long run. For firms such as Google and Microsoft, economic decision making is richer and so is the potential for profit making.

In the next three chapters, we explore markets in which competition is limited, either by the fewness of firms or by product differentiation. After a brief discussion of market structure in general, this chapter will focus on monopoly markets. Chapter 14 will cover oligopolies, while Chapter 15 will deal with monopolistic competition.

Imperfect Competition and Market Power: Core Concepts

In the competitive markets we have been studying all firms charge the same price. With many firms producing identical or homogeneous products, consumers have many choices, and those choices constrain the pricing of individual firms. This same competition also means that firms in the long run earn only a normal return on their capital. In **imperfectly competitive** markets, on the other hand, the absence of numerous competitors or the existence of product differentiation creates situations in which firms can at times raise their prices and not lose all their customers. These firms can be said to have **market power**. In these markets we may observe firms earning excess profits, and we may see firms producing different variants of a product and charging different prices for those variants. Studying these markets is especially interesting because we now have to think not only about pricing behavior, but also about how firms choose product quality and type.

imperfectly competitive industry   An industry in which individual firms have some control over the price of their output.

market power   An imperfectly competitive firm's ability to raise price without losing all of the quantity demanded for its product.

Forms of Imperfect Competition and Market Boundaries

Once we move away from perfectly competitive markets, with its assumption of many firms and undifferentiated products, there is a range of other possible market structures. At one extreme lies the monopoly. A *monopoly* is an industry with a single firm in which the entry of new firms is blocked. An *oligopoly* is an industry in which there is a small number of firms, each large enough so that its presence affects prices. Firms that differentiate their products in industries with many producers and free entry are called *monopolistic competitors*. We begin our discussion in this chapter with monopoly.

What do we mean when we say that a monopoly firm is the only firm in the industry? In practice, given the prevalence of branding, many firms, especially in the consumer products markets, are alone in producing a specific product. Procter & Gamble (P&G), for example, is the only producer of Ivory soap. Coca-Cola is the only producer of Coke Classic. And yet we would call neither firm monopolistic because for both, many other firms produce products that are *close substitutes*. Instead of drinking Coke, we could drink Pepsi; instead of washing with Ivory, we could wash with Dove. To be meaningful, therefore, our definition of a monopolistic industry must be more precise. We define a **pure monopoly** as an industry (1) with a single firm that produces a product for which there are *no close substitutes* and (2) in which significant barriers to entry prevent other firms from entering the industry to compete for profits.

As we think about the issue of product substitutes and market power, it is useful to recall the structure of the competitive market. Consider a firm producing an undifferentiated brand of hamburger meat, Brand X hamburger. As we show in Figure 13.1 the demand this firm faces is horizontal, perfectly elastic. The demand for hamburgers as a whole, however, likely slopes down. While there are substitutes for hamburgers, they are not perfect and some people will continue to consume hamburgers even if they cost more than other foods. As we broaden the category we are considering, the substitution possibilities *outside* the category fall, and demand becomes quite inelastic, as for example for food in general. If a firm were the only producer of Brand X hamburger, it would have no market power: If it raised its price, people would just switch to Brand Z hamburger. A firm that produced all the hamburgers in the United States, on the other hand, might have some market power: It could perhaps charge more than other beef-product producers and still sell hamburgers. A firm that controlled all of the food in the United States would likely have substantial market power since we all must eat!

In practice, figuring out which products are close substitutes for one another to determine market power can be difficult. Are hamburgers and hot dogs close substitutes so that a hamburger monopoly would have little power to raise prices? Are debit cards and checks close

pure monopoly An industry with a single firm that produces a product for which there are no close substitutes and in which significant barriers to entry prevent other firms from entering the industry to compete for profits.

▶ **FIGURE 13.1**

The Boundary of a Market and Elasticity

We can define an industry as broadly or as narrowly as we like. The more broadly we define the industry, the fewer substitutes there are; thus, the less elastic the demand for that industry's product is likely to be. A monopoly is an industry with one firm that produces a product for which there are *no close substitutes*. The producer of Brand X hamburger cannot properly be called a monopolist because this producer has no control over market price and there are many substitutes for Brand X hamburger.

substitutes for credit cards so that credit card firms have little market power? The courts in a recent antitrust case said no. Is Microsoft a monopoly, or does it compete with Linux and Apple for software users? These are questions that occupy considerable time for economists, lawyers, and the antitrust courts. The *Economics in Practice* on p. 287 discusses the antitrust rules that pertain to the National Football League.

Price and Output Decisions in Pure Monopoly Markets

Consider a market with a single firm producing a good for which there are few substitutes. How does this profit-maximizing monopolist choose its output levels? At this point we assume the monopolist cannot price-discriminate. It sells its product to all demanders at the same price. (*Price discrimination* means selling to different consumers or groups of consumers at different prices and will be discussed later in this chapter.)

Assume initially that our pure monopolist buys in competitive input markets. Even though the firm is the only one producing for its product market, it is only one among many firms buying factors of production in input markets. The local telephone company must hire labor like any other firm. To attract workers, the company must pay the market wage; to buy fiber-optic cable, it must pay the going price. In these input markets, the monopolistic firm is a price-taker.

On the cost side of the profit equation, a pure monopolist does not differ from a perfect competitor. Both choose the technology that minimizes the cost of production. The cost curve of each represents the minimum cost of producing each level of output. The difference arises on the revenue, or demand, side of the equation, where we begin our analysis.

Demand in Monopoly Markets

A perfectly competitive firm, you will recall, can sell all it wants to sell at the market price. The firm is a small part of the market. The demand curve facing such a firm is thus a horizontal line. Raising the price of its product means losing all demand because perfect substitutes are available. The perfectly competitive firm has no incentive to charge a lower price either since it can sell all it wants at the market price.

A monopolist is different. It does not constitute a small part of the market; it *is* the market. The firm no longer looks at a market price to see what it can charge; it sets the market price. How does it do so? Even a firm that is a monopolist in its own market will nevertheless compete with other firms in other markets for a consumer's dollars. Even a monopolist thus loses some customers when it raises its price. The monopolist sets its price by looking at the trade-off in terms of profit earned between getting more money for each unit sold versus selling fewer units.

Shortly we will look at exactly how a monopolist thinks about this trade-off. But before we become more formal, it is interesting to think about the business decisions of the competitive firm versus a monopolist. For a competitive firm, the market provides a lot of information; in effect, all the firm needs to do is figure out if, given its costs, it can make money at the current market price. A monopolist needs to learn about the demand curve for its product. When the iPod first came out, Apple had to figure out how much individuals would be willing to pay for this new product. What did its demand curve look like? Firms like Apple have quite sophisticated marketing departments that survey potential consumers, collect data from related markets, and even do a bit of trial and error to learn what their demand curves really look like.

Marginal Revenue and Market Demand   We learned in Chapter 7 that the competitive firm maximizes its profit by continuing to produce output so long as marginal revenue exceeds marginal cost. Under these conditions, incremental units add more to the plus, or revenue, side than they add to the minus, or cost, side. The same general rule is true for the monopolist: A monopolist too will maximize profits by expanding output so long as marginal revenue exceeds marginal cost. The key difference in the two cases lies in the definition of marginal revenue.

For a competitive firm marginal revenue is simply the price, as we discussed in Chapter 7. Every unit that the firm sells, it sells at the going market price. The competitive firm is a very small part of the overall market, and its behavior has no effect on the overall market price. So the incremental or marginal revenue from each new unit sold is simply the price. In the case of a monopolist, however, the monopolist is the market. If that firm decides to double its output, market output will double, and it is easy to see that the only way the firm will be able to sell twice the output is to lower its price. The fact that a monopolist's output decisions influence market prices means that price and marginal revenue will diverge. The simplest way to see this is via a bit of arithmetic.

Consider the hypothetical demand schedule in Table 13.1. Column 3 lists the total revenue that the monopoly would take in at different levels of output. If it were to produce 1 unit, that unit would sell for $10, and total revenue would be $10. Two units would sell for $9 each, in which case total revenue would be $18. As column 4 shows, marginal revenue from the second unit would be $8 ($18 minus $10). Notice that the marginal revenue from increasing output from 1 unit to 2 units ($8) is *less* than the price of the second unit ($9).

TABLE 13.1 Marginal Revenue Facing a Monopolist

(1) Quantity	(2) Price	(3) Total Revenue	(4) Marginal Revenue
0	$11	0	—
1	10	$10	$10
2	9	18	8
3	8	24	6
4	7	28	4
5	6	30	2
6	5	30	0
7	4	28	−2
8	3	24	−4
9	2	18	−6
10	1	10	−8

Now consider what happens when the firm considers setting production at 4 units instead of 3. The fourth unit would sell for $7, but because the firm cannot price discriminate, it must sell *all 4* units for $7 each. Had the firm chosen to produce only 3 units, it could have sold those 3 units for $8 each. Thus, offsetting the revenue gain of $7 is a revenue loss of $3—that is, $1 for each of the 3 units that would have sold at the higher price. The marginal revenue of the fourth unit is $7 minus $3, or $4, which is considerably below the price of $7. (Remember, unlike a monopoly, a perfectly competitive firm does not have to charge a lower price to sell more. Thus, $P = MR$ in competition.) For a monopolist, an increase in output involves not only producing more and selling it, but also reducing the overall price of its output.

Marginal revenue can also be derived by looking at the change in total revenue as output changes by 1 unit. At 3 units of output, total revenue is $24. At 4 units of output, total revenue is $28. Marginal revenue is the difference, or $4.

Moving from 6 to 7 units of output actually reduces total revenue for the firm. At 7 units, marginal revenue is negative. Although it is true that the seventh unit will sell for a positive price ($4), the firm must sell all 7 units for $4 each (for a total revenue of $28). If output had been restricted to 6 units, each would have sold for $5. Thus, offsetting the revenue gain of $4 is a revenue loss of $6—that is, $1 for each of the 6 units that the firm would have sold at the higher price. Increasing output from 6 to 7 units actually decreases revenue by $2. Figure 13.2

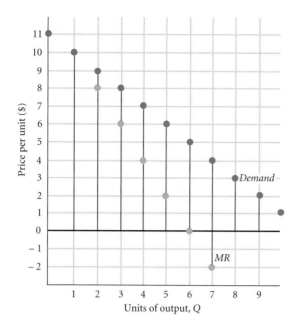

▲ FIGURE 13.2 Marginal Revenue Curve Facing a Monopolist

At every level of output except 1 unit, a monopolist's marginal revenue (*MR*) is below price. This is so because (1) we assume that the monopolist must sell all its product at a single price (no price discrimination) and (2) to raise output and sell it, the firm must lower the price it charges. Selling the additional output will raise revenue, but this increase is offset somewhat by the lower price charged for all units sold. Therefore, the increase in revenue from increasing output by 1 (the marginal revenue) is less than the price.

graphs the marginal revenue schedule derived in Table 13.1. Notice that at every level of output except 1 unit, marginal revenue is *below* price. Marginal revenue turns from positive to negative after 6 units of output. When the demand curve is a straight line, the marginal revenue curve bisects the quantity axis between the origin and the point where the demand curve hits the quantity axis, as in Figure 13.3.

Look carefully at Figure 13.3. The marginal revenue curve shows the change in total revenue that results as a firm moves along the segment of the demand curve that lies directly above it. Consider starting at a price in excess of point A per period in the top panel of Figure 13.3. Here total revenue (shown in the bottom panel) is zero because nothing is sold. To begin selling, the firm must lower the product price. Marginal revenue is positive, and total revenue begins to increase. To sell increasing quantities of the good, the firm must lower its price more and more. As output increases between zero and Q^* and the firm moves down its demand curve from point A to point B, marginal revenue remains positive and total revenue continues to increase. The quantity of output (Q) is rising, which tends to push total revenue ($P \times Q$) *up*. At the same time, the price of output (P) is falling, which tends to push total revenue ($P \times Q$) *down*. Up to point B, the effect of increasing Q dominates the effect of falling P and total revenue rises: Marginal revenue is positive (above the quantity axis).[1]

What happens as we look at output levels greater than Q^*—that is, farther down the demand curve from point B toward point C? We are still lowering P to sell more output, but at levels greater than Q^*, marginal revenue is negative, and total revenue in the bottom panel starts to fall. Beyond Q^*, the effect of cutting price on total revenue is larger than the effect of

---

[1] Recall from Chapter 4 that if the percentage change in Q is greater than the percentage change in P as you move along a demand curve, the absolute value of elasticity of demand is greater than 1. Thus, as we move along the demand curve in Figure 13.3 between point A and point B, demand is *elastic*.

▶ **FIGURE 13.3**

Marginal Revenue and Total Revenue

A monopoly's marginal revenue curve bisects the quantity axis between the origin and the point where the demand curve hits the quantity axis. A monopoly's *MR* curve shows the change in total revenue that results as a firm moves along the segment of the demand curve that lies exactly above it.

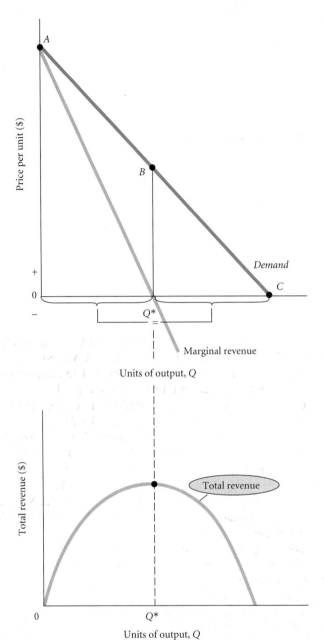

increasing quantity. As a result, total revenue ($P \times Q$) falls. At point *C*, revenue once again is at zero, this time because price has dropped to zero.[2]

The Monopolist's Profit-Maximizing Price and Output   We have spent much time defining and explaining marginal revenue because it is an important factor in the monopolist's choice of profit-maximizing price and output. Figure 13.4 superimposes a demand curve and the marginal revenue curve derived from it over a set of cost curves. In determining price and output, a monopolistic firm must go through the same basic decision process that a competitive firm goes through. Any profit-maximizing firm will raise its production as long as the added revenue from the increase outweighs the added cost. All firms, including monopolies, raise output as long as marginal revenue is greater than marginal cost. Any positive difference between marginal revenue and marginal cost can be thought of as marginal profit.

---

[2] Beyond Q^*, between points *B* and *C* on the demand curve in Figure 13.3, the decline in price must be bigger in percentage terms than the increase in quantity. Thus, the absolute value of elasticity beyond point *B* is less than 1: Demand is inelastic. At point *B*, marginal revenue is zero; the decrease in *P* exactly offsets the increase in *Q*, and elasticity is unitary or equal to −1.

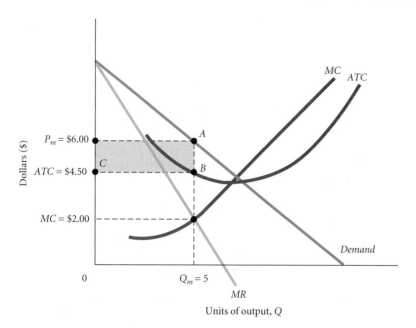

◀ **FIGURE 13.4 Price and Output Choice for a Profit-Maximizing Monopolist**

A profit-maximizing monopolist will raise output as long as marginal revenue exceeds marginal cost. Maximum profit is at an output of 5 units per period and a price of $6. Above 5 units of output, marginal cost is greater than marginal revenue; increasing output beyond 5 units would reduce profit. At 5 units, $TR = P_m A Q_m 0$, $TC = CBQ_m 0$, and profit = $P_m ABC$.

The optimal price/output combination for the monopolist in Figure 13.4 is $P_m = \$6$ and $Q_m = 5$ units, the quantity at which the marginal revenue curve and the marginal cost curve intersect. At any output below 5, marginal revenue is greater than marginal cost. At any output above 5, increasing output would reduce profits because marginal cost exceeds marginal revenue. This leads us to conclude that the profit-maximizing level of output for a monopolist is the one at which marginal revenue equals marginal cost: $MR = MC$.

Because marginal revenue for a monopoly lies below the demand curve, the final price chosen by the monopolist will be above marginal cost. ($P_m = \$6.00$ is greater than $MC = \$2.00$.) At 5 units of output, price will be fixed at $6 (point A on the demand curve), which is as much as the market will bear, and total revenue will be $P_m \times Q_m = \$6 \times 5 = \$30$ (area $P_m A Q_m 0$). Total cost is the product of average total cost and units of output, $\$4.50 \times 5 = \$22.50$ (area $CBQ_m 0$). Total profit is the difference between total revenue and total cost, $\$30 - \$22.50 = \$7.50$. In Figure 13.4, total profit is the area of the gray rectangle $P_m ABC$.

Our discussion about the optimal output level for a monopolist points to a common misconception. Even monopolists face constraints on the prices they can charge. Suppose a single firm controlled the production of bicycles. That firm would be able to charge more than could be charged in a competitive marketplace, but the power to raise prices has limits. As the bike price rises, we will see more people buying inline skates or walking. A particularly interesting case comes from monopolists who sell durable goods, goods that last for some period of time. Microsoft is the only producer for Windows, the operating system that dominates the personal computer (PC) market. But when Microsoft tries to sell a new version of that operating system (for example, Windows 7, which it introduced in 2010), its price is constrained by the fact that many of the potential consumers it seeks already have an old operating system. If the new price is too high, consumers will stay with the older version. Some monopolists may face quite elastic demand curves as a result of the characteristics of the product they sell.

The Absence of a Supply Curve in Monopoly   In perfect competition, the supply curve of a firm in the short run is the same as the portion of the firm's marginal cost curve that lies above the average variable cost curve. As the price of the good produced by the firm changes, the perfectly competitive firm simply moves up or down its marginal cost curve in choosing how much output to produce.

As you can see, however, Figure 13.4 contains nothing that we can point to and call a supply curve. The amount of output that a monopolist produces depends on its marginal cost curve *and* on the shape of the demand curve that it faces. In other words, the amount of output that a monopolist supplies is not independent of the shape of the demand curve. A monopoly firm has no supply curve that is independent of the demand curve for its product.

To see why, consider what a firm's supply curve means. A supply curve shows the quantity of output the firm is willing to supply at each price. If we ask a monopolist how much output she is willing to supply at a given price, the monopolist will say that her supply behavior depends not only on marginal cost but also on the marginal revenue associated with that price. To know what that marginal revenue would be, the monopolist must know what her demand curve looks like.

In sum, in perfect competition, we can draw a firm's supply curve without knowing anything more than the firm's marginal cost curve. The situation for a monopolist is more complicated: A monopolist sets both price and quantity, and the amount of output that it supplies depends on its marginal cost curve and the demand curve that it faces.

Perfect Competition and Monopoly Compared

One way to understand monopoly is to compare equilibrium output and price in a perfectly competitive industry with the output and price that would be chosen if the same industry were organized as a monopoly. To make this comparison meaningful, let us exclude from consideration any technological advantage that a single large firm might enjoy.

We begin our comparison with a perfectly competitive industry made up of a large number of firms operating with a production technology that exhibits constant returns to scale in the long run. (Recall that *constant returns to scale* means that average cost is the same whether the firm operates one large plant or many small plants.) Figure 13.5 shows a perfectly competitive industry at long-run equilibrium, a condition in which price is equal to long-run average costs and in which there are no profits.

Suppose the industry were to fall under the control of a single price monopolist. The monopolist now owns one firm with many plants. However, technology has not changed, only the location of decision-making power has. To analyze the monopolist's decisions, we must derive the consolidated cost curves now facing the monopoly.

The marginal cost curve of the new monopoly will be the horizontal sum of the marginal cost curves of the smaller firms, which are now branches of the larger firm. That is, to get the large firm's *MC* curve, at each level of *MC*, we add together the output quantities from each separate plant. To understand why, consider this simple example. Suppose there is perfect competition and the industry is made up of just two small firms, A and B, each with upward-sloping marginal cost curves. Suppose for firm A, *MC* = $5 at an output of 10,000 units and for firm B, *MC* = $5 at an output of 20,000 units. If these firms were merged, what would be the marginal cost of the 30,000th unit of output per period? The answer is $5 because the new larger firm

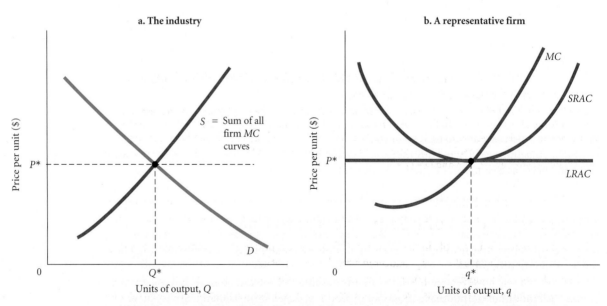

▲ **FIGURE 13.5 A Perfectly Competitive Industry in Long-Run Equilibrium**
In a perfectly competitive industry in the long run, price will be equal to long-run average cost. The market supply curve is the sum of all the short-run marginal cost curves of the firms in the industry. Here we assume that firms are using a technology that exhibits constant returns to scale: *LRAC* is flat. Big firms enjoy no cost advantage.

would produce 10,000 units in plant A and 20,000 in plant B. This means that the marginal cost curve of the new firm is *exactly the same curve* as the supply curve in the industry when it was competitively organized. (Recall from Chapter 9 that the industry supply curve in a perfectly competitive industry is the sum of the marginal cost curves [above average variable cost] of all the individual firms in that industry.)[3]

Figure 13.6 illustrates the cost curves, marginal revenue curve, and demand curve of the consolidated monopoly industry. If the industry were competitively organized, total industry output would have been $Q_c = 4,000$ and price would have been $P_c = \$3$. These price and output decisions are determined by the intersection of the competitive supply curve, S_c, and the market demand curve.

No longer faced with a price that it cannot influence, however, the monopolist can choose any price/quantity combination along the demand curve. The output level that maximizes profits to the monopolist is $Q_m = 2,500$—the point at which marginal revenue intersects marginal cost. Output will be priced at $P_m = \$4$. To increase output beyond 2,500 units or to charge a price below $4 (which represents the amount consumers are willing to pay) would reduce profit. Relative to a perfectly competitive industry, a monopolist restricts output, charges higher prices, and earns positive profits. In the long run, the monopolist will close plants.

Also remember that all we did was transfer decision-making power from the individual small firms to a consolidated owner. The new firm gains nothing technologically by being big.

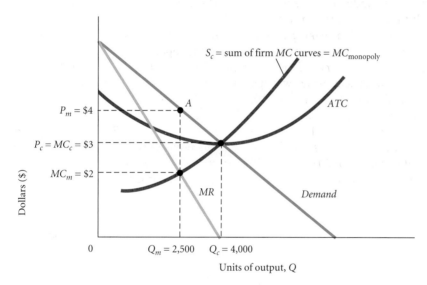

▲ **FIGURE 13.6 Comparison of Monopoly and Perfectly Competitive Outcomes for a Firm with Constant Returns to Scale**
In the newly organized monopoly, the marginal cost curve is the same as the supply curve that represented the behavior of all the independent firms when the industry was organized competitively. Quantity produced by the monopoly will be less than the perfectly competitive level of output, and the monopoly price will be higher than the price under perfect competition. Under monopoly, $P = P_m = \$4$ and $Q = Q_m = 2,500$. Under perfect competition, $P = P_c = \$3$ and $Q = Q_c = 4,000$.

Monopoly in the Long Run: Barriers to Entry

What will happen to a monopoly in the long run? Of course, it is possible for a monopolist to suffer losses. Just because a firm is the only producer in a market does not guarantee that anyone will buy its product. Monopolists can end up going out of business just like competitive firms. If, on the contrary, the monopolist is earning positive profits (a rate of return above the normal return to capital), as in Figure 13.4, we would expect other firms to enter as they do in competitive markets. In fact,

---

[3] The same logic will show that the average cost curve of the consolidated firm is the sum of the average cost curves of the individual plants.

many markets that end up competitive begin with an entrepreneurial idea and a short-lived monopoly position. In the mid-1970s, a California entrepreneur named Gary Dahl "invented" and marketed the Pet Rock. Dahl had the market to himself for about 6 months, during which time he earned millions before scores of competitors entered, driving down the price and profits. (In the end, this product, perhaps not surprisingly, disappeared). *For a monopoly to persist, some factor or factors must prevent entry.* We turn now to a discussion of those factors, commonly termed **barriers to entry**.

barriers to entry Factors that prevent new firms from entering and competing in imperfectly competitive industries.

Return for a moment to Figure 13.4 on p. 275. In that graph, we see that the monopolist is earning a positive economic profit. Such profits can persist only if other firms cannot enter this industry and compete them away. The term *barriers to entry* is used to describe the set of factors that prevent new firms from entering a market with excess profits. Monopoly can persist only in the presence of entry barriers.

Economies of Scale   In Chapter 9, we described production technologies in which average costs fall with output increases. In situations in which those scale economies are very large relative to the overall market, the cost advantages associated with size can give rise to monopoly power.

Scale economies come in a number of different forms. Providing cable service requires laying expensive cable; conventional telephones require the installation of poles and wires. For these cases, there are clear cost advantages in having only one set of physical apparatuses. Once a firm has laid the wire, providing service to one more customer is very inexpensive. The semiconductor industry is another case in which production favors the large firms. In 2007, Intel, the world leader in production of semiconductors for the PC, estimated that it would spend $6.2 billion for new production facilities and another $6 billion to support its research efforts to improve the speed of its chips. For Intel, physical production and the importance of research favor the large firm.

In some cases, scale economies come from marketing and advertising. Breakfast cereal can be produced efficiently on a small scale, for example; large-scale production does not reduce costs. However, to compete, a new firm would need an advertising campaign costing millions of dollars. The large front-end investment requirement in advertising is risky and likely to deter would-be entrants to the cereal market.

When scale economies are so large relative to the size of the market that costs are minimized with only one firm in the industry, we have a **natural monopoly**.

natural monopoly An industry that realizes such large economies of scale in producing its product that single-firm production of that good or service is most efficient.

Although Figure 13.7 presents an exaggerated picture, it does serve to illustrate our point. One large-scale plant (Scale 2) can produce 500,000 units of output at an average unit cost of $1. If the industry were restructured into five firms, each producing on a smaller scale (Scale 1), the industry could produce the same amount, but average unit cost would be five times as high ($5). Consumers potentially see a considerable gain when economies of scale are realized. The critical point here is that for a natural monopoly to exist, economies of scale must be realized at a scale that is close to total demand in the market.

▶ **FIGURE 13.7**

A Natural Monopoly

A natural monopoly is a firm in which the most efficient scale is very large. Here, average total cost declines until a single firm is producing nearly the entire amount demanded in the market. With one firm producing 500,000 units, average total cost is $1 per unit. With five firms each producing 100,000 units, average total cost is $5 per unit.

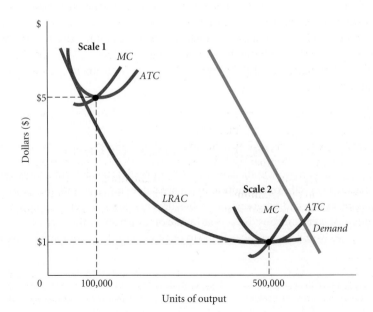

Notice in Figure 13.7 that the long-run average cost curve continues to decline until it almost hits the market demand curve. If at a price of $1 market demand is 5 *million* units of output, there would be no reason to have only one firm in the industry. Ten firms could each produce 500,000 units, and each could reap the full benefits of the available economies of scale.

Historically, natural monopolies in the United States have been regulated by the state. Public utility commissions in each state monitor electric companies and locally operating telephone companies, regulating prices so that the benefits of scale economies are realized without the inefficiencies of monopoly power. The *Economics in Practice* on p. 280 describes the current debate over the regulation of cable television.

Patents   **Patents** are legal barriers that prevent entry into an industry by granting exclusive use of the patented product or process to the inventor. Patents are issued in the United States under the authority of Article I, Section 8, of the Constitution, which gives Congress the power to "promote the progress of science and the useful arts, by securing for limited times to authors and inventors the exclusive right to their respective writings and discoveries." Patent protection in the United States is currently granted for a period of 20 years.

> **patent** A barrier to entry that grants exclusive use of the patented product or process to the inventor.

Patents provide an incentive for invention and innovation. New products and new processes are developed through research undertaken by individual inventors and by firms. Research requires resources and time, which have opportunity costs. Without the protection that a patent provides, the results of research would become available to the general public quickly. If research did not lead to expanded profits, less research would be done. On the negative side though, patents do serve as a barrier to competition and they slow down the benefits of research flowing through the market to consumers.

The expiration of patents after a given number of years represents an attempt to balance the benefits of firms and the benefits of households: On the one hand, it is important to stimulate invention and innovation; on the other hand, invention and innovation do society less good when their benefits to the public are constrained.[4]

In recent years, public attention has been focused on the high costs of health care. One factor contributing to these costs is the high price of many prescription drugs. Equipped with newly developed tools of bioengineering, the pharmaceutical industry has been granted thousands of patents for new drugs. When a new drug for treating a disease is developed, the patent holder can charge a high price for the drug. The drug companies argue that these rewards are justified by high research and development costs; others say that these profits are the result of a monopoly protected by the patent system.

Government Rules   Patents provide one example of a government-enforced regulation that creates monopoly. For patents, the justification for such intervention is to promote innovation. In some cases, governments impose entry restrictions on firms as a way of controlling activity. In most parts of the United States, governments restrict the sale of alcohol. In fact, in some states (Iowa, Maine, New Hampshire, and Ohio), liquor can be sold only through state-controlled and managed stores. Most states operate lotteries as monopolists. However, when large economies of scale do not exist in an industry or when equity is not a concern, the arguments in favor of government-run monopolies are much weaker. One argument is that the state wants to prevent private parties from encouraging and profiting from "sin," particularly in cases in which society at large can be harmed. Another argument is that government monopolies are a convenient source of revenues.

Ownership of a Scarce Factor of Production   You cannot enter the diamond-producing business unless you own a diamond mine. There are not many diamond mines in the world, and most are already owned by a single firm, the DeBeers Company of South Africa. At one time, the Aluminum Company of America (now Alcoa) owned or controlled virtually 100 percent of the known bauxite deposits in the world and until the 1940s monopolized the production and distribution of aluminum. Obviously, if production requires a particular input and one firm owns the entire supply of that input, that firm will control the industry. Ownership alone is a barrier to entry.

---

[4] Another alternative is *licensing*. With licensing, the new technology is used by all producers and the inventor splits the benefits with consumers. Because forcing the non-patent-holding producers to use an inefficient technology results in waste, some analysts have proposed adding mandatory licensing to the current patent system. A key question here involves determining the right licensing fee.

ECONOMICS IN PRACTICE

Managing the Cable Monopoly

Many people subscribe to cable television. Cable systems bundle a collection of network and cable stations and offer them to viewers as packages, ranging from a basic service with only a modest number of offerings to much-expanded premium services. In the last 20 years, the cable system has grown to a multibillion dollar industry covering most of the country.

What you might not realize about the cable system is that it consists of a network of local monopolies. In any given area, typically just one cable company is in operation. Historically, this monopoly was justified as a natural monopoly, reflecting the expensive cable that needed to be laid to serve the population and the fact that once the cable was laid, the costs of providing service to a new consumer was modest.

What you also may not realize is that when you pay your cable bill, part of your payment goes to your home city. In fact, cities negotiate with the various cable companies to give one of them the right to be the monopoly supplier of cable service in return for a fee that is typically on the order of 5 percent of the cable revenues. Once a firm has bought the right to be a local cable company, it must follow a set of rules, particularly with regard to the availability and price of the basic cable.

One of the hot debates in 2008 was in the cable industry. Cable companies offer programs bundled rather than à la carte programs. Keith Martin, the commissioner of the Federal Communications Commission, which oversees cable, pushed to have cable unbundled, largely in response to parents who were concerned about inappropriate television shows coming into their homes as part of a bundle. What economic logic would justify bundling programs in this way?

Here it is helpful to think about costs again. Once a television show is produced, distributing it to another customer has a zero marginal cost up to the capacity level of the cable. Thus, from a cable company's point of view, having a large customer base for the various shows is typically a profitable strategy. Suppose

100 viewers valued doctor shows at $2 a week each and lawyer shows at $1.50 each, while another 100 viewers had the opposite preference. To maximize revenue with à la carte pricing, the cable company would charge $1.50 for each show, giving it 200 viewers per show for a revenue of $600 (200 viewers × 2 shows each × $1.50). If the cable company sells the bundle for $3.50, all viewers buy and it earns $700. If the cable company sells the bundle for $3, its revenue is still the original $600 but now all of its customers are better off and can watch two programs instead of one. When the cost of distributing a good with high fixed costs is zero, bundling is often a way to make both producers and consumers better off.

Network Effects   How much value do you get from a telephone or a fax machine? It will depend on how many other people own a machine that can communicate with yours. Products such as these, in which benefits of ownership are a function of how many other people are part of the network, are subject to **network externalities**. For phones and faxes, the network effects are direct. For products such as the Windows operating system and the Xbox, network effects may be indirect. Having a large consumer base increases consumer valuation by encouraging the development of complementary goods. When many people own an Xbox, game developers have an incentive to create games for the system. Good games increase the value of the system. In the case of online interactive games like Zygna's Farmville, some observers have argued that the size of the playing community creates large network effects.

How does the existence of network effects create a barrier to entry? In this situation, a firm that starts early and builds a large product base will have an advantage over a newcomer. Microsoft's dominant position in the operating system market reflects network effects in this business. The high concentration in the game console market (Microsoft, Nintendo, and Sony control this market) also comes from network effects.

network externalities
The value of a product to a consumer increases with the number of that product being sold or used in the market.

The Social Costs of Monopoly

So far, we have seen that a monopoly produces less output and charges a higher price than a competitively organized industry if no large economies of scale exist for the monopoly. We have also seen the way in which barriers to entry can allow monopolists to persist over time. You are probably thinking at this point that producing less and charging more to earn positive profits is not likely to be in the best interests of consumers, and you are right.

Inefficiency and Consumer Loss

In Chapter 12, we argued that price must equal marginal cost ($P = MC$) for markets to produce what people want. This argument rests on two propositions: (1) that price provides a good approximation of the social value of a unit of output and (2) that marginal cost, in the absence of externalities (costs or benefits to external parties not weighed by firms), provides a good approximation of the product's social opportunity cost. In a pure monopoly, price is above the product marginal cost. When this happens, the firm is underproducing from society's point of view. Society would be better off if the firm produced more and charged a lower price. Monopoly leads to an inefficient mix of output.

A slightly simplified version of the monopoly diagram appears in Figure 13.8, which shows how we might make a rough estimate of the size of the loss to social welfare that arises from monopoly. (For clarity, we will ignore the short-run cost curves and assume constant returns to scale in the long run.) Under competitive conditions, firms would produce output up to $Q_c =$ 4,000 units and price would ultimately settle at $P_c = \$2$, equal to long-run average cost. Any price above \$2 will mean positive profits, which would be eliminated by the entry of new competing firms in the long run. (You should remember all this from Chapter 9.)

A monopoly firm in the same industry, however, would produce only $Q_m =$ 2,000 units per period and charge a price of $P_m = \$4$ because $MR = MC$ at $Q_m =$ 2,000 units. The monopoly would make a profit equal to total revenue minus total cost, or $P_m \times Q_m$ minus $ATC \times Q_m$. Profit

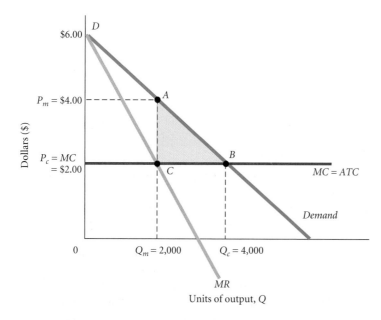

▲ **FIGURE 13.8 Welfare Loss from Monopoly**
A demand curve shows the amounts that people are willing to pay at each potential level of output. Thus, the demand curve can be used to approximate the benefits to the consumer of raising output above 2,000 units. *MC* reflects the marginal cost of the resources needed. The triangle *ABC* roughly measures the net social gain of moving from 2,000 units to 4,000 units (or the loss that results when monopoly decreases output from 4,000 units to 2,000 units).

to the monopoly is thus equal to the area P_mACP_c, or \$4,000. [(\$4 $\times$ 2,000) $-$ (\$2 $\times$ 2,000) $=$ \$8,000 $-$ \$4,000 $=$ \$4,000. Remember that $P_c = ATC$ in this example.]

Now consider the gains and losses associated with increasing price from \$2 to \$4 and cutting output from 4,000 units to 2,000 units. As you might guess, the winner will be the monopolist and the loser will be the consumer, but let us see how it works out.

At P_c = \$2, the price under perfect competition, there are no profits. Consumers are paying a price of \$2, but the demand curve shows that many are willing to pay more than that. For example, a substantial number of people would pay \$4 or more. Those people willing to pay more than \$2 are receiving what we earlier called a *consumer surplus*. Consumer surplus is the difference between what households are willing to pay for a product and the current market price. The demand curve shows approximately how much households are willing to pay at each level of output. Thus, the area of triangle DBP_c gives us a rough measure of the "consumer surplus" being enjoyed by households when the price is \$2. Consumers willing to pay exactly \$4 get a surplus equal to \$2. Those who place the highest value on this good—that is, those who are willing to pay the most (\$6)—get a surplus equal to DP_c, or \$4.

Now the industry is reorganized as a monopoly that cuts output to 2,000 units and raises price to \$4. The big winner is the monopolist, who ends up earning profits equal to \$4,000. The big losers are the consumers. Their "surplus" now shrinks from the area of triangle DBP_c to the area of triangle DAP_m. Part of that loss (which is equal to $DBP_c - DAP_m$, or the area P_mABP_c) is covered by the monopolist's gain of P_mACP_c, but not all of it. The loss to consumers exceeds the gain to the monopoly by the area of triangle ABC ($P_mABP_c - P_mACP_c$), which roughly measures the net loss in social welfare associated with monopoly power in this industry. Because the area of a triangle is half its base times its height, the welfare loss is 1/2 $\times$ 2,000 $\times$ \$2 = \$2,000. If we could push price back down to the competitive level and increase output to 4,000 units, consumers would gain more than the monopolist would lose and the gain in social welfare would approximate the area of ABC, or \$2,000.

In this example, the presence of a monopoly also causes an important change in the distribution of real income. In Figure 13.8, area P_mACP_c is a profit of \$4,000 flowing every period to the monopolist. If price were pushed down to \$2 by competition or regulation, those profits would pass to consumers in the form of lower prices. Society may value this resource transfer on equity grounds in addition to efficiency grounds.

Of course, monopolies may have social costs that do not show up on these graphs. Monopolies, which are protected from competition by barriers to entry, may not face the same pressures to cut costs and innovate as competitive firms do. A competitive firm that does not use the most efficient technology will be driven out of business by firms that do. One of the significant arguments against tariffs and quotas to protect such industries as automobiles and steel from foreign competition is that protection lessens the incentive to be efficient and competitive.

Rent-Seeking Behavior

Economists have another concern about monopolies. Triangle ABC in Figure 13.8 represents a real net loss to society, but part of rectangle P_mACP_c (the \$4,000 monopoly profit) may also end up lost. To understand why, we need to think about the incentives facing potential monopolists.

The area of rectangle P_mACP_c shows positive profits. If entry into the market were easy and competition were open, these profits would eventually be competed to zero. Owners of businesses earning profits have an incentive to prevent this development. In fact, the graph shows how much they would be willing to pay to prevent it. A rational owner of a monopoly firm would be willing to pay any amount less than the entire rectangle. Any portion of profits left over after expenses is better than zero, which would be the case if free competition eliminated all profits.

Potential monopolists can do many things to protect their profits. One obvious approach is to push the government to impose restrictions on competition. A classic example is the behavior of taxicab driver organizations in New York and other large cities. To operate a cab legally in New York City, you need a license. The city tightly controls the number of licenses available. If entry into the taxi business were open, competition would hold down cab fares to the cost of operating cabs. However, cab drivers have become a powerful lobbying force and have muscled the city into restricting the number of licenses issued. This restriction keeps fares high and preserves monopoly profits.

There are countless other examples. The steel industry and the automobile industry spend large sums lobbying Congress for tariff protection.[5] Some experts claim that establishment of the now-defunct Civil Aeronautics Board in 1937 to control competition in the airline industry and extensive regulation of trucking by the I.C.C. prior to deregulation in the 1970s came about partly through industry efforts to restrict competition and preserve profits.

This kind of behavior, in which households or firms take action to preserve positive profits, is called **rent-seeking behavior**. Recall from Chapter 10 that rent is the return to a factor of production in strictly limited supply. Rent-seeking behavior has two important implications.

rent-seeking behavior
Actions taken by households or firms to preserve positive profits.

First, this behavior consumes resources. Lobbying and building barriers to entry are not costless activities. Lobbyists' wages, expenses of the regulatory bureaucracy, and the like must be paid. Periodically faced with the prospect that the city of New York will issue new taxi licenses, cab owners and drivers have become so well organized that they can bring the city to a standstill with a strike or even a limited job action. Indeed, positive profits may be completely consumed through rent-seeking behavior that produces nothing of social value; all it does is help to preserve the current distribution of income.

Second, the frequency of rent-seeking behavior leads us to another view of government. So far, we have considered only the role that government might play in helping to achieve an efficient allocation of resources in the face of market failure—in this case, failures that arise from imperfect market structure. Later in this chapter we survey the measures government might take to ensure that resources are efficiently allocated when monopoly power arises. However, the idea of rent-seeking behavior introduces the notion of **government failure**, in which the government becomes the tool of the rent seeker and the allocation of resources is made even less efficient than before.

government failure Occurs when the government becomes the tool of the rent seeker and the allocation of resources is made even less efficient by the intervention of government.

This idea of government failure is at the center of **public choice theory**, which holds that governments are made up of people, just as business firms are. These people—politicians and bureaucrats—can be expected to act in their own self-interest, just as owners of firms do. We turn to the economics of public choice in Chapter 16.

public choice theory An economic theory that the public officials who set economic policies and regulate the players act in their own self-interest, just as firms do.

Price Discrimination

So far in our discussion of monopoly, we have assumed that the firm faces a known downward-sloping demand curve and must choose a *single price* and a single quantity of output. Indeed, the reason that price and marginal revenue are different for a monopoly and the same for a perfectly competitive firm is that if a monopoly decides to sell more output, it must lower price in order to do so.

In the real world, however, there are many examples of firms that charge different prices to different groups of buyers. Charging different prices to different buyers is called **price discrimination**. The motivation for price discrimination is fairly obvious: If a firm can identify those who are willing to pay a higher price for a good, it can earn more profit from them by charging a higher price. The idea is best illustrated using the extreme case where a firm knows what each buyer is willing to pay. A firm that charges the maximum amount that buyers are willing to pay for each unit is practicing **perfect price discrimination**.

price discrimination
Charging different prices to different buyers.

perfect price discrimination
Occurs when a firm charges the maximum amount that buyers are willing to pay for each unit.

Figure 13.9 is similar to Figure 13.8. For simplicity, assume a firm with a constant marginal cost equal to $2 per unit. A non-price-discriminating monopolist would have to set one and only one price. That firm would face the marginal revenue curve shown in the diagram and would produce as long as *MR* is above *MC*: Output would be Q_m, and price would be set at $4 per unit. The firm would earn an economic profit of $2 per unit for every unit up to Q_m. Consumers would enjoy a consumer surplus equal to the shaded area. Consumer A, for example, is willing to pay $5.75 but has to pay only $4.00.

Now consider what would happen if the firm could charge each consumer the maximum amount that that consumer was willing to pay. In Figure 13.9(a), if the firm could charge consumer A a price of $5.75, the firm would earn $3.75 in profit on that unit and the consumer would get no consumer surplus. Going on to consumer B, if the firm could determine B's

---

[5] A tariff is a tax on imports designed to give a price advantage to domestic producers.

▶ **FIGURE 13.9**

Price Discrimination

In Figure 13.9(a), consumer A is willing to pay $5.75. If the price-discriminating firm can charge $5.75 to A, profit is $3.75. A monopolist who cannot price discriminate would maximize profit by charging $4. At a price of $4.00, the firm makes $2.00 in profit and consumer A enjoys a consumer surplus of $1.75. In Figure 13.9(b), for a perfectly price-discriminating monopolist, the demand curve is the same as marginal revenue. The firm will produce as long as $MR > MC$, up to Q_c. At Q_c, profit is the entire shaded area and consumer surplus is zero.

a. Consumer surplus if the firm charges a single price of $4 per unit.

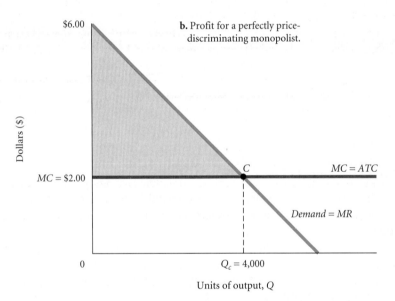

b. Profit for a perfectly price-discriminating monopolist.

maximum willingness to pay and charge $5.50, profit would be $3.50 and consumer surplus for B would again be zero. This would continue all the way to point C on the demand curve, where total profit would be equal to the entire area under the demand curve and above the $MC = ATC$ line, as shown in Figure 13.9(b).

Another way to look at the diagram in Figure 13.9(b) is to notice that the demand curve actually becomes the same as the marginal revenue curve. When a firm can charge the maximum that anyone is willing to pay *for each unit*, that price *is* marginal revenue. There is no need to draw a separate *MR* curve as there was when the firm could charge only one price to all consumers. Once again, profit is the entire shaded area and consumer surplus is zero.

It is interesting to note that a perfectly price-discriminating monopolist will actually produce the *efficient* quantity of output—Q_c in Figure 13.9(b), which is the same as the amount that would be produced had the industry been perfectly competitive. The firm will continue to produce as long as benefits to consumers exceed marginal cost; it does not stop at Q_m in Figure 13.9(a). But when a monopolist can perfectly price discriminate, it reaps all the net benefits from higher production. There is no deadweight loss, but there is no consumer surplus either.

Examples of Price Discrimination

Examples of price discrimination are all around us. It used to be that airlines routinely charged those who stayed over Saturday nights a much lower fare than those who did not. Business travelers generally travel during the week, often are unwilling to stay over Saturdays, and generally are willing to pay more for tickets.

Airlines, movie theaters, hotels, and many other industries routinely charge a lower price for children and the elderly. The reason is that children and the elderly generally have a lower willingness to pay. Telephone companies have so many ways of targeting different groups that it is difficult to know what they are really charging.

In each case, the objective of the firm is to segment the market into different identifiable groups, with each group having a different elasticity of demand. Doing so requires firms to ensure that different customers are kept separated, so that they cannot trade with one another. It can be shown, although we will not present the analysis here, that the optimal strategy for a firm that can sell in more than one market is to charge higher prices in markets with low demand elasticities.

Remedies for Monopoly: Antitrust Policy

As we have just seen, the exercise of monopoly power can bring with it considerable social costs. On the other hand, as our discussion of entry barriers suggested, at times, monopolies may bring with them benefits associated with scale economies or innovation gains. Sometimes monopolies result from the natural interplay of market and technological forces, while at other times firms actively and aggressively pursue monopoly power, doing their best to eliminate the competition. In the United States, the rules set out in terms of what firms can and cannot do in their markets are contained in two pieces of antitrust legislation: the Sherman Act passed in 1890 and the Clayton Act passed in 1914.

Major Antitrust Legislation

The following are some of the major antitrust legislation that have been passed in the United States.

 The Sherman Act of 1890   The substance of the Sherman Act is contained in two short sections:

> *Section 1.* Every contract, combination in the form of trust or otherwise, or conspiracy, in restraint of trade or commerce among the several States, or with foreign nations, is hereby declared to be illegal....
>
> *Section 2.* Every person who shall monopolize, or attempt to monopolize, or combine or conspire with any other person or persons, to monopolize any part of the trade or commerce among the several States, or with foreign nations, shall be deemed guilty of a misdemeanor, and, on conviction thereof, shall be punished by fine not exceeding five thousand dollars, or by imprisonment not exceeding one year, or by both said punishments, in the discretion of the court.

For our treatment of monopoly, the relevant part of the Sherman Act is Section 2, the rule against monopolization or attempted monopolization. The language of the act is quite broad, so it is the responsibility of the courts to judge conduct that is legal and conduct that is illegal. As a firm competes in the hopes of winning business, what kind of behavior is acceptable hard competition and what is not? Two different administrative bodies have the responsibility for initiating actions on behalf of the U.S. government against individuals or companies thought to be in violation of the antitrust laws. These agencies are the Antitrust Division of the Justice Department and the Federal Trade Commission (FTC). In addition, private citizens can initiate antitrust actions. *[handwritten: Exec Branch]*

In 1911, two major antitrust cases were decided by the Supreme Court. The two companies involved, Standard Oil and American Tobacco, seemed to epitomize the textbook definition of monopoly, and both appeared to exhibit the structure and the conduct outlawed by the Sherman Act. Standard Oil controlled about 91 percent of the refining industry, and although the exact figure is still disputed, the American Tobacco Trust probably controlled between 75 percent and 90 percent of the market for all tobacco products except cigars. Both companies had used tough tactics to swallow up competition or to drive it out of business. Not surprisingly, the Supreme Court found both firms guilty of violating Sections 1 and 2 of the Sherman Act and ordered their dissolution.[6]

rule of reason The criterion introduced by the Supreme Court in 1911 to determine whether a particular action was illegal ("unreasonable") or legal ("reasonable") within the terms of the Sherman Act.

The Court made clear, however, that the Sherman Act did not outlaw every action that seemed to restrain trade, only those that were "unreasonable." In enunciating this **rule of reason**, the Court seemed to say that structure alone was not a criterion for unreasonableness. Thus, it was possible for a near-monopoly not to violate the Sherman Act as long as it had won its market using "reasonable" tactics.

Subsequent court cases confirmed that a firm could be convicted of violating the Sherman Act only if it had exhibited *unreasonable conduct.* Between 1911 and 1920, cases were brought against Eastman Kodak, International Harvester, United Shoe Machinery, and United States Steel. The first three companies controlled overwhelming shares of their respective markets, and the fourth controlled 60 percent of the country's capacity to produce steel. Nonetheless, all four cases were dismissed on the grounds that these companies had shown no evidence of "unreasonable conduct."

New technologies have also created challenges for the courts in defining reasonable conduct. Perhaps the largest antitrust case recently has been the case launched by the U.S. Department of Justice against Microsoft. By the 1990s, Microsoft had more that 90 percent of the market in operating systems for PCs. The government argued that Microsoft had achieved this market share through illegal dealing, while Microsoft argued that the government failed to understand the issues associated with competition in a market with network externalities and dynamic competition. In the end, the case was settled with a *consent decree* in July 1994. A consent decree is a formal agreement between a prosecuting government and defendants that must be approved by the courts. Such decrees can be signed before, during, or after a trial and are often used to save litigation costs. In the case of Microsoft, under the consent decree, it agreed to give computer manufacturers more freedom to install software from other software companies. In 1997, Microsoft found itself charged with violating the terms of the consent decree and was back in court. In 2000, the company was found guilty of violating the antitrust laws and a judge ordered it split into two companies. But Microsoft appealed; and the decision to split the company was replaced with a consent decree requiring Microsoft to behave more competitively, including a provision that computer makers would have the ability to sell competitors' software without fear of retaliation. In the fall of 2005, Microsoft finally ended its antitrust troubles in the United States after agreeing to pay RealNetworks $761 million to settle one final lawsuit.

In 2005, Advanced Micro Devices (AMD) brought suit against Intel, which has an 80 percent share of the x-86 processors used in most of the world's PCs. AMD alleged anticompetitive behavior and attempted monopolization. At present in the United States, private antitrust cases, brought by one firm against another, are 20-plus times more common than government-led cases.

The Clayton Act and the Federal Trade Commission, 1914 Designed to strengthen the Sherman Act and to clarify the rule of reason, the **Clayton Act** of 1914 outlawed a number of specific practices. First, it made *tying contracts* illegal. Such contracts force a customer to buy one product to obtain another. Second, it limited mergers that would "substantially lessen competition or tend to create a monopoly." Third, it banned *price discrimination*—charging different customers different prices for reasons other than changes in cost or matching competitors' prices.

Clayton Act Passed by Congress in 1914 to strengthen the Sherman Act and clarify the rule of reason, the act outlawed specific monopolistic behaviors such as tying contracts, price discrimination, and unlimited mergers.

Federal Trade Commission (FTC) A federal regulatory group created by Congress in 1914 to investigate the structure and behavior of firms engaging in interstate commerce, to determine what constitutes unlawful "unfair" behavior, and to issue cease-and-desist orders to those found in violation of antitrust law.

The **Federal Trade Commission (FTC)**, created by Congress in 1914, was established to investigate "the organization, business conduct, practices, and management" of companies that engage in interstate commerce. At the same time, the act establishing the commission added another vaguely worded prohibition to the books: "Unfair methods of competition in commerce are hereby declared unlawful." The determination of what constituted "unfair" behavior was left up to the commission. The FTC was also given the power to issue "cease-and-desist orders" where it found behavior in violation of the law.

---

[6] *United States v. Standard Oil Co. of New Jersey*, 221 U.S. 1 (1911); *United States v. American Tobacco Co.*, 221 U.S. 106 (1911).

ECONOMICS IN PRACTICE

Antitrust Rules Cover the NFL

Most people recognize that a sports league like the National Football League is big business, but not everyone realizes that it is subject to antitrust laws. But, as the article below indicates, one of the biggest cases facing the Supreme Court in 2009–2010 involved the NFL.

The NFL's practice had been to negotiate as a single unit with apparel companies that wished to sell apparel like hats and T-shirts with football logos. Of course this meant that apparel companies could not play the New York Giants against the Indianapolis Colts in signing deals. American Needle, a large apparel company, sued. In its defense, the NFL argued that in its negotiations with companies like Reebok and American Needle, it faced competition from baseball and basketball leagues that kept it from extracting too high a price for its logos. In essence, the NFL argued that in the sports-logo hat market a New York Yankees hat was a pretty good substitute for a New York Giants hat. The court saw it differently.

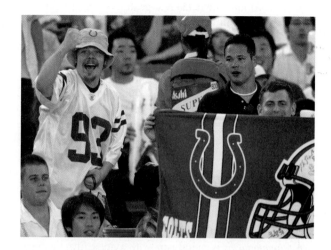

American Needle: High Court Delivers 9–0 Shutout Against NFL

The Wall Street Journal

Wow. Turns out the big antitrust case of the 2009–2010 Supreme Court term, American Needle v. NFL, didn't provide much of a matchup.

American Needle clobbered the league, in a unanimous 9-0 decision penned by Justice John Paul Stevens. We had no dissents and no concurrences. This was an unadulterated blowout. This was the 1940 NFL Championship game; the 1986 Super Bowl.

The case pitted American Needle, Inc., an apparel manufacturer, against the NFL. The dispute started back in 2000 when the NFL signed an exclusive apparel licensing deal with Reebok International, now a unit of Adidas AG.

American Needle, which had individual licensing deals with NFL teams, sued, arguing the NFL's exclusive deal

with Reebok violated antitrust rules. The NFL argued that it is a single entity with 32 teams that compete with each other in football but not in business, where the teams collectively compete with other sports and forms of entertainment. American Needle countered by arguing that the league was actually a collection of 32 independent entities—i.e., all the teams.

The Seventh Circuit in 2008 ruled for the NFL, prompting the appeal.

The Supreme Court on Monday essentially ruled that the NFL is composed of 32 separate business entities.

Source: The Wall Street Journal, from "American Needle: High Court Delivers 9–0 Shutout Against NFL" by Ashby Jones. Copyright 2010 by *Dow Jones & Company, Inc.* Reproduced with permission of *Dow Jones & Company, Inc.* via Copyright Clearance Center.

Nonetheless, the legislation of 1914 retained the focus on *conduct*; thus, the rule of reason remained central to all antitrust action in the courts.

Imperfect Markets: A Review and a Look Ahead

A firm has *market power* when it exercises some control over the price of its output or the prices of the inputs that it uses. The extreme case of a firm with market power is the pure monopolist. In a pure monopoly, a single firm produces a product for which there are no close substitutes in an industry in which all new competitors are barred from entry.

Our focus in this chapter on pure monopoly (which occurs rarely) has served a number of purposes. First, the monopoly model describes a number of industries quite well. Second, the monopoly case illustrates the observation that imperfect competition leads to an inefficient allocation of resources. Finally, the analysis of pure monopoly offers insights into the more commonly encountered market models of monopolistic competition and oligopoly, which we discussed briefly in this chapter and will discuss in detail in the next two chapters.

SUMMARY

1. A number of assumptions underlie the logic of perfect competition. Among them: (1) A large number of firms and households are interacting in each market; (2) firms in a given market produce undifferentiated, or homogeneous, products; and (3) new firms are free to enter industries and compete for profits. The first two imply that firms have no control over input prices or output prices; the third implies that opportunities for positive profit are eliminated in the long run.

IMPERFECT COMPETITION AND MARKET POWER: CORE CONCEPTS *p. 269*

2. A market in which individual firms have some control over price is imperfectly competitive. Such firms exercise *market power*. The three forms of *imperfect competition* are monopoly, oligopoly, and monopolistic competition.

3. A *pure monopoly* is an industry with a single firm that produces a product for which there are no close substitutes and in which there are significant *barriers to entry*.

4. Market power means that firms must make four decisions instead of three: (1) how much to produce, (2) how to produce it, (3) how much to demand in each input market, and (4) *what price to charge for their output*.

5. Market power does not imply that a monopolist can charge any price it wants. Monopolies are constrained by market demand. They can sell only what people will buy and only at a price that people are willing to pay.

PRICE AND OUTPUT DECISIONS IN PURE MONOPOLY MARKETS *p. 271*

6. In perfect competition, many firms supply homogeneous products. With only one firm in a monopoly market, however, there is no distinction between the firm and the industry—the firm *is* the industry. The market demand curve is thus the firm's demand curve, and the total quantity supplied in the market is what the monopoly firm decides to produce.

7. For a monopolist, an increase in output involves not just producing more and selling it but also reducing the price of its output to sell it. Thus, marginal revenue, to a monopolist, is not equal to product price, as it is in competition. Instead, marginal revenue is lower than price because to raise output 1 unit *and to be able to sell* that 1 unit, the firm must lower the price it charges to all buyers.

8. A profit-maximizing monopolist will produce up to the point at which marginal revenue is equal to marginal cost ($MR = MC$).

9. Monopolies have no identifiable supply curves. They simply choose a point on the market demand curve. That is, they choose a price and quantity to produce, which depend on both the marginal cost and the shape of the demand curve.

10. In the short run, monopolists are limited by a fixed factor of production, just as competitive firms are. Monopolies that do not generate enough revenue to cover costs will go out of business in the long run.

11. Compared with a competitively organized industry, a monopolist restricts output, charges higher prices, and earns positive profits. Because *MR* always lies below the demand curve for a monopoly, monopolists always charge a price higher than *MC* (the price that would be set by perfect competition).

12. Barriers to entry prevent new entrants from competing away industry excess profits.

13. Forms of barriers to entry include economies of scale, patents, government rules, ownership of scarce factors, and network effects.

14. When a firm exhibits economies of scale so large that average costs continuously decline with output, it may be efficient to have only one firm in an industry. Such an industry is called a *natural monopoly*.

THE SOCIAL COSTS OF MONOPOLY *p. 281*

15. When firms price above marginal cost, the result is an inefficient mix of output. The decrease in consumer surplus is larger than the monopolist's profit, thus causing a net loss in social welfare.

16. Actions that firms take to preserve positive profits, such as lobbying for restrictions on competition, are called rent seeking. *Rent-seeking behavior* consumes resources and adds to social cost, thus reducing social welfare even further.

PRICE DISCRIMINATION *p. 283*

17. Charging different prices to different buyers is called *price discrimination*. The motivation for price discrimination is fairly obvious: If a firm can identify those who are willing to pay a higher price for a good, it can earn more profit from them by charging a higher price.

18. A firm that charges the maximum amount that buyers are willing to pay for each unit is practicing *perfect price discrimination*.

19. A perfectly price-discriminating monopolist will actually produce the *efficient* quantity of output.

20. Examples of price discrimination are all around us. Airlines routinely charge travelers who stay over Saturday nights a much lower fare than those who do not. Business travelers generally travel during the week, often are unwilling to stay over Saturdays, and generally are willing to pay more for tickets.

REMEDIES FOR MONOPOLY: ANTITRUST POLICY *p. 285*

21. Governments have assumed two roles with respect to imperfectly competitive industries: (1) They *promote* competition and restrict market power, primarily through antitrust laws and other congressional acts; and (2) they *restrict* competition by regulating industries.

22. In 1914, Congress passed the *Clayton Act*, which was designed to strengthen the Sherman Act and to clarify what specific forms of conduct were "unreasonable" restraints of trade. In the same year, the *Federal Trade Commission* was established and given broad power to investigate and regulate unfair methods of competition.

───── REVIEW TERMS AND CONCEPTS ─────

barrier to entry, *p. 278*
Clayton Act, *p. 286*
Federal Trade Commission (FTC), *p. 286*
government failure, *p. 283*
imperfectly competitive industry, *p. 269*

market power, *p. 269*
natural monopoly, *p. 278*
network externalities, *p. 280*
patent, *p. 279*
perfect price discrimination, *p. 283*

price discrimination, *p. 283*
public choice theory, *p. 283*
pure monopoly, *p. 270*
rent-seeking behavior, *p. 283*
rule of reason, *p. 286*

───── PROBLEMS ─────

All problems are available on www.myeconlab.com

1. Do you agree or disagree with each of the following statements? Explain your reasoning.
   a. For a monopoly, price is equal to marginal revenue because a monopoly has the power to control price.
   b. Because a monopoly is the only firm in an industry, it can charge virtually any price for its product.
   c. It is always true that when demand elasticity is equal to −1, marginal revenue is equal to 0.

2. Explain why the marginal revenue curve facing a competitive firm differs from the marginal revenue curve facing a monopolist.

3. Assume that the potato chip industry in the Northwest in 2009 was competitively structured and in long-run competitive equilibrium; firms were earning a normal rate of return. In 2010, two smart lawyers quietly bought up all the firms and began operations as a monopoly called "Wonks." To operate efficiently, Wonks hired a management consulting firm, which estimated long-run costs and demand. These results are presented in the following figure.

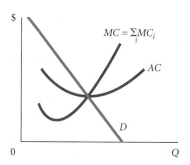

($\sum_i MC_i$ = the horizontal sum of the marginal cost curves of the individual branches/firms.)
   a. Indicate 2009 output and price on the diagram.
   b. By assuming that the monopolist is a profit-maximizer, indicate on the graph total revenue, total cost, and total profit after the consolidation.
   c. Compare the perfectly competitive outcome with the monopoly outcome.
   d. In 2010, an old buddy from law school files a complaint with the Antitrust Division of the Justice Department claiming that Wonks has monopolized the potato chip industry.

Justice concurs and prepares a civil suit. Suppose you work in the White House and the president asks you to prepare a brief memo (two or three paragraphs) outlining the issues. In your response, be sure to include:
   (1) The economic justification for action.
   (2) A proposal to achieve an efficient market outcome.

4. Willy's Widgets, a monopoly, faces the following demand schedule (sales in widgets per month):

PRICE	$20	$30	$40	$50	$60	$70	$80	$90	$100
QUANTITY DEMANDED	40	35	30	25	20	15	10	5	0

Calculate marginal revenue over each interval in the schedule—for example, between $q = 40$ and $q = 35$. Recall that marginal revenue is the added revenue from an additional *unit* of production/sales and assume that *MR* is constant within each interval.

If marginal cost is constant at $20 and fixed cost is $100, what is the profit-maximizing level of output? (Choose one of the specific levels of output from the schedule.) What is the level of profit? Explain your answer using marginal cost and marginal revenue.

Repeat the exercise for *MC* = $40.

5. The following diagram illustrates the demand curve facing a monopoly in an industry with no economies or diseconomies of scale and no fixed costs. In the short and long run *MC* = *ATC*. Copy the diagram and indicate the following:

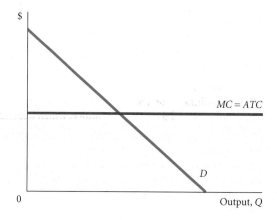

a. Optimal output
b. Optimal price
c. Total revenue
d. Total cost
e. Total monopoly profits
f. Total "excess burden" or "welfare costs" of the monopoly (briefly explain)

6. The following diagram shows the cost structure of a monopoly firm as well as market demand. Identify on the graph and calculate the following:
a. Profit-maximizing output level   10,000
b. Profit-maximizing price   4
c. Total revenue   40,000
d. Total cost   50,000
e. Total profit or loss   10,000 loss

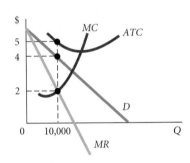

7. Consider the following monopoly that produces paperback books:

$$\text{fixed costs} = \$1,000$$
$$\text{marginal cost} = \$1 \text{ (and is constant)}$$

a. Draw the average total cost curve and the marginal cost curve on the same graph.
b. Assume that all households have the same demand schedule given by the following relationship:

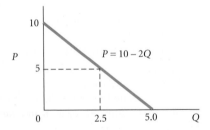

Assuming 400 households are in the economy, draw the market demand curve and the marginal revenue schedule facing the monopolist.
c. What is the monopolist's profit-maximizing output? What is the monopolist's price?
d. What is the "efficient price," assuming no externalities?
e. Suppose the government "imposed" the efficient price by setting a ceiling on price at the efficient level. What is the long-run output of the monopoly?
f. Suggest an alternative approach for achieving an efficient outcome.

*8. In Taiwan, there is only one beer producer, a government-owned monopoly called Taiwan Beer. Suppose that the company were run in a way to maximize profit for the government. That is, assume that it behaved like a private profit-maximizing monopolist. Assuming demand and cost conditions are given on the following diagram, at what level would Taiwan Beer target output and what price would it charge?

Now suppose Taiwan Beer decided to begin competing in the highly competitive American market. Assume further that Taiwan maintains import barriers so that American producers cannot sell in Taiwan but that they are not immediately reciprocated. Assuming Taiwan Beer can sell all that it can produce in the American market at a price $P = P_{US}$ indicate the following:
a. Total output
b. Output sold in Taiwan
c. New price in Taiwan
d. Total sold in the United States
e. Total profits
f. Total profits on U.S. sales
g. Total profits on Taiwan sales

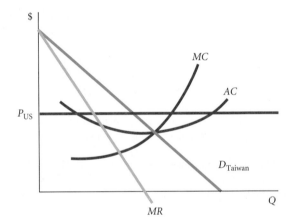

9. One of the big success stories of recent years has been Google. Research the firm and write a memorandum to the head of the Antitrust Division of the Justice Department presenting the case for and against antitrust action against Google. In what ways has Google acted to suppress competition? What private suits have been brought? What are the benefits of a strong, profitable Google?

10. [Related to the *Economics in Practice* on *p. 280*] When cable television was first introduced, there were few substitutes for it, particularly in areas with poor reception of network TV. In the current environment, a number of companies from outside the industry (for example, AT&T) have begun to develop new ways to compete with cable. What effect should we expect this to have on the cable companies?

11. [Related to the *Economics in Practice* on *p. 287*] Explain how the Supreme Court ruling in American Needle v. NFL exemplifies the "rule of reason" provision of the Sherman Act of 1890.

*Note: Problems marked with an asterisk are more challenging.

12. Black Eyed Peas was a rock band that stood at the top of the charts for sales in 2010 when its song "I Gotta Feeling" was downloaded over 7 million times. The path to success for a rock band involves reducing the elasticity of demand that it faces and building barriers to entry. That sounds like economic babble, but it has a lot of meaning. Using the language of economics and the concepts presented in this chapter, explain why lowering the elasticity of demand and building barriers to entry are exactly what Black Eyed Peas is trying to do.

13. The diagram below shows a firm (industry) that earns a normal return to capital if organized competitively. Price in the market place is P_c under competition. We assume at first that marginal cost is fixed at $50 per unit of output and that there are no economies or diseconomies of scale. [The equation of the demand curve facing the industry is $P = 100 - 1/180\ Q$].

Calculate the total revenue to the competitive firms, assuming free entry. What is total cost under competition? Calculate consumer surplus under competition.

Now assume that you bought all the firms in this industry, combining them into a single-firm monopoly protected from entry by a patent. Calculate the profit-maximizing price, P_m, total revenue from the monopoly, total cost, profit, and consumer surplus. Also compare the competitive and monopoly outcomes. Calculate the dead weight loss from monopoly. What potential remedies are available?

14. Explain why a monopoly faces no supply curve.

15. Suppose Gloria has the only franchise for a McDonald's restaurant in Laughlin, Nevada, a city with a population of roughly 8,100. Does the fact that Gloria has the only McDonald's in town necessarily mean this represents a monopoly? Explain.

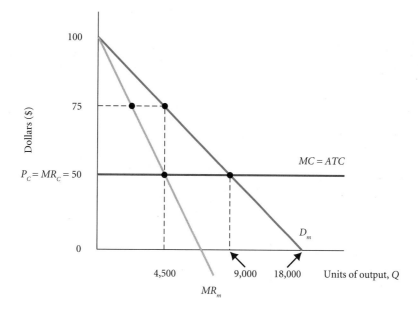

Oligopoly 14

We have now examined two "pure" market structures. At one extreme is *perfect competition*, a market structure in which many firms, each small relative to the size of the market, produce undifferentiated products and have no market power at all. Each competitive firm takes price as given and faces a perfectly elastic demand for its product. At the other extreme is *pure monopoly*, a market structure in which only one firm is the industry. The

oligopoly A form of industry (market) structure characterized by a few dominant firms. Products may be homogenous or differentiated.

monopoly holds the power to set price and is protected against competition by barriers to entry. Its market power would be complete if it did not face the discipline of the market demand curve. Even a monopoly, however, must produce a product that people want and are willing to pay for.

Most industries in the United States fall somewhere between these two extremes. In the next two chapters, we focus on two types of industries in which firms exercise some market power but at the same time face competition: oligopoly and monopolistic competition. In this chapter, we cover oligopolies, and in Chapter 15, we turn to monopolistic competition.

An **oligopoly** is an industry dominated by a few firms that, by virtue of their individual sizes, are large enough to influence the market price. Oligopolies exist in many forms. Consider the following cases:

In the United States, 90 percent of the music produced and sold comes from one of four studios: Universal, Sony, Warner, or EMI. The competition among these four firms is intense, but most of it involves the search for new talent and the marketing of that talent. Although studios compete less on price, Radiohead's 2007 campaign to have consumers set their own price in buying its new CD may result in a shake-up of the industry.

Stents are small metal devices used to prop open coronary arteries once they have been unblocked by angioplasty surgery. In the United States, the $1 billion stent market is dominated by three firms: Boston Scientific, Johnson & Johnson, and Medtronic. Among the three, there is fierce competition in the area of research and development (R&D) as they try to develop new, improved products. In 2007, Johnson & Johnson tried marketing its stents directly to patients, with an advertisement during the Dallas Cowboys–New York Jets Thanksgiving Day football game. On the other hand, we see very little price competition among these firms.

Airlines are another oligopolistic industry, but price competition can be fierce. When Southwest enters a new market, travelers often benefit from large price drops.

In 2010 Amazon found its position in the market for handheld readers threatened as the Kindle was joined by both the Nook and the iPad.

What we see in these examples is the complexity of competition among oligopolists. Oligopolists compete with one another not only in price but also in developing new products, marketing and advertising those products, and developing complements to use with the products.

At times, in some industries, competition in any of these areas can be fierce; in the other industries, there seems to be more of a "live and let live" attitude. The complex interdependence among oligopolists combined with the wide range of strategies that they use to compete makes them difficult to analyze. To find the right strategy, firms need to anticipate the reactions of their customers and their rivals to what the firms do. If I raise my price, will my rivals follow me? If they do not, will my customers leave, or are they attracted enough to what I produce that they will continue to purchase from me? If Universal decides to dramatically cut prices of its music and redo its contracts with artists so that they earn more revenue from concerts, will Sony imitate that strategy? If Sony does, how will that affect Universal? As you can see, these are hard, although interesting, questions. This chapter will introduce you to a range of different models from the fields of game theory and competitive strategy to help you answer these questions.

The four cases just described differ not only in how firms compete but also in some of the fundamental features of their industries. Before we describe the formal models of the way oligopoly firms interact, it is useful to provide a few tools that can be used to analyze the *structure* of the industries to which those firms belong. Knowing more of the structure of an industry can help us figure out which of the models we describe will be most helpful. For this exercise, we will rely on some of the tools developed in the area of competitive strategy used in business schools and in management consulting.

Market Structure in an Oligopoly

Five Forces model A model developed by Michael Porter that helps us understand the five competitive forces that determine the level of competition and profitability in an industry.

One of the standard models used in the competitive strategy area to look at the structure of an oligopoly industry is the **Five Forces model** developed by Michael Porter of Harvard University. Figure 14.1 illustrates the model.

The five forces help us explain the relative profitability of an industry and identify in which area firm rivalry is likely to be most intense.

The center box of the figure focuses on the competition among the existing firms in the industry. In the competitive market, that box is so full of competitors that no individual firm needs to think strategically about any other individual firm. In the case of monopoly, the center box has only one firm. In an oligopoly, there are a small number of firms and each of those firms will spend time thinking about how it can best compete against the other firms.

What characteristics of the existing firms should we look at to see how that competition will unfold? An obvious structural feature of an industry to consider is the number and size distribution of those firms. Do the top two firms have 90 percent of the market or only 20 percent? Is there one very large firm and a few smaller competitors, or are firms similar in size? Table 14.1 shows the distribution of market shares in a range of different U.S. industries, based on census data using value of shipments. Market share can also be constructed using employment data. We can see that even within industries that are highly *concentrated*, there are differences. Ninety percent of U.S. beer is made by the top four firms (Anheuser-Busch itself produces 50 percent of the beer sold in the

▶ **FIGURE 14.1**
Forces Driving Industry Competition

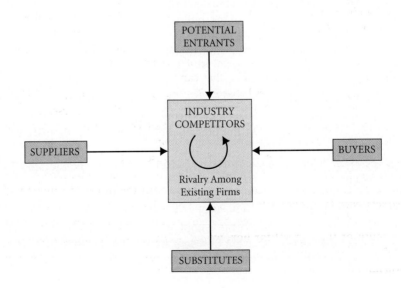

TABLE 14.1	Percentage of Value of Shipments Accounted for by the Largest Firms in High-Concentration Industries, 2002		
Industry Designation	Four Largest Firms	Eight Largest Firms	Number of Firms
Primary copper	99	100	10
Cigarettes	95	99	15
Household laundry equipment	93	100	13
Cellulosic man-made fiber	93	100	8
Breweries	90	94	344
Electric lamp bulbs	89	94	57
Household refrigerators and freezers	85	95	18
Small arms ammunition	83	89	109
Cereal breakfast foods	82	93	45
Motor vehicles	81	91	308

Source: U.S. Department of Commerce, Bureau of the Census, 2002 Economic Census, *Concentration Ratios: 2002* ECO2-315R-1, May 2006.

United States), but there is a relatively large fringe of much smaller firms. In the copper industry, we find only large firms. As we will see shortly in the models, with fewer firms, all else being equal competition is reduced.

We are also interested in the size distribution of firms among the top firms. Again, looking at the beer industry, while Anheuser-Busch produces half of the U.S. beer consumed, MillerCoors (a recently merged pair) is now up to 30 percent of the market, giving us a two-firm **concentration ratio** of 80 percent. In the market for conventional DVD players, Sony controls 20 percent of the market, but the next three or four firms in the industry have similar shares. When we discuss the price leadership model of oligopoly, we will highlight this question of size distribution. In our discussion of government merger policy, we will discuss measures other than the concentration ratio that can be used to measure firm shares.

concentration ratio The share of industry output in sales or employment accounted for by the top firms.

The final feature of existing firms that we want to look at is the amount of product differentiation we see in the industry. Are the firms all making the same product, or are the products very different from one another? This takes us back to the issue of how close products are as substitutes, a topic introduced in Chapter 13 in the description of monopoly. How different are Actavision's Guitar Hero and Electronic Arts' Rock Band? Does Farmville compete, or are there really different markets for casual and dedicated gamers as some claim? The more differentiated products made by oligopolists are, the more their behavior will resemble that of the monopolist.

Now look at the boxes to the north and south of the competitive rivalry box in Figure 14.1. To the north, we see potential entrants. In the last chapter, we described the major sources of entry barriers. When entry barriers are low, new firms can come in to compete away any excess profits that existing firms are earning. In an oligopoly, we find that the threat of entry by new firms can play an important role in how competition in the industry unfolds. In some cases, the threat alone may be enough to make an industry with only a few firms behave like a perfectly competitive firm. Markets in which entry and exit are easy so that the threat of potential entry holds down prices to a competitive level are known as **contestable markets.**

contestable markets Markets in which entry and exit are easy.

Consider, for example, a small airline that can move its capital stock from one market to another with little cost. Cape Air flies between Boston, Martha's Vineyard, Nantucket, and Cape Cod during the summer months. During the winter, the same planes are used in Florida, where they fly up and down that state's west coast between Naples, Fort Meyers, Tampa, and other cities. A similar situation may occur when a new industrial complex is built at a fairly remote site and a number of trucking companies offer their services. Because the trucking companies' capital stock is mobile, they can move their trucks somewhere else at no great cost if business is not profitable. Existing firms in this market are continuously faced with the threat of competition. In contestable markets, even large oligopolistic firms end up behaving like perfectly competitive firms. Prices are pushed to long-run average cost by competition, and positive profits do not persist.

To the south of the competitor box, we see substitutes. For oligopolists—just like the monopolists described in the last chapter—the availability of substitute products outside the industry will limit the ability of firms to earn high profits.

Why Are Record Labels Losing Key Stars Like Madonna?

How can we use the Five Forces model to help us understand the competition record labels face? Notice first that the defectors from the labels—Madonna, Radiohead, and Nine Inch Nails—are well-known stars. For the record labels, these stars are suppliers. As these stars gain in popularity, they can drive harder bargains with the record labels. (This is one reason record labels sign artists to multiple record contracts, but no contract lasts forever.) While the supply of unknown singers is likely quite elastic, the supply of branded stars like Madonna is much more inelastic. Some people would argue that venues such as YouTube reduce the power of the record labels, even for young artists, by providing low-cost exposure. Here, YouTube serves as a *substitute* for the record labels from the perspective of the unknown artists. Buyers are also gaining power. With easy access to downloaded music, often pirated, listeners are willing to spend less on music and concerts play a bigger role in generating revenue for artists. Most observers think that the sum of these changes brought by new technology will be negative for record label profits.

Madonna (and the Internet) Disrupts Another Business

Wall Street Journal

Madonna has always had a keen eye for the latest trends and her new megadeal is no exception. But this time it's not due to the latest musical styles she's embracing. It's the fact that the Internet is disrupting traditional business models.

Rather than renewing her contract with her longtime record label Warner Bros., the Material Girl is signing a 10-year, $120-million deal with a concert-promotion company, the *Journal* reports. The promoter, Live Nation, probably won't make that back by selling the three albums worth of music Madonna's agreed to record for them. Instead, it intends to make a profit by selling everything from concert tickets to Madonna-brand perfumes to corporate sponsorships.

It's a textbook example of how the Internet is disrupting an industry. The record labels used to be the key players in the music industry. Getting music to fans meant negotiating a complex supply chain that included printing records and delivering them to stores. Looking at it this way, the record labels are more or less distribution companies. Yes, it's a simplified view, but it also makes it easier to see the broader implications, because most successful companies have had to master two skills: making stuff and distributing stuff.

The Internet is the world's most efficient distribution channel, which makes it a threat to any business whose business model relies on getting product to customers. In the case of the music industry, anyone can now distribute their music over the Internet for little or no cost. This, in turn, changes the value of recorded music. Madonna and bands like Radiohead and Nine Inch Nails realize that the best way to make money is to use their music as a way to promote their overall brands.

The music industry is just the most obvious example of the way the Internet is changing the way an industry distributes, values, and indeed defines its product. Newspapers—including the Business Technology Blog's employer—are going through their own version of this disruption right now. And it's just a matter of time before it impacts other industries.

Now take a look at the horizontal boxes in Figure 14.1. One of the themes in this book has been the way in which input and output markets are linked. Firms that sell in the product market also buy in the input market. Conditions faced by firms in their input markets are described in the left-hand box, suppliers. The circular flow diagram in Chapter 3 emphasizes this point. We see this same point in the Five Forces horizontal boxes. Airlines, which have some market power in the airline industry, face strong oligopolists when they try to buy or lease airplanes. In the airplane market, Boeing and Airbus control almost the entire market for commercial airplanes. In the market for leasing planes, GE has a dominant position. When a firm with market power faces another firm with market power in the input markets, interesting bargaining dynamics may result in terms of who ends up with the profits.

Finally, on the right side of the Five Forces diagram, we see the buyer or consumer—in some ways the most important part of the schema. Buyer preferences, which we studied as we looked at individual demand and utility functions—help to determine how successful a firm will be when it tries to differentiate its products. Some buyers can also exert bargaining power, even when faced with a relatively powerful seller. When people think of buyers, they usually think of the retail buyer of consumer goods. These buyers typically have little power. But many products in the U.S. economy are sold to other firms, and in many of these markets firms face highly concentrated buyers. Intel sells its processors to the relatively concentrated personal computer market, in which Dell has a large share. Proctor & Gamble (P&G) sells its consumer products to Wal-Mart, which currently controls 25 percent of the retail grocery market. Wal-Mart's power has enormous effects on how P&G can compete in its markets.

We have now identified a number of the key features of an oligopolistic industry. Understanding these features will help us predict the strategies firms will use to compete with their rivals for business. We turn now to some of the models of oligopolistic behavior.

Oligopoly Models

Because many different types of oligopolies exist, a number of different oligopoly models have been developed. The following provides a sample of the alternative approaches to the behavior (or conduct) of oligopolistic firms. As you will see, all kinds of oligopolies have one thing in common: The behavior of any given oligopolistic firm depends on the behavior of the other firms in the industry composing the oligopoly.

The Collusion Model

In Chapter 13, we examined what happens when a perfectly competitive industry falls under the control of a single profit-maximizing firm. We saw that when many competing firms act independently, they produce more, charge a lower price, and earn less profit than if they had acted as a single unit. If these firms get together and agree to cut production and increase price—that is, if firms can agree *not* to price compete—they will have a bigger total-profit pie to carve up. When a group of profit-maximizing oligopolists colludes on price and output, the result is the same as it would be if a monopolist controlled the entire industry. That is, the colluding oligopoly will face market demand and produce only up to the point at which marginal revenue and marginal cost are equal ($MR = MC$) and price will be set above marginal cost.

A group of firms that gets together and makes price and output decisions jointly is called a **cartel**. Perhaps the most familiar example of a cartel today is the Organization of Petroleum Exporting Countries (OPEC). The OPEC cartel consists of 13 countries, including Saudi Arabia and Kuwait, that agree on oil production levels. As early as 1970, the OPEC cartel began to cut petroleum production. Its decisions in this matter led to a 400 percent increase in the price of crude oil on world markets during 1973 and 1974.

OPEC is a cartel of governments. Cartels consisting of firms, by contrast, are illegal under U.S. antitrust laws described in Chapter 13. Price fixing has been defined by courts as any agreement among individual competitors concerning prices. All agreements aimed at fixing prices or output levels, regardless of whether the resulting prices are high, are illegal. Moreover, price fixing is a criminal offense, and the penalty for being found guilty can involve jail time as well as fines. In the 1950s, a group of 12 executives from five different companies in the electrical equipment industry were found guilty of a price-fixing scheme to rotate winning bids among the firms. All were fined and sentenced to jail. In 2005, a former executive from Bayer AG, a major German pharmaceutical company, was sentenced to four months in jail and given a $50,000 fine for price fixing. In 2007, the U.S. government launched suits charging price fixing against a number of firms in industries ranging from car rentals to board game manufacturers. Despite the clear illegality of price fixing, the lure of profits seems to attract some executives to agree on prices.

For a cartel to work, a number of conditions must be present. First, demand for the cartel's product must be inelastic. If many substitutes are readily available, the cartel's price increases may become self-defeating as buyers switch to substitutes. Here we see the importance of understanding the substitutes box in Figure 14.1. Second, the members of the cartel must play by the rules. If

cartel A group of firms that gets together and makes joint price and output decisions to maximize joint profits.

a cartel is holding up prices by restricting output, there is a big incentive for members to cheat by increasing output. Breaking ranks can mean huge profits.

Incentives of the various members of a cartel to "cheat" on the cartel rather than cooperate highlights the role of the size distribution of firms in an industry. Consider an industry with one large firm and a group of small firms that has agreed to charge relatively high prices. For each firm, the price will be above its marginal cost of production. Gaining market share by selling more units is thus very appealing. On the other hand, if every firm drops prices to gain a market share, the cartel will collapse. For small players in an industry, the attraction of the added market share is often hard to resist, while the top firms in the industry have more to lose if the cartel collapses and have less added market share to gain. In most cartels, it is the small firms that begin pricing at below cartel prices.

Collusion occurs when price- and quantity-fixing agreements are explicit, as in a cartel. **Tacit collusion** occurs when firms end up fixing prices without a specific agreement or when such agreements are implicit. A small number of firms with market power may fall into the practice of setting similar prices or following the lead of one firm without ever meeting or setting down formal agreements. The fewer and more similar the firms, the easier it will be for tacit collusion to occur. As we will see later in this chapter, antitrust laws also play a role in trying to discourage tacit collusion.

tacit collusion Collusion occurs when price- and quantity-fixing agreements among producers are explicit. *Tacit collusion* occurs when such agreements are implicit.

The Price-Leadership Model

price leadership A form of oligopoly in which one dominant firm sets prices and all the smaller firms in the industry follow its pricing policy.

In another form of oligopoly, one firm dominates an industry and all the smaller firms follow the leader's pricing policy—hence its name **price leadership**. If the dominant firm knows that the smaller firms will follow its lead, it will derive its own demand curve by subtracting from total market demand the amount of demand that the smaller firms will satisfy at each potential price.

The price-leadership model is best applied when the industry is made up of one large firm and a number of smaller competitive firms. Under these conditions, we can think of the dominant firm as maximizing profit subject to the constraint of market demand *and* subject to the behavior of the smaller competitive firms. Smaller firms then can essentially sell all they want at this market price. The difference between the quantity demanded in the market and the amount supplied by the smaller firms is the amount that the dominant firm will produce.

Under price leadership, the quantity demanded in the market will be produced by a mix of the smaller firms and the dominant firm. Contrast this situation with that of the monopolist. For a monopolist, the only constraint it faces comes from consumers, who at some price will forgo the good the monopolist produces. In an oligopoly, with a dominant firm practicing price leadership, the existence of the smaller firms (and their willingness to produce output) is also a constraint. For this reason, the output expected under price leadership lies between that of the monopolist and the competitive firm, with prices also set between the two price levels.

The fact that the smaller firms constrain the behavior of the dominant firm suggests that that firm might have an incentive to try to push those smaller firms out of the market by buying up or merging with the smaller firms. We have already seen in the monopoly chapter how moving from many firms to one firm can help a firm increase profits, even as it reduces social welfare. Antitrust rules governing mergers, discussed later in this chapter, reflect the potential social costs of such mergers. An alternative way for a dominant firm to reduce the number of smaller firms in its industry is through aggressive price setting. Rather than accommodate the small firms, as is done in the price-leadership situation, the dominant firm can try cutting prices aggressively until the smaller firms leave. The practice by which a large, powerful firm tries to drive smaller firms out of the market by temporarily selling at an artificially low price is called *predatory pricing*. Such behavior can be very expensive for the larger firm and is often ineffective. Changing prices below average variable costs to push other firms out of an industry in the expectation of later recouping through price increases is also illegal under antitrust laws.

The Cournot Model

A very simple model that illustrates the idea of interdependence among firms in an oligopoly is the Cournot model, introduced in the 19th century by the mathematician Antoine Augustin Cournot. The model is based on Cournot's observations of competition between two producers of spring water. Despite the age of the model and some if its restrictive assumptions, the intuition that emerges from it has proven to be helpful to economists and policy makers.

The original Cournot model focused on an oligopoly with only two firms producing identical products and not colluding. A two-firm oligopoly is known as a **duopoly**. The key feature of an oligopoly, compared to the competitive firm, is that a firm's optimal decisions depend on the actions of the other individual firms in its industry. In a duopoly, the right output choice for each of the two firms will depend on what the other firm does. Cournot provides us with one way to model how firms take each other's behavior into account.

duopoly A two-firm oligopoly.

Return to the monopoly example that we used in the previous chapter in Figure 13.8 on p. 281, reproduced here as Figure 14.2(a). Marginal cost is constant at $2, and the demand curve facing the monopolist firm is the downward-sloping market demand curve. Recall that the marginal revenue curve lies below the demand curve because in order to increase sales the monopoly firm must lower its per-unit price. In this example, the marginal revenue curve hits zero at an output of 3,000 units. In this market, the monopolist maximizes profits at a quantity of 2,000 units and a price of $4 as we saw in the last chapter. What happens in this market if, instead of having one monopoly firm, we have a Cournot duopoly? What does the duopoly equilibrium look like?

In choosing the optimal output, the monopolist had only to consider its own costs and the demand curve that it faced. The duopolist has another factor to consider: how much output will its rival produce? The more the rival produces, the less market is left for the other firm in the duopoly. In the Cournot model, each firm looks at the market demand, subtracts what it expects the rival firm to produce, and chooses its output to maximize its profits based on the market that is left.

Let's illustrate the Cournot duopoly solution to this problem with two firms, Firm A and Firm B. Recall the key feature of the duopoly: Firms must take each other's output into account when choosing their own output. Given this feature, it is helpful to look at how each firm's optimal output might vary with its rival's output. In Figure 14.2(b), we have drawn two *reaction functions*, showing each firm's optimal, profit-maximizing output as it depends on its rival's output. The Y-axis shows levels of Firm A's output, denoted q_A, and the X-axis shows Firm B's output, denoted as q_B.

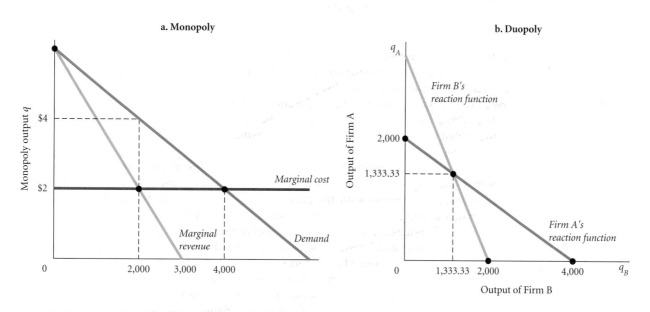

▲ **FIGURE 14.2 Graphical Depiction of the Cournot Model**
The left graph shows a profit-maximizing output of 2,000 units for a monopolist with marginal cost of $2. The right graph shows output of 1,333.33 units *each* for two duopolists with the same marginal cost of $2, facing the same demand curve. Total industry output increases as we go from the monopolist to the Cournot duopolists, but it does not rise as high as the competitive output (here 4,000 units).

Several of the points along Firm A's reaction function should look familiar. Consider the point where Firm A's reaction function crosses the vertical axis. At this point, Firm A's task is to choose the optimal output assuming Firm B produces 0. But we know what this point is from solving the monopoly problem. If Firm B produces nothing, then Firm A is a monopolist and it optimally produces 2,000 units. So *if* Firm A expects Firm B to produce 0, it should produce 2,000 to maximize its profits.

Look at the point at which Firm A's reaction function crosses the horizontal axis. At this point Firm B is producing 4,000 units. Look back at Figure 14.2(a). At an output level of 4,000 units the market price is $2, which is the marginal cost of production. If Firm A expects Firm B to produce 4,000 units, there is no profitable market left for Firm A and it will produce 0. If you start there, where the output of Firm B (measured on the horizontal axis) is 4,000 units each period, and you let Firm B's output fall moving to the left, Firm A will find it in its interest to increase output. If you carefully figure out what Firms A's profit-maximizing output is at every possible level of output for Firm B, you will discover that Firm A's reaction function is just a downward-sloping line between 2,000 on the Y-axis and 4,000 on the X-axis. The downward slope reflects the way in which firm A chooses its output. It looks at the market demand, subtracts its rival's output, and then chooses its own optimal output. The more the rival produces, the less market is profitably left for the other firm in the duopoly.

Next, we do the same thing for Firm B. How much will Firm B produce if it maximizes profit and accepts Firm A's output as given? Since the two firms are exactly alike in costs and type of product, Firm B's reaction function looks just like Firm A's: When Firm B thinks it is alone in the market (Firm A's output on the vertical axis is 0) it produces the monopoly output of 2,000; when Firm B thinks Firm A is going to produce 4,000 units, it chooses to produce 0.

As you can see, the two reaction functions cross. Each firm's reaction function shows what it wants to do, conditional on the other firm's output. At the point of intersection, each firm is doing the best it can, given the actual output of the other firm. This point is sometimes called the *best response equilibrium*. As you can see from the graph, the Cournot duopoly equilibrium to this problem occurs when each firm is producing 1,333.33 units for an industry total of 2,666.66. This output is more than the original monopolist produced in this market, but less than the 4,000 units that a competitive industry would produce.

It turns out that the crossing point is the only equilibrium point in Figure 14.2(b). To see why, consider what happens if you start off with a monopoly and then let a second firm compete. Suppose, for example, Firm A expected Firm B to stay out of the market, to produce nothing, leaving Firm A as a monopolist. With that expectation, Firm A would choose to produce 2,000 units. But now look at Firm B's reaction function. If Firm A is now producing 2,000 units, Firm B's profit-maximizing output is not zero, it is 1,000 units. Draw a horizontal line from Firm A's output level of 2,000 to Firm B's reaction function and then go down to the X-axis and you will discover that Firm B's optimal output lies at 1,000 units. So an output level for Firm A of 2,000 units is not an equilibrium because it was predicated on a production level for Firm B that was incorrect. Going one step further, with Firm B now producing 1,000 units, Firm A will cut back from 2,000. This will in turn lead to a further increase in Firm B's output and the process will go on until both are producing 1,333.33.

As we have seen, the output level predicted by the Cournot model is between that of the monopoly and that of a perfectly competitive industry. Later extensions of the Cournot model tell us that the more firms we have, behaving as Cournot predicted, the closer output (and thus prices) will be to the competitive levels. This type of intuitive result is one reason the Cournot model has been widely used despite its simplified view of firm interaction. The field of game theory, to which we now turn, offers a more sophisticated and complete view of firm interactions.

Game Theory

The firms in Cournot's model do not anticipate the moves of the competition. Instead, they try to guess the output levels of their rivals and then choose optimal outputs of their own. But notice, the firms do not try to anticipate or influence what the rival firms will do in response to their own actions. In many situations, it does not seem realistic for firms to just take their rival's output as independent of their own. We might think that Intel, recognizing how important Advanced Micro Devices (AMD) is in the processor market, would try to influence AMD's business decisions. **Game theory** is a subfield of economics that analyzes the choices made by rival firms, people, and even governments when they are trying to maximize their own well-being while anticipating and reacting to the actions of others in their environment.

Game theory began in 1944 with the work of mathematician John von Neumann and economist Oskar Morgenstern who published path-breaking work in which they analyzed a set of problems, or *games*, in which two or more people or organizations pursue their own interests and in which neither one of them can dictate the outcome. Game theory has become an increasingly popular field of study and research. The notions of game theory have been applied to analyses of firm behavior, politics, international relations, nuclear war, military strategy, and foreign policy. In 1994, the Nobel Prize in Economic Science was awarded jointly to three early game theorists: John F. Nash of Princeton University, John C. Harsanyi of the University of California at Berkeley, and Reinhard Selten of the University of Bonn. You may have seen the movie *A Beautiful Mind* about John Nash and his contribution to game theory.

Game theory begins by recognizing that in all conflict situations, there are decision makers (or players), rules of the game, and payoffs (or prizes). Players choose strategies without knowing with certainty what strategy the opposition will use. At the same time, though, some information that indicates how their opposition may be "leaning" may be available to the players. Most centrally, understanding that the other players are also trying to do their best will be helpful in predicting their actions.

Figure 14.3 illustrates what is called a payoff matrix for a simple game. Each of two firms, A and B, must decide whether to mount an expensive advertising campaign. If each firm decides not to advertise, it will earn a profit of $50,000. If one firm advertises and the other does not, the firm that does will increase its profit by 50 percent (to $75,000) while driving the competition into the loss column. If both firms decide to advertise, they will each earn profits of $10,000. They may generate a bit more demand by advertising, but not enough to offset the expense of the advertising.

If firms A and B could collude (and we assume that they cannot), their optimal strategy would be to agree not to advertise. That solution maximizes the joint profits to both firms. If both firms do not advertise, joint profits are $100,000. If both firms advertise, joint profits are only $20,000. If only one of the firms advertises, joint profits are $75,000 − $25,000 = $50,000.

We see from Figure 14.3 that each firm's *payoff* depends on what the other firm does. In considering what firms should do, however, it is more important to ask whether a firm's *strategy* depends on what the other firm does. Consider A's choice of strategy. Regardless of what B does, it pays A to advertise. If B does not advertise, A makes $25,000 more by advertising than by not advertising. Thus, A will advertise. If B does advertise, A must advertise to avoid a loss. The same logic holds for B. Regardless of the strategy pursued by A, it pays B to advertise. A **dominant strategy** is one that is best no matter what the opposition does. In this game, both players have a dominant strategy, which is to advertise.

> **game theory** Analyzes the choices made by rival firms, people, and even governments when they are trying to maximize their own well-being while anticipating and reacting to the actions of others in their environment.

> **dominant strategy** In game theory, a strategy that is best no matter what the opposition does.

> ◀ **FIGURE 14.3 Payoff Matrix for Advertising Game**
>
> Both players have a dominant strategy. If B does not advertise, A will because $75,000 beats $50,000. If B does advertise, A will also advertise because a profit of $10,000 beats a loss of $25,000. A will advertise regardless of what B does. Similarly, B will advertise regardless of what A does. If A does not advertise, B will because $75,000 beats $50,000. If A does advertise, B will too because a $10,000 profit beats a loss of $25,000.

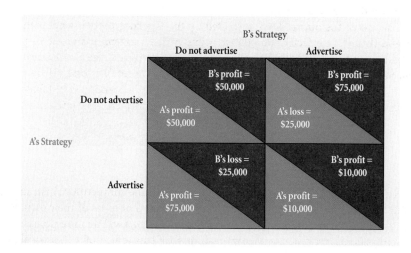

prisoners' dilemma A game in which the players are prevented from cooperating and in which each has a dominant strategy that leaves them both worse off than if they could cooperate.

The result of the game in Figure 14.4 is an example of what is called a **prisoners' dilemma**. The term comes from a game in which two prisoners (call them Ginger and Rocky) are accused of robbing the local 7-Eleven together, but the evidence is shaky. If both confess, they each get 5 years in prison for armed robbery. If each one refuses to confess, they are convicted of a lesser charge, shoplifting, and get 1 year in prison each. The problem is that the district attorney has offered each of them a deal independently. If Ginger confesses and Rocky does not, Ginger goes free and Rocky gets 7 years. If Rocky confesses and Ginger does not, Rocky goes free and Ginger gets 7 years. The payoff matrix for the prisoners' dilemma is given in Figure 14.4.

By looking carefully at the payoffs, you may notice that both Ginger and Rocky have dominant strategies: to confess. That is, Ginger is better off confessing regardless of what Rocky does and Rocky is better off confessing regardless of what Ginger does. The likely outcome is that both will confess even though they would be better off if they both kept their mouths shut. There are many cases in which we see games like this one. In a class that is graded on a curve, all students might consider agreeing to moderate their performance. But incentives to "cheat" by studying would be hard to resist. In an oligopoly, the fact that prices tend to be higher than marginal costs provides incentives for firms to "cheat" on output—restricting agreements by selling additional units.

Is there any way out of this dilemma? There may be, under circumstances in which the game is played over and over. Look back at Figure 14.3. The best joint outcome is not to advertise. But the power of the dominant strategy makes it hard to get to the top-left corner. Suppose firms interact over and over again for many years. Now opportunities for cooperating are richer. Suppose firm A decided not to advertise for one period to see how firm B would respond. If firm B continued to advertise, A would have to resume advertising to survive. Suppose B decided to match A's strategy. In this case, both firms might—with no explicit collusion—end up not advertising after A figures out what B is doing. We return to this in the discussion of repeated games, which follows.

There are many games in which one player does not have a dominant strategy, but in which the outcome is predictable. Consider the game in Figure 14.5(a) in which C does not have a dominant strategy. If D plays the left strategy, C will play the top strategy. If D plays the right strategy, C will play the bottom strategy. What strategy will D choose to play? If C knows the options, it will see that D has a dominant strategy and is likely to play that same strategy. D does better playing the right-hand strategy regardless of what C does. D can guarantee a $100 win by choosing right and is guaranteed to win nothing by playing left. Because D's behavior is predictable (it will play the right-hand strategy), C will play bottom. When all players are playing their best strategy *given* what their competitors are doing, the result is called a **Nash equilibrium**, named after John Nash. We have already seen one example of a Nash equilibrium in the Cournot model.

Nash equilibrium In game theory, the result of all players' playing their best strategy given what their competitors are doing.

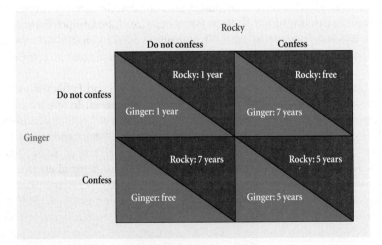

▲ FIGURE 14.4 **The Prisoners' Dilemma**

Both players have a dominant strategy and will confess. If Rocky does *not* confess, Ginger will because going free beats a year in jail. Similarly, if Rocky *does* confess, Ginger will confess because 5 years in the slammer is better than 7. Rocky has the same set of choices. If Ginger does *not* confess, Rocky will because going free beats a year in jail. Similarly, if Ginger *does* confess, Rocky also will confess because 5 years in the slammer is better than 7. Both will confess *regardless* of what the other does.

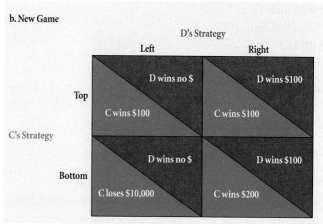

▲ FIGURE 14.5 **Payoff Matrixes for Left/Right–Top/Bottom Strategies**
In the original game (*a*), C does not have a dominant strategy. If D plays left, C plays top; if D plays right, C plays bottom. D, on the other hand, *does* have a dominant strategy: D will play right regardless of what C does. If C believes that D is rational, C will predict that D will play right. If C concludes that D will play right, C will play bottom. The result is a Nash equilibrium because each player is doing the best that it can *given* what the other is doing.
In the new game (*b*), C had better be very sure that D will play right because if D plays left and C plays bottom, C is in big trouble, losing $10,000. C will probably play top to minimize the potential loss if the probability of D's choosing left is at all significant.

Now suppose the game in Figure 14.5(a) were changed. Suppose all the payoffs are the same except that if D chooses left and C chooses bottom, C loses $10,000, as shown in Figure 14.5(b). While D still has a dominant strategy (playing right), C now stands to lose a great deal by choosing bottom on the off chance that D chooses left instead. When uncertainty and risk are introduced, the game changes. C is likely to play top and guarantee itself a $100 profit instead of playing bottom and risk losing $10,000 in the off chance that D plays left. A **maximin strategy** is a strategy chosen by a player to maximize the minimum gain that it can earn. In essence, one who plays a maximin strategy assumes that the opposition will play the strategy that does the most damage.

maximin strategy In game theory, a strategy chosen to maximize the minimum gain that can be earned.

Repeated Games

Clearly, games are not played once. Firms must decide on advertising budgets, investment strategies, and pricing policies continuously. Pepsi and Coca-Cola have competed against each other for 100 years, in countries across the globe. While explicit collusion violates the antitrust statutes, strategic reaction does not. Yet strategic reaction in a repeated game may have the same effect as tacit collusion.

Consider the game in Figure 14.6. Suppose British Airways and Lufthansa were competing for business on the New York to London route during the off-season. To lure travelers, they were offering low fares. The question is how much to lower fares. Both airlines were considering a deep reduction to a fare of $400 round-trip or a moderate one to $600. Suppose costs are such that each $600 ticket produces profit of $400 and each $400 ticket produces profit of $200.

Clearly, demand is sensitive to price. Assume that studies of demand elasticity have determined that if *both* airlines offer tickets for $600, they will attract 6,000 passengers per week (3,000 for each airline) and each airline will make a profit of $1.2 million per week ($400 dollar profit times 3,000 passengers). However, if both airlines offer deeply reduced fares of $400, they will attract 2,000 additional customers per week for a total of 8,000 (4,000 for each airline). While they will have more passengers, each ticket brings in less profit and total profit falls to $800,000 per week ($200 profit times 4,000 passengers). In this example, we can make some inferences about demand elasticity. With a price cut from $600 to $400, revenues fall from $3.6 million (6,000 passengers times $600) to $3.2 million (8,000 passengers times $400). We know from Chapter 5 that if a price cut reduces revenue, we are operating on an *inelastic* portion of the demand curve.

▶ **FIGURE 14.6**

Payoff Matrix for Airline Game

In a single play, both British Airways (BA) and Lufthansa Airlines (LA) have dominant strategies. If LA prices at $600, BA will price at $400 because $1.6 million beats $1.2 million. If, on the other hand, LA prices at $400, BA will again choose to price at $400 because $800,000 beats zero. Similarly, LA will choose to price at $400 regardless of which strategy BA chooses.

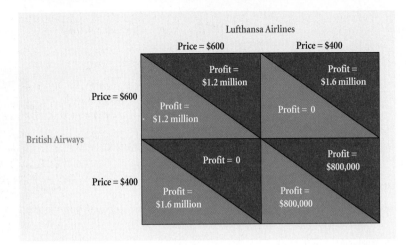

What if the two airlines offer different prices? To keep things simple, we will ignore brand loyalty and assume that whichever airline offers the lowest fare gets all of the 8,000 passengers. If British Airways offers the $400 fare, it will sell 8,000 tickets per week and make $200 profit each, for a total of $1.6 million. Since Lufthansa holds out for $600, it sells no tickets and makes no profit. Similarly, if Lufthansa were to offer tickets for $400, it would make $1.6 million per week while British Airways would make zero.

Looking carefully at the payoff matrix in Figure 14.6, do you conclude that either or both of the airlines have a dominant strategy? In fact, both do. If Lufthansa prices at $600, British Airways will price at the lower fare of $400, because $1.6 million per week is more than $1.2 million. On the other hand, if Lufthansa offers the deep price cut, British Airways must do so as well. If British Airways does not, it will earn nothing, and $800,000 beats nothing! Similarly, Lufthansa has a dominant strategy to offer the $400 fare because it makes more regardless of what British Airways does.

The result is that both airlines will offer the greatly reduced fare and each will make $800,000 per week. This is a classic prisoners' dilemma. If they were permitted to collude on price, they would both charge $600 per ticket and make $1.2 million per week instead—a 50 percent increase.

It was precisely this logic that led American Airlines President Robert Crandall to suggest to Howard Putnam of Braniff Airways in 1983, "I think this is dumb as hell...to sit here and pound the @#%* out of each other and neither one of us making a @#%* dime." ... "I have a suggestion for you, raise your @#%* fares 20 percent. I'll raise mine the next morning."

Since competing firms are prohibited from even talking about prices, Crandall got into trouble with the Justice Department when Putnam turned over a tape of the call in which these comments were made. But could they have colluded without talking to each other? Suppose prices are announced each week at a given time. It is like playing the game in Figure 14.6 a number of times in succession, a repeated game. After a few weeks of making $800,000, British Airways raises its price to $600. Lufthansa knows that if it sits on its $400 fare, it will double its profit from $800,000 to $1.6 million per week. But what is British Airways up to? It must know that its profit will drop to zero unless Lufthansa raises its fare too. The fare increase could just be a signal that both firms would be better off at the higher price and that if one leads and can count on the other to follow, they will both be better off. The strategy to respond in kind to a competitor is called a **tit-for-tat strategy**.

tit-for-tat strategy A repeated game strategy in which a player responds in kind to an opponent's play.

If Lufthansa figures out that British Airways will play the same strategy that Lufthansa is playing, both will end up charging $600 per ticket and earning $1.2 million instead of charging $400 and earning only $800,000 per week even though there has been no explicit price fixing.

 ## A Game with Many Players: Collective Action Can Be Blocked by a Prisoner's Dilemma

Some games have many players and can result in the same kinds of prisoners' dilemmas as we have just discussed. The following game illustrates how coordinated collective action in everybody's interest can be blocked under some circumstances.

Suppose I am your professor in an economics class of 100 students. I ask you to bring $10 to class. In front of the room I place two boxes marked Box A and Box B. I tell you that you must put the sum of $10 split any way you would like in the two boxes. You can put all $10 in Box A and nothing in Box B. You can put all $10 in Box B and nothing in Box A. On the other hand, you can put $2.50 in Box A and $7.50 in Box B. Any combination totaling $10 is all right, and I am the only person who will ever know how you split up your money.

At the end of the class, every dollar put into Box A will be returned to the person who put it in. You get back exactly what you put in. But Box B is special. I will add 20 cents to Box B for every dollar put into it. That is, if there is $100 in the box, I will add $20. But here is the wrinkle: The money that ends up in Box B, *including* my 20 percent contribution, will be divided equally among everyone in the class regardless of the amount that an individual student puts in.

You can think of Box A as representing a private market where we get what we pay for. We pay $10, and we get $10 in value back. Think of Box B as representing something we want to do collectively where the benefits go to all members of the class regardless of whether they have contributed. In Chapter 12, we discussed the concept of a *public good*. People cannot be excluded from enjoying the benefits of a public good once it is produced. Examples include clean air, a lower crime rate from law enforcement, and national defense. You can think of Box B as representing a public good.

Now where do you put your money? If you were smart, you would call a class meeting and get everyone to agree to put his or her entire $10 in Box B. Then everybody would walk out with $12. There would be $1,000 in the box, I would add $200, and the total of $1,200 would be split evenly among the 100 students.

But suppose you were not allowed to get together, in the same way that Ginger and Rocky were kept in separate cells in the jailhouse? Further suppose that everyone acts in his or her best interest. Everyone plays a strategy that maximizes the amount that he or she walks out with. If you think carefully, the dominant strategy for each class member is to put all $10 in Box A. *Regardless of what anyone else does*, you get more if you put all your money into Box A than you would get from any other split of the $10. And if you put all your money into A, no one will walk out of the room with more money than you will!

How can this be? It is simple. Suppose everyone else puts the $10 in B but you put your $10 in A. Box B ends up with $990 plus a 20 percent bonus from me of $198, for a grand total of $1,188, just $12 short of the maximum possible of $1,200. What do you get? Your share of Box B—which is $11.88, *plus* your $10 back, for a total of $21.88. Pretty slimy but clearly optimal for you. If you had put all your money into B, you would get back only $12. You can do the same analysis for cases in which the others split up their income in any way, and the optimal strategy is still to put the whole $10 in Box A.

Here is another way to think about it is: What part of what you ultimately get out is linked to or dependent upon what you put in? For every dollar you put in A, you get a dollar back. For every dollar *you yourself* put in B, you get back only 1 cent, one one-hundredth of a dollar, because your dollar gets split up among all 100 members of the class.

Thus, the game is a classic prisoners' dilemma, where collusion if it could be enforced would result in an optimal outcome but where dominant strategies result in a suboptimal outcome.

How do we break this particular dilemma? We call a town meeting (class meeting) and pass a law that requires us to contribute to the production of public goods by paying taxes. Then, of course, we run the risk that government becomes a player. We will return to this theme in Chapters 16 and 18.

To summarize, oligopoly is a market structure that is consistent with a variety of behaviors. The only necessary condition of oligopoly is that firms are large enough to have some control over price. Oligopolies are concentrated industries. At one extreme is the cartel, in which a few firms get together and jointly maximize profits—in essence, acting as a monopolist. At the other extreme, the firms within the oligopoly vigorously compete for small, contestable markets by moving capital quickly in response to observed profits. In between are a number of alternative models, all of which emphasize the interdependence of oligopolistic firms.

Price Fixing in Digital Music

In 2010 the Second Circuit Court of Appeals decided to reinstate a case from several years ago alleging that the major music labels had colluded to keep the prices of digital downloads higher than they otherwise would be. Earlier cases had found no direct evidence of any price conspiracy. In contrast to some price fixing cases, there was no trail of secret meetings or phone calls, no "smoking gun" as the lawyers often say. Instead, as the following article makes clear, the court relied on economic evidence: the failure of the major record labels to markedly reduce music prices despite the drastic reductions in costs associated with moving from compact discs to digital music.

RIAA Digital Music Price-Fixing Case Reinstated

ZeroPaid.com

It's been an open secret that record labels have long colluded with one another to ensure maximum profits with limited competition and consumer choice. A group of plaintiffs has taken the RIAA to court over the matter, and after initially having to watch the case dismissed at the District Court level back in 2008, has now convinced a three-judge panel at the Second Circuit Court of Appeals to reinstate the case.

One of the major points of evidence of collusion is that the price of digital music is still too similar to physical CDs despite the obviously drastic reduction in price associated with distributing it, something file-sharers have argued all along.

The judges note:

Moreover, the pricing of CDs accounted for costs such as copying the compact discs; producing the CD case, labels and anti-shoplifting packaging; shipping, both to the distributor and then to record stores; labor, such as shelving CDs and staffing cash registers; and damaged and unsold inventory. All of these costs were eliminated with Internet Music. However, these dramatic cost reductions were not accompanied by dramatic price reductions for Internet Music, as would be expected in a competitive market.

In other words, an album that once fetched $15 on store shelves should now cost much less being that the label has much fewer costs to recoup.

Source: Reprinted with permission from Zeropaid, Inc.

Oligopoly and Economic Performance

How well do oligopolies perform? Should they be regulated or changed? Are they efficient, or do they lead to an inefficient use of resources? On balance, are they good or bad?

With the exception of the contestable-markets model, all the models of oligopoly we have examined lead us to conclude that concentration in a market leads to pricing above marginal cost and output below the efficient level. When price is above marginal cost at equilibrium, consumers are paying more for the good than it costs to produce that good in terms of products forgone in other industries. To increase output would be to create value that exceeds the social cost of the good, but profit-maximizing oligopolists have an incentive not to increase output.

Entry barriers in many oligopolistic industries also prevent new capital and other resources from responding to profit signals. Under competitive conditions or in contestable markets, positive profits would attract new firms and thus increase production. This does not happen in most oligopolistic industries. The problem is most severe when entry barriers exist and firms explicitly or tacitly collude. The results of collusion are identical to the results of a monopoly. Firms jointly maximize profits by fixing prices at a high level and splitting up the profits.

On the other hand, it is useful to ask why oligopolies exist in an industry in the first place and what benefits larger firms might bring to a market. When there are economies of scale, larger and fewer firms bring cost efficiencies even as they reduce price competition.

Vigorous product competition among oligopolistic competitors may produce variety and lead to innovation in response to the wide variety of consumer tastes and preferences. The connection between market structure and the rate of innovation is the subject of some debate in research literature.

Industrial Concentration and Technological Change

One of the major sources of economic growth and progress throughout history has been technological advance. Innovation, both in methods of production and in the creation of new and better products, is one of the engines of economic progress. Much innovation starts with R&D efforts undertaken by firms in search of profit.

Several economists, notably Joseph Schumpeter and John Kenneth Galbraith, argued in works now considered classics that industrial concentration, where a relatively small number of firms control the marketplace, actually increases the rate of technological advance. As Schumpeter put it in 1942:

> As soon as we...inquire into the individual items in which progress was most conspicuous, the trail leads not to the doors of those firms that work under conditions of comparatively free competition but precisely to the doors of the large concerns ...and a shocking suspicion dawns upon us that big business may have had more to do with creating that standard of life than keeping it down.[1]

This interpretation caused the economics profession to pause and take stock of its theories. The conventional wisdom had been that concentration and barriers to entry insulate firms from competition and lead to sluggish performance and slow growth.

The evidence concerning where innovation comes from is mixed. Certainly, most small businesses do not engage in R&D and most large firms do. When R&D expenditures are considered as a percentage of sales, firms in industries with high concentration ratios spend more on R&D than firms in industries with low concentration ratios.

Many oligopolistic companies do considerable research. In the opening segment of this chapter, we noted three firms dominated the medical devices market—Johnson & Johnson, Boston Scientific, and Medtronic. Each of these firms spends more than 10 percent of its revenues on R&D. Johnson & Johnson alone spent $8 billion on R&D in 2007. Microsoft spends a similar amount.

However, the "high-tech revolution" grew out of many tiny start-up operations. Companies such as Sun Microsystems, Cisco Systems, and even Microsoft barely existed only a generation ago. The new biotechnology firms that are just beginning to work miracles with genetic engineering are still tiny operations that started with research done by individual scientists in university laboratories.

Significant ambiguity on this subject remains. Indeed, there may be no right answer. Technological change seems to come in fits and starts, sometimes from small firms and sometimes from large ones.

The Role of Government

As we suggested earlier, one way that oligopolies increase the market concentration is through mergers. Not surprisingly, the government has passed laws to control the growth of market power through mergers.

---

[1] J. A. Schumpeter, *Capitalism, Socialism, and Democracy* (New York: Harper, 1942); and J. K. Galbraith, *American Capitalism* (Boston: Houghton Mifflin, 1952).

Regulation of Mergers

Celler-Kefauver Act
Extended the government's authority to control mergers.

The Clayton Act of 1914 (as mentioned in Chapter 13) had given government the authority to limit mergers that might "substantially lessen competition in an industry." The **Celler-Kefauver Act** (1950) enabled the Justice Department to monitor and enforce these provisions. In the early years of the Clayton Act, firms that wanted to merge knew there was a risk of government opposition. Firms could spend large amounts of money on lawyers and negotiation. Firms could spend resources on negotiations only to have the government take the firms to court.

In 1968, the Justice Department issued its first guidelines designed to reduce uncertainty about the mergers it would find acceptable. The 1968 guidelines were strict. For example, if the largest four firms in an industry controlled 75 percent or more of a market, an acquiring firm with a 15 percent market share would be challenged if it wanted to acquire a firm that controlled as little as an additional 1 percent of the market.

**Herfindahl-Hirschman Index
(HHI)** An index of market concentration found by summing the square of percentage shares of firms in the market.

In 1982, the Antitrust Division—in keeping with President Reagan's hands-off policy toward big business—issued a new set of guidelines. Revised in 1984, they remain in place today. The standards are based on a measure of market structure called the **Herfindahl-Hirschman Index (HHI)**. The HHI is calculated by expressing the market share of each firm in the industry as a percentage, squaring these figures, and summing. For example, in an industry in which two firms each control 50 percent of the market, the index is

$$50^2 + 50^2 = 2,500 + 2,500 = 5,000$$

For an industry in which four firms each control 25 percent of the market, the index is

$$25^2 + 25^2 + 25^2 + 25^2 = 625 + 625 + 625 + 625 = 2,500$$

Table 14.2 shows HHI calculations for several hypothetical industries. The Justice Department's courses of action, summarized in Figure 14.7, are as follows: If the Herfindahl-Hirschman Index is less than 1,000, the industry is considered unconcentrated and any proposed merger will go unchallenged by the Justice Department. If the index is between 1,000 and 1,800, the department will challenge any

TABLE 14.2	Calculation of a Simple Herfindahl-Hirschman Index for Four Hypothetical Industries, Each with No More Than Four Firms				
	Percentage Share of:				Herfindahl Hirschman Index
	Firm 1	Firm 2	Firm 3	Firm 4	
Industry A	50	50	–	–	$50^2 + 50^2 = 5,000$
Industry B	80	10	10	–	$80^2 + 10^2 + 10^2 = 6,600$
Industry C	25	25	25	25	$25^2 + 25^2 + 25^2 + 25^2 = 2,500$
Industry D	40	20	20	20	$40^2 + 20^2 + 20^2 + 20^2 = 2,800$

▶ **FIGURE 14.7**

Department of Justice Merger Guidelines (revised 1984)

merger that would increase the index by over 100 points. Herfindahl indexes above 1,800 mean that the industry is considered concentrated already, and the Justice Department will challenge any merger that pushes the index up more than 50 points.

You should be able to see that the HHI combines two features of an industry that we identified as important in our Five Forces discussion: the number of firms in an industry and their relative sizes.

In the previous arithmetic example, we looked at the share of the market controlled by each of several firms. Before we can make these calculations, however, we have to answer another question: How do we define the market? What are we taking a share of? Think back to our discussion of market power in Chapter 13. Coca-Cola has a "monopoly" in the production of Coke but is one of several firms making cola products, one of many more firms making soda in general, and one of hundreds of firms making beverages. Coca-Cola's market power depends on how much substitutability there is among cola products, among sodas in general, and among beverages in general. Before the government can calculate an HHI, it must *define the market*, a task that involves figuring out which products are good substitutes for the products in question.

An interesting example of the difficulty in defining markets and the use of the HHI in merger analysis comes from the 1997 opposition by the FTC to the proposed merger between Staples and Office Depot. At that time, Office Depot and Staples were the number one and number two firms, respectively, in terms of market share in dedicated sales of office supplies. The FTC argued that in sales of office supplies, office superstores such as Office Depot and Staples had a strong advantage in the mind of the consumer. As a result of the one-stop shopping that they offered, it was argued that other stores selling stationery were not good substitutes for the sales of these two stores. So the FTC defined the market over which it intended to calculate the HHI to decide on the merger as the sale of office supplies in office superstores. Practically, this meant that stationery sold in the corner shop or in Wal-Mart was not part of the market, not a substantial constraint on the pricing of Office Depot or Staples. Using this definition, depending on where in the United States one looked, the HHI resulting from the proposed merger was between 5,000 and 10,000, clearly above the threshold. Economists working for Staples, on the other hand, argued that the market should include all sellers of office supplies. By that definition, a merger between Office Depot and Staples would result in a HHI well below the threshold since these two firms together controlled only 5 percent of the total market and the HHI in the overall market was well below 1,000. In the end, the merger was not allowed.

In Table 14.3, we present HHIs for a few different markets. Notice in one case—Las Vegas gaming—that the market has both a product and a geographic component. This definition, which was used by the government in one merger case, assumes that casinos in Las Vegas do not effectively compete with casinos in Atlantic City, for example. Other markets (for example, beer) are national markets. In general, the broader the definition of the market, the lower the HHI.

TABLE 14.3	
Industry Definition	Some Sample HHIs
Beer	3,525
Ethanol	326
Las Vegas gaming	1,497
Critical care patient monitors	2,661

In 1997, the Department of Justice and the FTC issued joint *Horizontal Merger Guidelines*, updating and expanding the 1984 guidelines. The most interesting part of the new provisions is that the government examines each potential merger to determine whether it enhances the firms' power to engage in "coordinated interaction" with other firms in the industry. The guidelines define "coordinated interaction" as

actions by a group of firms that are profitable for each of them only as the result of the accommodating reactions of others. This behavior includes tacit or express collusion, and may or may not be lawful in and of itself. [2]

---

[2] U.S. Department of Justice, Federal Trade Commission, *Horizontal Merger Guidelines*, 2005.

A Proper Role?

Certainly, there is much to guard against in the behavior of large, concentrated industries. Barriers to entry, large size, and product differentiation all lead to market power and to potential inefficiency. Barriers to entry and collusive behavior stop the market from working toward an efficient allocation of resources.

For several reasons, however, economists no longer attack industry concentration with the same fervor they once did. First, even firms in highly concentrated industries can be pushed to produce efficiently under certain market circumstances. Second, the benefits of product differentiation and product competition are real. After all, a constant stream of new products and new variations of old products comes to the market almost daily. Third, the effects of concentration on the rate of R&D spending are, at worst, mixed. It is true that large firms do a substantial amount of the total research in the United States. Finally, in some industries, substantial economies of scale simply preclude a completely competitive structure.

In addition to the debate over the desirability of industrial concentration, there is a never-ending debate concerning the role of government in regulating markets. One view is that high levels of concentration lead to inefficiency and that government should act to improve the allocation of resources—to help the market work more efficiently. This logic has been used to justify the laws and other regulations aimed at moderating noncompetitive behavior.

An opposing view holds that the clearest examples of effective barriers to entry are those created by government. This view holds that government regulation in past years has been ultimately anticompetitive and has made the allocation of resources less efficient than it would have been with no government involvement. Recall from Chapter 13 that those who earn positive profits have an incentive to spend resources to protect themselves and their profits from competitors. This *rent-seeking* behavior may include using the power of government.

Complicating the debate further is international competition. Increasingly, firms are faced with competition from foreign firms in domestic markets at the same time they are competing with other multinational firms for a share of foreign markets. We live in a truly global economy today. Thus, firms that dominate a domestic market may be fierce competitors in the international arena. This has implications for the proper role of government. Some contend that instead of breaking up AT&T, the government should have allowed it to be a bigger, stronger international competitor. We will return to this debate in a later chapter.

SUMMARY

MARKET STRUCTURE IN AN OLIGOPOLY *p. 294*

1. An *oligopoly* is an industry dominated by a few firms that, by virtue of their individual sizes, are large enough to influence market price. The behavior of a single oligopolistic firm depends on the reactions it expects of all the other firms in the industry. Industrial strategies usually are very complicated and difficult to generalize about.

2. The Five Forces model is a helpful way to organize economic knowledge about the structure of oligopolistic industries. By gathering data on an industry's structure in terms of the existing rivals, new entrants, substitutes, and buyer and supplier characteristics, we can better understand the sources of excess profits in an industry.

OLIGOPOLY MODELS *p. 297*

3. When firms collude, either explicitly or tacitly, they jointly maximize profits by charging an agreed-to price or by setting output limits and splitting profits. The result is the same as it would be if one firm monopolized the industry: The firm will produce up to the point at which $MR = MC$, and price will be set above marginal cost.

4. The *price-leadership* model of oligopoly leads to a result similar but not identical to the collusion model. In this organization, the dominant firm in the industry sets a price and allows competing firms to supply all they want at that price. An oligopoly with a dominant price leader will produce a level of output between what would prevail under competition and what a monopolist would choose in the same industry. An oligopoly will also set a price between the monopoly price and the competitive price.

5. The *Cournot model* of oligopoly is based on three assumptions: (1) that there are few firms in an industry, (2) that each firm takes the output of the other as a given, and (3) that firms maximize profits. The model holds that a series of output-adjustment decisions leads to a final level of output between that which would prevail under perfect competition and that which would be set by a monopoly.

GAME THEORY *p. 300*

6. *Game theory* analyzes the behavior of firms as if their behavior were a series of strategic moves and counter-moves. It helps us understand the problem of oligopoly

but leaves us with an incomplete and inconclusive set of propositions about the likely behavior of individual oligopolistic firms.

OLIGOPOLY AND ECONOMIC PERFORMANCE *p. 306*

7. Concentration in markets often leads to price above marginal cost and output below the efficient level. Market concentration, however, can also lead to gains from economies of scale and may promote innovation.

THE ROLE OF GOVERNMENT *p. 307*

8. The *Clayton Act* of 1914 (see Chapter 13) gave the government the authority to limit mergers that might "substantially lessen competition in an industry." The *Celler-Kefauver Act* (1950) enabled the Justice Department to move against a proposed merger. Currently, the Justice Department uses the *Herfindahl-Hirschman Index* to determine whether it will challenge a proposed merger.

9. Some argue that the regulation of mergers is no longer a proper role for government.

REVIEW TERMS AND CONCEPTS

PROBLEMS

All problems are available on www.myeconlab.com

1. Which of the following industries would you classify as an oligopoly? Which would you classify as monopolistically competitive? Explain your answer. If you are not sure, what information do you need to know to decide?
   a. Athletic shoes
   b. Restaurants
   c. Watches
   d. Aircraft
   e. Ice cream

2. [Related to the *Economics in Practice* on p. 296] In the last decade, many movie theaters have closed and others have seen a fall in yearly revenues. Use the Five Forces apparatus to analyze why this might have occurred.

3. Which of the following markets are likely to be perfectly contestable? Explain your answers.
   a. Shipbuilding
   b. Trucking
   c. Housecleaning services
   d. Wine production

4. Assume that you are in the business of building houses. You have analyzed the market carefully, and you know that at a price of $120,000, you will sell 800 houses per year. In addition, you know that at any price above $120,000, no one will buy your houses because the government provides equal-quality houses to anyone who wants one at $120,000. You also know that for every $20,000 you lower your price, you will be able to sell an additional 200 units. For example, at a price of $100,000, you can sell 1,000 houses; at a price of $80,000, you can sell 1,200 houses; and so on.
   a. Sketch the demand curve that your firm faces.

   b. Sketch the effective marginal revenue curve that your firm faces.
   c. If the marginal cost of building a house is $100,000, how many will you build and what price will you charge? What if *MC* = $85,000?

5. The matrix in Figure 1 on the following page shows payoffs based on the strategies chosen by two firms. If they collude and hold prices at $10, each firm will earn profits of $5 million. If A cheats on the agreement, lowering its price, but B does not, A will get 75 percent of the business and earn profits of $8 million and B will lose $2 million. Similarly, if B cheats and A does not, B will earn $8 million and A will lose $2 million. If both firms cut prices, they will end up with $2 million each in profits.

   Which strategy minimizes the maximum potential loss for A and for B? If you were A, which strategy would you choose? Why? If A cheats, what will B do? If B cheats, will A do? What is the most likely outcome of such a game? Explain.

6. The payoff matrixes in Figure 2 on the following page show the payoffs for two games. The payoffs are given in parentheses. The figure on the left refers to the payoff to A; the figure on the right refers to the payoff to B. Hence, (2, 25) means a $2 payoff to A and a $25 payoff to B.
   a. Is there a dominant strategy in each game for each player?
   b. If game 1 were repeated a large number of times and you were A and you could change your strategy, what might you do?
   c. Which strategy would you play in game 2? Why?

7. Between 2008 and 2010, dozens of lawsuits were brought or reinstated against U.S. firms for conspiracy to fix prices of things as diverse as pharmaceuticals, baby products, digital music, and eggs. Choose one of these lawsuits or cases and

describe the economic and legal issues. What are the details of the case? What law was allegedly violated? How was the case settled? Was justice done? Explain your answer.

8. Suppose we have an industry with two firms producing the same product. Firm A produces 90 units, while firm B produces 10 units. The price in the market is $100, and both firms have marginal costs of production of $50. What incentives do the two firms have to lower prices as a way of trying to get consumers to switch the firm they buy from? Which firm is more likely to lower its price?

9. For each of the following, state whether you agree or disagree. Explain your reasoning.
   a. Oligopolies are always bad for society.
   b. The beer industry has a few large firms and many small firms. Therefore, we would not call it an oligopoly.

10. The following table represents the market share percentage for each firm in a hypothetical industry.

Firm	A	B	C	D	E	F	G
Market Share	12	8	20	25	4	25	6

   a. Calculate the four-firm concentration ratio for this industry.
   b. Calculate the Herfindahl-Hirschman Index (HHI) for this industry.
   c. Would the Justice Department consider this industry as unconcentrated, moderately concentrated, or concentrated? Why?

d. Suppose firms E and G wanted to merge. What would be the value of the HHI following this merger? Would the Justice Department most likely challenge this merger? Why or why not?

11. Bernie and Leona were arrested for money laundering and were interrogated separately by the police. Bernie and Leona were each presented with the following independent offers. If one confesses and the other doesn't, the one who confesses will go free and the other will receive a 20-year prison sentence; if both confess, each will receive a 10-year prison sentence. Bernie and Leona both know that without any confessions, the police only have enough evidence to convict them of the lesser crime of tax evasion, and each would then receive a 2-year prison sentence.
   a. Use the above information to construct a payoff matrix for Bernie and Leona.
   b. What is the dominant strategy for Bernie and for Leona? Why?
   c. Based on your response to the previous question, what prison sentence will each receive?

12. Explain whether you agree or disagree with the following statement. If all firms in an industry successfully engage in collusion, the resulting profit-maximizing price and output would be the same as if the industry was a monopoly.

13. What is the *Cournot* model? How does the output decision in the *Cournot* model differ from the output decision in a monopoly?

▲ FIGURE 1

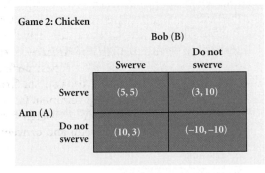

▲ FIGURE 2

Monopolistic Competition

We come now to our last broad type of market structure: *monopolistic competition*. Like perfect competition, a monopolistically competitive industry is an industry in which entry is easy and many firms are the norm. In contrast to the perfectly competitive firm, however, firms in this industry type do not produce homogeneous goods. Rather, each firm produces a slightly different version of a product. These product differences give rise to some market power. In the monopolistically competitive industry, a firm can charge a higher price than a competitor and not lose all of its customers. We will spend some time in this chapter looking at pricing in these industries.

But pricing is only one part of the story in these industries. When we look at firms in an industry characterized by monopolistic competition, we naturally focus on how firms make decisions about what kinds of products to sell and how to market and advertise them. Why do we see a dozen different types of shampoo in a store? Is a dozen too many, too few, or just the right amount? Why are beverages and automobiles advertised a great deal but semiconductors and economics textbooks are not? Advertising is expensive: Is it a waste of money, or does it serve some social function? In this chapter, we will also explore briefly some ideas from *behavioral economics*. Can consumers ever be offered too many choices? Why does nutritional cereal sell better in the extra large size while candy sells better by the bar?

By the end of this chapter, we will have covered the four basic types of market structure. Figure 15.1 summarizes the four types: perfect competition, monopoly, oligopoly, and monopolistic competition. The behavior of firms in an industry, the key decisions facing firms, and the key policy issues government faces in dealing with those firms differ depending on the market structure we are in. Although not every industry fits neatly into one of these categories, they do provide a useful and convenient framework for thinking about industry structure and behavior.

	Number of firms	Products differentiated or homogeneous	Price a decision variable	Easy entry	Distinguished by	Examples
Perfect competition	Many	Homogeneous	No	Yes	Market sets price	Wheat farmer Textile firm
Monopoly	One	One version or many versions of a product	Yes	No	Still constrained by market demand	Public utility Patented drug
Monopolistic competition	Many	Differentiated	Yes, but limited	Yes	Price and quality competition	Restaurants Hand soap
Oligopoly	Few	Either	Yes	Limited	Strategic behavior	Automobiles Aluminum

▲ **FIGURE 15.1** **Characteristics of Different Market Organizations**

Industry Characteristics

monopolistic competition
A common form of industry (market) structure in the United States, characterized by a large number of firms, no barriers to entry, and product differentiation.

A **monopolistically competitive industry** has the following characteristics:

1. A large number of firms
2. No barriers to entry
3. Product differentiation

While pure monopoly and perfect competition are rare, monopolistic competition is common in the United States, for example, in the restaurant business. In a Yahoo search of San Francisco restaurants, there are 8,083 listed in the area. Each produces a slightly different product and attempts to distinguish itself in consumers' minds. Entry to the market is not blocked. At one location near Union Square in San Francisco, five different restaurants opened and went out of business in 5 years. Although many restaurants fail, small ones can compete and survive because there are few economies of scale in the restaurant business.

The feature that distinguishes monopolistic competition from monopoly and oligopoly is that firms that are monopolistic competitors cannot influence market price by virtue of their size. No one restaurant is big enough to affect the market price of a prime rib dinner even though all restaurants can control their *own* prices. Instead, firms gain control over price in monopolistic competition by *differentiating* their products. You make it in the restaurant business by producing a product that people want that others are not producing or by establishing a reputation for good food and good service. By producing a unique product or establishing a particular reputation, a firm becomes, in a sense, a "monopolist"—that is, no one else can produce the exact same good.

The feature that distinguishes monopolistic competition from pure monopoly is that good substitutes are available in a monopolistically competitive industry. With 8,083 restaurants in the San Francisco area, there are dozens of good Italian, Chinese, and French restaurants. San Francisco's Chinatown, for example, has about 50 small Chinese restaurants, with over a dozen packed on a single street. The menus are nearly identical, and they all charge virtually the same prices. At the other end of the spectrum are restaurants, with established names and prices far above the cost of production, that are always booked. That is the goal of every restaurateur who ever put a stockpot on the range.

Table 15.1 presents some data on nine national manufacturing industries that have the characteristics of monopolistic competition. Each of these industries includes hundreds of individual firms, some larger than others, but all small relative to the industry. The top four firms in book printing, for example, account for 33 percent of total shipments. The top 20 firms account for 68 percent of the market, while the market's remaining 41 percent is split among almost 540 separate firms.

Firms in a monopolistically competitive industry are small relative to the total market. New firms can enter the industry in pursuit of profit, and relatively good substitutes for the firms' products are available. Firms in monopolistically competitive industries try to achieve a degree of market power by differentiating their products—by producing something new, different, or better or by creating a unique identity in the minds of consumers. To discuss the behavior of such firms, we begin with product differentiation and advertising.

TABLE 15.1 Percentage of Value of Shipments Accounted for by the Largest Firms in Selected Industries, 2002			
Industry Designation	Four Largest Firms	Eight Largest Firms	Twenty Largest Firms	Number of Firms
Travel trailers and campers	38	45	58	733
Games, toys	39	48	63	732
Wood office furniture	34	43	56	546
Book printing	33	54	68	560
Curtains and draperies	17	25	38	1,778
Fresh or frozen seafood	14	24	48	529
Women's dresses	18	23	48	528
Miscellaneous plastic products	6	10	18	6,775

Source: U.S. Department of Commerce, Bureau of the Census, 2002 Census of Manufacturers, *Concentration Ratios in Manufacturing.* Subject Ec02 315R, May 2006.

Product Differentiation and Advertising

Monopolistically competitive firms achieve whatever degree of market power they command through **product differentiation**. But what determines how much differentiation we see in a market and what form it takes?

product differentiation A strategy that firms use to achieve market power. Accomplished by producing products that have distinct positive identities in consumers' minds.

 ## How Many Varieties?

As you look around your neighborhood, notice the sidewalks that connect individual homes with the common outside walk. In some areas, you will see an occasional brick or cobblestone walk, but in most places in the United States, these sidewalks are made of concrete. In almost every case, that concrete is gray. Now look at the houses that these sidewalks lead up to. Except in developments with tight controls, house colors vary across the palette. Why do we have one variety of concrete sidewalk while we have multiple varieties of house colors?

Whenever we see limited varieties of a product, a first thought might be that all consumers—here homeowners—have similar preferences. Perhaps everyone has a natural affection for gray, at least in concrete. The wide variety in the colors of the houses that these sidewalks lead up to might make you skeptical of this explanation, but it is possible. Another possible explanation for the common gray sidewalks might be a desire for coordination: Maybe everyone wants his or her sidewalk to look like the neighbor's, and the fact that the sidewalk connecting the houses—often provided by the city—is gray serves to make gray a focal point. In fashion, for example, coordination and conformity play an enormous role. There is no inherent reason that oversized jeans should be more or less attractive than narrow-cut, low-rise jeans except that they are made so at certain times by the fact that many people are wearing them. Again, you might wonder why conformity is important in sidewalk color but not in house color, something even more visible to the neighbors.

In explaining the narrow variety of concrete sidewalks, a better explanation may come from a review of the material we covered in Chapter 8 when we looked at cost structures. As you know, concrete is made in large mixer trucks. The average capacity of these trucks is 9 or more cubic yards, well more than you would need for a sidewalk. An obvious way to color this concrete is to mix a coloring agent in the mixer truck along with the cement and other ingredients. When done this way, however, we need to find several neighbors who want the same color cement that we want at the same time—concrete is not storable. Even doing it this way is potentially problematic because the inside of the mixer unit can be affected, leaving a residue of our purple concrete, for example, for the next customer. Alternatively, we could add dye after the concrete comes out of the truck, which is done in some places, but the resulting colors are limited, and the process is expensive. So the lack of variety in concrete and not in houses may reflect the scale economies in homogeneous production of concrete not found in house painting.

The example of the sidewalks versus the houses helps explain the wide variety in some product areas and the narrowness in others. In some cases, consumers may have very *different tastes.* It should be no surprise that immigration brings with it an increase in the variety of restaurant types in an area and in the food offerings at the local grocery store. Immigration typically increases the heterogeneity of consumer tastes. Product variety is narrower when there are gains to coordination. In Chapter 13, we described products in which there are network externalities. Here *coordination needs* can dramatically narrow product choice. For example, it will be more important to most people to use the same word-processing program their friends use than to use one that suits them perfectly. Finally, scale economies that make producing different varieties more expensive than a single type can reduce variety. People prefer a relatively inexpensive standardized good over a more expensive custom product that perfectly suits them. The development of the Levitt house in the postwar period in Pennsylvania and New York was a testament to the cost savings in housing that came from standardization, creating uniform tract houses for affordable prices.

In sum, in well-working markets, the level of product variety reflects the underlying heterogeneity of consumers' tastes in that market, the gains if any from coordination, and cost economies from standardization. In industries that are monopolistically competitive, differences in consumer tastes, lack of need for coordination, and modest or no scale economies from standardization give rise to a large number of firms, each of which has a different product. Even within this industry structure, however, these same forces play a role in driving levels of variety.

In recent years, quite a few people have taken up the sport of running. The market has responded in a big way. Now there are numerous running magazines; hundreds of orthotic shoes designed specifically for runners with particular running styles; running suits of every color, cloth, and style; weights for the hands, ankles, and shoelaces; tiny radios to slip into sweatbands; and so on. Even physicians have differentiated their products: Sports medicine clinics have diets for runners, therapies for runners, and doctors specializing in shin splints or Morton's toe.

Why has this increase in variety in the running market taken place? More runners—each with a different body, running style, and sense of aesthetics—increase consumer heterogeneity. The increased market size also tells us that if you produce a specialized running product, it is more likely you will sell enough to cover whatever fixed costs you had in developing the product. So market size allows for more variety. New York has a wider range of ethnic restaurants than does Eden Prairie, Minnesota, not only because of the difference in the heterogeneity of the populations but also because of the sheer size of the two markets.

How Do Firms Differentiate Products?

We have learned that differentiation occurs in response to demands by consumers for products that meet their individual needs and tastes, constrained by the forces of costs of coordination and scale economies. We can go one step further and characterize the kinds of differentiation we see in markets.

Return to the restaurant example we brought up earlier. Of the 8,083 restaurants in San Francisco, some are French, some are Chinese, and some are Italian. Economists would call this form of differentiation across the restaurants **horizontal differentiation**. Horizontal differentiation is a product difference that improves the product for some people but makes it worse for others. If we were to poll San Francisco residents, asking for the best restaurant in town, we would undoubtedly get candidates from a number of different categories. Indeed, many people might not even consider this to be a legitimate question.

horizontal differentiation
Products differ in ways that make them better for some people and worse for others.

If you add sea salt and vinegar to potato chips, that makes them more attractive to some people and less attractive to others. Horizontal differentiation creates variety to reflect differences in consumers' tastes in the market.

For some products, people choose a type and continue with it for a long time. For many of us, breakfast cereals have this feature. Day after day we eat Cheerios or corn flakes. Brand preference for mayonnaise has the same stability. For dinner, however, most of us are *variety-seeking*. Even small cities can support some variety in restaurant types because people get tired of eating at the same place every week.

People who visit planned economies often comment on the lack of variety. Before the Berlin Wall came down in 1989 and East and West Germany were reunited in 1990, those who were allowed passed from colorful and exciting West Berlin into dull and gray East Berlin; variety seemed to vanish. As the wall came down, thousands of Germans from the East descended on the department stores of the West. Visitors to China since the economic reforms of the mid-1980s claim that the biggest visible sign of change is the increase in the selection of products available to the population.

Recent work in the area of *behavioral economics* suggests, however, that there may be times in which too much variety is a bad thing.[2] **Behavioral economics** is a branch of economics that uses the insight of psychology and economics to investigate decision making.

Researchers set up an experiment in an upscale grocery, Draeger's, located in Menlo Park, California. Draeger's is known for its large selection, carrying, for example, 250 varieties of mustard. A tasting booth was set up in the store on two consecutive Saturdays. On one day, consumers were offered one of six exotic jams to taste, while on the other day, 24 varieties were offered. The results of the experiment were striking. While more customers approached the 24-jam booth for a taste than approached the booth with a limited selection, almost none of the tasters at the 24-jam booth bought anything; in contrast, almost 30 percent of tasters at the six-jam booth made a purchase.[3] The researchers conclude that while some choice is highly valued by people, too much choice can reduce purchases.

The jam experiment offers a case in which individuals react to a wide range of choices by not making a choice at all. Behavioral economists also note that when the number of choices is large, individuals may avoid the decision-making burden by using a rule of thumb or by reverting to the default option. In the area of retirement savings, for example, some studies have found a tendency for people to allocate savings evenly across a range of investment options without paying much attention to the earnings characteristics of those funds. In other cases, people appear to favor whatever option is the default designated by the government body or by the firm offering the plan. For this reason, some economists have argued that one way to increase consumer savings (if that is desirable) is to make participation rather than no participation the default in pension plans. In this way, individuals would be enrolled in a retirement plan unless they chose not to be. These plans are called opt-out plans rather than opt-in plans.

Behavioral economics also has something to say about another form of horizontal differentiation—package size and pricing form.[4] Many consumer goods come in small, large, and extra large packages. Many goods (for example, health club visits and magazines) can be bought per visit or issue or via membership or subscription. Many of us think of these differences as matters of convenience. Firms can use these differences to create products targeted at consumer types. Small households buy small boxes of cereals, and large families purchase extra large sizes. Occasional readers buy *Us Weekly* on the newsstand, and fans subscribe to the magazine. Clearly, these kinds of differences play a role. But behavioral economists have also suggested that some of these differences survive in the market because some consumers are interested in trying to control their purchasing behavior. People buy small containers of ice cream but large bottles of vitamins. Why? Because they want to *commit* themselves to taking a vitamin every day but only occasionally eating ice cream. People buy memberships to health clubs as an incentive to work out; they make the marginal cost of a visit zero even though in the end, they may pay more than they would have by paying a per-visit fee. We subscribe to *The Economist* but buy *Us Weekly* on the newsstand at high per-issue prices in the hopes that we will read more of *The Economist* and less of *Us Weekly*. Some students choose classes that reward attendance as a way of ensuring that they go to class. Firms can be creative about using product differentiation to offer consumers commitment devices that help them control their own impulses. A **commitment device** is an action taken by an individual now to try to control his or her behavior in the future.

Behavioral economics is an exciting new field that is challenging and deepening our understanding of a number of areas of economics. New ideas from behavioral economics have entered both microeconomics and macroeconomics.

behavioral economics
A branch of economics that uses the insights of psychology and economics to investigate decision making.

commitment device Actions that individuals take in one period to try to control their behavior in a future period.

---

[2] The classic paper that describes the study reported here is I. Yengar and L. Epper, "When Choice Is Demotivating: Can One Desire Too Much of a Good Thing?" *Journal of Personality and Social Psychology*, 2000, 995–1006.

[3] The subsample of six brands was carefully selected to be neither the best nor the worst of the flavors, and to actually buy, consumers had to go to a shelf that contained all the varieties of jam.

[4] Papers described in this paragraph include Klaus W. Ertenbroch, "Self-Rationing: Self-Control in Consumer Choice," INSEAD Working Paper, 2001, on the package size topic; Ulrike Malmendier and Stefano Della Vigna, "Paying Not to Go to the Gym," *AER*, June 2006, 694–719, on health club memberships; and Sharon Oster and Fiona Scott Morton, "Behavioral Biases Meet the Market," *BEPress Journal of Economic Advance and Policy*, 2005, on magazines.

ECONOMICS IN PRACTICE

An Economist Makes Tea

You have probably seen Honest Tea, a slightly sweetened bottled iced tea made from green, black, and herbal blends in your local grocery store. It is probably not the only iced tea on the shelf. In addition to the popular brands Lipton and Snapple, you may also see SoBe, Tazo, and Turkey Hill, depending on where you live. Bottled iced tea is a classic example of a monopolistically competitive market. None of the brands are exactly alike. Honest Tea, for example, prides itself on being made with high-end tea leaves and only a hint of sweetener, while Snapple uses lower-quality leaves and a hefty dose of sweetener. Nor are the teas priced the same. In a typical store, the retail price of Honest Tea and SoBe are likely to be about $1.89, while Snapple would likely cost about $1.39. If you spend time in the beverage aisle of a grocery store, you will notice that despite the higher price of Honest Tea, some consumers choose it over the alternatives.

What you may not know about Honest Tea is that it was started a decade ago by Seth Goldman, an entrepreneur, and Barry Nalebuff, an economist. In figuring out how to differentiate his tea from others in the industry, Nalebuff used some of the economic theory that we covered in Chapter 6 of this book. Look at the following graph, which shows the placement of one of Honest Tea's most popular flavors, Green Dragon. The graph shows how taste varies with sugar for Goldman and Nalebuff's potential customers. Tea taste improves for the first few grams of sugar, but shortly begins to flatten out and then fall. Note that Green Dragon is somewhat to the left of the taste peak. Some economists looking at this graph criticized Nalebuff for choosing too little sugar content for his tea. What were the critics thinking, and why were they wrong?

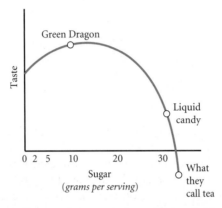

The critics clearly noticed that Green Dragon is not at the peak of the taste curve. That is, a little more sugar would improve the taste of the tea. Why did Nalebuff stop short of that point? This is product differentiation at its best. Goldman and Nalebuff are out to produce a new product that will attract demand. That is, at a reasonable price they must attract consumers away from other products. Goldman and Nalebuff discovered that sugar beyond some point adds little taste, yet comes at a health cost—more calories. Given consumers' new awareness of healthy and natural foods, Honest Tea became an overnight success. Since Nalebuff is an economist, he couldn't resist a graph on the label of the tea bottles.

vertical differentiation A product difference that, from everyone's perspective, makes a product better than rival products.

Products can be differentiated not only horizontally but also **vertically**. A new BMW with GPS is better than one without for almost everyone. A hard drive with more capacity is better than one with less. The Hilton is better than a Motel 6 if they are located in the same place. How can a product survive in a competitive marketplace when another better product is available? The answer, of course, is in the price. The better products cost more, and only some people find it worthwhile to pay the higher price to get a better product. So differences among people also give rise to vertical differentiation. Some people value quality in a specific product more than others do and are willing to pay for that quality. If you are on a special date, it might be worthwhile to go to the best restaurant in town. On the other hand, while at a casual dinner with friends, watching your budget might be more important.

We have described the forces that help determine how much differentiation we will see in a market and the major forms that differentiation can take. We turn now to advertising, which plays a special role in the area of monopolistic competition.

Advertising

Advertising fits into the differentiation story in two different ways. One role advertising plays is to inform people about the real differences that exist among products. Advertising can also *create* or contribute to product differentiation, creating a brand image for a product that has little to do with its physical characteristics. We can all think of examples of each type.

Recent Coca-Cola ads trumpeting the "Coke Side of Life" have little to do with Coke's taste, for example. The dancers in iPod's ads create an image of hip and happy people rather than describe the technical features of the device. On the other hand, the advertising circulars in local newspapers carry specific information about what products are on sale that week in the local grocery store.

In 2006, firms spent about $250 billion on advertising, as Table 15.2 shows. Advertising reaches us through every medium of communication. Table 15.3 shows national advertising expenditures by major industrial category. The automobile industry leads the pack with expenditures of nearly $20 billion advertising in 2006. In 2008, 30 seconds of prime commercial advertising time during Super Bowl XLII cost $2.7 million.

TABLE 15.2	Total Advertising Expenditures in 2006
	Billions of Dollars
Newspapers	$49.0
Television	66.8
Direct mail	59.6
Yellow pages	14.4
Internet	15.0
Radio	19.1
Magazines	24.0
Total	247.9

Source: www.plunkettresearch.com

Many observers believe that the Internet is rapidly changing the way advertising works. Traditionally, companies have targeted their advertisements in both print and media. Beer commercials are shown during televised sporting events, toy commercials air during children's programs, and so on. The Internet has dramatically improved the ability of advertising to target a specific market. Consider advertising on Google. Under Google's AdWords system, which is a click-and-pay system, advertisers pay only when a Web surfer clicks

TABLE 15.3	Domestic Advertising Spending by Category in 2006 in Billions of Dollars	
Rank	Category	2006
1	Automotive	$19.8
2	Retail	19.1
3	Telecommunications	11.0
4	Medicine and Remedies	9.2
5	General services	8.7
6	Financial services	8.7
7	Food, beverages, and candy	7.2
8	Personal care	5.7
9	Airlines, hotels, car rental, travel	5.4
10	Movies, recorded video, and music	5.4
11	Restaurants	5.3
12	Media	5.1
13	Government, politics, religion	3.5
14	Insurance	3.5
15	Real estate	3.1
16	Apparel	2.9
17	Computers, software	2.5
18	Home furnishings	2.2
19	Beer, wine, and liquor	2.1
20	Education	1.9

Source: TNS Media Intelligence.

to their site. In this way, advertisers are sure that people who see their advertisements are interested in the product. In 2006, Google earned over $6 billion from this form of targeted advertising.

YouTube, another new entrant into the advertising business, offers firms the opportunity to actively interact with customers. In addition to the standard video ads, firms can create online contests and brand channels to learn from customers about their preferences. Advertising as information has become more of a transparent two-way street as a result of the Internet.

The effects of product differentiation in general (and advertising in particular) on the allocation of resources have been hotly debated for years. Advocates claim that these forces give the market system its vitality and power. Critics argue that they cause waste and inefficiency. Before we proceed to the models of monopolistic competition and oligopoly, let us look at this debate.

The Case for Advertising   For product differentiation to be successful, consumers must know about product quality and availability. In perfect competition, where all products are alike, we assume that consumers have perfect information; without it, the market fails to produce an efficient allocation of resources. Complete information is even more important when we allow for product differentiation. Consumers get this information through advertising, at least in part. The basic function of advertising, according to its proponents, is to assist consumers in making informed, rational choices. When we think of advertising, many of us think of the persuasive ads shown on television geared to changing our image of a product. Over the years, Budweiser has developed a reputation for clever ads of this sort, especially those delivered during the Super Bowl. But much advertising is entirely informational. In most parts of the country, one day a week the newspaper grows in size. On this day, stores advertise and promote their food sales. For many newspapers, advertisements are a big source of revenue; and it is all informational, helping consumers figure out where to buy their orange juice and chicken, for example. During the holiday season, toy advertising, both in print and on television, increases dramatically. For toys, which have a high rate of new product introduction, publicizing them is very important.

Supporters of advertising also note that it can promote competition. New products can compete with old, established brands only when promoters can get their messages through to consumers. The standard of living rises when we have product *innovation*, when new and better products come on the market. Think of all the products today that did not exist 20 years ago: iPods, video games like Guitar Hero, and hybrid cars, to name a few. When consumers are informed about a wide variety of potential substitutes, their market choices help discipline older firms that may have lost touch with consumers' tastes.

Even advertising that seems to function mostly to create and reinforce a brand image can have efficiency effects. Creating a brand name such as Coca-Cola or Tide requires a huge investment in marketing and advertising. The stronger the brand name and the more a firm has invested in creating that name, the more the firm will invest in trying to protect that name. In many cases, those investments provide benefits for consumers. In reacting to the 2007 news about lead in children's toys made in China, large toy companies such as Hasbro and Mattel spent millions in new testing of those toys. Restoring parental trust in the face of the toy recalls is vital to the future of the firms.

Differentiated products and advertising give the market system its vitality and are the basis of its power. Product differentiation helps to ensure high quality and variety, and advertising provides consumers with valuable information on product availability, quality, and price that they need to make efficient choices in the marketplace.

The Case Against Product Differentiation and Advertising   Product differentiation and advertising waste society's scarce resources, argue critics. They say enormous sums of money are spent to create minute, meaningless differences among products.

ECONOMICS IN PRACTICE

Can Information Reduce Obesity?

Policy makers have been working to increase the level of information that consumers have about products. In the early 1990s, the Food and Drug Administration passed rules requiring most processed foods sold in grocery stores to carry nutrition labels. The current hot topic in the labeling area involves restaurant meals. With obesity growing in the United States, many policy makers think that one way to fight the problem is to require calorie and fat labeling in restaurants. The following article from *The Wall Street Journal* discusses a recent law requiring chain restaurants to post calorie counts.

Coming to the Menu: Calorie Counts

The Wall Street Journal

Chowing down on calorie-laden food at chain restaurants is going to become more of a guilt trip.

The health bill President Barack Obama signed into law Tuesday requires that restaurant chains post calorie counts for all the food items they sell. The law covers any chain with at least 20 outlets, amounting to more than 200,000 restaurants nationwide.

"Dining out no longer has to be a nutritional guessing game," said Margo G. Wootan, director of nutrition policy with the Center for Science in the Public Interest, a nonprofit health-advocacy group based in Washington. "People could cut hundreds, thousands, of calories from their diet."

Calorie counts must be listed on menus, menu boards, drive-through displays and vending machines under the law. Additional information—such as sodium levels, carbohydrates and saturated fats—must be available on request. Temporary specials and custom orders are exempted.

A growing number of state, county and local regulations already require similar disclosures, and those rules will be superceded by the federal law.

There has been debate about whether such menu labeling actually affects consumers' behavior. Some recent studies have found that such labeling leads to healthier eating: The New York City health department examined the behavior of 12,000 customers of 13 chain restaurants in 275 locations in the city before and after menu labeling was implemented in the city in 2008.

Preliminary results show that one in six fast-food customers report using the calorie-count information. Consumers who said they used the information bought items with 106 fewer calories compared with those who didn't see or use the information.

Separate studies have shown weak or inconsistent effects of menu labeling on consumer behavior, according to a 2008 review of the literature published in the *International Journal of Behavioral Nutrition and Physical Activity*.

"Calorie posting in and of itself is not going to change obesity per se, but it's all of these kinds of layering opportunities that we're doing for public health all across the country that are going to make the difference," said Cathy Nonas, director of physical activity and nutrition for the health department in New York City, a pioneer in adopting menu labeling.

The National Center for Health Statistics reported in January that 34 percent of Americans age 20 and older were obese in 2007–2008.

The restaurant industry is required to come up with a labeling proposal in one year, but the bill leaves it to Food and Drug Administration officials to determine specific regulations, including the printing fonts and their sizes to be used in calorie displays. Ms. Wootan said it could take three to four years before diners see the new information in restaurants.

One concern about the rules is accuracy. Researchers from Tufts University who looked into caloric disclosure from 29 quick-serve and sit-down restaurants found that restaurants underreported calories by an average of 18 percent.

Some restaurant owners and groups have supported labeling regulations, in part because they don't think such disclosures deter patrons from ordering what they want.

Drugs, both prescription and nonprescription, are an example. Companies spend millions of dollars to promote brand-name drugs that contain the same compounds as those available under the generic names. The antibiotics erythromycin and erythrocin have the same ingredients, yet erythrocin is half as expensive as erythromycin. Aspirin is aspirin, yet we pay twice the price for an advertised brand because the manufacturer has convinced us that there is a tangible—or intangible—difference.

Do we really need 50 different kinds of soap, some of whose prices are increased by the cost of advertising? For a firm producing a differentiated product, advertising is part of the everyday cost of doing business. Its price is built into the average cost curve and thus into the price of the product in the short run and the long run. Thus, consumers pay to finance advertising.

Critics also argue that the information content of advertising is minimal at best and deliberately deceptive at worst. Advertising is meant to change our minds, to persuade us, and to create brand images. Try to determine how much real information there is in the next 10 advertisements you see on television. U.S. firms spend about $250 billion a year on advertising. Critics argue that firms waste a substantial portion of this money if the advertising does not clearly convey information to consumers.

Competitive advertising can also easily turn into unproductive warfare. Suppose there are five firms in an industry and one firm begins to advertise heavily. To survive, the others respond in kind. Advertising of this sort may not increase demand for the product or improve profitability for the industry. Instead, it is often a "zero sum game"—a game in which the sum of the gains equals the sum of the losses.

Advertising may also reduce competition by creating a barrier to the entry of new firms into an industry. One famous case study taught at the Harvard Business School calculates the cost of entering the brand-name breakfast cereal market. To be successful, a potential entrant would have to start with millions of dollars in an extensive advertising campaign to establish a brand name recognized by consumers. Entry to the breakfast cereal game is not completely blocked, but such financial requirements make entry very difficult.

Finally, some argue that advertising, by its very nature, imposes a cost on society. We are continuously bombarded by bothersome jingles and obtrusive images. When driving home from school or work, we may pass 50 billboards and listen to 15 minutes of news and 20 minutes of advertising on the radio. When we get home, we throw away 10 pieces of unsolicited junk mail, glance at a magazine containing 50 pages of writing and 75 pages of advertisements, and perhaps watch a television show that is interrupted every 5 minutes for a "message."

The bottom line, critics of product differentiation and advertising argue, is waste and inefficiency. Enormous sums are spent to create minute, meaningless, and possibly nonexistent differences among products. Advertising raises the cost of products and frequently contains very little information. Often, it is merely an annoyance. Advertising can lead to unproductive warfare and may serve as a barrier to entry, thus reducing real competition.

Open Questions   You will see over and over as you study economics that many questions remain open. There are strong arguments on both sides of the advertising debate, and even the empirical evidence yields to conflicting conclusions. Some studies show that advertising leads to concentration and positive profits; others, that advertising improves the functioning of the market.

Price and Output Determination in Monopolistic Competition

Recall that monopolistically competitive industries are made up of a large number of firms, each small relative to the size of the total market. Thus, no one firm can affect market price by virtue of its size alone. Firms do differentiate their products, however, in ways we have been discussing. By doing so, they gain some control over price.

Product Differentiation and Demand Elasticity

Perfectly competitive firms face a perfectly elastic demand for their product: All firms in a perfectly competitive industry produce exactly the same product. If firm A tried to raise prices, buyers would go elsewhere and firm A would sell nothing. When a firm can distinguish its product from all others in the minds of consumers, as we assume it can under monopolistic competition, it probably can raise its price without losing all quantity demanded. Figure 15.2 shows how product differentiation might make demand somewhat less elastic for a hypothetical firm.

A monopoly is an industry with a single firm that produces a good for which there are no close substitutes. A monopolistically competitive firm is like a monopoly in that it is the only producer of its unique product. Only one firm can produce Cheerios or Wheat Thins or Johnson's Baby Shampoo or Oreo cookies. However, unlike the product in a monopoly market, the product of a monopolistically competitive firm has many close substitutes competing for the consumer's favor. Although the demand curve that a monopolistic competitor faces is likely to be less elastic than the demand curve that a perfectly competitive firm faces, it is likely to be more elastic than the demand curve that a monopoly faces.

Price/Output Determination in the Short Run

A profit-maximizing, monopolistically competitive firm behaves much like a monopolist in the short run. First, marginal revenue is not equal to price because the monopolistically competitive firm is different enough from its rivals that small price increases over those rivals do not eliminate all customers. This firm sees its price respond to its output decisions. The monopolistic competitor's marginal revenue curve lies *below* its demand curve, intersecting the quantity axis midway between the origin and the point at which the demand curve intersects it. (If necessary, review Chapter 13 to make sure you understand this idea.) The firm chooses the output/price combination that maximizes profit. To maximize profit, the monopolistically competitive firm will increase production until the marginal revenue from increasing output and selling it no longer exceeds the marginal cost of producing it. This occurs at the point at which marginal revenue equals marginal cost: $MR = MC$.

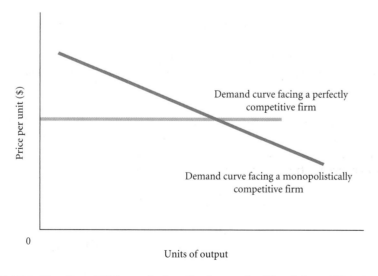

▲ **FIGURE 15.2 Product Differentiation Reduces the Elasticity of Demand Facing a Firm**

The demand curve that a monopolistic competitor faces is likely to be less elastic than the demand curve that a perfectly competitive firm faces. Demand is more elastic than the demand curve that a monopolist faces because close substitutes for the products of a monopolistic competitor are available.

In Figure 15.3(a), the profit-maximizing output is $q_0 = 2{,}000$, where marginal revenue equals marginal cost. To sell 2,000 units, the firm charges $6, which is the most it can charge and still sell the 2,000 units. Total revenue is $P_0 \times q_0 = \$12{,}000$, or the area of P_0Aq_00. Total cost is equal to average total cost times q_0, which is $10,000, or CBq_00. Total profit is the difference, $2,000 (the gray-shaded area P_0ABC).

Nothing guarantees that a firm in a monopolistically competitive industry will earn positive profits in the short run. Figure 15.3(b) shows what happens when a firm with similar cost curves faces a weaker market demand. Even though the firm does have some control over price, market demand is insufficient to make the firm profitable.

As in perfect competition, such a firm minimizes its losses by producing up to the point where marginal revenue is equal to marginal cost. Of course, as in perfect competition, the price that the firm charges must be sufficient to cover average variable costs. Otherwise, the firm will shut down and suffer losses equal to total fixed costs instead of increasing losses by producing more. In Figure 15.3(b), the loss-minimizing level of output is $q_1 = 1{,}000$ at a price of $5. Total revenue is $P_1 \times q_1 = \$5{,}000$, or P_1Bq_10. Total cost is $ATC \times q_1 = \$6{,}000$, or CAq_10. Because total cost is greater than revenue, the firm suffers a loss of $1,000, equal to the pink-shaded area, $CABP_1$.

Price/Output Determination in the Long Run

Under monopolistic competition, entry and exit are easy in the long run. Firms can enter an industry when there are profits to be made, and firms suffering losses can go out of business. However, entry into an industry of this sort is somewhat different from entry into perfect competition because products are differentiated in monopolistic competition. A firm that enters a monopolistically competitive industry is producing a close substitute for the good in question, *but not the same good.*

Let us begin with a firm earning positive profits in the short run, as shown on the left-hand side of Figure 15.3. Those profits provide an incentive for new firms to enter the industry. This entry creates new substitutes for the profit-making firm, which, in turn, drives down demand for its product. For example, if several restaurants seem to be doing well in a particular location, others may start up and take business from the existing restaurants. While firms are not perfect substitutes, they are similar enough to take business from one another.

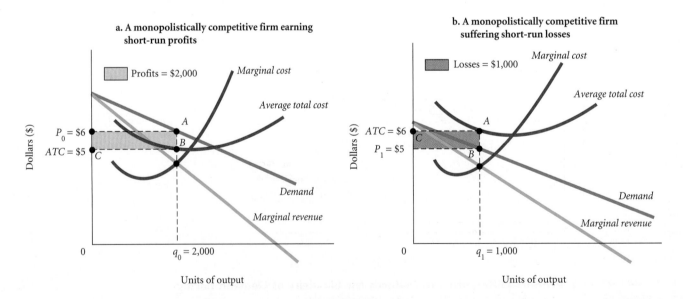

▲ **FIGURE 15.3 Monopolistic Competition in the Short Run**

In the short run, a monopolistically competitive firm will produce up to the point $MR = MC$. At $q_0 = 2{,}000$ in panel a, the firm is earning short-run profits equal to $P_0ABC = \$2{,}000$. In panel b, another monopolistically competitive firm with a similar cost structure is shown facing a weaker demand and suffering short-run losses at $q_1 = 1{,}000$, equal to $CABP_1 = \$1{,}000$.

In profitable markets, new firms continue to enter the market until profits are eliminated. As the new firms enter, the demand curve facing each old firm begins to shift to the left, pushing the marginal revenue curve along with it. With more entrants, less demand is left for older firms. This shift continues until profits are eliminated, which occurs when the demand curve slips down to the average total cost curve. Graphically, this is the point at which the demand curve and the average total cost curve are tangent (the point at which they just touch and have the same slope). Figure 15.4 shows a monopolistically competitive industry in long-run equilibrium. At q^* and P^*, price and average total cost are equal; so there are no profits or losses.

Look carefully at the tangency, which in Figure 15.4, is at output level q^*. The tangency occurs at the profit-maximizing level of output. At this point, marginal cost is equal to marginal revenue. At any level of output other than q^*, ATC lies above the demand curve. This means that at any other level of output, ATC is greater than the price that the firm can charge. (Recall that the demand curve shows the price that can be charged at every level of output.) Hence, price equals average total cost at q^* and profits equal zero.

This equilibrium must occur at the point at which the demand curve is *just tangent* to the average total cost curve. If the demand curve cuts across the average cost curve, intersecting it at two points, the demand curve would be *above* the average total cost curve at some levels of output. Producing at those levels of output would mean positive profits. Positive profits would attract entrants, shifting the market demand curve to the left and lowering profits. If the demand curve were always *below* the average total cost curve, all levels of output would produce losses for the firm. This would cause firms to exit the industry, shifting the market demand curve to the right and increasing profits (or reducing losses) for those firms still in the industry. The firm's demand curve must end up tangent to its average total cost curve for profits to equal zero. This is the condition for long-run equilibrium in a monopolistically competitive industry.

There is something else to notice about Figure 15.4: The monopolistically competitive firm is not operating at the lowest point on its average total cost curve. It is producing at a scale smaller than the one that minimizes its average total cost. In some ways this is the cost of product differentiation: The industry consists of firms that serve individualized tastes of customers, but serving those different tastes results in higher production costs than we would see if everyone liked the same thing. Remember our example of the gray sidewalks early in the chapter. Uniform gray sidewalks allows us to lower costs, but the cost is a gray undifferentiated product. In other cases, we see a rainbow of products, but the firms producing them are all operating at too small a scale.

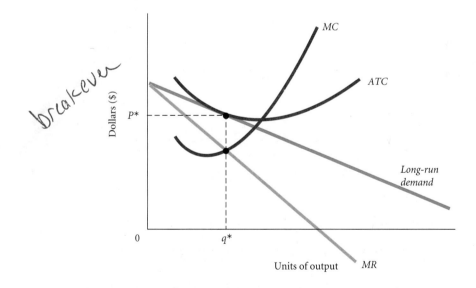

▲ **FIGURE 15.4**

Monopolistically Competitive Firm at Long-Run Equilibrium

As new firms enter a monopolistically competitive industry in search of profits, the demand curves of existing profit-making firms begin to shift to the left, pushing marginal revenue with them as consumers switch to the new close substitutes. This process continues until profits are eliminated, which occurs for a firm when its demand curve is just tangent to its average total cost curve.

Economic Efficiency and Resource Allocation

We have already noted some of the similarities between monopolistic competition and perfect competition. Because entry is easy and economic profits are eliminated in the long run, we might conclude that the result of monopolistic competition is efficient. There are two problems, however.

First, once a firm achieves any degree of market power by differentiating its product (as is the case in monopolistic competition), its profit-maximizing strategy is to hold down production and charge a price above marginal cost, as you saw in Figure 15.3 and Figure 15.4. Remember from Chapter 12 that price is the value that society places on a good and that marginal cost is the value that society places on the resources needed to produce that good. By holding production down and price above marginal cost, monopolistically competitive firms prevent the efficient use of resources. More product could be produced at a resource cost below the value that consumers place on the product.

Second, as Figure 15.4 shows, the final equilibrium in a monopolistically competitive firm is necessarily to the left of the low point on its average total cost curve. That means a typical firm in a monopolistically competitive industry will not realize all the economies of scale available. (In perfect competition, you will recall, firms are pushed to the bottom of their long-run average cost curves, and the result is an efficient allocation of resources.)

Suppose a number of firms enter an industry and build plants on the basis of initially profitable positions. As more firms compete for those profits, individual firms find themselves with smaller market shares; eventually, they end up with "excess capacity." The firm in Figure 15.4 is not fully using its existing capacity because competition drove its demand curve to the left. In monopolistic competition, we end up with many firms, each producing a slightly different product at a scale that is less than optimal. Would it not be more efficient to have a smaller number of firms, each producing on a slightly larger scale?

The costs of less-than-optimal production, however, need to be balanced against the gains that can accrue from aggressive competition among products. If product differentiation leads to the introduction of new products, improvements in old products, and greater variety, an important gain in economic welfare may counteract (and perhaps outweigh) the loss of efficiency from pricing above marginal cost or not fully realizing all economies of scale.

Most industries that comfortably fit the model of monopolistic competition are very competitive. Price competition coexists with product competition, and firms do not earn incredible profits and do not violate any of the antitrust laws that we discussed in the last chapter. Monopolistically competitive firms have not been a subject of great concern among economic policy makers. Their behavior appears to be sufficiently controlled by competitive forces, and no serious attempt has been made to regulate or control them.

SUMMARY

INDUSTRY CHARACTERISTICS *p. 314*

1. A monopolistically competitive industry has the following structural characteristics: (1) a large number of firms, (2) no barriers to entry, and (3) *product differentiation*. Relatively good substitutes for a monopolistic competitor's products are available. Monopolistic competitors try to achieve a degree of market power by differentiating their products.

PRODUCT DIFFERENTIATION AND ADVERTISING *p. 315*

2. The amount of product differentiation in an industry depends on a number of features of the industry. How different are customers' tastes? Are there gains to customers in buying a product that is identical to one bought by everyone else? Are there large-scale economies associated with making only one variety of a good? Industries with many different products reflect strong heterogeneity of consumers, low gains from coordination, and small cost gains from standardization.

3. Products can be differentiated horizontally or vertically. Horizontal differentiation produces different types of a good with different appeals to different types of people. In vertical differentiation, people agree that one product is better than another; they just may not be willing to pay for the better good.

4. *Behavioral economics* suggests that there may be times when too much variety reduces consumers' purchases.

5. Behavioral economics also suggests that there may be times when consumers prefer one form of a good over another as a way to commit themselves to different actions in the future than they would otherwise take.

6. Advocates of free and open competition believe that differentiated products and advertising give the market system its vitality and are the basis of its power. Critics argue that product differentiation and advertising are wasteful and inefficient.

PRICE AND OUTPUT DETERMINATION IN MONOPOLISTIC COMPETITION *p. 322*

7. By differentiating their products, firms hope to be able to raise prices without losing all demand. The demand curve facing a monopolistic competitor is less elastic than the demand curve faced by a perfectly competitive firm but more elastic than the demand curve faced by a monopoly.

8. To maximize profit in the short run, a monopolistically competitive firm will produce as long as the marginal revenue from increasing output and selling it exceeds the marginal cost of producing it.

9. When firms enter a monopolistically competitive industry, they introduce close substitutes for the goods being produced. This attracts demand away from the firms already in the industry. Demand faced by each firm shifts left, and profits are ultimately eliminated in the long run. This long-run equilibrium occurs at the point where the demand curve is just tangent to the average total cost curve.

ECONOMIC EFFICIENCY AND RESCOURCE ALLOCATION *p. 326*

10. Monopolistically competitive firms end up pricing above marginal cost. This is inefficient, as is the fact that monopolistically competitive firms do not realize all economies of scale available. There may be offsetting gains from increased variety.

REVIEW TERMS AND CONCEPTS

PROBLEMS

All problems are available on www.myeconlab.com

1. For each of the following, state whether you agree or disagree. Explain your answer.
   a. Monopolistically competitive firms produce their economic profits protected by barriers to entry.
   b. Monopolistically competitive firms are efficient because in the long run, price falls to equal marginal cost.

2. Consider the local music scene in your area. Name some of the local live bands that play in clubs and music halls, both on and off campus. Look in your local newspaper for advertisements of upcoming shows or performances. How would you characterize the market for local musicians? Is there product differentiation? In what specific ways do firms (individual performers or bands) compete? To what degree are they able to exercise market power? Are there barriers to entry? How profitable do you think the musicians are?

3. Write a brief essay explaining this statement: The Beatles were once a monopolistically competitive firm that became a monopolist.

4. In a market in which there is vertical differentiation, we always see price differences among the products. In markets with horizontal differentiation, sometimes the products differ but prices are very much the same. Why does vertical differentiation naturally bring with it price differences?

5. [Related to *Economics in Practice* on p. 318] If you look at the prices listed in the *Economics in Practice* on p. 318, you will see that the more well-known brands are being sold for a lower price than the less well-known brands. Is this pattern always true? Explain your answer.

6. [Related to *Economics in Practice* on p. 321] The news story tells us that some restaurant owners oppose the labeling requirement. Why? Since restaurants compete with one another, would you not expect some of the healthier restaurants to come out in favor of the rule? Explain.

7. The table shows the relationship for a hypothetical firm between its advertising expenditures and the quantity of its output that it expects it can sell at a fixed price of $5 per unit.

ADVERTISING EXPENDITURES (MILLIONS)	QUANTITY SOLD AT *P* = $5/IN MILLION UNITS
$1	8
$1.2	9
$1.4	9.4
$1.6	9.6
$1.8	9.7

   a. In economic terms, why might the relationship between advertising and sales look the way it does?

b. Assume that the marginal costs of producing this product (not including the advertising costs) are a constant $4. How much advertising should this firm be doing? What economic principle are you using to make this decision?

8. In the area around a local university, a number of food vendors gather each lunchtime to sell food to university students who are tired of dorm food. The university and the town have no license fees that apply to food vendors, preferring to let the market dictate how many and which vendors show up.

   Many different cuisines are represented on the street corner, including a cart sponsored by Madame Defarge selling gumbo and jambalaya. Madame Defarge sells a plate of either gumbo or jambalaya for $5. The food is made in the morning at her nearby restaurant, when the kitchen is otherwise unoccupied. Her crew of three, each of whom earns $15 per hour, takes 2 hours to make the 100 meals required by Madame Defarge. In creating these meals, they use ingredients equal to $100. Madame Defarge hires another worker to load her cart with food and sell it during the lunch hours. That worker costs $10 per hour and typically sells out the entire cart of 100 meals in 2 hours. The cart is rented for $100 per 5-day week. (The carts are not in operation on the weekends, when Madame Defarge is too busy at her restaurant.)

   a. What market structure does this business most resemble? What characteristics lead you to this conclusion?

   b. What would you expect to see happen in this business? Use the data in the problem to support your conclusions.

   c. How would your calculations change if Madame Defarge were to develop a weekday lunch business that used the kitchen's capacity?

9. Conduct an online search for "Chicago restaurants." You will find over 40 million entries. Now try "Chicago Chinese Restaurants." You will find nearly half a million entries. Try to estimate the total number of Chinese restaurants in Chicago. Pick some random locations and see how many are listed nearby. See if you can find some advertisements with menus and prices. How much variation does there seem to be in the price of standard spring rolls or fried rice? Make the case that the restaurant industry is or is not

well described by the model of monopolistic competition presented in this chapter. Be specific.

10. The following diagram shows the structure of cost and demand facing a monopolistically competitive firm in the short run.
    a. Identify the following on the graph and calculate each one.
       i.   Profit-maximizing output level
       ii. Profit-maximizing price
       iii. Total revenue
       iv. Total cost
       v.   Total profit or loss
    b. What is likely to happen in this industry in the long run?

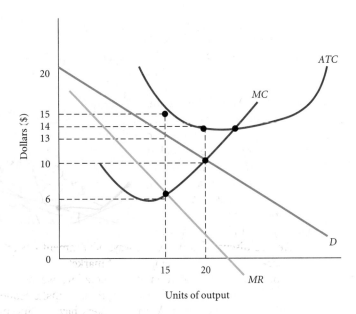

11. Explain the relationship between price and marginal revenue for a purely competitive firm and for a monopolistically competitive firm. Why is the relationship different for these markets?

Externalities, Public Goods, and Social Choice

16

In Chapters 6 through 12, we built a complete model of a perfectly competitive economy under a set of assumptions. By Chapter 12, we had demonstrated that the allocation of resources under perfect competition is efficient and we began to relax some of the assumptions on which the perfectly competitive model is based. We introduced the idea of **market failure**, and in Chapters 13, 14, and 15, we talked about three kinds of imperfect markets: monopoly, oligopoly, and monopolistic competition. We also discussed some of the ways government has responded to the inefficiencies of imperfect markets and to the development of market power.

As we continue our examination of market failure, we look first at *externalities* as a source of inefficiency. Often when we engage in transactions or make economic decisions, second or third parties suffer consequences that decision makers have no incentive to consider. For example, for many years, manufacturing firms and power plants had no reason to worry about the impact of smoke from their operations on the quality of the air we breathe. Now we know that air pollution—an externality—harms people.

Next, we consider a second type of market failure that involves products that private firms find unprofitable to produce even if members of society want them. These products are called *public goods* or *social goods*. Public goods yield collective benefits, and in most societies, governments produce them or arrange to provide them. The process of choosing what social goods to produce is very different from the process of private choice.

Finally, while the existence of externalities and public goods are examples of market failure, it is not necessarily true that government involvement always improves matters. Just as markets fail, so too can governments. When we look at the incentives facing government decision makers, we find several reasons behind government failure.

Externalities and Environmental Economics

An **externality** exists when the actions or decisions of one person or group impose a cost or bestow a benefit on second or third parties. Externalities are sometimes called *spillovers* or *neighborhood effects*. Inefficient decisions result when decision makers fail to consider social costs and benefits.

The presence of externalities is a significant phenomenon in modern life. Examples are everywhere: Air, water, land, sight, and sound pollution; traffic congestion; automobile accidents; abandoned housing; nuclear accidents; and secondhand cigarette smoke are only a few. For most of the spring and summer of 2010, people watched as the oil spill from BP's disastrous well explosion spread throughout the Gulf. The study of externalities is a major concern of *environmental economics*.

---

market failure Occurs when resources are misallocated or allocated inefficiently.

externality A cost or benefit imposed or bestowed on an individual or a group that is outside, or external to, the transaction.

The growth of China and India has put increased pressure on the environment. As new countries industrialize, strains on global air and water systems are inevitable. Problems of externalities have increasingly become global problems.

Marginal Social Cost and Marginal-Cost Pricing

In the absence of externalities, when a firm weighs price and marginal cost to decide output, it is weighing the full benefits to society of additional production against the full costs to society of that production. Those who benefit from the production of a product are the people or households who end up consuming it. The price of a product is a good measure of what an additional unit of that product is "worth" because those who value it more highly already buy it. People who value it less than the current price are not buying it. If marginal cost includes all costs—that is, all costs *to society*—of producing a marginal unit of a good, additional production will be efficient, provided P is greater than MC. Up to the point where $P = MC$, each unit of production yields benefits in excess of cost. Figure 16.1(a) shows a firm and an industry in which no externalities exist.

Suppose, however, that the production of the firm's product imposes external costs on society as well. A firm producing detergent may dump wastewater into a local river as a by-product of its detergent production. If the firm does not factor those additional costs into its decisions, it is likely to overproduce. Figure 16.1(b) shows what happens graphically when we add in those costs. The curve labeled MSC, **marginal social cost**, is the sum of the marginal costs of producing the product and the correctly measured damage costs imposed in the process of production.

marginal social cost (MSC)
The total cost to society of producing an additional unit of a good or service. *MSC* is equal to the sum of the marginal costs of producing the product and the correctly measured damage costs involved in the process of production.

If the firm is allowed to dump its wastewater and does not have to pay for resulting damage costs, it will produce exactly the same level of output (q^*) as before and price (P^*) will continue to reflect only the costs that the firm actually pays to produce its product. The firms in this industry will continue to produce, and consumers will continue to consume their product, but the market price of the detergent will not reflect wastewater costs. At equilibrium (q^*), marginal social costs are considerably greater than *price*. (Recall that *price* is a measure of the full value to consumers of a unit of the product at the margin.)

Consider what happens as the detergent plant freely dumps untreated toxic waste into a river. The waste imposes specific costs on people who live downstream: It kills the fish in the river, it makes the river ugly to look at and rotten to smell, and it destroys the river for recreational use. There may also be health hazards depending on what chemicals the firm is dumping. Obviously, the plant's product provides certain benefits. Its soap is valuable to consumers who are willing and able to pay for it. The firm employs people and capital. The issue is how the *net benefits* produced by the plant compare with the damage that it does. You do not need an economic model to know that *someone* should consider the costs of those damages.

Acid Rain and the Clean Air Act   Acid rain is an excellent example of an externality and of the issues and conflicts involved in dealing with externalities. When manufacturing firms and power plants in the Midwest burn coal with a high sulfur content, smoke from those plants mixes with moisture in the atmosphere. The result is a dilute acid that is windblown north to Canada and east to New York and New England, where it falls to Earth as rain.

How does the acid rain problem look to the different parties involved? For manufacturing firms and public utilities generating the sulfur dioxide that creates acid rain, burning high-sulfur coal delivers cheap power and employment to residents of the Midwest. Paying to clean up the damage or changing the fuel mix to reduce sulfur would result in higher electricity prices. Some firms would likely go out of business, and jobs would be lost. For residents in other parts of the United States and Canada, particularly those near wildlife areas, the burning of high-sulfur coal and the resulting acid rain results in fish kills and deforestation. Often these citizens are far enough away from the power plants producing the sulfur dioxide that they are not even benefiting from the cheaper power. As in many areas of economics, the hard issue here is how to balance benefits to one set of claimants with costs to another.

In complex cases of externalities, like acid rain, often governments get involved. The United States began its work in reducing acid rain with the Clean Air Act in 1990. Since then, the United

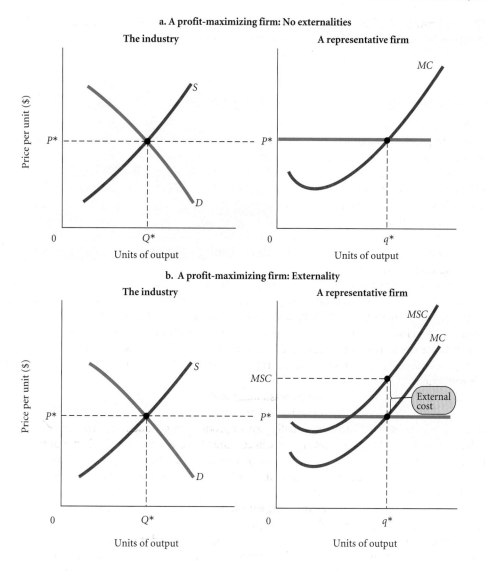

a. A profit-maximizing firm: No externalities

The industry

A representative firm

b. A profit-maximizing firm: Externality

The industry

A representative firm

◀ **FIGURE 16.1**

Profit-Maximizing Perfectly Competitive Firms Will Produce Up to the Point That Price Equals Marginal Cost ($P = MC$)

If we assume that the current price reflects what consumers are willing to pay for a product at the margin, firms that create external costs without weighing them in their decisions are likely to produce too much. At q^*, marginal social cost exceeds the price paid by consumers.

States has made substantial progress in reducing the problem of acid rain, and many acidified lakes and streams now once again support fish life. Recently, the United States has employed an innovative "cap and trade" program to control emissions, which we will discuss later in this chapter. For acid rain, which travels across national boundaries, agreements between Canada and the United States have also played an important role.

Other Externalities   Clearly, the most significant and hotly debated issue of externalities is global warming. The 2007 Nobel Peace Prize was awarded to former Vice President Al Gore and the Intergovernmental Panel on Climate Change, a group of 2,500 researchers from 130 nations that issued a number of reports linking human activity to the recent rise of the average temperature on Earth. Although there is considerable disagreement, many people are convinced that strong measures must be taken to prevent major adverse consequences such as dramatically rising sea levels. We will return to this topic later.

Individual actions can also create externalities. When I drive during rush hour, I increase congestion faced by other drivers. If I smoke, your health may be compromised. Again the key issue is weighing the costs and benefits to all parties.

Some Examples of Positive Externalities   Thus far we have described a series of negative externalities. But externalities can also be positive. In some cases, when other people or firms engage in an activity, there are side *benefits* from that activity. From an economics perspective, there are problems with positive externalities as well.

ECONOMICS IN PRACTICE

Ban on Oil Drillers

In April 2010, one of BP's deep water wells exploded, killing 10 people and creating what would become one of the largest environmental disasters in the United States. The article below describes what was known about the damage by the summer of 2010.

The effect of this disaster on economic and environmental policy is likely to also be substantial. Oil still provides a substantial portion of U.S. energy, and many of the oil reserves lie offshore. The recent disaster has made some of the trade-offs between environmental security and energy security considerably more salient.

New Ban Hits Oil Drillers

The Wall Street Journal

WASHINGTON—The Obama administration on Monday issued a new order banning most new deepwater-drilling activities until Nov. 30, setting up a fresh round of conflict with the oil industry over when it will be safe to drill again offshore.

The latest round in the clash over the ban on new drilling got under way as BP installed a new cap on its blown-out undersea well that company and government officials hope will capture all the spewing oil. BP officials have said they are also aiming to finish drilling a relief well that will allow them to permanently stanch the flow. Even after the well is sealed, BP and the Gulf Coast face a lengthy process of cleaning up the huge slick that has fouled beaches and wetlands from Texas to Florida.

In moving to reinstate the drilling ban, President Barack Obama again sided with environmental groups and many voters in big coastal states such as Florida and California who support a halt to new deepwater drilling until the causes of the catastrophic BP PLC well blowout are known.

"We know that that is not without some economic consequences to the region," White House Press Secretary Robert Gibbs said Monday. "But it's imperative that we have a sense of what happened before we continue to do this again."

But public officials and many residents of Gulf states directly affected by the spill say the ban threatens thousands of jobs in the offshore oil industry.

Source: The Wall Street Journal by Siobhan Hughes and Stephen Power. Copyright 2011 by *Dow Jones & Company, Inc.* Reproduced with permission of *Dow Jones & Company, Inc.* via Copyright Clearance Center.

Ian Ayres and Steve Levitt have studied a fascinating example of a product with positive externalities, LoJack. LoJack is a device that allows police to track a car when it is stolen. When a car has a LoJack device installed, the gains to stealing that car are sharply reduced. These devices not only help recover cars but also help catch car thieves. Suppose that 90 percent of the cars in a community had LoJack installed. If all LoJack cars were identified—the way houses are that have burglar alarms—potential thieves could look for the unmarked cars. As it happens, LoJack does not come with any identifying mark. From a thief's perspective, any car has a 90 percent chance of having a LoJack installed. As a result, the benefits from stealing *any* car are reduced. With reduced benefits, fewer thefts occur. Ayres and Levitt have found that the size of these positive externalities are very large; they estimate that the purchaser of a LoJack captures, as an individual, only 10 percent of the value of the device.[1]

We also see positive externalities in the case of vaccinations. The more people who are vaccinated, the less likely a disease will become prevalent. But the less likely the disease, the lower the private benefits to people from getting a vaccination. With communicable diseases, health precautions taken by an individual have positive external benefits to the rest of the community.

The problem with positive externalities should now be clear. For this type of externality, the individuals in charge have too little incentive to engage in the activity. Too few LoJacks are bought; too few people wash their hands often; too few people would vaccinate their children unless forced to do so by school systems.

---

[1] Ian Ayres and Steve Levitt, "Measuring Positive Externalities from Unobservable Victim Precautions: An Empirical Analysis of Lojack," *Quarterly Journal of Economics* 108, (1), 1998.

Private Choices and External Effects

To help us understand externalities and to see how one might make trade-offs in the situations we have described, let us use a simple two-person example. Harry lives in a dormitory at a big public college in the Southwest, where he is a first-year student. Harry is a serious gamer, with a particular fondness for "Call of Duty," a popular but noisy game. Unfortunately, the walls of Harry's dorm are made of quarter-inch drywall over 3-inch aluminum studs. You can hear people sleeping four rooms away. Because of a hearing loss after an accident on the Fourth of July some years ago, Harry often does not notice the volume of his game. Jake, who lives next door to Harry, is a pre-med student trying hard to steer clear of video games.

Let us assume that there are no further external costs or benefits to anyone other than Harry and Jake from Harry's play. Figure 16.2 illustrates the decision process that the two dorm residents face. The downward-sloping curve labeled *MB* represents the value of the marginal benefits that Harry derives from gaming. Of course, Harry does not sit down to draw this curve, any more than anyone else (other than an economics student) sits down to draw actual demand curves. Curves like this are simply abstract representations of the way people behave. If you think about it, such a curve must exist. To ask how much an hour of gaming is worth to you is to ask how much you would be willing to pay to have it. Start at $0.01 and raise the "price" slowly in your mind. Presumably, you must stop at some point. Where you stop depends on your taste for games and your income.

You can think about the benefits Harry derives from gaming as the maximum amount of money that he would be willing to pay for an hour of play. For the first hour, for instance, the value for *MB* is $0.50. We assume diminishing marginal utility, of course. The more hours Harry plays, the lower the additional benefits from each successive hour. As the graph shows, the *MB* curve falls below $0.05 per hour after 8 hours of playing.

We call the cost that Harry must pay for each additional hour of gaming the **marginal private cost**, labeled *MPC* in Figure 16.2. In the present example, this cost is primarily the cost of electricity. This cost is constant at $0.05 per hour.

Then there is Jake. Although Harry's gaming does not poison Jake, give him lung cancer, or even cause him to lose money, it damages him nonetheless: He gets a headache, loses sleep, and cannot concentrate on his work. Jake is harmed, and it is possible (at least conceptually) to measure that harm in terms of the maximum amount that he would be willing to pay to avoid it. The damage, or cost, imposed on Jake is represented in Figure 16.2 by the curve labeled *MDC*. Formally, **marginal damage cost (MDC)** is the additional harm done by increasing the level of an externality-producing activity by 1 unit. By assuming Jake would be willing to pay some amount of money to avoid the noise, it is reasonable to assume the amount increases each successive hour. His headache gets worse with each additional hour he is forced to listen.

marginal private cost (MPC)
The amount that a consumer pays to consume an additional unit of a particular good.

marginal damage cost (MDC)
The additional harm done by increasing the level of an externality-producing activity by 1 unit. If producing product *X* pollutes the water in a river, *MDC* is the additional cost imposed by the added pollution that results from increasing output by 1 unit of *X* per period.

◀ **FIGURE 16.2**
Externalities in a College Dormitory
The marginal benefits to Harry exceed the marginal costs he must bear to play his game system for a period of up to 8 hours. When the noise of the game occurs, a cost is being imposed on Jake. When we add the costs borne by Harry to the damage costs imposed on Jake, we get the full cost of the game play to the two-person society made up of Harry and Jake. Playing more than 5 hours is inefficient because the benefits to Harry are less than the social cost for every hour above 5. If Harry considers only his private costs, he will play for too long a time from society's point of view.

In the simple society of Jake and Harry, it is easy to add up social benefits and costs. At every level of output (playing time), total social cost is the sum of the private costs borne by Harry and the damage costs borne by Jake. In Figure 16.2, *MPC* (constant at $0.05 per hour) is added to *MDC* to get *MSC*. The social optimum occurs where the marginal social benefit equals the marginal social cost.

Now consider what would happen if Harry simply ignored Jake.[2] If Harry decides to continue gaming, Jake will be damaged. As long as Harry gains more in personal benefits from an additional hour of play than he incurs in costs, the system will stay on. He will play it for 8 hours (the point where Harry's *MB = MPC*). This result is inefficient; for every hour of play beyond 5, the marginal social cost borne by society—in this case, a society made up of Harry and Jake—exceeds the marginal benefits to Harry—that is, *MSC* > Harry's *MB*. It is generally true that when economic decisions ignore external costs, whether those costs are borne by one person or by society, those decisions are likely to be inefficient. We will return to Harry and Jake to see how they deal with their problem. First, we need to discuss the general problem of correcting for externalities.

Internalizing Externalities

A number of mechanisms are available to provide decision makers with incentives to weigh the external costs and benefits of their decisions, a process called *internalization*. In some cases, externalities are internalized through bargaining and negotiation without government involvement. In other cases, private bargains fail and the only alternative may be government action of some kind.

Five approaches have been taken to solving the problem of externalities: (1) private bargaining and negotiation, (2) legal rules and procedures, (3) government-imposed taxes and subsidies, (4) sale or auctioning of rights to impose externalities, and (5) direct government regulation. While each is best suited for a different set of circumstances, all five provide decision makers with an incentive to weigh the external effects of their decisions.

Private Bargaining and Negotiation Return to Harry and Jake. Most of you have likely been in this situation at one time or another. For most people in this situation, the first step is obvious: Knock on Harry's door and ask him to turn down the volume or reduce his play time during your study hours. In fact, good manners are a societal reaction to incipient externalities. As societies increase in population density, more and more activities fall under the category of "not done in public." Consider what has happened over time to the social acceptability of smoking, for example. In 2010, in anticipation of its Expo, the Chinese government cracked down on the tendency of its citizens in Shanghai to wear their pajamas outside the home, believing that this dress has negative externalities for their international guests.

Even when there are no social norms against an activity, private bargains and negotiation can often solve an externality problem. The formal model describing how private negotiations work was described first by Ronald Coase, in 1960.[3] Indeed the **Coase theorem** describing the process by which individual actions can solve externalities without government is a staple topic in both law and economics classes around the world.

> **Coase theorem** Under certain conditions, when externalities are present, private parties can arrive at the efficient solution without government involvement.

To see how the Coase theorem works, let us return to Jake and Harry's dorm rooms. Suppose Jake has been unsuccessful in his mannerly plea to Harry. What next? At this point one might want to know what the rules are. Indeed, Coase tells us that, while it does not matter *what* the rules are in situations like this, it is very important that there be rules that are known to all parties. Negotiations are difficult when the two parties don't agree on who has what rights. Let us assume, at least at first, that in this college, there are no rules against video games and everyone in the dorm is aware of this lenient policy. Harry can play his games as much as he likes, which we see from Figure 16.2 is 8 hours a day. In a system with no rules and an unmannerly neighbor, does Jake have any recourse?

Look back at Figure 16.2 and put yourself in Jake's position. With Harry playing his game 8 hours a day, the value of the last hour of play to Harry is pretty small. In fact, as you see at the eighth hour, playing is worth only $0.05 per hour. After 8 hours of listening to the sounds of battle, however, Jake is going wild. He would pay more than $0.25 per hour for some relief. There is room for a deal! As Harry cuts back on play, the value of the marginal hour of play goes up, and the marginal damage to Jake of listening begins to fall. For hours of play in excess of 5, Jake's

---

[2] It may be easier for individuals to ignore the social costs imposed by their actions when those costs fall on large numbers of other people whom they do not have to look in the eye or they do not know personally. For the moment, however, we assume that Harry takes no account of Jake.

[3] See Ronald Coase, "The Problem of Social Cost," *Journal of Law and Economics*, 1960.

incremental damage exceeds Harry's incremental value of playing. Again, look back at Figure 16.2. As Coase would tell us, for all hours greater than 5 per day, Jake realizes enough benefits from silence to be able to bribe Harry into being quiet. Notice, however, what happens at 5 hours of play per day. To cut back below 5 hours per day, Harry's marginal benefit from play rises to above $0.25 per hour. Electricity costs him $0.05 per hour. So to make him stop, Jake would have to bribe him with at least $0.20. But as the graph shows, at less than 5 hours per day, Jake's damage per hour is less than $0.20. Five hours is the efficient playing time. More hours or fewer hours reduce total benefits to Harry and Jake.

Coase tells us that under certain conditions, private negotiations will push society to the right level of output even with externalities. What features of the Harry–Jake situation matter for this type of solution to work? First, as noted, the basic rights must be understood by all parties. In this situation Jake knows he has to bribe Harry because Harry has the right to make noise if he wants to. If rights are not spelled out, arguments about who has what right interfere with the bargaining process. A second condition is that people must be able to bargain without impediment or costs. The fact that Jake and Harry lived next to each other made the bargaining a lot easier. Finally, private negotiation works best when the number of parties involved is few in number. If one party to a bargain is a large group, such as all residents of a town or an area as in the earlier acid rain example, private negotiations work less well.

Coase also pointed out that bargaining will bring the contending parties to the right solution regardless of where rights are initially assigned. Suppose that the dorm rules state that Jake has the right to silence. This being the case, Jake can go to the dorm administrators and have them enforce the rule. Now when Harry plays the game and Jake asks him to turn it off, Harry must comply. Now the tables are turned. Accepting the dorm rules (as he must), Harry knocks on Jake's door. Jake's damages from the first hour are only $0.15. This means that if Jake was compensated by more than $0.15, he would allow the gaming. Now the stage is set for bargaining. Harry gets $0.45 in net benefit from the first hour of playing ($0.50 minus private cost of $0.05). Thus, he is willing to pay up to $0.45 for the privilege. If there are no impediments to bargaining, money will change hands. Harry will pay Jake some amount between $0.15 and $0.45, and just as before, gaming will continue. Jake has, in effect, sold his right to have silence to Harry. As before, bargaining between the two parties will lead to 5 hours of gaming. At exactly 5 hours, Jake will stop taking compensation and tell Harry to turn the system off. (Look again at Figure 16.2 to see that this is true.)

In both cases, the offer of compensation might be made in some form other than cash. Jake may offer Harry goodwill, a favor or two, or the use of his Harley-Davidson for an hour. Indeed, in this example, if Harry has the right to play as much as he wants (our Case 1), Jake may offer to buy Harry a headset that allows him to game quietly. Jake's willingness to do this would, of course, depend on how much a headset costs and how long Jake expected to live next door to Harry.

Coase's critics are quick to point out that the conditions required for bargaining to produce the efficient result are not always present. The biggest problem with Coase's system is also a common problem. Very often one party to a bargain is a large group of people, and our reasoning may be subject to a fallacy of composition.

Suppose a power company in Pittsburgh is polluting the air. The damaged parties are the 100,000 people who live near the plant. Let us assume the plant has the right to pollute. The Coase theorem predicts that the people who are damaged by the smoke will get together and offer a bribe (as Jake offered a bribe to Harry). If the bribe is sufficient to induce the power plant to stop polluting or reduce the pollutants with air scrubbers, it will accept the bribe and cut down on the pollution. If the bribe is not sufficient, the pollution will continue, but the firm will have weighed all the costs (just as Harry did when he continued to play the game) and the result will be efficient.

However, not everyone will contribute to the bribe. First, each contribution is so small relative to the whole that no single contribution makes much of a difference. Making a contribution may seem unimportant or unnecessary to some. Second, all people get to breathe the cleaner air whether they contribute to the bribe or not. Many people will not participate simply because they are not compelled to, and the private bargain breaks down—the bribe that the group comes up with will be less than the full damages unless everyone participates. (We discuss these two problems—the *drop-in-the-bucket* and the *free-rider*—later in this chapter.) When the number of damaged parties is large, government taxes or regulation may be the only avenue to a remedy.

injunction   A court order forbidding the continuation of behavior that leads to damages.

liability rules   Laws that require A to compensate B for damages imposed.

Legal Rules and Procedures   As we have just seen, for bargaining to result in an efficient outcome, the initial assignment of rights must be clear to both parties. When rights are established by law, more often than not some mechanism to protect those rights is also built into the law. In some cases where a nuisance exists, for example, there may be legal remedies. In such cases, the victim can go to court and ask for an **injunction** that forbids the damage-producing behavior from continuing. If the dorm rules specifically give Jake the right to silence, Jake's getting the resident adviser to speak to Harry is something like getting an injunction.

Injunctive remedies are irrelevant when the damage has already been done. Consider accidents. If your leg has already been broken as the result of an automobile accident, enjoining the driver of the other car from drinking and driving will not work—it is too late. In these cases, rights must be protected by **liability rules**, rules that require A to compensate B for damages imposed. In theory, such rules are designed to do the same thing that taxing a polluter is designed to do: provide decision makers with an incentive to weigh all the consequences, actual and potential, of their decisions. Just as taxes do not stop all pollution, liability rules do not stop all accidents.

However, the threat of liability actions does induce people to take more care than they might otherwise. Product liability is a good example. If a person is damaged in some way because a product is defective, the producing company is, in most cases, held liable for the damages, even if the company took reasonable care in producing the product. Producers have a powerful incentive to be careful. If consumers know they will be generously compensated for any damages, however, they may not have as powerful an incentive to be careful when using the product.

Taxes and Subsidies   When private negotiations fail, economists have traditionally advocated marginal taxes and subsidies as a direct way of forcing firms to consider external costs or benefits. When a firm imposes an external social cost, the reasoning goes, a per-unit tax should be imposed equal to the damages of each successive unit of output produced by the firm—the tax should be *exactly equal* to marginal damage costs.[4]

Figure 16.3 repeats Figure 16.1(b), but this time the damage costs are paid by the firm in the form of a per-unit tax—that is, the tax = MDC. The firm now faces a marginal cost curve that is the same as the marginal social cost curve ($MC_1 = MSC$). Remember that the industry supply curve is the sum of the marginal cost curves of the individual firms. This means that as a result of the tax, the industry supply curve shifts to the left, driving up price from P_0 to P_1. The efficient level of output is q_1, where $P = MC_1$. (Recall our general equilibrium analysis from Chapter 12.)

▶ **FIGURE 16.3**

Tax Imposed on a Firm Equal to Marginal Damage Cost

If a per-unit tax exactly equal to marginal damage costs is imposed on a firm, the firm will weigh the tax, and thus the damage costs, in its decisions. At the new equilibrium price, P_1, consumers will be paying an amount sufficient to cover full resource costs as well as the cost of damage imposed. The efficient level of output for the firm is q_1.

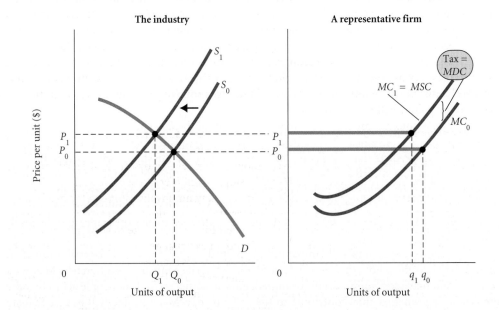

4 As we discuss later in this chapter, damage costs are difficult to measure. It is often assumed that they are proportional to the volume of pollutants discharged into the air or water. Instead of taxes, governments often impose *effluent charges*, which make the cost to polluters proportional to the amount of pollution caused. We will use "tax" to refer to both taxes and effluent charges.

Because a profit-maximizing firm equates price with marginal cost, the new price to consumers covers the resource costs of producing the product and the damage costs. The consumer decision process is once again efficient at the margin because marginal social benefit as reflected in market price is equal to the full social marginal cost of the product.

An interesting example of the use of taxes to reduce pollution is the tax that London has placed on cars driving into the central part of the city. New York's Mayor Bloomberg considered a similar policy.

Measuring Damages   The biggest problem with using taxes and subsidies is that damages must be estimated in financial terms. For the detergent plant polluting the nearby river to be properly taxed, the government must evaluate the damages done to residents downstream in money terms. This evaluation is difficult but not impossible. When legal remedies are pursued, judges are forced to make such estimates as they decide on compensation to be paid. Surveys of "willingness to pay," studies of property values in affected versus nonaffected areas, and sometimes the market value of recreational activities can provide basic data.

The monetary value of damages to health and loss of life is, naturally, more difficult to estimate, and any measurement of such losses is controversial. Even here, policy makers frequently make judgments that implicitly set values on life and health. Tens of thousands of deaths and millions of serious injuries result from traffic accidents in the United States every year, yet Americans are unwilling to give up driving or to reduce the speed limit to 40 miles per hour—the costs of either course of action would be too high. If most Americans are willing to increase the risk of death in exchange for shorter driving times, the value we place on life has its limits.

Keep in mind that taxing externality-producing activities may not eliminate damages. Taxes on these activities are not designed to eliminate externalities; they are simply meant to force decision makers to consider the full costs of their decisions. Even if we assume that a tax correctly measures all the damage done, the decision maker may find it advantageous to continue causing the damage. The detergent manufacturer may find it most profitable to pay the tax and go on polluting the river. It can continue to pollute because the revenues from selling its product are sufficient to cover the cost of resources used *and to compensate the damaged parties fully*. In such a case, producing the product in spite of the pollution is "worth it" to society. It would be inefficient for the firm to stop polluting. In our earlier example, the optimal level of Harry's gaming was 5 hours per day, not 0. Only if damage costs were very high would it make sense to have no pollution. Thus, you can see the importance of proper measurement of damage costs.

Reducing Damages to an Efficient Level   Taxes also provide firms with an incentive to use the most efficient technology for dealing with damage. If a tax reflects true damages and it is reduced when damages are reduced, firms may choose to avoid or reduce the tax by using a different technology that causes less damage. Suppose our soap manufacturer is taxed $10,000 per month for polluting the river. If the soap plant can ship its waste to a disposal site elsewhere at a cost of $7,000 per month and thereby avoid the tax, it will do so. If a plant belching sulfides into the air can install smoke scrubbers that eliminate emissions for an amount less than the tax imposed for polluting the air, it will do so.

The Incentive to Take Care and to Avoid Harm   You should understand that all externalities involve at least two parties and that it is not always clear which party is "causing" the damage. Take our friends Harry and Jake. Harry enjoys games; Jake enjoys quiet. If Harry plays, he imposes a cost on Jake. If Jake can force Harry to stop, he imposes a cost on Harry.

Often, the best solution to an externality problem may not involve stopping the externality-generating activity. Suppose Jake and Harry's dormitory has a third resident, Pete. Pete hates silence. The resident adviser on Harry's floor arranges for Pete and Jake to switch rooms. What was once an external cost has been transformed into an external benefit. Everyone is better off. Harry and Pete get to listen to sounds of war, and Jake gets his silence.

Sometimes the most efficient solution to an externality problem is for the damaged party to avoid the damage. However, if full compensation is paid by the damager, damaged parties may have no incentive to do so. Consider a laundry located next to the exhaust fans from the kitchen of a Chinese restaurant. Suppose damages run to $1,000 per month because the laundry must use special air filters in its dryers so that the clothes will not smell of Szechuan spices. The laundry looks around and finds a perfectly good alternative location away from the restaurant that rents for only $500 per month above its current rent. Without any compensation from the Chinese restaurant, the

ECONOMICS IN PRACTICE

Externalities Are All Around Us

Externalities arise from many sources. The most common examples involve smoking factories and the automobile. But externalities are everywhere. Here are two examples of externalities that you may have experienced.

THE CRYING BABY

Peter Scott, once employed as a research assistant on this book and now a writer in Hollywood, wrote the following lines about crying babies on airplanes:

"The best example of this [an externality] is on airplanes. For most of my life, a crying baby on an airplane felt like some kind of torture method used to get spies to reveal national secrets. There was actually a deleted scene in *Goldfinger* where Goldfinger locks James Bond in a room with crying babies. The problem was that Bond then shot himself, thus destroying the franchise. So they rewrote the scene and had Goldfinger try and slice Bond in half with a laser. Bond could easily escape from that because lasers are obviously less terrifying than crying babies."[1]

John Tierney wrote about the same externality in the *New York Times*:[2] "If you think of a screaming child as an environmental disturbance, then giving a child a discount is like offering subsidy to a polluter. A child should at least pay full fare, and the fairest policy would be to impose a surcharge."

CHRISTMAS DECORATIONS

Abominable Snowmen: The War on Lawn Decorations

Wall Street Journal

Jim McDilda's holiday display last year included a 28-foot lighted arch, 50-foot tree, 50,000 lights, and dozens of animated silhouettes. The spectacle—he needed a crane to set it all up—lit up the sky and drew thousands of gawking visitors to his Redding, Calif., house.

But nearby neighbors weren't so thrilled. Cars, limos, and tour buses clogged the cul-de-sac, and trash was strewn across lawns. Christmas music blasting from Mr. McDilda's display kept neighbors awake. They complained to the city, which required that Mr. McDilda get a special-events permit and demanded that he remove the nearby cargo containers he used to store the display most of the year. After months of sniping between Mr. McDilda and the city, he decided to throw in the towel. This year, his house is unadorned.

Source: The Wall Street Journal, excerpted from "Abominable Snowmen: The War on Lawn Decorations" by Sara Schaefer Munoz. Copyright 2007 by *Dow Jones & Company, Inc.* Reproduced with permission of *Dow Jones & Company, Inc.* via Copyright Clearance Center.

[1] Peter Scott, *There's a Spouse in My House: A Humorous Journey Through the First Years of Marriage.* Copyright© 2007–2008 Peter Scott. All Rights Reserved.
[2] John Tierney, *"The Big City: Urban Menace Stalks Streets in Diapers,"* The New York Times, *June 24, 2000.*

laundry will move and the total damage will be the $500 per month extra rent that it must pay. But if the restaurant compensates the laundry for damages of $1,000 a month, why should the laundry move? Under these conditions, a move is unlikely even though it would be efficient.

Subsidizing External Benefits   Sometimes activities or decisions generate external benefits instead of costs, as in the case of Harry and Pete, or in the LoJack example. Real estate investment provides another example. Investors who revitalize a downtown area—an old theater district in a big city, for example—provide benefits to many people, both in the city and in surrounding areas.

Activities that provide such external social benefits may be subsidized at the margin to give decision makers an incentive to consider them. Just as ignoring social costs can lead to inefficient decisions, so too can ignoring social benefits. Government subsidies for housing and other development, either directly through specific expenditure programs or indirectly through tax exemptions, have been justified on such grounds.

Selling or Auctioning Pollution Rights   We have already established that not all externality-generating activities should be banned. Around the world, the private automobile has become the clearest example of an externality-generating activity whose benefits (many believe) outweigh its costs.

Many externalities are imposed when we drive our cars. First, congestion is an externality. Even though the marginal "harm" imposed by any one driver is small, the sum total is a serious cost to all who spend hours in traffic jams. Second, most of the air pollution in the United States comes from automobiles. The problem is most evident in Los Angeles, where smog loaded with harmful emissions (mostly from cars) blankets the city virtually every day. Finally, driving increases the likelihood of accidents, raising insurance costs to all.

While we do not ignore these costs from the standpoint of public policy, we certainly have not banned driving. Athens, Greece, however, has instituted an even-odd system in which inner city driving is restricted to alternative days depending on a person's license plate number. (In a development that some economists predicted, however, this rule has led some people to buy two cars and simply switch off.) In many cases, we have also consciously opted to allow ocean dumping, river pollution, and air pollution within limits.

The right to impose environmental externalities is beneficial to the parties causing the damage. In a sense, the right to dump in a river or to pollute the air or the ocean is a resource. Thinking of the privilege to dump in this way suggests an alternative mechanism for controlling pollution: selling or auctioning the pollution rights to the highest bidder. The Clean Air Act of 1990 takes this cap-and-trade approach to controlling the emissions from our nation's power plants. Emissions from each plant are capped; that is, emissions are limited to a specified level. The lower the level specified, the more air quality will improve. The plant is issued a permit allowing it to emit only at that level. This permit can be used or can be traded to another firm in what has developed into a large auction market. For a firm with low costs of abating pollution, it is often in the firm's best interest to cut back below its permit levels and sell its unused permits to a firm with higher abatement costs. In this way, the given level of emissions chosen by the government will be achieved at the lowest possible costs as a result of market trades. Environmentalists can also buy up permits and leave them unused, resulting in improvements in air quality beyond what the government mandated. These cap-and-trade programs are being used around the world in an attempt to reduce greenhouse gases responsible for global warming.

A simple example will help illustrate the potential gains from a cap-and-trade system. Table 16.1 shows the situation facing two firms, both of which are polluting. Assume that each firm emits 5 units of pollution and the government wants to reduce the total amount of pollution from the current level of 10 to 4. To do this, the government caps each firm's allowed pollution level at 2. Thus, each firm must pay to cut its pollution levels by 3 units. The process of reducing pollution is sometimes called *pollution abatement*. The table shows the marginal cost of abatement for each firm and the total costs. For Firm A, for example, the first unit of pollution reduced or abated costs only $5. As the firm tries to abate more pollution, doing so becomes more difficult; the marginal costs of reducing pollution rise. If Firm A wants to reduce its pollution levels from 5 units to 2, as the government requires, it must spend $21, $5 for the first unit, $7 for the second unit, and $9 for the third unit. Firm B finds reducing pollution to be more difficult. If it tries to reduce pollution by 3 units, it will have costs of $45. A cap-and-trade policy gives each of these firms two permits and allows them to trade permits if they so choose. What will the firms want to do?

Firm A can reduce its emissions from 2 units to 1 unit by spending $12 more on abatement. It would then have a permit to sell to Firm B. How much would Firm B be willing to pay for this permit? At the moment, the firm is abating 3 units, and the marginal cost of that third

TABLE 16.1		Permit Trading			
Firm A	Firm A	Firm A	Firm B	Firm B	Firm B
Reduction of pollution by Firm A (in units of pollution)	MC of reducing pollution for Firm A	TC of reducing pollution for Firm A	Reduction of pollution by Firm B (in units of pollution)	MC of reducing pollution for Firm B	TC of reducing pollution for Firm B
1	$ 5	$ 5	1	$ 8	$ 8
2	7	12	2	14	22
3	9	21	3	23	45
4	12	33	4	35	80
5	17	50	5	50	130

unit is $23. This tells us that Firm B would be willing to pay up to $23 to buy a permit to allow it to continue polluting up to a level of 3. So there is room for a deal. Indeed, the permit price will be somewhere between the $12 demanded by Firm A and the $23 that Firm B is willing to spend. Because Firm A's marginal costs of abatement are lower than Firm B's, we expect Firm A to do more abatement and sell its extra permit to B. You should be able to see from the numbers that Firm A will not sell its last permit to B. To abate another unit, Firm A would have marginal costs of $17. To avoid abatement, however, Firm B would pay only $14. There is no room for a deal. Once the trade of one permit by A to B has occurred, there are still only 4 units of pollution, but now Firm A is emitting 1 unit and Firm B is emitting 3 units. What are the total costs of this pollution reduction? When both firms were reducing their emission levels equally, the total costs were $21 for Firm A and $45 for Firm B, for a total of $66. Now costs are $33 for A and $22 for B, for a total of $55. (Of course, A will also be receiving a payment for the permit.)

Europe took the problem of global warming seriously by implementing the world's first mandatory trading scheme for carbon dioxide emissions in 2005. Carbon dioxide emissions are a major source of global warming. The first phase of the plan, which was over at the end of 2007, involved around 12,000 factories and other facilities. The participating firms were oil refineries; power generation facilities; and glass, steel, ceramics, lime, paper, and chemical factories. These 12,000 plants represented 45 percent of total European Union (EU) emissions. The EU set an absolute cap on carbon dioxide emissions and then allocated allowances to governments. The nations in turn distributed the allowances to the separate plants. In the second phase from 2008 through 2012, a number of large sectors will be added, including agriculture and petrochemicals.

In both the United States and Europe, the allowances are given out to the selected plants free of charge even though the allowances will trade at a high price once they are distributed. Many are now questioning whether the government should sell them in the market or collect a fee from the firms. As it is, many of the firms that receive the allocations get a huge windfall. During the second phase in Europe, the governments are allowed to auction over 10 percent of the allowances issued.

Another example of selling externality rights comes from Singapore, where the right to buy a car is auctioned each year. Despite very high taxes and the need for permits to drive in downtown areas, the roads in Singapore have become congested. The government decided to limit the number of new cars on the road because the external costs associated with them (congestion and pollution) were becoming very high. With these limits imposed, the decision was made to distribute car ownership rights to those who place the highest value on them. It seems likely that taxi drivers, trucking companies, bus lines, and traveling salespeople will buy the licenses; families who drive for convenience instead of taking public transportation will find the licenses too expensive. Congestion and pollution are not the only externalities that Singapore takes seriously: In 2005 the fine for littering was as high as $1,000; for failing to flush a public toilet, over $100; and for eating on a subway, $300.

Direct Regulation of Externalities

Direct Regulation of Externalities   Taxes, subsidies, legal rules, and public auctions are all methods of indirect regulation designed to induce firms and households to weigh the social costs of their actions against their benefits. The actual size of the external cost/benefit depends on the reaction of households and firms to the incentives provided by the taxes, subsidies, and rules.

For obvious reasons, many externalities are too important to be regulated indirectly. Dumping cancer-causing chemicals into the ground near a public water supply is simply illegal, and those who do it can be prosecuted and sent to jail.

Direct regulation of externalities takes place at federal, state, and local levels. The Environmental Protection Agency (EPA) is a federal agency established by an act of Congress in 1970. Since the 1960s, Congress has passed a great deal of legislation that sets specific standards for permissible discharges into the air and water. Every state has a division or department charged with regulating activities that are likely to harm the environment. Most airports in the United States have landing patterns and hours that are regulated by local governments to minimize noise.

Many criminal penalties and sanctions for violating environmental regulations are like the taxes imposed on polluters. Not all violations and crimes are stopped, but violators and criminals face "costs." For the outcome to be efficient, the penalties they expect to pay should reflect the damage that their actions impose on society.

ECONOMICS IN PRACTICE

Climate Change

Global warming has become one of the most difficult environmental policy challenges of our time. The science is complex, the effects are long lasting, the nations involved are many, and the costs and benefits to different nations are highly varied. Island nations in areas that are already warm will experience very different effects from landlocked colder nations. Substantial reductions of greenhouse gases are likely to be very expensive. For all these reasons, international accord has been hard to achieve. In December 2010 the international community tried again with a set of meetings in Cancun, Mexico. The article below describes a meeting of the developing nations (and leading up to the Cancun meeting) that took place in May 2010 in China. The article illustrates some of the complex international issues in the global warming debate.

China, India Doubt Climate Deal Is Near

The Wall Street Journal

BEIJING—Top climate-change officials from China and India expressed pessimism at a Beijing conference this weekend about reaching a binding global deal at a United Nations Climate Summit in Cancun, Mexico, at the end of the year.

China hosted the high profile global-warming forum that brought together key negotiating blocs in the developing world, including fellow basic group members Brazil, South Africa, and India.

Beijing is trying to strengthen its role as leader of the developing world in climate-change talks after accusations it sabotaged efforts to reach a binding deal at a U.N.-backed summit in Copenhagen last December. The composition of the forum participants served to send "a signal to the world of the role China wants to play," said Li Yan, a climate-change specialist at Greenpeace.

China's climate-change czar said at the conference that a binding pact on tackling global warming remains out of reach until several big issues are settled, including how to handle $100 billion in funds for developing nations to rein in greenhouse gases over the next decade.

The Beijing meeting didn't result in any conclusive statement, but it aimed to provide a channel to promote larger climate-change talks, said former Chinese Vice Premier Zeng Peiyan, who was in charge of the conference.

Analysts say Beijing also wanted to use the conference to send a strong signal to the nation's local governments that it is serious about reaching energy-efficiency targets.

Such a signal is especially urgent after news that China's infrastructure and housing-led economic recovery increased the country's energy intensity 3.2% in the first quarter compared with a year earlier, reversing a steady decline in the amount of energy used to produce each dollar of gross domestic product.

China, the world's largest emitter of greenhouse gases in absolute terms, has said it would cut energy intensity 20% by the end of this year, a goal that is closely tied to the country's pledge to reduce its carbon intensity—the amount of carbon emitted per dollar of GDP—by 40% to 45% by 2020.

—*Wan Xu contributed to this article.*

Source: The Wall Street Journal, excerpted from "China, India Doubt Climate Deal is Near" by Shai Oster. Copyright 2010 by *Dow Jones & Company, Inc.* Reproduced with permission of *Dow Jones & Company, Inc.* via Copyright Clearance Center.

Public (Social) Goods

Another source of market failure lies in **public goods**, often called **social** *or* **collective goods**. Public goods are defined by two closely related characteristics: They are nonrival in consumption, and/or their benefits are nonexcludable. As we will see, these goods represent a market failure because they have characteristics that make it difficult for the private sector to produce them profitably. In an unregulated market economy with no government to see that they are produced, public goods would at best be produced in insufficient quantity and at worst not produced at all.

public goods (social *or* **collective goods)** Goods that are nonrival in consumption and/or their benefits are nonexcludable.

The Characteristics of Public Goods

A good is **nonrival in consumption** when A's consumption of it does not interfere with B's consumption of it. This means that the benefits of the goods are collective—they accrue to everyone. National defense, for instance, benefits us all. The fact that I am protected in no way detracts from

nonrival in consumption A characteristic of public goods: One person's enjoyment of the benefits of a public good does not interfere with another's consumption of it.

the fact that you are protected; every citizen is protected just as much as every other citizen. If the air is cleaned up, my breathing that air does not interfere with your breathing it, and (under ordinary circumstances) that air is not used up as more people breathe it. Private goods, in contrast, are *rival in consumption.* If I eat a hamburger, you cannot eat it too.

Goods can sometimes generate collective benefits and still be rival in consumption. This happens when crowding occurs. A park or a pool can accommodate many people at the same time, generating collective benefits for everyone. However, when too many people crowd in on a hot day, they begin to interfere with each other's enjoyment.

Most public goods are also **nonexcludable**. Once the good is produced, people cannot be excluded for any reason from enjoying its benefits. Once a national defense system is established, it protects everyone.

Before we go on, it is very important to note that goods are either public or private by virtue of their characteristics (nonrival and nonexcludable) and *not* by virtue of whether they are produced by the public sector. If the government decided to make it a law that hamburgers were an entitlement (that is, all people could have all the hamburgers they wanted at government expense), that decision would not make hamburgers into public goods. It is an example of the government's providing a private good free of charge to all. The government's decision not to exercise the power to exclude doesn't change the nature of a hamburger.

The real problem with public goods is that private producers may simply not have any incentive to produce them or to produce the right amount. For a private profit-making firm to produce a good and make a profit, it must be able to withhold that good from those who do not pay. McDonald's can make money selling chicken sandwiches only because customers do not get the chicken sandwich unless they pay for it first. If payment were voluntary, McDonald's would not be in business for long.

Consider an entrepreneur who decides to offer better police protection to the city of Metropolis. Careful (and we assume correct) market research reveals that the citizens of Metropolis want high-quality protection and are willing to pay for it. Not everyone is willing to pay the same amount. Some can afford more, others less. People also have different preferences and different feelings about risk. Our entrepreneur hires a sales force and begins to sell his service. Soon he encounters a problem. Because his company is private, payment is voluntary. He cannot force anyone to pay. Payment for a hamburger is voluntary too, but a hamburger can be withheld for nonpayment. The good that our new firm is selling, however, is by nature a public good.

As a potential consumer of a public good, you face a dilemma. You want more police protection, and let us say that you are even willing to pay $50 a month for it. But nothing is contingent on your payment. First, if the good is produced, the crime rate falls and all residents benefit. You get that benefit whether or not you pay for it. You get a free ride. That is why this dilemma is called the **free-rider problem**. Second, your payment is very small relative to the amount that must be collected to provide the service. Thus, the amount of police protection actually produced will not be significantly affected by how much you contribute or whether you contribute at all. This is the **drop-in-the-bucket problem**. Consumers acting in their own self-interest have no incentive to contribute voluntarily to the production of public goods. Some will feel a moral responsibility or social pressure to contribute, and those people indeed may do so. Nevertheless, the economic incentive is missing, and most people do not find room in their budgets for many voluntary payments. The public goods problem can also be thought of as a large-number, prisoners' dilemma game theory problem. (For a full discussion, see Chapter 14.)

Public Provision of Public Goods

All societies, past and present, have had to face the problem of providing public goods. When members of society get together to form a government, they do so to provide themselves with goods and services that will not be provided if they act separately. Like any other good or service, a body of laws (or system of justice) is produced with labor, capital, and other inputs. Law and the courts yield social benefits, and they must be set up and administered by some sort of collective, cooperative effort.

Notice that we are talking about public *provision*, not public *production*. Once the government decides what service it wants to provide, it often contracts with the private sector to produce the good. Much of the material for national defense is produced by private defense contractors. Highways, government offices, data processing services, and so on, are usually produced by private firms.

One of the immediate problems of public provision is that it frequently leads to public dissatisfaction. It is easy to be angry at government. Part, but certainly not all, of the reason for this dissatisfaction lies in the nature of the goods that government provides. Firms that produce or sell

---

nonexcludable A characteristic of most public goods: Once a good is produced, no one can be excluded from enjoying its benefits.

free-rider problem A problem intrinsic to public goods: Because people can enjoy the benefits of public goods whether or not they pay for them, they are usually unwilling to pay for them.

drop-in-the-bucket problem A problem intrinsic to public goods: The good or service is usually so costly that its provision generally does not depend on whether any single person pays.

private goods post a price—we can choose to buy any quantity we want, or we can walk away with nothing. It makes no sense to get angry at a shoe store because no one can force you to shop there.

You cannot shop for collectively beneficial public goods. When it comes to national defense, the government must choose one and only one kind and quantity of (collective) output to produce. Because none of us can choose how much should be spent or what it should be spent on, we are all dissatisfied. Even if the government does its job with reasonable efficiency, at any given time, about half of us think we have too much national defense and about half of us think we have too little.

Optimal Provision of Public Goods

In the early 1950s, economist Paul Samuelson, building on the work of Richard Musgrave, demonstrated that there exists an *optimal*, or a *most efficient*, level of output for every public good.[5] The discussion of the Samuelson and Musgrave solution that follows leads us straight to the thorny problem of how societies, as opposed to individuals, make choices.

The Samuelson–Musgrave Theory An efficient economy produces what people want. Private producers, whether perfect competitors or monopolists, are constrained by the market demand for their products. If they cannot sell their products for more than it costs to produce them, they will be out of business. Because private goods permit exclusion, firms can withhold their products until households pay. Buying a product at a posted price reveals that it is "worth" at least that amount to you and to everyone who buys it.

Market demand for a private good is the sum of the quantities that each household decides to buy (as measured on the horizontal axis) at each price. The diagrams in Figure 16.4 review the derivation of a market demand curve. Assume that society consists of two people, A and B. At a price of $1, A demands 9 units of the private good and B demands 13. Market demand at a price of $1 is 22 units. If price were to rise to $3, A's quantity demanded would drop to 2 units and B's would drop to 9 units; market demand at a price of $3 is 2 + 9 = 11 units. The point is that the price mechanism forces people to reveal what they want, and it forces firms to produce only what people are willing to pay for, but it works this way only because exclusion is possible.

People's preferences and demands for public goods are conceptually no different from their preferences and demands for private goods. You may want fire protection and be willing to pay for it in the same way you want to listen to a CD. To demonstrate that an efficient level of production exists, Samuelson assumes that we know people's preferences. Figure 16.5 shows demand curves

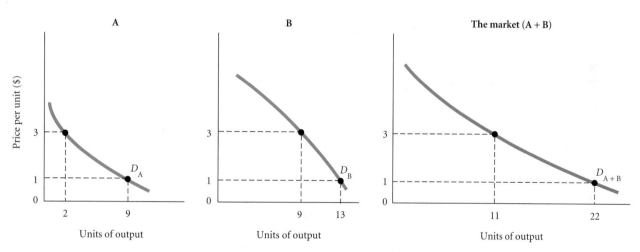

▲ **FIGURE 16.4 With Private Goods, Consumers Decide What Quantity to Buy; Market Demand Is the Sum of Those Quantities at Each Price**

At a price of $3, A buys 2 units and B buys 9 for a total of 11. At a price of $1, A buys 9 units and B buys 13 for a total of 22. We all buy the quantity of each private good that we want. Market demand is the horizontal sum of all individual demand curves.

---

[5] Paul A. Samuelson, "Diagrammatic Exposition of a Theory of Public Expenditure," *Review of Economics and Statistics*, 37, 1955, 350–56. For Musgrave's original version based on the work of Eric Lindahl, see "The Voluntary Exchange Theory of Public Economy," *Quarterly Journal of Economics 53 (2)*, 213-237, February 1938.

for buyers A and B. If the public good were available in the private market at a price of $6, A would buy X_1 units. Put another way, A is willing to pay $6 per unit to obtain X_1 units of the public good. B is willing to pay only $3 per unit to obtain X_1 units of the public good.

Remember, public goods are nonrival and/or nonexcludable—benefits accrue simultaneously to everyone. One and only one quantity can be produced, and that is the amount that everyone gets. When X_1 units are produced, A gets X_1 and B gets X_1. When X_2 units are produced, A gets X_2 and B gets X_2.

To arrive at market demand for public goods, we do not sum quantities. Instead, *we add the amounts that individual households are willing to pay for each potential level of output*. In Figure 16.5, A is willing to pay $6 per unit for X_1 units and B is willing to pay $3 per unit for X_1 units. Thus, if society consists only of A and B, society is willing to pay $9 per unit for X_1 units of public good X. For X_2 units of output, society is willing to pay a total of $4 per unit.

For private goods, market demand is the horizontal sum of individual demand curves—we add the different *quantities* that households consume (as measured on the *horizontal* axis). For public goods, market demand is the vertical sum of individual demand curves—we add the different *amounts* that households are willing to pay to obtain each level of output (as measured on the *vertical* axis).

▶ **FIGURE 16.5**

With Public Goods, There Is Only One Level of Output and Consumers Are Willing to Pay Different Amounts for Each Level

A is willing to pay $6 per unit for X_1 units of the public good. B is willing to pay only $3 for X_1 units. Society—in this case A and B—is willing to pay a total of $9 for X_1 units of the good. Because only one level of output can be chosen for a public good, we must add A's contribution to B's to determine market demand. This means adding demand curves vertically.

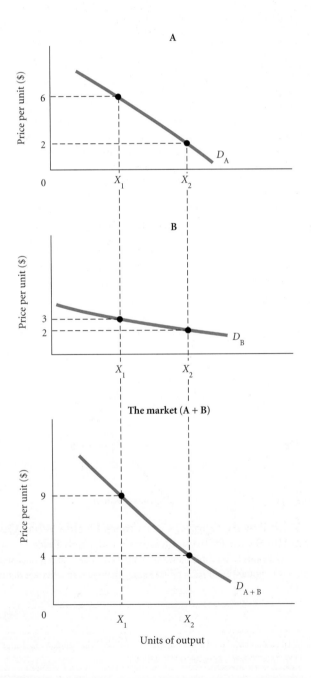

Samuelson argued that once we know how much society is willing to pay for a public good, we need only compare that amount to the cost of its production. Figure 16.6 reproduces A's and B's demand curves and the total demand curve for the public good. As long as society (in this case, A and B) is willing to pay more than the marginal cost of production, the good should be produced. If A is willing to pay $6 per unit of public good and B is willing to pay $3 per unit, society is willing to pay $9.

Given the *MC* curve as drawn in Figure 16.6, the efficient level of output is X_1 units. If at that level A is charged a fee of $6 per unit of *X* produced and B is charged a fee of $3 per unit of *X*, everyone should be happy. Resources are being drawn from the production of other goods and services only to the extent that people want the public good and are willing to pay for it. We have arrived at the **optimal level of provision for public goods**. At the optimal level, society's total willingness to pay per unit is equal to the marginal cost of producing the good.

optimal level of provision for public goods The level at which society's total willingness to pay per unit is equal to the marginal cost of producing the good.

The Problems of Optimal Provision

One major problem exists, however. To produce the optimal amount of each public good, the government must know something that it cannot possibly know—everyone's preferences. Because exclusion is impossible, nothing forces households to reveal their preferences. Furthermore, if we ask households directly about their willingness to pay, we run up against the same problem encountered by our protection-services salesperson mentioned earlier. If your actual payment depends on your answer, you have an incentive to hide your true feelings. Knowing that you cannot be excluded from enjoying the benefits of the good and that your payment is not likely to have an appreciable influence on the level of output finally produced, what incentive do you have to tell the truth—or to contribute?

How does society decide which public goods to provide? We assume that members of society want certain public goods. Private producers in the market cannot make a profit by producing these goods, and the government cannot obtain enough information to measure society's demands accurately. No two societies have dealt with this dilemma in the same way. In some countries, dictators simply decide for the people. In other countries, representative political bodies speak for the people's preferences. In still other countries, people vote directly. None of these solutions works perfectly. We will return to the problem of social choice at the end of the chapter.

Local Provision of Public Goods: Tiebout Hypothesis

In 1956, economist Charles Tiebout made this point: To the extent that local governments are responsible for providing public goods, an efficient market-choice mechanism may exist. Consider a set of towns that are identical except for police protection. Towns that choose to spend a great deal of money on police are likely to have a lower crime rate. A lower crime rate will attract households who are risk-averse and who are willing to pay higher taxes for a lower risk of being a crime victim. Those who are willing to bear greater risk may choose to live in the low-tax/high-crime

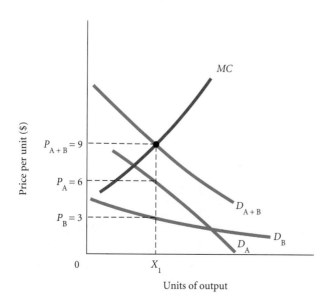

◀ **FIGURE 16.6**

Optimal Production of a Public Good

Optimal production of a public good means producing as long as society's total willingness to pay per unit (D_{A+B}) is greater than the marginal cost of producing the good.

towns. Also, if some town is efficient at crime prevention, it will attract residents—given that each town has limited space, property values will be bid up in this town. The higher home price in this town is the "price" of the lower crime rate.

According to the **Tiebout hypothesis**, an efficient mix of public goods is produced when local prices (in the form of taxes or higher housing costs) come to reflect consumer preferences just as they do in the market for private goods. What is different in the Tiebout world is that people exercise consumer sovereignty not by "buying" different combinations of goods in a market, but by "voting with their feet" (choosing among bundles of public goods and tax rates produced by different towns and participating in local government).

Tiebout hypothesis   An efficient mix of public goods is produced when local land/housing prices and taxes come to reflect consumer preferences just as they do in the market for private goods.

Social Choice

One view of government, or the public sector, holds that it exists to provide things that "society wants." A society is a collection of individuals, and each has a unique set of preferences. Defining what society wants, therefore, becomes a problem of **social choice**—of somehow adding up, or aggregating, individual preferences.

It is also important to understand that government is made up of individuals—politicians and government workers—whose *own* objectives in part determine what government does. To understand government, we must understand the incentives facing politicians and public servants, as well as the difficulties of aggregating the preferences of the members of a society.

social choice   The problem of deciding what society wants. The process of adding up individual preferences to make a choice for society as a whole.

The Voting Paradox

Democratic societies use ballot procedures to determine aggregate preferences and to make the social decisions that follow from them. If all votes could be unanimous, efficient decisions would be guaranteed. Unfortunately, unanimity is virtually impossible to achieve when hundreds of millions of people, with their own different preferences, are involved.

The most common social decision-making mechanism is majority rule, but it is not perfect. In 1951, economist Kenneth Arrow proved the **impossibility theorem**[6]—that it is impossible to devise a voting system that respects individual preferences and gives consistent, nonarbitrary results.

One example of a seemingly irrational result emerging from majority-rule voting is the voting paradox. Suppose that faced with a decision about the future of the institution, the president of a major university opts to let its top three administrators vote on the following options: Should the university (A) increase the number of students and hire more faculty, (B) maintain the current size of the faculty and student body, or (C) cut back on faculty and reduce the student body? Figure 16.7 represents the preferences of the three administrators diagrammatically.

The vice president for finance (VP1) wants growth, preferring A to B and B to C. The vice president for development (VP2), however, does not want to rock the boat, preferring the maintenance of the current size of the institution, option B, to either of the others. If the status quo is out of the question, VP2 would prefer option C. The dean believes in change, wanting to shake the place up and not caring whether that means an increase or a decrease. The dean prefers C to A and A to B.

impossibility theorem   A proposition demonstrated by Kenneth Arrow showing that no system of aggregating individual preferences into social decisions will always yield consistent, nonarbitrary results.

▶ **FIGURE 16.7**

Preferences of Three Top University Officials

VP1 prefers A to B and B to C. VP2 prefers B to C and C to A. The dean prefers C to A and A to B.

	Option A — Hire more faculty	Option B — No change	Option C — Reduce the size of the faculty
Ranking			
1	X (VP1)	X (VP2)	X
2	X	X	X
3	X	X (Dean)	X

---

[6] Kenneth Arrow, *Social Choice and Individual Values* (New York: John Wiley, 1951).

Table 16.2 shows the results of the vote. When the three vote on A versus B, they vote in favor of A—to increase the size of the university instead of keeping it the same size. VP1 and the dean outvote VP2. Voting on B and C produces a victory for option B; two of the three would prefer to hold the line than to decrease the size of the institution. After two votes, we have the result that A (an increase) is preferred to B (no change) and that B (no change) is preferred to C (a decrease).

TABLE 16.2	Results of Voting on University's Plans: The Voting Paradox			
		Votes of:		
Vote	VP1	VP2	Dean	Result[a]
A versus B	A	B	A	A wins: A > B
B versus C	B	B	C	B wins: B > C
C versus A	A	C	C	C wins: C > A

[a]A > B is read "A is preferred to B."

The problem arises when we have the three vote on A against C. Both VP2 and the dean vote for C, giving it the victory; C is actually preferred to A. Nevertheless, if A beats B and B beats C, how can C beat A? The results are inconsistent.

The **voting paradox** illustrates several points. Most important is that when preferences for public goods differ among individuals, any system for adding up, or aggregating, those preferences can lead to inconsistencies. In addition, it illustrates just how much influence the person who sets the agenda has. If a vote had been taken on A and C first, the first two votes might never have occurred. This is why rules committees in both houses of Congress have enormous power; they establish the rules under which, as well as the order in which, legislation will be considered.

Another problem with majority-rule voting is that it leads to logrolling. **Logrolling** occurs when representatives trade votes—D helps get a majority in favor of E's program; in exchange, E helps D get a majority on D's program. It is not clear whether any bill could get through any legislature without logrolling. It is also not clear whether logrolling is, on balance, a good thing or a bad thing from the standpoint of efficiency. On the one hand, a program that benefits one region or group of people might generate enormous net social gains, but because the group of beneficiaries is fairly small, it will not command a majority of delegates. If another bill that is likely to generate large benefits to another area is also awaiting a vote, a trade of support between the two sponsors of the bills should result in the passage of two good pieces of efficient legislation. On the other hand, logrolling can also turn out unjustified, inefficient pork barrel legislation.

A number of other problems also follow from voting as a mechanism for public choice. For one, voters do not have much of an incentive to become well informed. When you go out to buy a car or, on a smaller scale, an MP3 player, you are the one who suffers the full consequences of a bad choice. Similarly, you are the beneficiary of the gains from a good choice. This is not so in voting. Although many of us believe that we have a civic responsibility to vote, no one really believes that his or her vote will actually determine the outcome of an election. The time and effort it takes just to get to the polls are enough to deter many people. Becoming informed involves even more costs, and it is not surprising that many people do not do it.

Beyond the fact that a single vote is not likely to be decisive is the fact that the costs and benefits of wise and unwise social choices are widely shared. If the congressperson whom you elect makes a big mistake and wastes a billion dollars, you bear only a small fraction of that cost. Even though the sums involved are large in aggregate, individual voters find little incentive to become informed.

Two additional problems with voting are that choices are almost always limited to *bundles* of publicly provided goods and that we vote infrequently. Many of us vote for Republicans or Democrats. We vote for president only every 4 years. We elect senators for 6-year terms. In private markets, we can look at each item separately and decide how much of each item we want. We also can shop daily. In the public sector, though, we vote for a platform or a party that takes a particular position on a whole range of issues. In the public sector it is very difficult, or impossible, for voters to unbundle issues.

There is, of course, a reason why bundling occurs in the sphere of public choice. It is difficult enough to convince people to go to the polls once a year. If we voted separately on every appropriation bill, we would spend our lives at the polls. This is one reason for representative democracy. We elect officials who we hope will become informed and represent our interests and preferences.

voting paradox A simple demonstration of how majority-rule voting can lead to seemingly contradictory and inconsistent results. A commonly cited illustration of the kind of inconsistency described in the impossibility theorem.

logrolling Occurs when congressional representatives trade votes, agreeing to help each other get certain pieces of legislation passed.

Government Inefficiency: Theory of Public Choice

Recent work in economics has focused not just on the government as an extension of individual preferences but also on government officials as people with their own agendas and objectives. That is, government officials are assumed to maximize their own utility, not the social good. To understand the way government functions, we need to look less at the preferences of individual members of society and more at the incentive structures that exist around public officials.

The officials whom we seem to worry about are the people who run government agencies—the Social Security Administration, the Department of Housing and Urban Development, and state registries of motor vehicles, for example. What incentive do these people have to produce a good product and to be efficient? Might such incentives be lacking?

In the private sector, where firms compete for profits, only efficient firms producing goods that consumers will buy survive. If a firm is inefficient—if it is producing at a higher-than-necessary cost—the market will drive it out of business. This is not necessarily so in the public sector. If a government bureau is producing a necessary service or one that is mandated by law, it does not need to worry about customers. No matter how bad the service is at the registry of motor vehicles, everyone with a car must buy its product.

The efficiency of a government agency's internal structure depends on the way incentives facing workers and agency heads are structured. If the budget allocation of an agency is based on the last period's spending alone, for example, agency heads have a clear incentive to spend more money, however inefficiently. This point is not lost on government officials, who have experimented with many ways of rewarding agency heads and employees for cost-saving suggestions.

However, critics say such efforts to reward productivity and punish inefficiency are rarely successful. It is difficult to punish, let alone dismiss, a government employee. Elected officials are subject to recall, but it usually takes gross negligence to rouse voters into instituting such a measure. Also, elected officials are rarely associated with problems of bureaucratic mismanagement, which they decry daily.

Critics of "the bureaucracy" argue that no set of internal incentives can ever match the discipline of the market. They point to studies of private versus public garbage collection, airline operations, fire protection, mail service, and so on, all of which suggest significantly lower costs in the private sector. One theme of the Reagan and first Bush administrations was "privatization." If the private sector can possibly provide a service, it is likely to do so more efficiently—so the public sector should allow the private sector to take over.

One concern regarding wholesale privatization is the potential effect it may have on distribution. Late in his administration, President Reagan suggested that the federal government sell its entire stock of public housing to the private sector. Would the private sector continue to provide housing to poor people? The worry is that it would not because it may not be profitable to do so.

Like voters, public officials suffer from a lack of incentive to become fully informed and to make tough choices. Consider an elected official. If the real objective of an elected official is to get reelected, then the real incentive must be to provide visible goods for that official's constituency while hiding the costs or spreading them thin. Self-interest may easily lead to poor decisions and public irresponsibility.

Looking at the public sector from the standpoint of the behavior of public officials and the potential for inefficient choices and bureaucratic waste rather than in terms of its potential for improving the allocation of resources has become quite popular. This is the viewpoint of what is called the *public choice* field in economics that builds heavily on the work of Nobel laureate James Buchanan.

Rent-Seeking Revisited

Another problem with public choice is that special-interest groups can and do spend resources to influence the legislative process. As we said before, individual voters have little incentive to become well informed and to participate fully in the legislative process. Favor-seeking special-interest groups have a great deal of incentive to participate in political decision making. We saw in Chapter 13 that a monopolist would be willing to pay to prevent competition from eroding its economic profits. Many—if not all—industries lobby for favorable treatment, softer regulation, or antitrust exemption. This, as you recall, is *rent-seeking*.

Rent-seeking extends far beyond those industries that lobby for government help in preserving monopoly powers. Any group that benefits from a government policy has an incentive to use its resources to lobby for that policy. Farmers lobby for farm subsidies, oil producers lobby for oil import taxes, and the American Association of Retired Persons lobbies against cuts in Social Security.

In the absence of well-informed and active voters, special-interest groups assume an important and perhaps critical role. But there is another side to this story. Some have argued that favorable legislation is, in effect, for sale in the marketplace. Those willing and able to pay the most are more successful in accomplishing their goals than those with fewer resources. Theory may suggest that unregulated markets fail to produce an efficient allocation of resources. This should not lead you to the conclusion that government involvement necessarily leads to efficiency. There are reasons to believe that government attempts to produce the right goods and services in the right quantities efficiently may fail.

Government and the Market

There is no question that government must be involved in both the provision of public goods and the control of externalities. No society has ever existed in which citizens did not get together to protect themselves from the abuses of an unrestrained market and to provide for themselves certain goods and services that the market did not provide. The question is not *whether* we need government involvement. The question is *how much* and *what kind* of government involvement we should have.

Critics of government involvement correctly say that the existence of an "optimal" level of public-goods production does not guarantee that governments will achieve it. It is easy to show that governments will generally fail to achieve the most efficient level. There is no reason to believe that governments are capable of achieving the "correct" amount of control over externalities. Markets may fail to produce an efficient allocation of resources, but governments may make it worse. Measurement of social damages and benefits is difficult and imprecise. For example, estimates of the costs of acid rain range from practically nothing to incalculably high amounts.

Just as critics of government involvement must concede that the market by itself fails to achieve full efficiency, defenders of government involvement must acknowledge government's failures. Many on both sides agree that we get closer to an efficient allocation of resources by trying to control externalities and by doing our best to produce the public goods that people want with the imperfect tools we have than we would by leaving everything to the market.

─── **SUMMARY** ───

EXTERNALITIES AND ENVIRONMENTAL ECONOMICS *p. 329*

1. Often when we engage in transactions or make economic decisions, second or third parties suffer consequences that decision makers have no incentive to consider. These are called *externalities*. A classic example of an external cost is pollution.

2. When external costs are not considered in economic decisions, we may engage in activities or produce products that are not "worth it." When external benefits are not considered, we may fail to do things that are indeed "worth it." The result is an inefficient allocation of resources.

3. A number of alternative mechanisms have been used to control externalities: (1) government-imposed taxes and subsidies, (2) private bargaining and negotiation, (3) legal remedies such as *injunctions* and *liability rules*, (4) sale or auctioning of rights to impose externalities, and (5) direct regulation.

PUBLIC (SOCIAL) GOODS *p. 341*

4. In an unfettered market, certain goods and services that people want will not be produced in adequate amounts. These *public goods* have characteristics that make it difficult or impossible for the private sector to produce them profitably.

5. Public goods are *nonrival in consumption* (their benefits fall collectively on members of society or on groups of members), and/or their benefits are *nonexcludable* (it is generally impossible to exclude people who have not paid from enjoying the benefits of public goods). An example of a public good is national defense.

6. One of the problems of public provision is that it leads to public dissatisfaction. We can choose any quantity of private goods that we want, or we can walk away without buying any. When it comes to public goods such as national defense, the government must choose one and only one kind and quantity of (collective) output to produce.

7. Theoretically, there exists an *optimal level of provision* for each public good. At this level, society's willingness to pay per unit equals the marginal cost of producing the good. To discover such a level, we would need to know the preferences of each individual citizen.

8. According to the *Tiebout hypothesis*, an efficient mix of public goods is produced when local land/housing prices and taxes come to reflect consumer preferences just as they do in the market for private goods.

SOCIAL CHOICE *p. 346*

9. Because we cannot know everyone's preferences about public goods, we are forced to rely on imperfect *social choice* mechanisms such as majority rule.

10. The theory that unfettered markets do not achieve an efficient allocation of resources should not lead us to conclude that government involvement necessarily leads to efficiency. Governments also fail.

GOVERNMENT AND THE MARKET *p. 349*

11. Defenders of government involvement in the economy acknowledge its failures but believe we get closer to an efficient allocation of resources with government than without it. By trying to control externalities and by doing our best to provide the public goods that society wants, we do better than we would if we left everything to the market.

REVIEW TERMS AND CONCEPTS

Coase theorem, *p. 334*

drop-in-the-bucket problem, *p. 342*

externality, *p. 329*

free-rider problem, *p. 342*

impossibility theorem, *p. 346*

injunction, *p. 336*

liability rules, *p. 336*

logrolling, *p. 347*

marginal damage cost (*MDC*), *p. 333*

marginal private cost (*MPC*), *p. 333*

marginal social cost (*MSC*), *p. 330*

market failure, *p. 329*

nonexcludable, *p. 342*

nonrival in consumption, *p. 341*

optimal level of provision for public goods, *p. 345*

public goods (social *or* collective goods), *p. 341*

social choice, *p. 346*

Tiebout hypothesis, *p. 346*

voting paradox, *p. 347*

PROBLEMS

All problems are available on www.myeconlab.com

1. If government imposes on the firms in a polluting industry penalties (taxes) that exceed the actual value of the damages done by the pollution, the result is an inefficient and unfair imposition of costs on those firms and on the consumers of their products. Discuss that statement. Use a graph to show how consumers are harmed.

2. It has been proposed that toll collection on the Massachusetts Turnpike, a key commuter route into Boston from the west, be discontinued. Proponents argue that tolls have long ago paid for the cost of building the road; now they just provide cash for a fat bureaucracy. A number of economists are opposing the repeal of tolls on the grounds that they serve to internalize externalities. Explain their argument briefly.

3. Many people are concerned with the problem of urban sprawl. As the development of new housing tracts and suburban shopping malls continues over time, metropolitan areas have become more congested and polluted. Open space disappears, and the quality of life changes. Think of your own metropolitan area, city, or town. Using the concept of externalities, consider the issue of land use and development. What are the specific decisions made in the development process that lead to externalities? On whom are the externalities imposed? Do you think that they are measurable? In what specific ways can decision makers be given the incentive to consider them? One of the cities that has paid the most attention to urban sprawl is Portland, Oregon. Search the Web to see what you can find out about Portland's approach.

4. The existence of "public goods" is an example of potential market failure and suggests that a government or public sector can *improve* the outcome of completely free markets. Write a brief summary of the arguments *for* government provision of public goods. (Make sure you consider the discussion of a prisoners' dilemma in the last chapter.) The following three arguments suggest that government may not improve the outcome as much as we might anticipate.
    a. *Public goods theory:* Because public goods are collective, the government is constrained to pick a single level of output for all of us. National defense is an example. The government must pick one level of defense expenditure. Some will think it is too much, some will think it is too little, and no one is happy.

    b. *Problems of social choice:* It is impossible to choose collectively in a rational way that satisfies voters/consumers of public goods.

    c. *Public choice and public officials:* Once elected or appointed, public officials tend to act in accordance with their own preferences and not out of concern for the public.

5. Which of the three arguments do you find to be most persuasive?

    It has been argued that the following are examples of "mixed goods." They are essentially private but partly public. For each example, describe the private and public components and discuss briefly why the government should or should not be involved in their provision.
    a. Elementary and secondary education
    b. Higher education
    c. Medical care
    d. Air traffic control

6. A paper factory dumps polluting chemicals into the Snake River. Thousands of citizens live along the river, and they bring suit, claiming damages. You are asked by the judge to testify at the trial as an impartial expert. The court is considering four possible solutions, and you are asked to comment on the potential efficiency and equity of each. Your testimony should be brief.
    a. Deny the merits of the case and affirm the polluter's right to dump. The parties will achieve the optimal solution without government.
    b. Find in favor of the plaintiff. The polluters will be held liable for damages and must fully compensate citizens for all past and future damages imposed.
    c. Order an immediate end to the dumping, with no damages awarded.
    d. Refer the matter to the Environmental Protection Agency, which will impose a tax on the factory equal to the marginal damage costs. Proceeds will not be paid to the damaged parties.

7. [Related to the *Economics in Practice* on p. 338] The *Economics in Practice* suggests that children impose negative externalities. What does that imply about discounts for children's meals at restaurants and discount tickets for children at museums? Provide three examples of activities that may, in fact, generate positive externalities.

8. Explain why you agree or disagree with each of the following statements:
   a. The government should be involved in providing housing for the poor because housing is a "public good."
   b. From the standpoint of economic efficiency, an unregulated market economy tends to overproduce public goods.

9. Society is made up of two individuals, A and B, whose demands for public good X are given in Figure 1. Assuming that the public good can be produced at a constant marginal cost of $6, what is the optimal level of output? How much would you charge A and B?

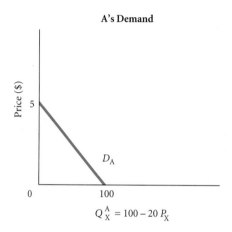

A's Demand

$$Q^A_X = 100 - 20\, P_X$$

B's Demand

$$Q^B_X = 100 - 10\, P_X$$

▲ **FIGURE 1**

10. Government involvement in general scientific research has been justified on the grounds that advances in knowledge are public goods—once produced, information can be shared at virtually no cost. A new production technology in an industry could be made available to all firms, reducing costs of production, driving down price, and benefiting the public. The patent system, however, allows private producers of "new knowledge" to exclude others from enjoying the benefits of that knowledge. Inventors would have little incentive to produce new knowledge if there was no possibility of profiting from their inventions. If one company holds exclusive rights to an advanced production process, it produces at lower cost but can use the exclusion to acquire monopoly power and hold price up.
    a. On balance, is the patent system a good or bad thing? Explain.
    b. Is government involvement in scientific research a good idea? Discuss.

11. The Coase theorem implies that we never need to worry about regulating externalities because the private individuals involved will reach the efficient outcome through negotiations. Is that statement true or false? Justify your answer and use examples.

12. The recent economic growth resulting from government policies of newly industrializing nations such as India and China has increased environmental strains on global air and water systems. The negative externalities associated with this economic growth demonstrate that the best economic system is one in which *all* economic decisions are made by individual households and firms without *any* government involvement. Comment briefly.

13. [Related to the *Economics in Practice* on *p. 341*] The United Nations Climate Change Conference was scheduled to be held in Cancun, Mexico, from November 29–December 10, 2010. Search the Internet to find information about this conference. Write a brief essay on any binding deals concerning global warming which were reached at the conference. If no deals were reached, discuss which nations prevented any binding resolutions and what issues stood in the way of reaching these deals.

14. The following diagram represents the profit-maximizing price and output for a firm in a perfectly competitive industry with no externalities. Use this diagram to explain what will happen if the production of the product imposes external costs on society and these costs are not factored into production decisions.

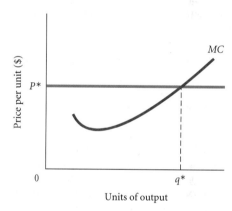

Units of output

15. Refer to the previous question but assume that the government has imposed a per-unit tax on this product which is exactly equal to the marginal damage costs. Use the diagram to show what will happen to production, output, and price.

16. Suppose the nation of Valencia must decide which project to fund: public transportation, construction of a seaport, or a national Wi-Fi network. The nation has the available funds to finance only one of these projects, and the decision is up to Valencia's three-person finance committee. The order of preference of the finance committee members is shown in the table. Explain whether the information in the table will lead to a voting paradox.

PROJECT	DELIA	ANDREW	MALIKA
Public transportation	1	3	2
Seaport construction	2	1	3
Wi-Fi network	3	2	1

17. Two firms, Cappcore and Tradiola, are each emitting 6 units of pollution, and the government wants to reduce the total level of pollution from the current level of 12 to 4. To do this, the government caps each firm's allowed pollution level at 2. Each firm must now pay to cut pollution levels by 4 units. A cap-and-trade policy gives each of these firms two permits and allows them to trade permits if they choose. Based on the table below which represents the situation faced by these two firms, what will the firms want to do?

	CAPPCORE			TRADIOLA	
POLLUTION REDUCTION, UNITS	*MC* OF REDUCING POLLUTION	*TC* OF REDUCING POLLUTION	POLLUTION REDUCTION, UNITS	*MC* OF REDUCING POLLUTION	*TC* OF REDUCING POLLUTION
1	$ 7	$ 7	1	$ 3	$ 3
2	10	17	2	4	7
3	14	31	3	6	13
4	19	50	4	9	22
5	26	76	5	14	36
6	35	111	6	21	57

18. Sammy, a drummer in a local band, and Dean, a librarian at a local university, share a condo in San Diego. Sammy enjoys playing his drums at home, and Dean enjoys reading in silence. Dean is willing to pay Sammy $125 if he will stop playing the drums at home. Sammy offers Dean $75 per week to find some place else to read. If Dean has the right to read in silence, explain why the condo will be free of drum playing. If Sammy has the right to play his drums, explain why the condo will still be free of drum playing.

Uncertainty and Asymmetric Information

17

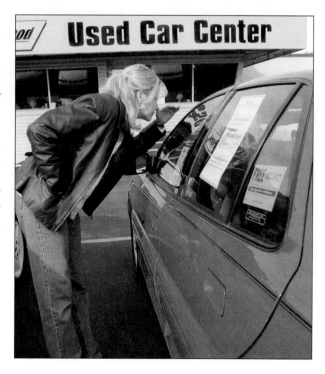

In previous chapters, we assumed that consumers and firms made choices based on perfect information. When consumers choose between two products, we assume that they know the qualities of those products, and as a result their choices reveal their true preferences. Similarly, when firms choose how many workers to hire or how much capital to use, we assume that they know the productivity of those workers or that capital. Of course, in many settings, perfect information seems to be a reasonable assumption to make. Every day you may choose whether to have cereal or eggs for breakfast. Every evening you may decide what to have for dinner and whether to go to the movies or stay home and study. Even for these choices, a little uncertainty can creep in; perhaps a new cereal is on the market or a new movie has been released. But assuming that these choices are made with perfect information does not seem too far a stretch.

In some markets, however, consumers and firms clearly make decisions with quite limited information. When you decide to insure your car against theft, you don't know whether the car will be stolen. When you decide to buy a used car, it is not easy to figure out how good that car really is. If you are choosing between a sales job that pays a flat salary and one that pays a commission for every sale you make, you have to predict how good your sales skills will be to determine which is the better offer. In many markets, including some very important markets, consumers as well as firms make decisions while having only some of the information they need. In this chapter, we will explore the economics of these markets. As we go through this chapter, you will see how both the recent health care reform discussion and the 2008–2009 banking crisis can be understood using economic tools.

Decision Making Under Uncertainty: The Tools

In Chapter 6, we laid out the fundamental principles of consumer choice assuming perfect information. To adapt this model to cases in which there is uncertainty, we need to develop a few more tools.

Expected Value

Suppose I offer you the following deal: You flip a coin 100 times. Every time the coin is a head, you pay me $1. Whenever the coin lands on tails, I pay you a dollar. We call the amount that one player—in this case, me—receives in each of the situations the **payoff**. Here my payoff is +$1 for heads and –$1 for tails. In the case of a coin toss, the probability of heads is ½, as is the probability of tails. This tells us that the financial value of this deal to me, or its expected value, is $0. Half the time I win a dollar, and half the time I lose a dollar. Formally, we define the **expected value** of an uncertain situation or deal as the sum of the payoffs associated with each possible outcome multiplied by the probability that outcome will occur. Again, in the case of a coin toss with the payoffs described, the expected value (EV) is

$$EV = 1/2 (\$1) + 1/2 (-\$1) = 0$$

The coin toss is an easy example, in part because there are only two outcomes. But the definition of expected value holds for any deal in which I can describe both the payoffs and the probabilities of all possible outcomes. If I play a game in which I receive $1 every time I roll a die and end up with an even number and I pay $1 every time the die comes up odd, this deal also has an expected value of $0. Half the time (3 of 6 possible outcomes) I receive $1, and half the time (3 of 6 possible outcomes) I pay $1.

The two games just described are known as **fair games** or **fair bets**. A fair game has an expected value of $0. The expected financial gains from playing a fair game are equal to the financial costs of that game. In the two fair games we described, the stakes are quite low. Suppose instead of $1 payoffs, we made the payoffs $1,000 for heads and –$1,000 for tails. As you can see, the expected value of that deal is $0 just as it was in the $1 game. But we have learned in watching people's behavior that while some people might be willing to play a fair game with $1 payoffs, very few people will play $1,000-payoff fair games. What is it about people that makes them change their minds about taking a fair bet when the stakes get high? We will explore this question next using some of the tools already covered in Chapter 6.

Expected Utility

Recall from Chapter 6 that consumers make choices to maximize utility. The idea of maximizing utility will also help us understand the way in which those consumers make choices in risky situations.

Chapter 6 introduced you to the idea of **diminishing marginal utility**—the more of any one good consumed in a period, the less incremental satisfaction (utility) will be generated by each additional (marginal) unit of that good. Review Figure 6.3 on p. 127 and notice the form the utility curve takes when we have diminishing marginal utility for a good. The curve flattens as we increase units of the good consumed. Now think about what happens to your utility level when we increase not the number of units of a particular good, but your overall income. Figure 17.1 graphs the total utility of a typical consumer, Jacob, as a function of his income. On the Y-axis, we have assigned units of total utility, while on the X-axis we have annual income. The shape of the utility curve tells us that Jacob has diminishing marginal utility from income. The first $20,000 of income is very important to Jacob, moving him from a total utility level of 0 to 10; this first $20,000 might allow him to buy food and shelter, for example. Moving from $20,000 to $40,000 brings an increase in well-being from 10 to 15. Notice that the second $20,000 adds 5 to the total utility level, while the first $20,000 adds 10. And the pattern continues as we add $20,000 increments to income. Each dollar increases total utility, but at a decreasing rate. The result is a curve as shown in Figure 17.1 that flattens as we move from left to right, with smaller gains in total utility from equal gains in income.

You should see that the assumption of diminishing marginal utility of income reflects the diminishing marginal utility of goods that we talked about in Chapter 6. Income counts for less the more we have because the value of what we can buy with that money on the margin falls as we buy more.

As you think about Figure 17.1, remember that we are describing the relationship between utility and income for a *given individual*. The figure does not tell us that rich people get less utility from an incremental dollar than do poor people. Indeed, it might be argued that one reason some rich people work so hard to make money is that they get a great deal of utility from increases in income relative to the average person. But rich or poor, Figure 17.1 tells us that as your income increases, the marginal utility of another dollar falls.

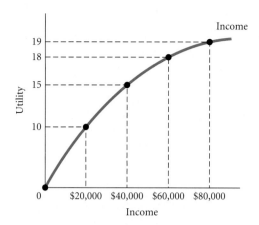

◀ **FIGURE 17.1 The Relationship Between Utility and Income**
The figure shows the way in which utility increases with income for a hypothetical person, Jacob. Notice that utility increases with income but at a decreasing rate: the curve gets flatter as income increases. This curve shows diminishing marginal utility of income.

How does Figure 17.1 help us explain people's unwillingness to play fair games with larger stakes? Suppose Jacob, the individual whose preferences are shown in Figure 17.1, is currently earning $40,000. We see that $40,000 corresponds to a total utility level of 15. Now a firm offers Jacob a different type of salary structure. Rather than earning $40,000 for sure, at the end of the year, a manager will toss a coin. If it is heads, Jacob will earn $60,000; but if the coin turns up tails, his earnings will fall to $20,000. This is a high stakes game of the sort described earlier. Notice that the expected value of the two salaries is the same. With one, Jacob earns $40,000 with certainty. With the second, he earns $20,000 half the time and $60,000 half the time, for an expected value of

$$EV = 1/2(\$20,000) + 1/2 (60,000) = \$40,000$$

From an expected value perspective, the two salary offers are identical. So if we simply looked at the expected values, we might expect Jacob to be indifferent between the two wage offers. But if you put yourself in Jacob's shoes, probably you would not find the coin-tossing salary to be as attractive as the fixed $40,000 wage. If we think back to the model introduced in Chapter 6, we can see why. Consumers make choices not to maximize income per se but to maximize their utility levels. Figure 17.1 tells us that while utility increases with income, the relationship is not linear. So to decide what Jacob will do, we need to look at his utility under the two contracts.

What can we say about Jacob's utility under the two salary contracts? With a fixed $40,000 salary, total utility is at a level of 15, as we saw earlier. If his income falls to $20,000, that utility level falls from 15 to 10, a substantial drop. With a possible earnings level of $60,000, the total utility level goes up; but notice that it only increases from 15 to only 18. The drop in income causes a bigger loss in utility than comes from a gain in income. Of course, this results from the diminishing marginal utility of income. In fact, we can define **expected utility** as the sum of the utilities coming from all possible outcomes of a deal, weighted by the probability of each occurring. You can see that the expected utility is like the expected value, but the payoffs are in utility terms rather than in dollars. In the coin-toss salary offer, if you look again at Figure 17.1, the expected utility (EU) is

expected utility The sum of the utilities coming from all possible outcomes of a deal, weighted by the probability of each occurring.

$$EU = 1/2 \ U(\$20,000) + 1/2 \ U(60,000), \text{ which reduces to}$$

$$EU = 1/2 \ (10) + 1/2 \ (18) = 14$$

Since Jacob's utility from a fixed salary of $40,000 is 15, he will not take the coin-toss salary alternative.

Of course, in practice, workers are not paid wages based on the toss of a coin. Nevertheless, many wage contracts contain some uncertainty. Many of you have probably had jobs where your wages were uncertain in ways you could not control. Understanding the difference between expected value maximization and expected utility maximization helps us understand these and other similar contracts.

In uncertain situations, consumers make choices to maximize their expected utility. Looking at Figure 17.1, you should now see why people may take small fair bets but will avoid fair games with high stakes. For small games, people are making choices within a very small region of the utility curve. The utility of gaining one more dollar or losing it is almost identical. When we compare outcomes at very different points on the utility curve, the differences in marginal utility become more pronounced. This makes large fair bets quite unattractive.

Attitudes Toward Risk

We have now seen that diminishing marginal utility of income means that the typical individual will not play a large stakes fair game. Individuals, like Jacob, who prefer a certain payoff to an uncertain payoff with an equal expected value are called **risk-averse**. Risk aversion thus comes from the assumption of diminishing marginal utility of income and can be seen in the shape of the utility curve. You are unwilling to take a risk because the costs of losing in terms of your well-being or utility exceed the gains of possibly winning. People who are willing to take a fair bet, one that has an expected value of zero, are known as **risk-neutral**. For these individuals, the marginal utility of income is constant so that the relationship between total utility and income in a graph like Figure 17.1, for example, would be a straight, upward-sloping line. Again, we have seen that some people will be risk-neutral when the stakes are low. Finally, some people, in some circumstances, may actually prefer uncertain games to certain outcomes. Individuals who pay to play a game with an expected value of zero or less are known as **risk-loving**. Since most people are risk-averse in most situations, we will concentrate on this case.

The fact that people are, in general, risk-averse is seen in many markets. Most people who own houses buy fire insurance even when not required to do so. In general, a fire insurance policy costs a homeowner more than it is worth in terms of expected value; this is how insurance companies make money. People pay for this insurance because they are risk-averse: The possible loss of their home is very important relative to the value of the premiums they have to pay to protect it. When people invest in a risky business, there has to be some chance that they will "make it big" to induce them to put up their money. The riskier the business in the sense that it may fail, the bigger the upside potential needs to be. This too is an indication of risk aversion.

The presence of risk and uncertainty do not by themselves pose a problem for the workings of the market. The risk that your house might burn down does not prevent you from buying a house; it simply encourages you, if you are risk-averse, to buy insurance. In fact, many markets are designed to allow people to trade risk. Individuals who are risk-averse seek out other individuals (or more commonly firms) who are willing to take on those risks for a price.

The **risk premium** is the maximum price a risk-averse person will pay to avoid taking a risk. Figure 17.2 gives us another look at the same individual, Jacob, we examined in Figure 17.1. Suppose Jacob is currently earning $40,000 but faces a 50 percent chance of suffering an unpreventable disability that will reduce his income level to $0. Thus, the expected value of Jacob's income is

$$EV = .5(\$40,000) + .5(\$0) = \$20,000$$

Suppose further that there are many individuals just like Jacob. On average, in any year, half would become disabled and half would not. If an insurance company offered policies to all of them, offering to replace their $40,000 salaries should they become disabled, on average, this policy would cost the company $20,000 per person. In other words, the expected value tells us what, on average, it would cost a firm that pooled large numbers of identical people to offer them insurance against an income loss of this size. If the individuals are willing to pay the insurance company more than this expected value, there is a potential deal to be made. In fact, looking at Figure 17.2 shows us that the deal offered by the insurance company to cover earnings losses in the case of a disability is worth more than $20,000 to a risk-averse individual like Jacob. Uninsured, Jacob faces a 50 percent chance of earning $0 and a 50 percent chance of earning $40,000. Looking at the graph, we see that the expected utility of Jacob in his uninsured state is

$$EU = .5 \, U \, (\$0) + .5 \, U(\$40,000)$$

$$EU = .5(0) + .5(15) = 7.5$$

risk-averse Refers to a person's preference of a certain payoff over an uncertain one with the same expected value.

risk-neutral Refers to a person's willingness to take a bet with an expected value of zero.

risk-loving Refers to a person's preference for an uncertain deal over a certain deal with an equal expected value.

risk premium The maximum price a risk-averse person will pay to avoid taking a risk.

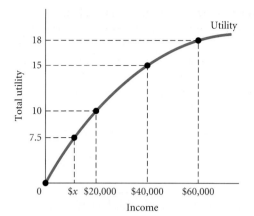

◀ **FIGURE 17.2**

Risk Aversion and Insurance Markets

With a 50 percent chance of earning $40,000 and a 50 percent chance of becoming disabled and earning $0, Jacob has an EV of income of $20,000. But his expected utility is halfway between the utility of $40,000 (15) and the utility of 0 (0), or 7.5. $x is the amount of certain earnings Jacob would accept to avoid a 50 percent chance of earning $0.

But a utility level of 7.5 corresponds, as we look at Figure 17.2, to a certain income level of x, which is below the $20,000 level. In other words, Jacob would be indifferent between a certain income of $x and remaining uninsured. But notice that $x is less than $20,000, which tells us that Jacob is willing to pay more than $20,000 to avoid this disability risk. So there is room for a deal between the insurance company and risk-averse individuals. Because insurance companies can pool risks across many different people, they will be risk-neutral, willing to take on the risks of individuals for a price. In this example, the distance between $20,000, the expected value of the risk, and $x tells us the risk premium.

You may now be wondering how economists explain gambling. Every day people throughout the United States buy lottery tickets even though they know that lotteries are not a fair bet. The Powerball lottery in Connecticut is one example. The winning number is generated by choosing 5 numbers out of a pool of 49, then choosing another number from a pool of 42. The probability of getting all 6 numbers correct and winning the lottery's top prize is 1 in 80 million. The top prize in the lottery varies but is typically in the $10 million to $150 million range. The prize is taxable, and winning the top prize would push a winner into the top tax bracket with a tax rate of almost 40 percent. When the prize level is very high, many people play the lottery and there is a risk of multiple winners, with prize sharing. Thus, in almost all cases, the expected value of the typical lottery is highly negative. Playing the slots at a casino also has a negative expected value, as do all professional games of chance. If this were not true, casinos would go out of business. Nevertheless, individuals buy lottery tickets and gamble in a range of forms. One explanation for this risk-taking behavior may, of course, be that some people find gambling fun and gamble not just in the hopes of winning but for the experience. For other people, gambling may be an addiction. Trying to understand more fully why people gamble while they seem to be risk-averse in most other ways remains an interesting research area in economics.

Asymmetric Information

In the discussion so far, we have described the way people behave in situations in which everyone involved in the deal is equally uncertain. Again, the coin toss is a classic case. When you offer me a coin toss game, neither you nor I know how the coin will fall. It is an unknowable game of chance. Under these situations, we have seen how to use the idea of expected utility to understand choices and we have seen how markets arise to enable risk trading. In other situations, though, the playing field may be less even, with one party to the transaction having more information relevant to the transaction than the other party. Economists refer to these circumstances as ones of **asymmetric information**. Asymmetric information creates possibilities of market failure by making it harder for individuals to make deals that would otherwise be attractive.

We are surrounded by situations with asymmetric information. A homeowner has better information than does his or her insurance company about how careful his or her family is, how often family members use candles, and whether anyone smokes. All of these factors are

asymmetric information One of the parties to a transaction has information relevant to the transaction that the other party does not have.

important to an insurance company trying to set an insurance price. When you applied to college, you likely knew more about your work ethic than did the colleges to which you applied.

In this section, we will explore several classic types of asymmetric situations. We will look at the nature of the market failure that arises when we have asymmetric information, and we will consider some of the mechanisms that individuals and markets use to deal with these problems.

Adverse Selection

A common saying in the car market is that once you drive a new car off the lot, it loses a substantial part of its original value. Why might this be true? Physical depreciation is likely small after only a few miles, for example. The answer can be found in the theory of adverse selection, a theory whose development was cited by the Nobel Committee in its award to George Akerlof in 2001. **Adverse selection** is a category of asymmetric information problems. In adverse selection, the quality of what is being offered in a transaction matters and is not easily demonstrated. For example, consumers might be willing to pay for high-quality used cars. But it is hard to tell which cars are good and which cars are not, and sellers will not, in general, have an incentive to be completely truthful. Insurance companies might be willing to offer inexpensive health insurance to people who take good care of themselves. But it is not easy to figure out who those people are, and insurance buyers are not likely to want to tell the company about their bad habits. As we will see, under these conditions, high-quality products and high-quality consumers are often squeezed out of markets, giving rise to the term *adverse selection*. In the *Economics in Practice* on page 360, we will explore some issues in adverse selection and genetic testing. But first we will explore the used car market, the setting Akerlof first wrote about.

adverse selection A situation in which asymmetric information results in high-quality goods or high-quality consumers being squeezed out of transactions because they cannot demonstrate their quality.

Adverse Selection and Lemons   Suppose you were in the market for a slightly used car of a particular make, perhaps from 2005. Having read a number of automotive magazines, you learned that half of these cars are lemons (bad cars) and half are peaches (good cars). Given your own tastes, a peach of this model year is worth $12,000 to you while a lemon is worth only $3,000. What would you pay if you were unable to tell a peach from a lemon?

One possible solution to this problem might involve thinking back to the lesson on expected value. The data we described suggest that the expected value of this type of used car is $7,500, which we calculate as ½($12,000) + ½($3,000). From expected utility theory, you might conclude that you would pay somewhat less than this—let's say $7,000.

The problem with this calculation, however, is that you have forgotten that you will be trying to buy this car from a rational, utility-maximizing car seller. Under these circumstances, it will not be equally likely that the car offered will be a peach or a lemon. Let us see how a potential seller of a used car sees the situation.

Suppose you offer current owners of a random 2005 car the $7,000 that we calculated. Which owners will want to sell? Owners of cars likely know whether they have peaches or lemons. After all, they have been driving these cars for a while. The game we are playing here is very different from the coin toss. Owners of the peaches will not, on average, find your offer attractive because their cars are worth $12,000 and you are offering only $7,000. Owners of lemons, on the other hand, will leap at the chance of unloading their cars at that price. In fact, with an offer of only $7,000, only lemon owners will offer their cars for sale. Over time, buyers come to understand that the probability of getting a lemon on the used market is greater than the probability of getting a peach and the price of the used cars will fall. In fact, in this situation, since you know with certainty that only lemons will be offered for sale, the most you will offer for the 2005 car is $3,000, the value to you of a lemon. In the end, Akerlof suggests, only lemons will be left in the market. Indeed, Akerlof called his paper "The Market for Lemons."

The used car example highlights the market failure associated with adverse selection. Because one party to the transaction—the seller here—has better information than the other party and because people behave opportunistically, owners of high-quality cars will have difficulty selling them. Buyers who are interested in peaches will find it hard to buy one because they cannot tell a lemon from a peach and thus are not willing to offer a high enough price to make the transaction. Thus, while there are buyers who value a peachy car more than it is valued by its current seller, no transaction will occur. The market, which is normally so good at moving goods from consumers who place a lower value on a good to consumers with higher values, does not work properly.

You should now see why the simple act of driving a car off the lot reduces its price dramatically: Potential buyers assume you are selling the car because you must have bought a lemon, and it is hard for you to prove otherwise.

Adverse Selection and Insurance   Adverse selection is a problem in a number of markets. Consider the very important market for insurance. We have already seen that risk aversion causes people to want to buy health insurance. But individuals often know more about their own health than anyone else, even with required medical exams. For a given premium level, those who know themselves to be most in need of medical care will be most attracted to the insurance. As unhealthy people swell the ranks of the insured, premiums will rise. The higher the rates, the less attractive healthy people will find such insurance. Similar problems are likely in markets for insurance on auto theft and fire. As with used cars, it will be difficult for insurance companies to transact business with lower-risk (high-quality) individuals.

Reducing Adverse Selection Problems   In practice, there are a number of ways in which individuals and markets try to respond to adverse selection problems. Mechanics offer would-be used car buyers an inspection service that levels the information playing field a bit. Of course, these inspection services have a price. Buyers can also look for other clues to quality. Some buyers have come to recognize that the best used cars to buy are from individuals who have to relocate to another state. Many students buy used cars from graduating seniors for example. People who need to relocate, like graduating seniors, often want to sell their cars even if they are peaches, and they may be willing to do so at prices that do not quite reflect what they know to be the high quality of the car they are selling. If a car is being sold by a dealer, he or she can offer a warranty that covers repairs for the first few years. The fact that a dealer is willing to offer a warranty tells the potential buyer that the car is not likely to be a lemon. Dealers also develop reputations for selling peaches or lemons. The government also plays a role in trying to reduce adverse selection problems in the used car market. All states have lemon laws that allow buyers to return a used car for a full refund within a few days of purchase on the grounds that some major problems can be detected after modest driving.

Insurance markets also employ strategies to reduce the problem of adverse selection. Companies require medical exams, for example, and often impose restrictions on their willingness to pay for treatment for preexisting conditions. Some companies offer better prices to people based on verifiable health-related behavior such as not smoking.

Understanding the problem of adverse selection is also useful when we think about the policy issue of universal health coverage. In the United States, health coverage is provided by a mix of the private sector (through employers and private purchase) and by the government through Medicare and Medicaid programs. Under the U.S. system currently in use, many people have a choice about what, if any, kind of health insurance they want to purchase given the premiums that insurers offer. By contrast, in some countries, including much of Western Europe, everyone receives health insurance, typically through a government program. A government program in which everyone is covered, at least at some level, is known as *universal health coverage*. The Health Care Reform Act of 2010 is moving the United States toward universal health coverage. While there is considerable debate about the merits of moving to a universal health coverage system, most economists agree that universal coverage reduces problems of adverse selection. When individuals can choose whether to be covered, on average, those who expect to most need medical care will be most attracted to the insurance offer. To the extent that universal coverage reduces choice, it reduces the adverse selection problem.

ECONOMICS IN PRACTICE

Adverse Selection in the Health Care Market

Health care is one area in which insurers worry about the problem of adverse selection. A recent study on long-term care insurance and Huntington's disease (HD) illustrates the issue.[1]

Huntington's disease is a degenerative neurological disorder. It is caused by a genetic mutation and affects 1 in 10,000 individuals. Onset typically occurs between ages 30 and 50 and individuals become increasingly disabled as the disease progresses. Death typically occurs about 20 years after onset.

Given the inheritability of HD, any individual with a parent who has the disease knows they have a 50 percent chance of having HD. Moreover, since 1993, there has been a test that perfectly predicts HD. Thus, individuals—because they know their family history and because they can be tested—have or could have substantial information about their likelihood of eventually suffering from HD. Insurers, on the other hand, while they can and typically do ask about health status, do not ask about family history and are not at this point permitted to inquire about the results of genetic tests. The health care reform bill of 2010 similarly requires the government to provide a long-term care option with premiums based only on age, not family or genetic history. Thus we have clear conditions of asymmetric information favoring potential insurance buyers. As indicated, HD also results in a prolonged period of severe disability, so that there is considerable benefit to owning insurance.

In a long-term study of HD patients, Oster et al. found that individuals who carry the HD genetic mutation are up to five

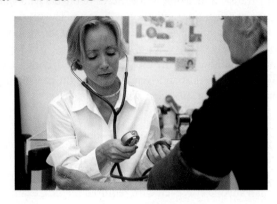

times as likely as the general population to buy long-term care insurance, indicating that adverse selection is both present and strong. For this population, the study finds that at current premiums, long-term care insurance is a bargain: For an individual who knows for sure that he or she will contract HD, the payout is almost $4 for every $1 of premiums paid. As genetic testing increases, situations of adverse selection in the health care area are likely to increase and we will be confronted with harder choices on how much genetic testing to reveal.

[1] Emily Oster, Kimberly Quaid, Ira Shoulson, E. Ray Dorsey, "Genetic Adverse Selection: Evidence from Long-Term Care Insurance and Huntington Disease," *Journal of Public Economics*, forthcoming.

Market Signaling

We have discussed how asymmetric information between buyers and sellers can lead to adverse selection. However, there are many things that can be done to overcome or at least reduce the information problem. Michael Spence, who shared the Nobel Prize in Economics with George Akerlof and Joseph Stiglitz in 2001, defined the concept of **market signaling** to help explain how buyers and sellers communicate quality in a world of uncertainty.

The college admission process is a good example of how signaling works. In the year 2008–2009, the age group applying to college in the United States peaked. This is the result of 4.1 million births in 1990, record immigration, and an economy that provided young people with an incentive to get a good education. Thus, the demand for spaces at the top schools far exceeded the spaces available. Harvard University alone received over 27,000 applications for membership in a class with fewer than 2,000 students. At the same time, many schools are far less selective and some cannot even fill the chairs in their classrooms.

In selective admissions, the student is clearly "selling" in the admissions process and the colleges and universities are buying. Signaling results because the matching between students and colleges involves communicating quality in a world of uncertainty.

The selective colleges and universities have uncertain information about the students that they admit. While schools have concrete information such as test scores and grades, they do not have concrete measures for other qualities that they are seeking. Thus, schools must look for *signals* of those characteristics.

First, selective schools want students who are likely to be successful. They are seeking students who are willing to work hard and who will do well academically. But schools also want students who will contribute to society by becoming good scientists, artists, humanists, dancers, musicians, businesspeople, and leaders. In their admissions forms, brochures, and Web sites, many selective colleges and universities explain that they are "seeking students who will make a difference."

market signaling Actions taken by buyers and sellers to communicate quality in a world of uncertainty.

ECONOMICS IN PRACTICE

How to Read Advertisements

Many high-end magazines, including alumni magazines for colleges, have a section at the back with advertisements for rentals of vacation homes. Consider the following ad recently found in one of those magazines.

St. Thomas Rental: "Lovely villa on the Caribbean island of St. Thomas. Sleeps 6. Beautiful garden and pool area. Covered veranda and barbecue. Available by the week or month."

What conclusion should a discerning reader of this ad draw about the property beyond what is written? The obvious conclusion to be drawn from this ad by anyone who has studied economics is that the property is not on or even near the beach.

Why do we conclude this? Ads are designed by people who want to attract customers. So a first step in our deduction is to recognize that the villa owner will mention any attractive and important positive feature that the villa has. On a Caribbean island, beachfront is a key attraction; thus, no mention of the beach tells us that this villa is not on or near the beach. Recognizing that profit-seeking individuals place the ad lets us draw conclusions about the information they do not provide.

This same logic can be used in a corporate setting. In 2002, Congress and the president passed new accounting rules that require firms to inform shareholders of the stock options they give to their

executives and the effect of those options on the firms' costs. Information could be embedded in the financial statements or placed in the footnotes. Not surprisingly, those firms—typically the dot-com firms—for whom options costs were large chose the less transparent method of putting the information in the footnotes, while more traditional firms, with fewer options to disclose, were more forthcoming.

Sometimes the lack of information serves as a signal.

Developing a set of signals for identifying quality in admissions candidates is a difficult task, but there are some generally accepted signals that the colleges and universities look at. Clearly, they look beyond grades and standardized tests. "Quality of the program" is a term used to describe the difficulty of the classes that the applicant took in high school. How many advanced placement courses did the student take? How many years of math, science, and foreign language? Did the student challenge himself or herself?

In addition to courses, extracurricular activities serve as a signal for future success. Admissions professionals also see hours of practicing the violin or piano or soccer as signals of students who dedicate energy to difficult challenges. Admissions professionals make these assumptions about students because they have imperfect information.

Even without knowing about the theory of signals, most high school students recognize that colleges reward extracurricular activities. Not surprisingly, this knowledge increases the incentive of all students to engage in such activities. But how can extracurricular activities be a good signal of interests and productivity if everyone begins to do them? If every high school senior belongs to the French Club, membership ceases to have a signaling effect.

For extracurricular activities to remain useful as a good signal, they must be more easily done by well-rounded and productive students than by other students. If a student who is truly interested in writing and is well-organized about time management finds it easier to write for the school paper, colleges can correctly infer that the newspaper writer is more likely to be interested in writing and is a good manager. It would be too costly in terms of lost time and fun for someone who dislikes writing and is disorganized to join the newspaper staff just to signal colleges. For signals to work, they must be costly and the cost of using them must be less for people who have the trait that is valued. College admissions committees are, for this reason, beginning to think about things like how many hours a given activity takes. Time-intensive activities are more painful if a student does not really like the activity, and they involve more of a trade-off with other academic pursuits.

For a signal to reduce the problem of adverse selection, then, it must be less costly for the high quality-type person to obtain. Extracurricular activities work as a signal when the most committed and brightest students are most able to do the activities and do well at school. Under those conditions, these activities are thought of as a *strong signal*. In the job market, education is a strong signal.

Of course, education improves your life in many ways, as a consumer, a citizen, and a worker. Education can directly improve your productivity in most jobs. But it can also signal a potential employer that you are a productive person. Why is education a good signal? Education, like extracurricular activities, is most easily attained by people who are disciplined, bright, and hard-working. All of those qualities are valued in the workplace but are hard to certify—hence, the need for a signal.

Signals are everywhere. Return for a moment to the used car example and the discussion of warranties. We argued that a car for which a dealer offered a warranty was likely to be a peach. Why? A warranty is a promise to pay for repairs for any defects. For a dealer, the warranty is expensive to live up to only if the car is a lemon. Because a lemon will require more repairs than a peach, providing a warranty for it will end up costing the dealer more. So the fact that a seller offers a warranty is a strong signal that the car is a peach.

Under some conditions, a firm's name can signal quality to consumers. Many airports now have nail salons offering manicures to travelers with spare time. On the surface, though, it appears that there might be a problem with adverse selection in the nail salon business. In a community, a nail salon that does a poor job for the money it charges is likely to go out of business. The salon will have few return visitors, and word of mouth of its poor quality is likely to spread. In an airport salon, return business is infrequent; thus, one might think that low-quality nail salons would not be forced out of business. Given that quality is more expensive in terms of labor costs and that consumers do not know whether a salon is good before they have a manicure, one might expect bad salons to crowd out good salons in airports. Savvy consumers would come to realize that only the desperate or those unconcerned with quality should get their nails done in an airport. In fact, there is an offset to this story about the crowding out of good salons. What we see in many airports is a shop that is part of a large chain of salons. The firm that owns the chain recognizes that providing good care in a shop at the Dallas-Fort Worth airport, for example, will have positive reputation effects in the same-named shop at the St. Louis airport. This gives the firm an incentive to provide better quality care at each airport. As a result, airport visitors can view the brand name of the salon as a signal of its quality. One of the economic advantages of a chain is its ability to provide some assurance to customers who are not local of a common level of product quality at different locations. Next time you are traveling along the interstate, look at the hotel and food choices at the rest stops. Most are chains for the reasons we just described.

Moral Hazard

Another information problem that arises in insurance markets is *moral hazard*. Often people enter into contracts in which the result of the contract, at least in part, depends on one of the parties' future behavior. A **moral hazard** problem arises when one party to a contract changes behavior in response to that contract and thus passes the cost of its behavior on to the other party to the contract. For example, accident insurance policies are contracts that agree to pay for repairs to your car if it is damaged in an accident. Whether you have an accident depends in part on whether you drive cautiously. Similarly, apartment leases may specify that the landlord will perform routine maintenance around the apartment. If you punch the wall every time you get angry, your landlord ultimately pays the repair bill.

Such contracts can lead to inefficient behavior. The problem is like the externality problem in which firms and households have no incentive to consider the full costs of their behavior. If your car is fully insured against theft, why should you lock it? If health insurance provides new glasses whenever you lose a pair, it is likely that you will be less careful.

In 2009, the U.S. government "bailed out" a number of firms in danger of failing: many of the largest banks, AIG, and General Motors. Many economists who looked at these bailouts warned about moral hazard. If the government is around to bail out banks when they fail, what will govern the risks those banks will take? If General Motors and AIG are kept from bankruptcy, will they too behave imprudently? "Moral hazard" became part of many headlines in 2009.

Like adverse selection, the moral hazard problem is an information problem. Contracting parties cannot always determine the future behavior of the person with whom they are

moral hazard Arises when one party to a contract changes behavior in response to that contract and thus passes on the costs of that behavior change to the other party.

contracting. If all future behavior could be predicted, contracts could be written to try to eliminate undesirable behavior. Sometimes this is possible. Life insurance companies do not pay off in the case of suicide during the first two years the policy is in force. Fire insurance companies will not write a policy unless you have smoke detectors. If you cause unreasonable damage to an apartment, your landlord can retain your security deposit. It is impossible to know everything about behavior and intentions. If a contract absolves one party of the consequences of his or her action and people act in their own self-interest, the result is inefficient.

Incentives

The discussion of moral hazard provides us with a number of examples in which individuals who buy insurance may have the wrong *incentives* when they make decisions. Incentives play an important role in other areas of life as well. When firms hire, they want to make sure that their workers have the incentive to work hard. Many employers provide bonuses for exemplary performance to create incentives for their employees. In class, teachers try to provide incentives in the form of positive feedback and grades to encourage students to learn the material. In designing policies to deal with unemployment, poverty, and even international relations, governments constantly worry about designing appropriate incentives.

In fact, most of our interest in incentives comes because of uncertainty. Because your teacher or employer cannot always see how hard you are working, he or she wants to design incentives to ensure that you work even when no one is watching. Grades and salary bonuses play this role. Because insurance companies cannot monitor whether you lock your car door, they would like to create incentives to encourage you to lock your doors even though you have theft insurance.

Within economics, the area of **mechanism design** explores how transactions and contracts can be designed so that, even under conditions of asymmetric information, self-interested people have the incentive to behave properly. In 2007, Leonid Hurwicz, Roger Myerson, and Eric Maskin won the Nobel Prize for their work in this area. While the field of mechanism design is a complex one, a simple idea in the field is that different incentive schemes can cause people to reveal the truth about themselves. In the following discussion, we will look at a few examples in the labor market and the health care market to see how incentives can help reduce both adverse selection and moral hazard in this way.

mechanism design A contract or an institution that aligns the interests of two parties in a transaction. A piece rate, for example, creates incentives for a worker to work hard, just as his or her superior wants. A co-pay in the health care industry encourages more careful use of health care, just as the insurance company wants.

Labor Market Incentives

In the section on expected utility versus expected value, we described an employee trying to choose between a job that offered a wage of $40,000 versus a coin toss that could bring him either $20,000 or $60,000. We suggested that few employees would take such a deal, given risk aversion. And yet many people do have wage contracts that contain some uncertainty. For many CEOs of large U.S. companies, less than half of their compensation is in the form of a fixed salary. Most of their pay comes from bonuses based on the firm's profits or its stock market performance. Many factory jobs pay piece wages that depend on how fast the worker is. Some of you may have had summer jobs selling magazines where wages were uncertain. Why do we see these contracts, given the risk aversion of most people?

These types of contracts occur because variable compensation can help firms get better performance from their workforce. Suppose you are hiring one individual as a salesperson and have two candidates, George and Harry. Both men seem to be affable, good with people, and hard-working. How can you tell who will be a better salesperson? In this case, incentives can play a powerful role. Suppose you offer George and Harry the following deal: The base pay for this job is $25,000, but for every sale made beyond a certain level, a large commission is paid. How valuable is this salary offer? That depends on how good George and Harry are as salespeople. If George knows he is an excellent salesperson, while Harry recognizes that despite his good nature, he is lazy, only George will want to take this salary offer. The way the incentive package is designed has caused the right person, the better salesperson, to *select* into the job.

Notice that in contrast to the problem of adverse selection described earlier in this chapter, this incentive scheme creates *beneficial* selection dynamics. One reason that many companies design compensation with a component that varies with performance is that they want to attract the right kind of employees. In this case, the compensation scheme has *screened out* the poor worker. Harry has revealed his own laziness by his job choice, as a result of the design of the incentive.

Performance compensation plays another role as well. Once George has taken the job, the fact that some of his salary depends on his hard work will encourage him to work even harder. Of course, it is important that his compensation depend on things he can, in part, control. This is one reason that in most companies, the CEO's compensation is tied more to firm profitability than is the salary of his or her executive assistant. Because the CEO has more control over profitability, he or she should face the strongest performance incentives.

At the top levels in the investment banking industry, most compensation is performance-based. In 2008, just before the financial meltdown, Lloyd Blankfein, the CEO of Goldman Sachs, received $73 million in compensation. Of that, $600,000 was in base pay! Many have argued that compensation in the financial industry can be traced to excess risk taking.

In recent years, there have been efforts in some states to use more incentive compensation for public school teachers. In some cases, bonuses have been tied to student performance on standardized tests. In a related set of experiments, New York City has a pilot program to reward students who earn good grades with gifts such as cell phones. There has been a lot of debate about the efficacy of both programs. Some people think that public school teachers are already highly motivated and that monetary compensation is not likely to have much effect. Others worry that teachers will "teach to the test," suggesting that the wrong behavior will be stimulated. Some worry that incentive pay will screen out committed teachers, while other people believe it will improve retention of hard-working teachers. In the case of public school students, critics worry that these incentives will turn learning from a matter of love to one of commerce. These issues will likely be debated for some time to come.

SUMMARY

DECISION MAKING UNDER UNCERTAINTY: THE TOOLS *p. 353*

1. To find the expected value of a deal, you identify all possible outcomes of the deal and find the payoffs associated with those outcomes. *Expected value* is the weighted average of those payoffs where the weights are the probability of each payoff occurring.

2. In general, people do not accept uncertain deals with the same expected value as certain deals.

3. *Risk aversion* exists when people prefer a certain outcome to an uncertain outcome with an equal expected value. *Risk-neutral* people are indifferent between these two deals, and *risk-loving* people prefer the uncertain deal to its certain equivalent.

4. Most people are risk-averse unless the payoffs are very small.

5. Income is subject to *diminishing marginal utility*, and this diminishing marginal utility helps explain risk aversion.

ASYMMETRIC INFORMATION *p. 357*

6. Choices made in the presence of imperfect information may not be efficient. In the face of incomplete information, consumers and firms may encounter the problem of *adverse selection*. When buyers or sellers enter into market exchanges with other parties who have more information, low-quality goods are exchanged in greater numbers than high-quality goods. *Moral hazard* arises when one party to a contract passes the cost of its behavior on to the other party to the contract. If a contract absolves one party of the consequences of its actions and people act in their own self-interest, the result is inefficient. *Asymmetric information* occurs when one of the parties to a transaction has information relevant to the transaction that the other party does not have.

7. In many cases, the market provides solutions to information problems. Profit-maximizing firms will continue to gather information as long as the marginal benefits from continued search are greater than the marginal costs. Consumers will do the same: More time is afforded to the information search for larger decisions. In other cases, government must be called on to collect and disperse information to the public.

8. Market signaling is a process by which sellers can communicate to buyers their quality. For a signal to be meaningful, it must be less expensive for high-quality types to acquire the signal than for low-quality types.

INCENTIVES *p. 363*

9. Correct incentive design can improve the selection mechanism along with reducing the moral hazard problem.

10. Performance contracts in the labor market and co-pays in the health insurance market are two examples of incentive contracts.

—— REVIEW TERMS AND CONCEPTS ——

adverse selection, *p. 358*

asymmetric information, *p. 357*

diminishing marginal utility, *p. 354*

expected utility, *p. 355*

expected value, *p. 354*

fair game *or* fair bet, *p. 354*

market signaling, *p. 360*

mechanism design, *p. 363*

moral hazard, *p. 362*

payoff, *p. 354*

risk-averse, *p. 356*

risk-loving, *p. 356*

risk-neutral, *p. 356*

risk premium, *p. 356*

—— PROBLEMS ——

All problems are available on www.myeconlab.com

1. Explain how imperfect information problems such as adverse selection and moral hazard might affect the following markets or situations:
   a. Workers applying for disability benefits from a company
   b. The market for used computers
   c. The market for customized telephone systems for college offices and dorms
   d. The market for automobile collision insurance

2. Figure 17.1 (p. 355) and Figure 17.2 (p. 357) show a utility curve for a person who is risk-averse. Draw a similar curve for an individual who is risk-neutral and for someone who is risk-loving.

*3. Your current salary is a fixed sum of $50,625 per year. You have an offer for another job. The salary there is a flat $25,000 plus a chance to earn $150,000 if the company does well. Assume that your utility from income can be expressed as $U = \sqrt{\text{Income}}$. So, for example, at an income level of $100, your utility level is 10; your utility level from the current salary of $50,625 is 225. How high does the probability of success for the company have to be to induce you to take this job?

4. Last January I bought life insurance; at the end of the year, I am still alive. Was my purchase a mistake? Explain.

5. Many colleges offer pass/fail classes. Use the ideas of adverse selection and moral hazard to explain why teachers in these classes find that pass/fail students rarely score at the top of the class.

6. Signals are also used in social settings. In a new place, what signals do you look for to find people who share your interests?

7. [Related to the *Economics in Practice* on p. 361] Find a product advertisement in a magazine for which the missing information tells you something important about the product.

8. [Related to the *Economics in Practice* on p. 360] Do you think companies that issue health insurance should be allowed to inquire about family medical history and the results of genetic testing before deciding to issue insurance policies? Why or why not?

9. Leopold Bloom runs a local United Parcel Service branch. At present, he pays his workers an hourly wage. He is considering changing to a piece rate, in which workers would be paid based on how many packages they process during a day. Assume on any given day that there are more packages than the work staff can handle. What effect would you expect this change in compensation to have on Bloom's operations?

10. The fast-food restaurants located on major highways are typically part of national chains. Why might this be the case?

11. Mary's local gym has two pricing options. If you pay by the day, the charge is $10 per day. Alternatively, you can pay an annual membership fee that allows you to exercise as often as you like for $1,000. On average, Mary predicts that she would use the gym once a week and the value of the 50 times per year she would go is not enough to warrant a membership. Instead, Mary decides to pay by the day.
   a. At the end of the year, Mary finds that she went to the gym only 25 times rather than the 50 she had predicted. She is still sure, however, that with a membership, she would go 50 times and insists that economic logic supports her prediction. What principle is she thinking about?
   b. Mary's employer has read a new health study that suggests that people who work out at least once a week perform better at work. The firm decides to give Mary and her coworkers a cash bonus of $40 per week to cover the costs of going to the health club four times a month. Do you think this policy would be effective? If not, suggest an alternative that would achieve the firm's goal.

12. Sondra wants to purchase a small, used car and sees a 2008 Honda Civic DX listed on Craigslist for $7,000. She is willing to pay $9,000 if the car is reliable, but only $5,000 if the car is not reliable. What additional information might Sondra find helpful in making her decision about the purchase?

13. One way insurance companies reduce adverse selection problems is by offering group medical coverage to large firms and requiring all employees to participate in the coverage. Explain how this reduces adverse selection.

14. Most casino game dealers in Las Vegas are paid minimum wage, and therefore rely on tips for a large portion of their income. Within the past few years, a majority of Las Vegas casinos have instituted tip-pooling policies for their dealers, whereby dealers are not allowed to keep the tips they earn; instead, they must pool all of their tips to be evenly distributed to all dealers. How would the tip-pooling system affect the productivity of the dealers?

15. Video poker is a very popular form of gambling in casinos, second only to slot machines. Some video poker games offer a "double-up" feature, where players receiving a paying hand are offered the chance to double their winnings. If a player chooses to play the double-up feature, the machine deals one card from a 52-card deck to the player and one to the "dealer." If the player's card is higher than the dealer's (with an ace being the highest card), the player doubles his or her winnings. If the player's card is lower than the dealer's card, the player loses his or her winnings. If both are dealt cards of the same value (a push), the player keeps his or her original bet. Explain whether the double-up feature is an example of a fair game.

*Note: Problems with an asterisk are more challenging.

Income Distribution and Poverty

18

What role should government play in the economy? Thus far we have focused only on actions the government might be called on to take to improve market efficiency. Even if we achieved markets that are perfectly efficient, would the result be fair? We now turn to the question of **equity**, or fairness.

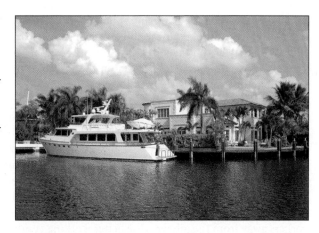

Somehow the goods and services produced in every society get distributed among its citizens. Some citizens end up with mansions in Palm Beach, ski trips to Gstaad, and Ferraris; other citizens end up without enough to eat, and they live in shacks. This chapter focuses on distribution. Why do some people get more than others? What are the sources of inequality? Should the government change the distribution generated by the market?

The Sources of Household Income

Why do some people and some families have more income than others? Before we turn to data on the distribution of income, let us review what we already know about the sources of inequality. Households derive their incomes from three basic sources: (1) from wages or salaries received in exchange for labor; (2) from property—that is, capital, land, and so on; and (3) from government.

Wages and Salaries

More than half of personal income in the United States in 2007 was received in the form of wages and salaries. If you add wage supplements, which include contributions for health insurance and pensions, the figure is 64 percent. Hundreds of different wage rates are paid to employees for their labor in thousands of different labor markets. As you saw in Chapter 10, perfectly competitive market theory predicts that all factors of production (including labor) are paid a return equal to their marginal revenue product—the market value of what they produce at the margin. There are reasons why one type of labor might be more productive than another and why some households have higher incomes than others.

Required Skills, Human Capital, and Working Conditions   Some people are born with attributes that translate into valuable skills. LeBron James and Kevin Garnett are great basketball players, partly because they happen to be very tall. They did not decide to go out and invest in height; they were born with the right genes. Some people have perfect pitch and beautiful voices; others are tone deaf. Some people have quick mathematical minds; others cannot add 2 and 2.

The rewards of a skill that is in limited supply depend on the demand for that skill. Men's professional basketball is extremely popular, and the top NBA players make millions of dollars

equity   Fairness.

per year. There are great women basketball players too, but because women's professional basketball has not become popular in the United States, these women's skills go comparatively unrewarded. In tennis, however, people want to see women play, so women therefore earn prize money similar to the money that men earn.

Some people with rare skills can make enormous salaries in an unfettered market economy. Luciano Pavarotti had a voice that millions of people were willing to pay to hear in person and on CDs. Some baseball players make tens of millions of dollars per year. Before Pablo Picasso died, he could sell small sketches for vast sums of money. Were they worth it? They were worth exactly what the highest bidder was willing to pay.

human capital The stock of knowledge, skills, and talents that people possess; it can be inborn or acquired through education and training.

Not all skills are inborn. Some people have invested in training and schooling to improve their knowledge and skills, and therein lies another source of inequality in wages. When we go to school, we are investing in **human capital** that we expect to yield dividends, partly in the form of higher wages, later on. Human capital, the stock of knowledge and skills that people possess, is also produced through on-the-job training. People learn their jobs and acquire "firm-specific" skills when they are on the job. Thus, in most occupations, there is a reward for experience. Pay scale often reflects numbers of years on the job, and those with more experience earn higher wages than those in similar jobs with less experience.

Some jobs are more desirable than others. Entry-level positions in "glamour" industries such as media tend to be low-paying. Because talented people are willing to take entry-level jobs in these industries at salaries below what they could earn in other occupations, there must be other, nonwage rewards. It may be that the job itself is more personally rewarding or that a low-paying apprenticeship is the only way to acquire the human capital necessary to advance. In contrast, less desirable jobs often pay wages that include **compensating differentials**. Of two jobs requiring roughly equal levels of experience and skills that compete for the same workers, the job with the poorer working conditions usually has to pay a slightly higher wage to attract workers away from the job with the better working conditions.

compensating differentials Differences in wages that result from differences in working conditions. Risky jobs usually pay higher wages; highly desirable jobs usually pay lower wages.

Compensating differentials are also required when a job is very dangerous. Those who take great risks are usually rewarded with high wages. High-beam workers on skyscrapers and bridges command premium wages. Firefighters in cities that have many old, run-down buildings are usually paid more than firefighters in relatively tranquil rural or suburban areas.

Multiple Household Incomes Another source of wage inequality among households lies in the fact that many households have more than one earner in the labor force. Second, and even third, incomes are becoming more the rule than the exception for U.S. families. In 1960, about 37 percent of women over the age of 16 were in the labor force. By 1978, the figure had increased to over 50 percent, and it continued to climb slowly but steadily to over 60 percent in 2007.

The Minimum Wage Controversy One strategy for reducing wage inequity that has been used for almost 100 years in many countries is the minimum wage. (The minimum wage and price floors were discussed in Chapter 4.) A **minimum wage** is the lowest wage firms are permitted to pay workers. The first minimum wage law was adopted in New Zealand in 1894. The United States adopted a national minimum wage with the passage of the Fair Labor Standards Act of 1938, although many individual states had laws on the books much earlier. The minimum wage was raised to $7.25 in the summer of 2009.

minimum wage The lowest wage that firms are permitted to pay workers.

In recent years, the minimum wage has come under increasing attack. Opponents argue that minimum wage legislation interferes with the smooth functioning of the labor market and creates unemployment. Proponents argue that it has been successful in raising the wages of the poorest workers and alleviating poverty without creating much unemployment.

These arguments can best be understood with a simple supply and demand graph. Figure 18.1 shows hypothetical demand and supply curves for unskilled labor. The equilibrium wage rate is $5.40. At that wage, the quantity of unskilled labor supplied and the quantity of unskilled labor demanded are equal. Now suppose that a law is passed setting a minimum wage of $6.55. At that wage rate, the quantity of labor supplied increases from the equilibrium level, L^*, to L_S. At the same time, the higher wage reduces the quantity of labor demanded by firms, from L^* to L_D. As a result, firms lay off $L^* - L_D$ workers.

It is true that those workers who remain on payrolls receive higher wages. With the minimum wage in effect, unskilled workers receive $6.55 per hour instead of $5.40. But is it worth it? Some workers gain while others (including those who had been employed at the equilibrium wage) suffer unemployment.

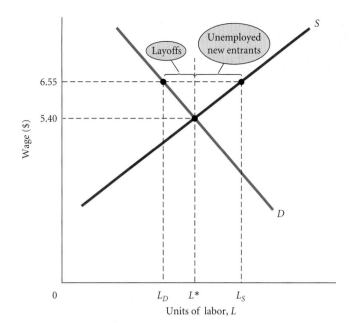

◀ **FIGURE 18.1**

Effect of Minimum Wage Legislation

If the equilibrium wage in the market for unskilled labor is below the legislated minimum wage, the result is likely to be unemployment. The higher wage will attract new entrants to the labor force (quantity supplied will increase from L^* to L_S), but firms will hire fewer workers (quantity demanded will drop from L^* to L_D).

In fact, the evidence on the extent to which the minimum wage causes jobs to be lost is unclear. Professor Finis Welch at Texas A&M and two colleagues estimated in a recent study that each 10 percent increase in the minimum wage produces job losses of about 1 percent of all minimum wage workers, or about 60,000 workers in total at the time of the study. But other studies find little or no effect on the number of jobs lost when the minimum wage increases. Two earlier studies by David Card of the University of California at Berkeley and one by Lawrence Katz of Harvard and Alan Krueger of Princeton University found that an increase in the minimum wage had virtually no effect on unemployment.

Unemployment   Before turning to property income, we need to mention another cause of inequality in the United States that is the subject of much discussion in macroeconomics: *unemployment*.

People earn wages only when they have jobs. In recent years, the United States has been through three severe recessions (economic downturns). In 1975, the unemployment rate hit 9 percent and over 8 million people were unable to find work. In 1982, the unemployment rate was nearly 11 percent and over 12 million were jobless. More recently, the recovery from the milder recession of 1990 to 1991 was slow at first. By 2000, the number of unemployed dropped below 5.5 million (an unemployment rate of 3.9 percent), but by 2008, it was back to 15.2 million, or 10 percent.

Unemployment hurts primarily those who are laid off, and thus its costs are narrowly distributed. For some workers, the costs of unemployment are lowered by unemployment compensation benefits paid out of a fund accumulated with receipts from a tax on payrolls.

Income from Property

Another source of income inequality is that some people have **property income**—from the ownership of real property and financial holdings—while many others do not. Some people own a great deal of wealth, and some have no assets at all. Overall, about 22 percent of personal income in the United States in 2007 came from ownership of property. The amount of property income that a household earns depends on (1) how much property it owns and (2) what kinds of assets it owns. Such income generally takes the form of profits, interest, dividends, and rents.

Households come to own assets through saving and through inheritance. Some of today's large fortunes were inherited from previous generations. The Rockefellers, the Kennedys, and the Fords, to name a few, still have large holdings of property originally accumulated by previous generations. Thousands of families receive smaller inheritances each year from their parents. (In 2010, taxation of these estates was an important political issue.) Most families receive little through inheritance; most of their wealth or property comes from saving.

Often fortunes accumulate in a single generation when a business becomes successful. The late Sam Walton built a personal fortune estimated at over $70 billion on a chain of retail stores including Wal-Mart. *Forbes* magazine estimated that Bill Gates, founder of Microsoft, was worth

property income   Income from the ownership of real property and financial holdings. It takes the form of profits, interest, dividends, and rents.

over $53 billion in 2009. Karl and Theo Albrecht made $20 billion, beginning with their mother's corner store in Germany and expanding to 8,500 stores in 2009 in Germany and 10 other countries. In the United States, they own the gourmet food-and-beverage chain Trader Joe's. *Forbes* estimated that there were over 1,011 billionaires in the world in 2009. The richest man in the world in 2009 was Mexican tycoon Carlos Slim Helu with an estimated $53.5 billion in wealth.

Income from the Government: Transfer Payments

transfer payments
Payments by government to people who do not supply goods or services in exchange.

About 14 percent of personal income in 2007 came from governments in the form of **transfer payments**. Transfer payments are payments made by government to people who do not supply goods or services in exchange. Some, but not all, transfer payments are made to people with low incomes precisely because they have low incomes. Transfer payments thus reduce the amount of inequality in the distribution of income. Not all transfer income goes to the poor. The biggest single transfer program at the federal level is Social Security. Transfer programs are by and large designed to provide income to those in need. They are part of the government's attempts to offset some of the problems of inequality and poverty.

The Distribution of Income

economic income The amount of money a household can spend during a given period without increasing or decreasing its net assets. Wages, salaries, dividends, interest income, transfer payments, rents, and so on are sources of economic income.

Economic income is defined as the amount of money a household can spend during a given period without increasing or decreasing its net assets. Economic income includes anything that enhances your ability to spend—wages, salaries, dividends, interest received, proprietors' income, transfer payments, rents, and so on. If you own an asset (such as a share of stock) that increases in value, that gain is part of your income whether or not you sell the asset to "realize" the gain. Normally, we speak of "before-tax" income, with taxes considered a use of income.

Income Inequality in the United States

Table 18.1 presents some estimates of the distribution of several income components and of total income for households in 2006. The measure of income used to calculate these figures is very broad; it includes both taxable and nontaxable items, as well as estimates of realized capital gains.

TABLE 18.1	Distribution of Total Income and Components in the United States, 2006 (Percentages)			
Households	Total Income	Labor Income	Property Income	Transfer Income
Bottom fifth	3.4	1.3	2.2	17.2
Second fifth	9.2	6.7	6.3	24.6
Third fifth	16.3	14.1	11.7	21.2
Fourth fifth	23.6	24.5	14.3	18.3
Top fifth	47.5	53.4	65.5	18.7
Top 1 percent	13.2	10.8	30.6	1.0

Source: Julie-Anne Cronin, U.S. Department of the Treasury, OTA paper 85, p. 19 and author's calculations.

The data are presented by "quintiles"; that is, the total number of households is first ranked by income and then split into five groups of equal size. In 2006, the top quintile earned 47.5 percent of total income while the bottom quintile earned just 3.4 percent. The top 1 percent (which is part of the top quintile) earned more than the bottom 40 percent. Labor income was less evenly distributed than total income.

Income from property is more unevenly distributed than wages and salaries. Property income comes from owning things: Land earns rent, stocks earn dividends and appreciate in value, bonds and deposit accounts earn interest, owners of small businesses earn profits, and so on. The top 20 percent of households earned 65.5 percent of property income, and the top 1 percent earned over 30 percent.

Transfer payments include Social Security benefits, unemployment compensation, and welfare payments, as well as an estimate of nonmonetary transfers from the government to households—food stamps and Medicaid and Medicare program benefits, for example. Transfers flow to low-income households, but not solely to them. Social Security benefits, for example, which account for about half of all transfer payments, flow to everyone who participated in the system for the requisite number of years and has reached the required age regardless of income.

Nonetheless, transfers represent a more important income component at the bottom of the distribution than at the top. Although not shown in Table 18.1, transfers account for more than 80 percent of the income of the bottom 10 percent of households, but only about 3 percent of income among the top 10 percent of households.

Changes in the Distribution of Income Table 18.2 presents the distribution of money income among U.S. households[1] at a number of points in time. **Money income**, the measure used by the Census Bureau in its surveys and publications, is slightly less complete than the income measure used in the calculations in Table 18.1. The measure does not include noncash transfer benefits, for example, and does not include capital gains.

money income The measure of income used by the Census Bureau. Because money income excludes noncash transfer payments and capital gains income, it is less inclusive than economic income.

TABLE 18.2	Distribution of Money Income of U.S. Households by *Quintiles*, 1967–2009 (Percentages)					
	1967	1975	1985	1995	2000	2009
Bottom fifth	4.0	4.3	3.9	3.7	3.6	3.4
Second fifth	10.8	10.4	9.8	9.1	8.9	8.6
Third fifth	17.3	17.0	16.2	15.2	14.8	14.6
Fourth fifth	24.2	24.7	24.4	23.3	23.0	23.2
Top fifth	43.6	43.6	45.6	48.7	49.8	50.3
Top 5%	17.2	16.4	17.6	21.6	22.1	21.7

Source: Bureau of the Census, Current Population Survey, Annual Social and Economic Supplements through 2010.

Since 1975, there has been a slow but steady drift toward more inequality. During those years, the share of income going to the top 5 percent has increased from 16.4 percent to 21.7 percent while the share going to the bottom 40 percent has fallen from 14.8 percent to 12 percent.

The Lorenz Curve and the Gini Coefficient The distribution of income can be graphed in several ways. The most widely used graph is the **Lorenz curve**, shown in Figure 18.2. Plotted along the horizontal axis is the percentage of households, and along the

Lorenz curve A widely used graph of the distribution of income, with cumulative percentage of households plotted along the horizontal axis and cumulative percentage of income plotted along the vertical axis.

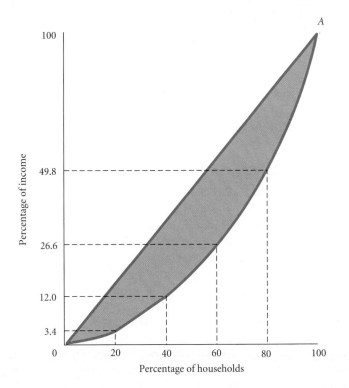

◀ **FIGURE 18.2**

Lorenz Curve for the United States, 2009

The Lorenz curve is the most common way of presenting income distribution graphically. The larger the shaded area, the more unequal the distribution. If the distribution were equal, the Lorenz curve would be the 45-degree line 0A.

[1] The term *household* includes unmarried individuals living alone and groups of people living together who are not related by blood, marriage, or adoption. In the United States in 2008, there was a total of 116.8 million households and 38.9 million nonfamily households.

vertical axis is the cumulative percentage of income. The curve shown here represents the year 2009, using data from Table 18.2.

During that year, the bottom 20 percent of households earned only 3.4 percent of total money income. The bottom 40 percent earned 12.0 percent (3.4 percent plus 8.6 percent), and so on. If income were distributed equally—that is, if the bottom 20 percent earned 20 percent of the income, the bottom 40 percent earned 40 percent of the income, and so on—the Lorenz curve would be a 45-degree line between 0 and 100 percent. More unequal distributions produce Lorenz curves that are farther from the 45-degree line.

The **Gini coefficient** is a measure of the degree of inequality in a distribution. It is the ratio of the shaded area in Figure 18.2 to the total triangular area below and to the right of the diagonal line 0A. If income is equally distributed, there is no shaded area (because the Lorenz curve and the 45-degree line are the same) and the Gini coefficient is zero. The Lorenz curves for distributions with more inequality are farther down to the right, their shaded areas are larger, and their Gini coefficients are higher. The maximum Gini coefficient is 1. As the Lorenz curve shifts down to the right, the shaded area becomes a larger portion of the total triangular area below 0A. If one family earned all the income (with no one else receiving anything), the shaded area and the triangle would be the same and the ratio would equal 1.

Gini coefficient A commonly used measure of the degree of inequality of income derived from a Lorenz curve. It can range from 0 to a maximum of 1.

Differences Among African-American Households, White Households, and Single-Person Households
Looking just at households without differentiating them in any way hides some needed distinctions. Income distribution differs significantly among African-American, Hispanic, and white households.

Table 18.3 presents data on the distribution of money income for different types of households. The differences among the groupings are dramatic. In 2008, the bottom 20 percent of white households had a mean household income that was twice that of the bottom 20 percent of African-American households. For the middle 20 percent of households, mean income for white households was 65 percent higher than mean income for African-American households. For Hispanics, the figure was 42 percent. The top 5 percent of white households averaged $310,032 of income. For African-Americans, it was $199,353; for Hispanics, $218,396.

TABLE 18.3	Mean Household Income Received by the Top, Middle, and Bottom Fifth of Households in 2008		
	White (non-Hispanic)	African-American	Hispanic
Bottom 20%	$ 13,540	$ 6,675	$ 9,629
Middle 20%	54,521	33,067	38,271
Top 20%	180,341	118,259	129,265
Top 5%	310,032	199,353	218,396

Source: U.S. Census Bureau, www.census.gov, Historical Income Tables, Table H3, 2009.

The World Distribution of Income

Data on the distribution of income across rich and poor nations reveal much more inequality, as shown in Table 18.4. The population of the world in 2008 was approximately 6.7 billion. Of that number, 1.0 billion, or 15 percent, live in what the World Bank classifies as low-income countries. The average income per capita in those countries was $524 in 2008. The same year about 1.1 billion, or 15 percent, lived in high-income countries, where per-capita income was $39,345. When you look at total national income, the rich countries with 15 percent of the population earn 73.0 percent of world income, while the poor countries with 15 percent of the population get only 1.0 percent of world income. The poorest country in the world in 2008 was Burundi, with 8 million people and a per-capita income of $140 per year. The richest country was Norway, with 5 million people and a per-capita income of $87,070.[2]

As we discussed earlier, income inequality has increased within the United States over the last several decades. The evidence also suggests that income inequality is increasing in most other advanced countries as well as in Asia and Latin America. Among the advanced economies, only

---

[2] U.S. Bureau of the Census, www.census.gov.

ECONOMICS IN PRACTICE

The New Rich Work!

Recent work by two economists, Thomas Piketty and Emmanuel Saez, documents the rise in income inequality in the United States described in the text and reports further that the bulk of the new inequality comes not from owners of capital, but from inequality in returns to the workforce.[1] As Piketty and Saez put it, "The working rich have now replaced the coupon-clipping rentiers."

In the recent recessionary period, there has been much media and public interest in executive compensation that further calls our attention to the returns to labor at the very top end of the workforce, the executives who run our major banks and corporations. There is considerable evidence that executive compensation has increased across a wide swath of firms, while the real wage of the average worker has stagnated. There is less consensus, however, as to why wages of executives have risen. Within economics there is debate about whether the rise in corporate pay comes from changes in the market, like growth of average firm size and the importance of scarce human capital, or from changes in corporate governance and social norms.

One interesting recent study of executive compensation by Carola Frydman at MIT traces the changes in executive compensation in one iconic American firm, General Electric. The chart shows the dramatic increases in real executive pay over the postwar period.

[1] Piketty, Thomas, and Emmanual Saez, "Income Inequality in the United States, 1913–1998," *Quarterly Journal of Economics*, February 2003, 1–39.

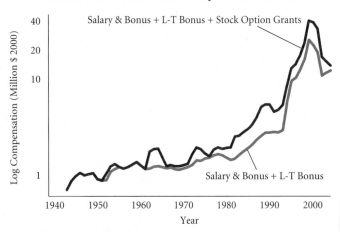

The Real Level of Total Executive Compensation at General Electric

Notes: Compensation is measured as the three-year moving-average for each measure of pay for the three highest-paid executives as reported in General Electric's proxy statements. Salary and Bonus is defined as the level of salaries and current bonuses both awarded and paid out in the year. Long-Term (L-T) Bonus measures the amount paid out in the year from long-term bonuses awarded in prior years. Stock Option Grants is defined as the Black-Scholes value of stock options granted in the given year. The real level of pay is calculated in millions of $2000, using the CPI.

Source: Carola Frydman, "Learning from the Past: Trends in Executive Compensation over the 20th Century," *CESifo Economic Studies*, 2009, volume 55: 458–481, by permission of Oxford University Press.

TABLE 18.4	Income and Income per Capita Across the World in 2008				
	Population		Gross National Income		Per-Capita Income
	Billions	%	Trillions of $	%	(Dollars)
World	6.7	100	57.6	100.0	8,613
Low-Income Countries	1.0	15	0.5	1.0	524
Middle-Income Countries	4.6	70	15.2	26.0	3,260
High-Income Countries	1.1	15	42.0	73.0	39,345

Source: World Bank, *World Development Report 2010*, Key development indicators Table 1.

France has seen decreasing inequality. Inequality has increased everywhere in the developing world except Africa and the Middle East.

Causes of Increased Inequality

The increased income inequality we see in the United States and in many other regions has become the subject of much political debate. Much of the debate concerns what we as a nation and as a member of the world community should do to improve the position of the poorest of our citizens. We will describe these economic issues in the next section of this chapter. But equally debated is the question of what has caused the rise in inequality. Is it the forces of free trade, immigration, and globalization all working together to worsen the position of the middle-income workers who find themselves competing with workers in lower-income countries? Is it the declining power of unions and deregulation that have opened up more labor markets to the forces of competition? Some have argued that a major force in increasing inequality has been technological change that has favored the well-educated worker at the expense of unskilled labor.

These are very difficult questions, questions that are becoming part of the political debate across the world. Consider the role that immigration plays, for example. Most immigrants to the United States come from lower-income countries. Movement of labor from low-income areas to higher-income areas is a natural economic phenomena, a manifestation of the forces of supply and demand in labor markets. Unchecked, these movements have the capacity to reduce costs of production in the high-wage country, increasing the return to capital, and to reduce world income inequality. Immigration also may play a role in increasing within-country inequality to the extent that it brings new group of less-skilled workers into a country, potentially competing for jobs with the lower-income population already in the country.

Empirical evidence of the extent to which immigration has in fact reduced wages of lower-income workers is mixed.

The Evidence: The Net Costs of Immigration   To determine whether the net benefits of immigration outweigh its net costs, we must ask one important question: To what extent does immigration reduce domestic wages and increase unemployment? A number of recent studies have found that metropolitan areas with greater numbers of immigrants seem to have only slightly lower wages and only slightly higher unemployment rates.

An influential study by economist David Card of the University of California, Berkeley, looks carefully at wages and employment opportunities in the Miami metropolitan area during and after the Mariel boat lift of 1980. Almost overnight about 125,000 Cubans arrived in Florida and increased the labor force in Miami by over 7 percent. Card looked at trends in wages and unemployment among Miami workers between 1980 and 1985 and found virtually no effect. In addition, the data he examined mirrored the experience of workers in Los Angeles, Houston, Atlanta, and similar cities that were not hit by the same shock.[3]

However, a more recent study by Borjas, Freeman, and Katz takes issue with much of the work done to date. They argue that immigrants do not stay in the cities at which they arrive, but rather move within the United States in response to job opportunities and wage differentials. Thus, they argue that the effects of immigration on wages and unemployment must be analyzed at the national level, not the city level. Their study points to the large decline in the wages of high school dropouts relative to workers with more education during the 1980s. Their results suggest that a third of the drop in the relative wages of high school dropouts can be attributed to lower-skilled immigrants.[4]

It is clear that immigration is not an issue simply for the United States. For someone in Guatemala, Mexico offers new opportunities. Per-capita income in Guatemala is $2,640 and is $7,870 in Mexico. Haiti, one of the poorest countries in the world, sends people to the Dominican Republic in search of work. In fact, the World Bank estimates that in 2007, 74 million migrants moved from one developing country to another. Here, too, there are lively debates about the effects of this migration on incomes and inequality.

Technological change also appears to play a role in the increases in inequality. In the last several decades, technological advances have played a strong role in development. In the United States and the developing world, more work is conducted with the aid of computers and less work requires large inputs of unskilled labor. The result has been a wage premium for skilled workers.[5] In fact, work by the International Monetary Fund (IMF) suggests that by looking at the growth in inequality in regions around the world, the central force has been technological change with its increased skill needs. The role of technology in increasing inequality appears to be especially large in Asia. The opening up of economies to free trade has played a modest role relative to technology. In fact, the IMF finds that in the advanced countries, free trade has decreased inequality by replacing low-paid manufacturing jobs with higher-paid jobs in the service sector.

The important role of technology in driving inequality suggests that going forward, education may be key to reducing inequality in the United States and across the world.

---

[3] David Card, "The Impact of the Mariel Boat Lift on the Miami Labor Market," *Industrial and Labor Relations Review,* January 1990, pp. 245–257.

[4] George Borjas, Richard Freeman, and Lawrence Katz, "On the Labor Market Effects of Immigration and Trade," in *Immigration and the Work Force: Economic Consequences for the United States and Source Areas,* eds. George Borjas and Richard Freeman (Chicago: University of Chicago Press, 1992).

[5] Nancy Birdsall, 2007. "Discussion of the Impact of Globalization on the World's Poor," Brookings.

Poverty

Most of the government's concern with income distribution and redistribution has focused on poverty. *Poverty* is a very complicated word to define. In simplest terms, it means the condition of people who have very low incomes. The dictionary defines the term simply as "lack of money or material possessions," but how low does your income have to be before you are classified as poor?

The Problem of Definition   Philosophers and social policy makers have long debated the meaning of "poverty." One school of thought argues that poverty should be measured by determining how much it costs to buy the "basic necessities of life." For many years, the Bureau of Labor Statistics published "family budget" data designed to track the cost of specific "bundles" of food, clothing, and shelter that were supposed to represent the minimum standard of living.

Critics argue that defining bundles of necessities is a hopeless task. Although it might be possible to define a minimally adequate diet, what is a "minimum" housing unit? Is a car a necessity? What about medical care? In reality, low-income families end up using what income they have in an enormous variety of ways.

Some say that poverty is culturally defined and is therefore a relative concept, not an absolute one. Poverty in Bangladesh is very different from poverty in the United States. Even within the United States, urban poverty is very different from rural poverty. If poverty is a relative concept, the definition of it might change significantly as a society accumulates wealth and achieves higher living standards.

Although it is difficult to define precisely, the word *poverty* is one that we all understand intuitively to some degree. It conveys images of run-down, overcrowded, rat-infested housing; homeless people; untreated illness; and so on. It is also a word that we have been forced to define formally for purposes of keeping statistics and administering public programs.

The Official Poverty Line   In the early 1960s, the U.S. government established an official poverty line. Because poor families tend to spend about one-third of their incomes on food, the official **poverty line** has been set at a figure that is simply three times the cost of the Department of Agriculture's minimum food budget.

The minimum food budget was only calculated once, in 1963. It has been updated with the Consumer Price Index since that year. Needless to say these figures are somewhat arbitrary, but they are still used to determine the official poverty rate. For 2007, the threshold for a family of four was $21,027.

After years of study and debate, the Department of Health and Human Services began publishing an alternative measure of poverty now called the Poverty Guidelines. The new and somewhat more complex methodology produces income limits that define eligibility for a number of programs including food stamps and Medicaid. The Department set the figure at $21,200 for a family of four in 2008.

> **poverty line** The officially established income level that distinguishes the poor from the nonpoor. It is set at three times the cost of the Department of Agriculture's minimum food budget.

Poverty in the United States Since 1960   In 1962, Michael Harrington published *The Other America: Poverty in the United States*, a book that woke the American people to the problem of poverty and stimulated the government to declare a "war on poverty" in 1964. In 1960, official figures had put the number of the poor in the United States at just under 40 million, or 22 percent of the total population. In his book, Harrington argued that the number had reached over 50 million.

By the late 1960s, the number living below the official poverty line had declined to about 25 million, where it stayed for over a decade. Between 1978 and 1983, the number of poor jumped nearly 45 percent, from 24.5 million to 35.3 million, the highest number since 1964. The figure stood at 43.6 million in 2009. As a percentage of the total population, the poor accounted for between 11 percent and 12.6 percent of the population throughout the 1970s. That figure increased sharply to 15.2 percent between 1979 and 1983. From 1983 to 1989, the rate dropped to 12.8 percent, rising back to 14.5 percent in 1995. The rate rose to 14.3 in 2009.

While the official 2009 figures put the poverty rate at 14.3 percent of the population, they also show that some groups in society experience more poverty than others. Table 18.5 shows the official poverty count for 1964 and 2009 by demographic group. One of the problems with the official count is that it considers only money income as defined by the census and is therefore somewhat inflated. Many federal programs designed to help people out of poverty include noncash benefits (sometimes called *in-kind benefits*) such as food stamps and public housing. If added to income, these benefits would reduce the number of those officially designated as below the poverty line to about 9 percent of the population.

TABLE 18.5	Percentage of Persons in Poverty by Demographic Group, 1964 and 2009	
	Official Measure 1964	Official Measure 2009
All	19.0	14.3
White (Non-Hispanic)	14.9	9.4
Black	49.6	25.8
Hispanic	NA	25.3
Female householder—no husband present	45.9	29.9
Elderly (65 +)	28.5	8.9
Children under 18	20.7	20.7

Source: U.S. Census Bureau. Income, Poverty and Health Insurance Coverage in the U.S., 2009.

The poverty rate among African-Americans is more than twice as high as the poverty rate among whites. Nearly one in four African-Americans live in poverty. In addition, a slightly lower proportion of Hispanics than African-Americans had incomes below the poverty line in 2009.

The group with the highest incidence of poverty in 2009 was women living in households with no husband present. In 1964, 45.9 percent of such women lived in poverty. By 2009, the figure was still 29.9 percent. During the 1980s, there was increasing concern about the "feminization of poverty," a concern that continues today.

Poverty rates among the elderly have been reduced considerably over the last few decades, dropping from 28.5 percent in 1964 to 8.9 percent in 2009. Certainly, Social Security, supplemental security income, and Medicare have played a role in reducing poverty among the elderly. In 1964, 20.7 percent of all children under 18 lived in poverty, and in 2009, the figure was 20.7 percent.

The Distribution of Wealth

Data on the distribution of wealth are not as readily available as data on the distribution of income. Periodically, however, the government conducts a detailed survey of the holdings that make up wealth. The results show that the top 10 percent of households held just under 70 percent of the total net worth in the United States in 2004 while the bottom 40 percent of households held only 2.6 percent.

The distribution of wealth is more unequal than the distribution of income. Part of the reason is that wealth is passed from generation to generation and accumulates. Large fortunes also accumulate when small businesses become successful large businesses. Some argue that an unequal distribution of wealth is the natural and inevitable consequence of risk taking in a market economy: It provides the incentive necessary to motivate entrepreneurs and investors. Others believe that too much inequality can undermine democracy and lead to social conflict. Many of the arguments for and against income redistribution, discussed in the next section, apply equally well to wealth redistribution.

The Utility Possibilities Frontier

Ideally, in discussing distribution, we should talk not about the distribution of income or goods and services, but about the distribution of well-being. In the nineteenth century, philosophers used the concept of *utility* as a measure of well-being. As they saw it, people make choices among goods and services on the basis of the utility those goods and services yield. People act to maximize utility. If you prefer a night at the symphony to a rock concert, the reason is that you expect to get more utility from the symphony. If we extend this thinking, we might argue that if household A gets more total utility than household B, A is better off than B.

Utility is not directly observable or measurable, but thinking about it as if it were can help us understand some of the ideas that underlie debates about distribution. Suppose society consisted of two people, I and J. Next, suppose that the line *PP'* in Figure 18.3 represents all the combinations of I's utility and J's utility that are possible, given the resources and technology available in their society. (This is an extension of the production possibilities frontier in Chapter 2.)

utility possibilities frontier
A graphic representation of a two-person world that shows all points at which I's utility can be increased only if J's utility is decreased.

Any point inside *PP'*, or the **utility possibilities frontier**, is inefficient because both I and J could be better off. A is one such point. B is one of many possible points along *PP'* that society should prefer to A because both members are better off at B than they are at A.

While point B is preferable to point A from everyone's point of view, how does point B compare with point C? Both B and C are efficient; I cannot be made better off without making J worse off, and vice versa. All the points along *PP'* are efficient, but they may not be equally desirable. If

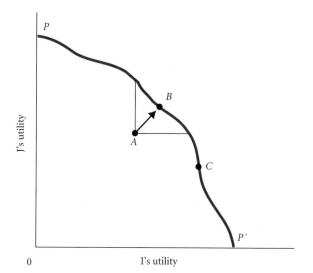

◀ **FIGURE 18.3**

**Utility Possibilities
Frontier**

If society were made up of two
people, I and J, and all the
assumptions of perfect competition held, the market system
would lead to some point along
PP'. Every point along *PP'* is
efficient; it is impossible to make
I better off without making J
worse off, and vice versa. Which
point is best? Is *B* better than *C*?

all the assumptions of perfectly competitive market theory held, the market system would lead to
one of the points along *PP'*. The actual point reached would depend on I's and J's initial endowments of wealth, skills, and so on.

In practice, however, the market solution leaves some people out. The rewards of a market
system are linked to productivity, and some people in every society are simply not capable of
being very productive or have not had the opportunity to become more productive. All societies
make some provision for the very poor. Most often, public expenditures on behalf of the poor are
financed with taxes collected from the rest of society. Society makes a judgment that those who
are better off should give up some of their rewards so that those at the bottom can have more
than the market system would allocate to them. In a democratic state, such redistribution is presumably undertaken because a majority of the members of that society think it is fair, or just.

Early economists drew analogies between social choices among alternative outcomes and
consumer choices among alternative outcomes. A consumer chooses on the basis of his or her
own unique utility function, or measure of his or her own well-being. Society, economists said,
chooses on the basis of a social welfare function that embodies the society's ethics.

Such theoretical discussions of fairness and equity focus on the distribution and redistribution
of utility. Because utility is neither observable nor measurable, most discussions of social policy center on the *distribution of income* or the *distribution of wealth* as indirect measures of well-being, as we
have done. It is important that you remember, however, that income and wealth are imperfect measures of well-being. Someone with a profound love of the outdoors may choose to work in a national
park for a low wage instead of a consulting firm in a big city for a high wage. The choice reveals that
she is better off even though her measured income is lower. As another example, think about five
people with $1 each. Now suppose that one of those people has a magnificent voice, and that the
other four give up their dollars to hear her sing. The exchange leads to inequality of measured
wealth—the singer has $5 and no one else has any—but all are better off than they were before.

Although income and wealth are imperfect measures we have of utility, they have no
observable substitutes and are therefore the measures we have used throughout this chapter.

The Redistribution Debate

Debates about the role of government in correcting for inequality in the distribution of income
revolve around philosophical and practical issues. *Philosophical* issues deal with the "ideal." What
should the distribution of income be if we could give it any shape we desired? What is "fair"?
What is "just"? *Practical* issues deal with what is and what is not possible. Suppose we wanted zero
poverty. How much would it cost, and what would we sacrifice? When we take wealth or income
away from higher-income people and give it to lower-income people, do we destroy incentives?
What are the effects of this kind of redistribution?

Policy makers must deal with both kinds of issues, but it seems logical to confront the philosophical issues first. If you do not know where you want to go, you cannot explain how to get there or how
much it costs. You may find that you do not want to go anywhere at all. Many respected economists
and philosophers argue quite convincingly that the government should *not* redistribute income.

Arguments Against Redistribution

Those who argue against government redistribution believe that the market, when left to operate on its own, is fair. This argument rests on the proposition that "one is entitled to the fruits of one's efforts."[6] Remember that if market theory is correct, rewards paid in the market are linked to productivity. In other words, labor and capital are paid in accordance with the value of what they produce.

This view also holds that property income—income from land or capital—is no less justified than labor income. All factors of production have marginal products. Capital owners receive profits or interest because the capital they own is productive.

The argument against redistribution also rests on the principles behind "freedom of contract" and the protection of property rights. When you agree to sell your labor or to commit your capital to use, you do so freely. In return, you contract to receive payment, which becomes your "property." When a government taxes you and gives your income to someone else, that action violates those two basic rights.

The more common arguments against redistribution are not philosophical. Instead, they point to more practical problems. First, it is said that taxation and transfer programs interfere with the basic incentives provided by the market. Taxing higher-income people reduces their incentive to work, save, and invest. Taxing the "winners" of the economic game also discourages risk taking. Furthermore, providing transfers to those at the bottom reduces their incentive to work as well. All of this leads to a reduction in total output that is the "cost" of redistribution.

Another practical argument against redistribution is that it does not work. Some critics see the rise in the poverty rate during the early 1980s, again in the early 1990s, and yet again between 2001 and 2004 as an indication that antipoverty programs simply drain money without really helping the poor out of poverty. Whether these programs actually help people out of poverty, the possibility of bureaucratic inefficiency in administration always exists. Social programs must be administered by people who must be paid. The Department of Health and Human Services employs over 120,000 people to run the Social Security system, process Medicaid claims, and so on. Some degree of waste and inefficiency is inevitable in any sizable bureaucracy.

Arguments in Favor of Redistribution

The argument most often used in favor of redistribution is that a society as wealthy as the United States has a moral obligation to provide all its members with the necessities of life. The Constitution does carry a guarantee of the "right to life." In declaring war on poverty in 1964, President Lyndon Johnson put it this way:

> There will always be some Americans who are better off than others. But it need not follow that the "poor are always with us."...It is high time to redouble and to concentrate our efforts to eliminate poverty....We know what must be done and this nation of abundance can surely afford to do it.[7]

Many people, often through no fault of their own, find themselves left out. Some are born with mental or physical problems that severely limit their ability to "produce." Then there are children. Even if some parents can be held accountable for their low incomes, do we want to punish innocent children for the faults of their parents and thus perpetuate the cycle of poverty? The elderly, without redistribution of income, would have to rely exclusively on savings to survive once they retire, and many conditions can lead to inadequate savings. Should the victims of bad luck be doomed to inevitable poverty? Illness is perhaps the best example. The accumulated savings of very few people can withstand the drain of extraordinary hospital and doctors' bills and the exorbitant cost of nursing home care.

Proponents of redistribution refute "practical" arguments against it by pointing to studies that show little negative effect on the incentives of those who benefit from transfer programs. For

---

[6] Powerful support for this notion of "entitlement" can be found in the works of the seventeenth-century English philosophers Thomas Hobbes and John Locke.

[7] *Economic Report of the President*, 1964.

many—children, the elderly, the mentally ill—incentives are irrelevant, they say, and providing a basic income to most of the unemployed does not discourage them from working when they have the opportunity to do so. We now turn briefly to several more formal arguments.

Utilitarian Justice First put forth by the English philosophers Jeremy Bentham and John Stuart Mill in the late eighteenth and early nineteenth centuries, the essence of the utilitarian argument in favor of redistribution is that "a dollar in the hand of a rich person is worth less than a dollar in the hand of a poor person." The rich spend their marginal dollars on luxury goods. It is easy to spend over $100 per person for a meal in a good restaurant in New York or Los Angeles. The poor spend their marginal dollars on necessities—food, clothing, and medical care. If the marginal utility of income declines as income rises, the value of a dollar's worth of luxury goods is worth less than a dollar's worth of necessities. Thus, redistributing from the rich to the poor increases total utility. To put this notion of **utilitarian justice** in everyday language: Through income redistribution, the rich sacrifice a little and the poor gain a great deal.

> **utilitarian justice** The idea that "a dollar in the hand of a rich person is worth less than a dollar in the hand of a poor person." If the marginal utility of income declines with income, transferring income from the rich to the poor will increase total utility.

The utilitarian position is not without problems. People have very different tastes and preferences. Who is to say that you value a dollar more or less than I do? Because utility is unobservable and unmeasurable, comparisons between individuals cannot be easily made. Nonetheless, many people find the basic logic of the utilitarians to be persuasive.

Social Contract Theory—Rawlsian Justice The work of Harvard philosopher John Rawls has generated a great deal of recent discussion, both within the discipline of economics and between economists and philosophers.[8] In the tradition of Hobbes, Locke, and Rousseau, Rawls argues that as members of society, we have a contract with one another. In the theoretical world that Rawls imagines, an original *social contract* is drawn up and all parties agree to it without knowledge of who they are or who they will be in society. This condition is called the "original position" or the "state of nature." With no vested interests to protect, members of society are able to make disinterested choices.

As we approach the contract, everyone has a chance to end up very rich or homeless. On the assumption that we are all "risk-averse," Rawls believes that people will attach great importance to the position of the least fortunate members of society because anyone could end up there. **Rawlsian justice** is argued from the assumption of risk aversion. Rawls concludes that any contract emerging from the original position would call for an income distribution that would "maximize the well-being of the worst-off member of society."

> **Rawlsian justice** A theory of distributional justice that concludes that the social contract emerging from the "original position" would call for an income distribution that would maximize the well-being of the worst-off member of society.

Any society bound by such a contract would allow for inequality, but only if that inequality had the effect of improving the lot of the very poor. If inequality provides an incentive for people to work hard and innovate, for example, those inequalities should be tolerated as long as some of the benefits go to those at the bottom.

The Works of Karl Marx For decades, a rivalry existed between the United States and the Soviet Union. At the heart of this rivalry was a fundamental philosophical difference of opinion about how economic systems work and how they should be managed. At the center of the debate were the writings of Karl Marx.

Marx did not write very much about socialism or communism. His major work, *Das Kapital* (published in the nineteenth century), was a three-volume analysis and critique of the capitalist system that he saw at work in the world around him. We know what Marx thought was wrong with capitalism, but he was not very clear about what should replace it. In one essay late in his life, he wrote, "from each according to his ability, to each according to his needs,"[9] but he was not specific about the applications of this principle.

Marx's view of capital income does have important implications for income distribution. In the preceding chapters, we discussed profit as a return to a productive factor: Capital, like labor, is productive and has a marginal product. However, Marx attributed all value to labor and none to capital. According to Marx's **labor theory of value**, the value of any commodity depends only on the amount of labor needed to produce it. The owners of capital are able to extract profit, or "surplus value," because labor creates more value in a day than it is paid for. Like any other good, labor power is worth only what it takes to "produce" it. In simple words, this means that under capitalism, labor is paid a subsistence wage.

> **labor theory of value** Stated most simply, the theory that the value of a commodity depends only on the amount of labor required to produce it.

---

[8] See John Rawls, *A Theory of Justice* (Cambridge, MA: Harvard University Press, 1972).

[9] Karl Marx, "Critique of the Gotha Program" (May 1875), in *The Marx-Engels Reader*, ed. Robert Tucker (New York: W. W. Norton), p. 388.

Marx saw profit as an illegitimate expropriation by capitalists of the fruits of labor's efforts. It follows that Marxians see the property income component of income distribution as the primary source of inequality in the United States today. Without capital income, the distribution of income would be more equal. (Refer again to Table 18.1 on p. 370.)

Income Distribution as a Public Good   Those who argue that the unfettered market produces a just income distribution do not believe private charity should be forbidden. Voluntary redistribution does not involve any violation of property rights by the state.

In Chapter 16, however, you saw that there may be a problem with private charity. Suppose people really do want to end the hunger problem. As they write their checks to charity, they encounter the classic public-goods problem. First, there are free riders. If hunger and starvation are eliminated, the benefits—even the merely psychological benefits—flow to everyone whether they contributed or not. Second, any contribution is a drop in the bucket. One individual contribution is so small that it can have no real effect.

With private charity, as with national defense, nothing depends on whether you pay. Thus, private charity may fail for the same reason that the private sector is likely to fail to produce national defense and other public goods. People will find it in their interest not to contribute. Thus, we turn to government to provide goods and services we want that will not be provided adequately if we act separately—in this case, help for the poor and hungry.

Redistribution Programs and Policies

The role of government in changing the *distribution of income* is hotly debated. The debate involves not only what government programs are appropriate to fight poverty but also the character of the tax system. Unfortunately, the quality of the public debate on the subject is low. Usually, the debate consists of a series of claims and counterclaims about what social programs do to incentives instead of a serious inquiry into what our distributional goal should be.

In this section, we talk about the tools of redistribution policy in the United States. As we do so, you will have a chance to assess for yourself some of the evidence about their effects.

Financing Redistribution Programs: Taxes

Redistribution always involves those who end up with less and those who end up with more. Because redistributional programs are financed by tax dollars, it is important to know who the donors and recipients are—who pays the taxes and who receives the benefits of those taxes. The issue of which households bear the burden of the taxes collected by government is quite complex and requires some analysis. Oftentimes households, firms, and markets react to the presence of taxes in ways that shift burdens off of those on whom they were intended to fall and onto others.

A perfect example is the corporation tax. At both the federal and state levels in most states, a special tax is levied on corporations in proportion to their profit or net income. Although this tax is levied on certain firms, the burden ultimately falls on households in one or more of a number of ways. The tax may result in higher prices for corporate products. The tax may result in lower wages for corporate employees, or the tax may result in lower profits for owners/shareholders of corporations. The ultimate impact of a tax, or set of taxes, on the distribution of income depends on which households end up bearing the burden after shifting has taken place.

The term *incidence* refers to the ultimate burden distribution of a tax. Chapter 19 illustrates the way in which economic analysis can be used to estimate the ultimate incidence of taxes.

The mainstay of the U.S. tax system is the individual income tax, authorized in 1913 by the Sixteenth Amendment to the Constitution. The income tax is *progressive*—those with higher incomes pay a higher percentage of their incomes in taxes. Even though the tax is subject to many exemptions, deductions, and so on that allow some taxpayers to reduce their tax burdens, all studies of the income tax show that its burden as a percentage of income rises as income rises.

With the passage of the Tax Reform Act of 1986, Congress initiated a major change in income tax rates and regulations. The reforms were to simplify the tax and make it easier for people to comply with and harder to avoid. In addition, the act reduced the number of tax brackets and the overall progressivity of the rates. The largest reduction was in the top rate, cut from 50 percent to 28 percent in 1986. The Act also substantially reduced the tax burdens of those at the very bottom by increasing the amount of income a person can earn before paying any tax at all.

In 1993, President Clinton signed into law a tax bill that increased the top rate to 36 percent for families with taxable incomes over $140,000 and individuals with taxable incomes over $115,000. In addition, families with incomes of over $250,000 paid a surtax (a tax rate on a tax rate) of 10 percent, bringing the marginal rate for those families to 39.6 percent. Families with low incomes received grants and credits under the plan. On May 28, 2003, President Bush signed a tax law that reduced the top rate to 35 percent and changed a number of other provisions of the tax code. (See Chapter 19 for details.)

The individual income tax is only one tax among many. More important to the individual is the *overall* burden of taxation, including all federal, state, and local taxes. Most studies of the effect of taxes on the distribution of income, both before and after the Tax Reform Act, have concluded that the overall burden is roughly proportional. In other words, all people pay about the same percentage of their income in total taxes.

Table 18.6 presents an estimate of effective tax rates paid in 2000 by families that have been ranked by income. Although some progressivity is visible, it is very slight. The bottom 20 percent of the income earners pay 28 percent of their total incomes in tax. The top 1 percent pay 37.0 percent. We can conclude from these data that the tax side of the equation produces very little change in the distribution of income. (For more on taxes, see Chapter 19.)

TABLE 18.6 Effective Rates of Federal, State, and Local Taxes, 2000 (Taxes as a Percentage of Total Income)		
	Federal	Total
Bottom 20%	5.9	28.1
Second 20	11.7	26.3
Third 20	17.4	29.2
Fourth 20	20.1	32.6
Top 20	24.6	33.9
Top 10	25.7	34.5
Top 5	26.6	34.9
Top 1	29.1	37.0

Source: Julie-Anne Cronin, U.S. Department of the Treasury, OTA paper 85, and authors' estimate.

Expenditure Programs

Some programs designed to redistribute income or to aid the poor provide cash income to recipients. Others provide benefits in the form of health care, subsidized housing, or food stamps. Still others provide training or help workers find jobs.

Social Security   By far the largest income redistribution program in the United States is Social Security. The **Social Security system** is three programs financed through separate trust funds. The *Old Age and Survivors Insurance (OASI) program*, the largest of the three, pays cash benefits to retired workers, their survivors, and their dependents. The *Disability Insurance (DI) program* pays cash benefits to disabled workers and their dependents. The third, *Health Insurance (HI)*, or Medicare, provides medical benefits to workers covered by OASI and DI and the railroad retirement program. The Social Security system has been credited with substantially reducing poverty among the elderly.

Most workers in the United States must participate in the Social Security system. For many years, federal employees and employees belonging to certain state and municipal retirement systems were not required to participate, but federal employees are now being brought into the system. Today, well over 90 percent of all workers in the United States contribute to Social Security.

Participants and their employers are required to pay a *payroll tax* to the *Federal Insurance Corporation Association (FICA)* to finance the Social Security system. The tax in 2008 was 7.65 percent paid by employers and 7.65 percent paid by employees on wages up to $102,000. Self-employed people assume the entire FICA burden themselves.

You are entitled to Social Security benefits if you participate in the system for 10 years. Benefits are paid monthly to you after you retire or, if you die, to your survivors. A complicated formula based on your average salary while you were paying into the system determines your benefit level. Those who earned more receive a higher level of benefits, but there are maximum and minimum monthly benefits. By and large, low-salaried workers get more out of the system

Social Security system
The federal system of social insurance programs. It includes three separate programs that are financed through separate trust funds: the Old Age and Survivors Insurance (OASI) program, the Disability Insurance (DI) program, and the Health Insurance (HI), or Medicare program.

than they paid into it while they were working. High-salaried workers usually get out of the system considerably less than they put in.

The Social Security system is self-financing, but it is different from funded retirement systems. In a *funded system*, deposits (by the employer, the employee, or both) are made to an account in the employee's name. Those funds are invested and earn interest or dividends that accumulate until the employee's retirement, when they are withdrawn. Funded retirement plans operate very much like a savings plan that you might set up independently, except that you cannot touch the contents until you retire.

In the U.S. Social Security system, the tax receipts from today's workers are used to pay benefits to retired and disabled workers and their dependents today. Currently, the system is collecting more than it is paying out, and the excess is accumulating in the trust funds. This is necessary to keep the system solvent because after the year 2010, there will be a large increase in the number of retirees and a relative decline in the number of workers. These demographic changes are the result of a high birth rate between 1946 and 1964—the so-called baby boom. In 2007, 31.5 million retired workers received Social Security benefits and 7.1 million received disability payments.

Public Assistance   Next to Social Security, the biggest cash transfer program in the United States is **public assistance**, more commonly called **welfare**. Aimed specifically at the poor, welfare falls into two major categories.

public assistance, *or* **welfare**
Government transfer programs that provide cash benefits to: (1) families with dependent children whose incomes and assets fall below a very low level and (2) the very poor regardless of whether they have children.

Most welfare is paid in the form of *temporary assistance for needy families*. Benefit levels are set by the states, and they vary widely. In January 2003, the maximum monthly payment to a one-parent family of three was $170 per month in Mississippi, $639 per month in Vermont, and $923 per month in Alaska. The average monthly payment in the United States was $423. To participate, a family must have a very low income and virtually no assets. In 2002, there were 5.1 million recipients of Temporary Assistance for Needy Families in the United States. Those who find jobs and enter the labor force lose benefits quickly as their incomes rise. This loss of benefits acts as a tax on beneficiaries, and some argue that it discourages welfare recipients from seeking jobs.

No topics raise passions more than welfare and welfare reform. The issue has been a focal point of "liberal/conservative" name-calling for more than three decades. In 1996, Congress passed and President Clinton signed a major overhaul of the welfare system in the United States. The name of the program was changed to Temporary Assistance for Needy Families from its former name, Aid to Families with Dependent Children, as of July 1997. The key change mandated that states limit most recipients to no more than five years of benefits over a lifetime. Some argue that the result will be a disaster, with some families left with nothing. Others argue that the previous system led to dependency and that there was no incentive to work.

The new legislation provides funds for added services to parents with young children but leaves a great deal of discretion in states' hands. Only time will tell how it turns out. However, remarkable declines in the Temporary Assistance for Needy Families program (TANF) caseloads occurred between 1994 and 2001. At the end of that year, the average monthly number of TANF recipients was 5.5 million, or 56 percent lower than the Aid to Families with Dependent Children (AFDC) caseload in 1996. From its peak of 14.4 million in March 1994, the number dropped by 64.6 percent to 5.1 million in 2002. Over three-fourths of the reduction in the U.S. average monthly number of recipients since March 1994 occurred following implementation of TANF. These are the largest caseload declines in the history of U.S. public assistance programs.

Supplemental Security Income   The *Supplemental Security Income program (SSI)* is a federal program that was set up under the Social Security Administration in 1974. The program is financed out of general revenues. That is, there is no trust fund and there are no earmarked taxes from which SSI benefits are paid out.

SSI is designed to take care of the elderly who end up very poor and have no or very low Social Security entitlement. In 2009, 8 million people received SSI payments, about half of whom also received some Social Security benefits. The average SSI payment was $498 per month. As with welfare, qualified recipients must have very low incomes and virtually no assets.

Unemployment Compensation   In the first quarter of 2005, governments paid out over $9.5 billion in benefits to 3.3 million recipients. The money to finance this benefit comes from taxes paid by employers into special funds. Companies that hire and fire frequently pay a higher tax rate, while companies with relatively stable employment levels pay a lower tax rate. Tax and benefit levels are determined by the states, within certain federal guidelines.

Workers who qualify for **unemployment compensation** begin to receive benefit checks soon after they are laid off. These checks continue for a period specified by the state. Most unemployment benefits continue for 20 weeks. In times of recession, the benefit period is often extended on a state-by-state basis. Average unemployed workers receive only about 36 percent of their normal wages, and not all workers are covered. To qualify for benefits, an unemployed person must have worked recently for a covered employer for a specified time for a given amount of wages. Recipients must also demonstrate willingness and ability to seek and accept suitable employment.

Unemployment benefits are not aimed at the poor alone, although many of the unemployed are poor. Unemployment benefits are paid regardless of a person's income from other sources and regardless of assets.

> **unemployment compensation**
> A state government transfer program that pays cash benefits for a certain period of time to laid-off workers who have worked for a specified period of time for a covered employer.

Health Care: Medicaid and Medicare

The largest in-kind transfer programs in the United States are Medicare and Medicaid. The **Medicaid** program provides health and hospitalization benefits to people with low incomes. Although the program is administered by the states, about 57 percent of the cost is borne by the federal government. In fiscal year 2011, the federal share was budgeted at $271 billion and growing rapidly. Both the federal share and the shares of each state are paid out of general revenue sources such as the income tax or the sales tax depending on the state.

Medicare, which is run by the Social Security Administration, is a health insurance program for the aged and certain disabled persons. Most U.S. citizens over age 65 receive Medicare hospital insurance coverage regardless of their income. In addition, Medicare recipients are able to purchase supplemental policies that cover things like the cost of prescription drugs.

Medicare is financed with the revenues from the Social Security payroll tax discussed above. Of the 7.65 percent flat rate tax paid by individuals who receive wages and salaries and an equal amount paid by their employers, 1.45 percent goes to Medicare. The self employed pay both halves or 15.3 percent. While the Social Security taxes apply only to income over a certain maximum, the Medicare tax is paid on *all* income without a cap. In fiscal year 2011, over $500 billion was budgeted for Medicare benefits payable to nearly 50 million recipients.

A major problem facing the system is the aging of the baby boom generation. The oldest of the baby boomers are now approaching the age of 65. Thus, a substantial number of people will be eligible for Medicare benefits precisely during the years that they are likely to need them. Projections are that the payroll tax will be insufficient to cover benefits and the system will be insolvent by the year 2020.

Despite the significant resources spent by the government, the Census Bureau reports that the number of people without health insurance grew to 50.7 million in 2009 from 46.3 million in 2008. The number of people covered by private insurance dropped during this period.

During the first term of the Obama administration the President put forward a major package of health care reform legislation. The Congress passed the Affordable Care Act bill by a razor thin vote in March 2010. The bill was designed to bring the United States closer to universal coverage by mandating that everyone buy health insurance coverage and setting up a government sponsored plan. The bill also made it illegal to drop coverage of people who become ill or deny coverage to people with preexisting conditions. The bill is very complex and it will take years to phase in. In addition, there was a great deal of public opposition to the reforms voiced during the mid-term elections of 2010. Much of the political opposition focused on the potential cost which would have to be added to an already high federal budget deficit.

> **Medicaid** *and* **Medicare**
> In-kind government transfer programs that provide health and hospitalization benefits: Medicare to the aged and their survivors and to certain of the disabled, regardless of income, and Medicaid to people with low incomes.

Food Stamps

The Food Stamp program is an antipoverty program fully funded out of general federal tax revenues, with states bearing 50 percent of the program's administrative costs. **Food stamps** are vouchers that have a face value greater than their cost and that can be used to purchase food at grocery stores. The amount by which the face value of the stamps exceeds their cost depends on income and family size. Only low-income families and single people are eligible to receive food stamps.

It is generally acknowledged that a thriving black market in food stamps exists. Families that want or need cash can sell their food stamps to people who will buy them for less than face value but more than the original recipient paid for them.

In 2009, there were 40 million participants in the Food Stamp program. The total cost of the program in 2009 was $54 billion.

> **food stamps** Vouchers that have a face value greater than their cost and that can be used to purchase food at grocery stores.

ECONOMICS IN PRACTICE

Does Price Matter in Charitable Giving?

In the United States, one of the ways in which people try to help the poor is through charity. Almost 90 percent of the population contributes each year to some charitable organization. Recent work in experimental economics has explored the factors that lead people to make these contributions. In experimental economics, experiments are conducted in a laboratory or in the field by using control groups to test economic theories. In some cases, the lessons learned have been put to use by charities as they try to raise funds.

One set of experiments looks at the effect of a matching gift on giving.[1] A matching gift is a commitment by a donor to give funds *conditioned on* another person's donation. A donor might say, for example, "For every dollar you raise up to $20,000, I will match with a dollar of my own." Why might an economist expect a matching gift commitment to increase the likelihood that another person will give to the charity?

There are at least two plausible explanations. In the previous chapter of this book, we described *signals*. In this situation, by offering a matching gift, in a public way, the original donor is telling other potential donors that he or she believes the charity to be worthy. If the donor is a well-known member of the community, this signal can be a powerful incentive to other givers.

Suppose that we think of "giving to charity" the same way we think of buying a good or a service. That is, we do it because we derive "utility" from it. If we do donate to charity, we are giving up the other things that the donation would buy. Now think of the "price of giving" as the amount you need to pay to deliver $10 in aid to a charity. With the matching grant, the price of giving falls to $5. If you give $5, the charity gets $10. If you give $100, the charity gets $200. So matching gifts are like reducing the "price" of a charitable gift.

Under the U.S. Income Tax, many taxpayers can deduct gifts to qualifying charities from their income in calculating their taxes each year. Suppose that a taxpayer were taxed at a marginal rate of 25 percent. Then a gift of $100 results in a tax saving of $25. The

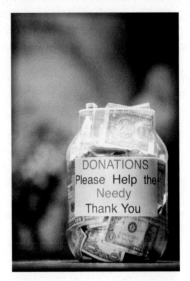

deduction reduces income by $100, and that $100 would have been taxed at 25 percent. Thus, just as in the case of the matching grant, the "price of giving" is reduced, in this case the price of giving $100 is reduced to $75. With deductibility, we reduce the price of charity from P to $P(1 - t)$ where t is the tax rate that applies to increases or decreases in income. Do you see why?

Whether a reduction in "price" leads people to give more depends on a lot of things. If it is a matching grant, you may give less and deliver more charity due to the match or you may give more to take advantage of the match. In the Karlan and List experiments, matching gift programs increased rates of giving.

[1] Dean Karlan and John List, "Does Price Matter in Charitable Giving" *American Economics Review*, 2008.

Housing Programs Over the years, the federal government and state governments have administered many different housing programs designed to improve the quality of housing for low-income people. The biggest is the Public Housing program, financed by the federal government but administered by local public housing authorities. Public housing tenants pay rents equal to no more than 30 percent of their incomes. In many cases, this means they pay nothing. The largest housing program, called "Section 8," provides housing assistance payments to tenants and slightly above-market rent guarantees to participating landlords.

In 2003, there were 33.5 million rental housing units in the United States, of which 1.9 million were in public housing projects. Another 2.2 million received a government rent subsidy.

The Earned Income Tax Credit An important program that is not well understood by most people is the earned income tax credit (EIC). The program is quite complex but essentially allows lower-income families with children a credit equal to a percentage of all wage and salary income against their income taxes. If the credit exceeds the amount of taxes due, the credit is refundable. To see roughly how the EIC works, consider a family made up of two adults and two children with an income of $11,000 per year, all earned as wages. After the standard deduction and exemptions, such a family would owe no taxes, but it would receive (subject to a number of restrictions) refundable credit of up to $3,800. That means the family would actually get a check for $3,800.

While not well known, the EIC program is very large. In 2009, the EIC was claimed by over 25 million households and totaled more than $57 billion.

Government or the Market? A Review

In Part II (Chapter 6 to 12), you were introduced to the behavior of households and firms in input and output markets. You learned that if all the assumptions of perfect competition held in the real world, the outcome would be perfectly efficient.

As we began to relax the assumptions of perfect competition in Part III (Chapter 13 to Chapter 19), we began to see a potential role for government in the economy. Some firms acquire market power and tend to underproduce and overprice. Unregulated markets give private decision makers no incentives to weigh the social costs of externalities. Goods that provide collective benefits may not be produced in sufficient quantities without government involvement. As we saw in this chapter, the final distribution of well-being determined by the unfettered market may not be considered equitable by society.

Remember, however, that government is not a cure for all economic woes. There is no guarantee that public-sector involvement will improve matters. Many argue that government involvement may bring about even more inequity and inefficiency because bureaucrats are often driven by self-interest, not public interest.

— S U M M A R Y —

THE SOURCES OF HOUSEHOLD INCOME p. 367

1. Households derive their incomes from three basic sources: (1) from wages or salaries received in exchange for labor (about 64 percent), (2) from property such as capital and land (about 22 percent), and (3) from government (about 14 percent).

2. Differences in wage and salary incomes across households result from differences in the characteristics of workers (skills, training, education, experience, and so on) and from differences in jobs (dangerous, exciting, glamorous, difficult, and so on). Household income also varies with the number of household members in the labor force, and it can decline sharply if members become unemployed.

3. The amount of property income that a household earns depends on the amount and kinds of property it owns. Transfer income from governments flows substantially but not exclusively to lower-income households. Except for Social Security, transfer payments are by and large designed to provide income to those in need.

THE DISTRIBUTION OF INCOME p. 370

4. The 20 percent of families at the top of the income distribution received 50.5 percent of the money income in the United States in 2006, while the bottom 20 percent earned just 3.4 percent. Income distribution in the United States has remained basically stable over a long period of time.

5. The Lorenz curve is a commonly used graphic device for describing the distribution of income. The Gini coefficient is an index of income inequality that ranges from 0 for perfect equality to 1 for total inequality.

6. Poverty is very difficult to define. Nonetheless, the official poverty line in the United States is fixed at three times the cost of the Department of Agriculture's minimum food budget. In 2006, the poverty line for a family of four was $17,628.

7. Between 1960 and 1970, the number of people officially classified as poor fell from 40 million to 25 million. That number did not change much between 1970 and 1978. Between 1978 and 1983, the number of poor people increased by nearly 45 percent to 35.3 million. In 2006, the figure was 36.5 million.

8. Data on the distribution of wealth are not as readily available as data on the distribution of income. The distribution of wealth in the United States is more unequal than the distribution of income. The wealthiest 10 percent of households own just under 70 percent of all household net worth in 2004.

THE UTILITY POSSIBILITIES FRONTIER p. 376

9. Even if all markets were perfectly efficient, the result might not be fair. Even in relatively unfettered market economies, governments redistribute income and wealth, usually in the name of fairness, or *equity*.

10. Because utility is neither directly observable nor measurable, most policy discussions deal with the distributions of income and wealth as imperfect substitutes for the concept of "the distribution of well-being."

THE REDISTRIBUTION DEBATE p. 377

11. The basic philosophical argument against government redistribution rests on the proposition that one is entitled to the fruits of one's efforts. The argument also rests on the principles of freedom of contract and protection of property rights. More common arguments focus on the negative effects of redistribution on incentives to work, save, and invest.

12. The basic philosophical argument in favor of redistribution is that a society as rich as the United States has a moral obligation to provide all its members with the basic necessities of life. More formal arguments can be found in the works of the utilitarians, Rawls, and Marx.

REDISTRIBUTION PROGRAMS AND POLICIES p. 380

13. In the United States, redistribution is accomplished through taxation and through a number of government transfer programs. The largest of these programs are Social Security, public assistance, supplemental security, unemployment compensation, Medicare and Medicaid, food stamps, and various housing subsidy programs (including public housing).

14. The increase in poverty during the 1980s and 1990s is at the center of a great debate over the effectiveness of antipoverty programs. One view holds that the best way to cure poverty

is with economic growth. Poverty programs are expensive and must be paid for with tax revenues. The high rates of taxation required to support these programs have eroded the incentive to work, save, and invest, thus slowing the rate of economic growth. In addition, the rise in poverty is cited as evidence that antipoverty programs do not work. The opposite view holds that without antipoverty programs, poverty would be much worse.

REVIEW TERMS AND CONCEPTS

compensating differentials, *p. 368*

economic income, *p. 370*

equity, *p. 367*

food stamps, *p. 383*

Gini coefficient, *p. 372*

human capital, *p. 368*

labor theory of value, *p. 379*

Lorenz curve, *p. 371*

Medicaid *and* Medicare, *p. 383*

minimum wage, *p. 368*

money income, *p. 371*

poverty line, *p. 375*

property income, *p. 369*

public assistance, *or* welfare, *p. 382*

Rawlsian justice, *p. 379*

Social Security system, *p. 381*

transfer payments, *p. 370*

unemployment compensation, *p. 383*

utilitarian justice, *p. 379*

utility possibilities frontier, *p. 376*

PROBLEMS

All problems are available on www.myeconlab.com

1. One of the issues that is debated in virtually every election is whether to raise the federal minimum wage, which stood at $7.25 per hour in 2010. Suppose that you are married with a child, working a 40 hour week in a minimum wage job. By assuming that you pay taxes of about 10 percent of your total pay, how much do you "take home" each month? How much does it cost to rent a "reasonable" apartment near where you live? How much would you have left after paying rent? How much would it cost for other items such as food? Work out a hypothetical "budget" for this family.

2. By using the data in the following table, create two graphs. The first graph should plot the Lorenz curves for African-American families and white families. The second graph should plot the Lorenz curve for the 1980 "all" data and the Lorenz curve for the 1995 "all" data.

   In each graph, which has the higher Gini coefficient? How do you interpret the result?

PERCENT OF INCOME

	AFRICAN-AMERICAN	WHITE	1995 ALL	1980 ALL
Lowest fifth	3.2	4.6	4.2	5.1
Second fifth	8.5	10.3	10.0	11.6
Third fifth	15.1	15.8	15.7	17.5
Fourth fifth	24.7	23.0	23.3	24.3
Highest fifth	48.7	46.3	46.9	41.6

3. Economists call education "an investment in human capital." Define *capital*. In what sense is education capital? Investments are undertaken to earn a rate of return. Describe the return to an investment in a college education. How would you go about measuring it? How would you decide if it is good enough to warrant the investment?

4. Following is a list of establishment categories and average weekly earnings for nonsupervisory employees in a recent year. Using the concepts of "human capital" and "compensating differentials," explain why they might be expected to differ in these areas:

Computer programming	$724.85
Heavy construction firms	535.29
Logging firms	447.02
Gas stations	218.13
Car washes	161.19

5. During the mid-1980s and again between 1995 and 2006, house values and rents rose sharply in California and in the northeastern United States. But starting in 2006, prices began to fall. Homeowners, who have higher incomes on average than renters, benefit from house-price increases and are protected from housing-cost increases. Falling house prices, on the other hand, make housing more affordable but inflict pain on homeowners. Renters experience rising rents and falling standards of living if incomes do not keep up with rents. Using the *Statistical Abstract of the United States*, other data sources, www.census.gov, www.ofheo.gov, or http://macromarkets.com, look up residential rent, home prices, and income levels for your area. What has happened in the last 10 years? Do you think the performance of the housing market in recent years has increased or decreased inequality in your area? Explain.

6. New PhDs in economics entering the job market find that academic jobs (jobs teaching at colleges and universities) pay about 30 percent less than nonacademic jobs such as working at a bank or a consulting firm. Those who take academic jobs are clearly worse off than those who take nonacademic jobs. Do you agree? Explain your answer.

7. Should welfare benefits be higher in California and New York than in Mississippi? Defend your answer.

8. Poverty among the elderly has been sharply reduced in the last quarter-century. How has this reduction been accomplished?

9. "Income inequality is evidence that our economic system is working well, not poorly." Do you agree or disagree? Defend your answer.

10. The official poverty line has been the subject of much debate over the last few decades. On Google or another search engine, look up and read the work of Molly Orshansky. Her work focused on finding a measure of poverty that reflected a bundle of goods that people in different circumstances must be able to purchase. Describe the debate and the resulting system for setting the poverty thresholds. How would you change them?

11. [Related to the *Economics in Practice* on p. 384] Some economists predict that an increase in the marginal income tax rate would increase the amount of charitable giving that people do even though this increase would require wealthier people to pay more taxes. Why do you think economists are predicting this effect?

12. Refer to the following Lorenz curve to answer the questions.

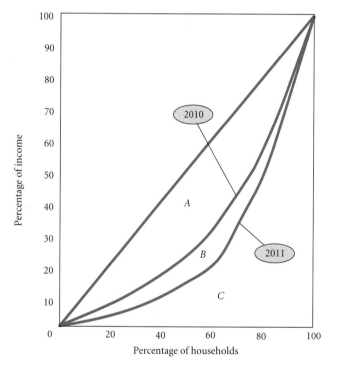

a. Explain whether the distribution of income was more equal in 2010 or 2011.

b. If area $A = 1,900$ and area $B = 300$, what is the value of area C? What is the value of the Gini coefficient for 2010 and for 2011?

13. The tiny island nation of Pong has five residents, and the table below lists the annual income of each of these people. Fill in the table and draw a Lorenz curve showing the distribution of income for the nation of Pong.

PERSON	ANNUAL INCOME	SHARE OF INCOME	CUMULATIVE SHARE OF INCOME
Angus	$15,000		
Belinda	25,000		
Coco	45,000		
Darius	70,000		
Eva	95,000		

14. Suppose the prevailing equilibrium wage in a labor market is $10.00 per hour. What would be the impact of a minimum wage law that sets the minimum wage in this market at $14.00 per hour? What if the minimum wage was set at $8.00 per hour?

15. Explain how a state government transfer program such as unemployment compensation may actually result in a higher unemployment rate than would occur if the program did not exist.

16. [Related to the *Economics in Practice* on p. 373] Executive compensation remains a much-debated topic in the United States. Over the past three decades, compensation for CEOs of U.S. corporations has risen dramatically, both in real dollars and in terms of worker's earnings, where in 1980 the average CEO of a major corporation earned 42 times the average pay of an hourly worker. The debate has reached Washington, where in 2009 President Obama imposed a pay limit of $500,000 for executives of companies that received federal bailout money. Write a brief essay discussing executive compensation, explaining whether you believe executive pay should be limited. Should the government be involved in compensation decisions of private corporations? What has happened to the ratio of CEO pay to hourly worker pay since 1980, and how does this compare to other countries?

Public Finance: The Economics of Taxation

19

The previous chapters in Part III have analyzed the potential role of government in the economy. Together those chapters discuss much of the field of *public economics*. In this chapter, we make the transition to *public finance*. No matter what functions we end up assigning to government, to do anything at all, government must first raise revenues. The primary vehicle that the government uses to finance itself is taxation.

Taxes may be imposed on transactions, institutions, property, meals, and other things, but in the final analysis they are paid by individuals or households.

tax base The measure or value upon which a tax is levied.

tax rate structure The percentage of a tax base that must be paid in taxes— 25 percent of income, for example.

The Economics of Taxation

To begin our analysis of the U.S. tax system, we need to clarify some terms. There are many kinds of taxes and tax analysts use a specific language to describe them.

Taxes: Basic Concepts

Every tax has two parts: a *base* and a *rate structure*. The **tax base** is the measure or value upon which the tax is levied. In the United States, taxes are levied on a variety of bases, including income, sales, property, and corporate profits. The **tax rate structure** determines the portion of the tax base that must be paid in taxes. A tax rate of 25 percent on income, for example, means that you pay a tax equal to 25 percent of your income.

Taxes on Stocks versus Taxes on Flows   Tax bases may be either stock measures or flow measures. The local property tax is a tax on the value of residential, commercial, or industrial property. A homeowner, for instance, is taxed on the current assessed value of his or her home. Current value is a *stock variable*—that is, it is measured or estimated at a point in time.

Other taxes are levied on *flows*. Income is a flow. Most people are paid on a monthly basis, and they have taxes taken out every month. Retail sales take place continuously, and a retail sales tax takes a portion of that flow. Figure 19.1 diagrams in simple form the important continuous payment flows between households and firms and the points at which the government levies six different taxes.

Although the individual income tax remained around 45 percent of total taxes through 2000, by 2009 it was down to 37.2 percent. The corporate tax has been around 10 percent since 1990. There has been a huge increase in the share of the social insurance tax, from 16.0 percent in 1960 to 42.7 percent in 2009. It is now the largest component of federal tax receipts.

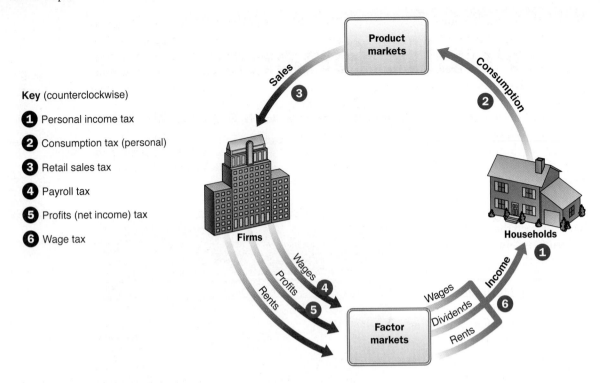

Key (counterclockwise)

1. Personal income tax
2. Consumption tax (personal)
3. Retail sales tax
4. Payroll tax
5. Profits (net income) tax
6. Wage tax

▲ **FIGURE 19.1 Taxes on Economic "Flows"**

Most taxes are levied on measurable economic flows. For example, a profits, or net income, tax is levied on the annual profits earned by corporations.

TABLE 19.1	Federal Government Receipts 1960–2009 (billions of dollars)					
	Individual Income Tax	Corporation Income Tax	Social Insurance Payroll Taxes	Excise Taxes	Other Receipts	Total
1960	41.8	21.4	16.0	13.1	1.6	93.9
%	**44.5**	**22.8**	**17.0**	**14.0**	**1.7**	**100**
1970	88.9	30.6	45.5	18.1	3.0	186.1
%	**47.8**	**16.4**	**24.4**	**9.7**	**1.6**	**100**
1980	250.0	70.3	163.6	33.7	15.2	532.8
%	**46.9**	**13.2**	**30.7**	**6.3**	**2.9**	**100**
1990	470.1	118.1	402.0	50.9	41.7	1,082.8
%	**43.4**	**10.9**	**37.1**	**4.7**	**3.9**	**100**
2000	995.6	219.4	698.6	87.3	56.2	2,057.1
%	**48.4**	**10.7**	**34.0**	**4.2**	**2.7**	**100**
2009	828.7	231.0	949.1	92.3	123.8	2,224.9
%	**37.2**	**10.4**	**42.7**	**4.1**	**5.6**	**100**

Source: Bureau of Economic Analysis. Percentages may not add to 100 due to rounding.

proportional tax A tax whose burden is the same proportion of income for all households.

progressive tax A tax whose burden, expressed as a percentage of income, increases as income increases.

regressive tax A tax whose burden, expressed as a percentage of income, falls as income increases.

Proportional, Progressive, and Regressive Taxes   All taxes are ultimately paid out of income. A tax whose burden is the same proportion of income for all households is a **proportional tax.** A tax of 20 percent on all forms of income, with no deductions or exclusions, is a proportional tax.

A tax that exacts a higher percentage of income from higher-income households than from lower-income households is a **progressive tax.** Because its rate structure increases with income, the U.S. individual income tax is a progressive tax. Under current law, a family with a taxable income of under $14,000 would pay a tax of 10 percent while a family with an income of $100,000 would pay about 19 percent.

A tax that exacts a lower percentage of income from higher-income families than from lower-income families is a **regressive tax.** *Excise taxes* (taxes on specific commodities such as gasoline and telephone calls) are regressive. The retail sales tax is also a regressive tax. Suppose the retail sales tax in your state is 5 percent. You might assume that it is a proportional tax because everyone pays 5 percent. But all people do not spend the same fraction of their income on taxable goods and services. In fact, higher-income households save a larger fraction of their incomes. Even though they spend more on expensive things and may pay more taxes in *dollars* than lower-income families, they end up paying a smaller *proportion* of their incomes in sales tax.

Table 19.2 shows this principle at work in three families. The lowest-income family saves 20 percent of its $10,000 income, leaving $8,000 for consumption. With a hypothetical 5 percent sales tax, the household pays $400, or 4 percent of total income, in tax. The $50,000 family saves 50 percent of its income, or $25,000, leaving $25,000 for consumption. With the 5 percent sales tax, the household pays $1,250, only 2.5 percent of its total income, in tax.

TABLE 19.2	The Burden of a Hypothetical 5% Sales Tax Imposed on Three Households with Different Incomes					
Household	Income	Saving Rate, %	Saving	Consumption	5% Tax on Consumption	Tax as a % of Income
A	$10,000	20	$ 2,000	$ 8,000	$ 400	4.0
B	20,000	40	8,000	12,000	600	3.0
C	50,000	50	25,000	25,000	1,250	2.5

Marginal versus Average Tax Rates   When discussing a specific tax or taxes in general, we should distinguish between average tax rate and marginal tax rates. Your **average tax rate** is the total amount of tax you pay divided by your total income. If you earned a total income of $15,000 and paid income taxes of $1,500, your average income tax rate would be 10 percent ($1,500 divided by $15,000). If you paid $3,000 in taxes, your average rate would be 20 percent ($3,000 divided by $15,000). Your **marginal tax rate** is the tax rate you pay on any additional income you earn.

Each year you must file a tax return with the Internal Revenue Service on or before April 15. On that form, you first figure out the total tax you are responsible for paying. Next, you determine how much was withheld from your income and sent to the IRS by your employer. If too much was withheld, you get a refund; if not enough was withheld, you have to write a check to the government for the difference.

In figuring out the total amount of tax you must pay, you first add up all your income. You are then allowed to subtract certain items from it. Among the things that virtually all taxpayers can subtract are the *personal exemption* and the *standard deduction*. After everything is subtracted, you are left with *taxable income*. Taxable income is then subject to a set of marginal rates that rise with income.

The *Economics in Practice* on p. 392 shows the income taxes that would be paid by two hypothetical single people earning $100,000 and $125,000, respectively. The discussion uses the actual 2009 U.S. tax rates. These calculations show that average and marginal tax rates are not the same in a progressive tax system. Which tax rate should you pay attention to? When talking about taxes, many people focus on average rates, the percent of one's income that goes to the government. But for most decisions, the marginal rate is more relevant. If you are thinking of working more hours, you will be paying the marginal (higher) rate on the incremental income earned; so that is the rate you should look at in thinking about whether to work. In thinking about whether to donate money (which has the effect of lowering adjusted income), the marginal rate is again the relevant one.

How Much Does a Deduction Save You in Taxes?   As you saw in the *Economics in Practice*, you were allowed to subtract $9,350 from your income as a single person before calculating taxes. However, you may be able to do better (that is, pay less tax) if you can come up with "itemized deductions" in excess of $9,350. Taxpayers may deduct income taxes paid to a state, charitable contributions to qualifying organizations, real estate taxes, and interest paid on a mortgage to finance the purchase of a home, as well as other items.

Some people complain that high-income households receive a bigger benefit from deductions. For example, if a single person with very high income—let's say over $400,000—gave a

average tax rate   Total amount of tax paid divided by total income.

marginal tax rate   The tax rate paid on any additional income earned.

ECONOMICS IN PRACTICE

Calculating Taxes

One way to get a sense of the structure of the U.S. income tax system is to actually calculate what you would owe assuming your income was at one level or another. Suppose you are single with no dependents and you rent rather than own. Assume your charitable contributions are relatively modest as well. In that case, you are likely to take a "standard deduction" when filing your taxes.

Consider what happens to your tax payments as you go from $100,000 per year to $125,000. We will use the 2009 tax schedule for this calculation. In 2009, single filers who were not claimed on anyone else's tax return (many students are still claimed on their parents' returns) and did not itemize were entitled to deduct $9,350 from their gross income before calculating their taxes. In our example, we will be comparing adjusted incomes of $90,650 versus $115,650. Notice that both before and after this adjustment the pretax incomes differ by $25,000.

The 2009 tax table is reproduced below. As you see, the tax rate increases with income, making it a *progressive* system. In the last two columns we calculate the taxes owed at the two income levels.

Notice your average tax rate goes up with income given that the tax system is progressive. Notice also that the marginal tax rate of

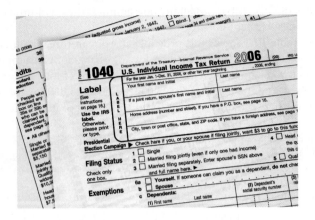

28 percent is higher than the average tax rate. Of the *added* $25,000 you earn, 28 percent goes to the government, and you net only $18,000 more than you had at a salary level of $100,000. (If you do the subtraction, you will see that your after-tax pay at $100,000 is $80,898, while at $125,000 it is $98,898.)

Rate	On income between	Amount owed on $100K ($90,650 taxed)	Amount owed on $125K ($115,650 taxed)
10%	$0-$8,350	$835	$835
15%	$8,350-$33,950	$3,840	$3,840
25%	$33,950-$82,250	$12,075	$12,075
28%	$82,250-$171,500	$2,352	$9,352
33%	$171,500-$372,950	0	0
35%	$372,950+	0	0
Tax owed (Sum)		$19,102	$26,102
Average tax rate (Tax/Income)		0.1910	0.2088
Marginal tax rate		0.28	0.28

contribution of $1,000, she would save $350 because her marginal tax rate is 35 percent, the highest marginal tax rate. If another person had a taxable income of $20,000, the same $1,000 charitable contribution would save her only $150 because she would face a marginal tax rate of 15 percent. You can see that higher income households, facing higher marginal tax rates, have more incentives to seek deductions of various sorts.

This discussion gives you a taste of the U.S. Individual Income Tax. It is a very complex tax, and most people need help in figuring out how to comply with the law. One of the top priorities of each of the past five U.S. presidents has been to simplify the tax code, and while the Tax Reform Act of 1986 made some progress, the code seems to get more complex with every passing year. Shortly after being elected, President Obama appointed a task force headed by Paul Volcker to streamline the tax code.

Tax Equity

One of the criteria for evaluating the economy that we defined in Chapter 1 (and returned to in Chapter 18) was fairness, or *equity*. Everyone agrees that tax burdens should be distributed fairly, that all of us should pay our "fair share" of taxes, but there is endless debate about what constitutes a fair tax system.

One theory of fairness is called the **benefits-received principle**. Dating back to the eighteenth-century economist Adam Smith and earlier writers, the benefits-received principle holds that taxpayers should contribute to government according to the benefits they derive from public expenditures. This principle ties the tax side of the fiscal equation to the expenditure side. For example, the owners and users of cars pay gasoline and automotive excise taxes, which are paid into the Federal Highway Trust Fund to build and maintain the federal highway system. The beneficiaries of public highways are thus taxed in rough proportion to their use of those highways.

The difficulty with applying the benefits principle is that many public expenditures are for public goods—national defense, for example. The benefits of public goods fall collectively on all members of society, and there is no way to determine what value individual taxpayers receive from them.

A different principle, and one that has dominated the formulation of tax policy in the United States for decades, is the **ability-to-pay principle**. This principle holds that taxpayers should bear tax burdens in line with their ability to pay. Here the tax side of the fiscal equation is viewed separately from the expenditure side. Under this system, the problem of attributing the benefits of public expenditures to specific taxpayers or groups of taxpayers is avoided.

Horizontal and Vertical Equity   If we accept the idea that ability to pay should be the basis for the distribution of tax burdens, two principles follow. First, the principle of *horizontal equity* holds that those with equal ability to pay should bear equal tax burdens. Second, the principle of *vertical equity* holds that those with greater ability to pay should pay more.

Although these notions seem appealing, we must have answers to two interdependent questions before they can be meaningful. First, how is ability to pay measured? What is the "best" tax base? Second, if A has a greater ability to pay than B, *how much* more should A contribute?

What Is the "Best" Tax Base?

The three leading candidates for best tax base are *income, consumption,* and *wealth*. Before we consider each as a basis for taxation, let us see what they mean.

Income—to be precise, *economic income*—is anything that enhances your ability to command resources. The technical definition of economic income is the value of what you consume plus any change in the value of what you own:

$$\text{Economic Income} = \text{Consumption} + \text{Change in Net Worth}$$

This broad definition is essentially consumption + saving, but it includes many items not counted by the Internal Revenue Service and some items the Census Bureau does not include in its definition of "money income." Economic income includes all money receipts, whether from employment, interest on savings, dividends, profits, or transfers from the government. It also includes the value of benefits not received in money form, such as medical benefits, employer retirement contributions, paid country club memberships, and so on. Increases or decreases in the value of stocks or bonds, whether or not they are "realized" through sale, are part of economic income. For income tax purposes, capital gains (increases in the value of assets, like shares of stock) count as income only when they are realized, but for purposes of defining economic income, all increases in asset values count, whether they are realized or not.

A few other items that we do not usually think of as income are included in a comprehensive definition of income. If you own your house outright and live in it rent free, income flows from your house just as interest flows from a bond or profit from a share of stock. By owning the house, you enjoy valuable housing benefits for which you would otherwise have to pay rent. You are your own landlord, and you are, in essence, earning your own rent. Other components of economic income include any gifts and bequests received and food grown at home. In economic terms, income is income regardless of source and use.

Consumption is the total value of goods and services that a household consumes in a given period.

Wealth, or *net worth*, is the value of all the goods and services you own after your liabilities are subtracted. If today you were to sell everything of value you own—stocks, bonds, houses, cars,

benefits-received principle   A theory of fairness holding that taxpayers should contribute to government (in the form of taxes) in proportion to the benefits they receive from public expenditures.

ability-to-pay principle   A theory of taxation holding that citizens should bear tax burdens in line with their ability to pay taxes.

and so on—at their current market prices and pay off all your debts—loans, mortgages, and so on—you would end up with your net worth.

Net worth = Assets − Liabilities

Remember, income and consumption are *flow* measures. We speak of income per month or per year. Wealth and net worth are *stock* measures at a point in time.

For years, conventional wisdom among economists held that income was the best measure of ability to pay taxes. Many who believe that consumption is a better measure have recently challenged that assumption. The following arguments are not just arguments about fairness and ability to pay; they are also arguments about the best base for taxation.

Remember as you proceed that the issue is which *base* is the best base, not which *tax* is the best tax or whether taxes ought to be progressive or regressive. Sales taxes are regressive, but it is possible to have a personal consumption tax that is progressive. Under such a system, individuals would report their income as they do now, but all documented saving would be deductible. The difference between income and saving is a measure of personal consumption that could be taxed with progressive rates.

Consumption as the Best Tax Base   The view favoring consumption as the best tax base dates back to at least the seventeenth-century English philosopher Thomas Hobbes, who argued that people should pay taxes in accordance with "what they actually take out of the common pot, not what they leave in." The standard of living, the argument goes, depends not on income, but on how much income is spent. If we want to redistribute well-being, therefore, the tax base should be consumption because consumption is the best measure of well-being. The value-added tax (VAT) used by most developed economies other than the United States is essentially a tax on consumption.

A second argument with a distinguished history dates back to work done by Irving Fisher in the early part of the last century. Fisher and many others have argued that a tax on income discourages saving by taxing savings twice. A story told originally by Fisher illustrates this theory nicely.[1]

Suppose Alex builds a house for Frank. In exchange, Frank pays Alex $10,000 and gives him an orchard containing 100 apple trees. Alex spends the $10,000 today, but he saves the orchard, and presumably he will consume or sell the fruit it bears every year in the future. At year's end, the state levies a 10 percent tax on Alex's total income, which includes the $10,000 and the orchard. First, the government takes 10 percent of the $10,000, which is 10 percent of Alex's consumption. Second, it takes 10 percent of the orchard—10 trees—which is 10 percent of Alex's saving. If this is all the government did, there would be no double taxation of saving. If, however, the income tax is also levied the following year, Alex will be taxed on the income generated by the 90 trees that he still owns. If the income tax is levied in the year after that, Alex will again be taxed on the income generated by his orchard, and so on. The income tax is thus taxing Alex's saving more than once. To tax the orchard fairly, the system should take 10 percent of the trees *or* 10 percent of the fruit going forward—*but not both!* To avoid the double taxation of savings, either the original savings of 100 trees should not be taxed or the income generated from the after-tax number of trees (90) should not be taxed.

The same logic can be applied to cash savings. Suppose the income tax rate is 25 percent and you earn $20,000. Out of the $20,000, you consume $16,000 and save $4,000. At the end of the year, you owe the government 25 percent of your total income, or $5,000. You can think of this as a tax of 25 percent on consumption ($4,000) and 25 percent on savings ($1,000). Why, then, do we say that the income tax is a double tax on savings? To see why, you have to think about the $4,000 that is saved.

If you save $4,000, you will no doubt put it to some use. Saving possibilities include putting it in an interest-bearing account or buying a bond. If you do either, you will earn interest that you can consume in future years. In fact, when we save and earn interest, we are spreading some of our present earnings over future years of consumption. Just as the orchard yields future fruit, the bond yields future interest, which is considered income in the year it is earned and is taxed as such. The only way you can earn that future interest income is by leaving your money tied up in the bond or the account. You can consume the $4,000 today, *or* you can have the future flow of interest; you can't have both. Yet both are taxed!

---

[1] Irving Fisher and Herbert Fisher, *Constructive Income Taxation: A Proposal for Reform* (New York: Harper, 1942), Ch. 8, p. 56.

Taxing consumption is also more efficient than taxing income. As you will see later, a tax that distorts economic choices creates *excess burdens*. By double-taxing savings, an income tax distorts the choice between consumption and saving, which is really the choice between present consumption and future consumption. Double-taxing also tends to reduce the saving rate and the rate of investment—and ultimately the rate of economic growth.

Income as the Best Tax Base   Your ability to pay is your ability to command resources, and many argue that your income is the best measure of your capacity to command resources today. According to proponents of income as a tax base, you should be taxed not on what you actually draw out of the common pot, but rather on the basis of your *ability* to draw from that pot. In other words, your decision to save or consume is no different from your decision to buy apples, to go out for dinner, or to give money to your mother. It is your *income* that enables you to do all these things, and it is income that should be taxed, regardless of its sources and regardless of how you use it. Saving is just another use of income.

If income is the best measure of ability to pay, the double taxation argument doesn't hold true. An income tax taxes savings twice only if consumption is the measure used to gauge a person's ability to pay. It does not do so if income is the measure used. Acquisition of the orchard enhances your ability to pay today; a bountiful crop of fruit enhances your ability to pay when it is produced. Interest income is no different from any other form of income; it too enhances your ability to pay. Taxing both is thus fair.

Wealth as the Best Tax Base   Still others argue that the real power to command resources comes not from any single year's income, but from accumulated wealth. Aggregate net worth in the United States is many times larger than aggregate income.

If two people have identical annual incomes of $10,000 but one of them also has an accumulated net worth of $1 million, is it reasonable to argue that these two people have the same ability to pay or that they should pay equal taxes? Most people would answer no.

Those who promote a wealth-based system also argue that the only real way to redistribute economic power is to tax the very high concentrations of wealth. Of course, it is important to note that if income is already taxed, a wealth tax, in essence, taxes the same dollars again.

No Simple Answer   Recall that these arguments are about the definition of "horizontal equity": What is the single best measure of ability to pay? In fact, policy debates about the system of taxes in the United States or in any other country involve much more. Virtually every country in the world has a system of taxation that taxes all three bases. In the United States, for example, there are sales and excise taxes (consumption taxes), the Federal Gift and Estate Tax (a wealth tax), the Individual Income Tax, and the local property tax (another wealth tax).

It is important to point out that for many U.S. taxpayers, the Individual Income Tax is probably closer to being a consumption tax than an income tax since much of household savings can be deducted from income before the tax is figured. The tax code (or law) is full of subsidies and incentives. Among the most significant incentives built into the system are provisions designed to encourage people to save. For example, an important exclusion from income for purposes of defining the income tax base is employers' contributions to employee pension accounts. For many workers, retirement is in part financed by payments from pension funds. As long as a person is working, many employers will make deposits or match employee deposits to retirement or pension accounts. Those contributions are part of a household's economic income and part of household savings, but they are not taxed. Recall that income is essentially consumption plus savings (change in net worth). In addition, deposits to specific kinds of accounts (such as Individual Retirement Accounts, or IRAs) can be excluded from income for tax purposes. A good portion of capital gains income (increases in the value of things that a household owns), such as increases in the value of corporate stocks or houses, is left out of the base or taxed at lower rates.

There is ongoing debate in the United States about whether it would be better to shift toward a more comprehensive consumption tax. In the fall of 2005, President Bush's Advisory Panel on Federal Tax Reform presented its report on reforming and simplifying the nation's tax code. The commission stopped short of full implementation of a consumption tax such as a national sales tax or a version of a national sales tax called a *value-added tax* (VAT) that is popular in Europe. But the panel did recommend moving to a system that rewards saving and discourages consumption more than the current one. An important goal of the commission was to recommend ways of simplifying the code.

ECONOMICS IN PRACTICE

The Yankees and the Estate Tax

As we indicated in the text, under a tax change passed in 2001, the gift and estate tax was phased out completely in 2010 for one year. By the fall of 2010, Congress had not yet reversed this phasing out, and articles began to appear about billionaires who had died in 2010 and whose heirs appear to have avoided the tax. George Steinbrenner, legendary owner of the New York Yankees, was one.

How Steinbrenner Saved His Heirs a $600 Million Tax Bill

The Wall Street Journal

Did George Steinbrenner save his heirs millions by dying in 2010?

Forbes recently estimated the Yankees owner's net worth at $1.1 billion, largely from the YES network. The New York Yankees, which he acquired in 1973 for $10 million, are now worth $1.6 billion but are 95% leveraged due to debt from the new Yankee Stadium, according to Forbes.

Because Steinbrenner died in a year when there is no federal estate tax, he potentially saved his heirs a 55% estate tax on his assets—or a tax bill of about $600 million. The 55% tax takes effect on January 1, 2011. If Steinbrenner had died in 2009 when the estate tax rate was 45%, his estate tax bill might have been nearer $500 million. Because the wealthy often do elaborate planning, putting assets into trusts taxed separately from the estate or into foundations that are tax-exempt, it is unclear how large his estate will be. Estate taxes may also be postponed on assets left to a spouse in years when there is an estate tax.

There is no estate tax this year due to changes made by Congress in 2001. Those changes eased the estate tax over several years and culminated with its repeal this year, followed by a return to high tax levels in 2011. Experts say few ever expected the tax's repeal, and its 2011 reinstatement, would actually take effect. Instead they believed lawmakers would smooth out the tax rates at some point between 2002 and the end of 2009.

Congress never got around to it, and the tax lapsed this year. Many still hope lawmakers will fix this year's law, which actually raises taxes on heirs of the merely affluent (with assets between $1.3 and $4 million). But they still haven't acted and have little time to do so.

Because of the huge chasm separating 2010's zero tax rate from 2011's 55% rate, some fear that Congress has provided the wealthy with an incentive for dying—or their relatives with an incentive for making sure they die—before the clock strikes midnight on Dec. 31.

Source: The Wall Street Journal Online, excerpted from "How Steinbrenner Saved His Heirs a $600 Million Tax Bill" by Laura Saunders. Copyright 2010 by *Dow Jones & Company, Inc.* Reproduced with permission of *Dow Jones & Company, Inc.* via Copyright Clearance Center.

The Gift and Estate Tax

estate The property that a person owns at the time of his or her death.

estate tax A tax on the total value of a person's estate.

One of the oldest and most common forms of taxation in the world is the taxation of property held by an individual at the time of his or her death. The property owned at the time of a person's death is called the person's **estate**. An **estate tax** is a tax on the total value of a person's estate regardless of how it is distributed. The United States levies a Gift and Estate Tax on gifts made over a person's lifetime and the value of the person's estate, for estates over a certain level. The Federal Gift and Estate Tax, which raises less than 2 percent of total tax revenues, was phased out for one year in 2010 under a law passed by Congress in 2001. In 2011, without further action, the tax will revert to its original 2001 level. The *Economics in Practice* discusses the picture in 2010.

Tax Incidence: Who Pays?

When a government levies a tax, it writes a law assigning responsibility for payment to specific people or specific organizations. To understand a tax, we must look beyond those named in the law as the initial taxpayers.

First, remember the principle of tax analysis: The burden of a tax is ultimately borne by individuals or households; institutions such as business firms and colleges have no real taxpaying capacity. Taxes paid by a firm ultimately fall on customers or owners or workers. Second, the burden of a tax is not always borne by those initially responsible for paying it. Directly or indirectly, tax burdens are often *shifted* to others. When we speak of the **incidence of a tax**, we are referring to the ultimate distribution of its burden.

tax incidence The ultimate distribution of a tax burden.

The simultaneous reactions of many households and/or firms to the presence of a tax may cause relative prices to change, and price changes affect households' well-being. Households may feel the impact of a tax on the sources side or on the uses side of the income equation. (We use the term *income equation* because the amount of income from all *sources* must be equal to the amount of income allocated to all *uses*—including saving—in a given period.) On the **sources side**, a household is hurt when the net wages or profits that it receives fall; on the **uses side**, a household is hurt when the prices of the goods and services that it buys rise. If your wages remain the same but the price of every item that you buy doubles, you are in the same position you would have been in if your wages had been cut by 50 percent and prices hadn't changed. In short, the imposition of a tax or a change in a tax can change behavior. Changes in behavior can affect supply and demand in markets and cause prices to change. When prices change in input or output markets, some households are made better off and some are made worse off. These final changes determine the ultimate burden of the tax.

Tax shifting takes place when households can alter their behavior and do something to avoid paying a tax. Such shifting is easily accomplished when only certain items are singled out for taxation. Suppose a heavy tax were levied on bananas. Initially, the tax would make the price of bananas much higher, but there are many potential substitutes for bananas. Consumers can avoid the tax by not buying bananas, and that is what many will do. But as demand drops, the market price of bananas falls and banana growers lose money. The tax shifts from consumers to the growers, at least in the short run.

A tax such as the retail sales tax, which is levied at the same rate on *all* consumer goods, is harder to avoid. The only thing consumers can do to avoid such a tax is to consume less of everything. If consumers consume less, saving will increase, but otherwise there are few opportunities for tax avoidance and therefore for tax shifting. Broad-based taxes are less likely to be shifted and more likely to "stick" where they are levied than "partial taxes" are.

sources side/uses side The impact of a tax may be felt on one or the other or on both sides of the income equation. A tax may cause net income to fall (damage on the sources side), or it may cause prices of goods and services to rise so that income buys less (damage on the uses side).

tax shifting Occurs when households can alter their behavior and do something to avoid paying a tax.

The Incidence of Payroll Taxes

In 2009, about 42.7 percent of federal revenues came from social insurance taxes, also called *payroll taxes*. The revenues from payroll taxes go to support Social Security, unemployment compensation, and other health and disability benefits for workers. Some of these taxes are levied on employers as a percentage of payroll, and some are levied on workers as a percentage of wages or salaries earned.

To analyze the payroll tax, let us take a tax levied on employers and sketch the reactions that are likely to follow. When the tax is first levied, firms find that the price of labor increases. Firms may react in two ways. First, they may substitute capital for the now more-expensive labor. Second, higher costs and lower profits may lead to a cut in production. Both reactions mean a lower demand for labor. Lower demand for labor reduces wages, and part of the tax is thus passed on (or *shifted to*) the workers, who end up earning less. The extent to which the tax is shifted to workers depends on how workers can react to the lower wages.

We can develop a more formal analysis of this situation with a picture of the market before the tax is levied. Figure 19.2 shows equilibrium in a hypothetical labor market with no payroll tax. Before we proceed, we should review the factors that determine the shapes of the supply and demand curves.

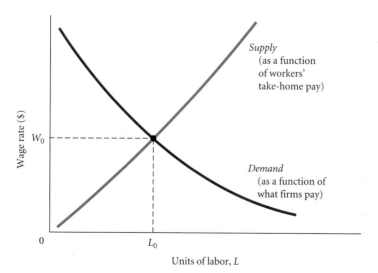

◀ **FIGURE 19.2**

Equilibrium in a Competitive Labor Market—No Taxes

With no taxes on wages, the wage that firms pay is the same as the wage that workers take home. At a wage of W_0, the quantity of labor supplied and the quantity of labor demanded are equal.

Labor Supply and Labor Demand Curves in Perfect Competition: A Review

Recall that the demand for labor in perfectly competitive markets depends on its productivity. As you saw in Chapter 10, a perfectly competitive, profit-maximizing firm will hire labor up to the point at which the market wage is equal to labor's marginal revenue product. The shape of the demand curve for labor shows how responsive *firms* are to changes in wages.

Recall from Chapter 6 that household behavior and thus the shape of the labor supply curve depend on the relative strengths of income and substitution effects. The labor supply curve represents the reaction of workers to changes in the wage rate. Household behavior depends on the *after-tax* wage that workers actually take home per hour of work. In contrast, labor demand is a function of the full amount that firms must pay per unit of labor, an amount that may include a tax if it is levied directly on payroll, as it is in our example. Such a tax, when present, drives a "wedge" between the price of labor that firms face and take-home wages.

Imposing a Payroll Tax: Who Pays?

In Figure 19.2, there were no taxes and the wage that firms paid was the same as the wage that workers took home. At a wage of W_0, quantity of labor supplied and quantity of labor demanded were equal and the labor market was in equilibrium.[2]

But suppose employers must pay a tax of T per unit of labor. Figure 19.3 shows a new curve that is parallel to the supply curve but above it by a distance T. The new curve, S_1, shows labor supply as a function of what firms pay. Note that S_1 is not really a new supply curve. Supply is still determined by what workers take home. S_1 simply adds T to the supply curve. Regardless of how the ultimate burden of the tax is shared, there is a difference between what firms pay and what workers take home.

If the initial wage is W_0 per hour, firms will face a price of $W_0 + T$ per unit of labor immediately after the tax is levied. Workers still receive only W_0, however. The higher wage rate—that is, the higher price of labor that firms now face—reduces the quantity of labor demanded from L_0 to L_d, and the firms lay off workers. Workers initially still receive W_0, so that amount of labor supplied does not change, and the result is an excess supply of labor equal to $(L_0 - L_d)$.

The excess supply applies downward pressure to the market wage, and wages fall, shifting some of the tax burden onto workers. The issue is how far wages will fall. Figure 19.3 shows that a new equilibrium is achieved at W_1, with firms paying $W_1 + T$. When workers take home W_1, they supply L_1 units of labor. If firms must pay $W_1 + T$, they will demand L_1 units of labor, and the market clears. Quantity supplied again equals quantity demanded.

In this case, then, employers and employees share the burden of the payroll tax. Initially, firms paid W_0; after the tax, they pay $W_1 + T$. Initially, workers received W_0; after the tax, they end up with

▶ **FIGURE 19.3**

Incidence of a Per-Unit Payroll Tax in a Perfectly Competitive Labor Market

With a tax on firms of T per unit of labor hired, the market will adjust, shifting the tax partially to workers. When the tax is levied, firms must first pay $W_0 + T$. This reduces the labor demand to L_d. The result is excess supply, which pushes wages down to W_1 and passes some of the burden of the tax on to workers.

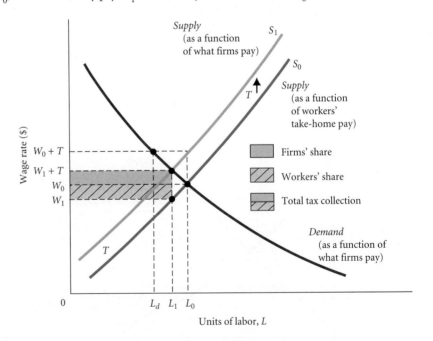

---

[2] Although the supply curve has a positive slope, that slope implies nothing about the actual shape of the labor supply curve in the United States.

the lower wage W_1. Total tax collections by the government are equal to $T \times L_1$. Geometrically, tax collections are equal to the entire shaded area in Figure 19.3. The workers' share of the tax burden is the lower portion, $(W_0 - W_1) \times L_1$. The firms' share is the upper portion, $[(W_1 + T) - W_0] \times L_1$.

The relative sizes of the firms' share and the workers' share of the total tax burden depend on the shapes of the demand and supply curves. Figure 19.4, parts a and b, show that the ultimate burden of a payroll tax depends, at least in part, on the *elasticity of labor supply*. If labor supply is very elastic (that is to say, responsive to price), take-home wages do not fall very much and workers bear only a small portion of the tax. But if labor supply is inelastic, or unresponsive to price, *most* of the burden is borne by workers. Workers bear the bulk of the burden of a payroll tax if labor supply is relatively inelastic, and firms bear the bulk of the burden of a payroll tax if labor supply is relatively elastic.

Empirical studies of labor supply behavior in the United States suggest that for most of the workforce, the elasticity of labor supply is close to zero. Therefore; most of the payroll tax in the United States is probably borne by workers. The result would be exactly the same if the tax were initially levied on workers rather than on firms. Go back to the equilibrium in Figure 19.3 on p. 398, with wages at W_0. But now assume that the tax of $\$T$ per hour is levied on workers rather than firms. The burden will end up being shared by firms and workers in the *exact same proportions*. Initially, take-home wages will fall to $W_0 - T$. Workers will supply less labor, creating excess demand and pushing market wages up. That shifts part of the burden back to employers. The "story" is different, but the result is the same.

Table 19.3 presents an estimate of the incidence of payroll taxes (Social Security taxes) in the United States in 2007. This estimate assumes that both the employers' share and employees' share of the payroll taxes are ultimately *borne by employees*.

The payroll tax is regressive at the top income levels for two reasons. First, in 2010, most of the tax (6.2 percent of total wage and salary income levied on both employers and employees) did not apply to wages and salaries above $106,800. The remainder of the total 7.65 percent tax—1.45 percent—

a.

b.

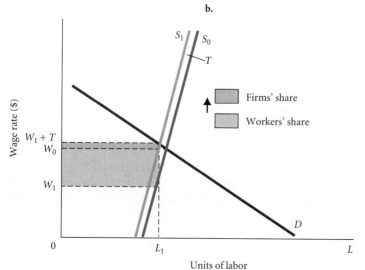

◀ **FIGURE 19.4**

Payroll Tax with Elastic (a) and Inelastic (b) Labor Supply
The ultimate burden of a payroll tax depends on the elasticities of labor supply and labor demand. For example, if supply is relatively elastic, as in part a, the burden falls largely on employers; if the supply is relatively inelastic, as in part b, the burden falls largely on workers.

TABLE 19.3	Estimated Incidence of Payroll Taxes in the United States in 2007
Population Ranked by Income	Tax as a % of Total Income
Bottom 20%	7.5
Second 20%	9.9
Third 20%	10.6
Fourth 20%	11.4
Top 20%	8.0
Top 10%	6.3
Top 5%	5.1
Top 1%	2.5

Source: Authors' estimate.

applied to all wage and salary income. Second, wages and salaries fell as a percentage of total income as we move up the income scale. Those with higher incomes earn a larger portion of their incomes from profits, dividends, rents, and so on, and these kinds of income are not subject to the payroll tax.

Some economists dispute the conclusion that the payroll tax is borne entirely by wage earners. Even if labor supply is inelastic, some wages are set in the process of collective bargaining between unions and large firms. If the payroll tax results in a higher gross wage in the bargaining process, firms may find themselves faced with higher costs. Higher costs either reduce profits to owners or are passed on to consumers in the form of higher product prices.

The Incidence of Corporate Profits Taxes

Another tax that requires careful analysis is the corporate profits tax that is levied by the federal government as well as by most states. The *corporate profits tax* or *corporation income tax*, is a tax on the profits of firms that are organized as corporations. *Corporations* are firms granted limited liability status by the government. Limited liability means that shareholders/owners can lose only what they have invested. The owners of *partnerships* and *proprietorships* do not enjoy limited liability and do not pay this tax; rather, they report their firms' income directly on their individual income tax returns.

We can think of the corporate tax as a tax on *capital income*, or profits, in one sector of the economy. For simplicity, we assume that there are only two sectors of the economy, corporate and noncorporate, and only two factors of production, labor and capital. Owners of capital receive profits, and workers (labor) are paid a wage.

Like the payroll tax, the corporate tax may affect households on the sources or the uses side of the income equation. The tax may affect profits earned by owners of capital, wages earned by workers, or prices of corporate and noncorporate products. Once again, the key question is how large these changes are likely to be.

When first imposed, the corporate profits tax initially reduces net (after-tax) profits in the corporate sector. Assuming the economy was in long-run equilibrium before the tax was levied, firms in both the corporate and noncorporate sectors were earning a *normal rate of return*; there was no reason to expect higher profits in one sector than in the other. Suddenly, firms in the corporate sector become significantly less profitable as a result of the tax. (In 2009, for example, the tax rate applicable to most corporations was 35 percent.)

In response to these lower profits, capital investment begins to favor the nontaxed sector because after-tax profits are higher there. Firms in the taxed sector contract in size or (in some cases) go out of business, while firms in the nontaxed sector expand and new firms enter its various industries. As this happens, the flow of capital from the taxed to the nontaxed sector reduces the profit rate in the nontaxed sector: More competition springs up, and product prices are driven down. Some of the tax burden shifts to capital income earners in the noncorporate sector, who end up earning lower profits.

As capital flows out of the corporate sector in response to lower after-tax profits, the profit rate in that sector rises somewhat because fewer firms means less supply, which means higher prices, and so on. Presumably, capital will continue to favor the nontaxed sector until the after-tax profit rates in the two sectors are equal. Even though the tax is imposed on just one sector, it eventually depresses after-tax profits in all sectors equally.

Under these circumstances, the products of corporations will probably become more expensive and products of proprietorships and partnerships will probably become less expensive. But because almost everyone buys both corporate and noncorporate products, these *excise effects* (that is, effects on the prices of products) are likely to have a minimal impact on the distribution of the tax burden. In essence, the price increases in the corporate sector and the price decreases in the noncorporate sector cancel each other out.

Finally, what effect does the imposition of a corporate income tax have on labor? Wages could actually rise or fall, but the effect is not likely to be large. Taxed firms will have an incentive to substitute labor for capital because capital income is now taxed. This could benefit labor by driving up wages. In addition, the contracting sector will use less labor *and* capital, but if the taxed sector is the capital-intensive corporate sector, the bulk of the effect will be felt by capital. The price of capital will fall more than the price of labor.

The Burden of the Corporate Tax   The ultimate burden of the corporate tax appears to depend on several factors: the relative capital/labor intensity of the two sectors, the ease with which capital and labor can be substituted in the two sectors, and elasticities of demand for the products of each sector. In 1962, economist Arnold Harberger, then of the University of Chicago, analyzed this and concluded that owners of corporations, proprietorships, and partnerships all bear the burden of the corporate tax in rough proportion to profits, even though it is directly levied only on corporations. Harberger also found that wage effects of the corporate tax were small and that excise effects, as we just noted, probably cancel each other out.[3]

Much has been written about the incidence of the corporate tax since Harberger, but the general conclusion that capital owners bear most of the tax burden is still viewed as correct by most economists.

One exception to this conclusion is corporate taxation of a monopolist. You might be tempted to conclude that because monopolists can control market price, they will simply pass on the profits tax in the form of higher prices to consumers of monopoly products. But theory predicts just the opposite: that the tax burden will remain with the monopolist.

Remember that monopolists are constrained by market demand. That is, they choose the combination of price and output that is consistent with market demand and that maximizes profit. If a proportion of that profit is taxed, the choice of price and quantity will not change. Why not? Quite simply, if you behave so as to maximize profit and then I come and take half of your profit, you maximize your half by maximizing the whole, which is exactly what you would do in the absence of the tax. Thus, your price and output do not change, the tax is shifted, and you end up paying the tax. In the long run, capital will not leave the taxed monopoly sector, as it did in the competitive case. Even with the tax, the monopolist is earning higher profits than are possible elsewhere.

Table 19.4 presents an estimate of the actual incidence of the U.S. corporate income tax in 2007. The burden of the corporate income tax is clearly progressive because profits and capital income make up a much bigger part of the incomes of high-income households.

TABLE 19.4   Estimated Burden of the U.S. Corporation Income Tax in 2007

Population Ranked by Income	Corporate Tax Burden as a % of Total Income
Bottom 20%	1.2
Second 20%	1.1
Third 20%	1.5
Fourth 20%	1.6
Top 20%	4.7
Top 10%	5.6
Top 5%	7.3
Top 1%	9.0

Source: Authors' estimate.

---

[3] Arnold Harberger, "The Incidence of the Corporate Income Tax," *Journal of Political Economy*, LXX, June 1962.

The Overall Incidence of Taxes in the United States: Empirical Evidence

Many researchers have done complete analyses under varying assumptions about tax incidence, and in most cases their results are similar. State and local taxes (with sales taxes playing a big role) seem as a group to be mildly regressive. Federal taxes, dominated by the individual income tax but increasingly affected by the regressive payroll tax, are mildly progressive. The overall system is mildly progressive.

Excess Burdens and the Principle of Neutrality

You have seen that when households and firms make decisions in the presence of a tax that differ from decisions they would make in its absence, the burden of the tax can be shifted from those for whom it was originally intended. Now we can take the same logic one step further. When taxes distort economic conditions, they impose burdens on society that, in aggregate, exceed the revenue collected by the government.

excess burden The amount by which the burden of a tax exceeds the total revenue collected. Also called deadweight loss.

The amount by which the burden of a tax exceeds the total revenue collected by the government is called the **excess burden** of the tax. The *total burden* of a tax is the sum of the revenue collected from the tax and the excess burden created by the tax. Because excess burdens are a form of waste, or lost value, tax policy should be written to minimize them. (Excess burdens are also called *deadweight losses*.)

The size of the excess burden imposed by a tax depends on the extent to which economic decisions are distorted. The general principle that emerges from the analysis of excess burdens is the **principle of neutrality**. *Ceteris paribus*, or all else equal,[4] a tax that is neutral with respect to economic decisions is preferred to one that distorts economic decisions.

principle of neutrality All else equal, taxes that are neutral with respect to economic decisions (that is, taxes that do not distort economic decisions) are generally preferable to taxes that distort economic decisions. Taxes that are not neutral impose excess burdens.

In practice, all taxes change behavior and distort economic choices. A product-specific excise tax raises the price of the taxed item, and people can avoid the tax by buying substitutes. An income tax distorts the choice between present and future consumption and between work and leisure. The corporate tax influences investment and production decisions—investment is diverted away from the corporate sector, and firms may be induced to substitute labor for capital.

How Do Excess Burdens Arise?

The idea that a tax can impose an extra cost, or excess burden, by distorting choices can be illustrated by example. Consider a perfectly competitive industry that produces an output, X, using the technology shown in Figure 19.5. Using technology A, firms can produce 1 unit of output with 7 units of capital (K) and 3 units of labor (L). Using technology B, the production of 1 unit of output requires 4 units of capital and 7 units of labor. A is thus the more capital-intensive technology.

If we assume labor and capital each cost $2 per unit, it costs $20 to produce each unit of output with technology A and $22 to produce each unit of output with technology B. Firms will choose technology A. Because we assume perfect competition, output price will be driven to cost of production and the price of output will in the long run be driven to $20 per unit.

Now let us narrow our focus to the distortion of technology choice that is brought about by the imposition of a tax. Assume that demand for the good in question is perfectly inelastic at

▶ **FIGURE 19.5**

Firms Choose the Technology That Minimizes the Cost of Production

If the industry is perfectly competitive, long-run equilibrium price will be $20 per unit of X. If 1,000 units of X are sold, consumers will pay a total of $20,000 for X.

Technology	Input requirements per unit of output X		Per-unit cost of X = $K(P_K) + L(P_L)$ $P_K = \$2$ $P_L = \$2$
	K	L	
A	7	3	$20 ⟶ Least cost
B	4	7	$22

---

[4] The phrase *ceteris paribus* (all else equal) is important. In judging the merits of a tax or a change in tax policy, the degree of neutrality is only one criterion among many, and it often comes into conflict with others. For example, tax A may impose a larger excess burden than tax B, but society may deem A more equitable.

	Input requirements per unit of output X		Per-unit cost of X $= K(P_K) + L(P_L)$ $P_K = \$2 + \$1 \text{ tax} = \$3$ $P_L = \$2$	
Technology	K	L		
A	7	3	$\longrightarrow \quad \$27$	
B	4	7	$\longrightarrow \quad \$26$	$\longrightarrow$ Least cost

◄ **FIGURE 19.6**

Imposition of a Tax on Capital Distorts the Choice of Technology

If the industry is perfectly competitive, price will be $26 per unit of X when a tax of $1 per unit of capital is imposed. If technology B is used and if we assume that total sales remain at 1,000 units, total tax collections will be 1,000 × 4 × $1 = $4,000. But consumers will pay a total of $26,000 for the good—$6,000 more than before the tax. Thus, there is an excess burden of $2,000.

1,000 units of output. That is, regardless of price, households will buy 1,000 units of the good. A price of $20 per unit means consumers pay a total of $20,000 for 1,000 units of X.

Now suppose the government levies a tax of 50 percent on capital. This has the effect of raising the price of capital, P_K, to $3. Figure 19.6 shows what would happen to unit cost of production after the tax is imposed. With capital now more expensive, the firm switches to the more labor-intensive technology B. With the tax in place, X can be produced at a cost of $27 per unit using technology A but for $26 per unit using technology B.

If demand is perfectly inelastic, buyers continue to buy 1,000 units of X regardless of its price. (We shall ignore any distortions of consumer choices that might result from the imposition of the tax.) Recall that the tax is 50 percent, or $1 per unit of capital used. Because it takes 4 units of capital to produce each unit of output, firms—which are now using technology B—will pay a total tax to the government of $4 per unit of output produced. With 1,000 units of output produced and sold, total tax collections amount to $4,000.

But if you look carefully, you will see that the burden of the tax exceeds $4,000. After the tax, consumers will be paying $26 per unit for the good. Twenty-six dollars is now the unit cost of producing the good using the best available technology in the presence of the capital tax. Consumers will pay $26,000 for 1,000 units of the good. This represents an increase of $6,000 over the previous total of $20,000. The revenue raised from the tax is $4,000, but its total burden is $6,000. There is an *excess burden* of $2,000.

How did this excess burden arise? Look back at Figure 19.5. You can see that technology B is less efficient than technology A. (Unit costs of production are $2 higher per unit using technology B.) But the tax on capital has caused firms to switch to this less efficient, labor-intensive mode of production. The result is a waste of $2 per unit of output. The total burden of the tax is equal to the revenue collected plus the loss due to the wasteful choice of technology, and the excess burden is $2 per unit times 1,000 units, or $2,000.

The same principle holds for taxes that distort consumption decisions. Suppose that you prefer to consume bundle X to bundle Y when there is no tax, but choose bundle Y when there is a tax in place. Not only do you pay the tax, you also end up with a bundle of goods that is worth less than the bundle you would have chosen had the tax not been levied. Again, we have the burden of an extra cost. The larger the distortion that a tax causes in behavior, the larger the excess burden of the tax. Taxes levied on broad bases tend to distort choices less and impose smaller excess burdens than taxes on more sharply defined bases. This follows from our discussion earlier in this chapter: The more partial the tax, the easier it is to avoid. An important part of the logic behind the recommendation of the president's tax reform commission in 2005 was that broader bases and lower rates reduce the distorting effects of the tax system and minimize excess burdens.

The only tax that has no excess burden is the lump-sum tax, where the tax you pay does not depend on your behavior or your income or your wealth. Everyone pays the same amount; there is no way to avoid the tax. In 1990, the government of Prime Minister Margaret Thatcher of Great Britain replaced the local property tax with a tax that was very similar to a lump-sum tax. Such a tax is highly regressive, and the perceived unfairness of it led her successor, John Major, to call for its repeal in 1991.

Measuring Excess Burdens

It is possible to measure the size of excess burdens if we know something about how people respond to price changes. Look at the demand curve in Figure 19.7. The product originally sold for a price, P_0, equal to marginal cost (which, for simplicity, we assume is constant). Recall that when input prices are determined in competitive markets, marginal cost reflects the real value of the resources used in producing the product.

▶ **FIGURE 19.7**

The Excess Burden of a Distorting Excise Tax

A tax that alters economic decisions imposes a burden that exceeds the amount of taxes collected. An excise tax that raises the price of a good above marginal cost drives some consumers to buy less desirable substitutes, reducing consumer surplus.

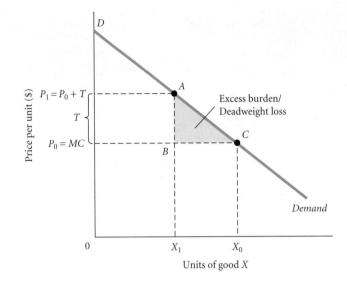

To measure the total burden of the tax, we need to recall the notion of consumer surplus from Chapter 4. At any price, some people pay less for a product than it is worth to them. All we reveal when we buy a product is that it is worth *at least* the price being charged. For example, if only 1 unit of product X were auctioned, someone would pay a price close to D in Figure 19.7. By paying only P_0, that person received a "surplus" equal to $(D - P_0)$. (For a review of consumer surplus and how it is measured, see Chapters 4 and 6.)

Consider what happens when an excise tax raises the price of X from P_0 to $P_1 = P_0 + T$, where T is the tax per unit of X. First, the government collects revenue. The amount of revenue collected is equal to T times the number of units of X purchased (X_1). You can see that $T \times X_1$ is equal to the area of rectangle $P_1 A B P_0$. Second, because consumers must now pay a price of P_1, the consumer surplus generated in the market is reduced from the area of triangle DCP_0 to the area of the smaller triangle DAP_1. The excess burden is equal to the original (pretax) consumer surplus *minus* the after-tax surplus *minus* the total taxes collected by the government.

In other words, the original value of consumer surplus (triangle DCP_0) has been broken up into three parts: the area of triangle DAP_1 that is still consumer surplus, the area of rectangle $P_1 A B P_0$ that is tax revenue collected by the government, and the area of triangle ACB that is lost. Thus, the area ACB is an approximate measure of the excess burden of the tax. The total burden of the tax is the sum of the revenue collected and the excess burden: the area of $P_1 A C P_0$.

Excess Burdens and the Degree of Distortion

The size of the excess burden that results from a decision-distorting tax depends on the degree to which decisions change in response to that tax. In the case of an excise tax, consumer behavior is reflected in elasticity of demand. The more elastic the demand curve, the greater the distortion caused by any given tax rate.

Figure 19.8 shows how the size of the consumer response determines the size of the excess burden. At price P_0, the quantity demanded by consumers is X_0. Now suppose that the government imposes a tax of $\$T$ per unit of X. The two demand curves (D_1 and D_2) illustrate two possible responses by consumers. The change in quantity demanded along D_1 (from X_0 to X_1) is greater than the change in quantity demanded along D_2 (from X_0 to X_2). In other words, the response of consumers illustrated by D_1 is more elastic than the response of consumers along D_2.

The excess burdens that would result from the tax under the two assumptions about demand elasticity are approximately equal to the areas of the shaded triangles in Figure 19.8. As you can see, where demand is more responsive (more elastic), the excess burden is larger.

If demand were perfectly inelastic, no distortion would occur and there would be no excess burden. The tax would simply transfer part of the surplus being earned by consumers to the government. That is why some economists favor uniform land taxes over other taxes. Because

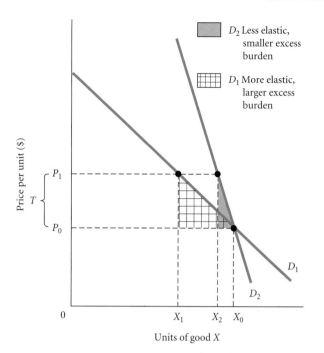

◀ **FIGURE 19.8**

The Size of the Excess Burden of a Distorting Excise Tax Depends on the Elasticity of Demand
The size of the excess burden from a distorting tax depends on the degree to which decisions or behaviors change in response to it.

land is in perfectly inelastic supply, a uniform tax on all land uses distorts economic decisions less than taxes levied on other factors of production that are in variable supply.

The Principle of Second Best

Now that we have established the connection between taxes that distort decisions and excess burdens, we can add more complexity to our earlier discussions. Although it may seem that distorting taxes always creates excess burdens, this is not necessarily the case. A distorting tax is sometimes desirable when other distortions already exist in the economy. This is called the **principle of second best**. At least two kinds of circumstances favor nonneutral (that is, distorting) taxes: the presence of externalities and the presence of other distorting taxes.

We already examined externalities at some length in Chapter 16. If some activity by a firm or household imposes costs on society that are not considered by decision makers, firms and households are likely to make economically inefficient choices. Pollution is the classic example of an externality, but there are thousands of others. An efficient allocation of resources can be restored if a tax is imposed on the externality-generating activity that is equal to the value of the damages caused by it. Such a tax forces the decision maker to consider the full economic cost of the decision.

Because taxing for externalities changes decisions that would otherwise be made, it does in a sense "distort" economic decisions. But its purpose is to force decision makers to consider real costs that they would otherwise ignore. In the case of pollution, for example, the distortion caused by a tax is desirable. Instead of causing an excess burden, it results in an efficiency gain. (Review Chapter 16 if this is not clear.)

A distorting tax can also improve economic welfare when other taxes are present that already distort decisions. Suppose there were only three goods, X, Y, and Z, and a 5 percent excise tax on Y and Z. The taxes on Y and Z distort consumer decisions away from those goods and toward X. Imposing a similar tax on X reduces the distortion of the existing system of taxes. When consumers face equal taxes on all goods, they cannot avoid the tax by changing what they buy. The distortion caused by imposing a tax on X corrects for a preexisting distortion—the taxes on Y and Z.

Let's return to the example described earlier in Figure 19.5 on p. 402 and Figure 19.6 on p. 403. Imposing the tax of 50 percent on the use of capital generated revenues of $4,000 but imposed a burden of $6,000 on consumers. A distortion now exists. But what would happen if the government imposed an additional tax of 50 percent, or $1 per unit, on labor? Such a tax would push our firm

principle of second best The fact that a tax distorts an economic decision does not always imply that such a tax imposes an excess burden. If there are previously existing distortions, such a tax may actually improve efficiency.

back toward the more efficient technology A. In fact, the labor tax would generate a total revenue of $6,000, but the burden it imposes on consumers would be only $4,000. (It is a good idea for you to work these figures out yourself.)

Optimal Taxation

The idea that taxes work together to affect behavior has led tax theorists to search for optimal taxation systems. Knowing how people will respond to taxes would allow us to design a system that would minimize the overall excess burden. For example, if we know the elasticity of demand for all traded goods, we can devise an optimal system of excise taxes that are heaviest on those goods with relatively inelastic demand and lightest on those goods with relatively elastic demands.

Of course, it is impossible to collect all the information required to implement the optimal tax systems that have been suggested. This point brings us full circle, and we end up where we started, with the *principle of neutrality*: All else equal, taxes that are neutral with respect to economic decisions are generally preferable to taxes that distort economic decisions. Taxes that are not neutral impose excess burdens.

SUMMARY

THE ECONOMICS OF TAXATION *p. 389*

1. Public finance is one of the major subfields of applied economics. A major interest within this subfield is the economics of taxation.

2. Taxes are ultimately paid by people. Taxes may be imposed on transactions, institutions, property, and all kinds of other things, but in the final analysis, taxes are paid by individuals or households.

3. The *base* of a tax is the measure or value upon which the tax is levied. The *rate structure* of a tax determines the portion of the base that must be paid in tax.

4. A tax whose burden is a constant proportion of income for all households is a *proportional tax*. A tax that exacts a higher proportion of income from higher-income households is a *progressive tax*. A tax that enacts a lower proportion of income from higher-income households is a *regressive tax*. In the United States, income taxes are progressive and sales and excise taxes are regressive.

5. Your average tax rate is the total amount of tax you pay divided by your total income. Your marginal tax rate is the tax rate that you pay on any additional income that you have earned. Marginal tax rates have the most influence on behavior.

6. There is much disagreement over what constitutes a fair tax system. One theory contends that people should bear tax burdens in proportion to the benefits that they receive from government expenditures. This is the *benefits-received principle*. Another theory contends that people should bear tax burdens in line with their ability to pay. This *ability-to-pay principle* has dominated U.S. tax policy.

7. The three leading candidates for best tax base are income, consumption, and wealth.

TAX INCIDENCE: WHO PAYS? *p. 396*

8. As a result of behavioral changes and market adjustments, tax burdens are often not borne by those initially responsible for paying them. When we speak of the *incidence of a tax*, we are referring to the ultimate distribution of its burden.

9. Taxes change behavior, and changes in behavior can affect supply and demand in markets, causing prices to change. When prices change in input markets or in output markets, some people may be made better off and some worse off. These final changes determine the ultimate burden of a tax.

10. *Tax shifting* occurs when households can alter their behavior and do something to avoid paying a tax. In general, broad-based taxes are less likely to be shifted and more likely to stick where they are levied than partial taxes are.

11. When labor supply is more elastic, firms bear the bulk of a tax imposed on labor. When labor supply is more inelastic, workers bear the bulk of the tax burden. Because the elasticity of labor supply in the United States is close to zero, most economists conclude that most of the payroll tax in the United States is probably borne by workers.

12. The payroll tax is regressive at top incomes for two reasons. First, in 2009, most of the tax (6.2 percent of total income levied on both employers and employees) did not apply to wages and salaries above $106,800. The remainder of the total 7.65 percent—only 1.45 percent—applied to all wage and salary income. Second, wages and salaries fall as a percentage of total income as we move up the income scale. Those with higher incomes earn a larger portion of their incomes from profits, dividends, rents, and so on, and these kinds of income are not subject to the payroll tax.

13. The ultimate burden of the corporate tax appears to depend on several factors. One generally accepted study shows that the owners of corporations, proprietorships, and partnerships all bear the burden of the corporate tax in rough proportion to profits, even though it is directly levied only on corporations, that wage effects are small, and that excise effects are roughly neutral. However, there is still much debate about whom the corporate tax "hurts." The burden of the corporate tax is progressive because profits and capital income make up a much bigger part of the incomes of the high-income households.

14. Under a reasonable set of assumptions about tax shifting, state and local taxes seem as a group to be mildly regressive. Federal taxes, dominated by the individual income tax but increasingly affected by the regressive payroll tax, are mildly progressive. The overall system is mildly progressive.

EXCESS BURDENS AND THE PRINCIPLE OF NEUTRALITY *p. 402*

15. When taxes distort economic decisions, they impose burdens that, in aggregate, exceed the revenue collected by the government. The amount by which the burden of a tax exceeds the revenue collected by the government is called the *excess burden*. The size of excess burdens depends on the degree to which economic decisions are changed by the tax. The

principle of neutrality holds that the most efficient taxes are broad-based taxes that do not distort economic decisions.

16. The excess burden imposed by a tax is equal to the pre-tax consumer surplus minus the after-tax consumer surplus minus the total taxes collected by the government. The more elastic the demand curve, the greater the distortion caused by any given tax rate.

THE PRINCIPLE OF SECOND BEST *p. 405*

17. The *principle of second best* holds that a tax that distorts economic decisions does not necessarily impose an excess burden. If previously existing distortions or externalities exist, such a tax may actually improve efficiency.

REVIEW TERMS AND CONCEPTS

ability-to-pay principle, *p. 393*

average tax rate, *p. 391*

benefits-received principle, *p. 393*

estate, *p. 396*

estate tax, *p. 396*

excess burden, *p. 402*

marginal tax rate, *p. 391*

principle of neutrality, *p. 402*

principle of second best, *p. 405*

progressive tax, *p. 390*

proportional tax, *p. 390*

regressive tax, *p. 390*

sources side/uses side, *p. 397*

tax base, *p. 389*

tax incidence, *p. 396*

tax rate structure, *p. 389*

tax shifting, *p. 397*

PROBLEMS

All problems are available on www.myeconlab.com

1. Suppose that in 2011, Congress passed and the president signed a new simple income tax with a flat rate of 25 percent on all income over $25,000 (no tax on the first $25,000). Assume that the tax is imposed on every individual separately. For each of the following total income levels, calculate taxes due and compute the average tax rate. Plot the average tax rate on a graph with income along the horizontal axis. Is the tax proportional, progressive, or regressive? Explain why.
   a. $25,000
   b. $35,000
   c. $45,000
   d. $60,000
   e. $80,000
   f. $100,000

2. [Related to the *Economics in Practice* on **p. 392**] Using the tax brackets and rates for 2009 on p. 392, compute the total tax for each of the following income levels for a single taxpayer. In each case, calculate average and marginal tax rates. Assume that in each case the taxpayer chooses the standard deduction and qualifies for a single exemption.
   a. Gross income = $30,000
   b. Gross income = $50,000
   c. Gross income = $100,000
   d. Gross income = $190,000

3. During the debate over tax policy following the land slide victory of the Republicans in the midterm elections in 2010, most thought the Federal Government was headed for gridlock. Both the Republicans and members of the new "Tea Party" favored tax provisions primarily beneficial to high income tax payers, while the Democrats tended to favored middle class tax cuts and increases

for people in the highest income groups. How did this debate turn out? Did the federal system become more regressive or progressive after the dust settled in 2011? How serious was the gridlock?

4. A citizens' group in the Pacific Northwest has the following statement in its charter:
   "Our goal is to ensure that large, powerful corporations pay their fair share of taxes in this country."
   To implement this goal, the group has recommended and lobbied for an increase in the corporation income tax and a reduction in the individual income tax. Would you support such a petition? Explain your logic.

5. Taxes on necessities that have low demand elasticities impose large excess burdens because consumers can't avoid buying them. Do you agree or disagree with that statement? Explain.

6. For each of the following statements, do you agree or disagree? Why?
   a. Economic theory predicts unequivocally that a payroll tax reduction will increase the supply of labor.
   b. Corporation income taxes levied on a monopolist are likely to be regressive because the monopoly can pass on its burden to consumers.
   c. All nonneutral taxes are undesirable.

7. In calculating total faculty compensation, the administration of Doughnut University includes payroll taxes (Social Security taxes) paid as a *benefit* to faculty. After all, those tax payments are earning future entitlements for the faculty under Social Security. However, the American Association of University Professors has argued that, far from being a benefit, the employer's contribution is simply a tax and that its burden falls on the faculty even though it is paid by the university. Discuss both sides of this debate.

8. Developing countries rarely have a sophisticated income tax structure like that in the United States. The primary means of raising revenues in many developing countries is through commodity taxes. What problems do you see with taxing particular goods in these countries? (*Hint:* Think about elasticities of demand.)

9. Suppose a special tax was introduced that used the value of one's automobile as the tax base. Each person would pay taxes equal to 10 percent of the value of his or her car. Would the tax be proportional, regressive, or progressive? What assumptions do you make in answering this question? What distortions do you think would appear in the economy if such a tax were introduced?

10. You are given the following information on a proposed "restaurant meals tax" in the Republic of Olympus. Olympus collects no other specific excise taxes, and all other government revenues come from a neutral lump-sum tax. (A lump-sum tax is a tax of a fixed sum paid by all people regardless of their circumstances.) Assume further that the burden of the tax is fully borne by consumers.

    Now consider the following data:
    - Meals consumed before the tax: 12 million
    - Meals consumed after the tax: 10 million
    - Average price per meal: $15 (not including the tax)
    - Tax rate: 10 percent

    Estimate the size of the excess burden of the tax. What is the excess burden as a percentage of revenues collected from the tax?

11. [Related to *Economics in Practice* on p. 396] As of 2010, Congress had not reversed the tax change of 2001 which phased out the gift and estate tax. Do you think the gift and estate tax should be reinstated? Why or why not? Using the key words "Federal Gift and Estate Tax", search the Internet to find the current status of this tax. Has the tax change now been reversed; if so, what are the new rates? What amount of assets can be passed on to one's children tax-free this year?

12. The graph below represents equilibrium in a competitive labor market both before and after a payroll tax which is levied on the employer has been implemented. Before the payroll tax, the equilibrium quantity of labor was 55 units. Supply curve S_1 represents supply as a function of what firms pay, including the tax. S_0 represents labor supply as a function of what workers take home.
    a. What is the amount of the per-unit payroll tax?
    b. What is the per-unit price of labor faced by firms immediately after the tax is levied?
    c. What wage will workers receive immediately after the tax is levied?

d. What are the quantity of labor demanded and the quantity of labor supplied immediately after the tax is levied?
e. If, after the tax is levied, the equilibrium quantity of labor settles at 40 units, what will be the new equilibrium wage?
f. If, after the tax is levied, the equilibrium quantity of labor settles at 40 units, what are the amounts of the workers' share of the tax burden, the firms' share of the tax burden, and the total tax collection?

13. Assume that at a price of $5 per pound, the quantity of coffee demanded is 20 pounds. Now assume that the government imposes an excise tax on coffee of $2 per pound. Draw a graph showing demand when consumers are relatively responsive to the tax and quantity demanded falls by 50 percent, and when consumers are relatively nonresponsive to the tax and quantity demanded falls by 10 percent. Calculate the amount of the excess burden of this tax for each situation and show this on the graph.

14. The market demand for product X is given by $Q_d = 8 - 1/3P$ and the market supply for good X is given by $Q_s = P - 8$, where P = price per unit.
    a. Draw a supply and demand graph with these curves. What are the equilibrium price and the equilibrium quantity?
    b. A per-unit excise tax is imposed on product X, and the market supply with the tax is now given by $Q_s = P - 12$. Add this supply curve to your graph and identify the new equilibrium price and equilibrium quantity. What is the value of the per-unit tax? How much of this per-unit tax will be paid by consumers and how much will be paid by the producer? What is the value of the excess burden of this tax? What is the value of the tax revenue?

15. In the United States, 41 states have passed legislation to legalize lotteries and the states use the lottery proceeds to raise revenue. If you view the price of a lottery ticket as a tax, do you think it would be a proportional, progressive, or regressive tax? What information would you need to definitively determine if it was proportional, progressive, or regressive?

16. Each year around April 15, discussions heat up regarding the tax system in the United States. A number of people are in favor of replacing the current federal income tax with either a flat tax or a consumption tax. Explain whether the current federal income tax is proportional, progressive, or regressive. Do the same for a flat tax and a consumption tax.

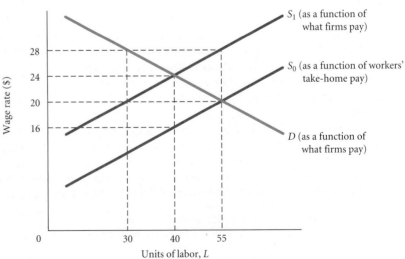

International Trade, Comparative Advantage, and Protectionism

20

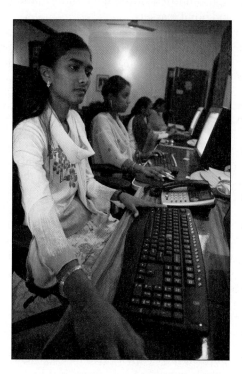

Over the last 40 years, international transactions have become increasingly important to the U.S. economy. In 1970, imports represented only about 7 percent of U.S. gross domestic product (GDP). The share is now around 15 percent. In 2010, the United States imported about $180 billion worth of goods and services each month. The increased trade we observe in the United States is mirrored throughout the world. From 1980 to 2009, world trade in real terms grew more than sixfold. This trend has been especially rapid in the newly industrialized Asian economies, but many developing countries such as Malaysia and Vietnam have been increasing their openness to trade.

The "internationalization" or "globalization" of the U.S. economy has occurred in the private and public sectors, in input and output markets, and in firms and households. Once uncommon, foreign products are now everywhere, from the utensils we eat with to the cars we drive. Chinese textiles and Indian software are commonplace. It might surprise you to learn that many of the cut flowers sold in the United States are grown in Africa and South America. In fact, most products today are made in a number of countries. Back in Chapter 1, we presented an *Economics in Practice* that described the production of Apple's iPod. An iPod contains 451 parts made in countries scattered around the world including Korea, Japan, China, and the United States. The bottom of the iPod has the following information: "Assembled in China; Designed in California." Suzuki makes cars in Hungary and employs workers from Romania and Slovakia. Honda started producing Japanese motorcycles in Ohio in 1977 with 64 employees in Marysville. The company now employs over 12,000 workers who assemble Honda automobiles. Bose is based in the United States but has its electronic components assembled in Mexico.

At the same time, the United States exports billions of dollars' worth of agricultural goods, aircraft, and industrial machinery. Korea imports substantial amounts of U.S. beef. In addition, the United States exports and imports large quantities of services. When a Pakistani student enrolls in an American college or university, or a sick woman from Chile seeks medical attention in a U.S. hospital, or a Kenyan hires a lawyer in Miami to help him with a real estate deal, or a

	Exports Minus Imports
1929	+0.4
1933	+0.1
1945	−0.8
1955	+0.5
1960	+4.2
1965	+5.6
1970	+4.0
1975	+16.0
1976	−1.6
1977	−23.1
1978	−25.4
1979	−22.5
1980	−13.1
1981	−12.5
1982	−20.0
1983	−51.7
1984	−102.7
1985	−115.2
1986	−132.5
1987	−145.0
1988	−110.1
1989	−87.9
1990	−77.6
1991	−27.0
1992	−32.8
1993	−64.4
1994	−92.7
1995	−90.7
1996	−96.3
1997	−101.4
1998	−161.8
1999	−262.1
2000	−382.1
2001	−371.0
2002	−427.2
2003	−504.1
2004	−618.7
2005	−722.7
2006	−769.3
2007	−713.8
2008	−707.8
2009	−392.4

Source: U.S. Department of Commerce, Bureau of Economic Analysis.

trade surplus The situation when a country exports more than it imports.

trade deficit The situation when a country imports more than it exports.

tourist from Indonesia eats at a restaurant in New York City, the United States is exporting a service. Similarly, when a student from the United States takes her junior year abroad in Scotland, or a tourist stays in a hotel in Singapore or gets a massage at a spa in Jamaica, the United States is importing a service.

Nor are the patterns of trade that we observe in one period set in stone. Consider the case of textiles and apparel. As recently as 2000, Mexico was the major supplier to the United States of textiles and apparel with almost 15 percent of total U.S. imports in this category. By 2006, China had overtaken Mexico's lead with 29 percent of the share of U.S. textile and apparel imports. The Dominican Republic and Honduras, which had been the fourth and fifth largest sources of U.S. imports, respectively, had been replaced by Bangladesh and Indonesia. In 2004, for the first time, India became one of the top five exporters to the United States in this category.

In addition to the fact that goods and services (outputs) flow easily across borders, so too do inputs: capital and labor. Certainly, it is very easy to buy financial assets abroad. Millions of Americans own shares in foreign stocks or have invested in bonds issued by foreign countries. At the same time, millions of foreigners have put money into the U.S. stock and bond markets.

A new phenomenon, outsourcing, is also changing the nature of the global labor market. It is now simple and very common for a customer service call to a software company from a user of its product in Bend, Oregon, to be routed to Bangalore, India, where a young, ambitious Indian man or woman provides assistance to a customer over the Internet. The Internet has in essence made it possible for labor to flow smoothly across international borders.

The inextricable connection of the U.S. economy to the economies of the rest of the world has had a profound impact on the discipline of economics and is the basis of one of its most important insights: All economies, regardless of their size, depend to some extent on other economies and are affected by events outside their borders.

To get you more acquainted with the international economy, this chapter discusses the economics of international trade. First, we describe the recent tendency of the United States to import more than it exports. Next, we explore the basic logic of trade. Why should the United States or any other country engage in international trade? Finally, we address the controversial issue of protectionism. Should a country provide certain industries with protection in the form of import quotas or tariffs, which are taxes imposed on imports? Should a country help a domestic industry compete in international markets by providing subsidies?

Trade Surpluses and Deficits

Until the 1970s, the United States generally exported more than it imported. When a country exports more than it imports, it runs a **trade surplus**. When a country imports more than it exports, it runs a **trade deficit**. Table 20.1 shows that before 1976 the United States generally ran a trade surplus. This changed in 1976, and since 1976 the United States has run a trade deficit. The deficit reached a local peak of $145.0 billion in 1987, fell to $27.0 billion in 1991, and then rose dramatically to over $700 billion by 2005. By 2009, the trade deficit had fallen to just under $400 billion, as U.S. imports declined more than U.S. exports during the recession.

The large trade deficits in the middle and late 1980s sparked political controversy that continues today. Foreign competition hit U.S. markets hard. Less expensive foreign goods—among them steel, textiles, and automobiles—began driving U.S. manufacturers out of business, and thousands of jobs were lost in important industries. Cities such as Pittsburgh, Youngstown, and Detroit had major unemployment problems. In more recent times, the outsourcing of software development to India has caused complaints from white-collar workers.

The natural reaction to trade-related job dislocation is to call for protection of U.S. industries. Many people want the president and Congress to impose taxes and import restrictions that would make foreign goods less available and more expensive, protecting U.S. jobs. This argument is not new. For hundreds of years, industries have petitioned governments for protection and societies have debated the pros and cons of free and open trade. For the last century and a half, the principal argument against protection has been the theory of comparative advantage, first discussed in Chapter 2.

The Economic Basis for Trade: Comparative Advantage

Perhaps the best-known debate on the issue of free trade took place in the British Parliament during the early years of the nineteenth century. At that time, the landed gentry—the landowners—controlled Parliament. For a number of years, imports and exports of grain had been subject to a set of tariffs, subsidies, and restrictions collectively called the **Corn Laws**. Designed to discourage imports of grain and to encourage exports, the Corn Laws' purpose was to keep the price of food high. The landlords' incomes, of course, depended on the prices they got for what their land produced. The Corn Laws clearly worked to the advantage of those in power.

Corn Laws The tariffs, subsidies, and restrictions enacted by the British Parliament in the early nineteenth century to discourage imports and encourage exports of grain.

With the Industrial Revolution, a class of wealthy industrial capitalists emerged. The industrial sector had to pay workers at least enough to live on, and a living wage depended greatly on the price of food. Tariffs on grain imports and export subsidies that kept grain and food prices high increased the wages that capitalists had to pay, cutting into their profits. The political battle raged for years. However, as time went by, the power of the landowners in the House of Lords was significantly reduced. When the conflict ended in 1848, the Corn Laws were repealed.

On the side of repeal was David Ricardo, a businessman, economist, member of Parliament, and one of the fathers of modern economics. Ricardo's principal work, *Principles of Political Economy and Taxation*, was published in 1817, two years before he entered Parliament. Ricardo's **theory of comparative advantage**, which he used to argue against the Corn Laws, claimed that trade enables countries to specialize in producing the products they produce best. According to the theory specialization and free trade will benefit all trading partners (real wages will rise), even those that may be absolutely less efficient producers. This basic argument remains at the heart of free-trade debates even today, as policy makers argue about the effects of tariffs on agricultural development in sub-Saharan Africa and the gains and losses from outsourcing software development to India.

theory of comparative advantage Ricardo's theory that specialization and free trade will benefit all trading partners (real wages will rise), even those that may be absolutely less efficient producers.

The easiest way to understand the theory of comparative advantage is to examine a simple two-person society. Suppose Bill and Colleen, stranded on a deserted island in Chapter 2, have only two tasks to accomplish each week: gathering food to eat and cutting logs to construct a house. If Colleen could cut more logs than Bill in a day and Bill could gather more berries and fruits, specialization would clearly benefit both of them.

But suppose Bill is slow and clumsy and Colleen is better at cutting logs *and* gathering food. Ricardo's point is that it still pays for them to specialize. They can produce more in total by specializing than they can by sharing the work equally. We now turn to look at the application of the powerful idea of comparative advantage to international trade.

Absolute Advantage versus Comparative Advantage

A country enjoys an **absolute advantage** over another country in the production of a good if it uses fewer resources to produce that good than the other country does. Suppose country A and country B produce wheat, but A's climate is more suited to wheat and its labor is more productive. Country A will produce more wheat per acre than country B and use less labor in growing it and bringing it to market. Country A enjoys an absolute advantage over country B in the production of wheat.

absolute advantage The advantage in the production of a good enjoyed by one country over another when it uses fewer resources to produce that good than the other country does.

A country enjoys a **comparative advantage** in the production of a good if that good can be produced at lower cost *in terms of other goods*. Suppose countries C and D both produce wheat and corn and C enjoys an absolute advantage in the production of both—that is, C's climate is better than D's and fewer of C's resources are needed to produce a given quantity of both wheat and corn. Now C and D must each choose between planting land with either wheat or corn. To produce more wheat, either country must transfer land from corn production; to produce more corn, either country must transfer land from wheat production. The cost of wheat in each country can be measured in bushels of corn, and the cost of corn can be measured in bushels of wheat.

comparative advantage The advantage in the production of a good enjoyed by one country over another when that good can be produced at lower cost in terms of other goods than it could be in the other country.

Suppose that in country C, a bushel of wheat has an opportunity cost of 2 bushels of corn. That is, to produce an additional bushel of wheat, C must give up 2 bushels of corn. At the same time, producing a bushel of wheat in country D requires the sacrifice of only 1 bushel of corn. Even though C has an *absolute* advantage in the production of both products, D enjoys a *comparative* advantage in the production of wheat because the *opportunity cost* of producing wheat is lower in D. Under these circumstances, Ricardo claims, D can benefit from trade if it specializes in the production of wheat.

Gains from Mutual Absolute Advantage   To illustrate Ricardo's logic in more detail, suppose Australia and New Zealand each have a fixed amount of land and do not trade with the rest of the world. There are only two goods—wheat to produce bread and cotton to produce clothing. This kind of two-country/two-good world does not exist, but its operations can be generalized to many countries and many goods.

To proceed, we have to make some assumptions about the preferences of the people living in New Zealand and the people living in Australia. If the citizens of both countries walk around naked, there is no need to produce cotton, so all the land can be used to produce wheat. However, assume that people in both countries have similar preferences with respect to food and clothing: The populations of both countries use both cotton and wheat, and preferences for food and clothing are such that both countries consume equal amounts of wheat and cotton.

Finally, we assume that each country has only 100 acres of land for planting and that land yields are as given in Table 20.2. New Zealand can produce 3 times the wheat that Australia can on 1 acre of land, and Australia can produce 3 times the cotton that New Zealand can in the same space. New Zealand has an absolute advantage in the production of wheat, and Australia has an absolute advantage in the production of cotton. In cases like this, we say the two countries have *mutual absolute advantage.*

TABLE 20.2 Yield per Acre of Wheat and Cotton

	New Zealand	Australia
Wheat	6 bushels	2 bushels
Cotton	2 bales	6 bales

If there is no trade and each country divides its land to obtain equal units of cotton and wheat production, each country produces 150 bushels of wheat and 150 bales of cotton. New Zealand puts 75 acres into cotton but only 25 acres into wheat, while Australia does the reverse (Table 20.3).

TABLE 20.3 Total Production of Wheat and Cotton Assuming No Trade, Mutual Absolute Advantage, and 100 Available Acres

	New Zealand	Australia
Wheat	25 acres × 6 bushels/acre = 150 bushels	75 acres × 2 bushels/acre = 150 bushels
Cotton	75 acres × 2 bales/acre = 150 bales	25 acres × 6 bales/acre = 150 bales

We can organize the same information in graphic form as production possibility frontiers for each country. In Figure 20.1, which presents the positions of the two countries before trade, each country is constrained by its own resources and productivity. If Australia put all its land into cotton, it would produce 600 bales of cotton (100 acres × 6 bales/acre) and no wheat; if it put all its land into wheat, it would produce 200 bushels of wheat (100 acres × 2 bushels/acre) and no cotton. The opposite is true for New Zealand. Recall from Chapter 2 that a country's production possibility frontier represents all combinations of goods that can be produced, given the country's resources and state of technology. Each country must pick a point along its own production possibility curve.

When both countries have an absolute advantage in the production of one product, it is easy to see that specialization and trade will benefit both. Australia should produce cotton, and New Zealand should produce wheat. Transferring all land to wheat production in New Zealand yields 600 bushels, while transferring all land to cotton production in Australia yields 600 bales. An agreement to trade 300 bushels of wheat for 300 bales of cotton would double both wheat and cotton consumption in both countries. (Remember, before trade, both countries produced 150 bushels of wheat and 150 bales of cotton. After trade, each country will have 300 bushels of wheat and 300 bales of cotton to consume. Final production and trade figures are provided in Table 20.4 and Figure 20.2.) Trade enables both countries to move beyond their previous resource and productivity constraints.

The advantages of specialization and trade seem obvious when one country is technologically superior at producing one product and another country is technologically superior at producing another product. However, let us turn to the case in which one country has an absolute advantage in the production of *both* goods.

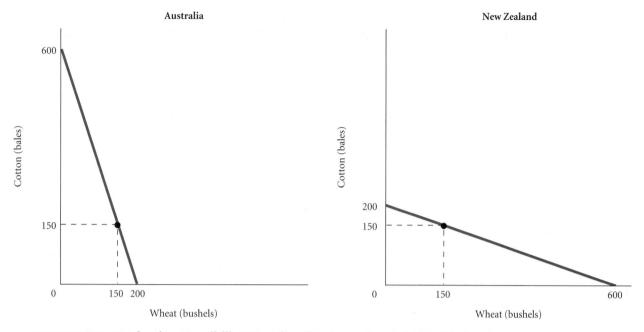

▲ **FIGURE 20.1 Production Possibility Frontiers for Australia and New Zealand Before Trade**

Without trade, countries are constrained by their own resources and productivity.

TABLE 20.4 Production and Consumption of Wheat and Cotton After Specialization

	Production			Consumption	
	New Zealand	Australia		New Zealand	Australia
Wheat	100 acres × 6 bushels/acre 600 bushels	0 acres 0	Wheat	300 bushels	300 bushels
Cotton	0 acres 0	100 acres × 6 bales/acre 600 bales	Cotton	300 bales	300 bales

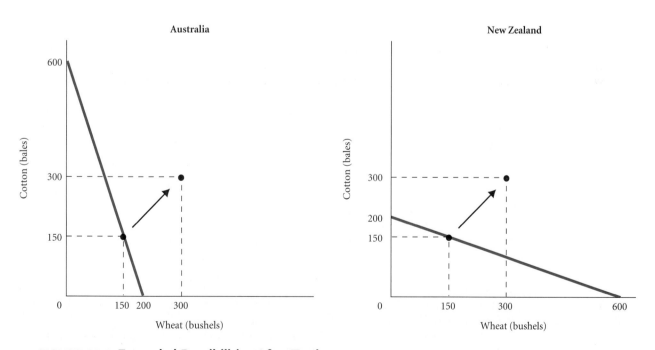

▲ **FIGURE 20.2 Expanded Possibilities After Trade**

Trade enables both countries to move beyond their own resource constraints—beyond their individual production possibility frontiers.

Gains from Comparative Advantage Table 20.5 contains different land yield figures for New Zealand and Australia. Now New Zealand has a considerable absolute advantage in the production of both cotton and wheat, with 1 acre of land yielding 6 times as much wheat and twice as much cotton as 1 acre in Australia. Ricardo would argue that *specialization and trade are still mutually beneficial.*

TABLE 20.5 Yield per Acre of Wheat and Cotton		
	New Zealand	Australia
Wheat	6 bushels	1 bushel
Cotton	6 bales	3 bales

Again, preferences imply consumption of equal units of cotton and wheat in both countries. With no trade, New Zealand would divide its 100 available acres evenly, or 50/50, between the two crops. The result would be 300 bales of cotton and 300 bushels of wheat. Australia would divide its land 75/25. Table 20.6 shows that final production in Australia would be 75 bales of cotton and 75 bushels of wheat. (Remember, we are assuming that in each country, people consume equal amounts of cotton and wheat.) Again, before any trade takes place, each country is constrained by its own domestic production possibility curve.

TABLE 20.6 Total Production of Wheat and Cotton Assuming No Trade and 100 Available Acres		
	New Zealand	Australia
Wheat	50 acres × 6 bushels/acre	75 acres × 1 bushel/acre
	300 bushels	75 bushels
Cotton	50 acres × 6 bales/acre	25 acres × 3 bales/acre
	300 bales	75 bales

Imagine we are at a meeting of trade representatives of both countries. As a special adviser, David Ricardo is asked to demonstrate that trade can benefit both countries. He divides his demonstration into three stages, which you can follow in Table 20.7. For Ricardo to be correct about the gains from specialization, it must be true that moving resources around in the two countries generates more than the 375 bushels of wheat and bales of cotton that we had before specialization. To see how this is managed, we move in stages.

TABLE 20.7 Realizing a Gain from Trade When One Country Has a Double Absolute Advantage					
	STAGE 1			STAGE 2	
	New Zealand	Australia		New Zealand	Australia
Wheat	50 acres × 6 bushels/acre 300 bushels	0 acres 0	Wheat	75 acres × 6 bushels/acre 450 bushels	0 acres 0
Cotton	50 acres × 6 bales/acre 300 bales	100 acres × 3 bales/acre 300 bales	Cotton	25 acres × 6 bales/acre 150 bales	100 acres × 3 bales/acre 300 bales

	STAGE 3	
	New Zealand	Australia
	100 bushels (trade) →	
Wheat	350 bushels	100 bushels
	(after trade)	
	200 bales (trade) ←	
Cotton	350 bales	100 bales
	(after trade)	

In Stage 1, let Australia move all its land into cotton production, where it is least disadvantaged. Australia would then produce 300 bales of cotton, as we see Stage 1 of Table 20.7. Now the question is whether Ricardo can help us use New Zealand's land to add at least 75 bales of cotton to the total while producing more than the original 375 bushels of wheat. In Stage 2, Ricardo tells New Zealand to use 25 acres to produce cotton and 75 acres for wheat production. With that allocation of land, New Zealand produces 450 bushels of wheat (far more than the total produced in the nonspecialization case by both countries) and 150 bales of cotton, leaving us with 450 bales of cotton as well. Specialization has increased the world production of both wheat and cotton by 75 units! With trade, which we show in Stage 3 for the case in which both countries prefer equal consumption of the two goods, both countries can be better off than they were earlier.

Why Does Ricardo's Plan Work?   To understand why Ricardo's scheme works, let us return to the definition of comparative advantage.

The real cost of producing cotton is the wheat that must be sacrificed to produce it. *When we think of cost this way, it is less costly to produce cotton in Australia than to produce it in New Zealand, even though an acre of land produces more cotton in New Zealand.* Consider the "cost" of 3 bales of cotton in the two countries. In terms of opportunity cost, 3 bales of cotton in New Zealand cost 3 bushels of wheat; in Australia, 3 bales of cotton cost only 1 bushel of wheat. Because 3 bales are produced by 1 acre of Australian land, to get 3 bales, an Australian must transfer 1 acre of land from wheat to cotton production. Because an acre of land produces a bushel of wheat, losing 1 acre to cotton implies the loss of 1 bushel of wheat. *Australia has a comparative advantage in cotton production* because its opportunity cost, in terms of wheat, is lower than New Zealand's. This is illustrated in Figure 20.3.

Conversely, New Zealand has a comparative advantage in wheat production. A unit of wheat in New Zealand costs 1 unit of cotton, while a unit of wheat in Australia costs 3 units of cotton. When countries specialize in producing goods in which they have a comparative advantage, they maximize their combined output and allocate their resources more efficiently.

Terms of Trade

Ricardo might suggest a number of options for exchanging wheat and cotton to the trading partners. The one we just examined benefited both partners; in percentage terms, Australia made out slightly better. Other deals might have been more advantageous to New Zealand.

The ratio at which a country can trade domestic products for imported products is the **terms of trade**. The terms of trade determine how the gains from trade are distributed among trading partners. In the case just considered, the agreed-to terms of trade were 1 bushel of wheat for 2 bales of cotton. Such terms of trade benefit New Zealand, which can get 2 bales of cotton for each bushel of wheat. If it were to transfer its own land from wheat to cotton, it would get only 1 bale of cotton. The same terms of trade benefit Australia, which can get 1 bushel of wheat for 2 bales of cotton. A direct transfer of its own land would force it to give up 3 bales of cotton for 1 bushel of wheat.

terms of trade   The ratio at which a country can trade domestic products for imported products.

◀ **FIGURE 20.3**
Comparative Advantage Means Lower Opportunity Cost

The real cost of cotton is the wheat sacrificed to obtain it. The cost of 3 bales of cotton in New Zealand is 3 bushels of wheat (a half acre of land must be transferred from wheat to cotton—refer to Table 20.5). However, the cost of 3 bales of cotton in Australia is only 1 bushel of wheat. Australia has a comparative advantage over New Zealand in cotton production, and New Zealand has a comparative advantage over Australia in wheat production.

If the terms of trade changed to 3 bales of cotton for every bushel of wheat, only New Zealand would benefit. At those terms of trade, *all* the gains from trade would flow to New Zealand. Such terms do not benefit Australia at all because the opportunity cost of producing wheat domestically is *exactly the same* as the trade cost: A bushel of wheat costs 3 bales of cotton. If the terms of trade went the other way—1 bale of cotton for each bushel of wheat—only Australia would benefit. New Zealand gains nothing because it can already substitute cotton for wheat at that ratio. To get a bushel of wheat domestically, however, Australia must give up 3 bales of cotton, and one-for-one terms of trade would make wheat much less costly for Australia.

Both parties must have something to gain for trade to take place. In this case, you can see that both Australia and New Zealand will gain when the terms of trade are set between 1:1 and 3:1, cotton to wheat.

Exchange Rates

The examples used thus far have shown that trade can result in gains to both parties. When trade is free—unimpeded by government-instituted barriers—patterns of trade and trade flows result from the independent decisions of thousands of importers and exporters and millions of private households and firms.

Private households decide whether to buy Toyotas or Chevrolets, and private firms decide whether to buy machine tools made in the United States or machine tools made in Taiwan, raw steel produced in Germany or raw steel produced in Pittsburgh.

But how does this trade actually come about? Before a citizen of one country can buy a product made in another country or sold by someone in another country, a currency swap must take place. Consider Shane, who buys a Toyota from a dealer in Boston. He pays in dollars, but the Japanese workers who made the car receive their salaries in yen. Somewhere between the buyer of the car and the producer, a currency exchange must be made. The regional distributor probably takes payment in dollars and converts them into yen before remitting the proceeds to Japan.

To buy a foreign-produced good, a consumer, or an intermediary, has to buy foreign currency. The price of Shane's Toyota in dollars depends on the price of the car stated in yen and the dollar price of yen. You probably know the ins and outs of currency exchange very well if you have ever traveled in another country.

In June 2010, the British pound was worth $1.48. Now suppose you are in London having dinner. On the menu is a nice bottle of wine for 15 pounds. How can you figure out whether you want to buy it? You know what dollars will buy in the United States, so you have to convert the price into dollars. Each pound will cost you $1.48, so 15 pounds will cost you $1.48 × 15 = $22.20.

exchange rate The ratio at which two currencies are traded. The price of one currency in terms of another.

The attractiveness of foreign goods to U.S. buyers and of U.S. goods to foreign buyers depends in part on the **exchange rate**, the ratio at which two currencies are traded. In May 2008, the British pound was worth $1.97, and that same bottle of wine would have cost $29.55.

To understand the patterns of trade that result from the actions of hundreds of thousands of independent buyers and sellers—households and firms—we must know something about the factors that determine exchange rates. Exchange rate determination is very complicated. Here, however, we can demonstrate two things. First, for any pair of countries, there is a range of exchange rates that can lead automatically to both countries' realizing the gains from specialization and comparative advantage. Second, within that range, the exchange rate will determine which country gains the most from trade. In short, exchange rates determine the terms of trade.

Trade and Exchange Rates in a Two-Country/Two-Good World Consider first a simple two-country/two-good model. Suppose both the United States and Brazil produce only two goods—raw timber and rolled steel. Table 20.8 gives the current prices of both goods as domestic buyers see them. In Brazil, timber is priced at 3 reals (R) per foot and steel is priced at 4 R per meter. In the United States, timber costs $1 per foot and steel costs $2 per meter.

TABLE 20.8 Domestic Prices of Timber (per Foot) and Rolled Steel (per Meter) in the United States and Brazil		
	United States	Brazil
Timber	$1	3 Reals
Rolled steel	$2	4 Reals

Suppose U.S. and Brazilian buyers have the option of buying at home or importing to meet their needs. The options they choose will depend on the exchange rate. For the time being, we will ignore transportation costs between countries and assume that Brazilian and U.S. products are of equal quality.

Let us start with the assumption that the exchange rate is $1 = 1 R. From the standpoint of U.S. buyers, neither Brazilian steel nor Brazilian timber is competitive at this exchange rate. A dollar buys a foot of timber in the United States, but if converted into a real, it will buy only one-third of a foot. The price of Brazilian timber to an American is $3 because it will take $3 to buy the necessary 3 R. Similarly, $2 buys a meter of rolled steel in the United States, but the same $2 buys only half a meter of Brazilian steel. The price of Brazilian steel to an American is $4, twice the price of domestically produced steel.

At this exchange rate, however, Brazilians find that U.S.-produced steel and timber are less expensive than steel and timber produced in Brazil. Timber at home—Brazil—costs 3 R, but 3 R buys $3, which buys 3 times as much timber in the United States. Similarly, steel costs 4 R at home, but 4 R buys $4, which buys twice as much U.S.-made steel. At an exchange rate of $1 = 1 R, Brazil will import steel and timber and the United States will import nothing.

However, now suppose the exchange rate is 1 R = $0.25. This means that 1 dollar buys 4 R. At this exchange rate, the Brazilians buy timber and steel at home and the Americans import both goods. At this exchange rate, Americans must pay a dollar for a foot of U.S. timber, but the same amount of timber can be had in Brazil for the equivalent of $0.75. (Because 1 R costs $0.25, 3 R can be purchased for $0.75.) Similarly, steel that costs $2 per meter in the United States costs an American half as much in Brazil because $2 buys 8 R, which buys 2 meters of Brazilian steel. At the same time, Brazilians are not interested in importing because both goods are cheaper when purchased from a Brazilian producer. In this case, the United States imports both goods and Brazil imports nothing.

So far we can see that at exchange rates of $1 = 1 R and $1 = 4 R, we get trade flowing in only one direction. Let us now try an exchange rate of $1 = 2 R, or 1 R = $0.50. First, Brazilians will buy timber in the United States. Brazilian timber costs 3 R per foot, but 3 R buys $1.50, which is enough to buy 1.5 feet of U.S. timber. Buyers in the United States will find Brazilian timber too expensive, but Brazil will import timber from the United States. At this same exchange rate, however, both Brazilian and U.S. buyers will be indifferent between Brazilian and U.S. steel. To U.S. buyers, domestically produced steel costs $2. Because $2 buys 4 R, a meter of imported Brazilian steel also costs $2. Brazilian buyers also find that steel costs 4 R, whether domestically produced or imported. Thus, there is likely to be no trade in steel.

What happens if the exchange rate changes so that $1 buys 2.1 R? While U.S. timber is still cheaper to both Brazilians and Americans, Brazilian steel begins to look good to U.S. buyers. Steel produced in the United States costs $2 per meter, but $2 buys 4.2 R, which buys more than a meter of steel in Brazil. When $1 buys more than 2 R, trade begins to flow in both directions: Brazil will import timber, and the United States will import steel.

If you examine Table 20.9 carefully, you will see that trade flows in both directions as long as the exchange rate settles between $1 = 2 R and $1 = 3 R. Stated the other way around, trade will flow in both directions if the price of a real is between $0.33 and $0.50.

TABLE 20.9 Trade Flows Determined by Exchange Rates		
Exchange Rate	Price of Real	Result
$1 = 1 R	$ 1.00	Brazil imports timber and steel.
$1 = 2 R	.50	Brazil imports timber.
$1 = 2.1 R	.48	Brazil imports timber; United States imports steel.
$1 = 2.9 R	.34	Brazil imports timber; United States imports steel.
$1 = 3 R	.33	United States imports steel.
$1 = 4 R	.25	United States imports timber and steel.

Exchange Rates and Comparative Advantage
If the foreign exchange market drives the exchange rate to anywhere between 2 and 3 R per dollar, the countries will automatically adjust and comparative advantage will be realized. At these exchange rates, U.S. buyers

begin buying all their steel in Brazil. The U.S. steel industry finds itself in trouble. Plants close, and U.S. workers begin to lobby for tariff protection against Brazilian steel. At the same time, the U.S. timber industry does well, fueled by strong export demand from Brazil. The timber-producing sector expands. Resources, including capital and labor, are attracted into timber production.

The opposite occurs in Brazil. The Brazilian timber industry suffers losses as export demand dries up and Brazilians turn to cheaper U.S. imports. In Brazil, lumber companies turn to the government and ask for protection from cheap U.S. timber. However, steel producers in Brazil are happy. They are not only supplying 100 percent of the domestically demanded steel but also selling to U.S. buyers. The steel industry expands, and the timber industry contracts. Resources, including labor, flow into steel.

With this expansion-and-contraction scenario in mind, let us look again at our original definition of comparative advantage. If we assume that prices reflect resource use and resources can be transferred from sector to sector, we can calculate the opportunity cost of steel/timber in both countries. In the United States, the production of a meter of rolled steel consumes twice the resources that the production of a foot of timber consumes. Assuming that resources can be transferred, the opportunity cost of a meter of steel is 2 feet of timber (Table 20.8). In Brazil, a meter of steel uses resources costing 4 R, while a unit of timber costs 3 R. To produce a meter of steel means the sacrifice of only four-thirds (or one and one-third) feet of timber. Because the opportunity cost of a meter of steel (in terms of timber) is lower in Brazil, we say that Brazil has a comparative advantage in steel production.

Conversely, consider the opportunity cost of timber in the two countries. Increasing timber production in the United States requires the sacrifice of half a meter of steel for every foot of timber—producing a meter of steel uses $2 worth of resources, while producing a foot of timber requires only $1 worth of resources. Nevertheless, each foot of timber production in Brazil requires the sacrifice of three-fourths of a meter of steel. Because the opportunity cost of timber is lower in the United States, the United States has a comparative advantage in the production of timber. If exchange rates end up in the right ranges, the free market will drive each country to shift resources into those sectors in which it enjoys a comparative advantage. Only in a country with a comparative advantage will those products be competitive in world markets.

The Sources of Comparative Advantage

Specialization and trade can benefit all trading partners, even those that may be inefficient producers in an absolute sense. If markets are competitive and if foreign exchange markets are linked to goods-and-services exchange, countries will specialize in producing products in which they have a comparative advantage.

So far, we have said nothing about the sources of comparative advantage. What determines whether a country has a comparative advantage in heavy manufacturing or in agriculture? What explains the actual trade flows observed around the world? Various theories and empirical work on international trade have provided some answers. Most economists look to **factor endowments**—the quantity and quality of labor, land, and natural resources of a country—as the principal sources of comparative advantage. Factor endowments seem to explain a significant portion of actual world trade patterns.

factor endowments The quantity and quality of labor, land, and natural resources of a country.

The Heckscher-Ohlin Theorem

Heckscher-Ohlin theorem A theory that explains the existence of a country's comparative advantage by its factor endowments: A country has a comparative advantage in the production of a product if that country is relatively well endowed with inputs used intensively in the production of that product.

Eli Heckscher and Bertil Ohlin, two Swedish economists who wrote in the first half of the twentieth century, expanded and elaborated on Ricardo's theory of comparative advantage. The **Heckscher-Ohlin theorem** ties the theory of comparative advantage to factor endowments. It assumes that products can be produced using differing proportions of inputs and that inputs are mobile between sectors in each economy but that factors are not mobile *between* economies. According to this theorem, a country has a comparative advantage in the production of a product if that country is relatively well endowed with inputs used intensively in the production of that product.

This idea is simple. A country with a great deal of good fertile land is likely to have a comparative advantage in agriculture. A country with a large amount of accumulated capital is likely to have a comparative advantage in heavy manufacturing. A country well-endowed with human capital is likely to have a comparative advantage in highly technical goods.

Other Explanations for Observed Trade Flows

Comparative advantage is not the only reason countries trade. It does not explain why many countries import and export the same kinds of goods. The United States, for example, exports and imports automobiles.

Just as industries within a country differentiate their products to capture a domestic market, they also differentiate their products to please the wide variety of tastes that exists worldwide. The Japanese automobile industry, for example, began producing small, fuel-efficient cars long before U.S. automobile makers did. In doing so, the Japanese auto industry developed expertise in creating products that attracted a devoted following and considerable brand loyalty. BMWs, made mostly in Germany, and Volvos, made mostly in Sweden, also have their champions in many countries. Just as product differentiation is a natural response to diverse preferences within an economy, it is also a natural response to diverse preferences across economies. Paul Krugman did some of the earliest work in this area, sometimes called New Trade Theory.

New trade theory also relies on the idea of comparative advantage. If the Japanese developed skills and knowledge that gave them an edge in the production of fuel-efficient cars, that knowledge can be thought of as a very specific kind of capital that is not currently available to other producers. The Volvo company invested in a form of intangible capital called *goodwill*. That goodwill, which may come from establishing a reputation for safety and quality over the years, is one source of the comparative advantage that keeps Volvos selling on the international market. Some economists distinguish between gains from *acquired comparative advantages* and gains from *natural comparative advantages*.

Trade Barriers: Tariffs, Export Subsidies, and Quotas

Trade barriers—also called *obstacles to trade*—take many forms. The three most common are tariffs, export subsidies, and quotas. All are forms of **protection** shielding some sector of the economy from foreign competition.

A **tariff** is a tax on imports. The average tariff on imports into the United States is less than 5 percent. Certain protected items have much higher tariffs. For example, in 2009 President Obama imposed a tariff of 35 percent on tire imports from China.

Export subsidies—government payments made to domestic firms to encourage exports—can also act as a barrier to trade. One of the provisions of the Corn Laws that stimulated Ricardo's musings was an export subsidy automatically paid to farmers by the British government when the price of grain fell below a specified level. The subsidy served to keep domestic prices high, but it flooded the world market with cheap subsidized grain. Foreign farmers who were not subsidized were driven out of the international marketplace by the artificially low prices.

Farm subsidies remain a part of the international trade landscape today. Many countries continue to appease their farmers by heavily subsidizing exports of agricultural products. The political power of the farm lobby in many countries has had an important effect on recent international trade negotiations aimed at reducing trade barriers. The prevalence of farm subsidies in the developed world has become a major rallying point for less developed countries as they strive to compete in the global marketplace. Many African nations, in particular, have a comparative advantage in agricultural land. In producing agricultural goods for export to the world marketplace, however, they must compete with food produced on heavily subsidized farms in Europe and the United States. Countries such as France have particularly high farm subsidies,

protection   The practice of shielding a sector of the economy from foreign competition.

tariff   A tax on imports.

export subsidies   Government payments made to domestic firms to encourage exports.

which, it argues, helps preserve the rural heritage of France. One side effect of these subsidies, however, is to make it more difficult for some of the poorer nations in the world to compete. Some have argued that if developed nations eliminated their farm subsidies, this would have a much larger effect on the economies of some African nations than is currently achieved by charitable aid programs.

dumping A firm's or an industry's sale of products on the world market at prices below its own cost of production.

Closely related to subsidies is **dumping**. Dumping occurs when a firm or industry sells its products on the world market at prices lower than its cost of production. Charges of dumping are often brought by a domestic producer that believes itself to be subject to unfair competition. In the United States, claims of dumping are brought before the International Trade Commission. In 2007, for example, a small manufacturer of thermal paper charged China and Germany with dumping. In 2006, the European Union charged China with dumping shoes. In 2009, China brought a dumping charge against U.S. chicken producers. Determining whether dumping has actually occurred can be difficult. Domestic producers argue that foreign firms will dump their product in the United States, drive out American competitors, and then raise prices, thus harming consumers. Foreign exporters, on the other hand, claim that their prices are low simply because their costs are low and that no dumping has occurred. Figuring out the costs for German thermal paper or Chinese shoes is not easy. In the case of the Chinese shoe claim, for example, the Chinese government pointed out that shoes are a very labor-intensive product and that given China's low wages, it should not be a surprise that it is able to produce shoes very cheaply. In other words, the Chinese claim that shoes are an example of the theory of comparative advantage at work rather than predatory dumping.

quota A limit on the quantity of imports.

A **quota** is a limit on the quantity of imports. Quotas can be mandatory or voluntary, and they may be legislated or negotiated with foreign governments. The best-known voluntary quota, or "voluntary restraint," was negotiated with the Japanese government in 1981. Japan agreed to reduce its automobile exports to the United States by 7.7 percent, from the 1980 level of 1.82 million units to 1.68 million units. Many quotas limit trade around the world today. Perhaps the best-known recent case is the textile quota imposed in August 2005 by the European Union on imports of textiles from China. Because China had exceeded quotas that had been agreed to earlier in the year, the EU blocked the entry of Chinese-produced textiles into Europe; as a result, more than 100 million garments piled up in European ports.

U.S. Trade Policies, GATT, and the WTO

Smoot-Hawley tariff The U.S. tariff law of the 1930s, which set the highest tariffs in U.S. history (60 percent). It set off an international trade war and caused the decline in trade that is often considered one of the causes of the worldwide depression of the 1930s.

The United States has been a high-tariff nation, with average tariffs of over 50 percent, for much of its history. The highest were in effect during the Great Depression following the **Smoot-Hawley tariff**, which pushed the average tariff rate to 60 percent in 1930. The Smoot-Hawley tariff set off an international trade war when U.S. trading partners retaliated with tariffs of their own. Many economists say the decline in trade that followed was one of the causes of the worldwide depression of the 1930s.[1]

General Agreement on Tariffs and Trade (GATT) An international agreement signed by the United States and 22 other countries in 1947 to promote the liberalization of foreign trade.

In 1947, the United States, with 22 other nations, agreed to reduce barriers to trade. It also established an organization to promote liberalization of foreign trade. The **General Agreement on Tariffs and Trade (GATT)** proved to be very successful in helping reduce tariff levels and encourage trade. In 1986, GATT sponsored a round of world trade talks known as the Uruguay Round that were focused on reducing trade barriers further. After much debate, the Uruguay Round was signed by the U.S. Congress in 1993 and became a model for multilateral trade agreements.

World Trade Organization (WTO) A negotiating forum dealing with rules of trade across nations.

In 1995, the **World Trade Organization (WTO)** was established as a negotiating forum to deal with the rules of trade established under GATT and other agreements. It remains the key institution focused on facilitating freer trade across nations and negotiating trade disputes. The WTO consists of 153 member nations and serves as a negotiating forum for countries as they work through complexities of trade under the Uruguay Round and other agreements. At this time, the WTO is the central institution for promoting and facilitating free trade.

Doha Development Agenda An initiative of the World Trade Organization focused on issues of trade and development.

While the WTO was founded to promote free trade, its member countries clearly have different incentives as they confront trade cases. In recent years, differences between developed and developing countries have come to the fore. In 2001, at a WTO meeting in Doha, Qatar, the WTO launched a new initiative, the **Doha Development Agenda**, to deal with some of the issues that intersect the areas of trade and development. In 2007, the Doha Development Agenda continued to struggle over

---

[1] See especially Charles Kindleberger, *The World in Depression 1929–1939* (London: Allen Lane, 1973).

the issue of agriculture and farm subsidies that were described earlier in this chapter. The less developed countries, with sub-Saharan Africa taking the lead, seek to eliminate all farm subsidies currently paid by the United States and the European Union. The EU has, for its part, tried to push the less developed countries toward better environmental policies as part of a broader free trade package. As of 2010, the Doha declaration remained stalled.

The movement in the United States has been away from tariffs and quotas and toward freer trade. The Reciprocal Trade Agreements Act of 1934 authorized the president to negotiate trade agreements on behalf of the United States. As part of trade negotiations, the president can confer *most-favored-nation status* on individual trading partners. Imports from countries with most-favored-nation status are taxed at the lowest negotiated tariff rates. In addition, in recent years, several successful rounds of tariff-reduction negotiations have reduced trade barriers to their lowest levels ever.

Despite this general trend toward freer trade, most American presidents in the last 50 years have made exceptions to protect one economic sector or another. Eisenhower and Kennedy restricted imports of Japanese textiles; Johnson restricted meat imports to protect Texas beef producers; Nixon restricted steel imports; Reagan restricted automobiles from Japan. In early 2002, President George W. Bush imposed a 30 percent tariff on steel imported from the EU. In 2003, the WTO ruled that these tariffs were unfair and allowed the EU to slap retaliatory tariffs on U.S. products. Shortly thereafter, the steel tariffs were rolled back, at least on EU steel. At present, the United States has high tariffs on sugar-based ethanol, an energy source competitive with corn-based ethanol, and on tires imported from China.

Economic Integration   **Economic integration** occurs when two or more nations join to form a free-trade zone. In 1991, the European Community (EC, or the Common Market) began forming the largest free-trade zone in the world. The economic integration process began that December, when the 12 original members (the United Kingdom, Belgium, France, Germany, Italy, the Netherlands, Luxembourg, Denmark, Greece, Ireland, Spain, and Portugal) signed the Maastricht Treaty. The treaty called for the end of border controls, a common currency, an end to all tariffs, and the coordination of monetary and political affairs. The **European Union (EU)**, as the EC is now called, has 27 members (for a list, see the Summary, p. 429). On January 1, 1993, all tariffs and trade barriers were dropped among the member countries. Border checkpoints were closed in early 1995. Citizens can now travel among member countries without passports.

The United States is not a part of the EU. However, in 1988, the United States (under President Reagan) and Canada (under Prime Minister Mulroney) signed the **U.S.-Canadian Free Trade Agreement**, which removed all barriers to trade, including tariffs and quotas, between the two countries in 1998.

During the last days of the George H. W. Bush administration in 1992, the United States, Mexico, and Canada signed the **North American Free Trade Agreement (NAFTA)**, with the three countries agreeing to establish all of North America as a free-trade zone. The agreement eliminated all tariffs over a 10- to 15-year period and removed restrictions on most investments. During the presidential campaign of 1992, NAFTA was hotly debated. Both Bill Clinton and George Bush supported the agreement. Industrial labor unions that might be affected by increased imports from Mexico (such as those in the automobile industry) opposed the agreement, while industries whose exports to Mexico might increase as a result of the agreement—for example, the machine tool industry—supported it. Another concern was that Mexican companies were not subject to the same environmental regulations as U.S. firms, so U.S. firms might move to Mexico for this reason.

NAFTA was ratified by the U.S. Congress in late 1993 and went into effect on the first day of 1994. The U.S. Department of Commerce estimated that as a result of NAFTA, trade between the United States and Mexico increased by nearly $16 billion in 1994. In addition, exports from the United States to Mexico outpaced imports from Mexico during 1994. In 1995, however, the agreement fell under the shadow of a dramatic collapse of the value of the peso. U.S. exports to Mexico dropped sharply, and the United States shifted from a trade surplus to a large trade deficit with Mexico. Aside from a handful of tariffs, however, all of NAFTA's commitments were fully implemented by 2003, and an 8-year report signed by all three countries declared the pact a success. The report concludes, "Eight years of expanded trade, increased employment and investment, and enhanced opportunity for the citizens of all three countries have demonstrated that NAFTA works and will continue to work." In 2007, trade among the NAFTA nations reached $930 billion.

---

economic integration
Occurs when two or more nations join to form a free-trade zone.

European Union (EU)   The European trading bloc composed of 27 countries (of the 27 countries in the EU, 16 have the same currency—the euro).

U.S.-Canadian Free Trade Agreement   An agreement in which the United States and Canada agreed to eliminate all barriers to trade between the two countries by 1998.

North American Free Trade Agreement (NAFTA)   An agreement signed by the United States, Mexico, and Canada in which the three countries agreed to establish all North America as a free-trade zone.

Tariff Wars

In the recent recession we have again seen political pressure aimed at imposing tariffs. These pressures have been especially strong in the case of China, whose export growth to the United States and the EU has been very strong. In the case of the EU's tariff on Chinese shoes, pressure from Italian shoemakers played a substantial role.

China Complains to WTO About EU Tariffs

The Wall Street Journal

China filed a complaint against European Union shoe tariffs at the World Trade Organization on Thursday, as Beijing continued its legal assault on what it says is unfair Western protectionism.

China's exports have been growing since the 1990s, particularly after the country joined the WTO in 2001. Eight years later, China passed Germany to become the world's top exporter. That status comes with a price: China is now the leading target for protectionist measures, according to Global Trade Alert, an independent monitor.

As the fitful economic recovery has put some domestic jobs and profits at risk, the EU and the U.S. have sought to stem the flow of Chinese imports with special duties. Added to existing tariffs, the duties are meant to make Chinese goods too expensive for consumers to afford.

China isn't taking the restrictions lying down. From a new office near WTO headquarters in Geneva, Beijing is playing hardball. It is paying top dollar to engage premium counsel, some trade lawyers say.

In September, China reacted to President Barack Obama's tariffs on tire imports with a complaint against the U.S. China has also put restrictions on imports of U.S. poultry and auto parts.

Early Friday, China's Commerce Ministry said it had made a preliminary decision to impose antidumping duties on some U.S. chicken products from Feb. 13, the eve of the Lunar New Year, China's biggest holiday. Companies named in the statement include Pilgrim's Pride and Tyson Foods Inc.

In the EU case, China is taking on one of the most important tariff increases ever levied, which has taken a bite out of its expansive shoe industry. The 16.5% tariffs are antidumping duties, meant to punish goods that are sold below cost and hurt the sales of domestic producers.

The EU duties were inaugurated in 2006 and extended for 15 months in December 2009. At the same time, shoe imports from Vietnam were hit with a 10% tariff.

The EU tariffs were passed after fierce lobbying by Italy on behalf of its domestic shoemakers. Italy traded votes in other debates with EU members in exchange for support for the tariffs, EU officials say.

Source: The Wall Street Journal, excerpted from "China Complains to WTO About EU Tariffs" by John W. Miller. Copyright 2010 by *Dow Jones & Company, Inc.* Reproduced with permission of *Dow Jones & Company, Inc.* via Copyright Clearance Center.

Free Trade or Protection?

One of the great economic debates of all time revolves around the free-trade-versus-protection controversy. We briefly summarize the arguments in favor of each.

The Case for Free Trade

In one sense, the theory of comparative advantage *is* the case for free trade. Trade has potential benefits for all nations. A good is not imported unless its net price to buyers is below the net price of the domestically produced alternative. When the Brazilians in our earlier example found U.S. timber less expensive than their own, they bought it, yet they continued to pay the same price for homemade steel. Americans bought less expensive Brazilian steel, but they continued to buy domestic timber at the same lower price. Under these conditions, *both Americans and Brazilians ended up paying less and consuming more.*

At the same time, resources (including labor) move out of steel production and into timber production in the United States. In Brazil, resources (including labor) move out of timber production and into steel production. The resources in both countries are used more efficiently.

Tariffs, export subsidies, and quotas, which interfere with the free movement of goods and services around the world, reduce or eliminate the gains of comparative advantage.

We can use supply and demand curves to illustrate this. Suppose Figure 20.4 shows domestic supply and demand for textiles. In the absence of trade, the market clears at a price of $4.20. At equilibrium, 450 million yards of textiles are produced and consumed.

Assume now that textiles are available at a world price of $2. This is the price in dollars that Americans must pay for textiles from foreign sources. If we assume that an unlimited quantity of textiles is available at $2 and there is no difference in quality between domestic and foreign textiles, no domestic producer will be able to charge more than $2. In the absence of trade barriers, the world price sets the price in the United States. As the price in the United States falls from $4.20 to $2.00, the quantity demanded by consumers increases from 450 million yards to 700 million yards, but the quantity supplied by domestic producers drops from 450 million yards to 200 million yards. The difference, 500 million yards, is the quantity of textiles imported.

The argument for free trade is that each country should specialize in producing the goods and services in which it enjoys a comparative advantage. If foreign producers can produce textiles at a much lower price than domestic producers, they have a comparative advantage. As the world price of textiles falls to $2, domestic (U.S.) quantity supplied drops and resources are transferred to other sectors. These other sectors, which may be export industries or domestic industries, are not shown in Figure 20.4a. It is clear that the allocation of resources is more efficient at a price of $2. Why should the United States use domestic resources to produce what foreign producers can produce at a lower cost? U.S. resources should move into the production of the things it produces best.

Now consider what happens to the domestic price of textiles when a trade barrier is imposed. Figure 20.4b shows the effect of a set tariff of $1 per yard imposed on imported textiles. The tariff raises the domestic price of textiles to $2 + $1 = $3. The result is that some of the gains from trade are lost. First, consumers are forced to pay a higher price for the same good. The quantity of

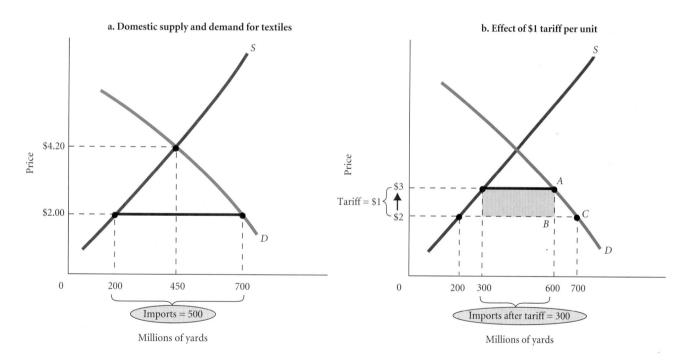

▲ **FIGURE 20.4 The Gains from Trade and Losses from the Imposition of a Tariff**
A tariff of $1 increases the market price facing consumers from $2 per yard to $3 per yard. The government collects revenues equal to the gray shaded area in **b**. The loss of efficiency has two components. First, consumers must pay a higher price for goods that could be produced at lower cost. Second, marginal producers are drawn into textiles and away from other goods, resulting in inefficient domestic production. The triangle labeled ABC in **b** is the dead weight loss or excess burden resulting from the tariff.

textiles demanded drops from 700 million yards under free trade to 600 million yards because some consumers are not willing to pay the higher price. Notice in Figure 20.4b the triangle labeled ABC. This is the deadweight loss or excess burden resulting from the tariff. Absent the tariff, these 100 added units of textiles would have generated benefits in excess of the $2 that each one cost.

At the same time, the higher price of textiles draws some marginal domestic producers who could not make a profit at $2 into textile production. (Recall that domestic producers do not pay a tariff.) As the price rises to $3, the quantity supplied by domestic producers rises from 200 million yards to 300 million yards. The result is a decrease in imports from 500 million yards to 300 million yards.

Finally, the imposition of the tariff means that the government collects revenue equal to the shaded area in Figure 20.4b. This shaded area is equal to the tariff rate per unit ($1) times the number of units imported after the tariff is in place (300 million yards). Thus, receipts from the tariff are $300 million.

What is the final result of the tariff? Domestic producers receiving revenues of only $2 per unit before the tariff was imposed now receive a higher price and earn higher profits. However, these higher profits are achieved at a loss of efficiency. Trade barriers prevent a nation from reaping the benefits of specialization, push it to adopt relatively inefficient production techniques, and force consumers to pay higher prices for protected products than they would otherwise pay.

The Case for Protection

A case can also be made in favor of tariffs and quotas. Over the course of U.S. history, protectionist arguments have been made so many times by so many industries before so many congressional committees that it seems all pleas for protection share the same themes. We describe the most frequently heard pleas next.

Protection Saves Jobs   The main argument for protection is that foreign competition costs Americans their jobs. When Americans buy imported Toyotas, U.S. produced cars go unsold. Layoffs in the domestic auto industry follow. When Americans buy Chinese textiles, American workers may lose their jobs. When Americans buy shoes or textiles from Korea or Taiwan, the millworkers in Maine and Massachusetts, as well as in South Carolina and Georgia, lose their jobs.

It is true that when we buy goods from foreign producers, domestic producers suffer. However, there is no reason to believe that the workers laid off in the contracting sectors will not ultimately be reemployed in expanding sectors. Foreign competition in textiles, for example, has meant the loss of U.S. jobs in that industry. Thousands of textile workers in New England lost their jobs as the textile mills closed over the last 40 years. Nevertheless, with the expansion of high-tech industries, the unemployment rate in Massachusetts fell to one of the lowest in the country in the mid-1980s, and New Hampshire, Vermont, and Maine also boomed. By the 1990s, New England had suffered another severe downturn, due partly to high-technology hardware manufacturing that had moved abroad. But by the late 1990s, its economy was booming again, this time on the back of what was called a "New Industrial Revolution": the rise of Internet-based business.

The adjustment is far from costless. The knowledge that some other industry, perhaps in some other part of the country, may be expanding is of little comfort to the person whose skills become obsolete or whose pension benefits are lost when his or her company abruptly closes a plant or goes bankrupt. The social and personal problems brought about by industry-specific unemployment, obsolete skills, and bankruptcy as a result of foreign competition are significant.

These problems can be addressed in two ways. We can ban imports and give up the gains from free trade, acknowledging that we are willing to pay premium prices to save domestic jobs in industries that can produce more efficiently abroad, or we can aid the victims of free trade in a constructive way, helping to retrain them for jobs with a future. In some instances, programs to relocate people in expanding regions may be in order. Some programs deal directly with the transition without forgoing the gains from trade.

ECONOMICS IN PRACTICE

A Petition

While most economists argue in favor of free trade, it is important to recognize that some groups are likely to lose from freer trade. Arguments by the losing groups against trade have been around for hundreds of years. In the following article, you will find an essay by a French satirist of the nineteenth century, Frederic Bastiat, complaining about the unfair competition that the sun provides to candle makers. You see that the author proposes a quota, as opposed to a tariff, on the sun.

From the Manufacturers of Candles, Tapers, Lanterns, Sticks, Street Lamps, Snuffers, and Extinguishers, and from Producers of Tallow, Oil, Resin, Alcohol, and Generally of Everything Connected with Lighting.

To the Honourable Members of the Chamber of Deputies.

Gentlemen:

You are on the right track. You reject abstract theories and [have] little regard for abundance and low prices. You concern yourselves mainly with the fate of the producer. You wish to free him from foreign competition, that is, to reserve the *domestic market* for *domestic industry*.

We come to offer you a wonderful opportunity for your— what shall we call it? Your theory? No, nothing is more deceptive than theory. Your doctrine? Your system? Your principle? But you dislike doctrines, you have a horror of systems, as for principles, you deny that there are any in political economy; therefore we shall call it your practice—your practice without theory and without principle.

We are suffering from the ruinous competition of a rival who apparently works under conditions so far superior to our own for the production of light that he is *flooding* the *domestic market* with it at an incredibly low price; for the moment he appears, our sales cease, all the consumers turn to him, and a branch of French industry whose ramifications are innumerable is all at once reduced to complete stagnation. This rival, which is none other than the sun, is waging war on us so mercilessly we suspect he is being stirred up against us by perfidious Albion (excellent diplomacy nowadays!), particularly because he has for that haughty island a respect that he does not show for us. [A reference to Britain's reputation as a foggy island.]

We ask you to be so good as to pass a law requiring the closing of all windows, dormers, skylights, inside and outside

Screening out the sun would increase the demand for candles. Should candlemakers be protected from unfair competition?

shutters, curtains, casements, bull's-eyes, deadlights, and blinds—in short, all openings, holes, chinks, and fissures through which the light of the sun is wont to enter houses, to the detriment of the fair industries with which, we are proud to say, we have endowed the country, a country that cannot, without betraying ingratitude, abandon us today to so unequal a combat.

Source: An Open Letter to the French Parliament by Frederic Bastiat (1801–1850), originally published in 1845.

Some Countries Engage in Unfair Trade Practices   Attempts by U.S. firms to monopolize an industry are illegal under the Sherman and Clayton acts. If a strong company decides to drive the competition out of the market by setting prices below cost, it would be aggressively prosecuted by the Antitrust Division of the Justice Department. However, the argument goes, if we will not allow a U.S. firm to engage in predatory pricing or monopolize an industry or a market, can we stand by and let a German firm or a Japanese firm do so in the name of free trade? This is a legitimate argument and one that has gained significant favor in recent years. How should we respond when a large international company or a country behaves strategically against a domestic firm or industry? Free trade may be the best solution when everybody plays by the rules, but sometimes we have to fight back. The WTO is the vehicle currently used to negotiate disputes of this sort.

Cheap Foreign Labor Makes Competition Unfair   Let us say that a particular country gained its "comparative advantage" in textiles by paying its workers low wages. How can U.S. textile companies compete with companies that pay wages that are less than a quarter of what U.S. companies pay? Questions like this are often asked by those concerned with competition from China and India.

First, remember that wages in a competitive economy reflect productivity: a high ratio of output to units of labor. Workers in the United States earn higher wages because they are more productive. The United States has more capital per worker; that is, the average worker works with better machinery and equipment and its workers are better trained. Second, trade flows not according to *absolute* advantage, but according to *comparative* advantage: All countries benefit, even if one country is more efficient at producing everything.

Protection Safeguards National Security   Beyond saving jobs, certain sectors of the economy may appeal for protection for other reasons. The steel industry has argued for years with some success that it is vital to national defense. In the event of a war, the United States would not want to depend on foreign countries for a product as vital as steel. Even if we acknowledge another country's comparative advantage, we may want to protect our own resources.

Virtually no industry has ever asked for protection without invoking the national defense argument. Testimony that was once given on behalf of the scissors and shears industry argued that "in the event of a national emergency and imports cutoff, the United States would be without a source of scissors and shears, basic tools for many industries and trades essential to our national defense." The question lies not in the merit of the argument, but in just how seriously it can be taken if *every* industry uses it.

Protection Discourages Dependency   Closely related to the national defense argument is the claim that countries, particularly small or developing countries, may come to rely too heavily on one or more trading partners for many items. If a small country comes to rely on a major power for food or energy or some important raw material in which the large nation has a comparative advantage, it may be difficult for the smaller nation to remain politically neutral. Some critics of free trade argue that larger countries, such as the United States, Russia, and China have consciously engaged in trade with smaller countries to create these kinds of dependencies.

Therefore, should small, independent countries consciously avoid trading relationships that might lead to political dependence? This objective may involve developing domestic industries in areas where a country has a comparative disadvantage. To do so would mean protecting that industry from international competition.

Environmental Concerns   In recent years, concern about the environment has led some people to question advantages of free trade. Some environmental groups, for example, argue that the WTO's free trade policies may harm the environment. The central argument is that poor countries will become havens for polluting industries that will operate their steel and auto factories with few environmental controls.

These issues are quite complex, and there is much dispute among economists about the interaction between free trade and the environment. One relatively recent study of sulphur dioxide, for example, found that in the long run, free trade reduces pollution, largely by increasing the income of countries; richer countries typically choose policies to improve the environment.[2] Thus, while free trade and increased development initially may cause pollution levels to rise, in the long run, prosperity is a benefit to the environment. Many also argue that there are complex trade-offs to be made between pollution control and problems such as malnutrition and health for poor countries. The United States and Europe both traded off faster economic growth and income against cleaner air and water at earlier times in their development. Some argue that it is unfair for the developed countries to impose their preferences on other countries facing more difficult trade-offs.

Nevertheless, the concern with global climate change has stimulated new thinking in this area. A recent study by the Tyndall Centre for Climate Change Research in Britain found that in 2004, 23 percent of the greenhouse gas emissions produced by China were created in the production of

---

[2] Werner Antweiler, Brian Copeland, and M. Scott Taylor, "Is Free Trade Good for the Environment?" *AER*, September, 2001.

exports. In other words, these emissions come not as a result of goods that China's population is enjoying as its income rises, but as a consequence of the consumption of the United States and Europe, where most of these goods are going. In a world in which the effects of carbon emissions are global and all countries are not willing to sign binding global agreements to control emissions, trade with China may be a way for developed nations to avoid their commitments to pollution reduction. Some have argued that penalties could be imposed on high-polluting products produced in countries that have not signed international climate control treaties as a way to ensure that the prices of goods imported this way reflect the harm that those products cause the environment.[3] Implementing these policies is, however, likely to be very complex, and some have argued that it is a mistake to bundle trade and environmental issues. As with other areas covered in this book, there is still disagreement among economists as to the right answer.

Protection Safeguards Infant Industries   Young industries in a given country may have a difficult time competing with established industries in other countries. In a dynamic world, a protected **infant industry** might mature into a strong industry worldwide because of an acquired, but real, comparative advantage. If such an industry is undercut and driven out of world markets at the beginning of its life, that comparative advantage might never develop.

infant industry   A young industry that may need temporary protection from competition from the established industries of other countries to develop an acquired comparative advantage.

Yet efforts to protect infant industries can backfire. In July 1991, the U.S. government imposed a 62.67 percent tariff on imports of active-matrix liquid crystal display screens (also referred to as "flat-panel displays" used primarily for laptop computers) from Japan. The Commerce Department and the International Trade Commission agreed that Japanese producers were selling their screens in the U.S. market at a price below cost and that this dumping threatened the survival of domestic laptop screen producers. The tariff was meant to protect the infant U.S. industry until it could compete head-on with the Japanese.

Unfortunately for U.S. producers of laptop computers and for consumers who purchase them, the tariff had an unintended (although predictable) effect on the industry. Because U.S. laptop screens were generally recognized to be of lower quality than their Japanese counterparts, imposition of the tariff left U.S. computer manufacturers with three options: (1) They could use the screens available from U.S. producers and watch sales of their final product decline in the face of *higher-quality* competition from abroad, (2) they could pay the tariff for the higher-quality screens and watch sales of their final product decline in the face of *lower-priced* competition from abroad, or (3) they could do what was most profitable for them to do—move their production facilities abroad to avoid the tariff completely. The last option is what Apple and IBM did. In the end, not only were the laptop industry and its consumers hurt by the imposition of the tariff (due to higher costs of production and to higher laptop computer prices), but the U.S. screen industry was hurt as well (due to its loss of buyers for its product) by a policy specifically designed to help it.

The case for free trade has been made across the world as increasing numbers of countries have joined the world marketplace. Figure 20.5 traces the path of tariffs across the world from

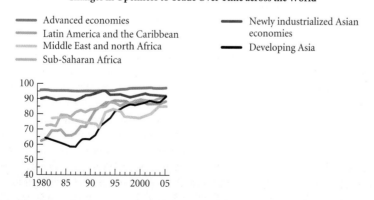

Changes in Openness to Trade Over Time across the World

— Advanced economies
— Latin America and the Caribbean
— Middle East and north Africa
— Sub-Saharan Africa
— Newly industrialized Asian economies
— Developing Asia

Source: International Monetary Fund, *2007 World Economic Outlook.*
Trade openness is measured as 100 minus the average effective tariff rate in the region.

◀ **FIGURE 20.5 Trade Openness Across the World (Index is 100 minus the average effective tariff rate in the region.)**

[3] Judith Chevalier, "A Carbon Cap That Starts in Washington," *New York Times*, December 16, 2007.

1980–2005. The lines show an index of trade openness, calculated as 100 minus the tariff rate. (So higher numbers mean lower tariffs.) We see rapid reductions in the last 25 years across the world, most notably in countries in the emerging and developing markets.

An Economic Consensus

You now know something about how international trade fits into the structure of the economy.

Critical to our study of international economics is the debate between free traders and protectionists. On one side is the theory of comparative advantage, formalized by David Ricardo in the early part of the nineteenth century. According to this view, all countries benefit from specialization and trade. The gains from trade are real, and they can be large; free international trade raises real incomes and improves the standard of living.

On the other side are the protectionists, who point to the loss of jobs and argue for the protection of workers from foreign competition. Although foreign competition can cause job loss in specific sectors, it is unlikely to cause net job loss in an economy and workers will, over time, be absorbed into expanding sectors. Foreign trade and full employment can be pursued simultaneously. Although economists disagree about many things, the vast majority of them favor free trade.

——— SUMMARY ———

1. All economies, regardless of their size, depend to some extent on other economies and are affected by events outside their borders.

TRADE SURPLUSES AND DEFICITS *p. 410*

2. Until the 1970s, the United States generally exported more than it imported—it ran a *trade surplus*. In the mid-1970s, the United States began to import more merchandise than it exported—a *trade deficit*.

THE ECONOMIC BASIS FOR TRADE: COMPARATIVE ADVANTAGE *p. 411*

3. The *theory of comparative advantage*, dating to David Ricardo in the nineteenth century, holds that specialization and free trade will benefit all trading partners, even those that may be absolutely less efficient producers.

4. A country enjoys an *absolute advantage* over another country in the production of a product if it uses fewer resources to produce that product than the other country does. A country has a *comparative advantage* in the production of a product if that product can be produced at a lower cost in terms of other goods.

5. Trade enables countries to move beyond their previous resource and productivity constraints. When countries specialize in producing those goods in which they have a comparative advantage, they maximize their combined output and allocate their resources more efficiently.

6. When trade is free, patterns of trade and trade flows result from the independent decisions of thousands of importers and exporters and millions of private households and firms.

7. The relative attractiveness of foreign goods to U.S. buyers and of U.S. goods to foreign buyers depends in part on *exchange rates*, the ratios at which two currencies are traded for each other.

8. For any pair of countries, there is a range of exchange rates that will lead automatically to both countries realizing the gains from specialization and comparative advantage. Within that range, the exchange rate will determine which country gains the most from trade. This leads us to conclude that exchange rates determine the terms of trade.

9. If exchange rates end up in the right range (that is, in a range that facilitates the flow of goods between nations), the free market will drive each country to shift resources into those sectors in which it enjoys a comparative advantage. Only those products in which a country has a comparative advantage will be competitive in world markets.

THE SOURCES OF COMPARATIVE ADVANTAGE *p. 418*

10. The *Heckscher-Ohlin theorem* looks to relative *factor endowments* to explain comparative advantage and trade flows. According to the theorem, a country has a comparative advantage in the production of a product if that country is relatively well endowed with the inputs that are used intensively in the production of that product.

11. A relatively short list of inputs—natural resources, knowledge capital, physical capital, land, and skilled and unskilled labor—explains a surprisingly large portion of world trade patterns. However, the simple version of the theory of comparative advantage cannot explain why many countries import and export the same goods.

12. Some theories argue that comparative advantage can be acquired. Just as industries within a country differentiate their products to capture a domestic market, they also differentiate their products to please the wide variety of tastes that exists worldwide. This theory is consistent with the theory of comparative advantage.

TRADE BARRIERS: TARIFFS, EXPORT SUBSIDIES, AND QUOTAS *p. 419*

13. Trade barriers take many forms. The three most common are *tariffs, export subsidies*, and *quotas*. All are forms of *protection* through which some sector of the economy is shielded from foreign competition.

14. Although the United States has historically been a high-tariff nation, the general movement is now away from tariffs and quotas. The *General Agreement on Tariffs and Trade (GATT)*, signed by the United States and 22 other countries in 1947, continues in effect today; its purpose is to reduce barriers to world trade and keep them down. Also important are the *U.S.-Canadian Free Trade Agreement*, signed in 1988, and the *North American Free Trade Agreement*, signed by the United States, Mexico, and Canada in the last days of the George H. W. Bush administration in 1992, taking effect in 1994.

15. The World Trade Organization (WTO) was set up by GATT to act as a negotiating forum for trade disputes across countries.

16. The *European Union (EU)* is a free-trade bloc composed of 27 nations: Austria, Belgium, Bulgaria, Cyprus, the Czech Republic, Denmark, Estonia, Finland, France, Germany, Greece, Hungary, Ireland, Italy, Latvia, Lithuania, Luxembourg, Malta, the Netherlands, Poland, Portugal, Romania, Slovakia, Slovenia, Spain, Sweden, and the United Kingdom. Many economists believe that the advantages of free trade within the bloc, a reunited Germany, and the ability to work well as a bloc will make the EU the most powerful player in the international marketplace in the coming decades.

FREE TRADE OR PROTECTION? *p. 422*

17. In one sense, the theory of comparative advantage is the case for free trade. Trade barriers prevent a nation from reaping the benefits of specialization, push it to adopt relatively inefficient production techniques, and force consumers to pay higher prices for protected products than they would otherwise pay.

18. The case for protection rests on a number of propositions, one of which is that foreign competition results in a loss of domestic jobs, but there is no reason to believe that the workers laid off in the contracting sectors will not be ultimately reemployed in other expanding sectors. This adjustment process is far from costless, however.

19. Other arguments for protection hold that cheap foreign labor makes competition unfair; that some countries engage in unfair trade practices; that free trade might harm the environment; and that protection safeguards the national security, discourages dependency, and shields *infant industries*. Despite these arguments, most economists favor free trade.

REVIEW TERMS AND CONCEPTS

absolute advantage, *p. 411*

comparative advantage, *p. 411*

Corn Laws, *p. 411*

Doha Development Agenda, *p. 420*

dumping, *p. 420*

economic integration, *p. 421*

European Union (EU), *p. 421*

exchange rate, *p. 416*

export subsidies, *p. 419*

factor endowments, *p. 418*

General Agreement on Tariffs and Trade (GATT), *p. 420*

Heckscher-Ohlin theorem, *p. 418*

infant industry, *p. 427*

North American Free Trade Agreement (NAFTA), *p. 421*

protection, *p. 419*

quota, *p. 420*

Smoot-Hawley tariff, *p. 420*

tariff, *p. 419*

terms of trade, *p. 415*

theory of comparative advantage, *p. 411*

trade deficit, *p. 410*

trade surplus, *p. 410*

U.S.-Canadian Free Trade Agreement, *p. 421*

World Trade Organization (WTO), *p. 420*

PROBLEMS

All problems are available on www.myeconlab.com

1. Suppose Germany and France each produce only two goods, guns and butter. Both are produced using labor alone. Assuming both countries are at full employment, you are given the following information:

    Germany: 10 units of labor required to produce 1 gun
    5 units of labor required to produce 1 pound of butter
    Total labor force: 1,000,000 units

    France: 15 units of labor required to produce 1 gun
    10 units of labor required to produce 1 pound of butter
    Total labor force: 750,000 units

    a. Draw the production possibility frontiers for each country in the absence of trade.
    b. If transportation costs are ignored and trade is allowed, will France and Germany engage in trade? Explain.
    c. If a trade agreement was negotiated, at what rate (number of guns per unit of butter) would they agree to exchange?

2. The United States and Russia each produce only bearskin caps and wheat. Domestic prices are given in the following table:

	RUSSIA	UNITED STATES	
Bearskin caps	10 Ru	$ 7	Per hat
Wheat	15 Ru	$10	Per bushel

On April 1, the Zurich exchange listed an exchange rate of $1 = 1 Ru.

  a. Which country has an absolute advantage in the production of bearskin caps? wheat?
  b. Which country has a comparative advantage in the production of bearskin caps? wheat?
  c. If the United States and Russia were the only two countries engaging in trade, what adjustments would you predict assuming exchange rates are freely determined by the laws of supply and demand?

3. The following table shows imports and exports of goods during 2009 for the United States:

	EXPORTS	IMPORTS
Total	1,068.0	1,575.0
Civilian aircraft	35.0	10.0
Apparel, household goods—textile	5.0	74.0
Crude oil	1.0	189.0
Vehicles, parts, and engines	82.0	158.0
Foods, feeds, and beverages	94.0	81.0

All figures are rounded to the nearest billion dollars.
Source: www.census.gov.

What, if anything, can you conclude about the comparative advantage that the United States has relative to its trading partners in the production of goods? What stories can you tell about the wide disparities in apparel and aircraft?

4. The following table gives recent figures for yield per acre in Illinois and Kansas:

	WHEAT	SOYBEANS
Illinois	48	39
Kansas	40	24

Source: U.S. Department of Agriculture, *Crop Production.*

  a. If we assume that farmers in Illinois and Kansas use the same amount of labor, capital, and fertilizer, which state has an absolute advantage in wheat production? soybean production?
  b. If we transfer land out of wheat into soybeans, how many bushels of wheat do we give up in Illinois per additional bushel of soybeans produced? in Kansas?
  c. Which state has a comparative advantage in wheat production? in soybean production?
  d. The following table gives the distribution of land planted for each state in millions of acres in the same year.

	TOTAL ACRES UNDER TILL	WHEAT	SOYBEANS
Illinois	22.9	1.9 (8.3%)	9.1 (39.7%)
Kansas	20.7	11.8 (57.0%)	1.9 (9.2%)

Are these data consistent with your answer to part c? Explain.

5. You can think of the United States as a set of 50 separate economies with no trade barriers. In such an open environment, each state specializes in the products that it produces best.
  a. What product or products does your state specialize in?
  b. Can you identify the source of the comparative advantage that lies behind the production of one or more of these products (for example, a natural resource, plentiful cheap labor, or a skilled labor force)?
  c. Do you think that the theory of comparative advantage and the Heckscher-Ohlin theorem help to explain why your state specializes the way that it does? Explain your answer.

6. Australia and the United States produce white and red wines. Current domestic prices for each wine are given in the following table:

	AUSTRALIA	UNITED STATES
White wine	5 AU$	10 US$
Red wine	10 AU$	15 US$

Suppose the exchange rate is 1 AU$ = 1 US$.
  a. If the price ratios within each country reflect resource use, which country has a comparative advantage in the production of red wine? white wine?
  b. Assume that there are no other trading partners and that the only motive for holding foreign currency is to buy foreign goods. Will the current exchange rate lead to trade flows in both directions between the two countries? Explain.
  c. What adjustments might you expect in the exchange rate? Be specific.
  d. What would you predict about trade flows between Australia and the United States after the exchange rate has adjusted?

7. Some empirical trade economists have noted that for many products, countries are both importers and exporters. For example, the United States both imports and exports shirts. How do you explain this?

8. [Related to the *Economics in Practice* on *p. 422*] Review the *Economics in Practice* on p. 422. Despite the reduction in tariffs brought about by the passage of trade agreements such as GATT, the recent recession has generated political pressure in many countries to again impose import tariffs, with this pressure especially strong in the case of imports from China. Why would a recession create pressure to impose tariffs? Who is likely to be in favor of imposing these tariffs, and who might be in favor of reducing or eliminating them? Do some research on the imposition of tariffs during the recent recession. Did many countries actually impose new tariffs on imports? What has been the response of the WTO and countries like China to the imposition of these tariffs?

9. [Related to the *Economics in Practice* on *p. 425*] When a president presents a trade agreement for ratification to Congress, many domestic industries fight the ratification. In 2005, the United States was negotiating the Central America-Dominican Republic Free Trade Agreement (CAFTA-DR). Write a brief essay on the U.S. political opposition to CAFTA-DR in 2004 and 2005. What industries in the United States opposed the trade agreement? Is it fair to compare the arguments of these industries to the arguments posed by the candle makers?

10. The following graph represents the domestic supply and demand for coffee a number of years ago.
  a. In the absence of trade, what is the equilibrium price and equilibrium quantity?

b. The government opens the market to free trade, and Columbia enters the market, pricing coffee at $1 per pound. What will happen to the domestic price of coffee? What will be the new domestic quantity supplied and domestic quantity demanded? How much coffee will be imported from Columbia?

c. After numerous complaints from domestic coffee producers, the government imposes a $0.50 per pound tariff on all imported coffee. What will happen to the domestic price of coffee? What will be the new domestic quantity supplied and domestic quantity demanded? How much coffee will now be imported from Columbia?

d. How much revenue will the government receive from the $0.50 per pound tariff?

e. Who ultimately ends up paying the $0.50 per pound tariff? Why?

11. Refer to the previous problem. Assume the market is opened to trade and Columbia still enters the market by pricing coffee at $1.00 per pound. But as a response to complaints from domestic coffee producers, instead of imposing a $0.50 per pound tariff, the government imposes an import quota of 50 million pounds on Columbian coffee. How will the results of the quota differ from the results of the tariff?

12. The nation of Pixley has an absolute advantage in everything it produces compared to the nation of Hooterville. Could these two nations still benefit by trading with each other? Explain.

13. Evaluate the following statement: If lower exchange rates increase a nation's exports, the government should do everything in its power to ensure that the exchange rate for its currency is as low as possible.

14. Since the 1960s, the United States has had an embargo in place on Cuba, virtually eliminating all trade between the two countries. Suppose the United States decided to lift the embargo on exports to Cuba while maintaining the embargo on Cuban imports. Explain whether this one-sided change would benefit neither country, just one country, or both countries?

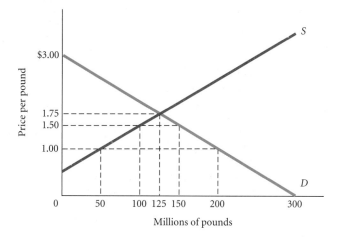

Economic Growth in Developing and Transitional Economies

21

Our primary focus in this text has been on countries with modern industrialized economies that rely heavily on markets to allocate resources, but what about the economic problems facing countries such as Somalia and Haiti? Can we apply the same economic principles that we have been studying to these less developed nations?

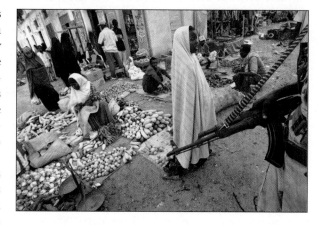

Yes. All economic analysis deals with the problem of making choices under conditions of scarcity, and the problem of satisfying people's wants and needs is as real for Somalia and Haiti as it is for the United States, Germany, and Japan. The universality of scarcity is what makes economic analysis relevant to all nations, regardless of their level of material well-being or ruling political ideology.

The basic tools of supply and demand, theories about consumers and firms, and theories about the structure of markets all contribute to an understanding of the economic problems confronting the world's developing nations. However, these nations often face economic problems quite different from those that richer, more developed countries face. In developing nations, an economist may have to worry about chronic food shortages, explosive population growth, and hyperinflations that reach triple, and even quadruple, digits. The United States and other industrialized economies rarely encounter such difficulties.

The instruments of economic management also vary from nation to nation. The United States has well-developed financial market institutions and a strong central bank (the Federal Reserve) through which the government can control the macroeconomy to some extent. Even limited intervention is impossible in some of the developing countries. In the United States, tax laws can be changed to stimulate saving, to encourage particular kinds of investments, or to redistribute income. In most developing countries, there are neither meaningful personal income taxes nor effective tax policies.

Even though economic problems and the policy instruments available to tackle them vary across nations, economic thinking about these problems can be transferred easily from one setting to another. In this chapter, we discuss several of the economic problems specific to developing nations in an attempt to capture some of the insights that economic analysis can offer.

Life in the Developing Nations: Population and Poverty

In 2010, the population of the world reached over 6.8 billion people. Most of the world's more than 200 nations belong to the developing world, in which about three-fourths of the world's population lives.

In the early 1960s, the nations of the world could be assigned rather easily to categories: The *developed countries* included most of Europe, North America, Japan, Australia, and New Zealand; the *developing countries* included the rest of the world. The developing nations were often referred to as the *Third World* to distinguish them from the Western industrialized nations (the *First World*) and the former Socialist bloc of Eastern European nations (the *Second World*).

In 2010, the world did not divide easily into three neat parts. Rapid economic progress brought some developing nations closer to developed economies. Countries such as Argentina and Chile, still considered to be "developing," are often referred to as middle-income or newly industrialized countries. Other countries, such as those in much of sub-Saharan Africa and some in South Asia, have stagnated and fallen so far behind the economic advances of the rest of the world that the term *Fourth World* has been used to describe them. China and India, while usually labeled developing countries, are fast becoming economic superpowers. It is not clear yet where some of the republics of the former Soviet Union and other formerly Communist countries of Eastern Europe will end up. Production fell sharply in many of them in the early transition stage to a market economy. Post-2000, however, the Russian economy began growing more rapidly.

Although the countries of the developing world exhibit considerable diversity in both their standards of living and their particular experiences of growth, marked differences continue to separate them from the developed nations. The developed countries have a higher average level of material well-being (the amount of food, clothing, shelter, and other commodities consumed by the average person). Comparisons of gross national income (GNI) are often used as a crude index of the level of material well-being across nations. GNI is a new measure of a nation's income, computed using a more accurate way of converting purchasing power into dollars. See Table 21.1, where GNI per-capita in the industrial

Country Group	Population, 2006	Gross National Income per Capita, 2006 (dollars)	Literacy Rate (percent over 15 years of age)	Infant Mortality, 2006 (deaths before age 5 per 1,000 births)	Internet Users per 1,000 people, 2005
Low-income	2.4 billion	650	60.8	114	44
Lower middle-income	2.3 billion	1,778	88.9	39.8	86
Upper middle-income	810 million	5,913	93.1	29.9	194
High-income	1.0 billion	36,487	98.7	6.9	523

TABLE 21.1 Indicators of Economic Development

Source: International Bank for Reconstruction and Development / The World Bank: *World Development Report* 2002.

market economies significantly exceeds GNI of both the low- and middle-income developing economies.

Other characteristics of economic development include improvements in basic health and education. The degree of political and economic freedom enjoyed by individual citizens might also be part of what it means to be a developed nation. Some of these criteria are easy to quantify. Table 21.1 presents data for different types of economies according to some of the more easily measured indexes of development. As you can see, the industrial market economies enjoy higher standards of living according to whatever indicator of development is chosen.

Behind these statistics lies the reality of the very difficult life facing the people of the developing world. For most people, meager incomes provide only the basic necessities. Many people share a small room, usually with an earthen floor and no sanitary facilities. The great majority of the population lives in rural areas where agricultural work is hard and extremely time-consuming. Productivity (output produced per worker) is low because household plots are small and only the crudest of farm implements are available. Low productivity means farm output per person is barely sufficient to feed a farmer's own family. School-age children may receive some formal education, but illiteracy remains chronic for young and old. Infant mortality runs 20 times higher than in the United States. Although parasitic infections are common and debilitating, there is only one physician per 5,000 people. In addition, many developing nations are engaged in civil and external warfare.

Life in the developing nations is a continual struggle against the circumstances of poverty, and prospects for dramatic improvements in living standards for most people are dim. As with all generalizations, there are exceptions. Some nations are better off than others, and in any given nation an elite group always lives in considerable luxury. India is on the World Bank's list of low-income countries, yet Mumbai, a state capital, is one of the top 10 centers of commerce in the world, home to Bollywood, the world's largest film industry.

Poverty—not affluence—dominates the developing world. Recent studies suggest that 40 percent of the population of the developing nations has an annual income insufficient to provide for adequate nutrition. While the developed nations account for only about one-quarter of the world's population, they are estimated to consume three-quarters of the world's output. This leaves the developing countries with about three-fourths of the world's people but only one-fourth of the world's income. The simple result is that most of our planet's population is poor.

In the United States in 2005, the poorest one-fifth (bottom 20 percent) of the families received 3.4 percent of total income; the richest one-fifth received 50 percent. Inequality in the world distribution of income is much greater. When we look at the world population, the poorest one-fifth of the families earns about .5 percent and the richest one-fifth earns 79 percent of total world income.

Economic Development: Sources and Strategies

Economists have been trying to understand economic growth and development since Adam Smith and David Ricardo in the eighteenth and nineteenth centuries, but the study of development economics as it applies to the developing nations has a much shorter history. The geopolitical struggles that followed World War II brought increased attention to the developing nations and their economic problems. During this period, the new field of development economics asked simply: Why are some nations poor and others rich? If economists could understand the barriers to economic growth that prevent nations from developing and the prerequisites that would help them to develop, economists could prescribe strategies for achieving economic advancement.

The Sources of Economic Development

Although a general theory of economic development applicable to all nations has not emerged, some basic factors that limit a poor nation's economic growth have been suggested. These include insufficient capital formation, a shortage of human resources and entrepreneurial ability, and a lack of social overhead capital.

Capital Formation   One explanation for low levels of output in developing nations is insufficient quantities of necessary inputs. Developing nations have diverse resource endowments—Congo, for instance, is abundant in natural resources, while Bangladesh is resource-poor. Almost all developing nations have a scarcity of capital relative to other resources, especially labor. The small stock of physical capital (factories, machinery, farm equipment, and other productive capital) constrains labor's productivity and holds back national output.

vicious-circle-of-poverty hypothesis   Suggests that poverty is self-perpetuating because poor nations are unable to save and invest enough to accumulate the capital stock that would help them grow.

Nevertheless, citing capital shortages as the cause of low productivity does not explain much. We need to know why capital is in such short supply in developing countries. There are many explanations. One, the **vicious-circle-of-poverty hypothesis**, suggests that a poor nation must consume most of its income just to maintain its already low standard of living. Consuming most of national income implies limited saving, and this implies low levels of investment. Without investment, the capital stock does not grow, the income remains low, and the vicious circle is complete. Poverty becomes self-perpetuating.

The difficulty with the vicious-circle argument is that if it were true, no nation would ever develop. Japanese GDP per capita in 1900 was well below that of many of today's developing nations, yet today it is among the affluent, developed nations. Among the many nations with low levels of capital per capita, some—like China—have managed to grow and develop in the last 20 years, while others remain behind. In even the poorest countries, there remains some capital surplus that could be harnessed if conditions were right. Many current observers believe that scarcity of capital in some developing countries may have more to do with a lack of incentives for citizens to save and invest productively than with any absolute scarcity of income available for capital accumulation. Many of the rich in developing countries invest their savings in Europe or in the United States instead of in their own country, which may have a riskier political climate. Savings transferred to the United States do not lead to physical capital growth in the developing countries. The term **capital flight** refers to the fact that both human capital and financial capital (domestic savings) leave developing countries in search of higher expected rates of return elsewhere or returns with less risk. Government policies in the developing nations—including price ceilings, import controls, and even outright appropriation of private property—tend to discourage investment. There has been increased attention to the role that financial institutions, including accounting systems and property right rules, play in encouraging domestic capital formation.

capital flight   The tendency for both human capital and financial capital to leave developing countries in search of higher expected rates of return elsewhere with less risk.

Whatever the causes of capital shortages, it is clear that the absence of productive capital prevents income from rising in any economy. The availability of capital is a necessary, but not a *sufficient*, condition for economic growth. The landscape of the developing countries is littered with idle factories and abandoned machinery. Other ingredients are required to achieve economic progress.

Human Resources and Entrepreneurial Ability   Capital is not the only factor of production required to produce output. Labor is equally important. First of all, to be productive, the workforce must be healthy. Disease today is the leading threat to development in much of the world. In 2009, more than 1 million people died of malaria, almost all of them in Africa. The Gates Foundation has targeted malaria eradication as one of its key goals in the next decade.

HIV/AIDS was still responsible for more than 2 million deaths in 2009, again mostly in Africa, and has left Africa with more than 14 million AIDS orphans. Iron deficiency and parasites sap the strength of many workers in the developing world.

Health is not the only issue. Look back at Table 21.1 You will notice that low-income countries lag behind high-income countries not only in health but also in literacy rates. To be productive, the workforce must be educated and trained. Basic literacy as well as specialized training in farm management, for example, can yield high returns to both the individual worker and the economy. Education has grown to become the largest category of government expenditure in many developing nations, in part because of the belief that human resources are the ultimate determinant of economic advance. Nevertheless, in many developing countries, many children, especially girls, receive only a few years of formal education.

Just as financial capital seeks the highest and safest return, so does human capital. Thousands of students from developing countries, many of whom were supported by their governments, graduate every year from U.S. colleges and universities. After graduation, these people face a difficult choice: to remain in the United States and earn a high salary or to return home and accept a job at a much lower salary. Many remain in the United States. This **brain drain** siphons off many of the most talented minds from developing countries.

brain drain The tendency for talented people from developing countries to become educated in a developed country and remain there after graduation.

It is interesting to look at what happens to the flow of educated workers as countries develop. Increasingly, students who have come from China and India to study are returning to their home countries eager to use their skills in their newly growing economies. The return flow of this human capital stimulates growth and is a signal that growth is occurring. Indeed, development economists have found evidence that in India, schooling choices made by parents for their children respond quite strongly to changes in employment opportunities.[1] The connection between growth and human capital is in fact a two-way street.

Even when educated workers leave for the developed world, they may contribute to the growth of their home country. Recently, economists have begun studying *remittances*, compensation sent back from recent immigrants to their families in less developed countries. While measurement is difficult, estimates of these remittances are approximately $100 billion per year. Remittances fund housing and education for families left behind, but they also can provide investment capital for small businesses. In 2007, it appeared that remittances from illegal immigrants in the United States to Mexico, which had been growing by 20 percent per year, were beginning to fall with tightening of enforcement of immigration rules. Remittances fell further in 2008–2009 with the recession.

In recent years, we have become increasingly aware of the role of entrepreneurship in economic development. Many of the iconic firms in the nineteenth century that contributed so strongly to the early industrial growth of the United States—Standard Oil, U.S. Steel, Carnegie Steel—were begun by entrepreneurs starting with little capital. In China, one of the top search engines is Baidu, a firm started in 2000 by two Chinese nationals, Eric Xu and Robin Li, and now traded on NASDAQ. Providing opportunities and incentives for creative risk takers seems to be an increasing part of what needs to be done to promote development.

Social Overhead Capital Anyone who has spent time in a developing nation knows how difficult it can be to carry on everyday life. Problems with water supplies, poor roads, frequent electrical power outages—in the few areas where electricity is available—and often ineffective mosquito and pest control make life and commerce difficult.

---

[1] The classic work in this area was done by Kaivan Munshi and Mark Rosenzweig, "Traditional Institutions Meet the Modern World: Caste, Gender, and Schooling Choice in a Globalizing Economy," *American Economic Review*, September 2006, 1225–1252. More recent work includes Emily Oster and Bryce Millett, "Do Call Centers Promote School Enrollment? Evidence from India," Chicago Booth Working Paper, June 2010.

ECONOMICS IN PRACTICE

Corruption

Many people have argued that one barrier to economic development in a number of countries is the level of corruption and inefficiency in the government. Measuring levels of corruption and inefficiency can be difficult. Some researchers have tried surveys and experiments. Ray Fisman[1] had a more unusual way to measure the way in which political connections interfere with the workings of the market in Indonesia.

From 1967 to 1998, Indonesia was ruled by President Suharto. While Suharto ruled, his children and longtime allies were affiliated with a number of Indonesian companies. Fisman had the clever idea of looking at what happened to the stock market prices of those firms connected to the Suharto clan relative to unaffiliated firms when Suharto unexpectedly fell ill. Fisman found a large and significant reduction in the value of those affiliated firms on rumors of illness. What does this tell us? A firm's

stock price reflects investors' views of what earnings the firm can expect to have. In the case of firms connected to Suharto, the decline in their stock prices tells us that a large part of the reason investors think that those firms are doing well is because of the family connection rather than the firm's inherent efficiency. One reason corruption is bad for an economy is that it often leads to the wrong firms, the less efficient firms, producing the goods and services in the society.

The following chart shows the World Bank's rating of corruption levels in a number of countries around the world. The countries are ranked from those with the strongest controls on corruption—Germany and France—to those with the lowest controls—Pakistan and Nigeria. Indonesia, as you can see, is near the bottom of the list.

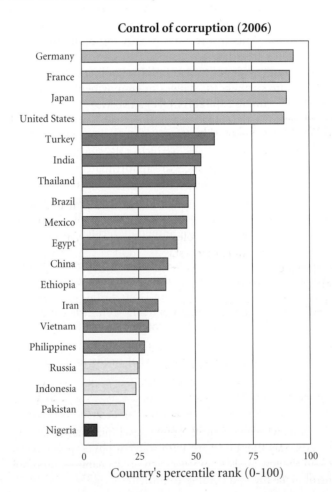

Control of corruption (2006)

Country's percentile rank (0-100)

Source: International Bank for Reconstruction and Development / The World Bank: *World Development Report* 2002.
Note: The governance indicators presented here aggregate the views on the quality of governance provided by a large number of enterprise, citizen, and expert survey respondents in industrial and developing countries. These data are gathered from a number of survey institutes, think tanks, nongovernmental organizations, and international organizations. The aggregate indicators do not reflect the official views of the World Bank, its executive directors, or the countries they represent.

[1] Raymond Fisman, "Estimating the Value of Political Connections," *The American Economic Review,* September 2001, 1095–1102.

In any economy, developing or otherwise, the government plays an investment role. In a developing economy, the government must create a basic infrastructure—roads, power generation, and irrigation systems. Such projects, referred to as **social overhead capital**, often cannot successfully be undertaken by the private sector. Many of these projects operate with economies of scale, which means they can be efficient only if they are very large, perhaps too large for any private company or group of companies to carry out. In other cases, the benefits from a development project, while extraordinarily valuable, cannot be easily bought and sold. The availability of clean air and potable water are two examples. Here government must play its role before the private sector can proceed. For example, some observers have recently argued that India's growth prospects are being limited by its poor rail transport system. Goods from Singapore to India move easily over water in less than a day, but they can take weeks to move from port cities to supply factories in the interior. China, by contrast, spent the bulk of its stimulus money in the 2008–2009 period trying to build new transportation networks in part because the government understood how key this social overhead capital was to economic growth.

To build infrastructure requires public funding. Many less developed countries struggle with raising tax revenues to support these projects. In 2010, Greece struggled to repay its debt partly because of widespread tax evasion by its wealthiest citizens. In many less developed countries, corruption limits the public funds available for productive government investments, as the *Economics in Practice* on p. 438 suggests.

Strategies for Economic Development

Just as no single theory appears to explain lack of economic advancement, no one development strategy will likely succeed in all nations. How active a role should government play in directing economic development? What sectors should be emphasized? Should one focus on new business as a growth engine? These questions are being debated by economists and governments across the globe.

Governments or Markets?   Soviet-style development was accomplished with detailed central planning, state ownership, and control of prices and output. Today in developing economies, the market plays a much stronger role. In most parts of the world, including nondemocratic countries like China, state ownership has declined and prices are mostly set in markets. International agencies like the **International Monetary Fund (IMF)**, whose primary goals are to stabilize international exchange rates and to lend money to countries with problems financing international transactions, and the **World Bank**, which lends money to countries for development projects, have pushed hard for market-oriented reforms.

Market-oriented reforms, however, have not eliminated the role of government. As indicated earlier, governments play a vital role in creating institutions that allow markets to work effectively—physical institutions like roads and schools, and business and legal institutions such as accounting systems and property rights. Many governments also use their taxing and expenditure policies to favor specific sectors over others as they try to grow. **Industrial policy**, in which governments actively pick industries to support as a base for economic development, is still carried on at some level in most developing nations. The greater central control of the economy in China was very evident during the recent recession in the speed with which China could direct its government expenditures as it sought to stimulate its economy.

Agriculture or Industry?   Consider the data in Table 21.2. The richest countries listed—the United States, Japan, and Korea—generate much of their GDP in services, with little value contributed by agricultural production. The poorest countries, on the other hand, have substantial agricultural sectors, although as you can see, the service sector is also

social overhead capital Basic infrastructure projects such as roads, power generation, and irrigation systems.

International Monetary Fund (IMF) An international agency whose primary goals are to stabilize international exchange rates and to lend money to countries that have problems financing their international transactions.

World Bank An international agency that lends money to individual countries for projects that promote economic development.

industrial policy A policy in which governments actively pick industries to support as a base for economic development.

large in a number of these economies. A casual look at the data might well lead one to conclude that moving out of agriculture was the path to development. And, indeed, industrialization was the path that Eastern Europe and other economies pursued in the post-World War II period.

TABLE 21.2	The Structure of Production in Selected Developed and Developing Economies, 2008			
Country	Per-Capita Gross National Income (GNI)	Percentage of Gross Domestic Product		
		Agriculture	Industry	Services
Tanzania	$ 440	45	17	38
Bangladesh	520	19	29	52
China	2,940	11	49	40
Thailand	3,670	12	44	44
Colombia	4,620	9	36	55
Brazil	7,300	7	28	65
Korea (Rep.)	21,530	3	37	60
Japan	38,130	1	29	70
United States	47,930	1	22	77

Source: International Bank for Reconstruction and Development / The World Bank: *World Development Report* 2002.

In many countries, however, industrialization has been unsuccessful. Some have argued that a move out of agriculture may be a result of development, rather than a cause. Others have suggested that industrialization worked for the Western economies but may not work as well for economies with other distributions of human and physical capital. Indeed, in the last several decades the agricultural sector has received more attention as a source of economic development. Many agricultural projects with large productivity enhancement potential have relatively low capital requirements and thus may better match the capital-poor developing world. Agricultural development also improves the lot of the rural population, where more of the poor typically live. Finally, improving agriculture may slow the move of the poor to cities, where infrastructure is inadequate for the growing population.

Experience over the last three decades suggests that some balance between industrialization and agricultural reform leads to the best outcome—that is, it is important and effective to pay attention to both industry and agriculture. The Chinese have referred to this dual approach to development as "walking on two legs."

Exports or Import Substitution? As developing nations expand their industrial activities, they must decide what type of trade strategy to pursue. Development economists discuss two alternatives: import substitution or export promotion.

Import substitution is a strategy used to develop local industries that can manufacture goods to replace imports. If fertilizer is imported, import substitution calls for a domestic fertilizer industry to produce replacements for fertilizer imports. This strategy gained prominence throughout South America in the 1950s. At that time, most developing nations exported agricultural and mineral products, goods that faced uncertain and often unstable international markets. Under these conditions, the call for import substitution policies was understandable. Special government actions, including tariff and quota protection and subsidized imports of machinery, were set up to encourage new domestic industries. Multinational corporations were also invited into many countries to begin domestic operations.

import substitution An industrial trade strategy that favors developing local industries that can manufacture goods to replace imports.

Most economists believe that import substitution strategies have failed almost everywhere they have been tried. With domestic industries sheltered from international competition by high tariffs (often as high as 200 percent), major economic inefficiencies were created. For example, Peru has a population of approximately 29 million, only a tiny fraction of whom can afford to buy an automobile. Yet at one time, the country had five or six different automobile manufacturers, each of which produced only a few thousand cars per year. Because there are substantial economies of scale in automobile production, the cost per car was much higher than it needed to be, and valuable resources that could have been devoted to another, more productive, activity were squandered producing cars.

Furthermore, policies designed to promote import substitution often encouraged capital-intensive production methods, which limited the creation of jobs and hurt export activities. A country such as Peru could not export automobiles because it could produce them only at a cost far greater than their price on the world market. Worse still, import substitution policies encouraged the use of expensive domestic products, such as tractors and fertilizer, instead of lower-cost imports. These policies taxed the sectors that might have successfully competed in world markets.

As an alternative to import substitution, some nations have pursued strategies of export promotion. **Export promotion** is the policy of encouraging exports. As an industrial market economy, Japan was a striking example to the developing world of the economic success that exports can provide. Japan had an average annual per-capita real GDP growth rate of roughly 6 percent per year from 1960–1990. This achievement was, in part, based on industrial production oriented toward foreign consumers.

Several countries in the developing world have attempted to emulate Japan's success. Starting around 1970, Hong Kong, Singapore, Korea, and Taiwan (the "four little dragons" between the two "big dragons," China and Japan) began to pursue export promotion of manufactured goods. Today their growth rates have surpassed Japan's. Other nations, including Brazil, Colombia, and Turkey, have also had some success at pursuing an outward-looking trade policy. China's growth has been mostly export-driven as well.

Government support of export promotion has often taken the form of maintaining an exchange rate favorable enough to permit exports to compete with products manufactured in developed economies. For example, many people believe China has kept the value of the yuan artificially low. Because a "cheap" yuan means inexpensive Chinese goods in the United States, sales of these goods increased dramatically.

A big issue for countries growing or trying to grow by selling exports on world markets is free trade. African nations in particular have pushed for reductions in tariffs imposed on their agricultural goods by Europe and the United States, arguing that these tariffs substantially reduce Africa's ability to compete in the world marketplace.

export promotion A trade policy designed to encourage exports.

Microfinance In the mid 1970s, Muhammad Yunus, a young Bangladeshi economist created the Grameen Bank in Bangladesh. Yunus, who trained at Vanderbilt University and was a former professor at Middle Tennessee State University, used this bank as a vehicle to introduce microfinance to the developing world. In 2006, Yunus received a Nobel Peace Prize for his work. Microfinance is the practice of lending very small amounts of money, with no collateral, and accepting very small savings deposits.[2] It is aimed at introducing entrepreneurs in the poorest parts of the developing world to the capital market. By 2002, more than 2,500 institutions were making these small loans, serving over 60 million people. Two-thirds of borrowers were living below the poverty line in their own countries, the poorest of the poor.

---

[2] An excellent discussion of microfinance is contained in Beatriz Armendariz de Aghion and Jonathan Morduch, *The Economics of Microfinance*, (MIT Press, 2005.)

ECONOMICS IN PRACTICE

Cell Phones Increase Profits for Fishermen in India

Kerala is a poor state in a region of India. The fishing industry is a major part of the local economy, employing more than one million people and serving as the main source of protein for the population. Every day fishing boats go out; and when they return, the captain of the ship needs to decide where to take the fish to sell. There is much uncertainty in this decision: How much fish will they catch; what other boats will come to a particular location; how many buyers will there be at a location? Moreover, fuel costs are high and timing is difficult, so that once a boat comes ashore, it does not pay for the fishermen to search for a better market-place. In a recent study of this area, Robert Jensen[1] found on a Tuesday morning in November 1997, 11 fishermen in Badagara were dumping their load of fish because they faced no buyers at the dock. However, unbeknownst to them, 15 kilometers away, 27 buyers were leaving their marketplace empty-handed, with unsatisfied demand for fish.

Beginning in 1997 and continuing for the next several years, mobile phone service was introduced to this region of India. By 2001, the majority of the fishing fleet had mobile phones, which they use to call various vendors ashore to confirm where the buyers are. What was the result? Once the phones were introduced, waste, which had averaged 5 to 8 percent of the total catch, was virtually eliminated. Moreover, just as we would have predicted from the simple laws of supply and demand, the prices of fish across the various villages along the fishing market route were closer to each other than they were before. Jensen found that with less waste fishermen's profits rose on average by 8 percent, while the average price of fish fell by 4 percent.

In fact, cell phones are improving the way markets in less developed countries work by providing price and quantity information so that both producers and consumers can make better economic decisions.

[1]Robert Jensen, "The Digital Provide: Information Technology, Market Performance, and Welfare in the South Indian Fisheries Sector," *The Quarterly Journal of Economics*, August 2007.

Yunus, while teaching economics in Bangladesh, began lending his own money to poor households with entrepreneurial ambitions. He found that with even very small amounts of money, villagers could start simple businesses: bamboo weaving or hair dressing. Traditional banks found these borrowers unprofitable: The amounts were too small, and it was too expensive to figure out which of the potential borrowers was a good risk. With a borrower having no collateral, information about his or her character was key but was hard for a big bank to discover. Local villagers, however, typically knew a great deal about one another's characters. This insight formed the basis for Yunus's microfinance enterprise. Within a village, people who are interested in borrowing money to start businesses are asked to join lending groups of five people. Loans are then made to two of the potential borrowers, later to a second two, and finally to the last. As long as everyone is repaying their loans, the next group receives theirs. But if the first borrowers fail to pay, all members of the group are denied subsequent loans. What does this do? It makes community pressure a substitute for collateral. Moreover, once the peer lending mechanism is understood, villagers have incentives to join only with other reliable borrowers. The mechanism of peer lending is a way to avoid the problems of imperfect information described in an earlier chapter.

The Grameen model grew rapidly. By 2002, Grameen was lending to two million members. Thirty countries and thirty U.S. states have microfinance lending copied from the Grameen model. Relative to traditional bank loans, microfinance loans are much smaller, repayment begins very quickly, and the vast majority of the loans are made to women (who, in many cases, have been underserved by mainstream banks). A growing set of evidence shows that providing opportunities for poor women has stronger spillovers in terms of improving the welfare of children than does comparable opportunities for men. While the field of microfinance has changed considerably since Yunus's introduction and some people question how big a role it will ultimately play in spurring major development and economic growth, it has changed many people's views about the possibilities of entrepreneurship for the poor of the world.

Two Examples of Development: China and India

China and India provide two interesting examples of rapidly developing economies. While low per-capita incomes still mean that both countries are typically labeled developing as opposed to developed countries, many expect that to change in the near future. In the 25-year period from 1978 to 2003, China grew, on average, 8 percent per year, a rate faster than any other country in the world. While India's surge has been more recent, in the last 5 years, it too has seen annual growth rates in the 8 to 9 percent range. Many commentators expect India and China to dominate the world economy in the twenty-first century.

How did these two rather different countries engineer their development? Consider institutions: India is a democratic country, has a history of the rule of law, and has an English-speaking heritage—all factors typically thought to provide a development advantage. China is still an authoritarian country politically, and property rights are still not well established—both characteristics that were once thought to hinder growth. Both China and India have embraced free market economics, with China taking the lead as India has worked to remove some of its historical regulatory apparatus.

What about social capital? Both India and China remain densely populated. While China is the most populous country in the world, India, with a smaller land mass, is the world's most densely populated country. Nevertheless, as is true in most developing nations, birth rates in both countries have fallen. Literacy rates and life expectancy in China are quite high, in part a legacy from an earlier period. India, on the other hand, has a literacy rate that is less than that of China's and a lower life expectancy. In terms of human capital, China appears to have the edge, at least for now.

What about the growth strategies used by the two countries? China has adopted a pragmatic, gradual approach to development, sharply in contrast to that adopted some years ago in Poland. China's approach has been called *moshi guohe*, or "Crossing the river by feeling for stepping stones." In terms of sector, most of China's growth has been fueled by manufacturing. The focus on manufacturing is one reason that China's energy consumption and environmental issues have increased so rapidly in the last decade. In India, services have led growth, particularly in the software industry. In sum, it is clear that there is no single recipe for development.

Development Interventions

To this point we have used the terms *growth* and *development* interchangeably, assuming that as an economy grows in its level of income, it will develop to provide benefits to most of its population. Since the 1970s at least, however, economists and policy makers have questioned the relationship between growth and development. A 1974 World Bank study concluded that "More than a decade of rapid growth in underdeveloped countries has been of little or no benefit to perhaps a third of their population." In the last 20 years, development economists have increasingly turned to much narrower, more microeconomically oriented programs to see if they can figure out which interventions do help the condition of the bottom of the income distribution in developing countries and how to replicate those successful programs.

Random and Natural Experiments: Some New Techniques in Economic Development

Suppose we were trying to decide whether it was worthwhile in terms of student achievement to hire another teacher to reduce the student-faculty ratio. One traditional way we might try to answer that question is to find two classrooms with different enrollments in otherwise similar school systems and look at the educational performance of the students. We see comparisons of this sort everyday in newspaper discussions of policies, and many research projects take a variant of this approach. But the approach is subject to serious criticism. It is possible that differences in the two classrooms beyond the enrollment numbers also matter to performance—differences we have failed to correct in the comparisons we make. Crowded classrooms may be in poorer areas (indeed, this may account for the crowding); they may have less effective teachers; they may lack other resources. In the social sciences, it is very difficult to ensure that we have comparisons that differ only in the one element in which we are interested. The fact that our interventions involve people makes even harder. In the case of the classrooms with small enrollment, it may well be that the most attentive parents have pushed to have their children in these classrooms, believing them to be better. Perhaps the best teachers apply to lead these classrooms, and their higher quality makes it more likely that they get their first choice of classrooms. If either of these things happens, the two classrooms will differ in systematic ways that bias the results in favor of finding better performance in the smaller classrooms. More attentive parents may provide home support that results in better test outcomes for their children even if the classrooms are crowded. Better teachers improve performance no matter how crowded the classrooms are. Problems of this sort, sometimes called selection bias, plague social science research.

In recent years, a group of development economists began using a technique borrowed from the natural sciences, the **random experiment**, to try to get around the selection problem in evaluating interventions. Instead of looking at results from classrooms that have made different choices about class size or textbooks, for example, the experimenters randomly assign otherwise identical-looking classes to follow an intervention or not. Students and teachers are not allowed to shift around. By comparing the outcomes of large numbers of randomly selected subjects with control groups, social scientists hope to identify effects of interventions in much the same way natural scientists evaluate the efficacy of various drugs.

The leading development group engaged in random experiments in the education and health areas is the Poverty Research Lab at MIT, run by Esther Duflo and Abhijit Banerjee. By working with a range of NGOs and government agencies in Africa, Latin America, and Asia, these economists have looked at a wide range of possible investments to help improve outcomes for the poorest of the poor.

Of course, not all policies can be evaluated this way. Experimenters do not always have the luxury of random assignment. An alternative technique is to rely on what have been called **natural experiments** to mimic the controlled experiment. Suppose I am interested in the effect of an increase in wealth on the likelihood that a poor family will enroll its daughters in school. Comparing school behavior of rich and poor families is obviously problematic because they are likely to differ in too many ways to control adequately. Nor does it seem feasible to substantially increase the wealth of a large number of randomly selected parents. But in an agrarian community we may observe random, annual weather occurrences that naturally lead to occasional years of plenty, and by observing behavior in those years versus other years, we may learn a good deal. The weather in this case has created a natural experiment.

Empirical development economics thus has added experimental methods to its tool kit as a way to answer some of the very difficult and important questions about what does and does not work to improve the lot of the poor in developing nations. We turn now to look at some of the recent work in the fields of education and health, focusing on this experimental work, to provide some sense of the exciting work going on in this field.

random experiment
(Sometimes referred to as a randomized experiment.) A technique in which outcomes of specific interventions are determined by using the intervention in a randomly selected subset of a sample and then comparing outcomes from the exposed and control group.

natural experiment Selection of a control versus experimental group in testing the outcome of an intervention is made as a result of an exogenous event outside the experiment itself and unrelated to it.

Education Ideas

As we suggested earlier, human capital is an important ingredient in the economic growth of a nation. As economies grow, returns to education also typically grow. As we move from traditional agrarian economies to more diversified and complex economies, the advantages to an individual from education rises. So if we want a nation's poor to benefit from growth, improving their educational outcomes is key. This leads us to one of the central preoccupations of development economists in the last decade or so: Of the many investments one could make in education, which have the highest payoffs? Is it better to invest in more books or more teachers? How much does the quality of teachers matter? Are investments most important in the first years of education or later? In a world with limited resources in which educational outcomes are very important, getting the right answers to these questions is vital.

For most middle-class American students, it may come as a surprise that in the developing world, teacher absenteeism is a serious problem. A recent study led by researchers from the World Bank found, for example, that on an average day, 27 percent of Ugandan and 25 percent of Indian teachers are not at work. Across six poor countries, teacher absences averaged 19 percent. The Poverty Research Lab has conducted a number of experiments in a range of developing countries to see how one might reduce these absences. The most successful intervention was introduced in Rajasthan, India, by an NGO called Seva Mandir. Each day when he or she arrived, the teachers in half of Seva Mandir's 160-single teacher schools were asked to have their picture taken with the children. Cameras were date-stamped. This evidence of attendance fed into the compensation of the teacher. Teacher absentee rates were cut in half relative to the seemingly identical classrooms in which no cameras were introduced.

Student absenteeism is also a problem throughout the developing world, reducing educational outcomes even when schools are well staffed with qualified teachers. Several countries, including Mexico, have introduced cash payments to parents for sending their children to school regularly. Since the Mexican government introduced these payments over time, in ways not likely to be related to educational outcomes, researchers could compare student absenteeism across seemingly identical areas with and without the cash incentives as a form of natural experiment. There is some evidence that cash payments do increase school attendance. Natural experiments have also been used to look at the effect of industrialization that improves educational returns as a way to induce better school attendance; the results have been positive.

Work using experiments, both natural and random, is still at an early stage in development economics. While many reform ideas have proven helpful in improving educational outcomes in different developing countries, it has proven hard up to now to find simple answers that work across the globe. Nevertheless, these new techniques appear to offer considerable promise as a way of tackling issues of improving education for the poor of the developing world.

Health Improvements

Poor health is a second major contributor to individual poverty. In the developing world, estimates are that one-quarter of the population is infected with intestinal worms that sap the energy of children and adults alike. Malaria remains a major challenge in Africa, as does HIV/AIDS.

In the case of many interventions to improve health, human behavior plays an important role, and here is where development economics has focused. For many diseases, we have workable vaccines. But we need to figure out how to encourage people to walk to health clinics or schools to get those vaccines. We want to know if charging for a vaccine will substantially reduce uptake. For many waterborne diseases, treatment of drinking water with bleach is effective, but the taste is bad and bleach is not free. How do we induce usage? Treated bed nets can reduce malaria, but only if they are properly used. In each of these cases, there are benefits to the individual from seeking treatment or preventive care, but also costs. In the last several years, a number of development economists have explored the way in which individuals in developing economies have responded to policies that try to change these costs and benefits.

Intestinal worms, quite common in areas of Africa with inadequate sanitation, are treatable with periodic drugs at a relatively low cost. Michael Kremer and Ted Miguel, working with the World Bank, used random experiments in Kenya to examine the effect of health education and user fees on families' take-up of treatment of their children. Kremer and Miguel found a number of interesting results, results very much in keeping with economic principles. First, a program of charging user fees—even relatively low ones—dramatically reduced treatment rates. The World Bank's attempts to make programs more financially self-sustaining, if used in this area, were likely to have large, averse public health effects. Elasticities were well above one. Kremer and Miguel also found that as the proportion of vaccinated people in a village grew, and thus the risk of contagion fell, fewer people wanted treatment, indicating some sensitivity to costs and benefit calculations by the villagers. Disappointingly, health education did not seem to make much difference.

As with the area of education, much remains for development economists to understand in the area of health and human behavior. Development economics continues to be one of the most exciting areas in economics.

Population Issues

The populations of the developing nations are estimated to be growing at about 1.7 percent per year. If the Third World's population growth remained at this level, within 41 years its population would double from its 1990 level of 4.1 billion to over 8 billion by the year 2031. For poor nations, rapid population growth can strain infrastructure and may impede development. For this reason, population control has at times been part of the development strategy of a number of nations.

Figure 21.1 provides the long historical record of population growth in the world. More than 200 years ago, the Reverend Thomas Malthus, England's first professor of political economy, expressed his fears about this record of population growth. Malthus believed that populations inexorably grew geometrically at a constant growth rate, while the diminishing productivity of land caused food supplies to grow more slowly. Looking at the two phenomena together led Malthus to predict the increasing impoverishment of the world's people unless population could be slowed.

Malthus's fears for Europe and America proved unfounded. Technological changes revolutionized agriculture so that food supplies grew despite the scarcity of land. At the same

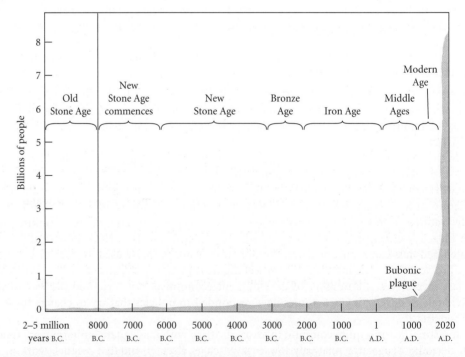

▲ FIGURE 21.1 **The Growth of World Population, Projected to A.D. 2020**

For thousands of years, population grew slowly. From A.D. 1 until the mid 1600s, population grew at about .04 percent per year. Since the Industrial Revolution, population growth has occurred at an unprecedented rate.

time, population growth fell dramatically in Europe and America. Nor did Malthus fully see the causal connection between technical change, economic growth, and population. As early as the mid 1960s, economist T. W. Schultz argued that technical progress increased the returns to education by making it harder for children to simply move into the jobs of their parents. Faced with this recognition, more parents in the developing world reduced their family sizes to better consolidate resources for education. Economists have referred to this reduction in family size and increase in child education levels as trading quantity of children for quality. In some countries, market forces pushing populations toward reduced family size have been helped along by government policies aimed at reducing populations.

Of course, there are parts of the developing world in which population growth continues at high levels. Uganda, with a GDP of $300 per capita, had a population growth rate in 2008 of 3.6 percent, one of the highest in the world. As an agrarian economy with high infant mortality rates, Uganda, as well as a number of other countries, still values large families. In agrarian societies, children are sources of farm labor and they may make significant contributions to household income. In societies without public old-age-support or social security programs, children may also provide a source of income for parents who are too old to support themselves. With the high value of children enhanced by high rates of infant mortality, it is no wonder that families try to have many children to ensure that a sufficient number will survive into adulthood.

Economic theories of population growth suggest that fertility decisions made by poor families should not be viewed as uninformed and uncontrolled. An individual family may find that having many children is a rational strategy for economic survival given the conditions in which it finds itself. Only when the relationship between the costs and benefits of having children changes, in places like Uganda, will fertility rates decline. This does not mean, however, that having many children is a net benefit to society as a whole. When a family decides to have a large number of children, it imposes costs on the rest of society; the children must be educated, their health provided for, and so on. In other words, what makes sense for an individual household may create negative effects for the nation as a whole.

The Transition to a Market Economy

In the last several decades, a number of countries have made the transition from a planned economy to a market economy. Russia and the formerly Communist countries of Eastern Europe led the way in this transition beginning in the late-1980s. For a number of these countries, the early transition period was difficult, and there has been considerable debate about the optimal speed of transitions and ways to manage the social upheaval that often comes with economic reform.

For example, between 1992 and 2002, while per-capita income grew by 51 percent in Poland, it shrank by 63 percent in the Ukraine. Countries of the former USSR seem to have had a particularly difficult transition to market economies. Economists have attributed differences in ease of transition to reform strategies (slow versus fast), resource endowments of the country, and differences in institutions.

In more recent years, China and Vietnam have joined the collection of transition economies, coming to rely less on central planning for economic decisions and more on the market. India too is sometimes thought to be a transition economy, as it has in the last decade dismantled much of its government ownership and elaborate rules governing market transactions.

Six Basic Requirements for Successful Transition

Economists generally agree on six basic requirements for a successful transition to a market-based system: (1) macroeconomic stabilization, (2) deregulation of prices and liberalization of trade, (3) privatization of state-owned enterprises and development of new private industry,

(4) establishment of market-supporting institutions such as property and contract laws and accounting systems, (5) a social safety net to deal with unemployment and poverty, and (6) external assistance. We now discuss each component.

Macroeconomic Stabilization   Many countries in transition have had a problem with inflation, but nowhere has it been worse than in Russia. As economic conditions worsened, the government found itself with serious budget problems. As revenue flows slowed and expenditure commitments increased, large budget deficits resulted. At the same time, each of the new republics established its own central bank. Each central bank began issuing "ruble credits" to keep important enterprises afloat and to pay the government's bills. The issuance of these credits, which were generally accepted as a means of payment throughout the country, led to a dramatic expansion of the money supply.

Almost from the beginning, the expanded money supply meant too much money was chasing too few goods. This was made worse by government-controlled prices set substantially below market-clearing levels. The combination of monetary expansion and price control was deadly. Government-run shops that sold goods at controlled prices were empty. People waited in line for days and often became violent when their efforts to buy goods at low official prices were thwarted. At the same time, suppliers found that they could charge much higher prices for their products on the black market—which grew bigger by the day, further exacerbating the shortage of goods at government shops. Over time, the ruble became worth less and less as black market prices continued to rise more rapidly. Russia found itself with near hyperinflation in 1992. To achieve a properly functioning market system, prices must be stabilized. To do so, the government must find a way to move toward a balanced budget and to bring the supply of money under control. China and India, in contrast to Russia and Eastern European states, initially suffered only modest inflation as they decontrolled their prices, though more recently inflation appears to be increasing in China.

Deregulation of Prices and Liberalization of Trade   To move successfully from central planning to a market system, individual prices must be deregulated. A system of freely moving prices forms the backbone of a market system. When people want more of a good than is currently being produced, its price will rise. This higher price increases producers' profits and provides an incentive for existing firms to expand production and for new firms to enter the industry. Conversely, if an industry is producing a good for which there is no market or a good that people no longer want in the same quantity, the result will be excess supply and the price of that good will fall. This outcome reduces profits or creates losses, providing an incentive for some existing firms to cut back on production and for others to go out of business. In short, an unregulated price mechanism ensures an efficient allocation of resources across industries. Until prices are deregulated, this mechanism cannot function. In practice, transition economies have moved at varying speeds in decontrolling prices. Vietnam, for example, decontrolled prices very quickly in moving to a market economy, as did Poland. China, on the other hand, took a slower path in freeing prices from state control.

Trade barriers must also be removed. Reform-minded countries must be able to import capital, technology, and ideas. In addition, it makes no sense to continue to subsidize industries that cannot be competitive on world markets. If it is cheaper to buy steel from an efficient West German steel mill than to produce it in a subsidized antiquated Russian mill, the Russian mill should be modernized or shut down. Ultimately, as the theory of comparative advantage suggests, liberalized trade will push each country to produce the products it produces best.

Deregulating prices and eliminating subsidies can bring serious political problems. Many products in Russia and the rest of the socialist world were priced below market-clearing levels for equity reasons. Housing, food, and clothing were considered by many to be entitlements. Making them more expensive, at least relative to their prices in previous times, is not likely to be popular. In 2008, rising rice prices in Southeast Asia caused considerable unrest in Vietnam, Thailand, and Cambodia. In addition, forcing inefficient firms to operate without subsidies will lead many of them to go out of business, and jobs will be lost. So while price deregulation and trade liberalization are necessary, they are very difficult politically.

Privatization   One problem with a system of central ownership is a lack of accountability. Under a system of private ownership, owners reap the rewards of their successes and suffer the consequences of their failures. Private ownership provides a strong incentive for efficient operation, innovation, and hard work that is lacking when ownership is centralized and profits are distributed to the people.

The classic story to illustrate this point is called the **tragedy of commons**, which is the idea that collective ownership may not provide the proper private incentives for efficiency because individuals do not bear the full costs of their own decisions but do enjoy the full benefits. Suppose an agricultural community has 10,000 acres of grazing land. If the land was held in common so that all farmers had unlimited rights to graze their animals, each farmer would have an incentive to overgraze. He or she would reap the full benefits from grazing additional calves while the costs of grazing the calves would be borne collectively. The system provides no incentive to manage the land efficiently. Similarly, if the efficiency and benefits of your hard work and managerial skills accrue to others or to the state, what incentive do you have to work hard or to be efficient?

> **tragedy of commons**
> The idea that collective ownership may not provide the proper private incentives for efficiency because individuals do not bear the full costs of their own decisions but do enjoy the full benefits.

One solution to the tragedy of commons attempted in eighteenth-century Britain was to divide up the land into private holdings. Today, many economists argue, the solution to the incentive problem encountered in state-owned enterprises is to privatize them and let the owners compete.

In addition to increasing accountability, privatization means creating a climate in which new enterprises can flourish. If there is market demand for a product not currently being produced, individual entrepreneurs should be free to set up a business and make a profit. During the last months of the Soviet Union's existence, private enterprises such as taxi services, car repair services, restaurants, and even hotels began to spring up all over the country.

Like deregulation of prices, privatization is difficult politically. Privatization means that many protected enterprises will go out of business because they cannot compete at world prices, resulting in a loss of jobs, at least temporarily.

Market-Supporting Institutions   Between 1991 and 1997, U.S. firms raced to Eastern Europe in search of markets and investment opportunities and immediately became aware of a major obstacle. The institutions that make the market function relatively smoothly in the United States did not exist in Eastern Europe. For example, the capital market, which channels private saving into productive capital investment in developed capitalist economies, is made up of hundreds of different institutions. The banking system, venture capital funds, the stock market, the bond market, commodity exchanges, brokerage houses, investment banks, and so on, have developed in the United States over hundreds of years, and they could not be replicated overnight in the formerly Communist world.

Similar problems exist in the Chinese economy. While the Chinese equity market has grown rapidly in the last decade, that growth has been accompanied by problems with weak governance and lack of transparency. These issues discourage investments by western firms.

Many market-supporting institutions are so basic that Americans take them for granted. The institution of private property, for example, is a set of rights that must be protected by laws that the government must be willing to enforce. Suppose the French hotel chain Novotel decides to build a new hotel in Moscow or Beijing. Novotel must first acquire land. Then it will construct a building based on the expectation of renting rooms to customers. These investments are made with the expectation that the owner has a right to use them and a right to the profits that they produce. For such investments to be undertaken, these rights must be guaranteed by a set of property laws. This is equally true for large business firms and for local entrepreneurs who want to start their own enterprises. China's ambiguous property rights laws may also be problematic. While farmers can own their own homes, for example, all rural land is collectively owned by villages. Farmers have the right to manage farmland, but not own it. As a result, transfer of land is difficult.

Similarly, the law must provide for the enforcement of contracts. In the United States, a huge body of law determines what happens if you break a formal promise made in good faith. Businesses exist on promises to produce and promises to pay. Without recourse to the law when a contract is breached, contracts will not be entered into, goods will not be manufactured, and services will not be provided.

Protection of intellectual property rights is also an important feature of developed market economies. When an artist puts out a record, the artist and his or her studio are entitled to reap revenues from it. When Apple developed the iPod, it too earned the right to collect revenue for its patent ownership. Many less developed countries lack laws and enforcement mechanisms to protect intellectual property of foreign investments and their own current and future investors. The lack of protection discourages trade and home-grown invention. For example, in late 2007, China, in recognition of some of these issues, began drafting a new set of laws for intellectual property protection.

Another seemingly simple matter that turns out to be quite complex is the establishment of a set of accounting principles. In the United States, the rules of the accounting game are embodied in a set of generally accepted accounting principles (GAAP) that carry the force of law. Companies are required to keep track of their receipts, expenditures, and liabilities so that their performance can be observed and evaluated by shareholders, taxing authorities, and others who have an interest in the company. If you have taken a course in accounting, you know how detailed these rules have become. Imagine trying to do business in a country operating under hundreds of different sets of rules. That is what happened in Russia during its transition.

Another institution is insurance. Whenever a venture undertakes a high-risk activity, it buys insurance to protect itself. Several years ago Amnesty International (a nonprofit organization that works to protect civil liberties around the world) sponsored a worldwide concert tour with a number of well-known rock bands and performers. The most difficult part of organizing the tour was obtaining insurance for the artists and their equipment when they played in the then-Communist countries of Eastern Europe.

Social Safety Net In a centrally planned socialist economy, the labor market does not function freely. Everyone who wants a job is guaranteed one somewhere. The number of jobs is determined by a central plan to match the number of workers. There is essentially no unemployment. This, it has been argued, is one of the great advantages of a planned system. In addition, a central planning system provides basic housing, food, and clothing at very affordable levels for all. With no unemployment and necessities available at very low prices, there is no need for unemployment insurance, welfare, or other social programs.

Transition to a free labor market and liberalization of prices means that some workers will end up unemployed and that everyone will pay higher prices for necessities. Indeed, during the early phases of the transition process, unemployment will be high. Inefficient state-owned enterprises will go out of business; some sectors will contract while others expand. As more and more people experience unemployment, popular support for reform is likely to drop unless some sort of social safety net is erected to ease the transition. This social safety net might include unemployment insurance, aid for the poor, and food and housing assistance. The experiences of the developed world have shown that such programs are expensive.

External Assistance　Very few believe that the transition to a market system can be achieved without outside support and some outside financing. Knowledge of and experience with capitalist institutions that exist in the United States, Western Europe, and Japan are of vital interest to the Eastern European nations. The basic skills of accounting, management, and enterprise development can be taught to developing nations; many say it is in everyone's best interest to do so.

There is little agreement about the extent of *financial* support that should be given, however. In the case of Russia, the United States pushed for a worldwide effort to provide billions of dollars in aid, to stabilize its macroeconomy, and to buy desperately needed goods from abroad. For China, no such aid was thought to be necessary.

Shock Therapy or Gradualism?　Although economists generally agreed on what the former socialist economies needed to do, they debated the sequence and timing of specific reforms.

The popular press described the debate as one between those who believe in "shock therapy" (sometimes called the Big Bang approach) and those who prefer a more gradual approach. Advocates of **shock therapy** believe that the economies in transition should proceed immediately on all fronts. They should stop printing money, deregulate prices and liberalize trade, privatize, develop market institutions, build a social safety net, and acquire external aid—all as quickly as possible. The pain will be severe, the argument goes, but in the end, it will be forgotten as the transition raises living standards. Advocates of a *gradualist* approach believe the best course is to build up market institutions first, gradually decontrol prices, and privatize only the most efficient government enterprises first.

Those who favor moving quickly point to the apparent success of Poland, which moved rapidly through the first phases of reform. Russia's experience during the first years of its transition demonstrated that, at least in that country, change must, to some extent, be gradual. In theory, stabilization and price liberalization can be achieved instantaneously. To enjoy the benefits of liberalization, a good deal of privatization must have taken place—and that takes time. One analyst has said that privatization means "selling assets with no value to people with no money." Some estimates suggest that half of Russian state-owned enterprises were incapable of making a profit at world prices. Simply cutting them loose would create chaos. In a sense, Russia had no choice but to move slowly.

shock therapy The approach to transition from socialism to market capitalism that advocates rapid deregulation of prices, liberalization of trade, and privatization.

─── **SUMMARY** ───

1. The economic problems facing the developing countries are often quite different from those confronting industrialized nations. The policy options available to governments may also differ. Nonetheless, the tools of economic analysis are as useful in understanding the economies of less developed countries as in understanding the U.S. economy.

LIFE IN THE DEVELOPING NATIONS: POPULATION AND POVERTY *p. 434*

2. The central reality of life in the developing countries is poverty. Although there is considerable diversity across the developing nations, most of the people in most developing countries are extremely poor by U.S. standards.

ECONOMIC DEVELOPMENT: SOURCES AND STRATEGIES *p. 435*

3. Almost all developing nations have a scarcity of physical capital relative to other resources, especially labor. The *vicious-circle-of-poverty hypothesis* says that poor countries cannot escape from poverty because they cannot afford to postpone consumption—that is, to save—to make investments. In its crude form, the hypothesis is wrong inasmuch as some prosperous countries were at one time poorer than many developing countries are today. However, it is often difficult to mobilize saving efficiently in many developing nations.

4. Human capital—the stock of education and skills embodied in the workforce—plays a vital role in economic development.

5. Developing countries are often burdened by inadequate *social overhead capital*, ranging from poor public health and sanitation facilities to inadequate roads, telephones, and court systems. Such social overhead capital is often expensive to provide, and many governments are not in a position to undertake many useful projects because they are too costly.

6. Inefficient and corrupt bureaucracies also play a role in retarding economic development in places.

7. Among the many questions governments in developing nations must answer as they seek a road to growth and development is how much to rely on free working markets versus central planning. In recent decades, the pendulum has shifted toward market based strategies, with governments playing more of a role in creating institutions supportive of markets.

8. Because developed economies are characterized by a large share of output and employment in the industrial sector, many developing countries seem to believe that development and industrialization are synonymous. In many cases, developing countries have pursued industry at the expense of agriculture, with mixed results. Recent evidence suggests that some balance between industry and agriculture leads to the best outcome.

9. *Import-substitution* policies, a trade strategy that favors developing local industries that can manufacture goods to replace imports, were once very common in developing nations. In general, such policies have not succeeded as well as those promoting open, export-oriented economies.

10. The failure of many central planning efforts has brought increasing calls for less government intervention and more market orientation in developing economies.

11. Microfinance—lending small amounts to poor borrowers using peer lending groups—has become an important new tool in encouraging entrepreneurship in developing countries.

12. China and India have followed quite different paths in recent development.

DEVELOPMENT INTERVENTIONS *p. 443*

13. Development economists have begun to use randomized experiments as a way to test the usefulness of various interventions.

In these experiments, modeled after the natural sciences, individuals or even villages are randomly assigned to receive various interventions and the outcomes they experience are compared with those of control groups. In the areas of education and health, random experiments have been most prevalent.

14. Development economists also rely on natural experiments to learn about the efficacy of various interventions. In a natural experiment, we compare areas with differing conditions that emerge as a consequence of an unrelated outside force.

15. Many of the newer economic studies focus on understanding how to motivate individuals to take actions that support policy interventions: to use health equipment properly, to attend schools, to receive vaccinations.

16. Rapid population growth is characteristic of many developing countries. Large families can be economically rational because parents need support in their old age or because children offer an important source of labor. However, having many children does not mean a net benefit to society as a whole. Rapid population growth can put a strain on already overburdened public services such as education and health.

THE TRANSITION TO A MARKET ECONOMY *p. 447*

17. Economists generally agree on six requirements for a successful transition from socialism to a market-based system: (1) macroeconomic stabilization, (2) deregulation of prices and liberalization of trade, (3) privatization, (4) establishment of market-supporting institutions, (5) a social safety net, and (6) external assistance.

18. Much debate exists about the sequence and timing of specific reforms. The idea of *shock therapy* is to proceed immediately on all six fronts, including rapid deregulation of prices and privatization. The *gradualist* approach is to build up market institutions first, gradually decontrol prices, and privatize only the most efficient government enterprises first.

———— REVIEW TERMS AND CONCEPTS ————

brain drain, *p. 437*

capital flight, *p. 436*

export promotion, *p. 441*

import substitution, *p. 440*

industrial policy, *p. 439*

International Monetary Fund (IMF), *p. 439*

natural experiment, *p. 444*

random experiment, *p. 444*

shock therapy, *p. 451*

social overhead capital, *p. 439*

tragedy of commons, *p. 449*

vicious-circle-of-poverty hypothesis, *p. 436*

World Bank, *p. 439*

PROBLEMS

All problems are available on www.myeconlab.com

1. One of the biggest problem facing developing countries across the globe in 2009 was disease. More than 1 million people died of malaria and over 2 million deaths were due to HIV/AIDS, with most of these deaths occurring in Africa. Describe the effects of these diseases on the economies of these countries. Make sure you discuss the sources of economic growth and the use of scarce resources.

2. For a developing country to grow, it needs capital. The major source of capital in most countries is domestic saving, but the goal of stimulating domestic saving usually is in conflict with government policies aimed at reducing inequality in the distribution of income. Comment on this trade-off between equity and growth. How would you go about resolving the issue if you were the president of a small, poor country?

3. The GDP of any country can be divided into two kinds of goods: capital goods and consumption goods. The proportion of national output devoted to capital goods determines, to some extent, the nation's growth rate.
   a. Explain how capital accumulation leads to economic growth.
   b. Briefly describe how a market economy determines how much investment will be undertaken each period.
   c. Consumption versus investment is a more painful conflict to resolve for developing countries. Comment on that statement.
   d. If you were the benevolent dictator of a developing country, what plans would you implement to increase per capita GDP?

4. The World Bank and the International Monetary Fund were scheduled to formally cancel the debts of 18 very poor countries in 2006, and the African Development Bank was committed to taking the same action during its 2006 annual meeting. Go online and find out whether these debts were indeed canceled. How much debt was forgiven during that year in each of the countries involved? What are the expected benefits to those countries?

5. Poor countries are trapped in a vicious circle of poverty. For output to grow, they must accumulate capital. To accumulate capital, they must save (consume less than they produce). Because they are poor, they have little or no extra output available for savings—it must all go to feed and clothe the present generation. Thus they are doomed to stay poor forever. Comment on each step in that argument.

6. Famines are acts of God resulting from bad weather or other natural disasters. There is nothing we can do about them except to send food relief after they occur. Explain why that position is inaccurate. Concentrate on agricultural pricing policies and distributional issues.

7. In China, rural property is owned collectively by the village while being managed under long-term contracts by individual farmers. Why might this be a problem in terms of optimal land managment, use, and allocation?

8. How does peer lending used in microfinance help to solve the problem of adverse selection?

9. [Related to the *Economics in Practice* on *p. 442*] Find another example of the use of cell phones as a way to improve market functioning in a developing economy.

10. [Related to the *Economics in Practice* on *p. 438*] Corruption in a government is often accompanied by inefficiency in the economy. Why should this be true?

11. The distribution of income in a capitalist economy is likely to be more unequal than it is in a socialist economy. Why is this so? Is there a tension between the goal of limiting inequality and the goal of motivating risk taking and hard work? Explain your answer in detail.

12. The following quote is from the *Encyclopedia of the Developing World*: "[Some scholars] suggest that poor people are not poor because they have large families, but rather they have large families because they are poor." Explain the logic behind this quote.

   Source: Thomas M. Leonard, editor, *Encyclopedia of the Developing World, Vol. 3*, p. 1297, 2006.

13. Explain how each of the following can limit the economic growth of developing nations.
   a. Insufficient capital formation
   b. A shortage of human resources
   c. A lack of social overhead capital

14. Of the roughly 7 billion people in the world, more than 75 percent live in developing countries, and one issue of economic concern in many of these countries is that of population growth. In the summary report of the Population Reference Bureau's *2008 World Population Data Sheet*, PRB president Bill Butz made the following comment: "Nearly all of world population growth is now concentrated in the world's poorer countries. Even the small amount of overall growth in the wealthier nations will largely result from immigration." Explain how rapid population growth can limit a nation's productivity. Are there any ways in which population growth can have a positive economic effect? Explain.

   Source: "2008 World Population Data Sheet," Population Reference Bureau, August 19, 2008.

15. You have been hired as an economic consultant for the nation of Ishtar. Ishtar is a developing nation that has recently emerged from a 10-year civil war; as a result, it has experienced appreciable political instability. Ishtar has a serious lack of capital formation, and capital flight has been a problem since before the civil war began. As an economic consultant, what policy recommendations would you make for the economic development of Ishtar?

Glossary

ability-to-pay principle   A theory of taxation holding that citizens should bear tax burdens in line with their ability to pay taxes. *p. 393*

absolute advantage   A producer has an absolute advantage over another in the production of a good or service if he or she can produce that product using fewer resources. *p. 28 p. 411*

adverse selection   A situation in which asymmetric information results in high-quality goods or high-quality consumers being squeezed out of transactions because they cannot demonstrate their quality. *p. 358*

asymmetric information   One of the parties to a transaction has information relevant to the transaction that the other party does not have. *p. 357*

average fixed cost (AFC)   Total fixed cost divided by the number of units of output; a per-unit measure of fixed costs. *p. 169*

average product   The average amount produced by each unit of a variable factor of production. *p. 154*

average tax rate   Total amount of tax paid divided by total income. *p. 391*

average total cost (ATC)   Total cost divided by the number of units of output. *p. 175*

average variable cost (AVC)   Total variable cost divided by the number of units of output. *p. 174*

barriers to entry   Factors that prevent new firms from entering and competing in imperfectly competitive industries. *p. 278*

behavioral economics   A branch of economics that uses the insights of psychology and economics to investigate decision making. *p. 317*

benefits-received principle   A theory of fairness holding that taxpayers should contribute to government (in the form of taxes) in proportion to the benefits they receive from public expenditures. *p. 393*

black market   A market in which illegal trading takes place at market-determined prices. *p. 84*

bond   A contract between a borrower and a lender, in which the borrower agrees to pay the loan at some time in the future, along with interest payments along the way. *p. 236*

brain drain   The tendency for talented people from developing countries to become educated in a developed country and remain there after graduation. *p. 437*

breaking even   The situation in which a firm is earning exactly a normal rate of return. *p. 190*

budget constraint   The limits imposed on household choices by income, wealth, and product prices. *p. 122*

capital   Things that are produced and then used in the production of other goods and services. *p. 25 p. 233*

capital flight   The tendency for both human capital and financial capital to leave developing countries in search of higher expected rates of return elsewhere with less risk. *p. 436*

capital income   Income earned on savings that have been put to use through financial capital markets. *p. 237*

capital market   The input/factor market in which households supply their savings, for interest or for claims to future profits, to firms that demand funds to buy capital goods. *p. 49 p. 236*

capital stock   For a single firm, the current market value of the firm's plant, equipment, inventories, and intangible assets. *p. 234*

capital-intensive technology   Technology that relies heavily on capital instead of human labor. *p. 152*

cartel   A group of firms that gets together and makes joint price and output decisions to maximize joint profits. *p. 297*

Cartesian coordinate system   A common method of graphing two variables that makes use of two perpendicular lines against which the variables are plotted. *p. 18 p. 22*

Celler-Kefauver Act   Extended the government's authority to control mergers. *p. 308*

***ceteris paribus, or* all else equal**   A device used to analyze the relationship between two variables while the values of other variables are held unchanged. *p. 11*

choice set *or* opportunity set   The set of options that is defined and limited by a budget constraint. *p. 123*

Clayton Act   Passed by Congress in 1914 to strengthen the Sherman Act and clarify the rule of reason, the act outlawed specific monopolistic behaviors such as tying contracts, price discrimination, and unlimited mergers. *p. 286*

Coase theorem   Under certain conditions, when externalities are present, private parties can arrive at the efficient solution without government involvement. *p. 334*

command economy   An economy in which a central government either directly or indirectly sets output targets, incomes, and prices. *p. 40*

commitment device   Actions that individuals take in one period to try to control their behavior in a future period. *p. 317*

comparative advantage   A producer has a comparative advantage over another in the production of a good or service if he or she can produce that product at a lower *opportunity cost*. *p. 29 p. 411*

compensating differentials   Differences in wages that result from differences in working conditions. Risky jobs usually pay higher wages; highly desirable jobs usually pay lower wages. *p. 368*

complements, complementary goods   Goods that "go together"; a decrease in the price of one results in an increase in demand for the other and vice versa. *p. 55*

concentration ratio   The share of industry output in sales or employment accounted for by the top firms. *p. 295*

constant returns to scale   An increase in a firm's scale of production has no effect on costs per unit produced. *p. 195*

constant-cost industry   An industry that shows no economies or diseconomies of scale as the industry grows. Such industries have flat, or horizontal, long-run supply curves. *p. 212 p. 213*

consumer goods   Goods produced for present consumption. *p. 32*

consumer sovereignty   The idea that consumers ultimately dictate what will be produced (or not produced) by choosing what to purchase (and what not to purchase). *p. 41*

consumer surplus   The difference between the maximum amount a person is willing to pay for a good and its current market price. *p. 89*

contestable markets   Markets in which entry and exit are easy. *p. 295*

Corn Laws   The tariffs, subsidies, and restrictions enacted by the British Parliament in the early nineteenth century to discourage imports and encourage exports of grain. *p. 411*

cross-price elasticity of demand   A measure of the response of the quantity of one good demanded to a change in the price of another good. *p. 110*

deadweight loss   The total loss of producer and consumer surplus from underproduction or overproduction. *p. 92*

decreasing returns to scale, *or* diseconomies of scale   An increase in a firm's scale of production leads to higher costs per unit produced. *p. 195*

decreasing-cost industry   An industry that realizes external economies—that is, average costs decrease as the industry grows. The long-run supply curve for such an industry has a negative slope. *p. 212 p. 213*

demand curve   A graph illustrating how much of a given product a household would be willing to buy at different prices. *p. 51*

demand schedule   A table showing how much of a given product a household would be willing to buy at different prices. *p. 51*

demand-determined price   The price of a good that is in fixed supply; it is determined exclusively by what households and firms are willing to pay for the good. *p. 224*

depreciation   The amount by which an asset's value falls in a given period. *p. 236*

depreciation of a currency   The fall in value of one currency relative to another. *p. 224*

derived demand   The demand for resources (inputs) that is dependent on the demand for the outputs those resources can be used to produce. *p. 215*

descriptive economics   The compilation of data that describe phenomena and facts. *p. 10*

diamond/water paradox   A paradox stating that (1) the things with the greatest value in use frequently have little or no value in exchange and (2) the things with the greatest value in exchange frequently have little or no value in use. *p. 129*

diminishing marginal utility   The more of any one good consumed in a given period, the less incremental satisfaction is generated by consuming a marginal or incremental unit of the same good. *p. 354*

Doha Development Agenda   An initiative of the World Trade Organization focused on issues of trade and development. *p. 420*

dominant strategy   In game theory, a strategy that is best no matter what the opposition does. *p. 301*

drop-in-the-bucket problem   A problem intrinsic to public goods: The good or service is usually so costly that its provision generally does not depend on whether any single person pays. *p. 342*

dumping   A firm's or an industry's sale of products on the world market at prices below its own cost of production. *p. 420*

duopoly   A two-firm oligopoly. *p. 299*

economic growth   An increase in the total output of an economy. It occurs when a society acquires new resources or when it learns to produce more using existing resources. *p. 14 p. 36*

economic income   The amount of money a household can spend during a given period without increasing or decreasing its net assets. Wages, salaries, dividends, interest income, transfer payments, rents, and so on are sources of economic income. *p. 370*

economic integration   Occurs when two or more nations join to form a free-trade zone. *p. 421*

economic theory   A statement or set of related statements about cause and effect, action and reaction. *p. 10*

economics   The study of how individuals and societies choose to use the scarce resources that nature and previous generations have provided. *p. 2*

efficiency   In economics, allocative efficiency. An efficient economy is one that produces what people want at the least possible cost. *p. 13 p. 254*

efficient market   A market in which profit opportunities are eliminated almost instantaneously. *p. 3*

elastic demand   A demand relationship in which the percentage change in quantity demanded is larger than the percentage change in price in absolute value (a demand elasticity with an absolute value greater than 1). *p. 100*

elasticity   A general concept used to quantify the response in one variable when another variable changes. *p. 97*

elasticity of labor supply   A measure of the response of labor supplied to a change in the price of labor. *p. 111*

elasticity of supply   A measure of the response of quantity of a good supplied to a change in price of that good. Likely to be positive in output markets. *p. 111*

empirical economics   The collection and use of data to test economic theories. *p. 13*

entrepreneur   A person who organizes, manages, and assumes the risks of a firm, taking a new idea or a new product and turning it into a successful business. *p. 48*

equilibrium   The condition that exists when quantity supplied and quantity demanded are equal. At equilibrium, there is no tendency for price to change. In the macroeconomic goods market, equilibrium occurs when planned aggregate expenditure is equal to aggregate output. *p. 66*

equity   Fairness. *p. 14 p. 367*

estate   The property that a person owns at the time of his or her death. *p. 396*

estate tax   A tax on the total value of a person's estate. *p. 396*

European Union (EU)   The European trading bloc composed of 27 countries. *p. 421*

excess burden   The amount by which the burden of a tax exceeds the total revenue collected. Also called deadweight loss. *p. 402*

excess demand *or* shortage   The condition that exists when quantity demanded exceeds quantity supplied at the current price. *p. 66*

excess supply *or* surplus   The condition that exists when quantity supplied exceeds quantity demanded at the current price. *p. 68*

expected rate of return   The annual rate of return that a firm expects to obtain through a capital investment. *p. 243*

expected utility   The sum of the utilities coming from all possible outcomes of a deal, weighted by the probability of each occurring. *p. 355*

expected value   The sum of the payoffs associated with each possible outcome of a situation weighted by its probability of occurring. *p. 354*

export promotion   A trade policy designed to encourage exports. *p. 441*

export subsidies   Government payments made to domestic firms to encourage exports. *p. 419*

external economies and diseconomies   When industry growth results in a decrease of long-run average costs, there are *external economies*; when industry growth results in an increase of long-run average costs, there are *external diseconomies*. *p. 210 p. 213*

externality   A cost or benefit imposed or bestowed on an individual or a group that is outside, or external to, the transaction. *p. 263 p. 329*

factor endowments   The quantity and quality of labor, land, and natural resources of a country. *p. 418*

factor substitution effect   The tendency of firms to substitute away from a factor whose price has risen and toward a factor whose price has fallen. *p. 222*

factors of production (*or* factors)   The inputs into the process of production. Another term for resources. Land, labor, and capital are the three key factors of production. *p. 25 p. 49*

fair game *or* fair bet   A game whose expected value is zero. *p. 354*

fallacy of composition   The erroneous belief that what is true for a part is necessarily true for the whole. *p. 13*

favored customers   Those who receive special treatment from dealers during situations of excess demand. *p. 84*

Federal Trade Commission (FTC)   A federal regulatory group created by Congress in 1914 to investigate the structure and behavior of firms engaging in interstate commerce, to determine what constitutes unlawful "unfair" behavior, and to issue cease-and-desist orders to those found in violation of antitrust law. *p. 286*

financial capital market   The complex set of institutions in which suppliers of capital (households that save) and the demand for capital (firms wanting to invest) interact. *p. 137 p. 237*

firm   An organization that comes into being when a person or a group of people decides to produce a good or service to meet a perceived demand. A firm transforms resources (inputs) into products (outputs). Firms are the primary producing units in a market economy. *p. 48 p. 148*

Five Forces model   A model developed by Michael Porter that helps us understand the five competitive forces that determine the level of competition and profitability in an industry. *p. 294*

fixed cost   Any cost that does not depend on the firms' level of output. These costs are incurred even if the firm is producing nothing. There are no fixed costs in the long run. *p. 168*

food stamps   Vouchers that have a face value greater than their cost and that can be used to purchase food at grocery stores. *p. 383*

free enterprise   The freedom of individuals to start and operate private businesses in search of profits. *p. 41*

free-rider problem   A problem intrinsic to public goods: Because people can enjoy the benefits of public goods whether or not they pay for them, they are usually unwilling to pay for them. *p. 342*

game theory   Analyzes the choices made by rival firms, people, and even governments when they are trying to maximize their own well-being while anticipating and reacting to the actions of others in their environment. *p. 301*

General Agreement on Tariffs and Trade (GATT)   An international agreement signed by the United States and 22 other countries in 1947 to promote the liberalization of foreign trade. *p. 420*

general equilibrium   The condition that exists when all markets in an economy are in simultaneous equilibrium. *p. 254*

Gini coefficient   A commonly used measure of the degree of inequality of income derived from a Lorenz curve. It can range from 0 to a maximum of 1. *p. 372*

government failure   Occurs when the government becomes the tool of the rent seeker and the allocation of resources is made even less efficient by the intervention of government. *p. 283*

graph   A two-dimensional representation of a set of numbers, or data. *p. 17 p. 22*

Heckscher-Ohlin theorem   A theory that explains the existence of a country's comparative advantage by its factor endowments: A country has a comparative advantage in the production of a product if that country is relatively well endowed with inputs used intensively in the production of that product. *p. 418*

Herfindahl-Hirschman Index (HHI)   An index of market concentration found by summing the square of percentage shares of firms in the market. *p. 308*

homogenous products   Undifferentiated products; products that are identical to, or indistinguishable from, one another. *p. 119 p. 179*

horizontal differentiation   Products differ in ways that make them better for some people and worse for others. *p. 316*

households   The consuming units in an economy. *p. 48*

human capital   A form of intangible capital that includes the skills and other knowledge that workers have or acquire through education and training and that yields valuable services to a firm over time. *p. 234 p. 368*

imperfect information   The absence of full knowledge concerning product characteristics, available prices, and so on. *p. 264*

imperfectly competitive industry   An industry in which individual firms have some control over the price of their output. *p. 269*

import substitution   An industrial trade strategy that favors developing local industries that can manufacture goods to replace imports. *p. 440*

impossibility theorem A proposition demonstrated by Kenneth Arrow showing that no system of aggregating individual preferences into social decisions will always yield consistent, nonarbitrary results. *p. 346*

income The sum of all a household's wages, salaries, profits, interest payments, rents, and other forms of earnings in a given period of time. It is a flow measure. *p. 54*

income elasticity of demand A measure of the responsiveness of demand to changes in income. *p. 110*

increasing returns to scale, *or* **economies of scale** An increase in a firm's scale of production leads to lower costs per unit produced. *p. 195*

increasing-cost industry An industry that encounters external diseconomies—that is, average costs increase as the industry grows. The long-run supply curve for such an industry has a positive slope. *p. 212 p. 213*

Indifference curve A set of points, each point representing a combination of goods X and Y, all of which yield the same total utility. *p. 141 p. 145*

industrial policy A policy in which governments actively pick industries to support as a base for economic development. *p. 439*

Industrial Revolution The period in England during the late eighteenth and early nineteenth centuries in which new manufacturing technologies and improved transportation gave rise to the modern factory system and a massive movement of the population from the countryside to the cities. *p. 4*

inelastic demand Demand that responds somewhat, but not a great deal, to changes in price. Inelastic demand always has a numerical value between zero and –1. *p. 100*

infant industry A young industry that may need temporary protection from competition from the established industries of other countries to develop an acquired comparative advantage. *p. 427*

inferior goods Goods for which demand tends to fall when income rises. *p. 54*

injunction A court order forbidding the continuation of behavior that leads to damages. *p. 336*

input *or* **factor markets** The markets in which the resources used to produce goods and services are exchanged. *p. 48*

inputs *or* **resources** Anything provided by nature or previous generations that can be used directly or indirectly to satisfy human wants. *p. 26*

intangible capital Nonmaterial things that contribute to the output of future goods and services. *p. 234*

interest The payments made for the use of money; The fee that borrowers pay to lenders for the use of their funds. *p. 237*

interest rate Interest payments expressed as a percentage of the loan. *p. 238*

International Monetary Fund (IMF) An international agency whose primary goals are to stabilize international exchange rates and to lend money to countries that have problems financing their international transactions. *p. 439*

investment The process of using resources to produce new capital; New capital additions to a firm's capital stock. Although capital is measured at a given point in time (a stock), investment is measured over a period of time (a flow). The flow of investment increases the capital stock. *p. 32 p. 235*

isocost line A graph that shows all the combinations of capital and labor available for a given total cost. *p. 163 p. 165*

isoquant A graph that shows all the combinations of capital and labor that can be used to produce a given amount of output. *p. 162 p. 165*

labor market The input/factor market in which households supply work for wages to firms that demand labor. *p. 49*

labor supply curve A curve that shows the quantity of labor supplied at different wage rates. Its shape depends on how households react to changes in the wage rate. *p. 134*

labor theory of value Stated most simply, the theory that the value of a commodity depends only on the amount of labor required to produce it. *p. 379*

labor-intensive technology Technology that relies heavily on human labor instead of capital. *p. 152*

laissez-faire economy Literally from the French: "allow [them] to do." An economy in which individual people and firms pursue their own self-interest without any central direction or regulation. *p. 40*

land market The input/factor market in which households supply land or other real property in exchange for rent. *p. 49*

law of demand The negative relationship between price and quantity demanded: As price rises, quantity demanded decreases; as price falls, quantity demanded increases. *p. 52*

law of diminishing marginal utility The more of any one good consumed in a given period, the less satisfaction (utility) generated by consuming each additional (marginal) unit of the same good. *p. 126*

law of diminishing returns When additional units of a variable input are added to fixed inputs after a certain point, the marginal product of the variable input declines. *p. 154*

law of supply The positive relationship between price and quantity of a good supplied: An increase in market price will lead to an increase in quantity supplied, and a decrease in market price will lead to a decrease in quantity supplied. *p. 61*

liability rules Laws that require A to compensate B for damages imposed. *p. 336*

logrolling Occurs when congressional representatives trade votes, agreeing to help each other get certain pieces of legislation passed. *p. 347*

long run That period of time for which there are no fixed factors of production: Firms can increase or decrease the scale of operation, and new firms can enter and existing firms can exit the industry. *p. 151*

long-run average cost curve (LRAC) The "envelope" of a series of short-run cost curves. *p. 197*

long-run competitive equilibrium When $P = SRMC = SRAC = LRAC$ and profits are zero. *p. 206*

long-run industry supply curve (LRIS) A graph that traces out price and total output over time as an industry expands. *p. 212 p. 213*

Lorenz curve A widely used graph of the distribution of income, with cumulative percentage of households plotted along the horizontal axis and cumulative percentage of income plotted along the vertical axis. *p. 371*

macroeconomics The branch of economics that examines the economic behavior of aggregates—income, employment, output, and so on—on a national scale. *p. 7*

marginal cost (MC) The increase in total cost that results from producing 1 more unit of output. Marginal costs reflect changes in variable costs. *p. 171*

marginal damage cost (MDC) The additional harm done by increasing the level of an externality-producing activity by 1 unit. If producing product X pollutes the water in a river, MDC is the additional cost imposed by the added pollution that results from increasing output by 1 unit of X per period. *p. 333*

marginal private cost (MPC) The amount that a consumer pays to consume an additional unit of a particular good. *p. 333*

marginal product The additional output that can be produced by adding one more unit of a specific input, *ceteris paribus.* *p. 153*

marginal product of labor (MP_L) The additional output produced by 1 additional unit of labor. *p. 216*

Marginal rate of substitution MU_X/MU_Y; the ratio at which a household is willing to substitute good Y for good X. *p. 141 p. 145*

marginal rate of technical substitution The rate at which a firm can substitute capital for labor and hold output constant. *p. 162 p. 165*

marginal rate of transformation (MRT) The slope of the production possibility frontier (ppf). *p. 35*

marginal revenue (MR) The additional revenue that a firm takes in when it increases output by one additional unit. In perfect competition, $P = MR$. *p. 180*

marginal revenue product (MRP) The additional revenue a firm earns by employing 1 additional unit of input, *ceteris paribus.* *p. 217*

marginal social cost (MSC) The total cost to society of producing an additional unit of a good or service. MSC is equal to the sum of the marginal costs of producing the product and the correctly measured damage costs involved in the process of production. *p. 330*

marginal tax rate The tax rate paid on any additional income earned. *p. 391*

marginal utility (MU) The additional satisfaction gained by the consumption or use of one more unit of a good or service. *p. 126*

marginalism The process of analyzing the additional or incremental costs or benefits arising from a choice or decision. *p. 3*

market The institution through which buyers and sellers interact and engage in exchange. *p. 40*

market demand The sum of all the quantities of a good or service demanded per period by all the households buying in the market for that good or service. *p. 58*

market failure Occurs when resources are misallocated, or allocated inefficiently. The result is waste or lost value. *p. 262 p. 329*

market power An imperfectly competitive firm's ability to raise price without losing all of the quantity demanded for its product. *p. 269*

market signaling Actions taken by buyers and sellers to communicate quality in a world of uncertainty. *p. 360*

market supply The sum of all that is supplied each period by all producers of a single product. *p. 65*

maximin strategy In game theory, a strategy chosen to maximize the minimum gain that can be earned. *p. 303*

mechanism design A contract or an institution that aligns the interests of two parties in a transaction. A piece rate, for example, creates incentives for a worker to work hard, just as his or her superior wants. A co-pay in the health care industry encourages more careful use of health care, just as the insurance company wants. *p. 363*

Medicaid *and* **Medicare** In-kind government transfer programs that provide health and hospitalization benefits: Medicare to the aged and their survivors and to certain of the disabled, regardless of income, and Medicaid to people with low incomes. *p. 383*

microeconomics The branch of economics that examines the functioning of individual industries and the behavior of individual decision-making units—that is, firms and households. *p. 6*

midpoint formula A more precise way of calculating percentages using the value halfway between P_1 and P_2 for the base in calculating the percentage change in price and the value halfway between Q_1 and Q_2 as the base for calculating the percentage change in quantity demanded. *p. 102*

minimum efficient scale (MES) The smallest size at which the long-run average cost curve is at its minimum. *p. 197*

minimum wage A price floor set for the price of labor; the lowest wage that firms are permitted to pay workers. *p. 86 p. 368*

model A formal statement of a theory, usually a mathematical statement of a presumed relationship between two or more variables. *p. 10*

money income The measure of income used by the Census Bureau. Because money income excludes noncash transfer payments and capital gains income, it is less inclusive than economic income. *p. 371*

monopolistic competition A common form of industry (market) structure in the United States, characterized by a large number of firms, no barriers to entry, and product differentiation. *p. 314*

moral hazard Arises when one party to a contract changes behavior in response to that contract and thus passes on the costs of that behavior change to the other party. *p. 362*

movement along a demand curve The change in quantity demanded brought about by a change in price. *p. 58*

movement along a supply curve The change in quantity supplied brought about by a change in price. *p. 63*

Nash equilibrium In game theory, the result of all players' playing their best strategy given what their competitors are doing. *p. 302*

natural experiment Selection of a control versus experimental group in testing the outcome of an intervention is made as a result of an exogenous event outside the experiment itself and unrelated to it. *p. 444*

natural monopoly An industry that realizes such large economies of scale in producing its product that single-firm production of that good or service is most efficient. *p. 278*

negative relationship A relationship between two variables, X and Y, in which a decrease in X is associated with an increase in Y and an increase in X is associated with a decrease in Y. *p. 19 p. 22*

network externalities The value of a product to a consumer increases with the number of that product being sold or used in the market. *p. 280*

nonexcludable A characteristic of most public goods: Once a good is produced, no one can be excluded from enjoying its benefits. *p. 342*

nonrival in consumption A characteristic of public goods: One person's enjoyment of the benefits of a public good does not interfere with another's consumption of it. *p. 341*

normal goods Goods for which demand goes up when income is higher and for which demand goes down when income is lower. *p. 54*

normal rate of return A rate of return on capital that is just sufficient to keep owners and investors satisfied. For relatively risk-free firms, it should be nearly the same as the interest rate on risk-free government bonds. *p. 149*

normative economics An approach to economics that analyzes outcomes of economic behavior, evaluates them as good or bad, and may prescribe courses of action. Also called *policy economics*. *p. 9*

North American Free Trade Agreement (NAFTA) An agreement signed by the United States, Mexico, and Canada in which the three countries agreed to establish all North America as a free-trade zone. *p. 421*

Ockham's razor The principle that irrelevant detail should be cut away. *p. 11*

oligopoly A form of industry (market) structure characterized by a few dominant firms. Products may be homogenous or differentiated. *p. 293*

opportunity cost The best alternative that we forgo, or give up, when we make a choice or a decision. *p. 2 p. 27*

optimal level of provision for public goods The level at which society's total willingness to pay per unit is equal to the marginal cost of producing the good. *p. 345*

optimal method of production The production method that minimizes cost. *p. 151*

optimal scale of plant The scale of plant that minimizes average cost. *p. 200*

origin On a Cartesian coordinate system, the point at which the horizontal and vertical axes intersect. *p. 18 p. 22*

output effect of a factor price increase (decrease) When a firm decreases (increases) its output in response to a factor price increase (decrease), this decreases (increases) its demand for all factors. *p. 224*

outputs Goods and services of value to households. *p. 26*

Pareto efficiency or **Pareto optimality** A condition in which no change is possible that will make some members of society better off without making some other members of society worse off. *p. 256*

partial equilibrium analysis The process of examining the equilibrium conditions in individual markets and for households and firms separately. *p. 254*

patent A barrier to entry that grants exclusive use of the patented product or process to the inventor. *p. 279*

payoff The amount that comes from a possible outcome or result. *p. 354*

perfect competition An industry structure in which there are many firms, each being small relative to the industry and producing virtually identical products, and in which no firm is large enough to have any control over prices. In perfectly competitive industries, new competitors can freely enter and exit the market. *p. 119 p. 179*

perfect knowledge The assumption that households possess a knowledge of the qualities and prices of everything available in the market and that firms have all available information concerning wage rates, capital costs, and output prices. *p. 119*

perfect price discrimination Occurs when a firm charges the maximum amount that buyers are willing to pay for each unit. *p. 283*

perfect substitutes Identical products. *p. 55*

perfectly elastic demand Demand in which quantity drops to zero at the slightest increase in price. *p. 99*

perfectly inelastic demand Demand in which quantity demanded does not respond at all to a change in price. *p. 99*

physical, *or* **tangible, capital** Material things used as inputs in the production of future goods and services. The major categories of physical capital are nonresidential structures, durable equipment, residential structures, and inventories. *p. 233*

positive economics An approach to economics that seeks to understand behavior and the operation of systems without making judgments. It describes what exists and how it works. *p. 9*

positive relationship A relationship between two variables, X and Y, in which a decrease in X is associated with a decrease in Y, and an increase in X is associated with an increase in Y. *p. 19 p. 22*

post hoc, ergo propter hoc Literally, "after this (in time), therefore because of this." A common error made in thinking about causation: If Event A happens before Event B, it is not necessarily true that A caused B. *p. 12*

poverty line The officially established income level that distinguishes the poor from the nonpoor. It is set at three times the cost of the Department of Agriculture's minimum food budget. *p. 375*

Preference map A consumer's set of indifference curves. *p. 142 p. 145*

present discounted value (PDV) *or* **present value (PV)** The present discounted value of R dollars to be paid t years in the future is the amount you need to pay today, at current interest rates, to ensure that you end up with R dollars t years from now. It is the current market value of receiving R dollars in t years. *p. 249 p. 251*

price ceiling A maximum price that sellers may charge for a good, usually set by government. *p. 82*

price discrimination Charging different prices to different buyers. *p. 283*

price elasticity of demand The ratio of the percentage of change in quantity demanded to the percentage of change in price; measures the responsiveness of quantity demanded to changes in price. *p. 99*

price floor A minimum price below which exchange is not permitted. *p. 86*

price leadership A form of oligopoly in which one dominant firm sets prices and all the smaller firms in the industry follow its pricing policy. *p. 298*

price rationing The process by which the market system allocates goods and services to consumers when quantity demanded exceeds quantity supplied. *p. 79*

principle of neutrality All else equal, taxes that are neutral with respect to economic decisions (that is, taxes that do not distort economic decisions) are generally preferable to taxes that distort economic decisions. Taxes that are not neutral impose excess burdens. *p. 402*

principle of second best The fact that a tax distorts an economic decision does not always imply that such a tax imposes an excess burden. If there are previously existing distortions, such a tax may actually improve efficiency. *p. 405*

prisoners' dilemma A game in which the players are prevented from cooperating and in which each has a dominant strategy that leaves them both worse off than if they could cooperate. *p. 302*

producer surplus The difference between the current market price and the full cost of production for the firm. *p. 90*

product differentiation A strategy that firms use to achieve market power. Accomplished by producing products that have distinct positive identities in consumers' minds. *p. 315*

product *or* output markets The markets in which goods and services are exchanged. *p. 48*

production The process that transforms scarce resources into useful goods and services. *p. 25 p. 147*

production function *or* total product function A numerical or mathematical expression of a relationship between inputs and outputs. It shows units of total product as a function of units of inputs. *p. 152*

production possibility frontier (ppf) A graph that shows all the combinations of goods and services that can be produced if all of society's resources are used efficiently. *p. 33*

production technology The quantitative relationship between inputs and outputs. *p. 152*

productivity of an input The amount of output produced per unit of that input. *p. 216*

profit The difference between revenues and costs. *p. 61 p. 148*

progressive tax A tax whose burden, expressed as a percentage of income, increases as income increases. *p. 390*

property income Income from the ownership of real property and financial holdings. It takes the form of profits, interest, dividends, and rents. *p. 369*

proportional tax A tax whose burden is the same proportion of income for all households. *p. 390*

protection The practice of shielding a sector of the economy from foreign competition. *p. 419*

public assistance, *or* welfare Government transfer programs that provide cash benefits to: (1) families with dependent children whose incomes and assets fall below a very low level, and (2) the very poor regardless of whether they have children. *p. 382*

public choice theory An economic theory that the public officials who set economic policies and regulate the players act in their own self-interest, just as firms do. *p. 283*

public goods, (or social *or* collective goods) Goods and services that bestow collective benefits on members of society. Generally, no one can be excluded from enjoying their benefits. The classic example is national defense. *p. 263 p. 341*

pure monopoly An industry with a single firm that produces a product for which there are no close substitutes and in which significant barriers to entry prevent other firms from entering the industry to compete for profits. *p. 270*

pure rent The return to any factor of production that is in fixed supply. *p. 224*

quantity demanded The amount (number of units) of a product that a household would buy in a given period if it could buy all it wanted at the current market price. *p. 50*

quantity supplied The amount of a particular product that a firm would be willing and able to offer for sale at a particular price during a given time period. *p. 61*

queuing Waiting in line as a means of distributing goods and services: a nonprice rationing mechanism. *p. 83*

quota A limit on the quantity of imports. *p. 420*

random experiment (Sometimes referred to as a randomized experiment.) A technique in which outcomes of specific interventions are determined by using the intervention in a randomly selected subset of a sample and then comparing outcomes from the exposed and control group. *p. 444*

ration coupons Tickets or coupons that entitle individuals to purchase a certain amount of a given product per month. *p. 84*

Rawlsian justice A theory of distributional justice that concludes that the social contract emerging from the "original position" would call for an income distribution that would maximize the well-being of the worst-off member of society. *p. 379*

real income The set of opportunities to purchase real goods and services available to a household as determined by prices and money income. *p. 124*

regressive tax A tax whose burden, expressed as a percentage of income, falls as income increases. *p. 390*

rent-seeking behavior Actions taken by households or firms to preserve positive profits. *p. 283*

risk premium The maximum price a risk-averse person will pay to avoid taking a risk. *p. 348*

risk-averse Refers to a person's preference of a certain payoff over an uncertain one with the same expected value. *p. 356*

risk-loving Refers to a person's preference for an uncertain deal over a certain deal with an equal expected value. *p. 356*

risk-neutral Refers to a person's willingness to take a bet with an expected value of zero. *p. 356*

rule of reason The criterion introduced by the Supreme Court in 1911 to determine whether a particular action was illegal ("unreasonable") or legal ("reasonable") within the terms of the Sherman Act. *p. 286*

scarce Limited. *p. 2*

shift of a demand curve The change that takes place in a demand curve corresponding to a new relationship between quantity demanded of a good and price of that good. The shift is brought about by a change in the original conditions. *p. 58*

shift of a supply curve The change that takes place in a supply curve corresponding to a new relationship between quantity supplied of a good and the price of that good. The shift is brought about by a change in the original conditions. *p. 64*

shock therapy The approach to transition from socialism to market capitalism that advocates rapid deregulation of prices, liberalization of trade, and privatization. *p. 451*

short run The period of time for which two conditions hold: The firm is operating under a fixed scale (fixed factor) of production, and firms can neither enter nor exit an industry. *p. 151*

short-run industry supply curve The sum of the marginal cost curves (above *AVC*) of all the firms in an industry. *p. 194*

shut-down point The lowest point on the average variable cost curve. When price falls below the minimum point on *AVC*, total revenue is insufficient to cover variable costs and the firm will shut down and bear losses equal to fixed costs. *p. 193*

slope A measurement that indicates whether the relationship between variables is positive or negative and how much of a response there is in *Y* (the variable on the vertical axis) when *X* (the variable on the horizontal axis) changes. *p. 19 p. 22*

Smoot-Hawley tariff The U.S. tariff law of the 1930s, which set the highest tariffs in U.S. history (60 percent). It set off an international trade war and caused the decline in trade that is often considered one of the causes of the worldwide depression of the 1930s. *p. 420*

social capital, *or* infrastructure Capital that provides services to the public. Most social capital takes the form of public works (roads and bridges) and public services (police and fire protection). *p. 234*

social choice The problem of deciding what society wants. The process of adding up individual preferences to make a choice for society as a whole. *p. 346*

social overhead capital Basic infrastructure projects such as roads, power generation, and irrigation systems. *p. 439*

Social Security system The federal system of social insurance programs. It includes three separate programs that are financed through separate trust funds: the Old Age and Survivors Insurance (OASI) program, the Disability Insurance (DI) program, and the Health Insurance (HI), or Medicare program. *p. 381*

sources side/uses side The impact of a tax may be felt on one or the other or on both sides of the income equation. A tax may cause net income to fall (damage on the sources side), or it may cause prices of goods and services to rise so that income buys less (damage on the uses side). *p. 397*

spreading overhead The process of dividing total fixed costs by more units of output. Average fixed cost declines as quantity rises. *p. 169*

stability A condition in which national output is growing steadily, with low inflation and full employment of resources. *p. 14*

stock A share of stock is an ownership claim on a firm, entitling its owner to a profit share. *p. 238*

substitutes Goods that can serve as replacements for one another; when the price of one increases, demand for the other increases. *p. 55*

sunk costs Costs that cannot be avoided because they have already been incurred. *p. 3*

supply curve A graph illustrating how much of a product a firm will sell at different prices. *p. 62*

supply schedule A table showing how much of a product firms will sell at alternative prices. *p. 61*

tacit collusion Collusion occurs when price- and quantity-fixing agreements among producers are explicit. *Tacit collusion* occurs when such agreements are implicit. *p. 298*

tariff A tax on imports. *p. 419*

tax base The measure or value upon which a tax is levied. *p. 389*

tax incidence The ultimate distribution of a tax burden. *p. 396*

tax rate structure The percentage of a tax base that must be paid in taxes—25 percent of income, for example. *p. 389*

tax shifting Occurs when households can alter their behavior and do something to avoid paying a tax. *p. 397*

technological change The introduction of new methods of production or new products intended to increase the productivity of existing inputs or to raise marginal products. *p. 228*

terms of trade The ratio at which a country can trade domestic products for imported products. *p. 415*

theory of comparative advantage Ricardo's theory that specialization and free trade will benefit all trading parties, even those that may be "absolutely" more efficient producers. *p. 28 p. 411*

Tiebout hypothesis An efficient mix of public goods is produced when local land/ housing prices and taxes come to reflect consumer preferences just as they do in the market for private goods. *p. 346*

time series graph A graph illustrating how a variable changes over time. *p. 17 p. 22*

tit-for-tat strategy A repeated game strategy in which a player responds in kind to an opponent's play. *p. 304*

total cost (TC) Total fixed costs plus total variable costs. *p. 168*

total cost (total economic cost) The total of (1) out-of-pocket costs and (2) opportunity cost of all factors of production. *p. 148*

total fixed costs (TFC) or overhead The total of all costs that do not change with output even if output is zero. *p. 168*

total revenue (TR) The amount received from the sale of the product; The price per unit times the quantity of output the firm decides to produce ($P \times q$). *p. 148 p. 180*

total utility The total amount of satisfaction obtained from consumption of a good or service. *p. 126*

total variable cost (TVC) The total of all costs that vary with output in the short run. *p. 169*

total variable cost curve A graph that shows the relationship between total variable cost and the level of a firm's output. *p. 170*

trade deficit Occurs when a country's exports of goods and services are less than its imports of goods and services in a given period. *p. 410*

trade surplus The situation when a country exports more than it imports. *p. 410*

tragedy of commons The idea that collective ownership may not provide the proper private incentives for efficiency because individuals do not bear the full costs of their own decisions but do enjoy the full benefits. *p. 449*

transfer payments Cash payments made by the government to people who do not supply goods, services, or labor in exchange for these payments. They include Social Security benefits, veterans' benefits, and welfare payments. *p. 370*

U.S.-Canadian Free Trade Agreement An agreement in which the United States and Canada agreed to eliminate all barriers to trade between the two countries by 1998. *p. 421*

unemployment compensation A state government transfer program that pays cash benefits for a certain period of time to laid-off workers who have worked for a specified period of time for a covered employer. *p. 383*

unitary elasticity A demand relationship in which the percentage change in quantity of a product demanded is the same as the percentage change in price in absolute value (a demand elasticity of –1). *p. 100*

utilitarian justice The idea that "a dollar in the hand of a rich person is worth less than a dollar in the hand of a poor person." If the marginal utility of income declines with income, transferring income from the rich to the poor will increase total utility. *p. 379*

utility The satisfaction a product yields. *p. 126*

utility possibilities frontier A graphic representation of a two-person world that shows all points at which I's utility can be increased only if J's utility is decreased. *p. 376*

utility-maximizing rule Equating the ratio of the marginal utility of a good to its price for all goods. *p. 129*

variable A measure that can change from time to time or from observation to observation. *p. 10*

variable cost A cost that depends on the level of production chosen. *p. 168*

vertical differentiation A product difference that, from everyone's perspective, makes a product better than rival products. *p. 318*

vicious-circle-of-poverty hypothesis Suggests that poverty is self-perpetuating because poor nations are unable to save and invest enough to accumulate the capital stock that would help them grow. *p. 436*

voting paradox A simple demonstration of how majority-rule voting can lead to seemingly contradictory and inconsistent results. A commonly cited illustration of the kind of inconsistency described in the impossibility theorem. *p. 347*

wealth or net worth The total value of what a household owns minus what it owes. It is a stock measure. *p. 54*

World Bank An international agency that lends money to individual countries for projects that promote economic development. *p. 439*

World Trade Organization (WTO) A negotiating forum dealing with rules of trade across nations. *p. 420*

X-axis On a Cartesian coordinate system, the horizontal line against which a variable is plotted. *p. 18 p. 22*

X-intercept The point at which a graph intersects the X-axis. *p. 18 p. 22*

Y-axis On a Cartesian coordinate system, the vertical line against which a variable is plotted. *p. 18 p. 22*

Y-intercept The point at which a graph intersects the Y-axis. *p. 18 p. 22*

Index

Photo Credits